ENCYCLOPEDIA OF BIBLICAL INTERPRETATION

לֹא יָמוּשׁ סֵפֶר הַתּוֹרָה הַזֶּה מִפִּיךָ
וְהָגִיתָ בּוֹ יוֹמָם וָלַיְלָה...

(יהושע א׳, ח׳)

This book of the law shall not de-
part out of thy mouth, but thou
shalt meditate therein day and
night . . .

JOSHUA 1:8

ENCYCLOPEDIA
of BIBLICAL
INTERPRETATION

תּוֹרָה שְׁלֵמָה

a millennial anthology

by MENAHEM M. KASHER

translated under the editorship of
RABBI DR. HARRY FREEDMAN, B.A., PH.D.

GENESIS: VOLUME III

AMERICAN BIBLICAL ENCYCLOPEDIA SOCIETY
New York

'Copyright 1957 by
AMERICAN BIBLICAL ENCYCLOPEDIA SOCIETY, INC.
114 Liberty Street, New York 6, N. Y.

Printed in the United States of America by
SHULSINGER BROS. LINOTYPING & PUBLISHING CO.
21 EAST 4TH STREET, NEW YORK 3, N. Y.

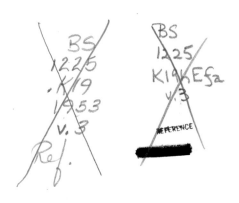
ENDOWED WITH WARM HEART AND LIBERAL SPIRIT, HUMANITARIAN
AND PHILANTHROPIST, INDUSTRIALIST AND COMMUNITY LEADER,
HE HAS LABORED NOBLY AND FAITHFULLY TO BRING SOLACE AND
RELIEF TO OUR PEOPLE EVERYWHERE, STRENGTH AND DIGNITY TO
THE BURGEONING STATE OF ISRAEL, CULTURE AND ENLIGHTENMENT
TO MANKIND.

IN RECOGNITION OF HIS DEVOTED AND CONSECRATED SERVICE TO
HUMANITY AND IN GRATEFUL APPRECIATION OF HIS BENEVOLENT
SPONSORSHIP OF HEBREW SCHOLARSHIP, THIS WORK IS RESPECTFULLY
AND AFFECTIONATELY DEDICATED TO

Israel Rogosin

WHOSE GENEROSITY MADE PUBLICATION OF THIS VOLUME POSSIBLE.

STATESMAN AND HUMANITARIAN, HE HAS CARVED A NICHE FOR HIMSELF IN THE ANNALS OF WORLD HISTORY AS AN UNSELFISH, BRILLIANT AND DEDICATED SERVANT OF HUMANKIND. SCION OF AN ARISTOCRATIC FAMILY, HIS PHILANTHROPY AND PUBLIC SERVICE HAVE SHED GLORY AND LUSTRE UPON THE AMERICAN JEWISH COMMUNITY. HIS GENTLE PERSONALITY, UNIMPEACHABLE INTEGRITY, UNSWERVING DEVOTION TO NOBLE PURPOSE, COURAGEOUS AND LIBERAL SPIRIT, HAVE EARNED FOR HIM THE RESPECT, ADMIRATION AND AFFECTION OF THE ENTIRE FREE WORLD.

THE AMERICAN BIBLICAL ENCYCLOPEDIA SOCIETY, THROUGH THE GENEROSITY OF THE GRACIOUS SPONSOR OF THIS VOLUME, TAKES PLEASURE IN PRESENTING THIS TRIBUTE TO

Herbert H. Lehman

FORMER GOVERNOR OF THE STATE OF NEW YORK; DIRECTOR GENERAL, UNRRA; UNITED STATES SENATOR FROM NEW YORK.

CONTENTS

FOREWORD

The Maecenas of this Volume, Israel Rogosin, shares several personality traits with its author, Dr. Menachem M. Kasher.

Israel Rogosin's phenomenally successful business empire has been built steadily on solid foundations of knowledge, versatility, diligence and, above all, integrity. Rabbi Kasher's international reputation as an outstanding scholar was achieved through the monumental BIBLICAL ENCYCLOPEDIA TORAH SHELEMAH, universally recognized as a work of thorough, exhaustive and reliable scholarship.

Israel Rogosin embarked on his career at a relatively tender age, when most youths are usually pre-occupied with frivolous pursuits. He is fond of telling young people: "Champions start young." Dr. Kasher followed a similar pattern. The dream of compiling a Biblical Encyclopedia, born in his fertile mind while he was still in his teens, enabled him to bring out, at this writing, seventeen volumes of "Torah Shelemah" and three volumes of the "Encyclopedia of Biblical Interpretation." Rabbi Kasher was an "illui" (prodigy) in Talmud, Israel Rogosin was an "illui" in business.

Finally, Rabbi Kasher's scholarship serves him not merely as a source of gratification and spiritual satisfaction. He is imbued with a sense of mission: to share his knowledge with the world, to make an abiding contribution to Biblical literature.

Israel Rogosin, too, is not the ordinary captain of industry bent on amassing a fortune in order to achieve a sense of power. He has a profound sense of mission. He feels that the Almighty's blessings have imposed upon him a dynamic obligation. He not only shares his wealth most generously, but gives of himself as well, of his vast knowledge and keen intelligence, for projects in behalf of the State of Israel, American Jewry, and the community at large. He is a creative philanthropist.

The American Biblical Encyclopedia Society salutes Israel Rogosin and congratulates him upon the significant contribution he has made to Biblical literature through the generous sponsorship of this volume.

LEO JUNG

INTRODUCTION

The third volume covers the Sidrahs Vayyera and Hayye Sarah. These carry the Biblical narrative forward from the prediction of the birth of Isaac to his marriage to Rebekah.

The first Sidrah is made up mainly of four narratives, each of which shows a different facet of the character of Abraham, particularly when viewed in the light of the rich Rabbinical interpretations contained in this volume. In the first narrative we see him sitting at the entrance to his tent, seeking a breeze to give him relief from the hot interior, yet at the same time mentally suffering more from the absence of wayfarers to whom he might offer hospitality than from the physical discomfort of the burning sun. He is scanning the horizon in the hope of finding some stray traveler in spite of the heat, when first God appears to him; and then, as though out of nowhere, three men—they are so described, although the narrative makes it clear that they are Divine messengers—are suddenly standing before him. He begs them to stay and partake of some refreshment—they will indeed be doing him a favor by granting him the privilege of exercising hospitality—after which they will proceed on their way. They immediately accede to his request, and Abraham becomes busy preparing for them.

This is, after all, a very ordinary, everyday story, one that might happen to anyone that loves his fellow-men. Nevertheless it is told in intimate detail, notwithstanding the Rabbinical axiom that the Torah is sparing of words. Nothing seems to be too unimportant: we see him running to the herd to choose the animal and giving it to "the lad," whom the Rabbis identify as his own son Ishmael, to prepare it. And here he hastens into Sarah's tent to bid her knead dough and bake bread for their visitors. And now he is standing over them while they are eating.

In all this, *personal* effort is stressed: he *himself* runs to the herd; his own son is to prepare it; his own wife, in spite of her age, is to knead and bake; and all in spite of the fact that he was able to muster three hundred and eighteen men of his own household in the war against the four kings (see Gen. 14:14). Hence the Rabbinic interpretations exalt the virtue of hospitality, even above communion with the Shechinah (Divine Presence). Another thread runs through the Anthology: how Abraham employed his hospitality in the service of bringing men to the understanding of God.

ii

The next narrative brings out another facet of his character—his insistence on Justice as the foundation of Divine government, which binds even God Himself; and pity and love for his fellows even when they are sinners, a love that is fitting for one who has been described as "the father of a multitude of nations." It is the story of the destruction of Sodom and Gomorrah on account of sin, and Abraham pleading for them that they be forgiven. A strong sense of justice leads all too frequently to an equally strong intolerance, which in the name of justice *demands* the punishment of the sinner. But although Abraham declares that God cannot be otherwise than just, he does not carry this to its logical sequel that the sinner must be punished; on the contrary, here love takes over, and he is concerned with nothing else but saving lives. Although he is no longer a might-be neighbor of ours—for the man next door cannot reason and plead with God as Abraham does here—but a man so spiritually exalted that he can argue and even battle with the Almighty, tenaciously and boldly using each gain in his fight for forgiveness as a stepping-stone for further demands—we feel very near to him none the less, for here he is at his most human.

iii

The faith of Abraham and Sarah during their long years of childlessness is now rewarded: the promise in the beginning of the Sidrah is fulfilled, and Isaac is born. When the child is weaned Abraham makes a great feast. Seeing Ishmael, Abraham's son by Hagar, mocking, Sarah insists on the expulsion of both mother and son, to which Abraham with heavy heart agrees, having been instructed by the Almighty to defer to Sarah, "for in Isaac shall seed be called to thee." In the wilderness Ishmael is brought near death when their water is gone; but God opens his mother's eyes and she espies a well which she had overlooked. At the same time the promise is repeated that a great nation will spring from him.

Of the numerous Rabbinic observations on this chapter we may single out their dicta that prayer is most efficacious when it is altruistically offered on behalf of another; the miracle of Sarah's release from barrenness was simultaneously wrought for many others; her demand for Ishmael's expulsion was due to the evil courses on which he had embarked, which would have corrupted Isaac; and finally, God judges man as he is, and not as he may become.

The fourth and last main episode of Sidrah Vayyera has a *motif* of obedient faith: it tells of Abraham's supreme trial—God's command to offer up Isaac as a sacrifice; and the man who wrestled so strenuously for the sinners of Sodom and Gomorrah does not utter one word on behalf of his own son! Rabbinic interpretation has woven a tapestry of elaboration around this trial, particularly in its account of Satan's efforts to dissuade Abraham or thwart him in his purpose; this may be taken as the allegorical description of the inner battle between a man's sense of duty and his natural feelings, when these clash.

Needless to say, Rabbinic comment on the Binding (Sacrifice) of Isaac exalts both Abraham for his obedience to God and Isaac for his willingness to be sacrificed; in the case of the latter the added virtue of parental honor is stressed, since he was old enough (by most views he was thirty-seven at the time) to object.

One more aspect of this episode is its role in prayer: "When your children sin and they seek My forgiveness," said the Almighty to Abraham, "let them remind Me how you suppressed your fatherly feelings to do My will; then will I suppress My anger at their sinning and do their will and grant them pardon." This has become an important *motif* in the liturgy of Rosh Hashanah and Yom Kippur (New Year and the Day of Atonement).

The second Sidrah, Hayye Sarah, commences with an account of the negotiations for the purchase of the Cave of Machpelah as a burial place for Sarah in the first instance, and later for the Patriarchs and their wives. This is told at great length, undoubtedly because it is the first land to become the property of Israel for all time.

The rest of the Sidrah is the story of the selection and wooing of Rebekah by Eliezer on behalf of Isaac. Many and varied are the comments of the Rabbis: in discussing the test by which Eliezer, Abraham's slave, chooses a wife for Isaac they naturally have much to say on the virtues of womanhood. This test is really a projection of the hospitality for which Abraham was famous: a wife for Abraham's son must be ready to exercise that same hospitality and love for her fellow creatures. Other observations of particular interest are the linking of Eliezer's gifts with the Two Tablets of Stone bearing the Ten Commandments, which Rebekah's descendants were to receive; the inference that when Eliezer is called "blessed," it shows us that by faithful service a man can change his destiny from cursed to blessed; marriage as predestined in heaven; and the institution of daily prayer. This of course is but a very short mention of only a few subjects out of a large variety suggested when the Rabbis examine every word of the text. A graceful note, as it were, is provided by their comparison between Sarah and Rebekah, which tells what a good wife means to her husband and their home.

As in the first and second volumes the ordinary reader has been mainly kept in mind, both in transliteration and in the annotations to the Anthology: the latter is directed to the plain elucidation of the text, in an humble attempt to follow the Biblical injunction "Write . . . all the words of this Torah very plainly (Deut. 27:8).

HARRY FREEDMAN

SIDRAHS VAYYERA AND HAYYE SARAH

(GENESIS 18:1 — 25:18)

GENESIS

Chapter XVIII

¹And the Lord appeared unto him by

COMMENTARY

¹**the Lord. a.** His glory.[1] **b.** The three angels (verse 2).[2] **c.** First the Lord appeared in a vision, and then he saw three men.[3] **the Lord appeared.** How, and for what purpose? **a.** By letting him see the angels.[4] **b.** Abraham apprehended His Presence through his intellectual and prophetic perception, but did not actually see Him with his eyes.[5] **c.** As a reward for his obedience and an indication that He was pleased with him.[6] **d.** By the manifestation of the Shechinah, in order to confirm the eternal nature of the Covenant (see 17:4 *et sqq.*).[7] **e.** He is in high spirits, for his is the joyfulness that flows from the fulfillment of a Mitzvah, and at this moment God becomes visible to him. This fact is of tremendous importance for the understanding of the true character of Jewish Prophecy: Prophecy has nothing to do with "rapture" or "ecstasy"; neither does one partake of Divine revelations by an "escape from life": men who are in the prime of their God-serving lives are selected by God as tools of His Prophecy.[8] **unto him. a.** Near him.[9] **b.** In his honor. This is closely connected with the narrative of his circumcision which immediately pre-

ANTHOLOGY

1. The Lord appeared to him.

Let our Master teach us:[1] How many benedictions must one recite every day? Our Rabbis taught: A man must recite eighteen benedictions every day.[2] The Holy One, blessed is He, said: Pay careful attention to prayer, for there is no finer practice; and even if a man does not deserve to be answered, yet will I show him loving-kindness, for all My ways are love.

R. Simlai said: Would you have proof that all His ways are love? At the beginning of the Torah we find Him adorning a bride, as it says, *And God plaited[3] the rib* (Gen. 2:22). At the end of the Torah too we see His love, viz., in burying the dead, as it says, *And He buried him [Moses] in the valley* (Deut. 34:6). In the middle we find Him visiting the sick, as our text says, *The Lord appeared to him.* It was taught: It was the third day after his circumcision, when he was in great pain. For all sickness reaches a climax on the third day, as it is written, *It came to pass on the third day, when they were in pain* (Gen. 34:25). Said the Holy One, blessed is He, to His ministering angels: "Let us go and visit Abraham." This teaches how greatly the Almighty esteems visiting the sick, and so we learn that it is a Biblical precept.

R. Hama b. R. Hanina said: What is meant by the text, *After the Lord your God shall you walk* (Deut. 13:5): but how can a man walk after the Shechinah, which is a consuming fire? Rather, it means, Imitate His deeds: He visited the sick, as our text states; so do you too visit the sick.

> Sot. 14a; Tan. Y. Vayyera; B.M. 30b; MhG *ad loc.* T.S. 18, 1 and note. 8.

2. THE LORD APPEARED TO HIM.

Abraham had complained: "Before I was circumcised travelers came to me; now that I am circumcised will they no longer come to me?" Said the Holy One, blessed is He, to him: "Before you were circumcised, uncircumcised mortals came to you; now I reveal Myself to you in all My glory." Thus it is written, *The Lord appeared to him.*

> Gen. R. 47. T.S. 18, 2.

3. THE LORD APPEARED TO HIM.

R. Levi commenced his exposition with the text: *Take ye . . . an ox and a ram for peace-offerings, to sacrifice before the Lord . . . for today the Lord*

---

§ 1   [1] Heb. *y'lamdenu.* This is a frequent opening in the Midrash Tanhuma, whence it is also known as Midrash Y'lamdenu.

[2] These Eighteen Benedictions (Heb. *sh'moneh esreh*), which are the most important element of the daily services, are known simply as *t'filah*, the prayer *par excellence.* A nineteenth was subsequently added, yet the original name, *shemoneh esreh,* was retained.

[3] This is the Rabbinical interpretation; cf. Vol. I, chap. 2, par. 169.

1

ANTHOLOGY

appears to you (Lev. 9:3-4). The Holy One blessed is He, said: "If I appear to and bless him who offers an ox and a ram for My sake, how much the more should I do it to Abraham, who circumcised himself for My sake."

R. Isaac Nappaha quoted: *An altar of earth you shall make to Me* (Exod. 20:21). The Holy One, blessed is He, said: "When one kills an ox or a sheep, shedding just a little blood, I come to him and bless him," as this text continues, *I will come to you and bless you.* "How much the more must I bless Abraham, from whose house flows a river of the blood of circumcision."

Gen. R. 48; Tan. Y. Vayyera 4.
T.S. 18, 3. 5.

4. THE LORD APPEARED TO HIM. It is written, *And when after my skin this is destroyed* (Job 19:26). Said Abraham: "After my circumcision many proselytes came and attached themselves to this covenant."[1] *Then through my flesh I see God* (ibid.):"had I not done this, how would God have revealed Himself to me?"[2] Therefore *the Lord appeared to him.*

R. Issi quoted: *If I did despise the cause of my manservant . . . what then shall I do when God rises up* (ibid. 31:13)? This alludes to Abraham, as it says, *And Abraham took Ishmael his son, and all that were born in his house, and all that were bought with his money . . . and circumcised the flesh of their foreskin* (17:23).[3] Said he: "Had I not done this, why should God have revealed Himself to me?"[4]

Gen. R. 48, 2. T.S. 18, 4 and note.

5. THE LORD APPEARED TO HIM. Abraham took all the foreskins which he had circumcised and made a hill of them in his house, whence a river of blood streamed forth. Then the Holy One, blessed is He, summoned the angels and proposed to them, "Let us go and visit the sick." "Sovereign of the Universe!" they protested, "*What is man, that Thou art mindful of him, and the son of man, that Thou shouldst visit him* (Ps. 8:5)? Yet Thou wouldst go to a place of blood and repulsive filth?" "Do you speak so?" He replied. "By your life! The odor of that blood is sweeter to Me than myrrh and frankincense. If you will not come with Me, I will go alone." In this vein spoke Solomon, *Until the day breathe, and the shadows flee away, I will get Me to the mountain of myrrh, and to the hill of frankincense* (Song 4:6): this alludes to Abraham,[1] as it says, *The Lord appeared to him.* Similarly, it is written, *And Joshua . . . circumcised the children of Israel at Gibeath ha-Araloth* (the hill of foreskins) (Josh. 5:3), which also is an allusion to Abraham's taking the foreskins and piling them up into a hill. Therefore the Lord revealed Himself to him. When the angels saw this they too went with Him. Hence the narrative continues, *And he lifted up his eyes and looked, and, lo,* three men *stood over against him* (verse 2).

When a disciple is sick and the master goes to visit him, the other disciples go first and the master follows. But when Abraham circumcised himself and was in great pain, the Holy One, blessed is He, proposed to the angels to go and visit him. Yet as they went He preceded them. For first it says, *The Lord appeared to him*; and after that, *he lifted up his eyes and looked, and, lo, three men stood over against him.*

Tan. Y. Vayyera 4; Tan. Ki Thissa 15.
T.S. 18, 6-7.

§ 4 [1] He connects *nikk'fu*, destroyed, with *hekkif*, to surround, encompass, and renders: After I removed my [fore]skin, they flocked to *this* covenant (cf. Gen. 17:10: *This is My* covenant . . . *every man among you shall be circumcised*) in such numbers as to surround me completely.
[2] Rendering: and through [circumcision performed in] my flesh I see God—before that I was not worthy of the Divine revelation.
[3] He did not despise the "cause" (i.e., rights) of his servants, but circumcised them too, this being their right and privilege.
[4] Rendering: If I did despise, etc., what could I do to earn such honor that God should rise before me in Self-manifestation?

§ 5 [1] I.e., when God said, "*I will get Me to the mountain of myrrh,*" etc., He meant Abraham.

ANTHOLOGY

6. THE LORD APPEARED TO HIM. Great is circumcision, for only when a child is circumcised does he enter into the count of generations, as it says, *A seed shall serve Him;*[1] *he shall be counted by the Lord in the generation* (Ps. 22:31). R. Isaac said: Service is stated in connection with both circumcision and sacrifices: now, just as the service mentioned in connection with sacrifices is a blood rite, so also is that in connection with circumcision. Hence, what is meant by, *a seed shall serve Him?* When a person loses a single drop of blood [through circumcision], it is as precious to the Lord as sacrifices. Therefore the Holy One, blessed is He, revealed Himself to Abraham when he circumcised himself, just as He did when sacrifices were offered, as it says, *Take ye . . . an ox and a ram for peace-offerings, to sacrifice before the Lord . . . for today the Lord appears to you* (Lev. 9:4).[2] Said He to him: "When you were uncircumcised and came to speak to Me, you fell," as it says, *And Abram fell on his face, and God talked with him* (17:3). But after his circumcision the Holy One, blessed is He, appeared to him, and He stood while Abraham sat, as it says, *The Lord appeared to him by the terebinths of Mamre, and he sat.*

Tan. Vayyera 6. T.S. 18, 9.

7. THE LORD APPEARED TO HIM. R. Hama b. Hanina said: It was the third day after his circumcision, and the Holy One, blessed is He, came to enquire after his welfare. This may be compared to a storekeeper in whose courtyard there was uncleanness. He had a friend, a priest. Said the latter to him: "If you desire me to enter your courtyard, you must first remove the uncleanness." When he did this, the priest entered his home. Now, the Holy One, blessed is He, was Abraham's Friend; yet He could not visit him because of his uncir-

cumcised state [which made him unclean]. But immediately he circumcised himself *the Lord appeared to him.*

Midrash Abakir. T.S. 18, 10.

8. THE LORD APPEARED TO HIM. *My beloved is like a deer* (Song 2:9). R. Isaac commented: Just as a deer leaps over the mountains and springs from tree to tree; so does the Holy One, blessed is He, speed from synagogue to synagogue and from school to school.[1] Why? In order to bless Israel. For whose sake? For the sake of him who sat by the terebinths of Mamre. Thus it is written, *The Lord appeared to him by the terebinths of Mamre, as he sat by the tent door.*

PRK 25. T.S. 18, 12.

9. THE LORD APPEARED TO HIM. But how could the Shechinah rest on him when he was in pain? Did we not learn: The spirit of prophecy does not rest upon a man when he is indolent or melancholy; and certainly not when he is sick? The truth is that the Holy One, blessed is He, signalled to the angels to heal him, which they did.

Midrash Hahefetz. T.S. 18, 13.

10. THE LORD APPEARED TO HIM. R. Simeon said: What does this mean? That just as the Holy One, blessed is He, showed Adam every generation and its rulers and leaders, so He did to Abraham, and He informed him: "In this generation there will be righteous, in that generation nondescripts, in yet another there will be wicked men."

Zohar Hadash Tikkunim 121. T.S. 18, 14.

11. THE LORD APPEARED TO HIM. He appeared to him in a prophetic vision to inform him what was to befall Sodom, as it is written, *For the Lord God will do nothing without revealing His counsel to His servants the prophets*

§ 6 [1] The service is assumed to be circumcision.
[2] Cf. par. 3.
§ 8 [1] The Song of Songs was allegorically interpreted as a poem describing the love uniting God and Israel. God is the Lover, and Israel the beloved.

the terebinths of Mamre, as he sat in

COMMENTARY

cedes: now that he was circumcised He appeared to him.[10] **by the terebinths of Mamre. a.** The plain of Mamre.[11] **b.** Mamre was one of the three men (see 14:13) with whom Abraham had a pact. He was his most faithful and reliable friend, and Abraham was now staying here as a precautionary measure, in case the defeated kings (see 14:15) seek to utilize his weakness through circumcision by attacking him.[12] **c.** Scripture states the location in order to let us know where he was circumcised.[13] **he sat.** Engaged neither in prayer nor in spiritual

ANTHOLOGY

(Amos 3:7); also, to give him the tidings of Isaac's birth and heal him of his sickness.

MhG. T.S. 18, 15.

12. THE LORD APPEARED TO HIM. R. Hiyya commenced his discourse with the verse *The flowers appear on the earth, the time of song is come, and the voice of the turtle is heard in our land* (Song 2:12). He said: When God created the world He endowed the earth with all the energy she needed, yet she did not yield fruit until man appeared. . . Similarly, the heaven did not impart strength to the earth until man came. . . As soon as man appeared *the flowers appeared on the earth,* all her latent powers being revealed; *the time of song was come,* the earth was now ripe to offer praises to the Almighty—which she could not do before man was created. *And the voice of the turtle was heard in our land:* this alludes to the word of God, which was not heard in the world till man was created. Thus, when man was there everything was there. Then man sinned, the earth was cursed, and all these good things left her, as it is written, *cursed is the earth for your sake* (Gen. 3:17); also, *when you till the ground it shall not henceforth give its strength to you* (ibid. 4:12); also *thorns and thistles it shall bring forth to you* (ibid. 3:18). When Noah came, he invented spades and hoes, but afterwards he sinned through drunkenness, and the rest of the world also sinned before God, and the strength of the earth deserted her. So matters continued until Abraham. When he came, *the blossoms appeared in the earth* once more and all the powers of the earth were restored and displayed themselves. . . . When at length the covenant was made with Abraham through circumcision, then the whole of this verse was fulfilled in him, the world was firmly established, and the word of the Lord came to him openly: hence it is written, *The Lord appeared to him.*

Zohar 1, 97a, b.

13. **To him.**

But not to the other circumcised. *The Lord [appeared to him]* indicates that He appeared as the God of mercy and as a Healer. Further, *the Lord* emphasizes that He is Sovereign over all living.

PZ; Sechel Tob. T.S. 18, 16 and note.

14. **By the terebinths of Mamre.**

Why did the Holy One, blessed is He, appear to him by[1] a terebinth? To intimate to him that as the terebinth yields both sweet fruit and bitter, so would there issue from Isaac two sons —one righteous and one wicked. Another reason is because Israel is likened to it, as it is written, *And if there be yet a tenth in it, it shall again be eaten up: as a terebinth, and as an oak* (Isa. 6:13): just as the terebinth and the oak, even when completely sere and bare, flourish again and blossom and bring forth fruit immediately they drink water, so is Israel: even if its children have descended to the lowest depths of iniquity, yet when the appointed time[2] comes and they repent, they will immediately burst into resplendent blossom, as it is

§ 14 [1] Or: in. Perhaps he renders: "The Lord appeared to him *in* the terebinths," just as He appeared to Moses *in* the burning bush.
[2] For their redemption — a technical term for the Messianic era.

the tent door in the heat of the day;

COMMENTARY

exercises to make himself fit to receive prophecy; nevertheless he was favored with the Divine Presence.[14] **in the tent door in the heat of the day. a.** This explains why he did not invite his guests to spend the night, as did Lot; daytime visitors were offered refreshments, but not lodgings.[15] **b.** This is said in praise of Abraham: notwithstanding the intense heat and his own sickness he still sat there to invite any stray passer-by. As a reward for such devotion to the ideal of hospitality he was privileged to attain to the spiritual heights of prophecy and Divine communion.[16] **c.** The Bible emphasizes that even in broad daylight, amid the turmoil and the distractions of passers-by, Abraham was still so intensely attached to the Almighty that he could

ANTHOLOGY

written, *His branches shall spread, and his beauty shall be as the olive-tree, and his fragrance as Lebanon* (Hos. 14:7). Therefore He appeared to him *by the terebinths of Mamre.*

MhG. T.S. 18, 17.

15. BY THE TEREBINTHS OF MAMRE. Why by a tree? To teach: just as a tree yields fruit after it is clipped, so when Abraham was circumcised he was privileged that *the fruit of the righteous,* [which] *is a tree of life* (Prov. 11:30), came forth from him. Again, just as a tree sends forth new shoots when it is cut down, as it is written, *For there is hope of a tree, if it be cut down, that it will sprout again* (Job 14:7), so did the sun of Abraham not set until the sun of Isaac rose. Again: why by a tree? Because the righteous are compared to it, as it is written, *The righteous shall flourish like the palm-tree* (Ps. 92:13).

MhG. T.S. 18, 18.

16. **As he sat in the tent door.**

Job boasted: "What did Abraham do that I did not do?" Said He [the Almighty] to him: "How long, Job, will you boast? If a poor man did not come to you, you had no compassion on him. But Abraham was not so: on the third day after circumcision he went and sat at the door of his tent [to offer hospitality to any passer-by]," as we read, *as he sat in the tent door in the heat of the day.* Was it then Abraham's practice to sit at the tent door? This, however, shows how much he loved to exercise hospitality. For when two days passed without any guests, he said: "They must think that they will cause me further pain." Without hesitation he went out and sat at the door, to invite travelers into his home.

R. Hama b. R. Hanina said: It was the third day after his circumcision, when the Holy One, blessed is He, came to pay him a visit. He brought the sun out of its sheathe [to make it too hot for traveling], to save that righteous man the trouble of wayfarers. Abraham thereupon sent out Eliezer, who, however, found none. "I do not believe you," he cried out. There [in Eretz Israel] it is proverbial that slaves are not trustworthy.

B.M. 86b; ARN (Codex 2) 14; MhG. T.S. 18, 20. 23. 25.

17. AS HE SAT IN THE TENT DOOR. When the Holy One, blessed is He, revealed Himself to him, he was sitting, as our text states. He was about to rise, when the Almighty said to him, "Do not suffer the pain of rising; remain seated." Thus it says, *The Lord saith unto my lord: "Sit at My right hand"* (Ps. 110:1). "Is it then mannerly," he protested, "that I should sit whilst Thou standest?" "Let it not grieve you," He assured him, "you are aged, a hundred years old. By your life! Because you sit and I stand, your children shall sit in their schools and synagogues when but three or four years old, and I will stand over them," as it says, *God stands in the congregation of God (ibid.* 82:1). Abraham then burst out into pæans to the Almighty, *Thou hast also given me Thy shield of salvation, and Thy right hand hath holden me up; and Thy condescension hath made me great (ibid.* 18:36)—by allowing me to sit whilst Thou didst stand.

Tan. Y. Vayyera 4.

2and he lifted up his eyes and looked, and, lo, three men stood over against

COMMENTARY

receive prophecy, even though that was not his purpose in sitting there.[17] 2**he lifted up his eyes.** After the Divine Presence (Shechinah) had revealed itself to him.[18] **looked.** Literally, i.e., he saw with his eyes ["looked" and "saw" in this verse is the same word].[19] **lo.** Heb. *v'hinneh.* This implies suddenness: three men suddenly were standing there, as though they had fallen from heaven.[20] **three men. a.** Prophets.[21] **b.** Both "men" and "angels" (19:1) are meant literally, for when they revealed themselves as men they were actually men.[22] **c.** Angels in the guise of men. They had assumed human form in his honor, that he might have the privilege of entertaining them as his guests; this was the reward for his circumcision.[23] **stood over against him. a.** Near, or before him.[24] **b.** Expec-

ANTHOLOGY

18. IN THE TENT DOOR. [The word "door" signifies that the Almighty commended him:] "You have opened a goodly door to wayfarers; you have opened a goodly door to proselytes.[1] But for you I had not created heaven and earth, the orb of the sun, or the moon."[2]

R. Levi said: In the Hereafter Abraham will sit at the door of Gehenna and suffer no circumcised Israelite to descend therein. But what will he do to those whose sins were too great [to escape punishment]? He will remove the foreskin from the babes who died before they were circumcised, set it upon them, and then allow them to go down into Gehenna. That is the significance of the verse, *He has sent forth his hands upon them that were whole;*[3] *he has profaned his covenant*[4] (Ps. 55:21). [This follows from our text,] *As he sat in the tent door in the heat of the day,* which hints at that day in the time to come which is described in the text, *For, behold, the day comes; it burns as a furnace* (Mal. 3:19).

Gen. R. 48, 8. T.S. 18, 22.

19. **In the heat of the day.**

R. Yannai said: The Holy One, blessed is He, made a hole in Gehenna to allow the heat to issue from it, and for a short while the world became a blazing inferno for its inhabitants. For, said He, shall the righteous suffer pain while the world is at ease?

[Further,] from this you can learn that heat is beneficial to a wound.[1]

Gen. R. 48, 8. T.S. 18, 26.

20. IN THE HEAT OF THE DAY. R. Judah said: The Holy One, blessed is He, reveals Himself to the Gentiles only at night . . . but to the prophets of Israel by day, as our text says, *In the heat of* the day.

Lev. R. 1, 13. T.S. 18, 27.

21. IN THE HEAT OF THE DAY. Our Rabbis taught: This is an allusion to the Great Day of Judgment, when the soul parts from the body. The righteous does not die before he sees the Shechinah, which is accompanied by three ministering angels to receive his soul. Thus *in the heat of the day* alludes to the Day of Judgment, which burns as a furnace in order to separate the soul from the body.

Midrash Haneelam Zohar Hadash 1, 98. T.S. 18, 29.

22. **He lifted up his eyes and saw.**

He saw the Shechinah and the angels.

Gen. R. 48. T.S. 18, 30.

§ 18   [1] See chap. 21, par. 100.
   [2] The sole purpose of creation was that man might know God; Abraham was the first to recognize and teach this great truth.
   [3] I.e., the circumcised wicked.
   [4] By setting the uncircumcised foreskin upon them.
§ 19   [1] Midrash Or Haafelah reverses it: Heat is harmful to a wound and therefore he went out to get relief. Presumably it had this reading in Gen. R. PRE 29 (quoted in T.S. 25) takes the same view, and regards his great pain as one of his trials.

ANTHOLOGY

23. HE LIFTED UP HIS EYES AND SAW. R. Helbo quoted: *Let their eyes be darkened, that they see not* (Ps. 69:24)—because what the wicked see hurls them down into Gehenna.[1] But what the righteous see lifts them up into Paradise, as it says, *He lifted up his eyes and saw, and, lo, three men stood over against him.*

He was one of the six who saw and rejoiced, viz.: Abraham, Isaac, Jacob, Moses, Phinehas and Joshua.

Est. R. 7, 9; MhG. T.S. 18, 31. 33.

24. Three men stood over against him.

"Sovereign of the Universe!" the angels protested, "how long wilt Thou honor him; how long wilt Thou stand while he sits?" Said He to them, "This is not yet enough. [Another three will stand before him] for the sake of the three righteous men, who, I foresee, will descend from him.[1] When the whole world falls and makes obeisance before an image, they will stand upright like a palm-tree and refuse to do so"; as it says, *This thy stature is like to a palm-tree* (Song 7:8). Therefore, now *three men stood over against him.*

AB 19. T.S. 18, 32.

25. THREE MEN STOOD OVER AGAINST HIM. Who were they? Michael, Gabriel, and Raphael. Michael came to give the tidings of Isaac's birth to Sarah; Raphael to heal Abraham;[1] and Gabriel went on to overturn Sodom.

R. Hanina said: The Holy One, blessed is He, revealed Himself, together with three angels, to the Patriarch Abraham, as this text states. One informed him of Sarah's conception, as it says, *At the set time I will return to you . . . and Sarah shall have a son* (verse 14). Another apprised him of the doom of Sodom and Gomorrah, as it says, *And the Lord said: "Verily, the cry of Sodom and Gomorrah is great"* (verse 20). Hence our Sages said: When a man wishes to tell his neighbor anything to his discredit, let him begin with something good and end with the bad. Whence do we learn it? From the Holy One, blessed is He: when He appeared to Abraham He first informed him of Sarah's conception and then told him of Sodom's doom.

B.M. 86a; PRE 25. T.S. 18, 34. 37.

26. THREE MEN. Here they are called men, whilst further on they are called angels.[1] R. Alexandri explained it: To Abraham they were men, because angels were frequent visitors in his home, as it says, *She looks well upon the frequenters of her house* (Prov. 31:27)—the frequenters of Abraham's house were angels.[2] For that reason they appeared to him as men. Seeing Abraham grieved at the absence of guests to enjoy his hospitality, the Holy One, blessed is He, bade the angels to visit him in the guise of travelers. For the Almighty invests angels with whatever appearance He desires. [Thus, when Manoah asked the angel who foretold Samson's birth his name, the angel of the Lord answered him:] *"Why do you ask my name"* (Judge 13:18)?—by which he implied: I do not know what guise I take, because He continually changes me, *for it is a wonder* (*ibid.*): He deals with me in a most wondrous fashion. At times I am but wind, as it says, *Who makest winds Thine angels* (Ps. 104:4); at others, I am fire, as the verse continues, [Thou makest] *the flaming fire Thy ministers.* Whereas, to Abraham they appeared as men, to Lot, a man of inferior status, they appeared as angels, as it says, *The two angels came to Sodom* (19:1).

Tan. Y. Vayyera 20; MA; Yalkut Shimoni quoting Yelamdenu. T.S. 18, 35 and note. 38 note.

§ 23 [1] They look on things that fill them with lust and desire, to which they yield and so incur the torments of hell.
§ 24 [1] Hananiah, Mishael, and Azariah.
§ 25 [1] Cf. par. 9.
§ 26 [1] 19:1: *And the two angels came to Sodom at even . . . and Lot saw them, and rose up to meet them.*
　　　 [2] To him they were not supernatural.

him; and when he saw them, he ran to meet them from the tent door,

COMMENTARY

tantly, as though waiting to speak to him.[25] **saw . . .**

ran. a. This second "saw" means understood: he saw them standing and understood that they did not desire to trouble him.[26] **b.** He saw that they were too important to be invited through a servant, and so he personally ran to them.[27] **he ran . . . from the tent door. a.** This indicates that he was still sitting there after the Divine Presence had

ANTHOLOGY

27. THREE MEN STOOD OVER AGAINST HIM. R. K'ruspedai said: When a man recites the laws of sacrifices in the synagogue or Beth Hamidrash with devout sincerity,[1] it is ordained[2] that the angels who would indict him for any evil deeds he may have committed are reduced to impotence and can speak nought but good of him. What is the proof? The present passage, which states, *Three men stood over against him.* Now, what does *against him* mean? To scrutinize his deeds, [which they do] whenever they see the souls of the righteous. Now, what follows? *Abraham hastened into the tent* (verse 6): *the tent* is an allusion to the Beth Hamidrash. What did he say there? *Make ready quickly three measures of fine meal,* whose esoteric meaning is that he recited the laws of sacrifices,[3] his soul devoutly willing this recital to count as actual sacrifices. In this same spirit Scripture writes that *Abraham ran to the herd* (verse 7).[4] This appeased his heavenly accusers, so that they could speak no evil against him.

Zohar 1, 100b. T.S. 18, 45.

28. **He ran to meet them.**

He was requited measure for measure. He ran three times before the angels, as it says, *He ran to meet them; and Abraham hastened into the tent to Sarah* (verse 6); *and Abraham ran to the herd* (verse 7). Therefore the Omnipresent too sped thrice before his descendants, as it says, *The Lord* came *from Sinai, and* rose *from Seir unto them; He* shone forth *from mount Paran* (Deut. 33:2).

T. Sot. 4. T.S. 18. 39.

29. HE RAN TO MEET THEM. R. Eliezer, R. Joshua and R. Zadok were reclining at the [wedding] banquet of R. Gamaliel's son. R. Gamaliel filled a glass for R. Eleazar, who would not accept it. He filled one for R. Joshua, who accepted it. Said R. Eleazar to him: "Joshua! what is this? We are reclining while R. Gamaliel stands and waits on us!"[1] Said R. Joshua to him: "Let him! Abraham, the greatest man in the world, waited on the angels, even though he thought them to be idolatrous Arabs;[2] as it says, *He lifted up his eyes and looked, and, lo, three men stood over against him, and . . . he ran to meet them.* Shall then R. Gamaliel not attend to our wants?"

Sifre Ekeb 38. T.S. 18, 40.

30. HE RAN TO MEET THEM. R. Levi said: One appeared to him as a Sarki,[1] the second as a Nabatean, and the third as an Arab [Bedouin].[2] Said he: "If I see the Shechinah waiting for them, I will know that they are great; and if they show respect to one another, I will

§ 27 [1] With the sincere thought that this recital is intended as a substitute for the actual sacrifice, which can no longer be offered since the destruction of the Temple.
[2] Lit., a covenant has been made.
[3] Some sacrifices consisted of fine meal and oil.
[4] "The herd" is likewise an esoteric allusion to the recital of the sacrificial laws, as many sacrifices were brought of "the herd."

§ 29 [1] It is beneath his dignity, for he is the *nasi* (the title of the head of Palestinian Jewry).
[2] See next par.

§ 30 [1] A nomadic tribe.
[2] Some commentaries render, respectively: a baker, a master-mariner, and an Arab.

and bowed down to the earth, [3]and

COMMENTARY

departed.[28] **b.** Thus showing how highly he prized the opportunity to offer hospitality; at the same time he indicated to them that they were honored guests.[29] **bowed down to the earth. a.** He either recognized them as angels, or thought they were royal messengers.[29a] **b.** He pleaded with them, as

ANTHOLOGY

know that they are distinguished." Seeing them indeed showing honor to one another, he recognized their nobility.

R. Abbahu said: Abraham's tent was open at both ends. R. Judan said: It was like a double-gated passage.[3] Said he [Abraham]: "If they go out of their way to approach hither, I will know that they are coming to me." When he saw them do this, he immediately *ran to meet them*.

Gen. R. 48. T.S. 18, 42.

31. HE RAN TO MEET THEM. The blood of the circumcision began to drip from the wound. Said the Holy One, blessed is He, to him: "By your life! For your sake I will have compassion on your descendants on two occasions of blood, and exact retribution of their enemies"; as it says, *And when I passed by you, and saw you wallowing in your bloods* (Ezek. 16:6): two bloods are meant, as the verse continues, *I said to you, "In your blood, live"*—the blood of the Passover sacrifice; *yea, I said to you, "In your blood, live"*—the blood of circumcision.

Tan. Vayyera 4. T.S. 18, 43.

32. **And bowed down to the earth.**

Even as the humble bow down to the great, for thus we find Jacob doing, when we read, *And he bowed himself to the ground seven times, until he came near to his brother* (33:3). The Holy One, blessed is He, said to him:

"You bowed down to My angels: by your life, kings will one day bow down to your descendants"; as it says, *And kings shall be your foster-fathers, and their queens your nursing mothers: they shall bow down to you* (Isa. 49:23). Thus in the very words of our text He foretold this to his descendants for the World to Come.[1]

Upon Abraham, Isaac, and Jacob were conferred various Powers, corresponding to the peculiar character of each. Upon Abraham was conferred the Power of Chesed,[2] because he practised *chesed* towards the angels; moreover, by bowing down to them he made his *chesed* complete. Therefore the Holy One, blessed is He, meted out his reward in appropriate measure, as it is written, *Thou wilt give Truth to Jacob, and* Chesed (AJV: *mercy*) *to Abraham* (Mic. 7:20).

T. Sot. 4; AB 19; Sechel Tob; Sefer Habahir 49. T.S. 18, 44 and note.

33. HE RAN TO MEET THEM. R. Judah said: When the soul of the righteous is about to depart it rejoices, for the righteous faces death confidently, knowing that he will receive his reward. That is the inner meaning of our text, *And when he saw them, he ran to meet them*—welcoming them with joy.[1] Whence did he speed?—*From the tent door*, as we have [recondite]ly] interpreted this.[2] *And he bowed down to the earth* means to the Shechinah.

Zohar 1, 98a. 99b. T.S. 18, 46.

---

[3] The exact meaning is uncertain. The general idea is that it was open on all sides, inviting wayfarers from whichever direction they came.

§ 32 [1] Here this phrase apparently means the Messianic era, and not the Hereafter, as it usually does.

[2] Love or mercy. In mystic literature the world was brought into being and is sustained by various Powers, e.g., Strength, Majesty, Beauty, Compassion, etc. (generally ten are enumerated), emanating from the Godhead as separate spheres of spiritual existence.

§ 33 [1] This is made to refer to the soul meeting the angels after death.

[2] "The tent" is interpreted as a metaphor for the human frame: the soul of the righteous runs from "the tent door"—its human habitation—toward the angels that come to greet it after death; at which time it bows in homage to the Shechinah.

said: "My lord, if now I have found

COMMENTARY

though they would do him a favor by accepting his hospitality and not the reverse.[30] [3]**My lord. a.** He addressed the chief of them; consequently the word does not signify God. Another interpretation: He spoke to God, praying Him to wait until he had attended to his guests.[31] **b.** He recognized that they were angels, and therefore called them by their Master's Name, *Lord*.[32] **c.** The word is both "sacred" (referring to God) and non-sacred (referring

ANTHOLOGY

34. **And said: "My lord, if now I have found favor in your sight."**

R. Hiyya the Great taught: He spoke to their chief, who was Michael.[1]

All [Divine] names occuring in the Torah in connection with Abraham are holy, save the present, which is non-holy.[2] Hanina, the son of R. Joshua's brother, and R. Eleazar b. Azariah, quoting R. Eleazar of Modai, maintained that this too is holy.[3] Rab Judah quoting Rab said: Hospitality is greater than welcoming the Shechinah, for it is written, *And he said: "My Lord, if now I have found favor in Thy sight, pass not away, I pray Thee, from Thy servant."*[4] (This interpretation agrees with the view of the two scholars above, that the Name here is holy). R. Eleazar said: Come and see how God's character differs from mortal man's. In human intercourse the lesser cannot say to the greater, "Wait until I come to you"; whereas in respect to the Holy One, blessed is He, it is written, *My Lord, if now I have found favor,* etc.[5]

> Shebu. 35b; Shab. 127a; Gen. R. 48, 9.
> T.S. 18, 47-9.

35. AND SAID: "MY LORD, IF NOW I HAVE FOUND FAVOR IN YOUR SIGHT." When Abraham saw the ministering angels, the Shechinah came and stood over him. Said he to them: "My masters, pray wait until I take leave of the Shechinah, which is greater than you"; as it says *My lord, if now I have found favor in thy sight, pass not away, I pray thee, from thy servant.*[1] When he had taken his leave of the Shechinah, he came, bowed down to them, and led them under the tree. Thus it says, *Let now a little water be brought, and wash your feet.* [Only] after that [he said], *"I will bring a morsel of bread."*[2] But what did Lot say? *"Tarry all night, and wash your feet"* (19:2).[3]

> DER 4. T.S. 18, 50.

36. AND SAID: "MY LORD, IF NOW I HAVE FOUND FAVOR IN YOUR SIGHT." Hence the Sages said: Let a man dine often with scholars, that he may learn Torah from them, but let him not dine often with the ignorant, for later they will slander him. We learn this from Abraham, who prepared food for the angels and they enjoyed his hospitality, as it says, *My lord . . . pass not away, I pray you, from your servant.* Whence they [the Sages] inferred also: A man must first receive permission to depart from his teacher, and then comply with

§ 34 [1] Hence the sing., although there were three.
[2] The name referred to is *adonai*, here rendered "lord." Wherever this occurs in the Abrahamic narrative it is holy, alluding to the Almighty. But here it is non-holy, as it means the angels.
[3] He spoke to God.
[4] See preceding note. He begged the Shechinah to remain until he discharged his duty of hospitality; thus he showed that the latter was more important even than attending upon the Shechinah.
[5] He asked Him to wait, as it were.

§ 35 [1] If this proof-text is correct, *pass not away,* etc., was a request that they should not go on but wait until he took leave of the Shechinah. Var. lec. quotes verse 33: *The Lord went His way, as soon as He had left off speaking to Abraham; [and Abraham returned to his place]*—after Abraham had taken leave and God had departed, he returned to the angels.
[2] Thinking them idolaters who worship the dust of their feet (see par. 42), he wished them first to remove that dust, and only after that should they enjoy his hospitality.
[3] He did not ask them to wash their feet *before* entering, as he did not object to their introducing the object of their idolatrous worship into his home.

favor in thy sight, pass not away, I pray thee, from thy servant. [4]Let now a little water be fetched, and

COMMENTARY

to man): it was addressed to his guests (hence non-sacred), and at the same time a petition to God (hence sacred) that they might accept his hospitality.[33] **pass not. a.** He spoke to the chief, on behalf of all.[34] **b.** He spoke only to him whom he perceived to be on his way to Sodom, for the other two showed clearly their intention of staying (one was to give the tidings of Isaac's birth, and the other to heal his wound).[35] **c.** Since this was a *negative* request the plural would be inappropriate, as it would only indicate that they should not *all* go on, whereas he desired that not even one should go.[36] **d.** He addressed each separately, as each came near to him.[37] **e.** He addressed them collectively, as one company.[38] **[4]Let now...be fetched.** By a servant: I have plenty of servitors, so you need

ANTHOLOGY

the desires of the disciples that follow him. This we learn from our text.[1]

SER 12, ancient MS. T.S. 18, 51.

37. Pass not away, I pray you, from your servant.

Some called themselves servants, and the Holy One, blessed is He, called them servants too. Others called themselves servants, but the Almighty did not call them servants. Some did not call themselves servants, but the Almighty did. Abraham called himself a servant, as we see in our text. The Holy One, blessed is He, called him a servant too, as it says, *for My servant Abraham's sake* (26:24).

Sifre Vaethchanan 27. T.S. 18, 52.

38. PASS NOT AWAY, I PRAY YOU, FROM YOUR SERVANT. Scripture writes, *With the loving Thou dost show Thyself loving* (Ps. 18:26). R. Judah referred the verse to Abraham. Because he showed love, the Holy One, blessed is He, showed him love. And when did he show love? When he said, *"Pass not away, I pray you, from your servant."*[1]

Lev. R. 11, 4. T.S. 18, 53.

39. Let now a little water be brought.

He was requited measure for measure. Abraham said, *Let now a little water be brought.*

Therefore the Holy One, blessed is He, gave his children the well in the wilderness, whence flowed water through the whole camp of Israel and watered the desolation, as it says, *The well ... [flowed] from Bamoth to the valley ... which looks down upon the desolation* (Num. 21:20).

Said the Almighty to him: "You said, *Let now a little water be brought*: By your life! I will repay your children for it in the wilderness, in the Land [Eretz Israel], and in the Messianic future." Thus: *Then sang Israel this song: "Spring up, O well—sing ye unto it"* (ibid. 17-8)—here you have the wilderness. In the Land: *For the Lord your God brings you into a good land, a land of brooks of water* (Deut. 8:7). In the Messianic future: *And it shall come to pass in that day, that the living waters shall go out from Jerusalem* (Zech. 14:8).

"Again, you said, *And wash your feet*: By your life! I will reward your descendants for it." In the wilderness: *Then I washed you with water* (Ezek. 16:9). In the Land: *Wash you, make you clean* (Isa. 1:16). In the future: *When the Lord shall have washed away the filth of the daughters of Zion* (ibid. 4:4).

"You said, *And recline yourselves under the tree*: As you live, I will requite your children for it." In the wilderness: *He spread a cloud*

§ 36 [1] The passage is obscure. The proof-text is apparently first used to show that a man should court the presence of scholars, as Abraham courted the angels (who are in the same category). The text is not intended to prove the inadvisability of associating with the ignorant. It must now be assumed that *"my lord,"* etc., refers to the angels. However, the second inference assumes it to be addressed to God: he requested that He pass not on, but permit him to leave Him, as it were, while he attended to the desire of his guests, the angels, who in their relationship to God are as disciples to their master.

§ 38 [1] He then showed his love for his fellow-creatures.

wash your feet, and recline your-

COMMENTARY

not fear that you will put me to any trouble.[39] **a little.** Since it is still morning and you will continue your journey, you do not need a thorough wash, but just enough to cool your feet; for this a little water will suffice, to provide which is no trouble at all. Further, it is good manners to belittle one's gift.[40] **recline yourselves. a.** For your meal [they used to eat reclining].[41] **b.** While the meal

ANTHOLOGY

for a screen (Ps. 105:39). In the Land: *You shall dwell in booths* (Lev. 23:42).[1] In the Messianic future: *And there shall be a pavilion for a shadow in the day-time from the heat* (Isa. 4:6).

> T. Sot. 4; Gen. R. 48, 10.
> T.S. 18, 54. 56.

40. LET NOW A LITTLE WATER BE BROUGHT. Rab Judah said, quoting Rab: Whatever Abraham *himself* did for the angels, the Holy One, blessed is He, *Himself* did for his descendants. But whatever Abraham did through a servant, the Almighty did for his descendants through a servant. E.g., *let now a little water be brought*—therefore God bade Moses, *And you shall smite the rock, and there shall come water out of it, that the people may drink* (Exod. 17:6).[1]

> B.M. 86b. T.S. 18, 55.

41. LET NOW A LITTLE WATER BE BROUGHT. "You said, *Let . . . be brought*: as a reward I will give your descendants the precept of the Passover sacrifice"; as it says, *They shall take* [same root] *for themselves every man a lamb* [for a sacrifice] (Exod. 12:3). "You said to them, *na* (AJV: now): I will give your children the precept of the Passover," of which it

is written, *Eat not of it* na (AJV: *raw*) (*ibid.* 9).[1] "You said, *a little*: I will drive out their enemies little by little"; as it says, *By little and little I will drive them out from before you* (*ibid.* 23:30). "You said, *water*: I will give them a well of water in the wilderness"; as it says, *Spring up, O well* (Num. 21:17). "You said, *And wash your feet*: I will wash them from all uncleanness"; as it says, *When the Lord shall have washed away the filth of the daughters of Zion* (Isa. 4:4). "You said, *And recline yourselves under the tree*: I will give them the precept of *sukkah* (booths)," as it is written, *Go forth to the mount, and fetch olive branches . . . and branches of thick trees, to make booths* (Neh. 8:15).[2]

"Again, you said, *Let . . . water be brought*: with those very words I will redeem you from Egypt"; as it says, *And I will take you to Me for a people* (Exod. 6:7). "You said, *na*: with that very word will I rebuke your descendants,"[3] as it says, *Come now* (na), *and let us reason together*, etc. (Isa. 1:18).

Abraham brought water before the angels, as our text states. It continues further, *And Abraham ran to the herd, and fetched a calf tender and good* (verse 7). Said the Holy One, blessed is He, to him: "Even so shall your descendants purify themselves: they will pour

---

§ 39   [1] The two verses quoted, like the next, indicate the same protection and grateful shade which Abraham now offered to his visitors.

§ 40   [1] Thus God gave his descendants water through an intermediary—Moses. Midrash Hahefetz comments: Abraham ordered water to be fetched because it is unfitting for a great man and a prophet to bring water himself. Sefer Hasidim p. 491 (Ms) writes: Why did he not say, I will fetch water, and wash your feet? Because one may not deliberately create a false impression, and Abraham knew that they would not permit him to do this himself. But he did say, "And I will fetch a morsel of bread" (verse 5), because it is the host's duty to break bread and recite the benediction. These comments justify Abraham's action. It is clear, however, that the present passage criticised him: complete hospitality requires a personal effort, which does not affect any man's dignity.

§ 41   [1] God's precepts are not a burden but a privilege.
    [2] It is strange that the explicit precept in Lev. 23:42 (*you shall dwell in booths*) is not quoted. Perhaps the present is quoted because here it relates (verses 16 *et sqq.*) that they did actually perform the precept.
    [3] God's rebuke too is a privilege, for it may lead to reconciliation with Him.

selves under the tree. ⁵And I will

COMMENTARY

was being prepared for them they could enjoy the

shade of the tree in front of his tent (see v. 1).[42] **the tree.** The well-known tree in the plain of Mamre.[43] **recline . . . under the tree. a.** I do not ask you into the tent, lest you fear that it would entail too much trouble.[44] **b.** I cannot ask you in

ANTHOLOGY

the ashes of the red heifer into water, besprinkle and so purify themselves."

He bade them, *Wash your feet.* The Holy One, blessed is He, assured his descendants that He would wash them of their iniquities and forgive their sins every year, as it says, *And this shall be an everlasting statute to you, to make atonement for the children of Israel because of all their sins once in the year* (Lev. 16:34).

Tan. Vayyera 4; Tan. Y. *ibid.* 5; PR 14; Midrash Hahefetz. T.S. 18, 57 and note.

42. Let now a little water be brought, and wash your feet.

R. Yannai b. R. Ishmael commented: They answered him, "Do you suspect us of being Arabs, who worship the dust of their feet?[1] Ishmael has already issued from you."[2]

B.M. 86b. T.S. 18, 58.

43. LET NOW A LITTLE WATER BE BROUGHT, AND WASH. After that *I will bring a morsel of bread.* Hence we learn that bread may not be eaten without first washing the hands.

Midrash Habiur. T.S. 18, 60.

44. And recline yourselves under the tree.

He had planted trees for travelers, that they might congregate there, as it says, *And Abraham planted an* eshel (AJV: *a tamarisk-tree*) *in Beer-sheba* (21:33). Some interpret *eshel* as an abbreviation of *achilah* (food), *shethiah* (drink), and *l'wiyah* (companionship).[1]

Midrash Hahefetz. T.S. 18, 63.

45. AND RECLINE YOURSELVES UNDER THE TREE. [As a reward for providing shade for these wayfarers] the Holy One, blessed is He, gave his descendants seven clouds—four on the four sides of their encampment in the wilderness, one above them, the cloud of the Shechinah among them, and the pillar of cloud which went before them, leveling the heights and raising the valleys, slaying snakes and scorpions, burning the briars and thorns, and straightening the path before them.

T. Sot. 4. T.S. 18, 61.

46. AND RECLINE YOURSELVES UNDER THE TREE. "Tree" is an allusion to the Torah, which is described as *a tree of life to them that lay hold upon her* (Prov. 3:18). It is therefore fitting that when guests visit a man, he should entertain them with a Torah discourse.

Or Haafelah. T.S. 18, 62.

47. AND RECLINE YOURSELVES UNDER THE TREE. R. Ananiel b. R. Sason said: The Holy One, blessed is He, declared: When I desire it, an angel, who is a third of the world,[1] stretches out his hand from heaven and touches the earth, as it says, *And the form of a hand was put forth, and I was taken by a lock of my head* (Ezek. 8:3).[2] Yet when I wished, I had three of them sit under a tree, as it says, *And recline yourselves under the tree.*

Exod. R. 3, 7. T.S. 18, 54.

48. AND RECLINE YOURSELVES UNDER THE TREE. Wherever Abraham came to live he planted a tree. But it never grew up properly, save when he dwelt in Canaan. Through that

§ 42 [1] Therefore you bid us wash our feet, because you do not desire us to bring it into your house, seeing that it is the object of idolatrous worship.
[2] He will be an idolater—therefore do not imply that others are idolaters.
§ 44 [1] He offered all these to wayfarers. Companionship here means to escort them on their travels.
§ 47 [1] This was an ancient tradition.
[2] Thus the angel's hand reached from heaven down to earth, where the prophet stood.

fetch a morsel of bread, and stay ye your heart; after that ye shall

because there are sick persons in the tent, still suffering pain from their circumcision. Or: because I

ANTHOLOGY

tree he knew who served the Almighty and who was an idol-worshiper. For the tree would spread its branches and grant grateful shade to the former; but would recoil from the latter, draw in its branches and point heavenward. In this way Abraham recognized the idolater, and earnestly harangued him, until he accepted the true faith. In the same way the tree accepted the clean, but spurned the unclean; perceiving this Abraham purified the latter with water. At the foot of this tree lay a well, whose water gushed up for him who was in need of purification, while at the same time the branches of the tree shrank away from him. So Abraham knew him to be unclean and in need of immediate purification. Otherwise its waters ran dry. By means of this Abraham knew. For that reason even when he invited the angels he bade them, *And recline yourselves under the tree*, his purpose being to test them. When he spoke of the tree he meant the Almighty, the life-giving Tree to all; thus he bade them, *Recline yourselves under the Tree*, and not under the protection of idols.

Zohar 1, 102b. T.S. 18, 67.

49. And I will bring a morsel of bread.

Say little and do much. Whence do we know that the righteous act thus? From Abraham. He said to the angels, "You will join me in a little bread," as our text states. Yet see how he treated them: he prepared three oxen[1] for them, and nine measures of fine meal.

ARN 13. T.S. 18, 68.

50. AND I WILL BRING A MORSEL OF BREAD. This teaches that with the same measure that a man metes out it is meted out to him. Abraham said, *And I will fetch a morsel of bread*. The Lord rewarded him by sending down manna for forty years, as it says, *Behold, I will rain down bread from heaven for you* (Exod. 16:4). Thus He rewarded him in the wilderness. He repaid him in the Holy Land too, as it says, *For the Lord your God brings you to a good land . . . a land of wheat and barley* (Deut. 8:7-8). In the Messianic era? —*He will be as a rich cornfield in the land*[1] (Ps. 72:16).

Gen. R. 48; Mechilta B'shallach 1. T.S. 18, 70-1.

51. AND I WILL BRING A MORSEL OF BREAD. R. Isaac said: We find in the Torah, the Prophets, and the Writings that bread is food for the heart. In the Torah we have our present text: *And I will fetch a morsel of bread, and refresh your hearts*. In the Prophets: *Stay your heart with a morsel of bread* (Judg. 19:5). In the Writings: *And bread that stays man's heart* (Ps. 104:15).

Gen. R. 48. T.S. 18, 69.

52. And stay your hearts.

R. Aha said: For "hearts" Scripture does not employ the usual form, *l'bab'chem*, but *lib'chem*;[1] this proves that angels are free from the Evil Impulse.[2] R. Hiyya had a similar view, for commenting on the verse, *Turn your hearts to the dance*[3] (Ps. 48:14), he observed: Scripture employs the shorter form, *lib'chem*,

§ 49   [1] See par. 70.
§ 50   [1] Here lies the fitness of the reward; for his hospitality with bread—made from wheat—his descendants received a land of wheat.
§ 52   [1] A shorter form, which is regarded as a limitation.
    [2] The longer form implies two hearts—for good and for evil. The shorter implies one only—to do good without thought of evil.
    [3] AJV: *Mark ye well* (lit., put your heart to) *her ramparts* (*l'helah*). He, however, read it *l'holah*, deriving it from *m'hol*, a dance, and makes it allude to the life of happiness—a dance, as it were—in the Messianic era.

pass on; forasmuch as ye are come to your servant." And they said: "So do, as thou hast said." [6]And

COMMENTARY

do not wish to detain you too long.[45] [5]**foreasmuch as ye are come to your servant. a.** Divine Providence has sent you to me at meal-time: it must be in order that you should eat here and honor me with your company.[46] **b.** Since you have turned aside from the road to me and it is meal-time, this must certainly have been your purpose.[47] **So do.** (The verb is in the future). May you always be able to offer such hospitality.[48] **as thou hast said. a.** Viz., a morsel of bread will suffice.[49] **b.** Let us

ANTHOLOGY

not *l'bab'chem*: this proves that the Evil Impulse will not return to man in the Messianic era.

Gen. R. 48. T.S. 18, 72.

53. After that you shall pass on.

R. Isaac said: The textual readings as laid down by the Soferim[1] and their embellishments go back to Moses at Sinai.[2] An example of the latter is our text: *After that you shall pass on.*[3]

Ned. 37b. T.S. 18, 73.

54. Forasmuch as you are come to your servant.

R. Joshua b. R. Nehemiah interpreted: From the very day that the Almighty created you you were destined to visit me, for the phrase *ki al ken* (forasmuch) has the same meaning as in the text, *So (ken) be the Lord with you* (Exod. 10:10).[1]

Gen. R. 48. T.S. 18, 75.

55. FORASMUCH AS YOU ARE COME TO YOUR SERVANT. It was Abraham's invariable practice to entertain all wayfarers with food and drink, never allowing a single person to pass without enjoying his hospitality. When he described himself as "your servant," he meant, I am happy to entertain you.[1]

Midrash Hahefetz; Lekach Tob; MhG. T.S. 18, 76 and note.

56. So do, as you have said.

Why did they accept Abraham's invitation immediately, whereas in the case of Lot it is written, *And he urged them greatly* (19:3)? Said R. Eleazar: From this we learn that you may decline the invitation of an inferior person, but not that of a great man.

B.M. 87a. T.S. 18, 77.

57. SO DO, AS YOU HAVE SAID. From this we learn that a guest must not thwart his host; also that you honor a person by acceding to his wish.

Midrash Habiur. T.S. 18, 79.

58. SO DO, AS YOU HAVE SAID. A guest must not give a child anything of what is placed before him, for it says, *So do, as you have said.*[1]

MhG MS. T.S. 18, 81.

59. SO DO, AS YOU HAVE SAID. "We neither eat nor drink," they replied. "But since you do, *so do yourself, as you have said*; and may you repeat it one day in celebration of the birth of a son." Thus Scripture does not write, So will we do, but *So do*, implying: Do what you will, and it will count as though we had partaken of your hospitality.

Gen. R. 48; MhG. T.S. 18, 78. 80.

§ 53 [1] The Scribes, whose work included the determining of the exact text, both in the orthography and in the reading, of the Bible.
[2] Lit., are a *halachah* (law) of Moses from Sinai.
[3] The meaning is not clear. Possibly "after" is superfluous, for only a *waw* ("and") is necessary; but it was added to "embellish" the style, as it were. Others hold that their punctuation is meant; for the text could also read: And stay your hearts after ye shall have passed on. See Nedarim, Sonc. ed., p. 117, n. 5.
§ 54 [1] I.e., you have passed so—for this very purpose of fulfilling your destiny.
§ 55 [1] Lit., who rejoices in good deeds.
§ 58 [1] Only you can offer us food; we may not offer one another of your hospitality, or to anyone else. Cf. Hul. 94a: Guests may not share their portions with their host's son or daughter without his permission.

Abraham hastened into the tent unto Sarah, and said: "Make ready quickly three measures of fine meal, knead

COMMENTARY

recline under the tree and then pass on, and do not press us to come into your house.[50] [6]**hastened.** Himself: he did not send a servant.[51] **unto Sarah. a.** In spite of her age he desired her to knead the dough herself as a mark of respect to their guests.[52]

b. That she should order her servants to prepare the meal.[53] **Make ready quickly.** Because the angels were anxious to continue their journey.[54] **three measures,** etc. **a.** This was a large quantity. Possibly other members of his household or some friends dined with them. The Heb. may also mean: sift three measures of ordinary, coarse flour (*kemah*) to obtain fine flour (*soleth*), and use the latter; that, of course, would be much less.[55] **fine meal. a.** The coarse flour (*kemah*) for cooking and the fine (*soleth*) for cakes.[56] **b.** Wheaten flour.[57] **c.** Sift the coarse flour to obtain fine.[58] **d.** Normally only coarse flour was used for cakes, the fine meal being

ANTHOLOGY

60. Abraham hastened into the tent.

Scripture writes, *The king is held captive in the tresses* (Song 7:6). The Holy One, blessed is He, declared to the Community of Israel: I am, if one might say so, held captive by you.[1] Why do you merit this? As a reward for Abraham's eager hospitality to Me,[2] as it says, *Abraham hastened into the tent ... and Abraham ran to the herd* (verse 7). See how Abraham and his household loved good deeds. When the three men appeared, *he ran to meet them* (verse 2), and now *he* hastened *into the tent*.[3] This teaches that the righteous always act with speed.

Midrash Hahefetz; Lekach Tob. T.S. 18, 82-3 and note.

61. Into the tent to Sarah.

This illustrates the text, *All glorious is the king's daughter within* (Ps. 45:14).[1]

PZ. T.S. 18, 85.

62. Make ready quickly.

Himself eager, he fired her too with eagerness for good deeds.

Lekach Tob. T.S. 18, 83 note.

63. Three measures meal, fine meal.

Our text teaches that she baked nine measures: "*Three*" has its plain meaning; "*meal*" implies another three, making six; "*fine meal*," yet another three, totaling nine in all.

This is the view of R. Abiathar. She baked three measures of plain cakes, three of honey cakes, and three of pastries.[1] But our Rabbis maintain that she baked three measures in all, one of each of these three.

Yet another explanation of the words, "*meal, fine meal*," is that she took three measures of coarse meal, which yielded one of fine meal.

Rab observed: This shows that a woman is more niggardly toward guests than a man.[2]

ARN 13; Gen. R. 48; B.M. 87a; PZ. T.S. 18, 86-9.

64. Knead it, and make cakes.

The narrative continues, *And he took curd, and milk, and the calf* (verse 8)—but no bread! Said Ephraim Makshaah,[1] a disciple of R. Meir, in his teacher's name: Abraham ate *hullin*[2] only when undefiled,[3] and on that day Sarah had her menses.[4] Our Rabbis hold that he gave them bread too. If he gave them even

§ 60 [1] Bound to answer your prayers. See par. 8, n. 1.
  [2] Lit., for Abraham's running before Me—hospitality to God's creatures is as hospitality to Himself.
  [3] Cf. par. 28.
§ 61 [1] Sarah modestly kept within the tent.
§ 63 [1] The rendering is conjectural.
  [2] Apparently he divides the verse: Abraham asked her to prepare fine meal, but she used coarse.
§ 64 [1] Probably a place-name.
  [2] Unsanctified food, in contrast to *t'rumah*, the priestly due.
  [3] As though it were consecrated, though *hullin* may be eaten when ritually unclean.
  [4] Thereby defiling the bread she had baked.

it, and make cakes." ⁷And Abraham ran unto the herd, and fetched a

COMMENTARY

sifted out first. Here, however, he told her to use it unsifted, because their guests were in a hurry.[59]

knead it, and make cakes. a. But the baking was done by a man.[60] b. The whole operation, grinding, kneading and baking, was done by women, as was common in the East.[61] cakes. Thin, for quick baking.[62] ⁷ran. a. Having spoken of a morsel of bread only, and seeing that they were in a hurry, he had to make haste, as he wished to do more than he had offered. This is related in his praise.[63]

ANTHOLOGY

what he had not offered, as it says, *And he took curd, and milk, and the calf which he had dressed, and set it before them* (verse 8); how much more what he had promised! The bread ("cakes") is not mentioned, because it is taken for granted.

B.M. 87a; Gen. R. 48; MA. T.S. 18, 90. 109 and note.

65. KNEAD IT, AND MAKE CAKES. Isaac was born in Nisan.[1] How do we know this? When the angels visited Abraham, he bade Sarah, Make *cakes* [i.e., of unleavened bread], because it was the Passover season. Now, the angel promised, *I will certainly return to you when the season comes round;*[2] and, lo, Sarah your wife shall have a son (verse 10).

In bidding her to make *cakes* he intimated that his descendants would make cakes when they departed from Egypt; so it is written, *And they baked unleavened* cakes *of the dough which they had brought out of Egypt* (Exod. 12:39).

Hence Abraham insisted that they should not be leavened, lest they be forbidden.[3]

PR 6; Lekah Tob. T.S. 18, 91 and note. 92.

66. KNEAD IT, AND MAKE CAKES. [Knead it yourself,] that you may have the credit for this hospitality. Thus the Scriptural text, *She girds her loins with strength and makes her arms strong* (Prov. 31:17), applies to Sarah, who ignored all her servants and baked the cakes herself.

[Centuries later Jeremiah rebuked the women of his time:] "Sarah kneaded dough and made cakes for the angels; but you women *knead dough and make cakes to the queen of heaven* (Jer. 7:18). Why do you not follow your ancestors' example? Oh, your perverseness!"

PR 31; Tan. Y. T.S. 18, 94 and note.

67. **Abraham ran to the herd.**

Hence we learn that the righteous run to perform good deeds.

"You ran after the herd" [said the Almighty to him]: "by your life! I will requite your descendants." Thus it says, *And there went out a wind from the Lord, and brought across quails from the sea* (Num. 11:31). This was in the wilderness. How do we know that He rewarded them in Eretz Israel? From the verse, *Now the children of Reuben and the children of Gad had a very great multitude of cattle; and when they saw the land of Jazer, and the land of Gilead, that, behold, the place was a place for cattle* [they requested and received it from Moses] (*ibid.* 32:1 *seq.*).[1] In the Messianic era?—*And it shall come to pass in that day, that a man shall rear a young cow and two sheep* (Isa. 7:21).

Rab Judah said, quoting Rab: Whatever Abraham himself did for the angels, the Holy One, blessed is He, Himself did for his children; but whatever he did through a servant, the Almighty too did for his children through

§ 65 [1] The first month of the year, generally corresponding to about mid-March-April. Passover commences on the fifteenth of the month.
[2] I.e., at this same time next year.
[3] Even though the prohibition had not yet been proclaimed. There is a tradition that Abraham fulfilled all the precepts of the Bible even before they were given (Yoma 28b); see par. 77.
§ 67 [1] This land on the east of the Jordan (Transjordan) was thus the first to be settled by the Israelites as part of Eretz Israel. Cf. pars. 39, 40 for this entire passage.

calf tender and good, and gave it unto the servant; and he hastened to dress it. ⁸And he took curd, and

COMMENTARY

b. Although possessing many servants and still weak

from circumcision, he ran himself in his eagerness to exercise hospitality.⁶⁴ **hastened.** Either, the servant; or, Abraham hastened to the servant.⁶⁵ ⁸**curd. a.** Only the food which he had not offered is mentioned, the bread being understood.⁶⁶ **b.** The verse may be understood as meaning that the guests were given curd and milk to slake their thirst and refresh themselves (cf. Judges 4:19), and then followed the

ANTHOLOGY

a servant. Thus, since *Abraham* [himself] *ran to the herd, there went forth a wind* from the Lord, etc.

> B.M. 86b; Gen. R. 48, 10; MA. T.S. 18, 97-9.

68. ABRAHAM RAN TO THE HERD. R. Levi said: He ran to anticipate that people of which we read, *Ephraim is a heifer well trained, that loves to thresh* (Hos. 10:11).¹

> Gen. R. 48, 13. T.S. 18, 95.

69. ABRAHAM RAN TO THE HERD. Abraham cultivated the friendship of the common people.¹ When the angels appeared he thought them ordinary guests, yet he ran to greet them. He desired to offer them a substantial meal, and requested Sarah to prepare it. While kneading the dough Sarah became menstruous;² therefore he did not offer them the cakes. He ran to fetch a young calf, which fled into the cave of Machpelah. He followed, and found Adam and Eve sleeping on their couches, candles burning above them, enveloped in fragrance as of incense. Therefore did he covet the possession of the Cave of Machpelah for a burial place.³

> PRE 36. T.S. 18, 96.

70. **Abraham ran to the herd, and brought a calf tender and good.**

Rab Judah said, quoting Rab: "A calf" means one; "tender" is another; and "good"

is a third. (Others interpret "to the herd" as one, totaling four in all.) ...But why three? One would have sufficed. Said R. Hanan b. Abba: He wished to give them three tongues with *hardal*.¹

Whoever possesses these three qualities shows himself a true disciple of our father Abraham, viz., generosity, humility, and modesty. Abraham displayed the first in the present case: "a calf" (lit., a young one of the herd) means a three-year old animal; "tender," a two-year old; while "good" refers to a yearling.

> B.M. 86b; ARN 13; ARN (Codex 2) 45. T.S. 18, 100-2.

71. ABRAHAM RAN TO THE HERD, AND BROUGHT A CALF TENDER AND GOOD. [For the consecration of Aaron, Moses was bidden,] *Take one young bullock*¹ (Exod. 29:1). This symbolized Abraham, of whom our text tells that he *ran to the herd.*

Again, Scripture says, *On this man will I look,* [saith the Lord,] *on him that is poor and of a contrite spirit, and trembles at My word* (Isa. 66:2). Who trembled at God's word? Abraham, who hastened to obey God's command to circumcise himself. If you want proof that the text alludes to Abraham, see what follows: *He kills an ox (ibid.* 3), which applies to Abraham, as we see in our text.

> Tan. Y. Vayyera 20; T'tsaveh 10. T.S. 18, 104 and note.

---

§ 68 ¹ His running to the herd symbolized in advance to his descendants atonement through sacrifice.
§ 69 ¹ Lit., had made a covenant with the people of the earth—*am ha-aretz.*
 ² Cf. par. 64.
 ³ See Gen. 23:8-20.
§ 70 ¹ A certain **relish**, esteemed as a great delicacy. Abraham thus showed his lavish hospitality.
§ 71 ¹ Lit., *one ox, son of herd.*

milk, and the calf which he had dressed, and set it before them; and he stood by them under the tree, and

COMMENTARY

meal proper, which consisted of the calf. This procedure would be quite in accord with the dietary laws.[67] **he stood by them.** In the East, the host

ANTHOLOGY

72. And gave it to the lad.

He gave it to his son Ishmael, to train him in good deeds.

[Others maintain that] it was Eliezer.[1] Hence we learn that ritual killing, when performed by slaves, is valid.[2]

ARN 13; Midrash Hahefetz; Midrash Habiur. T.S. 18, 105-7.

73. And he took curd, and milk, and the calf which he had dressed, and set it before them.

Each as it became ready.[1]

[Another interpretation:] From this we learn that the curd and milk must precede the meat, [but may not follow it].[2]

B.M. 86b; Midrash Hahafetz. T.S. 18, 110-11.

74. And he took curd, and milk, and the calf which he had dressed, and set it before them; and he stood over them under the tree.

The School of R. Ishmael taught: Because he did three things he was thrice rewarded. Because he offered curd and milk his descendants received the manna in the wilderness. Because he stood over them they were favored with the pillar of cloud which guided them. While as a reward for his saying, *"Let now a little water be brought"* (verse 4), they were granted Miriam's well.[1]

R. Joshua b. Karcha taught: The Holy One, blessed is He, said to Moses: Israel did not deserve the manna, but should have suffered hunger, thirst, and utter destitution. But what can I do? I must grant them the reward due to Abraham, My beloved, for his hospitality to My ministering angels.

Again, Scripture says, *For the churning of milk brings forth curd* (Prov. 30:33). This alludes to Edom [= Esau; Gen. 36:1], who was privileged to found a kingdom for the sake of Abraham, who entertained the angels with curd and milk.

We learn from this that a man is requited measure for measure. Because Abraham stood over them, the Almighty cast His protection over his descendants in Egypt, that the plague should not smite them, as it says, *The Lord will pass over the door, and will not suffer the destroyer to come into your houses to smite you* (Exod. 12:23).

[Said He to Abraham,] "By your life! I will requite you"; as it says, *And the Lord went before them by day in a pillar of cloud* (*ibid.* 13:21): thus He rewarded him in the wilderness. In Eretz Israel? *God stands in the congregation of God* (Ps. 82:1). In the Messianic future? *The breaker is gone up before them* (Micah 2:13).

B.M. 86b; Gen. R. 48, 10; Mechilta B'shallach 1; Mechilta of R. Simeon b. Yohai; Midrash Mishle 30, 13. T.S. 18, 112 and note. 114-5.

§ 72 [1] Two different sources are combined here. However, the two views are not necessarily mutually exclusive, in view of the statement in par. 70 that he took *three* animals; hence their preparation may have been divided.
[2] Eliezer was a slave; hence he would not have allowed him to prepare the animal if his killing were not ritually valid to make it fit for food (see par. 77).

§ 73 [1] Two interpretations are possible: (1) He offered them curd, milk, and the calf, in that order, as each was made ready. (2) In par. 70 it is stated that he prepared *three* animals, yet here the text states that he took "the calf" (sing.). The answer is given that he set each calf before them as it became ready.
[2] In accordance with the dietary laws: meat may be eaten after milk, but not *vice versa*.

§ 74 [1] According to tradition (Taan. 9a) a well followed the Israelites in the wilderness, for Miriam's sake, which left them when she died. For Scripture relates, *The people abode in Kadesh; and Miriam died there, and was buried there. And there was no water for the congregation* (Num. 20:1-2). Cf. par. 39 for the whole passage.

they did eat. ⁹And they said unto him: "Where is Sarah thy wife?" And he said: "Behold, in the tent."

does not sit with his guests, but stands and attends to their needs.⁶⁸ ⁹**Where is Sarah?** It was a rhetorical question, serving as an opening for their

ANTHOLOGY

75. He stood over them.

Rab Judah said, quoting Rab: Whatever Abraham *himself* did for the ministering angels, the Holy One, blessed is He, *Himself* did for his descendants. Because *he stood by them under the tree* [God promised Moses,] *"Behold, I will stand before you there upon the rock in Horeb"* (Exod. 17:6).

B.M. 86b. T.S. 18, 113.

76. HE STOOD OVER THEM. But earlier *they stood over him* (verse 2)? Before he did his duty by them, they stood over him;¹ but after he had done his duty [by his hospitality], he stood over them, inspiring them with awe: Michael trembled before him, Gabriel trembled before him.²

Gen. R. 48, 14; T.S. 18, 116.

77. HE STOOD OVER THEM. Rab—others say, R. Assi—said: Abraham fulfilled [every precept,] even *erube tabshilin*;¹ some say, even the prohibition of mixing meat and milk. They prove this from our text, *And he took curd, and milk, and the calf which he had dressed, and set it before them; and he stood over them,* lest they mix the meat with the milk.²

MhG Tol'doth 26, 5. T.S. 18, 117.

78. He stood over them under the tree (etz).

God bade Moses, *"And you shall make the altar of acacia-wood"* (etz) (Exod. 27:1).

This was a reward for Abraham's hospitality, as our text says, *He stood over them under the tree.*¹

Tan. T'rumah 7. T.S. 18, 118.

79. They ate.

R. Tanhum b. Hanilai said: When in Rome do as Rome does.¹ For Moses ascended on high, where there is no eating, and did not eat bread, while the ministering angels descended below, where men eat and drink, and ate. They ate! Can you really think so? Say rather, they seemed to eat and drink, removing each course in turn.

Abraham thus showed kindness to the angels, who did not really need it. How did the Almighty requite his children? The manna descended for them, the well came up, quails appeared, clouds of glory surrounded them, and the pillar of cloud preceded them. Now, if the Almighty thus requited the children of one who showed kindness to those who did not need it, how much the more will He reward when kindness is shown to one who does need it.

B.M. 86b; Gen. R. 48, 14; Lev. R. 34, 8. T.S. 18, 120 and note. 121.

80. THEY ATE. I.e., those who could eat [not the angels] ate, for Abraham, Ishmael, Aner, Eshcol and Mamre were present too.

MhG. T.S. 18, 124.

§ 76 ¹ As though his superiors.
² When man does his duty, he is superior even to angels.
§ 77 ¹ Lit., the combining of dishes. Cooking, baking, etc., are permitted on festivals, but only for the festival. When a festival falls on the eve of the Sabbath, a ritual ceremony, known as *erube tabshilin*, is performed, whereby one may cook, etc., on the festival for the Sabbath too. This ceremony consists of setting aside two dishes, e.g., bread and cooked fish, and declaring that in virtue thereof food needed on the Sabbath may be prepared on the festival.
² See, however, par. 82 for a different view.
§ 78 ¹ This is based on the word *etz* (which means both tree and wood) in both texts.
§ 79 ¹ Lit., a man should never deviate from the usual practice.

ANTHOLOGY

81. THEY ATE. Whoever maintains that the angels did not eat there is wrong. For the sake of that righteous man and the trouble he had taken the Holy One, blessed is He, opened their mouths and they ate, as our text states.[1]

TDER 13. T.S. 18, 122.

82. THEY ATE. When the Holy One, blessed is He, desired to write [the Ten Commandments] a second time, the angels would not let Him, [arguing, "But yesterday they transgressed its laws!"] Said He to them: "Do you then fulfill the Torah? A mere infant in Israel observes it more than you do! When he goes out of school and has meat and milk to eat, will he have the milk until he has washed his hands from the meat?[1] But when you were sent to Abraham he brought you meat and milk together, and you ate"; as it says, *and he took curd, and milk, and the calf which he had dressed . . . and they ate.*[2]

PR 25. T.S. 18, 123.

83. **They said to him (*elaw*): "Where is Sarah your wife?"**

The *alef, yod,* and *waw* in *elaw* are dotted, but not the *lamed.*[1] Said R. Simeon b. Eleazar: Wherever you find the [normally] written letters of the text exceeding the dotted ones, you interpret the former; where the dotted letters are more numerous you interpret them. Here that the dotted letters exceed the undotted, you interpret the dotted, which read *ayo,* meaning, Where is Abraham? R. Akiba said: Just as they asked, Where is Sarah, so they also asked Sarah, "Where is Abraham?"[2]

It was taught on R. Jose's authority: Why is the *ayo* in the word *elaw* dotted? The Torah gives a lesson in manners, that a man should enquire after his host's well-being. But Samuel said: You must not enquire about a woman's well-being at all? When it is asked of her own husband it is different.

Gen. R. 48, 15; B.M. 87a. T.S. 18, 125-6.

84. THEY SAID TO HIM: "WHERE IS SARAH YOUR WIFE?" All three asked, for had one only asked he would have cast suspicion upon himself. Subsequently, however, only Michael gave him the good tidings [that she would bear a son].

Sechel Tob. T.S. 18, 133.

85. WHERE IS SARAH YOUR WIFE? You might think that they really did not know. Therefore the letters of *ayeh* (where) are dotted, to show that they did know, but asked the question in order to conceal from Abraham that they were angels,[1] lest they hinder him in his exercise of hospitality.[2]

ARN (Codex 2) 37. T.S. 18, 127.

86. WHERE IS SARAH YOUR WIFE? [When Jethro's daughters told him, "An Egyptian delivered us out of the hand of the shepherd,] *he said to his daughters: And where is he?* (Exod. 2:19-20), hinting, Perhaps he is of the seed of her concerning whom it was asked, *"Where is Sarah your wife?"* — that seed through whom the whole world will be blessed.

Midrash Abakir. T.S. 18, 128.

87. **"Where is Sarah your wife?" And he said: "Behold, in the tent."**

This teaches that Sarah was modest. Rab

---

§ 81   [1] This and the next par. disagree with the preceding. Zohar 1, 102a states: They certainly ate whatever Abraham offered them, in the sense of fire invisibly devouring fire.

§ 82   [1] Midrash T'hillim 8 reads: When he comes home and his mother offers him bread and cheese and meat, he says to her, "Today my teacher taught us, *You shall not seethe a kid in its mother's milk*" (Exod. 34:26).

      [2] This disagrees with the view in par. 77.

§ 83   [1] In this verse אליו (*elaw,* to him) is traditionally written אֵלָיו.

      [2] Probably in the sense of "How is he?"

§ 85   [1] Had they not asked he might have recognized them as supernatural beings, since ordinary visitors would enquire after their hostess as a matter of politeness.

      [2] Lit., not to hinder the [performance of God's] precepts. Had he immediately known them to be angels, he would have felt that they did not need hospitality.

21

10And He said: "I will certainly return unto thee when the season cometh round; and, lo, Sarah thy

tidings.[69] **10He said: "I,"** etc. The angel, speaking in God's name; hence "I" refers to God.[70] **when the season cometh round.** (Heb. *kaeth hayyah,*

ANTHOLOGY

Judah said, quoting Rab—others say, R. Isaac: The angels knew that the Matriarch Sarah was in her tent, but they asked in order to enhance her in her husband's eyes.[1] R. Jose b. R. Hanina said: They asked the question in order to send her the cup of blessing.[2]

[Reverting to her modesty:] Scripture writes, *Your wife shall be as a fruitful vine* (Ps. 128:3). When will she be so? When she keeps herself *in the innermost parts of your house* (*ibid.*), then shall *your children* [be] *like olive plants* (*ibid.*). So you find this in the case of Sarah too: when he said, *"Behold, in the tent,"* then *he* [the angel] *said: "I will certainly return to you when the season comes round; and, lo, Sarah your wife shall have a son."*

B.M. 86a; Midrash T'hillim 128:3. T.S. 18, 129. 134.

88. WHERE IS SARAH YOUR WIFE? Did not the celestial angels know that she was in the tent? No: for angels do not know what is happening in this world save what is necessary for their mission. This is proved by the text, *For I will pass through the land of Egypt . . . I am the Lord* (Ex. 12:12), which indicates that although the Holy One had many messengers and angels to perform His work, yet they would not have been able to distinguish between the sperms of the first-born and those

born after—only the Almighty Himself could do this.

Zohar 1, 101b.

89. HE SAID: "BEHOLD, IN THE TENT." *An Ammonite or a Moabite shall not enter* [i.e., marry] *into the assembly of the Lord* (Deut. 23:4): an Ammonite, but not an Ammonitess.[1] This deduction follows from the reason given by Scripture: *Because they met you not with bread and with water in the way, when you came out of Egypt* (*ibid.* 5)—it is for a man to go out and meet [travelers], not for a woman.[2] But the men should have met the men, and the women the women? . . . Here [in Babylon] they quote, *All glorious is the king's daughter within*[3] (Ps. 45:14). In the West [Eretz Israel] they quote—others ascribe it to R. Isaac:—*They said to him: "Where is Sarah your wife?" And he said: "Behold, in the tent."*[4]

Yeb. 77a. T.S. 18, 130.

90. BEHOLD, IN THE TENT. Because Sarah examined herself and found that she was menstruous,[1] she is called virtuous. The angel immediately seized the opportunity to ask Abraham, *"Where is Sarah your wife?"* When Abraham replied, *"Behold, in the tent,"* the angel assured him, *"I will certainly return to you when the*

§ 87 [1] By hinting at her modesty in staying in her tent when visitors arrived.
  [2] A cup of wine over which a blessing has been recited. This would be an act of politeness and good will.
§ 89 [1] She is not forbidden.
  [2] The women did nothing wrong; hence the prohibition does not apply to them.
  [3] A woman's honor requires her to remain within, and not go out to meet even her own sex.
  [4] The commentator Rebid Hazahab enumerates several laws which flow from this principle: i) If a man dies, leaving young sons and daughters, and his estate is not sufficient for both, the daughters must be provided for first, even if the sons have to go begging (B.B. 139b). ii) A woman has the precedence over a man in respect of clothing out of charity funds and redemption from captivity (end of Horayoth). iii) A woman may not be summoned to a court of law, but the court's clerk takes her deposition in her home. iv) She may not be publicly sworn, but only in private.
§ 90 [1] See par. 64.

ANTHOLOGY

season comes round; and, lo, Sarah your wife shall have a son."

> B'raitha Nid. 3, 2. T.S. 18, 135.

91. I will certainly return.

An angel does not perform two missions. Only Michael came to inform Sarah. For it does not say, We will return, but, *"I will certainly return."* Having performed his mission, he departed.

> Tan. Y. Vayyera 20. T.S. 18, 136.

92. I WILL CERTAINLY RETURN. From this we know that he was an angel, for a human being does not know when his time will come, that he should say, *"I will certainly return."*

Now, the prophet Elisha told the Shunammite, *"At this season, when the time comes round, you shall embrace a son"* (2 Kings 4:16), but he did not promise to return. An angel, who lives for ever, could make such a promise; but Elisha could not determine for himself that he would still be alive. In this spirit it is written, *And the prophets, do they live for ever* (Zech. 1:5)?

> Lekach Tob; Midrash Hahefetz. T.S. 18, 137 and note.

93. I WILL CERTAINLY RETURN. But we do not find that he kept his word and returned? The scholars went and questioned R. Ishmael and R. Hanina about it: Would you say that the angel who informed Sarah of Isaac's birth returned, or not? Said R. Hanina: We find that the angel did return, but that he is then given the name of the Lord, for which reason the Torah mentions it only indirectly. What is the source of that statement?—*The Lord remembered Sarah as he*—viz., the angel—*had said, and the Lord did to Sarah as He*—viz., the Holy One, blessed is He—*had spoken* (21:1).

R. Isaac commented: Surely it should have said, "He [God] will certainly return," seeing that the key which unlocks barrenness is in God's hand, and not in the hand of any messenger; as we learned: Three keys were not entrusted to any messenger, viz., those of childbirth, resurrection, and rain? Hence it must have been God Himself who stood over him and said, "I will certainly return."

[Another interpretation:] *He said: I will certainly return*: but nowhere do we find the angel returning to give Abraham these tidings? The real meaning, however, is that he informed him, *I will certainly return* when the child's life is in danger. When did this happen? When his father bound him on mount Moriah for a sacrifice. Then *the angel of the Lord called to him out of heaven, and said: . . . "Lay not your hand upon the lad"* (22:11-12). It was this very angel, who now returned to save Isaac, and thus he kept his promise.

> B'raitha Nid. 3, 2; Zohar 1, 102b; Likutim in Sefer Hapardes (Rashi) 44. T.S. 18, 138 and note.

94. I WILL CERTAINLY RETURN, etc. Thus Scripture writes, *And also the Glory of Israel will not lie* (1 Sam. 15:29). Said the Holy One, blessed is He: Shall I be less than a mortal? Elisha was but a mere mortal, yet because the Shunammite fed him, as it says, *And she constrained him to eat bread* (2 Kings 4:8), he told her, *"At this season, when the time comes round, you shall embrace a son"* (ibid. 16). This promise was fulfilled, as it says, *The woman conceived and bore a son at that season, when the time came round* (ibid. 17). How much more so then must I fulfill My promise which I made to Abraham! Therefore did Balaam declare, *God is not a man, that He should lie*[1] (Num. 23:19).

> AB 28. T.S. 18, 139.

95. I WILL CERTAINLY RETURN. They acted with good taste. Before Abraham invited them to dine they said nothing to him, lest he appear to have invited them on account of their tid-

---

§ 94 [1] Perhaps he renders (in view of the foregoing): Is God not [as trustworthy as] a man, that He should lie?— when men have kept their word.

wife shall have a son." And Sarah heard in the tent door, which was behind him.—[11]Now Abraham and Sarah were old, and well stricken in

COMMENTARY

lit., as the time that lives). **a.** This time next year.[71] **b.** At this season—Sarah will then be alive.[72] **c.** When you will all be alive.[73] **Sarah heard.** Having heard him enquire after her, she came near the opening of the tent to listen to what he had to say about her.[74] **behind him. a.** Viz., the angel; hence she heard what he said.[75] **b.** Had it not been behind him (the angel), modesty would have prevented her from standing there.[76] **c.** Therefore he did not tell her directly, as Elisha did the Shunammite (2 Kings 4:15f).[77] **[11]Now Abraham and Sarah,** etc. This verse is parenthetical, to explain why Sarah laughed.[78] **well stricken in age. a.** Lit., "entered into the days," i.e., into those days (old age) when man knows that he must go the way of all flesh. The expression denotes that old age now weighed heavily upon them.[79] **b.** Coming after "old" this means that they were well advanced in old age, i.e., *very* old.[80] **c.** This phrase, added to "old," indicates that they were old because of the long time ("days") they had lived, but had not

ANTHOLOGY

ings. But only after they ate did they give him these tidings.

> Zohar 1, 102a. T.S. 18, 144.

96. When the season comes round.

Zabdi b. Levi said: He made a mark on the wall and said to him, "When the sun reaches this next year she will be visited with child." As soon as the sun reached that point she was visited, as it says, *And the Lord remembered Sarah as He had said ... And Sarah conceived and bore Abraham a son* (21:1-2).

> Tan. Vayyera 13. T.S. 18, 140.

97. And, lo, Sarah your wife shall have a son.

Why not "and *you* shall have a son"? Because Isaac was indeed a son to Sarah, since it was on his account that she died, on his account she suffered anguish of soul until her life departed, and, further, for his sake she is exalted when the Holy One sits in judgment on the world, for on that day we read the Scriptural lesson, *And the Lord remembered Sarah as He had said*, (21:1), mentioning Sarah for the sake of Isaac.

> Zohar 1, 103a.

98. Sarah heard in the tent-door, and he was behind him.

"He" means Ishmael, who stood behind the angel, lest the latter be privately closeted with Sarah. On his [the angel's] looking backward he perceived a light shining out from behind him.[1] Another interpretation: *And he was behind him* refers to Abraham, who was behind the Shechinah.

> Gen. R. 48; Zohar 1, 103a. T.S. 18, 142.

99. Now Abraham and Sarah were old.

R. Johanan said: Since our text states that they were old, why repeat later, *Now Abraham was old* (Gen. 24:1)? The reason is that God restored him his youth; therefore, *Abraham was old* must be repeated.[1] R. Ammi said: In his present old age he still enjoyed virility; but in his later old age he lacked virility.

> Gen. R. 48. T.S. 18, 145.

§ 98 [1] The reading and meaning are doubtful. Sechel Tob reads: He (Abraham) was behind the angel, to protect Sarah, because they had appeared in the guise of Arabs, who are steeped in immorality. The first half of our text will have a similar meaning, save that Ishmael is substituted for Abraham. When Sarah came to listen to the angels, her radiant beauty lit up the place; and the angel thus perceived the light behind him. This reads *orah*, light. But possibly it reads *orah*, a guest (the two words are very similar in Hebrew). The interpretation will then be quite different: Sarah understood that this was the guest for whom she had prepared. However, *orah* is also a euphemism for a woman's menses. As stated above (par. 64), Sarah had become menstruous, and therefore stayed at a distance, lest she defile anything by her inadvertent touch. The meaning will then be (although it is difficult to give an exact rendering): *She* remained behind it (the tent), desiring to isolate herself, because her menstrual flow had come.

§ 99 [1] That was a second old age. The second verse refers to a later time.

age; it had ceased to be with Sarah after the manner of women.—¹²And Sarah laughed within herself, say-

COMMENTARY

aged prematurely.[81] **it had ceased to,** etc. She no longer menstruated, and was therefore incapable of child-bearing.[82] **manner. a.** Lit., path. Heb. *orach*. Another word for path is *derech*: the latter connotes the broad highway, whereas the former means a side lane, infrequently used. The phrase therefore means that not only the regular but even the irregular menses which are usual later in life had ceased. This explains why *derech* is used in describing Rachel's menses (31:35), since she was a young woman.[83] **b.** "The manner of women," which is to menstruate only in the youthful years, had "ceased" with her, i.e., did not operate in her case, for she *continued* even in old age. (These interpretations are in keeping with the statement in Anthology par. 64 that she menstruated on that very day).[84] ¹²**Sarah laughed within herself. a.** In disbelief, because she did not recognize the visitors as angels, but thought her informant a prophet (whose prophecy she disbelieved).[84a] **b.** Derisively, for the laughter

ANTHOLOGY

100. Now Abraham and Sarah were old. The Bible ordained, *And you shall take you on the first day* [of the feast of Tabernacles] *the fruit of a glorious tree* (Lev. 23:40). This symbolized Sarah, whom the Holy One, blessed is He, made glorious with a good old age, as our text states.

Lev. R. 30. T.S. 18, 146.

101. Now Abraham and Sarah were old. From the beginning of the Book until here no man showed signs of old age, until Abraham came and pleaded: "Sovereign of the Universe! When a man and his son come into a place together, none knows whom to honor; if, however, Thou wilt crown the former with the venerability of old age, one will know whom to honor." Said the Holy One, blessed is He, to him: "You ask well, and with you will it commence." Thus it says, *Now Abraham and Sarah were old.*

Hizkuni.[1] T.S. 18, 146 note.

102. Coming in days.

That means that they had earned both worlds, this world and the Hereafter. *Days* alludes to the days of the hereafter, of which they had lost nought. *Coming in days* means that they were leaving the present dark world and entering the world to come.

Or Haafelah; MA.
T.S. 18, 148 and note.

103. Sarah laughed within herself.

He reveals the deep and secret things; He knows what is in the darkness, and the light dwells with Him (Dan. 2:22). For it says, *Sarah laughed within herself:* she laughed in her own heart, expressing nothing with her mouth. Yet through the Holy Spirit it was known.

MhG; PZ. T.S. 18, 152 and note.

104. Sarah laughed b'kirbah (within her). When the translators came to write this for King Ptolemy,[1] they altered it to, *Sarah laughed bik'robehah* (in the presence of the bystanders).[2]

Mechilta Bo 14. T.S. 18, 151.

105. Sarah laughed within herself, saying. She looked at herself and exclaimed: "Shall this body bear child, and these shrivelled breasts flow with milk? Yet even if I were so trans-

---

§ 101 [1] This passage is found in cur. edd. Gen. R. 68 on 24:1. Presumably Hizkuni had it in his edd. of Gen. R. on the present verse. Possibly the reason for its postponement in cur. edd. to 24:1 is the statement in the preceding par. that Abraham and Sarah were now rejuvenated; hence he did not really show signs of old age at the present moment.

§ 104 [1] Who according to tradition had the Pentateuch translated into Greek.
  [2] Rashi in Meg. 9a explains that the alteration was made in order to explain why God objected to Sarah's laughter and rebuked her for it, as the following verse relates, whereas He did not object when Abraham laughed (17:17). Hence they altered the text to indicate that her laughter was open, whereas he had kept it to himself. This passage disagrees with the preceding. See also par. 111.

ing: "After I am waxed old shall I have pleasure, my lord being old also?" [13]And the Lord said unto

COMMENTARY

of joy is expressed with the mouth.[85] **c.** Such a miraculous rejuvenation would be as great a miracle as resurrection, which only the assurance by God Himself could make credible.[86] **d.** She thought that

this was merely a courteous blessing by a guest, not a prophecy.[86a] **waxed old.** Lit., worn out, the opposite of new.[87] **pleasure. a.** The smooth unwrinkled flesh and the restored beauty of youth.[88] **b.** Menstruation and marital relations. The Heb. *ednah* means period; it is used of menstruation because this normally occurs at fixed periods.[89] **my lord being old.** No longer desirous of the marriage bed.[90] [13]**the Lord.** The angel; God's messenger is called here by the name of the Sender.[91] **Shall I of a surety...?** An expression of in-

ANTHOLOGY

formed, is not Abraham old?" as it says, *My lord being old.*

> Tan. Shof'tim, 18. T.S. 18, 153.

106. After I am waxed old, I have *ednah* (youth).[1]

R. Hisda interpreted: After my skin has aged and the wrinkles have multiplied, my skin is rejuvenated, the wrinkles are smoothed out, and my former beauty has returned.

Said she: "When a woman is young she has beautiful finery, whereas I, having waxed old, have *ednah*;" this means finery, as in the text, *I decked you also with* edi (*ornaments*) (Ezek. 16:11). "When a woman is young she has her regular periods, whereas I in my old age have *ednah*," — i.e., *idanin* (my periods). "A young woman can conceive (*idunin*), whereas I, though old, am capable of conception. It is, indeed, my time for child-bearing, but that *my lord is old.*" R. Judah said: He is virile, but impotent.

> B.M. 87a; Gen. R. 48. T.S. 18, 154-5.

107. AFTER I AM WAXED OLD, I HAVE YOUTH. In the world to come every righteous person ... will be physically rejuvenated and enjoy renewed youth, as it says, *They that hope in the Lord shall renew their strength* (Isa. 40:31); also, *They shall bring forth fruit in old age; they shall be full of sap and richness* (Ps. 92: 15): it does not say, they were full of sap, but,

they shall be, which indicates that their youth will be restored. Should you wonder at this, consider Abraham and Sarah, of whom it says, *After I am waxed old, I have youth.* It also says, *Who would have said to Abraham, that Sarah should give children suck* (21:7)? So too will it be with the righteous in the world to come.

> Midrash Alfa Beth. T.S. 18, 157.

108. AFTER I AM WAXED OLD, SHALL I HAVE PLEASURE? Our Rabbis maintained that she had despaired of children, since she wondered, *After I am waxed old, shall I have pleasure?* Said the Almighty: Lo, I will inform her that she will yet be built up: *At the set time I will return to you, when the season comes round, and Sarah shall have a son* (verse 14).[1]

> Tan. Vayyera 13. T.S. 18, 156.

109. My lord being old.

She should have said, I being old. This proves that women do not admit old age.

> Or Haafelah. T.S. 18, 159.

110. The Lord said.

From this we learn that angels know not what is in man's heart, which is known to none but the Lord, as it says, *No thought can be withholden from Thee* (Job 42:2).[1]

> Sechel Tob. T.S. 18, 160.

§ 106 [1] This rendering, upon which the interpretations that follow are based, assumes that she stated a fact, not a rhetorical question.
§ 108 [1] This would seem to add nothing to the text. Possibly the idea is that since she disbelieved the angels, God now assured her that He Himself would return. This interpretation of her words disagrees with that of the last par.
§ 110 [1] Cf. par. 103.

Abraham: "Wherefore did Sarah laugh, saying: Shall I of a surety bear a child, who am old? [14]Is any thing too hard for the Lord? At the set time I will return unto thee, when the season cometh round, and Sarah shall have a son." [15]Then Sarah denied, saying: "I laughed not"; for she was afraid. And He said: "Nay; but thou didst laugh." [16]And the

COMMENTARY

credulity, spoken of the impossible.[92] **I . . . who am old. a.** She had in fact said *after I am waxed old*; but what was omitted was that she had also said the same of Abraham.[93] **b.** It was unnecessary to quote her words about Abraham, since the wonder lay in *her* old age; old *men* do beget children.[94] **[14]too hard. a.** Is anything hidden from Me: do I not know that Sarah is old and no longer has her periods? In spite of that I have promised, and the promise will be fulfilled.[95] **b.** Is then Sarah's laughter hidden from Me?[96] **I will return. a.** Now *I* promise this, not the angel; therefore there is no room for the slightest doubt.[97] **b.** God repeated the promise lest Abraham think that in His anger He had withdrawn it.[98] **[15]she was afraid.** To admit that she had sinned, but at the same time she inwardly repented.[99] **He said: Nay.** "He"

ANTHOLOGY

111.   The Lord said to Abraham: "Wherefore did Sarah laugh?"

Why does Scripture rebuke Sarah, but not Abraham, of whom too it relates, *Then Abraham fell upon his face, and laughed* (17:17)? This is to teach that when two, a greater and a lesser, do something improper, only the lesser is rebuked, and then the greater will understand himself.[1]

[Another explanation:] Because Sarah is described as having laughed *within herself*, but not so Abraham. Now, what does "within herself" mean? She looked at her inner frame and exclaimed, "Shall these shrivelled breasts flow with milk?"[2] Therefore the Holy One, blessed is He, was wroth with her.

MhG; MA. T.S. 18, 161-2.

112.   Shall I of a surety bear a child, seeing that I am old?

R. Hanina said: Come and see how grievous even the breath of slander is! Even Scripture made a mis-statement in order to preserve peace between Abraham and Sarah. First we read,

And Sarah laughed within herself, saying: "After I am waxed old shall I have pleasure, my lord *being old?"* Yet God did not say this to Abraham, but, *Wherefore did Sarah laugh, saying: "Shall I of a surety bear a child, seeing that I am old?"* Not my lord is old, but *I am old.*

J. Peah 1:1. T.S. 18, 163.

113.   AND I AM OLD. R. Judah b. R. Simon said: The Holy One, blessed is He, said: You would have yourself young and your companion old, yet I am too old to perform miracles![1]

Gen. R. 48. T.S. 18, 164.

114.   Is anything too hard for the Lord?

R. Judah b. R. Simon said: This may be compared to a man who took a broken chain[1] to a smith and asked him: "Can you repair this?" "I can make a new one," he replied; "can I then not repair this?" So here too: "I can create *de novo*," said God, "yet cannot bring back men to their youth?"

Gen. R. 48. T.S. 18, 165.

§ 111   [1] This may seem strange; we might have expected the reverse. Yet it displays a delicacy of feeling: even a well-merited rebuke should be avoided if the same result can be achieved without it. When the lesser person is reproved, the greater will understand that it applies to himself with even more force. In the reverse case, however, the lesser may think himself exempt, precisely because one's very greatness imposes a greater responsibility—*noblesse oblige.*
       [2] By drawing attention to her withered frame she emphasized her utter disbelief.
§ 113   [1] This makes *"and I am old"* refer to God.
§ 114   [1] Or, two parts of a lock.

men rose up from thence, and looked out toward Sodom; and

COMMENTARY

refers to Abraham (hence should be written "he"): Abraham knew that God's accusation could not be untrue.[100] [16]**the men rose up.** Two of them went on to Sodom, but the chief remained with Abraham to inform him of Sodom's destruction. In the conversation with Abraham which follows it was he who spoke.[101] **from thence.** From the house where they had experienced kind hospitality.[102] **and looked out toward Sodom. a.** They discussed what they had to do to carry out their mission.[103] **b.** Which presented the strongest con-

ANTHOLOGY

115. At the festival[1] I will return to you.

Isaac was born on Passover. How do we know it? From our text: *at the festival I will return to you, and Sarah shall have a son.* Now, when was this spoken? Shall we say, on Passover, and he promised the child for Atzereth (the Feast of Weeks):[2] could she bear a child in fifty days? Or on Atzereth, and he meant in Tishri? But even then, she still could not bear in five months. Hence it must have been on Tabernacles, and he promised for Nisan.[3] Yet the question still remains, could she bear in six months? It was taught: It was an intercalated year.[4] Yet even so, when you deduct her days of uncleanness,[5] it is less than seven months. Mar Zutra answered: Even on the view that when a woman gives birth at nine months they cannot be incomplete months, but when she gives birth at seven months they can be incomplete.[6]

R.H. 11a. T.S. 18, 166.

116. Is anything too hard for the Lord? At the set time I will return to you ... and Sarah shall have a son.

What does *at the set time* mean? That time, known only to Myself, when the resurrection of the dead will take place. *Sarah shall have a son*: this teaches that he [the resurrected] will be renewed like a three-year old. R. Jose b. R. Simon said: Since the soul is nourished with the celestial luster, the Almighty will instruct the Angel Dumah [Silence], "Go and tell such and such a body that I will resurrect him at the appointed time in the Hereafter when I resurrect the righteous." He will answer, "*After I am waxed old, shall I have youth*": after I am dissolved in the earth, sleeping in the dust, after worms have consumed my flesh and my very body is dust, shall I have a renewal? The Almighty will reassure the soul: "Is anything too hard for the Lord? At the time of resurrection, known only to Myself, I shall restore[1] you your body, which is indeed holy, renewed with its pristine youth."

Zohar 1, 102a. T.S. 18, 169.

117. Sarah denied . . . for she was afraid.

Hence we learn that women deny the truth through fear. Therefore our Rabbis disqualified women as witnesses. Had not God promised Abraham a son from Sarah, she would not have borne child, because of her disbelief.

Yelamdenu. T.S. 18, 170.

118. He said: "Nay, but you did laugh."

R. Judah b. R. Johanan, quoting R. Eleazar b. R. Simeon, said: The Holy One, blessed is He, never entered into conversation with any woman save with that righteous one [Sarah], and even then it was only for a particular reason. R. Abba b. Kahana said, citing R. Biri: What a devious way He sought in order to speak to

§ 115   [1] AJV: *set time*. The Heb. *moed*, however, also means festival; cf. Lev. 23:4: *These are the appointed seasons* (moade) *of the Lord, holy convocations*—i.e., festivals.
  [2] Which is seven weeks after Passover.
  [3] On the fifteenth of which Passover commences.
  [4] When the month of Adar, which precedes Nisan, is repeated. Hence there were seven months.
  [5] Since she menstruated on that day; par. 64.
  [6] I.e., just over six months.
§ 116   [1] Regarding *ashub* (I shall return) as though it read *ashib*, I shall restore.

Abraham went with them to bring them on the way. ¹⁷And the Lord said: "Shall I hide from Abraham

COMMENTARY

trast to the house of Abraham.¹⁰⁴ **Abraham went with them. a.** The present tense is used here (lit., Abraham goes with them) because this is linked with the next verse: i.e., even while Abraham was accompanying them, God said, etc., without waiting for him to return home.¹⁰⁵ **b.** They accommodated their pace to his, that he might complete his hospitality by escorting them.¹⁰⁶ **c.** He escorted them in order to guard against a possible attack by the Sodomites.¹⁰⁷ ¹⁷**the Lord said. a.** God spoke to the host of Heaven, or to His angels; or perhaps *said* means "thought."¹⁰⁸ **b.** As a reward for his hospitality God said that He would not conceal His intentions from Abraham, so that *he may command his children*, etc., the reward of one good deed being another good deed (the reward for his hospitality would be the further good deed of giving his children charge to keep God's commandments).¹⁰⁹ **c.** It was for this purpose that *the Lord appeared to him* (verse 1).¹¹⁰ **Shall I hide from Abraham.**

ANTHOLOGY

her, as it says, *He said: "Nay, but you did laugh."*

Gen. R. 48, 20. T.S. 18, 171 note.

119. HE SAID: "NAY, BUT YOU DID LAUGH." The School of R. Haggai taught: The Matriarchs were prophetesses; this follows from the present text.¹

MhG. T.S. 18, 172.

120. **The men rose up from thence, etc.**

Because Abraham was righteous they are not called angels. All the time that they were with him Abraham did not realize that they were angels; therefore he now escorted them on their way.

R. Eleazar, however, maintained that he did know. Nevertheless he went to escort them, desiring to treat them just the same as he treated his human guests.¹

MA; Zohar 1, 104a. T.S. 18, 174 and note.

121. **The men rose up from thence, and looked out (*vayyashkifu*) toward Sodom.**

R. Eleazar b. Pedath, quoting R. Jose b. Zimra, said: The verb *hashkef* (to look out) is always used in connection with calamity. E.g., *He* [Abraham] *looked out toward Sodom and Gomorrah . . . and, lo, the smoke of the land went up as the smoke of a furnace* (19:28); our present text is another instance; again, *The Lord looked forth . . . and discomfited the host of the Egyptians* (Exod. 14:24). Yet we read: *Look forth from Thy holy habitation, from heaven, and bless Thy people Israel* (Deut. 26:15)! Thus you can indeed see that when Israel is worthy¹ even a curse is turned into a blessing.

Midrash.² T.S. 18, 175.

122. **Abraham went with them to bring them on the way.**

So runs the proverb: Having given your guest food and drink, escort him [on his way].

This teaches that a man is rewarded according to his deserts.¹ Abraham escorted the angels, as our text states. Therefore the Omnipresent escorted his descendants forty years in the wilderness, as it says, *And the Lord went before them by day in a pillar of cloud, to lead them the way*, etc. (Exod. 13:21).

Gen. R. 48, 20; Mechilta B'shallach 1. T.S. 18, 177-8.

123. **The Lord said: "Shall I hide from Abraham that which I am doing?"**

It is written, *The secret of the Lord is with them that fear Him* (Ps. 25:14). At first His

§ 119 ¹ I.e., from the fact that God spoke to her. It is interesting to note that according to this the essence of prophecy is direct communion with the Almighty.
§ 120 ¹ For the whole passage cf. *supra* par. 26.
§ 121 ¹ MA reads: Because the Israelites render tithes and priestly dues, the curse becomes a blessing.
   ² Quoted in Yalkut Hamakiri on Prov. 30:4.
§ 122 ¹ Lit., with the measure that a man metes out it is meted out to him. Cf. *supra* par. 39.

that which I am doing; ⁱ⁸seeing that Abraham shall surely become a great and mighty nation, and all the na-

COMMENTARY

a. It is fitting that I do not hide from Abraham My goodness, viz., that if there were any righteous

men among the wicked of Sodom, so that there was a hope of repentance, I would spare the wicked too, for I do not delight in the death of the wicked.[111] **b.** Should I hide what I am about to do through the agency of the very persons whom he has just entertained?[112] **c.** He deserves to know My most secret intentions.[113] **that which I am doing.** That Sodom's impending destruction is *My* work and none other's.[114] ⁱ⁸**seeing that Abraham . . . mighty nation. a.** Shall I hide it from him who is so

ANTHOLOGY

secret was with them that feared Him. Then it was revealed to the upright,[1] as it says, *His secret is with the upright* (Prov. 3:32). Then it was entrusted to the prophets, as we read, *For the Lord God will do nothing without revealing His secret to His servants the prophets* (Amos 3:7). Said the Holy One, blessed is He: This Abraham fears God, as it says, *Now I know that you are a God-fearing man* (22:12). He is upright, for of him it is written, *The upright love thee* (Song 1:4). He is also a prophet, as it says, *Now therefore restore the man's wife, for he is a prophet* (20:7). Shall I then not reveal My intentions to him? Hence *the Lord said: "Shall I hide from Abraham that which I am doing?"*

Gen. R. 49.   T.S. 18, 179.

124. SHALL I HIDE FROM ABRAHAM? etc. Why did God reveal His intentions to Abraham? R. Judah b. Levi said: This may be compared to a king who made a gift of an orchard to his friend. Some time later he found that he had to cut down five beams in it. Said he: Although it was mine, and it was I who gave it to my friend, it is not right for me to cut down anything in it without consulting him. Similarly, when Abraham went up to Eretz Israel, the Holy One, blessed is He, told him: *"Lift up now your eyes, and look from the place where you are, northward and southward and eastward and westward; for all the land which you see, to you will I give it"* (13:14-15). Therefore when He desired to destroy these five cities,[1]

He declared, "I cannot destroy them without Abraham's knowledge." Hence when He was actually about to overthrow them He took counsel with him, as our text states.

R. Hiyya said: The Almighty informs the righteous in advance so that they may call the wicked to repent and thereby avert their decreed punishment. Also, to leave no loophole for any complaint that He punishes unjustly. R. Eleazar said: If the Holy One, whose acts are truth and whose ways are just, does not execute His intentions before revealing them to the righteous, so that men may have no possibility of censuring His acts; how much more must mere mortals take care that their actions give no grounds for the spreading of evil reports about them. Thus it is written, *And you shall be clean before the Lord and before Israel* (Num. 32:22).

Tan. Vayyera 5; Zohar 1, 104b.   T.S. 18, 180.

125. SHALL I HIDE FROM ABRAHAM? etc. When the Sodomites sinned He revealed His resolve to Abraham, that he might plead on their behalf. Abraham did, indeed, speak in their defense, as it says, *And Abraham drew near and said: "Wilt Thou indeed sweep away the righteous with the wicked"* (verse 23)? Now, drawing near implies prayer, as in the text, *And it came to pass at the time of the offering of the evening prayer, that Elijah the prophet drew near, and said: "O Lord . . . let it be known this day that Thou art God in Israel"* (1 Kings 18:36).

Tan. Vayyera 8.   T.S. 18, 181.

§ 123   ¹ From the context it appears that God-fearers, the upright, and prophets, respectively, stand on progressively higher spiritual levels.
§ 124   ¹ Sodom and Gomorrah, and Admah, Zeboiim and Lasha (see 10:19), which, according to tradition, were also destroyed.

ANTHOLOGY

126. SHALL I HIDE FROM ABRAHAM? etc. R. Levi said: Why did the Holy One, blessed is He, reveal His intentions to Abraham? Because his mind was filled with doubt about the generation of the Flood: "It is impossible," thought he, "that there were no righteous men in that generation for whose sake their doom should have been averted."[1] The proof that this is so is seen in the fact that when God declared, "Shall I hide from Abraham?" etc., he immediately answered, "Wilt Thou indeed sweep away the righteous with the wicked" (verse 23)?[2]

Tan. Y. Vayyera 7. T.S. 18, 182.

127. SHALL I HIDE FROM ABRAHAM THAT WHICH I AM DOING? Let our Master teach us:[1] May the public translator of the Torah look into the Sefer Torah and translate?[2] Thus did our Masters teach: The translator may not look into the Sefer Torah when he translates, lest one think that the translation is written in the Torah itself.[3] The reader of the Torah must not look anywhere else but in the Torah, because the Torah was given in writing, as it says, And I will write on the tables the words that were on the first tables (Exod. 34:1).[4]

R. Judah b. Shalom said: Moses desired the Mishnah also to be in writing.[5] But the Holy One, blessed is He, foresaw that the nations would translate the Torah and read it in Greek,[6] and claim that they are the true Jews.[7] Said the Holy One, blessed is He, to Moses: If I should write the greater part of My Torah for them, they would be accounted as strangers (Hos. 8:12).[8] Now, why was so much care taken [to keep the Mishnah in its oral form]? Because the Mishnah is the esoteric teaching of the Almighty, which He entrusts only to the righteous, as it says, The secret of the Lord is with them that fear Him (Ps. 25:14). Similarly you find that even when the Sodomites angered the Lord and He desired to overthrow them, He consulted none but Abraham.

Tan. Vayyera 5. T.S. 18, 183.

128. THE LORD SAID: "SHALL I HIDE FROM ABRAHAM?" etc. Let our Master teach us:[1] If two sons are born to a person, one on the eve of the Sabbath and the other on the Sabbath, and he erroneously circumcises the eve-of-the-Sabbath-child on the Sabbath, or vice versa, is he culpable for the desecration of the Sabbath?[2]

---

§ 126 [1] Therefore God showed him that these wicked cities too did not possess sufficient righteous men to save them. In a MS Yalkut the reading is: Is it possible that there were not twenty or ten righteous men in that generation?

[2] Which shows that he had already been thinking along these lines before God spoke to him.

§ 127 [1] See par. 1, n. 1.

[2] In ancient times (and among the Yemenite Jews to this day) the Torah was publicly read and translated into Aramaic, the popular vernacular. The Sefer Torah is the sacred scroll from which the original is read.

[3] Nothing may be allowed to impair the purity of the text, not even the thought that anything whatsoever was added thereto.

[4] Therefore the Torah must not be recited by heart.

[5] The Mishnah is the interpretation of the laws contained in the Torah, the Five Books of Moses. It is known as the Oral Law, because originally it was not written down but transmitted orally from generation to generation. In its present form it is the work of R. Judah ha-Nasi (c. 220 C.E.), based upon oral compilations in the possession of the Rabbis before him. Scholars differ as to whether his compilation, which is accepted as definitive, was written or still in oral form only.

[6] An allusion to the Septuagint, the Greek translation, which was publicly read by the Greek-speaking Jews of Alexandria, instead of the Hebrew original.

[7] This Hellenizing process produced a generally changed outlook, which, however, according to the present passage, was claimed to represent the pure Jewish philosophy of life.

[8] "The greater part of My Torah" is understood here to mean the Mishnah, the Oral Law, which far exceeds the Written Law in volume and content. If these Hellenized Jews should possess this too, they could apparently substantiate their claim to be the true Jews, and so render the Palestinian Jews strangers, as it were. The possession of the Oral Law thus became the criterion whereby these claims could be judged. AJV: Though I write for him never so many things of My Law, they are accounted as a stranger.

§ 128 [1] See par. 1, n. 1.

[2] Circumcision takes place on the eighth day, even if it is the Sabbath. If, however, it is performed on a Sabbath which is not the eighth day, it constitutes a culpable desecration of the Sabbath. Here the problem is this: If a man has two sons, one of whom should have been circumcised on the eve of the Sabbath, but was not,

ANTHOLOGY

Our Rabbis taught thus: If two sons are born to a person, one on the eve of the Sabbath and the other on the Sabbath, and he inadvertently circumcises the Sabbath-eve-child on the Sabbath, or the Sabbath-child on Sabbath eve, he is culpable. Why? Because he has desecrated the Sabbath, whereas it is written, *And in the* eighth *day the flesh of his skin shall be circumcised* (Lev. 12:3); hence this man has transgressed the Torah by desecrating the Sabbath. Great indeed is circumcision that it overrides the Sabbath. And when the Holy One, blessed is He, came to overturn the five cities of Sodom,[3] He revealed His intentions to Abraham as a reward for circumcision, as it says, *The Lord said: "Shall I hide from Abraham?"* etc.

Tan. Vayyera 6.   T.S. 18, 184.

129. THE LORD SAID: "SHALL I HIDE FROM ABRAHAM?" etc. It is written, *So shall you find grace and good favor in the sight of God and man* (Prov. 3:4). This applies to Abraham, who was beloved by humans and angels: *Hear us, my Lord: you are a mighty prince among us* (23:6)—here you have his popularity amongst men. Where do we find it with God and angels? In our text: *The Lord said*, etc.

Tan. Vayyera 6.   T.S. 18, 185.

130. THE LORD SAID: "SHALL I HIDE?" etc. In this vein Scripture writes, *Then He opens the ears of men, and by their chastisement seals the decree* (Job. 33:16). *He opens the ears of men* applies to Abraham, as our text indicates. *By their chastisement seals the decree* applies to the Sodomites: when He found no righteous man amongst them, He sealed their decree.

Tan. Vayyera 6.   T.S. 18, 186.

131. **Seeing that Abraham shall surely become a great and mighty nation.**

R. Samuel b. Nahman said: We see that when the Holy One, blessed is He, mentions Israel, He blesses them, as it says, *The Lord has been mindful of us; He will bless . . . the house of Israel* (Ps. 115:12). We know this only of the six hundred thousand [who collectively form the house of Israel];[1] how do we know that He blesses every individual Israelite when He mentions him by name? From the text, *The Lord said: "Shall I hide from Abraham . . . Abraham shall surely become a great and mighty nation?"* Now Scripture need only have said, *The Lord said: Verily, the cry of Sodom and Gomorrah is great* (verse 20).[2] However, the Holy One blessed is He, said: Having mentioned this righteous man, shall I not bless him? [I declare,] *"Abraham shall surely become a great and mighty nation."*

Rabina asked one of our Rabbis who was arranging *aggadah* before him:[3] What is the authority for the Rabbinic dictum, "The memory of the righteous shall be for a blessing?" Surely, he replied, this is a Biblical verse (Prov. 10:7). But where do we find it in the Torah?[4] —In our text: *The Lord said: "Shall I hide from Abraham that which I am doing?"* which is immediately followed by, *"Abraham shall surely become a great and mighty nation."*[5]

Yoma 38b; Gen. R. 49, 1.
T.S. 18, 187 and note.

and he circumcises him on the Sabbath, is he still culpable in view of the fact that he has a child who is to be circumcised on that day, so that in his particular case circumcision does override the Sabbath? The same problem arises if, having inadvertently circumcised the Sabbath-child on the previous day, he now circumcises the eve-of-the-Sabbath-child; can we argue that since the Sabbath originally stood to be overridden in his case, he is not culpable?

[3] See par. 124 and note.

§ 131 [1] This number left Egypt (Exod. 12:37), and so it became a synonym for the whole nation. I.e., the verse quoted only shows that He blesses Israel when He mentions the whole nation.

[2] Without interposing, *Seeing that Abraham shall surely become*, etc.

[3] *Aggadah*, fr. *hagged*, to tell, narrate, is the non-legal part of Rabbinic teaching. "*Was arranging* aggadah" is the literal translation; its sense is not quite clear. It may mean either that he was expounding *aggadah*, or that he was arranging aggadic teaching in a certain order.

[4] I.e., the Pentateuch.

[5] Having mentioned Abraham, He immediately speaks of his blessing.

**tions of the earth shall be blessed
in him?** [19]**For I have known him,**

COMMENTARY

beloved by Me that I will make him a great nation
and a source of blessing to the families of the
earth?[115] **b.** Seeing that he will become a great
nation, future nations will ask, "How could God
have hidden this from him?" or, "How could Abraham have refrained from praying for them?"[116]

c. He deserves to be informed more than any other
prophet, because he devotes all his strength to im-
prove people, so much so that a great nation will
certainly arise from him.[117] **be blessed in him.**
a. For his sake.[118] **b.** In "him" means in the nation
that shall spring from him, that one nation will
bless another by saying, "God make you like the
nation descended from Abraham."[119] **c.** Because he
is to be a blessing to the nations, his rebuke will
have great value.[120] [19]**I have known him. a.** I
know that he will command, etc.[121] **b.** i.e., loved
him. This is a secondary meaning of "know," for

ANTHOLOGY

132. Seeing that Abraham shall surely
become, etc. R. Nahman said, quoting R.
Mana: The world cannot exist unless it contains
thirty men as righteous as Abraham. What is
the proof? *Seeing that Abraham shall surely
become*: the numerical value of *yihyeh* ("shall
become") is thirty.[1] At times a majority of
them are in Babylon and a minority in Eretz
Israel, and at others it is the reverse. When a
majority are in Eretz Israel it is a good augury
for the world.

J.A.Z. 2:1. T.S. 18, 188.

133. Seeing that Abraham shall surely
become, etc. It is written, *There was a certain
Jew . . . whose name was Mordecai* (Est. 2:5):
this teaches that he ranked with Abraham, of
whom it was written, *shall surely become*.[1]
Abraham sacrificed himself for the Sanctification of the Divine Name, and Mordecai did
likewise.[2]

Quoted in Yalkut Shimoni 2, 1053
as a Midrash. T.S. 18, 189.

134. Abraham shall surely become, etc.
It is written, *He that walks uprightly walks
securely* (Prov. 10:9). This applies to Ab-

raham, whom God assured, *I will make of you
a great nation* (Gen. 12:2), which promise
He kept, as we read, *Abraham shall surely
become a great and mighty nation*.[1]

Similarly, we read, *In keeping of them* [sc.
the ordinances of the Lord] *there is the reward
of greatness* (Ps. 19:12): Abraham kept them,
and therefore became great, as our text declares.

Midrash T'hillim 19:16; 119:3.
T.S. 18, 190-1.

135. Abraham shall surely become, etc.
When a man has sad news for his neighbor, let
him begin on a happy note, to set his mind at
ease. The Holy One, blessed is He, acted so.
Desiring to inform Abraham of Sodom's impending destruction, He first set his mind at
rest by good tidings, viz., *Abraham shall surely
become a great and mighty nation*.[1]

Or Haafelah. T.S. 18, 192.

136. Abraham shall surely become a
great and mighty nation. When the Almighty determined to execute judgment on
Sodom, He would not pronounce its doom save
after consultation with six hundred thousand
angels. [Yet He first spoke to Abraham before

§ 132 [1] Heb. letters are also numbers: ׳ = (10) + ה = (5) + ׳ = (10) + ה = (5): total 30. Whilst the interpretation, of course, is far-fetched, the idea is lofty: The only guarantee of human survival is righteousness.
§ 133 [1] In the original the same verb, *hayah*, is used in both verses.
  [2] Abraham allowed himself to be thrown into the fiery furnace rather than disavow God (see Vol. II, chap.
15, pars. 57-9). Mordecai risked his life in refusing to prostrate himself before Haman (Est. 3:2), because,
according to the Rabbis, the latter had fastened an idolatrous image on his breast. Every such act which
affirms the true God is called *Kiddush ha-Shem*, the Sanctification of the Divine Name.
§ 134 [1] Thus he walked secure in God's promise.
§ 135 [1] PRE 25 deduces this from the fact that first He informed him of the birth of Isaac and then told him of
Sodom's impending doom.

to the end that he may command his children and his household after

COMMENTARY

one who loves another brings him near to him and thus knows him. And why have I known him? *To the end*, etc.[122] **c.** I know he is aware that I am a God who loves righteousness and justice, and therefore he will charge his children and household to cultivate these virtues. Now, if it is possible to pardon the Sodomites on the basis of these qualifications, he will certainly beseech Me to do so. If, on the other hand, it is not possible, he too will

desire that I follow their dictates.[123] **d.** I have exalted him, in order that he may command, etc.[124] **e.** I have watched over him.[125] **f.** God's foreknowledge does not rob man of free will. Hence He said, "I have known him"—he will command his children, but only of his own free will, without constraint or compulsion on My part.[126] **to the end, that he may command his children, etc. a.** Since he will certainly command his children to keep My commandments, they will deserve to inherit this land; therefore I cannot destroy part of it without telling him of My intention.[127] **b.** I chose him not for his own sake alone but in order that he should charge his children to keep My ways.[128] **c.** I will inform him, because when he sees

ANTHOLOGY

carrying out the sentence, whereat] the angels protested, "Sovereign of the Universe! The celestial court consists of six hundred thousand, and Abraham is but one, yet wouldst Thou attach equal weight to him!" Said He to them, *"Abraham shall surely become a great and mighty nation"*; that is to say, six hundred thousand shall come forth from him.[1] This is hinted at in God's promise, *And I will make of you a great nation* (12:2), the last letters of which total sixty.[2]

> Quoted as a Midrash in the *D'rashoth Ibn Shoib ad. loc.* T.S. 18, 193.

137. **All the nations of the earth shall be blessed in him.**

Because he will teach them the right paths of life and make them comprehend Him who is Unique in the world.

R. Levi said: In the Generation of the Division the sea overflowed and swept away thirty families of the children of Ham, as it says, *So the Lord swept them away from there* (11:8).[1] The Holy One, blessed is He, said to Abraham: "From you I will raise up thirty families to replace them"; and that is the meaning of our text, *All the nations of the earth shall be blessed in him*. The Almighty, indeed, did so.

> Tan. Hayye Sarah 6; PZ. T.S. 18, 194.

138. **For I have known him, to the end that he may command his children and his household after him, that they may keep the way of the Lord.**

At the age of three Abraham recognized his Creator; he observed even the minutiae of the Torah, and taught his children to do likewise, as our text relates. Said the Holy One, blessed is He, to him: "In this world you taught Torah to your children; but in the Hereafter I Myself, in all My glory, will teach them"; as it says, *And all your children shall be taught of the Lord* (Isa. 54:13).

R. Simeon said: Happy are the righteous, who do not depart this world until they charge their children to keep the Torah. For so we find that the Patriarch Abraham did not depart this world until he had charged his children and his household to keep the ways of the Lord, as our text states. What did Abraham charge his children? To follow the golden mean in every virtue; that is the upright way which Abraham taught Isaac, and that is the way of the Lord.

Happy are the righteous: not only do they keep God's ways themselves, but they also charge others to do the same. And woe to the wicked: not only do they not observe His ways themselves, but they even hinder others from

§ 136   [1] See Exod. 12:37.
     [2] The original reads ואעשך לגוי גדול; the last letters of these three words are כ (=20), י (=10) and ל (=30): total 60.
§ 137   [1] Cf. Vol. II, chap. 11, par. 34.

him, that they may keep the way of the Lord, to do righteousness and

COMMENTARY

how merciful I am to the penitent, and how I execute justice upon the wicked, he will impress his children to keep the way of the Lord.[129] **d.** God's election of Abraham was not for his own sake alone, but that he might charge his children to keep His ways. So when he learned of Sodom's fate he would impress this even more strongly upon them.[130] **e.** The supreme task of the Patriarchs and their *raison d'être* was to raise up the people of Israel as the people of righteousness and equity.[131] **f.** Or, "charge his children." An important doctrine is here

taught in connection with the word "command" צוה, which has played a conspicuous part in Jewish life. It is the sacred duty of the Israelite to transmit the Jewish heritage to his children after him. The last injunction of the true Jewish father to his children is that they walk in "the way of the Lord" and live lives of probity and goodness. These injunctions were often put in writing; and this custom has given rise to a distinct type of literary production, the Jewish Ethical Will (צוואה).[132] **the way of the Lord, to do righteousness,** etc. The demands of justice and love cannot be realized unless men are ready to preserve "the way of God"; men must be willing to recognize God as Master of their lives whose Divine Will directs their individual lives before they are called upon to meet the Divine demands of justice and love in their (social)

ANTHOLOGY

them, as it says, *For they sleep not, except they have done evil; and their sleep is taken away, unless they cause some to fall* (Prov. 4:16).

> Gen. R. 95, 3; Midrash Tannaim beginning of D'barim; MhG; Midrash Habiur. T.S. 18, 195-7. 204 note.

139. THAT HE MAY COMMAND HIS CHILDREN etc. Chastise your son, even to excess. So did our Father Abraham: he beat his children and his household [to teach them to walk in God's paths]. How do we know that his fear lay upon his children and his household? From our text. Therefore let your fear be upon your children, and refrain not from beating them.[1]

> Alpha Betha of Ben Sira. T.S. 18, 199.

140. **That he may command his sons and his household after him . . . to do ts'dakah (AJV: righteousness) and justice.**

["His household" includes the womenfolk]. R. Hamnuna interpreted: He commanded his sons to exercise judgment; his household [i.e., his daughters], to perform *ts'dakah* (charity).[1]

> Sanh. 57b. T.S. 18, 200.

141. **That they may keep the way of the Lord, to do righteousness and justice.**

Scripture relates, *His [Jehoshaphat's] heart was lifted up in the ways of the Lord* (2 Chron. 17:6): was he then arrogant, that it says that his heart was lifted up? Rather, it means that he appointed judges who knew how to walk in the ways of the Lord.

When Israel executes justice the Holy One, blessed is He, casts down his enemies before them, as it says, *Oh that My people would hearken unto Me, that Israel would walk in My ways! I would soon subdue their enemies* (Ps. 81:14f). Now, what are God's ways? Righteousness and justice, as we read in our text.

The Holy One, blessed is He, seeks neither beauty nor wealth, but only the fear of sin, as it says, *A woman that fears the Lord, she shall be praised* (Prov. 31:30). For that Abraham too was praised, as our text says, *For I have known him, to the end that he may command his children . . . to keep the way of the Lord, to do righteousness and justice.* It is also written of him, *For now I know that you are a God-fearing man* (22:12).

[Walk in God's ways:] As He is righteous, so you be righteous; as He is compassionate, so

---

§ 139 [1] This is not in accord with accepted Jewish teaching. Cf. B.B. 21a: Rab said to R. Samuel b. Shilath: When you beat children, use only a light strap. Maim. Hilchoth Talmud Torah 12, 2.

§ 140 [1] "Ts'dakah" means both righteousness and charity, the latter being regarded as only a particular instance of the former. R. Hamnuna thus maintained that the "exercise of justice", i.e., judicial functions, is an obligation upon men only; whereas women too are bidden to give charity.

you be compassionate, as we read, *You shall . . . walk in His ways* (Deut. 28:9). [In our present text] "to do" means good deeds; *ts'dakah* has its literal meaning;[1] and "justice" means civil law.

R. Aha, quoting R. Alexandri, said: "*Ts'dakah*" refers to the provision of the mourner's meal.[2] Our Rabbis said: It refers to sick-visiting.

Scripture writes: *When you lend your neighbor any manner of loan* [and take a pledge therefor] *. . . you shall surely restore to him the pledge when the sun goes down, that he may sleep in his garment, and bless you;*] *and it shall be* ts'dakah (AJV *righteousness*) *to you* (Deut. 24:10-13). Why is this last clause added? Because it says, *That they may keep the way of the Lord, to do* ts'dakah *and justice*. Now, we do not know what *ts'dakah* actually is, but when it says, *you shall surely restore to him the pledge*, it points at one form of *ts'dakah* [viz., charity and kindness]. How do we know that all other precepts are likewise called *ts'dakah*? Because Scripture adds, *And it shall be* ts'dakah *to you*.[3]

> Tan. Shoftim 1, 26; Midrash T'hillim 112:1; Midrash Hahefetz; Midrash Tannaim D'barim 24:13; Gen. R. 49, 4. T.S. 18, 201-4; 207-8.

142. To DO TS'DAKAH. This people [Israel] possesses three distinguishing characteristics: they are compassionate, retiring,[1] and benevolent. The last follows from our text, *to do* ts'dakah. He who possesses these characteristics is worthy to join this people.

> Yeb. 79a. T.S. 18, 205.

143. To DO TS'DAKAH. It was said, citing the School of Elijah the Prophet: Great is *ts'dakah* (charity), for all who have given it since the very creation have been praised. Why did our Patriarchs merit this world, the Messianic era, and the hereafter? Because they practised charity. Abraham, Isaac, Jacob, Moses, Aaron, David, and Solomon were all praised only for their charity.

Charity, indeed, is found in the hand of the Holy One, blessed is He, as it says, *Thy right hand is full of* tsedek (Ps. 48:11). When Abraham saw this, he too practised it fervently, as our text says. Whereupon the Almighty declared to him, *Sit at My right hand . . . The rod of your strength the Lord will send out of Zion* (ibid. 110:1-2).

> SEZ MS. 1; AB 24. T.S. 18, 209 and note.

144. To DO TS'DAKAH. Until Abraham one could not distinguish between father and son.[1] The Holy One, blessed is He, gave him this crown [of venerable appearance], whereby a man is crowned in his old age. But when does one receive it? When one performs charity, as it says, *The hoary head is a crown of glory* (Prov. 16:31). Where do you find it? *It is found in the way of* ts'dakah (ibid.). To whom does this apply? To Abraham, as our text indicates.[2]

> Tan. Y. Hayye Sarah 4. T.S. 18, 210.

145. To DO TS'DAKAH AND JUSTICE. He would begin with charity and end with justice. How so? Abraham entertained travelers, and when they had dined he would bid them say Grace. They asked, "What shall we say?" and he would reply, "Say 'Blessed is the Eternal God of whose bounty we have partaken.'" If the guest agreed, he ate, drank and departed. But if he demurred, Abraham said, "Pay what you owe." "But what do I owe you?" objected

§ 141   [1] See preceding note.
  [2] The first meal eaten by a mourner must not be of his own, but provided by his neighbors. Th. reads: hospitality [to travelers].
  [3] This, strictly speaking, is superfluous. It is therefore interpreted as teaching that the very act of obedience to God's precept is *ts'dakah*. Cf. par. 140, note 1.
§ 142   [1] Lit., bashful.
§ 144   [1] Old age did not change one's countenance.
  [2] Cf. par. 101.

COMMENTARY

lives![133] **to do righteousness.** (Heb. צדקה, which also means charity.) We must carry out the precepts of charity more scrupulously than any other, because it is the characteristic of the true descendant of Abraham, as it says,—*to the end that he may command his children . . . to perform charity.*[134] **righteousness** (צדקה) and *justice.* משפט means just treatment from one's fellow-men. צדקה

ANTHOLOGY

the guest. He would reply: "One xestes[1] of wine is ten follera;[2] one pound of meat, ten follera; a round of bread, ten follera. Who will give you wine in the desert, or meat, or bread?" Finding himself thus hard pressed he would declare, "Blessed is the Eternal God of whose bounty we have eaten." Therefore Scripture writes *ts'dakah* first and then justice.

Gen. R. 49, 4. T.S. 18, 214.

146. To do ts'dakah and justice. When David saw how beloved *ts'dakah* and justice are by the Almighty he practised both, as it says, *And David executed justice and ts'dakah to all his people* (2 Sam. 8:15). "Sovereign of the Universe!" he cried out, "We have fulfilled our pledge; do Thou fulfill Thine. Of Abraham —peace be to him!—'tis written, *For I have known him, to the end that he may command his children and his household after him, that they may keep the way of the Lord, to do ts'dakah and justice; to the end that the Lord may bring upon Abraham that which He has spoken of him.*[1] So do Thou too fulfill Thy pledge"; as it says, *Fulfill Thy pledge to Thy servant for good* (Ps. 119:122), that is to say, Fulfill Thy pledge that we descend not into Gehenna.

Midrash Hashkem. T.S. 18, 215.

147. To do righteousness and justice. R. Simeon b. Halafta said: This may be compared to a king who married a lady of noble birth; her dowry included jewels, to which he added two jewels of his own.[1] But she lost hers, and so he took his away too. Later, seeking to regain his favor, she found them again for him; the king then brought his back too, and ordered, "Let a crown be made of all these for her head." Even so Abraham gave his sons two precious jewels, righteousness and justice. In return the Holy One, blessed is He, gave him two jewels, love and mercy, as it is written, *Then the Lord your God shall keep with you the* covenant *and the* mercy *which he swore to your fathers* (Deut. 7:12). But Israel having lost theirs, as we read, *You who turn* justice *to wormwood, and cast* righteousness *to the ground* (Amos 5:7), the Almighty took His back too, as it says, *I have taken away My peace from this people, saith the Lord, even* mercy *and* compassion (Jer. 16:5). Yet Israel will regain her virtues, as it says, *Zion shall be redeemed with* justice, *and they that return of her with* righteousness (Isa. 1:27). Then shall the Almighty restore His gifts, as it is written, *For the mountains may depart, and the hills be removed; but My* love *shall not depart from you, neither shall My covenant of peace be removed, saith the Lord that hath* mercy *upon you* (ibid. 54:10). Let a crown be made of all these, He will decree, and placed upon Israel's head, as it says, *I will betroth you to Me in* righteousness *and* justice, *in* love *and* mercy (Hos. 2:21).

Cited in Yalkut Shimoni 2, 295, as a Midrash. T.S. 18, 216.

148. To do righteousness and justice. Abraham himself was created only for Jacob's sake. For our text states, *I have known him, to*

§ 145 [1] Nearly a pint.
       [2] A small coin (Jast.).
§ 146 [1] This charge of Abraham becomes a pledge or debt which his descendants must discharge. Since David did perform them, he could claim that the debt was paid, and that God in turn must pay His.
§ 147 [1] To the bride's dowry which she brought to her husband the latter generally added an amount of his own; the combined sum was the settlement which she could subsequently claim in certain circumstances.

justice; to the end that the Lord may bring upon Abraham that which He

COMMENTARY

signifies love and charity which one cannot demand

but is entitled to expect in the name of God, because it is God who commands them; thus צדקה is a brotherly love which God demands from us![135] **that the Lord may bring upon Abraham. a.** I.e., on his seed after him.[136] **b.** It is a fundamental article of faith to know that every favor that God shows us is for the sake of the Patriarchs,

ANTHOLOGY

the end that he may command his children and his household after him, that they may keep the way of the Lord, to do righteousness and justice. Now, righteousness and justice are found in none but Jacob, as it says, *Thou hast executed justice and righteousness in Jacob* (Ps. 99:4).[1]

Lev. R. 36, 4. T.S. 18, 217.

149. THAT THEY MAY KEEP THE WAY OF THE LORD, TO DO TS'DAKAH AND JUSTICE. "The way of the Lord" is the exercise of love,[1] and "ts'dakah" has its literal meaning (charity).[2] "Justice" means civil laws. Hence our Sages said: Love is greater than charity, and charity is greater than justice.[3]

MhG. T.S. 18, 219.

150. THAT THEY MAY KEEP THE WAY OF THE LORD, TO FORGE[1] RIGHTEOUSNESS AND JUSTICE. Since it says, *That they may keep the way of the Lord*, why add, *to forge righteousness and justice*? To teach that he who keeps the way of the Torah "forges" righteousness and justice—if we could but speak thus. And what is this righteousness and justice? The Holy One, blessed is He. R. Simeon wept and declared: Unhappy are they who neither know nor care about their Master's honor. Who forges the

Holy name[2] daily? Surely, he who gives charity to the poor.

Zohar 3, 113. T.S. 18, 220.

151. **To the end that the Lord may bring upon Abraham that which He has spoken of him.**

R. Simeon b. Yohai taught: He who leaves a son after him who studies the Torah is as though he were not dead. For Scripture does not say, that which He has spoken *to* him, but, *that which He hath spoken of him.*[1]

Gen. R. 49, 4. T.S. 18, 221.

152. THAT WHICH HE HAS SPOKEN OF HIM. What He had spoken of him was the promise of *chesed* (love), as it says, *Thou wilt show faithfulness to Jacob,* chesed (love) *to Abraham, as Thou hast sworn to our fathers from the days of old* (Mic. 7:20). R. Jacob said: In the Torah (Pentateuch), the Prophets, and the Writings we find that whenever the Holy One, blessed is He, makes mention of justice (*mishpat*), He couples it with love (*chesed*) on one side, and charity (*ts'dakah*) on the other. Why so? Because it is hard.[1] Where do we find it in the Torah? In our text, *For I have known him, to the end that he may command his children and his household after him, that they may keep*

§ 148　[1] The general idea is that even Abraham's justification for existence lay only in the flowering of justice and righteousness in his descendants.

§ 149　[1] *Gemiluth chasadim*, which is generally and incorrectly rendered the exercise of charity. Rather, it is the practice of love. As the Talmud points out, charity can only be exercised by the rich toward the poor, whereas even the poor can exercise *gemiluth chasadim* toward the rich (Suc. 49b).
　　　[2] See par. 140 and note.
　　　[3] Lit., civil laws.

§ 150　[1] The Heb. means make or do. In view of the comment which follows "forge" is preferable here.
　　　[2] The thought expressed there is that God's name is forged, i.e., made complete, only through *ts'dakah*, now understood as charity.

§ 151　[1] "Of him" implies that God's promises of future greatness actually referred to Abraham himself. But since they were not fulfilled in his own lifetime, it follows that he is regarded as still in life—because his children and descendants studied the Torah, as he did.

§ 152　[1] Stern justice is hard and unfeeling. It must be tempered with and administered in a spirit of love and charity.

hath spoken of him." [20]And the Lord said: "Verily, the cry of Sodom and Gomorrah is great, and, verily, their sin is exceeding grievous. [21]I

COMMENTARY

that He may fulfill His promise to them.[137] [20]**the Lord said.** **a.** The angel of the Lord said to Abraham, "I am sending these, my messengers, to Sodom because *the cry of Sodom,*" etc.[188] **b.** God said this to Abraham when the angels were already in Sodom, verse 22 preceding the present one in time.[139] **c.** In His heart.[140] **d.** He spoke to the angels in Abraham's presence.[141] **e.** At this point commenced Prophecy, which is higher than the vision expressed in the words *The Lord appeared to him* (verse 1).[142] **the cry of Sodom. a.** Its cry of rebellion against God; or, the cry of the victims of its injustice and violence.[143] **b.** Sometimes the cry of the victims of oppression is greater than really warranted; here it is the reverse.[144] **verily, their sin is exceeding grievous. a.** More than

ANTHOLOGY

the way of the Lord, to do ts'dakah and justice; to the end that the Lord may bring upon Abraham that which He has spoken of him, which we interpreted as meaning *chesed.* In the Prophets?—*But let him that glories glory in this, that he understands and knows Me, that I am the Lord who exercises* love, *justice, and* charity *in the earth* (Jer. 9:23).

MhG. T.S. 18, 222.

153. THAT WHICH HE HAS SPOKEN OF HIM. This refers to the life of the Hereafter, to which He alluded when He said to him, *Your reward shall be exceeding great* (15:1).

Or Haafelah. T.S. 18, 224.

154. **The Lord (*Adonai*) said, etc.**

In this chapter on Sodom, *Adonai,* not *Elohim,* is written, as our text says, Adonai *said: "Verily, the cry of Sodom and Gomorrah is great."*[1]

Midrash Tadshe 20. T.S. 18, 226.

155. **The Lord said: "Verily, the cry of Sodom and Gomorrah is great."**

R. Eleazar said: From the blessing of the righteous you may learn [the cause of] the curse of the wicked. Thus it is written, *For I have known him,* etc., which is followed by, *The cry of Sodom and Gomorrah is great.*[1]

Yoma 38b. T.S. 18, 225.

156. THE CRY OF SODOM AND GOMORRAH IS GREAT, etc. It was great through the robbery committed there. [The verse continues:] *their sin [is exceedingly grievous]:* this refers to idolatry, adultery, and murder.

Whenever a stranger passed through they robbed him, in accordance with their laws, on the pretext that he was a rogue. They also despoiled the fatherless and the widow of their possessions, as it says, *They drive away the ass of the fatherless, they take the widow's ox for a pledge* (Job 24:3).

Midrash Hahefetz; Or Haafelah. T.S. 18, 230-1.

157. IS GREAT (*ki rabbah*). A maiden carried out bread to a poor man in a pitcher.[1] When it was discovered they daubed her with honey and placed her on the top of a wall; bees came and devoured her. This is the meaning of our text, *The cry of Sodom and Gomorrah ki rabbah,* which Rab Judah, citing Rab, interpreted: on account of the maiden (*ribah*).

Sanh. 109b. T.S. 18, 228.

§ 154 [1] According to Rabbinical interpretation *Adonai* (Lord) denotes Him as the God of mercy, *Elohim,* as the God of judgment. But the wicked force Him to turn to judgment even in His former capacity. Therefore the narrative of Sodom speaks of *Adonai*—even as the God of mercy their wickedness compelled Him to destroy them. Cf. par. 162.

§ 155 [1] The meaning is doubtful. Maharsha: Abraham is blessed because he will instruct his children to perform charity and justice, whence it follows that the Sodomites were cursed and destroyed because they lacked these, which made "*the cry of Sodom and Gomorrah great.*"

§ 157 [1] Because charity had been forbidden in Sodom; cf. par. 162.

will go down now, and see whether they have done altogether according

COMMENTARY

the earth can bear.[145] **b.** Grievous in its extent and heinousness.[146] **c.** Even though it is great and grievous, yet "I will go down now, and see," etc.[147] [21]**I will go down now. a.** I will descend from the judgment seat to see if it is still possible to show them mercy.[148] **b.** To test them yet once more, by sending two men to them [and seeing how they will treat them].[149] **c.** Here God informed Abraham that their doom was not yet finally decreed, to encourage him to pray on their behalf.[150] **d.** "Go down," because His Glory demeans itself by looking thus upon earthly beings.[151] **e.** An anthropomorphic expression, as in 11:7, to convey the idea that before God decided to punish the dwellers of the cities, "He descended," as it were, to obtain ocular proof of, or extenuation for, their crimes.[152] **whether they have done altogether. a.** If they have *all* acted in this way.[153] **b.** If they have indeed been as wicked as the cry suggests, and they persist in their rebellion against Me, then I will *altogether* destroy it; but *if not*, and they are prepared to cease their rebellious behavior, *I will know* how to pun-

ANTHOLOGY

158. Their sin is exceeding grievous.

R. Berechiah said: What was committed by Judah and Benjamin was not perpetrated even in Sodom. For concerning the sin of the latter we read, *Their sin is* exceeding *grievous*; whereas of the former it says, *The iniquity of the house of Israel and Judah is* most exceeding *great* (Ezek. 9:9). Yet whereas no remnant remained of the latter, a remnant was left of the former! The reason is this: the latter, *that was overthrown as in a moment* (Lam. 4:6), never did any good deeds, *and hands therein accepted no obligations (ibid.)*,[1] which R. Tanhuma interpreted, Hand was not stretched out to hand.[2] But the former did stretch out their hands to do their duty, as it says, *The hands of compassionate women have sodden their own children to comfort the sorrow-stricken (ibid. 10)*.[3]

Gen. R. 28, 5. T.S. 18, 229.

159. I will go down now.

Ten times the Shechinah (Divine Presence) went down into the world, one of which was the present.

ARN 34. T.S. 18, 232.

160. I will go down now, and see.

R. Abba b. Kahana said: This teaches that the Holy One, blessed is He, gave them an opportunity to repent. For it says, *I will go down now and see: if they have done according to the cry of it*, kalah—i.e., they deserve destruction (*k'liyah*). *If not, I will know*—i.e., I will let the world know that My attribute of Justice still functions.[1]

In the same vein the Bible relates, *Then the Lord rained down on Sodom and Gomorrah brimstone and fire* (19:24): if they repented, it was to be a rain [of blessing]; if not, it would be brimstone and fire. But though an extension of time was given them they did not repent, but on the contrary filled their measure of wickedness.

Gen. R. 49, 6; Mechilta, Parshath Hashirah 1. T.S. 18, 233-4.

161. I WILL GO DOWN NOW, AND SEE. Hence our Rabbis taught: Do not judge your neighbor until you come to his place.

Again, although it was fully manifest to Me that it was so, said He, yet I must carefully

§ 158 [1] AJV: *No hands fell upon her.*
[2] None helped one's neighbor.
[3] AJV: *They were their food.* The first meal a mourner eats after the funeral must be provided by his neighbors; this is known as *s'udath habraah*, the meal of comfort, and *l'baroth* in the text is connected with *habraah*. Lam. R. 3:10 explains: They gave their last morsel to provide this mourner's meal, even though they thereby hastened their own death and that of their children through starvation. Figuratively the Bible calls this seething their own children.

§ 160 [1] He interprets: *And if* [they are] *not* as evil as the cry which has come to Me in the past, *I will know* how to punish them, to vindicate the demands of Justice, but without destroying them. Thus they were given an opportunity to avert their doom by repentance.

to the cry of it, which is come unto Me; and if not, I will know." [22]And the men turned from thence, and

COMMENTARY

ish without destroying them.[154] **c.** Between "done" (עשׂו) and "altogether" (כלה) there is a *psik* (a strong disjunctive): hence it must be rendered, If they have done [thus], destruction (כליה) must be their fate.[155] **if not, I will know.** If they will not sin any more, I will know how to deal with them; or, "know" is used with the same sense as in verse 19: I will know them, and My Divine Providence will save them.[156] [22]**the men turned from thence. a.** From the place whither Abraham had escorted them.[157] **b.** The angel's [=God's] speech being ended, the narrative now returns to Abraham: from the time that the two angels departed from him until their arrival at Sodom Abraham stood before the remaining angel and pleaded.[158] **c.** When the angels saw Abraham in prophetic intercourse with God they departed without taking their leave, lest they hinder him in his prayers and intercession.[159]

ANTHOLOGY

consider their case in the presence of Gabriel and Rafael, and also Lot(?).[1]

Furthermore, He declared thus: I have most scrupulously examined their deeds and their posterity, hoping to find a righteous man amongst them for whose sake I could suspend their doom, but have found none.

MhG; Midrash Habiur; Sechel Tob. T.S. 18, 235-7.

162. According to the cry of it (her).

R. Levi said: Should I even desire to be silent, said the Almighty, the maiden's cry for justice would not permit Me. It once happened that two maidens went down to drink and draw water. "Why are you so pale?" one asked the other. She answered that all her food was gone and she was at death's door; thereupon the former filled her pitcher with flour and they exchanged their pitchers. When the Sodomites discovered this they burnt her.[1] Said the Holy One, blessed is He: Even if I desired to be silent, that maiden's cry for justice would not permit Me. Hence our text states, *according to the cry of her*: it does not say, according to the cry of them, but, *according to the cry of her*, viz., of that maiden.

R. Judah said: It was proclaimed in Sodom: Whoever assists the poor, the stranger, or the needy with bread shall be burnt alive. Now Palotis, Lot's daughter, was married to one of the foremost men of Sodom. She saw a poor man in the market place, emaciated, and was filled with pity for him. What did she do? Every day when she went out to draw water she would take food from her house in her pitcher, and so feed him. "How does this poor man live?" the Sodomites asked: and so the matter was discovered, and they led her out to be burnt. "God of the world!" she cried out, "Execute judgment for my wrongs on these Sodomites." Her cry ascended before the very Throne of Glory. Said the Holy One, blessed is He, I will go down and see: If the people of Sodom have done as this maiden has cried to Me, I will raze it to its very foundations.

Gen. R. 49, 6; PRE 25. T.S. 18, 238-9.

163. The men turned from thence.
This proves that angels have no back.[1]

Gen. R. 49, 7. T.S. 18, 242.

164. THE MEN TURNED FROM THENCE.
Completely drained of all mercy.[1]

MA. T.S. 18, 243.

§ 161 [1] Both the construction of the Hebrew and the thought are obscure. Perhaps we have an allusion to the crime against Palotis, the daughter of Lot (see next par.), with the latter as accuser.

§ 162 [1] Because they had strictly forbidden charity. See par. 157 and below.

§ 163 [1] This is rather obscure. M.M.K. explains: "From thence" is apparently superfluous, being obvious. Hence *vayyifnu*, they turned, is connected with *panim*, face, and the text is rendered: And the men (i.e., the angels) went toward Sodom, yet their faces still looked upon the place whence they came.

§ 164 [1] Stern justice was now imperative. *Vayyifnu* is now derived from *pinnah*, to clear out: They were cleared out, i.e., emptied, of all mercy.

went toward Sodom; but Abraham stood yet before the Lord. ²³And Abraham drew near, and said: "Wilt Thou indeed sweep away the righteous with the wicked? ²⁴Peradven-

COMMENTARY

d. All this was part of his prophetic vision, viz., that he escorted them on their way and they took leave of him.[160] **stood yet before the Lord. a.** Before the angel.[161] **b.** His prophetic vision was

not yet ended: he was still experiencing it.[162] **c.** Even though the two angels had already reached Sodom, Abraham still stood before God, beseeching mercy.[163] ²³**drew near. a.** Not in a *local* sense: he approached his task of wrestling with God in argument and intercession to spare the doomed cities.[164] **Wilt Thou indeed** (*ha-af*) **sweep away. a.** Abraham assumed that this was God's intention because He had spoken of Sodom collectively (*the cry of Sodom*).[165] **b.** *Af* means anger: God's anger is a figure of speech for His Justice. Abraham pleaded that His Mercy would demand that the whole city should be spared if it contained fifty righteous men. But even His Justice would demand that these righteous men should not be destroyed together with the wicked. Hence the next two

ANTHOLOGY

165. Abraham stood yet before the Lord.

R. Simeon said: This is an emendation of the Soferim, for the Shechinah was waiting for Abraham.[1]

Gen. R. 49, 7. T.S. 18, 244.

166. ABRAHAM STOOD YET BEFORE THE LORD. From this you learn that the Holy One, blessed is He, acceded to Abraham's request, *Pass not away, I pray Thee, from Thy servant* (verse 3).

MA. T.S. 18, 245.

167. Abraham approached.

R. Judah and R. Nehemiah interpreted this. R. Judah said: He approached to give battle,[1] as it says, *So Joab and the people that were with him* approached *to the* battle (2 Sam. 10:13). R. Nehemiah said: Approaching is for conciliation, as in the verse, *Then the children of Judah* approached *Joshua* (Josh. 14:6)—to conciliate him. Our Rabbis said: It means prayer, as in the verse, *And it came to pass at the time of the evening offering, that Elijah the prophet*

approached, *and said: "O Lord, the God of Abraham, of Isaac, and of Israel, let it be known this day that Thou art God in Israel"* (1 Kings 18:36). R. Eleazar interpreted: I come for battle, conciliation, or for prayer.[2]

Gen. R. 49, 8. T.S. 18, 246.

168. Wilt Thou indeed sweep away the righteous with the wicked?

It is written, *As a father has compassion on his children* (Ps. 103:13). R. Hiyya taught: That means, like the most compassionate of the Patriarchs. Who was that? Said R. Judah b. R. Simon: It was Abraham, who pleaded with the Almighty for Sodom, saying, "*Wilt Thou indeed sweep away?*" etc.

Was ever a father so compassionate as Abraham? When God said to Noah, *The end of all flesh is come before Me* (6:13), he remained silent and did not plead for mercy. But immediately God informed him, *Verily, the cry of Sodom and Gomorrah is great*, Abraham on the contrary approached Him and pleaded, *Wilt*

---

§ 165   [1] This does not mean that the Soferim (the Scribes and interpreters of the Torah in the time of Ezra and later) emended the text, but that their investigation revealed that it had been so written as to appear emended. For the text should logically have said: The Lord still stood before Abraham, since it was He who had revealed Himself to him, but that this would seem to be derogatory to His honor, for we speak of an inferior standing before his superior. Therefore our text appears to be emended.

§ 167   [1] He was ready to battle even with God Himself to save Sodom and Gomorrah.
   [2] He came "to battle," i.e., argue, with God: *That be far from Thee...to slay the righteous with the wicked... shall not the Judge of all the earth do justly?* (verse 25); to appease: *Behold, now, I have taken upon me to speak to the Lord*, etc. (verse 27); to pray: *Peradventure there are fifty righteous within the city— wilt Thou ... not forgive?* (verse 24). Mah.

COMMENTARY

verses contain both of these pleas.[166] **c.** Since the righteous obviously may not be destroyed, the wicked *must* be saved together with them (since God has spoken of the whole of Sodom sharing the same fate).[167] **d.** The remainder of the chapter forms one of the sublimest passages in the Bible or out of the Bible. Abraham's plea for Sodom is a signal illustration of his nobility of character. Amid the hatreds and feuds of primitive tribes who glorified brute force and despised pity, Abraham proves true to his new name and embraces in his sympathy all the children of men. Even the wicked inhabitants of Sodom were his brothers, and his heart overflows with sorrow over their doom. The unique dialogue between God and Abraham teaches two vital lessons: first, the supreme value of righteousness; and, se-

ANTHOLOGY

Thou indeed sweep away the righteous with the wicked?[1]

Midrash T'hillim 103; Zohar 1, 106a. T.S. 18, 247 note.

169. WILT THOU INDEED, etc. R. Phinehas the Priest b. Hama said: The Holy One, blessed is He, does not desire to condemn any creature, as it says, *For Thou art not a God that has pleasure in condemnation* (Ps. 5:4);[1] also, *For I have no pleasure in the death of him that dies, saith the Lord God* (Ezek. 18:32); also, *As I live, saith...God, I have no pleasure in the death of the wicked* (Ezek. 33:11). In what then does He delight? In vindicating His creatures, as it says, *The Lord is delighted in His vindication* [of wrongdoers] (Isa. 42:21).[2]

This is the proof: When His creatures sin and provoke Him, and He is angry with them, what does the Holy One, blessed is He, do? He seeks an advocate to plead in their defense, and opens a path to the advocate. And so when the Sodomites sinned He revealed it to Abraham, that he might plead on their behalf, as it says, *The Lord said: "Shall I hide from Abraham?"* etc.[3] There and then Abraham began to speak in their favor, as the text relates.

Tan. Vayyera 8. T.S. 18, 247.

170. WILT THOU INDEED? etc. All the righteous came with skillful pleading before the Holy One, blessed is He. What is written of Abraham? *How beautiful are thy steps in sandals, O prince's daughter . . . the work of the hands of a skilled workman* (Song 7:2):[1] he came before God with skillful intercession, as we see from our text.

Exod. R. 47, 9. T.S. 18, 248.

171. WILT THOU INDEED SWEEP AWAY (*ha-af tispeh*)? Rabbi and R. Jonathan commented. Rabbi interpreted: A mortal is dominated by his fury,[1] but the Holy One, blessed is He, dominates fury, as it says, *The Lord avenges and masters wrath* (Nah. 1:2). R. Jonathan said: A mortal is dominated by jealousy, but the Holy One, blessed is He, dominates jealousy, as it says, *The Lord is God* [i.e., master] *of jealousy and vengeance* (ibid.).

R. Huna, quoting R. Aha, interpreted: Sweep Thine anger (*af*) away: Thou conquerest anger, but anger cannot conquer Thee.

R. Joshua b. Nehemiah commented: Wouldst Thou destroy with the anger which Thou visitest upon Thy world both the righteous and the

§ 168 [1] Nevertheless, the Zohar concludes, Abraham too was not beyond censure, for he stopped at ten. The perfect advocate was Moses, who, when the Israelites sinned through the Golden Calf, pleaded for them unconditionally, even to the extent of offering himself: *Yet, now, if Thou wilt forgive their sin; and if not, blot me, I pray Thee, out of Thy book which Thou hast written* (Exod. 32:32).

§ 169 [1] AJV: *in wickedness.* But here it is understood in the sense of declaring one as wicked.
    [2] AJV: *for His righteousness' sake.*
    [3] On this interpretation He revealed this to Abraham in order to give him an opportunity to plead.

§ 170 [1] The Song of Songs was interpreted as a dialogue between God, the Lover, and Israel, the beloved. Hence there is nothing incongruous in making the "prince's daughter" allude to Abraham, Israel's ancestor. The "beautiful steps" are those he took to intercede for Sodom, the "sandals" fashioned by "a skilled workman," his arguments and pleas. He did not begin by pleading that the whole of Sodom be spared. First he argued that the righteous must not share the same fate as the wicked. Having gained his point, as it were, he pleaded that fifty righteous men should suffice to save the city, then gradually reduced the number to ten.

§ 171 [1] *Af*, rendered in the text, *Wilt* [Thou] *indeed*, also means anger, and it is so translated now.

43

ture there are fifty righteous within the city; wilt Thou indeed sweep away and not forgive the place for the fifty righteous that are therein? [25]That be far from Thee to do after

COMMENTARY

condly, God's readiness to pardon (Ezek. 33:11), if only He can do so consistently with justice.[168] [24]fifty righteous. a. There were five towns in all (see verse 29 and chap. 14:2); for the saving of each ten men were needed, so that if there were only forty, four would be saved; if thirty, three would be saved, and so on.[169] b. Throughout—even when he came down to ten—Abraham was pleading that *all* might be saved.[170] within the city. a. Sodom. If fifty were found in Sodom, the largest of the five cities, it is impossible that righteous men would not be found in the other cities too.[171] b. Even if they are only righteous "within the city," i.e., only by comparison with the rest of the people.[172] and not forgive the place. a. The whole, including the wicked, for the sake of the righteous?[174] b. He did not say, "the whole place," as in God's answer (verse 26), deliberately leaving it vague: his plea might cover the whole; or at least, if this was not possible, then the place where the righteous were.[175] [25]That be far (*halilah*) from Thee. a. It is inconceivable. Some connect *halilah* with *halul*,

ANTHOLOGY

wicked? Moreover, not only dost Thou not suspend the doom of the wicked for the sake of the righteous; Thou wouldst even destroy the righteous together with the wicked.

Gen. R. 49, 8.   T.S. 18, 249-50.

172. WILT THOU INDEED SWEEP AWAY THE RIGHTEOUS WITH THE WICKED? R. Levi said: [Job declared,] *It is all one—therefore I say, He destroys the innocent and the wicked* (Job 9:22). Abraham too said, "*Wilt Thou indeed sweep away the righteous with the wicked?*" but continued, "*That be far from Thee to do after this manner.*"[1]

Tan. Vayyera 5.   T.S. 18, 252.

173. **Peradventure there are fifty righteous.**

[He started with fifty] because five cities were involved, viz., Sodom, Gomorrah, Admah, Zeboiim, and Lasha, which would give ten for each. Because the Holy One, blessed is He, does not spurn the prayers of the multitude,[1] as it says, *Behold, God despises not the multitude* (Job 36:5);[2] also, [who answers] *as the Lord our God, whenever we call on Him?* (Deut. 4:7).[3]

Midrash Hahefetz.   T.S. 18, 254.

174. PERADVENTURE THERE ARE FIFTY RIGHTEOUS. Hence the Sages said: If there are fifty righteous in the world, the world endures for the sake of their righteousness. They inferred this from God's reply: "*If I find in Sodom fifty righteous men within the city, then I will forgive all the place for their sake*" (verse 26).

PRE 25; Or Haafelah.   T.S. 18, 255. 269.

175. **That be far (*halilah*) from thee, etc.**

Abraham pleaded, "Sovereign of the Universe! It is unworthy (*hulin*) of Thee, *to do after this manner, to slay the righteous with the wicked.*" Yet does He not? Surely it is written, *And I will cut off from thee the righteous and the wicked* (Ezek. 21:8)? That refers only to the semi-righteous.

R. Judan interpreted: It is a profanation

§ 172   [1] Job made it as a positive statement: metaphorically, he ate an unripe fig, one unfit for food—so was his assertion an unworthy one. But Abraham put it as a rhetorical question, answering it with a firm negative: the fruit of his faith was indeed ripe.
§ 173   [1] Technically ten constitute a "multitude," this being the quorum for public prayer. In all Abraham's pleas, until he came down to ten, it is assumed that ten righteous men were a minimum for *each* city, yet by various pleas the successively smaller numbers were to suffice for *all* the cities. Cf. pars. 195, 197.
   [2] AJV: *God is mighty, yet He despiseth not any.*
   [3] The point lies probably in the plural: when *we* call upon him—collectively, as a multitude.

ANTHOLOGY

(*halalah*) for Thee, it is foreign to Thee. R. Aha said: *Halilah* is written twice in that verse, implying, It would profane the Divine Name, it would desecrate the Divine Name.

Another reason for the repetition is this: Abraham pleaded, Far be it from Thee[1] not to forgive any creature, neither in this world nor in the next.

> A.Z. 4a; Gen. R. 49, 9;
> Tan. Y. Vayyera 11. T.S. 18, 256-8.

176. THAT BE FAR FROM THEE. R. Hiyya b. Abba said: We have here a blending of dialogue.[1] Abraham said: *"That be far from Thee . . . to slay the righteous with the wicked"*; to which the Almighty replied: *"Shall the righteous and the wicked be alike?* Is judgment to be suspended for the wicked on account of the righteous? Would that they were truly righteous! They are but counterfeit."[2]

> Gen. R. 49, 9. T.S. 18, 259.

177. THAT BE FAR FROM THEE. "Sovereign of the Universe!" he cried out, " 'twould profane Thy name. Let not men say, It is God's *métier* to destroy the generations in His cruelty: He destroyed the generation of Enosh, the generation of the Flood, and the generation of the Division, and He still does not abandon His craft." The Holy One, blessed is He, replied: "Say you thus? Come, and I will let you review all the generations which I destroyed, and show you that I did not exact [full] retribution from them. Yet if you still think that I did not do rightly, teach Me, and I will do!" . . . [The generations thus arraigned] exclaimed: "Sovereign of the Universe! That be far from Thee: Thou withholdest not the rights of any crea-ture"; as it says, *Therefore, hearken to me you men of understanding: Far be it from God, that He should do wickedness; and from the Almighty that He should commit iniquity* (Job 34:10).[1] Rather, *the work of a man will He requite to him (ibid.).* Therefore Abraham pleaded, *"That be far from Thee."*[2]

> Tan. Y. Vayyera 10. T.S. 18, 260.

178. THAT BE FAR FROM THEE, etc. Abraham pleaded: "Sovereign of the Universe! I see by Divine inspiration that one woman is destined to save an entire city. Am I then not worthy of saving these five towns?" Who was this woman? Serah the daughter of Asher. It happened when Sheba the son of Bichri revolted against David and entered Abel. For it says, *And they came and besieged him in Abel of Beth-maachah . . . and all the people that were with Joab battered the wall, to throw it down* (2 Sam. 20:15). On learning of this Serah demanded that Joab be summoned. When he appeared she said to him, "Have you not read in the Torah, *When you approach a city to fight against it, then proclaim peace to it* (Deut. 20:10)?" Joab answered: *"Far be it from me, far be it from me, that I should swallow up or destroy"* (2 Sam. 20:20).[1] "Thou, Who art compassionate," [continued Abraham,] "is it agreeable to Thee to destroy these? *That be far from Thee, to do after this manner."* Now, when Joab took the head of Sheba the son of Bichri, he withdrew immediately and harmed not the city. Said Abraham: "Joab, who took the head of a single man, who was indeed guilty, let the city alone. Wilt Thou, Who art compassionate, destroy all? *That be far from Thee."*

> Tan. Y. Vayyera 12, T.S. 18, 261.

§ 175   [1] Or as above: 'Twere unworthy of Thee, a profanation of Thy name.
§ 176   [1] The sentence is not wholly the speech of Abraham, but consists of plea and answer.
     [2] Even those who claim to be righteous are spurious, their righteousness a hypocritical pretense. This is based on the defective spelling of *tsaddikim* (righteous) in the present passage, where the second *yod* is missing: they are defective *tsaddikim*.
§ 177   [1] Or: that He should [unjustly] condemn.
     [2] It is, in fact, far from Thee and inconceivable.
§ 178   [1] See the whole chapter *ad loc.* for the complete narrative. According to an ancient tradition the "wise woman" of verse 16ff. was Serah, the daughter of Asher, who was supposed to have lived many centuries.

this manner, to slay the righteous with the wicked, that so the righteous should be as the wicked; that be far

COMMENTARY

empty, hollow: it would be empty, beneath Thy dignity and honor.[176] **b.** It would desecrate Thy name, connecting *halilah* with *hillul,* desecration.[177] **to slay the righteous with the wicked.** Even if Thou dost not forgive the whole city for their sake, surely Thou wilt not slay them too?[178] **that so the righteous should be as the wicked. a.** Men must then believe that there is no difference between the righteous and the wicked.[179] **b.** If the two are treated alike, Free Will and service of God

ANTHOLOGY

179. THAT BE FAR FROM THEE, etc. Speaks mortal man thus to the Holy One, blessed is He? This is to be explained by the text, *The God of Israel said, the Rock of Israel spoke to me: "Ruler in man is the righteous, ruling over the fear of God"* (2 Sam. 23:3). What does this mean? David said, "Come and hear what the Almighty has spoken"; as it says, *The God of Israel said.* "What did He tell you?" [they inquired]. Said he: "*The Rock of Israel spoke to me: Ruler in man is the righteous, ruling over the fear of God.*" How so? The Holy One, blessed is He, pronounces a decree with His awe, but the righteous rule over that awe.[1] Now, where do we find this? The Holy One, blessed is He, is about to overturn the five cities by His fear, but Abraham rules over His fear and says, Why dost Thou so? as it says, *That be far from Thee.* Blessed be the Name of the Holy One, blessed is He, who so loves the righteous for their humility that He calls them His princes, who rule over His fear, as it says, "*That be far from Thee.*"

AB 22, 1. T.S. 18, 262.

180. THAT BE FAR FROM THEE. Let our master teach us: May one stand and pray in a frivolous frame of mind? Thus did our masters teach: One may pray only in a solemn mood. David said: *Serve the Lord with fear, and rejoice with trembling* (Ps. 2:11). You will find that the fathers of the world[1] prayed in a spirit of awe. Moses said, *And I fell down before the Lord . . . for I was in dread,* etc. (Deut. 9:18-19). He was then beseeching compassion on Israel's behalf , as it says, *And Moses besought the Lord* (Exod. 32:11). He girded his loins in prayer to plead in Israel's favor. Said the Holy One, blessed is He, to him: "Moses, you know not how to intercede." What did He do? He wrapped Himself in a praying robe, even like the precentor at the lectern, and said to Moses: "Pray thus before Me: Say, *The Lord, the Lord, God, merciful and gracious,*" etc. (*ibid.* 34:6). For it says, *And the Lord passed before him* (*ibid.*). What does "passed" mean? Like one [the precentor] who stands before the reading desk.[2] See how the righteous seek to defend the world and plead for Israel. And not only for Israel but for the wicked too, as it says, *As I live, saith the Lord God, I have no pleasure in the death of the wicked* (Ezek. 33:11). Why [do they pray on their behalf]? Because they may repent. The proof is that when the Almighty desired to overturn these cities He took counsel with Abraham, as it says, *And the Lord said: Verily, the cry of Sodom and Gomorrah is great.* Abraham immediately interceded for them, hoping that perhaps they would repent. This we know from our text, "*That be far from Thee,*" etc.

Abba Saul said: When a man prays devoutly he may rest assured that his prayer will be heard, for it says, *Thou wilt direct their heart, Thou wilt cause Thine ear to attend* (Ps. 10:17). None prayed with such fervor as Abraham, when he urged, "*That be far from Thee to do after this manner.*" When the Holy One, blessed is He, saw how he pleaded that He should not destroy the world, He praised him: *You are*

§ 179   [1] And annul the decree.
§ 180   [1] The early ancestors and teachers of the Jewish people. For the opening phrase, see par. 1, note 1.
          [2] This is a technical phrase for leading a congregation in prayer.

from Thee; shall not the Judge of all the earth do justly?" ²⁶And the

COMMENTARY

must cease.¹⁸⁰ **c.** Of what value would proof of Divine Providence be?¹⁸¹ **the Judge of all the earth. a.** Shall not the Judge Who sent thee (the angel) on this mission, etc.¹⁸² **b.** Being Judge of all the earth Thou wilt certainly destroy it all if Thou wilt judge all by the majority, for the majority are wicked.¹⁸³ **c.** Thou judgest each man according to his ways: how then canst Thou include the righteous in a general punishment?¹⁸⁴ **d.** Abraham did not have the slightest doubt on the question: but he was filled with anxiety lest God's name be profaned among the nations.¹⁸⁵ **e.** These words have been well described as an "epochal sentence in the Bible". They make justice the main pillar of God's Throne; without it, the whole idea of the Divine totters. Justice, it is true, is not the only ethical quality in God or man, nor is it the highest quality; but it is the basis for all the others. . . . The boldness of the Patriarch's ringing challenge, the universality of the phrase "all the earth," and the absolute conviction that the infinite might of God must be controlled by the decrees

ANTHOLOGY

fairer than the children of men; grace is poured upon your lips (Ps. 45:3).

> Tan. Y. Vayyera 9; Tan. Hayye Sarah 1.
> T.S. 18, 263 and note.

181. To do after this manner.

R. Abba said: Scripture does not write, to do this, but, *to do after this manner,* which means neither this nor anything like it nor even anything of a lesser nature.

> Gen. R. 49, 9. T.S. 18, 264.

182. To slay the righteous with the wicked.

When Abraham the Patriarch stood to intercede on behalf of the Sodomites, what is written? *"That be far from Thee to do after this manner, to slay the righteous with the wicked,"* etc. R. Abba commented: Thou hast sworn not to bring another flood upon the world: wouldst Thou evade the oath—'tis incredible! Thou wilt not bring a flood of water, yet wouldst bring a flood of fire! Then Thou wilt not have kept Thine oath.

R. Levi observed: *Shall not the Judge of all the earth do justly?* If Thou desirest the world to endure, there can be no absolute justice;¹ if Thou desirest uncompromising justice, there can be no world. Wouldst Thou grasp the cord by both ends, desiring the world to exist and yet enforcing absolute justice? Take one of these only; for if Thou canst not forgo a little, the world cannot endure. Said the Holy One, blessed is He, to him: *You have loved vindication and hated condemnation; therefore God, your God, has anointed you with oil of gladness above your fellow-men* (Ps. 45:8). What does *"above your fellow-men"* mean? There were ten generations from Noah to yourself, and I spoke not to any of all these save yourself.

> Gen. R. 39, 6. T.S. 18, 265.

183. Shall not the judge of all the earth do justly?

R. Judah b. R. Simon commented: In the case of an [earthly] tribunal a decision may be appealed, from the commander to the prefect and from the prefect to the governor;¹ wilt Thou not act justly because none can appeal from Thy decision? R. Judah said: When Thou desirest to judge Thy world, Thou didst entrust it to two, e.g., Remus and Romulus,² and if one wished to do anything, the other could stop him. Wilt Thou, because none can prevent Thee, not do justly?

> Gen. R. 49, 9. T.S. 18, 266.

§ 182 ¹ I.e., justice untempered by mercy.
§ 183 ¹ The terms indicate Roman officials. It is doubtful if the appeal system operated in Jewish courts.
   ² The legendary founders of Rome. Their mention here is unexpected and surprising. Perhaps they were regarded as the rod in God's hand for punishing the nations. Th. suggests that we have a reference here to the early Roman system of dyarchy, wherein a duumvirate ruled, and a decision by one could be appealed to the other.

Lord said: "If I find in Sodom fifty righteous within the city, then I will forgive all the place for their sake."

COMMENTARY

of Justice—that, in fact, an unjust God would be a contradiction in terms—are truly extraordinary.[186] [26]**the Lord said.** He informed Abraham that He would deal with them with His Attribute of Mercy [This is based on the usual Rabbinic interpretation of "Lord"—the Tetragrammaton—as always referring to His merciful side. But even Mercy did not ultimately permit them to be saved.—Ed.].[187] **in Sodom. a.** Which was the chief place of the threatened area.[188] **b.** Sodom is mentioned because as the largest of the cities there was a greater possibility of finding fifty righteous men there.[189] **within the city. a.** I.e., who are *openly* God-fearing.[190] **b.** Even if they are strangers there. Abraham had Lot in mind.[191] **c.** Even if they are righteous only in the city, i.e., only by comparison with her other inhabitants.[192] **d.** These words are added to show that fifty righteous men, whether in Sodom or in any other city, would save it.[193] **all the place. a.** Cities and their suburbs.[194] **b.** Even those cities (of the five) which did not contain any righteous at all.[195] **c.** Not only the righteous.[196] **for their sake.** Heb. *baaburam,* fr. *abur,* for the sake of. This is not the same as *l'maan,* the word used by Abraham in verse 24: the latter implies for the benefit of: i.e., there Abraham pleaded for the

ANTHOLOGY

184. If I find in Sodom fifty righteous.

[One of the characteristics of a wise man is that] he does not interrupt his neighbor. An example of this is found in connection with Abraham. When he prayed on behalf of the people of Sodom the Holy One, blessed is He, said to him: *"If I find in Sodom fifty righteous within the city, then I will forgive all the place for their sake."* It was fully known to Him who spoke and the world existed,[1] that even if it had contained three or five righteous men, sin would not have mastered it. Nevertheless He waited until Abraham finished what he had to say, and then He answered him, as it says, *The Lord went His way, as soon as He had left off speaking to Abraham* (verse 33).

ARN 37. T.S. 18, 268.

185. Then I will forgive all the place for their sake.

An unbeliever[1] [has no portion in the Hereafter]. Who, for instance, is meant? Said R. Joseph: Those, for instance, who say, How do our rabbis benefit us? They study the Bible for themselves and the Mishnah for themselves. Said Abaye to him: This is insolence against the Bible too, for it is written, *Thus saith the Lord: But for My covenant* [studied] *day and night, I had not appointed the ordinances of heaven and earth* (Jer. 33:25).[2] R. Nahman b. Isaac said: You may infer it also from the text, *Then I will forgive all the place for their sake.*[3]

Sanh. 99b. T.S. 18, 270.

186. Then I will forgive all the place for their sake. R. Judah b. R. Simon and R. Joshua b. Levi interpreted the following text: *For it is for God to say: "I have forgiven"* (Job 34:31); that is as we read, *Then I will forgive the whole place for their sake.* The verse continues: *I will not take a pledge,*[1] which means, I will not take their lives in pledge [for their sins], as in the verse, *If you at all take your neighbor's garment in pledge* (Exod. 22:25).[2] Yet men abuse Me and say that I do not judge well. *Apart from Me, do you see* (Job 34:32) —without Me,[3] go and scrutinize My judgment,

§ 184   [1] I.e., whose Word created all. The phrase is now part of the morning prayers.
§ 185   [1] See Sanh. (Sonc. ed.) p. 602, n. 1.
          [2] I.e., the world endures only because the Torah is studied. To deny the value of the Rabbis, therefore, is insolently to deny the truth of what the Bible asserts.
          [3] Which likewise declares that a place is spared for the sake of the righteous. To the Rabbis the scholar was automatically assumed to be righteous—there was no value in scholarship otherwise.
§ 186   [1] AJV translates the complete verse: *For hath any said unto God: I have borne chastisement, though I offend not.*
          [2] In both verses there is the Heb. root *habal.*
          [3] I.e., without My all-encompassing knowledge. AJV translates vs. 32: *That which I see not teach Thou me,* etc.

[27]And Abraham answered and said: "Behold now, I have taken upon me to speak unto the Lord, who am but dust and ashes. [28]Peradventure there

COMMENTARY

wicked to be saved for the sake, i.e., the benefit, of the righteous, e.g., the wicked might be a near relation of the righteous. God answered that they would be saved *baaburam*, for their sake, even though no *personal* interests whatsoever were at stake.[197]   [27]**I have taken upon me to speak. a.** To resolve the doubts in my mind about the manner in which God's justice works.[198] **b.** It was I who commenced to speak: perhaps I set the target too high in naming fifty.[199] **dust and ashes. a.** I am from the dust, and will revert to ashes.[200] **b.** Though so lowly, yet would I speak and seek to understand

ANTHOLOGY

and if I have erred, *teach me* (ibid.). And *if I have wrought injustice* (ibid.) to the earlier generations, *I will do it no more* (ibid.) to the later generations.[4]

To him will I keep silence [and] *to his scions* (ibid. 41:4):[5] [The Almighty said to Abraham:] I will maintain silence before you and your scions. [He kept silent] before Abraham who said, *That be far from Thee*, etc.; before Moses, who implored, *Lord, Why does Thy wroth wax hot against Thy people?* (Exod. 32:11); before Joshua, who said, *Wherefore hast Thou at all brought this people over the Jordan?* (Josh. 7:7); and before David, who said, *Why standest Thou afar off, O Lord?* (Ps. 10:1).[6] *Or his proud talk, or his gracious array of words* (Job 41:4): with grace were the words of his lips crowned when he beseeched clemency for the Sodomites.

Gen. R. 49, 10.   T.S. 18, 271.

187.   **I am but dust and ashes.**

The righteous accept Divine judgment with resignation. Abraham was resigned, as it says, *I am but dust and ashes.*[1]

Torath Kohanim Sh'mini.   T.S. 18, 272.

188.   I AM BUT DUST AND ASHES. Mishnah: What is the order [of service] at fasts?[1] The Ark is taken out into the public square of the city, and burnt ashes are sprinkled on it.

Gemara: R. Judan b. R. Manasseh and R. Samuel b. Nahman disagreed. One maintained that the ashes were to recall the merit of Abraham; the other, to recall the merit of Isaac. On the former view either dust or ashes will do, in allusion to his saying, "*I am but* dust *and* ashes." But for the latter, it must be ashes, to symbolize that it was as though Isaac's ashes lay in a heap on the altar.[2]

J. Taan. 2, 1.   T.S. 18, 273.

189.   I AM BUT DUST AND ASHES. The Holy One, blessed is He, said to Israel: I delight in you, because even when I confer greatness upon you, you humble yourselves before Me. I conferred greatness upon Abraham: he said to Me, *I am but dust and ashes.* On Moses and Aaron: they declared, *Yet what are we* (Exod. 16:8)? On David: he declared, *But I am a worm, and no man* (Ps. 22:7).

Raba—others maintain, R. Johanan—said: Higher praise is given to Moses and Aaron than to Abraham. Of Abraham it says, *I am but*

---

[4] The "earlier" and "later" generations are those of the Flood and the Separation of Tongues, and the Sodomites, respectively. On this interpretation God is the speaker, defending Himself against the charge of injustice.

[5] Reading לו (to him) instead of לא (not), and deriving בדיו from בד, a branch, i.e., to his descendants. AJV: *Would I keep silence concerning his boastings?*

[6] All of these hinted doubt of God's justice.

§ 187   [1] This is best explained in the light of Sechel Tob: *Behold now, I have taken upon me to speak to the Lord, and I am but dust and ashes*: Since I have begun to speak to the Lord, even if He slay me (so that I become dust and ashes), I will not refrain from beseeching His compassion. Our passage may be explained similarly: Should God slay him for his presumption in arguing with Him, he accepted the justice of his fate.

§ 188   [1] Specially proclaimed for rain.
        [2] When he was placed thereon for a burnt-offering.

49

shall lack five of the fifty righteous; wilt Thou destroy all the city for lack of five?" And He said: "I will not destroy it, if I find there forty

COMMENTARY

God's justice.[201] **c.** Though I am but dust and ashes, yet hast Thou graciously desired me to speak before Thee.[202] [28]**I will not destroy.** He did not answer that the number would not be found there, for they were still on trial (see on verse 21, *I will go*

ANTHOLOGY

dust and ashes; but of Moses and Aaron it says, *Yet what are we?*[1]

Hul. 89a. T.S. 18, 275-6.

190. I AM BUT DUST AND ASHES. All who possess these three qualities are of the disciples of our Father Abraham: A generous eye, a lowly spirit, and a humble soul. Where did he display a humble soul? When he said, *"I am but dust and ashes."*

See how great was his humility. God had promised him the whole world, yet he said, *I am but dust and ashes!*

R. Tanhum b. Hanilai taught: *Your memorials are like ashes, your eminences are eminences of clay* (Job 13:12): If you are worthy, you are the children of Abraham, who compared himself to ashes; but if not, *your eminences are eminences of clay*: prepare for the servitude of Egypt [where you slaved in mortar and clay].

ARN Codex 2, Ch. 45; MhG;
Tan. Y. Thetse. T.S. 18, 277 and note.

191. I AM BUT DUST AND ASHES. Had Nimrod slain me, said he, would I not have been dust by now; and had he burnt me, would I not have been ashes?[1] Said the Holy One, blessed is He, to him: "You have declared, *I am but dust and ashes.* As you live, through these will I give your children a means of atonement"; as it says, *And a man that is clean shall gather up* the ashes *of the heifer . . . [and it shall be kept for the congregation of the children of Israel for a water of sprinkling; it is a purification*

from sin] (Num. 19:9); also, *And for the unclean they shall take of the* dust *of the burning of the purification from sin (ibid.* 17).

Gen. R. 49, 11. T.S. 18, 278.

192. I AM BUT DUST AND ASHES. Thus sang Hannah too, *He raises up the poor out of the dust* (1 Sam. 2:8), alluding to him who declared himself but dust and ashes [viz., Abraham]. Now, when He raises up the poor out of the dust, what does He do to him? He seats him on the throne of glory, as it says, *To make them sit with princes, and inherit the throne of glory* (*ibid.*).

Similarly it is written, *He . . . hangs the earth over nothingness* (Job 26:7). This teaches that the whole world stands only on him who makes himself as nothing. Which nation does that? Israel, as it says, *This people I formed for Myself, they tell of My praise* (Isa. 43:21).[1] What did Abraham say? *I am but dust and ashes.*

AB 18; Midrash Alpha Bethoth 111.
T.S. 18, 280-1.

193. **Perhaps there shall lack of the fifty righteous five.**

R. Hiyya b. Abba said: Abraham desired to go from fifty straight down to five.[1] Said the Holy One, blessed is He, to him: Go back to the beginning.[2] R. Levi said: This may be compared to a water-clock filled with water: the defending counsel may plead only as long as there is water in it.[3] Sometimes, however, the judge

§ 189 [1] Implying complete self-negation.
§ 191 [1] See Vol. II, chap. 15, pars. 57-8.
§ 192 [1] The relevance is not clear. Probably: they exist only for God, counting themselves as nought.
§ 193 [1] He renders: Peradventure the fifty righteous shall be lacking, and there be but five.
   [2] To a number nearer your first—it is too great a jump.
   [3] In Roman courts a time-limit was set for pleading.

and five." [29]And he spoke unto Him yet again, and said: "Peradventure there shall be forty found there." And He said: "I will not do it for the forty's sake." [30]And he said: "Oh, let not the Lord be angry, and I will speak. Peradventure there shall thirty be found there." And

He said: "I will not do it, if I find thirty there." [31]And he said: "Behold now, I have taken upon me to speak unto the Lord. Peradventure there shall be twenty found there." And He said: "I will not destroy it for the twenty's sake." [32]And he said: "Oh, let not the Lord be angry,

ANTHOLOGY

desires the counsel to plead further; he then orders more water to be added.[4]

Gen. R. 49, 12. T.S. 18, 282.

194. THE FIFTY RIGHTEOUS (tsaddikim). R. Johanan observed: Wherever tsaddikim occurs in the story of Sodom it is written defectively.[1] This corresponds to another observation of his, viz.: Z'kenenu in the verse, And z'kenenu (our elders) spoke to us (Josh. 9:11) is spelled defectively, intimating that they were elders in guilt, elders in evil.

R. Joshua b. Levi said: Abraham pleaded, Combine their good deeds, and they will amount to fifty.[2] R. Judah b. R. Simon said: [Abraham urged:] Art Thou not the Righteous of the Universe? Unite Thyself with them and they will amount to fifty.

Gen. R. 49, 9. T.S. 18, 283.

195. PERHAPS THERE SHALL LACK FIVE OF THE FIFTY RIGHTEOUS. Here the Torah taught us correct procedure: When a man would petition a king for anything, let him first ask for a small thing; if he finds the king gracious, and he grants his petition, then he may ask

what he wishes. Therefore Abraham first asked, "Perhaps there shall lack five of the fifty." Why so? This would give nine for each of the five cities, whilst the merit of Abraham's prayer would combine with each city separately, making the equivalent of ten righteous men in each.

Midrash Hahefetz. T.S. 18, 285.

196. **Perhaps forty shall be found there.**

This would give [ten] righteous men, more than in the generation of the Flood,[1] plus thirty, the number of righteous for whose sake the world endures.[2]

MA. T.S. 18, 286.

197. PERHAPS FORTY SHALL BE FOUND THERE.

These will atone for four cities, Sodom and Gomorrah, Admah and Zeboiim. As for Zoar: Since she has been but recently populated and her iniquities are but few,[1] forgive her for the sake of Thy compassion. The Holy One, blessed is He, assured him: "I will not destroy them if I find forty."

PERHAPS THIRTY SHALL BE FOUND THERE.

Ten for Sodom, ten for Gomorrah, and ten for Admah. For the sake of Thy compassion

---

[4] In the same way God desired Abraham to plead for Sodom, even though He knew the result in advance.

§ 194 [1] See par. 176, n. 2. However, Midrash Haseroth Viy'theroth (Defective and Plene Spellings) 1, 33, points out that with one exception (Exod. 23:8) the word is always spelled defectively in the Pentateuch.

[2] Everyone must have some good deed to his credit; if these are all combined they will total the good deeds to be expected from fifty righteous.

§ 196 [1] According to tradition there were eight righteous people in that generation—Noah and his wife, his three sons and their wives.

[2] See par. 132.

§ 197 [1] See chap. 19, par. 69.

and I will speak yet but this once. Peradventure ten shall be found there." And He said: "I will not destroy it for the ten's sake." [33]And the Lord went His way, as soon as He had left off speaking to Abraham;

COMMENTARY

down).[203] [32]**I will speak yet but this once.** He realized that if there were not even ten, no plea could save them. He did not ask on behalf of Lot, thinking that he must be destroyed together with them, since he had thrown in his lot with them.[204] **ten.** Knowing that God does not desire the death of the righteous, he was confident that if there were less, they at least would be saved, and that he need not intercede on their behalf.[205] [33]**the Lord went.**

ANTHOLOGY

forgive Zeboiim, Thou who art full of compassion and great [in merit].[2] To me, whose merit is small, grant Zoar, whose sins are light, because of my intercession. The Holy One, blessed is He, answered: "I will not destroy if I find thirty."

PERHAPS TWENTY SHALL BE FOUND THERE.

A "congregation" for Sodom and a "congregation" for Gomorrah.[3] Since Thou hast agreed to forgive Zeboiim for the sake of Thy compassion and Zoar because of my intercession, Admah is left but one, and the one should be ignored as against the many, for being in a minority it is of no account. The Lord said, *"I will not destroy for the twenty's sake."*

PERHAPS TEN SHALL BE FOUND THERE.

Why ten? That there might be enough for an assembly[4] [to make atonement] for all of them. Another reason: He thought that there were ten, viz., Lot and his wife, his four daughters, and his four sons-in-law. Another reason: Because in the generation of the Flood eight indeed had remained, yet the world was not spared on their account.[5]

R. Judah b. R. Simon and R. Hanin, quoting R. Johanan, said: Here ten were required, but in Jerusalem even one [would have saved the

city,] as it says, *Run to and fro in the streets of Jerusalem . . . and seek . . . if you can find a man . . . that does justly* (Jer. 5:1). Thus it also says, *One by one, to find out the account* (Eccl. 7:27), which R. Isaac interpreted: How far can an account be drained?[6] Down to one.

When Abraham reached ten he became silent. Ten can avert retribution, for the Sanctity of the [Divine] Name is found in [an assembly of] ten, as it says, *I will be hallowed among the children of Israel* (Lev. 22:32), and it also says, *Get you up from among this congregation* (Num. 17:10) [which consisted of ten,] since Joshua and Caleb had dissociated themselves from their counsel.[7]

Sechel Tob; Gen. R. 49, 13;
Midrash Hahefetz. T.S. 18, 287-290. 293.

198. **I will not destroy for the ten's sake.**

Hence our Sages said: If there are ten righteous in a place, the place is saved for their sake.

Said the Holy One, blessed is He: I will indeed not destroy the place for the sake of the ten, but it is fully known to Me that it contains less than a third of a congregation [of righteous],[1] viz., Lot and his two betrothed daughters, and these are so few that they are as nought.

PRE 25; Sechel Tob. T.S. 18, 292. 294.

---

[2] So canst Thou add Thine own merit to theirs; cf. par. 194.
[3] See par. 173 and notes *ad loc*. Ten constitute a congregation.
[4] Probably, the same as congregation.
[5] Hence he understood that it would be useless to go below ten.
[6] How few can save?
[7] The "congregation" there were the twelve spies sent by Moses to spy out the land, less Joshua and Caleb, leaving ten. This verse then, taken in conjunction with the previous one quoted, indicates that the "children of Israel" in whom God's Name is hallowed (here understood as meaning that His Name is peculiarly and intimately associated therewith) means a "congregation" of ten.
§ 198 [1] See last par. and n. 6 *ad loc*. This would seem to differ with the statement in par. 184 that it contained not even three.

and Abraham returned unto his place.

COMMENTARY

a. His glory departed.[206] **b.** Because God did not desire him to plead further; therefore the spirit of Prophecy, which had enabled him to intercede with God, now left him.[207] **unto his place. a.** Hebron. This vision had occurred at the point whither Abraham had escorted his visitors.[208] **b.** When God's glory departed it seemed to him that he returned to his place: immediately the prophetic vision ended he found himself sitting again in his home.[209] **c.** "His place" may mean his usual routine: he now resumed his wonted hospitality, seeking new wayfarers to enjoy the hospitality of his home.[210] **d.** To his usual humility.[211] **e.** Had the Divine Presence remained Abraham would have continued his intercession; seeing, however, that it had departed, he immediately returned home.[212]

ANTHOLOGY

199. The Lord went His way, as soon as He had left off speaking to Abraham.

As long as the defending counsel pleads the judge waits; when he becomes silent the judge rises. So it was here. [Conversely,] as long as the judge shows that he is willing to listen to him, the counsel pleads; but when the judge rises, he becomes silent. So it was here.

It is further written, *Abraham returned to his place.* As long as the defending counsel pleads and the judge is willing to listen, the accuser waits. But when the judge rises and the defending counsel becomes silent, the accuser goes forth to execute his mission. So, *the Lord went His way;* then it is written, *The two angels* came to Sodom (19:1).

Gen. R. 49, 14. T.S. 18, 295.

200. THE LORD WENT HIS WAY, etc. See the humility of the Holy One, blessed is He. R. Berechiah said: When two people who are conversing wish to part, the normal practice is for the inferior to seek permission from the greater. But when the Holy One, blessed is He, desired to part from Abraham after speaking to him, He sought permission—if we might speak thus—from Abraham, as it says, *And the Lord went His way.* When? *As soon as He had left off speaking to Abraham.*[1] Only after that do we read that *Abraham returned to his place.*

Tan. Vayyera 8. T.S. 18, 296.

201. Abraham returned to his place.

Scripture tells us that when the spirit of prophecy departs from them all prophets revert to their original state with its bodily needs, just like all other men. Moses, our Teacher, was an exception: he never reverted to his original state.

MhG. T.S. 18, 298.

§ 200 [1] The manner of the inference is not clear. Perhaps: The text implies that He was the last Speaker; hence He must have asked for leave.

GENESIS

CHAPTER XIX

¹And the two angels came to Sodom

COMMENTARY

¹the two angels. Viz., those who had visited Abraham.[1] **angels.** Only here and in v. 15, "*the angels hastened Lot,*" are they designated angels; everywhere else they are called men: where they acted as humans they are called men: where they acted as celestial messengers they were called angels.[2] **at**

ANTHOLOGY

1. The two angels came to Sodom.

Gabriel went to overturn Sodom. But it is written, *The* two *angels came to Sodom?*—Michael accompanied him to rescue Lot. This may also be inferred from the verse, *And he overthrew those cities* (verse 25).

Three visited Abraham, as it says, *And he lifted up his eyes and looked, and lo,* three *men stood over against him* (18:2); yet now there were only two?[1] The Holy One, blessed is He, sent three angels, each on his own mission, for one angel does not perform two missions, nor do two angels do one task. Michael came to inform Sarah. Having done his task, he departed; then the other two proceeded on their mission, as it says, *The* two *angels came to Sodom.*

It was taught: Michael came to inform Sarah [of Isaac's birth], Gabriel to overturn Sodom, and Rafael to heal Abraham [of the wound of circumcision]. Others maintain that Rafael came to inform Sarah and heal [Abraham], as it says, *And* Elohim *healed Abimelech, and his wife, and his maidservants; and they bore children* (20:17);[2] while Michael and Gabriel came to overturn Sodom.[3] What are the grounds for the first Tanna's view?—*And* he *overthrew those cities.* What is the basis of the second teacher's view? *The* two *angels came to Sodom.*

> B.M. 86b; Tan. Y. Vayyera 20; Kallah Rabbathi 7. T.S. 19, 1-3.

2. THE ANGELS. Here you call them angels, whereas earlier they are called men?[1] Earlier when the Shechinah was above them, they are called men; but as soon as the Shechinah departed from them they resumed their angelic status. R. Tanhum, quoting R. Levi, said: To Abraham, endowed with great spiritual qualities, they appeared as men; but to Lot, a man poor in spiritual qualities,[2] they appeared in the form of angels. R. Hanin said: Before doing their task they are called men; after they have done it they are called angels. R. Tanhuma said: This may be compared to one who receives a governorship from the king. Before coming to the seat of his authority he walks like an ordinary citizen; but when he comes to it he walks as a lord. Similarly, before they were to perform their mission they are called men; but when about to perform it[3] they are called angels.

> Gen. R. 50, 2. T.S. 19, 4.

3. THE TWO ANGELS CAME TO SODOM. Let our master teach us:[1] How many modes of ex-

---

§ 1   [1] The def. art. here, as well as the whole sequence of the narrative, shows that the same are meant.
[2] *Elohim* (AJV: God) is now understood to mean an angel. The text shows that one angel healed and made childbirth possible. Hence the same angel (Rafael) is now assumed to have healed and brought the tidings of Isaac's birth.
[3] This disagrees with the preceding par.

§ 2   [1] *Three* men *stood over against him* (Abraham) (18:2); see par. 1, n. 1.
[2] Lit., Abraham, whose strength was great . . . Lot, whose strength was poor.
[3] Lit., before they performed . . . when they had performed. But the comparison as well as the narrative itself makes the present rendering necessary.

§ 3   [1] See chap. 18, par. 1, n. 1.

at even; and Lot sat in the gate of

COMMENTARY

even. a. To give Lot an opportunity to offer hospitality, which would justify his being saved. Had they arrived by day, they might have been prevented from entering the city altogether.[3] **b.** They were particular to enter at even, as a test whether anyone would invite them into his home.[4] **the gate. a.** That was where he lived, not actually in Sodom but near the gate.[5] **b.** The passage beneath the

ANTHOLOGY

ecution is the Court of Law empowered to impose?—Four, viz., stoning, burning, slaying,[2] and strangling. Which is the most severe? Our Rabbis maintained, Stoning. R. Simeon b. Yohai said, Burning, since it is imposed upon a priest's daughter who commits incest.[3] See how heinous is incest, as it says, *So he that goes in to his neighbor's wife; whosoever touches her shall not go unpunished* (Prov. 6:29). R. Joshua b. Nehemiah said: The Sodomites too, because they were wildly immoral,[4] were condemned to die by fire, as it says, *Then the Lord rained upon Sodom and Gomorrah brimstone and fire* (verse 24). As soon as they were thus sentenced the Holy One, blessed is He, said to the angels, "Why do you stand? Go and destroy!" Forthwith they descended and obeyed their Creator's behest. Whence do you know this? From our text.

> Tan. Y. Vayyera 14. T.S. 19, 5.

4. THE TWO ANGELS CAME TO SODOM. It is written, *But He is at one with Himself, and who can turn Him? And what His soul desires, even that He does* (Job 23:13). What does *But He is at one with Himself* mean? Said R. Phinehas ha-Cohen b. R. Hanina: Because He is Unique in His world He knows the judgment of His creatures. Whomever He bids, "Go on My mission," the same must go. Thus the text continues, *and what His soul desires, even that He does.* So too in the case of Sodom, He carefully weighed their judgment and saw that they deserved extermination.[1] Then He sent the angels to overturn them.

> Tan. Y. Vayyera 21. T.S. 19, 6.

5. **At even.**

It is written, *And the living creatures ran (ratso) and returned as the appearance of a flash of lightning* (Ezek. 1:14). R. Aibu commented: It does not say *ratsoth* (running), but *ratso*: they are eager to perform their task.[1] *As the appearance of a flash of lightning:* R. Judah b. R. Simon observed, quoting R. Levi b. Parta: [Like the flames which leap up] when you scatter olive waste in a stove.[2] R. Hiyya b. Abba said: They were like a wind-fanned spark. Our Rabbis said: As the eye perceives a flash of lightning.[3] [Yet they leave Abraham at noon and only arrive in Sodom in the evening!⁴] The truth is that they were angels of mercy, so they waited, thinking that he might perhaps find something in their favor. When, however, he found nothing, *the two angels came to Sodom at even.*

> Gen. R. 50, 1. T.S. 19, 8.

6. AT EVEN. Evening had fallen upon Sodom;[1] her sun had set and her doom was sealed.

> Gen. R. 50, 3. T.S. 19, 9.

7. AT EVEN. R. Levi said: The Holy One, blessed is He, judges the nations only at night,

---

[2] Decapitation.
[3] Which includes adultery and forbidden sexual relations in general. The criterion of the severity of punishment is not the amount of pain it causes, but the greater or lesser nature of the crime for which it is inflicted.
[4] See par. 22.
§ 4   [1] Cf. chap. 18, pars. 160-1.
§ 5   [1] He derives *ratso* from *ratsah*, to be willing, desirous, rather than from *ruts*, to run.
     [2] He connects *bazak* (lightning) with the same verb meaning to scatter.
     [3] All these are similes of the swiftness with which they speed to their task.
     [4] How could it have taken so long, when they move like a flash of lightning?
§ 6   [1] *Baerev* (at even) is read *ba erev*, evening had come.

Sodom; and Lot saw them, and rose up to meet them; and he fell down on his face to the earth; [2]and he said:

COMMENTARY

city-wall, where people congregate in the East to converse, transact business, or have their disputes

adjudicated.[6] **rose up to meet them. a.** Abraham, seeing them in the distance, as it was daytime, "*ran to meet them*" (18:2); but Lot saw them only when they were quite near him, since it was **evening**, and so he rose up.[7] **b.** So that they should not spend the night in the streets, for he knew how unhospitable the people were and the dangers to which the visitors would be exposed.[8] **he fell down on his face. a.** He recognized them as beings of high rank.[9] **b.** Because they were of awe-inspiring

ANTHOLOGY

when they sleep from their sins.[1] Israel He judges only by day, when they are busy with His precepts. That is the meaning of the verse, *And He will judge the world in righteousness, He will minister judgment to the peoples in equity* (Ps. 9:9).[2]

[Another interpretation:] It is written, *Let their way be dark* (Ps. 35:6): because the wicked are wrapped in darkness, *and their works are in the dark* (Isa. 29:15), the Holy One, blessed is He, exacts retribution only at night. E.g., the Sodomites: *The two angels came to Sodom at even.*

> Gen. R. 50, 3; Yelamdenu.
> T.S. 19, 10 and note.

8. AT EVEN. When Lot came to Sodom he practised hospitality. But when its citizens proclaimed, "Whoever supports the poor with food shall be burnt to death," he was afraid to do it by day and did it at night, as it says, *The two angels came to Sodom at even, [and Lot sat in the gate of Sodom].*[1]

> PRE 25. T.S. 19, 11.

9. IN THE EVENING.[1] The well-known evening, viz., Passover eve,[2] as it is written, *He*

baked unleavened bread, and they ate (verse 3).

> Quoted as a Midrash in *D'rashoth Ibn Shoib* on Vayyera. T.S. 19, 12.

10. **Lot sat in the gate of Sodom.**

Yosheb (sat) is written defectively, intimating that only that very day had they appointed him Chief Justice.[1] There were five senior judges in Sodom: Out-and-out Liar, Master Liar, Master Perverter, Master Rogue, and Man-Stealer: Lot was their chief. When he said something which pleased them they would say, *Go on* (verse 9)—take a higher seat. But when he said something that displeased them they would jeer, *This one fellow came in to sojourn, and he will needs play the judge!* (ibid.)

> Gen. R. 50, 3. T.S. 19, 13.

11. **Lot saw them, and rose up to meet them.**

He saw the two angels, thought them ordinary travelers, ran to meet them . . . and invited them: "Come and spend the night in my house. Eat and drink, and then go your way in peace."

[He offered them hospitality] because he had learned the ways of Abraham, of whom it is written, *He saw, and ran to meet them*

§ 7   [1] He can be more lenient then.
     [2] "The world" is understood as a contrast to "the peoples," hence Israel. The verse is rendered: He judges "the world," i.e., Israel, when they are performing righteousness, viz., by day; but "the peoples" in equity, i.e., with grace, by night, when they cease from their wrong-doing.
§ 8   [1] The proof probably lies in the second half of the verse, added here. So Midrash Hagadol: What then was Lot doing in the gate of Sodom in the evening? He was looking for night travelers to invite secretly into his home. For the whole passage cf. chap. 18, par. 162.
§ 9   [1] Lit. translation. The noun has the def. art.
     [2] See chap. 18, par. 65; *infra* par. 18; chap. 21, par. 29.
§ 10   [1] Justice was dispensed "in the gate." Sitting in the gate is therefore interpreted to mean that he sat there as a judge. The defective form of *yosheb* (ישב instead of יושב) is interpreted as implying that he had not sat there previously.

"Behold now, my lords, turn aside, I pray you, into your servant's house, and tarry all night, and wash your feet, and ye shall rise up early, and go on your way." And they said: "Nay; but we will abide in the broad

COMMENTARY

appearance.[10] **2my lords.** Since you have passed by my house, you are *my lords* (i.e., I am at your service).[11] **turn aside. a.** He begged them to come into his home, knowing the danger they ran from the wicked Sodomites.[12] **b.** He felt certain that his position as a judge would deter the evil-minded.[13] **c.** The Heb. term *sur* is used wherever there is a cause to fear.[13a] **into your servant's house. a.** Where you will be safe.[14] **b.** Being a resident of a city, Lot dwelt in a "house," whereas Abraham's abode was a "tent."[15] **wash your feet.** This is the first thing which one invites a guest to do, even before eating and drinking.[16] **and ye shall rise up early, and go on your way.** Before the townspeople learn of your presence.[17] **Nay.** They declined in order to make his merit all the greater in insisting that they accept his hospitality.[18] **broad**

ANTHOLOGY

(18:2). Solomon said: *Train up a child in the way he should go* (Prov. 22:6). Because Lot was brought up in Abraham's home, he followed his pattern of behavior. So runs the proverb: "Come near people and you become like them."

R. Isaac asked: Why did Lot invite them? R. Hazekiah and R. Jesa disagreed. One maintained, Because he saw in them a likeness to Abraham. The other, Because he observed the Shechinah hovering over them. For of Abraham it says similarly, *He saw, and ran to meet them*: just as there it was the Shechinah that he saw,[1] so here too.

> Tan. Y. Vayyera 11. 15; PRE 25;
> Zohar 1, 106b. T.S. 19, 14-15. 16 note. 19.

12. AND ROSE UP TO MEET THEM. But in the case of Abraham it says, *And* ran *to meet them.* This teaches that they came upon him like a bird flying through the air.[1]

> PZ. T.S. 19, 16.

13. **My lords.**

Wherever "lord" occurs in connection with Abraham [and his visitors], it is holy;[1] when it occurs in connection with Lot, it is profane (not holy).

> PZ. T.S. 19, 17.

14. **Turn aside.**

R. Judan interpreted: Even if I do not deserve it, turn your path for my sake. R. Huna said: [He requested:] Take a roundabout way to my house, that you may not be seen coming to me.

> Gen. R. 50, 4. T.S. 19, 18.

15. **Tarry all night, and wash your feet.**

Abraham invited them first to wash and then enjoy his hospitality,[1] whereas Lot invited them first to spend the night there and then to wash. Abraham objected to the pollution of idolatry,[2] whereas Lot did not mind. Some say that he too acted with forethought, so that when they left the dust would be seen on their feet, lest the Sodomites ask, where did they spend the night?

> Gen. R. 50, 4. T.S. 19, 20.

16. **They said: "Nay, but we will abide in the broad place all night."**

You may refuse a lesser person, but not a great one.[1] They declined his invitation until he grasped and led them, unwilling, into his house.

> Gen. R. 50, 4; MhG. T.S. 19, 22-3.

§ 11   [1] Since the narrative begins with *"The Lord appeared to him."*
§ 12   [1] They came upon him so suddenly that he had no time to *run* to meet them.
§ 13   [1] It means God.
§ 15   [1] Lit., spend the night. Abraham did not invite them for the night; the word merely echoes the context.
　　　　[2] See chap. 18, par. 42.
§ 16   [1] They had accepted Abraham's invitation immediately, but Lot's they declined at first.

place all night." [3]And he urged them greatly; and they turned in unto him, and entered into his house; and he made them a feast, and did bake unleavened bread, and they did eat. [4]But before they lay down, the men of the city, even the

COMMENTARY

place. a. From this answer he might understand that they had no other place in view. How then could he leave them?[19] **b.** The "square" of the city; and the climate being warm, it would be a natural place where a homeless visitor would spend the night.[20] [3]**feast. a.** As it was night there was no time to kill an animal and offer meat.[21] **b.** The Heb. *mishteh* (fr. *shatoh,* to drink) means a meal at which one drinks wine, of which he was fond. Abraham did not make a *feast* for them, because he reserved feasts (with wine) for special occasions, as at the weaning of Isaac (21:8).[22] **and did bake.** What a contrast to the to the spirit of hospitality that prevailed in Abraham's house! Here neither wife nor children partake of the Mitzvah—Lot found himself quite alone.[23] **unleavened bread.** These could be baked quickly, so that he would not have to keep guests waiting.[24] **they did eat. a.** They seemed to Lot to be eating, the food and drink miraculously reverting to their original elements.[25] **b.** Although he had prepared a feast in their honor, they ate only the unleavened bread.[26] [4]**the men of the city, even the men of Sodom.** The plain meaning is:

ANTHOLOGY

17. He urged them greatly (*vayyiftsar*).

He filled them with anger (*af*) and distress (*tsarah*).[1] *And they turned aside to him, and entered into his house:* This supports R. Huna who said that he asked them: "Take a roundabout way to my house, that you may not be seen coming to me."[2] *He made them a feast:* he was reared in the house of Abraham, who entertained wayfarers. *Baked unleavened bread* (*matsoth*) *and they ate:* R. Isaac said: A fierce quarrel (*matsuth*) arose over the salt. He (Lot) asked his wife to give them a little salt, to which she replied, "Do you wish to introduce here this evil practice too?" R. Isaac said: [Her subsequent fate] was her punishment for sinning through salt. What did she do that night when the angels came to Lot? She went round to her neighbors and asked them, "Let me have some salt, as we have guests." Her purpose was to apprise the townspeople of this. Therefore she became a pillar of salt.

Gen. R. 50, 4; 51, 5. T.S. 19, 24. 154.

18. And baked unleavened bread.

Because Lot did this one good deed of receiving the angels at night, as our text says, Scripture writes, *Be not at enmity with Moab* (Deut. 2:9).[1]

[He baked unleavened bread] because it was the second night of Passover.[2]

Yelamdenu; Sechel Tob. T.S. 19, 26. 28.

19. They ate.

But surely angels neither eat nor drink? The Torah teaches manners: Do not deviate from the general practice.[1]

Tan. Y. Vayyera 11. T.S. 19, 25.

20. But before they lay down, etc.

They began questioning him, "What kind of people are they here?"[1] "Everywhere you have good and bad," he replied, "but here the majority by far are bad." *The men of the city, the men*

§ 17 [1] A play on *vayyiftsar*. They did not wish to accept his invitation, and were angered and distressed that he compelled them (see last par.). Y. M. renders: Through them he brought anger and trouble into his house —the anger of the Sodomites.
[2] Par. 14.
§ 18 [1] Lot was Moab's progenitor; see verses 36-7.
[2] Cf. par. 9.
§ 19 [1] Cf. chap. 18, par. 79.
§ 20 [1] Rendering: *But before they lay down* [they questioned him about] *the men of the city.*

men of Sodom, compassed the house round, both young and old, all the people from every quarter. [5]And they called unto Lot, and said unto him: "Where are the men that came in to thee this night? bring them out unto us, that we may know them." [6]And Lot went out unto them to the door, and shut the door after

COMMENTARY

The men of the city, true Sodomites, surrounded the house.[27] **both young and old.** The old were as evil as the young.[28] **all the people.** Emphasis is here laid on the fact that the inhabitants were all addicted to unnatural depravity. The rejection of Abraham's plea was, therefore, justified.[29] **from every quarter. a.** Even those who lived at a distance.[30] **b.** The spectacle of visitors was so unusual in that city, which travelers had learned to avoid, that all the inhabitants thronged to see them, determined to make them suffer for their temerity.[31] [5]**that we may know them. a.** Their purpose was to keep strangers away, that they might retain the entire wealth of the place for themselves.[32]

ANTHOLOGY

of Sodom, compassed the house round—not one sought to hinder them.

Gen. R. 50, 5.   T.S. 19, 29.

21.   **The men of the city, the men of Sodom, compassed the house round.**

Do not think that they were some wretched strangers, but *the men of the city*: the notables of the city surrounded the house first, then came *both young and old, and all the people from every quarter.*

It is written [further on,] *They smote the men that were at the door of the house with blindness* (verse 11): the first to do this evil were the first to suffer retribution.[1]

Sechel Tob; Sifre Zuta Naso 5, 21.
T.S. 19, 30-1.

22.   **Bring them out to us, that we may know them.**

R. Joshua b. Levi, quoting R. Padiah, said: That whole night Lot prayed for mercy on their behalf. [The angels] would have heeded him, but when [the Sodomites] demanded, *Bring them out to us, that we may know them* —for sexual abuse[1]—[the angels] said to him, *Have you yet a mouth* [to plead for them] (verse 12)?[2]

Gen. R. 50, 5.   T.S. 19, 32.

23.   THAT WE MAY KNOW THEM. They wished to abuse them carnally. R. Hiyya b. Abba said: From this you may learn how steeped in immorality they were. [Seeing their desires] he proposed, *Behold now, I have two daughters that have not known man,* etc.

A lad of Sodom espied [the angels]. He went and informed the people, whereupon they all gathered at the door of the house to treat them in the usual way. They called out to Lot, *Where are the men that came in to you this night? Bring them out to us, that we may know them*—we desire to follow our usual practice.

Tan. Y. Vayyera 22; PRE 25.   T.S. 19, 34-5.

24.   THAT WE MAY KNOW THEM. Some fountains produce strong men, others, weaklings; some rear chaste men, others dissolute. The fountain of Shittim promoted immorality,[1] and it was this fountain that watered Sodom. So you find its citizens demanding, *Bring them out to us, that we may know them.*

Num. R. 20, 22.   T.S. 19, 36.

25.   BRING THEM OUT TO US, THAT WE MAY KNOW THEM. If heathens demand: "Give us one of yourselves that we may murder him," or, "Give us So-and-So, that we may slay him;

§ 21   [1] Contrast par. 43.
§ 22   [1] For this rendering of "know" cf. 4:1: *The man* knew *Eve his wife, and she conceived.*
    [2] AJV: *Hast thou here* (poh) *any besides.* By a play on words *poh* is read *peh*, a mouth.
§ 24   [1] The passage is a comment on Num. 25:1, *q.v.*

him. [7]And he said: "I pray you, my brethren, do not so wickedly. [8]Behold now, I have two daughters that have not known man; let me, I pray you, bring them out unto you, and

COMMENTARY

b. That we may know who they are—perhaps they are spies. Thereupon he offered his

daughters as hostages if it should really be so.[33] [7]**my brethren.** You are my brethren and neighbors; out of respect for me do not molest them.[34] [8]**I have.** Only I have violated your laws, but not my guests, who, not being citizens, are not bound by them. Therefore I will pay the penalty myself.[35] **two daughters.** On whom you can satisfy your lust—or even slay them.[36] **bring them out. a.** While the narrative reveals Lot's hospitality, it also reveals his wickedness.[37] **b.** He was fighting for time. He knew that his sons-in-law would never agree to the proposal and would seek to rescue them. In the delay thus gained his guests would escape.[38]

ANTHOLOGY

otherwise we will kill all of you"—let them all die rather than deliver one person to them. The same is true of immorality.

Midrash Or Haafelah. T.S. 19, 37.

26. THAT WE MAY KNOW THEM. Scripture informs us that they were steeped in incest, pederasty, and bestiality. Of them the Writ declares, *For all his days are pains, and his occupation vexation* (Eccl. 2:23), which means that they pained and vexed the Omnipresent. *Yea, even in the night his heart takes no rest:* their hearts rested not from sin day or night. Said the Holy One, blessed is He, to them: "Your hearts take no rest from sin day or night; therefore will I too bring retribution upon you day and night"; as it is written, *Then the Lord rained upon Sodom and Gomorrah brimstone and fire* (verse 24).

MhG. T.S. 19, 38.

27. **And shut the door after him.**

I.e., Lot shut it. But our Rabbis maintained: It shut of its own accord.

PZ; Sechel Tob. T.S. 19, 39 and note.

28. **He said.**

"Saying" always implies supplication, as in

the present case: *He said: "I pray you, my brethren, do not so wickedly."*

Sifre B'haalothecha 99. T.S. 19, 40.

29. **My brethren.**

You are my kinsmen through my wife, for a husband is as his wife, and *vice versa*, in respect to the testimony of kinsmen.[1]

Sechel Tob. T.S. 19, 41.

30. **I pray you, my brethren, do not so wickedly.**

Do not do this thing, for it is great wickedness before the Holy One, blessed is He, as it says, *How then I can do this great wickedness, and sin against God* (39:9)?[1] The Almighty enjoined the children of Noah[2] likewise, *A man shall cleave to his wife, and they shall be one flesh* (2:24), but not to a male, with whom he cannot become one flesh.

Sechel Tob. T.S. 19, 42.

31. **Behold now, I have two daughters.**

How do we know that Lot chose to behave like the people of Sodom? Because he said to them, *"Behold now, I have two daughters,"* etc. Usually a man will fight to the death for the honor of his wife and daughters, and will slay

§ 29 [1] The testimony of relations is invalid. In that respect husband and wife are alike: i.e., one who could not testify in a matter concerning the husband on the grounds of relationship cannot testify where his wife is concerned, and *vice versa*. The comment seeks to show that they were literally "brethren" (i.e., kinsmen) through his wife; cf. par. 33.

§ 30 [1] There too it refers to immorality—adultery.
      [2] A technical term embracing all humanity other than the Jewish people, generally used in reference to obligations devolving upon all men and not only Jews.

do ye to them as is good in your eyes; only unto these men do nothing; forasmuch as they are come under the shadow of my roof." [9]And they said: "Stand back." And they said: "This one fellow came in

COMMENTARY

forasmuch as they are come under the shadow, etc. **a.** Their very purpose in entering my house was to avoid trouble.[39] **b.** They knew that I would protect them even with my life.[40] **[9]Stand back ... This one fellow,** etc. To the offer of his daughters they gently answered *Stand back;* but his attempt to protect his visitors they met with a furious *This one fellow,* etc.[41] **This one (ha-ehad).** The *he* is

ANTHOLOGY

or be slain. Yet this man offers his daughters to be dishonored! Said the Holy One, blessed is He, to him: "By your life! You keep them for yourself, and eventually schoolchildren will read, *Thus were both the daughters of Lot with child by their father*" (verse 36).[1]

Tan. Y. Vayyera 12. T.S. 19, 43.

32. BEHOLD NOW, I HAVE TWO DAUGHTERS. What did Lot do? Just as Moses offered his life for Israel, so did Lot sacrifice himself for his guests. He took his two daughters and offered them to the people in place of the two angels, as it says, *Behold now, I have two daughters;* but the people refused them.[1]

PRE 25. T.S. 19, 44.

33. BEHOLD NOW, I HAVE TWO DAUGHTERS THAT HAVE NOT KNOWN MAN. Even though they are betrothed.

Let me now, I pray you, bring them out to you. He actually implored them: "Let me bring them out to you, that you may make free with them."

And do to them as is good in your eyes. For had they even been given in marriage, but the

marriage was not consummated, they would count as unmarried and intimacy be permitted. *Only to the men of God:*[1] they came on a Divine mission. *Do nothing, forasmuch as they are come under the shadow of my roof:* but not under the shadow of my wife's roof, for she is your sister.[2]

Sechel Tob.[3] T.S. 19, 50.

34. **Forasmuch as they are come under the shadow of my roof.**

They came not for my sake, but for Abraham's.[1]

Another interpretation: This teaches that his wife protested, "The people of this city refrain from receiving visitors, and yet you invite them in! Do you want them to kill us both? If you insist on receiving them, divide the house with me and entertain the visitors in your half." Hence it says, *Under the shadow of my roof.*

Gen. R. 50, 6; MA. T.S. 19, 46-7.

35. UNDER THE SHADOW OF MY ROOF. Because Manoah's wife[1] saw an angel she was called Hazelelponi,[2] which means that she had looked upon (*ponah,* lit., turned) an angel, for *tselel*

§ 31 [1] See next par. for an opposite view.
§ 32 [1] *D'rashoth Ibn Shoib,* quoting R. Hananel, writes: Heaven forfend that he offered his daughters! Rather it is like one says, "My house is open—take whatever you wish." Or as one throws himself upon his attacker and cries out, "Kill me!," knowing that they will not. That is why they answered him, "Stand back," reviling and insulting him, because they saw that he did not in fact hand his guests over.
§ 33 [1] AJV: *these men.* But *ha-el* can also mean God, and it is so understood here.
[2] In her behavior; cf. par. 34. But see par. 29, according to which this is meant literally too.
[3] The passage adds: "These are the words of our Rabbis." Presumably a Midrash, no longer extant, is the source.
§ 34 [1] I was not privileged to have them through my own merit, but only on Abraham's account. *"Shadow"* is interpreted as a metaphor for protector: they are come for the sake of the protector of my roof, sc. Abraham (M.K.).
§ 35 [1] Samson's mother.
[2] See 1 Chron. 4:3. Apparently there was a tradition that they were identical.

to sojourn, and he will needs play
the judge; now will we deal worse
with thee, than with them." And
they pressed sore upon the man,
even Lot, and drew near to break
the door. [10]But the men put forth
their hand, and brought Lot into the

COMMENTARY

interrogative: Shall this one, who is but a stranger,
play the judge?[42] **to sojourn (la-gur). a.** Even

he is only a stranger (*ger*) and not a citizen, and
yet he would act as an authority and presume to
judge.[43] **b.** This man was a stranger and yet we
appointed him a judge [rendering: This one fellow
came in to sojourn, and now indeed he is a judge—
we appointed him.—Ed.], and now he presumes to
lord it over us.[44] **play the judge. a.** He presumes
to judge the validity of laws which have long ago
been judged and determined.[45] **b.** He would even
judge the judges! [This is based on the repetition
of the root-word for judging.—Ed.][46] **will we
deal worse with thee than with them.** We will
deal ill with them, as is our wont, but even worse
with you, since you have admitted yourself that you
have sinned more than they.[47] **pressed sore.** The
Hebrew verb denotes persuasion; they tried hard to
persuade him, and only when they failed did they

ANTHOLOGY

means angel, as it says, *Forasmuch as they are
come under the shadow* (tsel) *of my roof.* There,
where Lot was more righteous than his wife,
they came under the shadow of *his* roof, not
her roof. Here, however, because she was a
righteous woman and the angel came to *her*,
she was called Hazelel.

Num. R. 10, 5.   T.S. 19, 49.

36.   **This one fellow came in to sojourn, and
now he must needs play the judge.**

When they revealed their secret desires by
demanding, *Bring them out to us, that we may
know them,* Lot began speaking persuasively
to them: "*I pray you, my brethren, do not so
wickedly.*" "My brethren," said he to them,
"surely the generation of the Flood was destroyed precisely on account of these sins, yet
you would commit them anew!" To which
they replied: "Turn back! We would pay no
heed even to Abraham himself." That is what
our text says, *This one fellow came in to sojourn, and now he must needs play the judge.*

[Said they:] "You come to overthrow an
old-established law."[1] R. Menahma, quoting
R. Berechiah, said: The people of Sodom had
made this agreement among themselves: What-

ever visitor comes here, we will abuse him carnally and confiscate his money. Were it even he
of whom it is written [that he would command
his children to] *keep the way of the Lord, to
do righteousness and justice* (18:19), we would
so abuse and rob him.

Gen. R. 50, 7; MhG.   T.S. 19, 54-5.

37.   **Now we will deal worse with you than
with them.**

What we desire to do to these men, we will
do even in worse form to you. Their language
here was [indeed] coarse.[1]

Tan. Vayyera 12.   T.S. 19, 56.

38.   **They pressed sore upon the man, even
Lot.**

Why does Scripture say, *the man*? To teach
that with every word [that he spoke] he became
more exalted in their eyes, so that they feared
to harm him.[1] Seeing then that he refused to
listen to them, they sought to ensnare and cajole
him.

Sechel Tob.   T.S. 19, 58.

39.   **But the men put out their hand.**

Because he had put out his hand to take them

§ 36   [1] Perhaps the verse is rendered: And he would judge the judgments (laws)—of the past.
§ 37   [1] They declared plainly that they would force him to bestiality.
§ 38   [1] He became more and more a man in their eyes.

house to them, and the door they shut. [11]And they smote the men that were at the door of the house with blindness, both small and great; so that they wearied themselves to find the door. [12]And the men said unto Lot: "Hast thou here any besides? son-in-law, and thy sons, and thy daughters, and whomsoever thou hast in the city; bring them out of

COMMENTARY

approach to break the door.[48] [10]**they shut. a.** So that in wearying themselves to find the opening, these Sodomites would publicize their wickedness.[49] **b.** Although the crowd was smitten with blindness (verse 11) and unable to find the door in any case, the angels did not wish to rely on a miracle.[50] [11]**blindness.** The Heb. word occurs again only in 2 Kings 6:18, and denotes a temporary loss of sight.[51] **they wearied themselves to find the door. a.** They could not find the door and gave up the attempt.[52] **b.** Though smitten with blindness, they still sought the door to break it.[53] [12]**"Hast thou here any besides?" a.** Have you any other relations in the city in addition to those in your home?[54] **b.** What hope have you to live in such a wicked city?[55] **thy sons. a.** He had no sons, only daughters; the reference is to the sons of his married daughters.[56] **b.** Possibly he had grown-up married sons.[57] **son-in-law, and thy sons, and thy daughters.** Sons-in-law who are as dear to you as your sons and daughters.[58] **and whomsover thou hast in the city.** Cattle and wealth.[59] **bring**

ANTHOLOGY

into his house,[1] they put out their hand and took him in to them.

Or Haafelah. T.S. 19, 59.

40. And brought Lot into the house to them.

Scripture shows that the Holy One, blessed is He, does not deprive any creature of his just reward. The bite of food which he had given them saved him and his household from the Sodomites and their retribution. That is the implication of our text.

MhG. T.S. 19, 60.

41. The door they shut.

Lest they come to test the Name of God.[1]

Sechel Tob. T.S. 19, 61.

42. They smote with blindness.

I.e., with dazzling brightness.[1]

MhG. T.S. 19, 62.

43. Both small and great.

The small were the first to sin, as it says, *But before they lay down,* etc.; therefore they were smitten first, whilst the others too did not escape, as it says, *They smote the men that were at the door of the house.*[1]

T. Sot. 4. T.S. 19, 63.

44. Have you any here (*poh*) besides?

For *poh* read *peh* (a mouth): hitherto you were permitted to plead in their defense; henceforth you have no further permission to plead on their behalf.[1]

[The same may be deduced from] *od* (besides), which is written defectively, without a *waw* [so that it reads *ad* (until)]. Said they to him: [Only] "until this point might you speak."[2]

Gen. R. 50, 5; Midrash Haser V'yether. T.S. 19, 66-7.

§ 39 [1] See par. 16.
§ 41 [1] They had no need to shut the door, for their power was such that even had they left it open the Sodomites could not have entered. But they did not wish to test God by looking to a miracle.
§ 42 [1] Which (temporarily?) blinded them.
§ 43 [1] Cf. par. 21.
§ 44 [1] Cf. par. 22 and note 2.
[2] Possibly: Only until now might you plead. But now that they have shown the extent of their stubbornness, that even after being smitten with blindness they still grope for the door to carry out their nefarious designs, it is clearly hopeless to expect them to repent, and you may not plead any more.

the place; [13]for we will destroy this place, because the cry of them is waxed great before the Lord; and the Lord hath sent us to destroy it." [14]And Lot went out, and spoke unto his sons-in-law, who married his daughters, and said: "Up, get you out of this place; for the Lord will destroy the city." But he seemed unto his sons-in-law as one that jested. [15]And when the morning

COMMENTARY

them out of the place. Not only from the city but from the entire region.[60] [13]**destroy.** Sodom's doom was necessary for Eretz Israel, which as God's heritage could not abide such abominations.[61] **the cry of them.** The cry of the poor, the oppressed, and the wayfarers.[62] **to destroy it.** The city contained in this region.[63] [14]**Lot went out. a.** After the Sodomites, unable to find the door, had gone.[64] **b.** Now that he realized that the people outside could not harm him.[65] **his sons-in-law.** He had two married daughters in the city.[66] **who married his daughters.** *Other* sons-in-law, married to daughters who had died. The proof lies in the phrase "thy two daughters that are *here*," (next verse) which implies that there had been others who were no longer there, viz., alive.[67] **as one that jested.** A credulous fool.[68] [15]**when the morning arose. a.** For Abraham's sake they waited all night for

ANTHOLOGY

45. For we will destroy this place.

R. Levi, citing R. Nahman, said: For revealing God's secrets the ministering angels were banished from their precinct one hundred and thirty-eight years.[1] R. Tanhuma expressed it in the word *kelah*.[2] R. Hama b. Hanina said: [They were thus punished] because they boasted by saying, *For we will destroy this place.*

[Another version:] R. Tanhuma said: [This punishment lasted] one hundred and thirty years, this being the numerical value of *sulam*.[3]

Gen. R. 50, 9; Tan. Y. Vayyera 21. T.S. 19, 70-71.

46. FOR WE WILL DESTROY. Scripture informs us that twelve thousand destroying angels, captained by the angel Kemuel, descended and destroyed it in the twinkling of an eye. Therefore it says, *The Lord hath sent us to destroy it.*

MhG. T.S. 19, 73.

47. Because the cry of them is waxed great before the Lord, and the Lord has sent us to destroy it.

Why is "the Lord" mentioned twice? The Holy One, blessed is He, said: "It is I who punished sinners, and it is I who will give a goodly reward to him who resists the temptation to sin."[1]

Yelamdenu. T.S. 19, 74.

48. Lot . . . spoke to his sons-in-law [and] those who were taking his daughters.

He had four daughters, two betrothed and two married. For it does not say, *Who were taken of his daughters*, but, *who were taking his daughters*.[1]

Gen. R. 50, 9. T.S. 19, 75.

49. But he seemed to his sons-in-law as one that jested.

Grave indeed is the sin of scoffing. For retri-

§ 45 [1] They were expelled from their abode in the Divine presence, until they re-ascended at Beer Sheba, in Jacob's dream. For they were the angels whom Jacob saw ascending the ladder—to return to their former precincts.
[2] A stalk. The numerical value of *kelah* (all Hebrew letters are also numbers) is 138.
[3] Ladder; see n. 1. But see next par. for a different view.
§ 47 [1] Lit., who fences himself in from sin.
§ 48 [1] "Betrothed" here means married, but before the home-taking ceremony (*n'suin*) which made conjugal relations permissible. "*Sons-in-law*" is understood to mean those who were already fully married, the *n'suin* having already taken place, and "*those who were taking his daughters*" as different persons, who were in the process of taking, i.e., who had betrothed but not yet married, his daughters.

arose, then the angels hastened Lot, saying: "Arise, take thy wife, and thy two daughters that are here; lest thou be swept away in the iniquity

COMMENTARY

him.[69] **b.** Only then did they hasten him, because he could not have seen his way at night.[70] **the angels.** They are now called angels (God's messengers), because they had revealed the future and fulfilled their task of rescuing him.[71] **hastened.** So that Sodom's destruction might take place at sunrise, the sun being their chief deity (thus its impotence to save its worshippers would be demonstrated).[72] **that are here.** In the house, ready to be saved.[73] **in the iniquity of the city.** In the *punishment* of the city; since the punishment is on account of the iniquity, it is called iniquity.[74]

ANTHOLOGY

bution did not speed upon the Sodomites until they scoffed at Lot, as it says, *But he seemed to his sons-in-law as one that jested.* Said they to him: "What a unique fool you are! Harps, viols, and flutes are playing in the city, yet you say that Sodom shall be overthrown!"

Gen. R. 50, 9; MhG. T.S. 19, 76-7.

50. **As the dawn arose.**

R. Hanina said: From the first rays of dawn[1] until the east is alight a man can walk four mils,[2] and from the lighting up of the east until sunrise[3] a man can walk four mils. Now, how do we know that from the first rays of dawn until the east is alight a man can walk four mils? Because it says, *As the dawn arose, then the angels hastened Lot.*[4] But is it only four mils from Sodom to Zoar? Surely it is more! Said R. Zeira: The angel flattened the road before them.[5] How do we know that a man can walk four mils from the lighting up of the east until sunrise? *And as* intimates that one period equals the other.[6]

J. Yoma 3, 1. T.S. 19, 78.

51. As THE DAWN AROSE. When the people of Sodom began to awake, so that Lot might depart in their full view.[1]

Or Haafelah. T.S. 19, 80.

52. As THE DAWN AROSE. Most Gentiles are punished at night, as it says, *All darkness is laid up for his treasures* (Job 20:26).[1] Yet in connection with Sodom it is written, *As the dawn arose*, etc.[2] That was because they had already been smitten at night.

PZ Bo 11, 4. T.S. 19, 81.

53. **Your two daughters that are found here.**

R. Tobiah b. R. Isaac commented: Two "finds" [would issue from them]: Ruth the

---

§ 50 [1] Heb. *ayelath ha-shahar,* lit., hind of the dawn. The phrase is Biblical, occurring in the superscription to Ps. 22, where its meaning is very doubtful and obscure. Here apparently it refers to the first fingers of light which stab the darkness of the night, poetically conceived as the branches of a hind. However, a poetic simile is out of place here, and if the conjectured interpretation is correct we must assume that the phrase had passed into ordinary language.
[2] A mil = 2,000 cubits.
[3] Lit., until the sun sparkles, i.e., when it becomes fully visible over the horizon.
[4] In v. 23 it is stated that Lot reached Zoar when *"the sun was risen upon the earth,"* i.e., when the east was lit up. Hence he must have traveled that distance since dawn.
[5] It is more only because of the hills and slopes, but not over a level road. In Pes. 94a a different explanation is given: They covered this distance because the angel hurried them, but at a normal gait only four mils could be traveled.
[6] *"And as"* is regarded as extending the scope of the sentence to two periods, whilst *"as"* implies that these periods are similar.
§ 51 [1] And yet they were powerless to intervene.
§ 52 [1] The text deals with the fate of the wicked, and it is here interpreted: Darkness is laid up (i.e., appointed) for the retribution which awaits him and his ill-gotten treasures. Cf. par. 7.
[2] Implying that they were punished by day.

of the city." [16]But he lingered; and the men laid hold upon his hand, and upon the hand of his wife, and upon the hand of his two daughters;

COMMENTARY

[16]**he lingered.** Either to collect his valuables, or he was reluctant to leave. All that Scripture tells of Lot is characteristic of a weak, irresolute character.[75] **laid hold. a.** In his terror he was powerless to flee himself.[76] **b.** They took him forcibly;

ANTHOLOGY

Moabitess and Naamah the Ammonitess. R. Isaac, commenting on the text, *I have found David My servant* (Ps. 89:21), observed: Where did I find him? In Sodom.[1]

They were indeed saved for the sakes of David and the Messiah, as it says, *I have found David My servant*, David being descended from Ruth the Moabitess and Rehaboam[2] from Naamah the Amonitess, whilst the Messiah will be descended from both.

Gen. R. 50, 10; MA. T.S. 19, 83 and note.

54. YOUR TWO DAUGHTERS THAT ARE FOUND HERE. So far they are still righteous.[1]

MhG. T.S. 19, 84.

55. **Lest you be swept away in the iniquity of the city.**

Scripture tells us that Lot too deserved to be swept away with them, had not Abraham's merit preceded him.[1]

MhG. T.S. 19, 85.

56. LEST YOU BE SWEPT AWAY IN THE INIQUITY OF THE CITY. For the wealth of [even] the righteous in a condemned city is destroyed,[1] as the proverb goes, "Woe to the wicked, and woe to his neighbor."

[Another interpretation:] Once the Destroyer is given permission [to destroy], he does not differentiate between the righteous and the wicked.

Or Haafelah; Sechel Tob. T.S. 19, 86-7.

57. **But he lingered.**

In astonishment and amazement,[1] exclaiming, "What a loss of gold and silver and precious stones and pearls!" In this vein Scripture writes, *Riches kept by their owner to his hurt* (Eccl. 5:12), which R. Joshua b. Levi applied to Lot.

[He lingered] because he desired to take out his wealth.

Gen. R. 50, 11; MA. T.S. 19, 88-9.

58. **Then the men laid hold upon his hand, etc.**

Who was it [that saved them?—The angel] Rafael. An objection was raised: But it says, *And* they *brought him forth, and* they *set him outside the city, And it came to pass, when* they *had brought them forth.* Read what follows, he [this interpreter] replied: It does not say, *They* said: "Escape for your life," but, *He said*, etc. (verse 17). Then why does it say, *Then* the men *laid hold*, etc.? It means, Abraham's merit together with Rafael [saved him].

Gen. R. 50, 11. T.S. 19, 91.

59. THEN THE MEN LAID HOLD UPON HIS HAND. Everything is in due measure. Just as he had seized their hands against their will[1] and

§ 53 [1] He was descended from Ruth the Moabitess. Moab and Ammon spring from the union which took place after the overthrow of Sodom; see verses 37-8.
    [2] Solomon's son.
§ 54 [1] "Found" is interpreted as "found worthy"—still, although their subsequent behavior was reprehensible. Cf. chap. 18, pars. 184, 198.
§ 55 [1] See next par. for a different view.
§ 56 [1] See Deut. 13:13 *et sqq.* Everything therein is destroyed, even the property of the righteous (see par. 72 for the reason). Similarly Lot too would be swept away with the rest if he stayed there.
§ 57 [1] *Va-yithmahamah* (he lingered) is now by a play on words derived from *timahon*, astonishment, wonder.
§ 59 [1] See par. 16.

the Lord being merciful unto him. And they brought him forth, and set him without the city. [17]And it came to pass, when they had brought them forth abroad, that he said: "Escape for thy life; look not be-

COMMENTARY

cp. Exod. 12:33.[77] **the Lord being merciful unto him. a.** Not for his own merit, but through Divine mercy. Or, the angels sought to speed him while God was still merciful, lest His wrath go forth and he be consumed.[78] **b.** Although he was to be saved for Abraham's sake, through his lingering he might have forfeited this privilege but for God's mercy.[79] **they brought him forth.** To-

gether with his wife and daughters.[80] [17]**when they had brought.** Rather: As they brought, etc.: as they were taking them out they urged him to make haste and escape.[81] **them.** But not his possessions.[82] **abroad.** Far from the city.[83] **he said.** The angel whose mission it was to rescue Lot.[84] **Escape for thy life.** Be satisfied with your life; do not try to save your wealth also.[85] **look not behind thee. a.** You have sinned as much as they, and therefore it is not fitting that you should look upon their punishment.[86] **b.** Because it will increase your grief for the sons-in-law whom you have left in the city. Further, this would cause delay. It was also undesirable that he should look upon the angels performing their task.[87] **c.** The mere sight of the destroying agencies would have had a most harmful effect upon him, and even thinking about them would be dangerous.[88] **d.** Because the rain of fire and brimstone (verse 24) is spreading: if you pause even momentarily to look back it will engulf you.[89] **e.** Do not look back with regret upon the wealth

ANTHOLOGY

taken them into the house, so did they seize his hand, and the hands of his two daughters, and lead them out.

Said they to him: "Enough that you are saved." Therefore our Rabbis said that the wealth of the righteous in a condemned city is destroyed.

PRE 25; MA. T.S. 19, 92-3.

60. THE MEN LAID HOLD UPON HIS HAND, etc. Here Scripture calls the angels men, because they acted as men, seizing the hands of women, married, and betrothed.

Sechel Tob. T.S. 19, 94.

61. **The Lord being merciful to him.**

God spared Lot for Abraham's sake: because when Abraham went to Egypt and said that Sarah was his sister Lot did not reveal the secret. Therefore the Holy One, blessed is He, had compassion on him and saved him.

MA. T.S. 19, 95.

62. **Look not behind you.**

He [the angel] said to them: "Do not look hind you," because the Shechinah (Divine

Presence) of the Holy One, blessed is He, has descended to rain brimstone and fire upon Sodom and Gomorrah.

PRE 25. T.S. 19, 97.

63. LOOK NOT BEHIND YOU. As when you look upon harlots, as it says, *For on account of a harlot a man is brought to a loaf of bread, and the adulteress hunts for the precious life* (Prov. 6:26). "What shall I do?" he asked them. "Go to Abraham," they answered. For it says, *Escape to the mountain,* by which is meant Abraham, who was called mountain, as it says, *Hear, O mountains,* etc. (Micah 6:2).[1]

[Another interpretation:] Because the Shechinah is descending to Sodom, and he whose heart desires whoredom may not see the Shechinah.

AB 25; MA. T.S. 19, 98-9.

64. LOOK NOT BEHIND YOU. Then it says, *His wife looked back from behind him, and she became a pillar of salt* (verse 26). From this we learn that the Bible does not punish without first forbidding.

Midrash Habiur. T.S. 19, 100.

§ 63   [1] It is understood figuratively as a call to the Patriarchs to hear God's controversy with their descendants.

hind thee, neither stay thou in all the Plain; escape to the mountain, lest thou be swept away." [18]And Lot said unto them: "Oh, not so, my lord; [19]behold now, thy servant hath found grace in thy sight, and thou hast magnified thy mercy, which thou hast shown unto me in saving my life; and I cannot escape to the mountain, lest the evil overtake me, and I die. [20]Behold now, this city is

COMMENTARY

you have left behind. But he did not actually forbid him to gaze upon the destruction.[90] **neither stay thou in all the Plain.** Thinking that you may save something here or there: everything is doomed.[91] **to the mountain. a.** To Abraham who dwells in the mountain.[92] **b.** Of Moab, to the east of the Dead Sea.[93] [18]**unto them.** He addressed them both, although only one had spoken to him, in order to show respect for both.[94] [19]**thy servant.** ("thy" is in the sing.). **a.** He said this to him whom he considered the chief, for angels too are of various ranks.[95] **b.** He spoke to him who had urged him to escape to the mountain.[96] **I cannot. a.** I am too old and weak to go so far.[97] **b.** Terror had weakened him, and he felt that he should not speed such a distance.[98] **lest the evil overtake me.** While I am still in the plain.[99] **the evil.** The fire

ANTHOLOGY

65. Oh, not so, my lord.

Wherever "lord" occurs in connection with Lot it is profane, except the present instance, which is holy.[1] For it says, *But Lot said to them: Oh, not so, my Lord. Behold now, Thy servant has found grace in Thy sight, and Thou hast magnified Thy mercy, which Thou hast shown to me* in giving life *to my soul.* This must refer to Him who can put to death and give life, viz., the Holy One, blessed is He.

Sheb. 35a. T.S. 19, 103.

66. Behold now, thy servant has found grace in your sight, etc.

Said Lot: "Before I went to Abraham the Holy One, blessed is He, saw my deeds and those of my fellow-citizens, and by comparison I was righteous. But if I go to Abraham, whose [good] deeds exceed mine, I cannot stand in his flame."[1]

Gen. R. 50, 11. T.S. 19, 104.

67. I cannot escape to the mountain.

R. Berechiah, quoting R. Levi, said: What is the source of what we learned: Just as a bad dwelling tries a person so does a good one?[1] The present text: *I cannot escape to the mountain, lest the evil overtake me, and I die,* Sodom being in a valley. He lives in a valley and they tell him to go to the mountain, and he answers thus![2] This proves that [changing] even from a poor dwelling to a good one [may be dangerous]; hence a good dwelling puts one to the test.

Gen. R. 50, 11. T.S. 19, 106.

68. I CANNOT ESCAPE TO THE MOUNTAIN. When the angels were overturning Sodom and rescuing him for Abraham's sake, what did they say to him? *Escape to the mountain, lest you be swept away:* you have been saved for the sake of that great mountain, Abraham;[1] then go to him. I cannot, he replied, because he already

§ 65 [1] It is referred to God. According to this we must render: But Lot said to them: "Oh, not so." (Then, addressing himself to God:) "Oh, my Lord! Behold now," etc.

§ 66 [1] See pars. 63 and 68, according to which the angel bade Lot to go to Abraham. Lot now pleaded: "Until now I found grace in God's sight, by comparison; but I will lose it if I go to Abraham."

§ 67 [1] Mishnah Keth. 110b: A husband can compel his wife to accompany him when he moves from an inferior to a superior dwelling, but not the reverse. R. Simeon b. Gamaliel maintains that he cannot compel her even in the former case, because even such a change is a test, i.e., a trial, to one's health. R. Berechiah asks the source of R. Simeon's view.

[2] Mountain air is certainly healthier, yet he pleads that it may harm him!

§ 68 [1] Cf. par. 63.

near to flee unto, and it is a little one; oh, let me escape thither—is it not a little one?—and my soul shall live." [21]And he said unto him: "See, I have accepted thee concerning this thing also, that I will not overthrow the city of which thou hast spoken. [22]Hasten thou, escape thither; for I cannot do anything till thou be come thither."—Therefore the name of the city was called

COMMENTARY

and brimstone.[100] [20]**a little one.** It is so insignificant in size; it is but a small favor to spare it.[101] [21]**he said unto him,** etc. This proves that God's messenger is authorized to add or subtract somewhat from his task.[102] **concerning this thing also.** Not only have you saved your own life, but the inhabitants of this town will also be spared.[103] [22]**for I cannot do anything. a.** Thus were the angels punished for saying, *for we will destroy this place* (verse 13), implying that it depended upon them. They were now forced to admit their powerlessness.[104] **b.** For thus have I been commanded.[105] **c.** This is a human figure of speech, for the speaker is God, who can do all.[106] **d.** This angel who spoke was not the destroyer; he means that he cannot permit the destroying angel to proceed with the destruction.[107] **I cannot.** In the singular, for only one angel was to destroy, the other's task being to

ANTHOLOGY

told me to part from him;[2] therefore *I cannot escape to the mountain.*

PR 3. T.S. 19, 107.

69. Behold now, this city is near.

Raba b. Mehasia, quoting R. Hama b. Guria, said on Rab's authority: Let a person always endeavor to live in a recently-settled (lit., near) city, because since it was but recently settled its sins are [but] few. For it says, *Behold now, this city is near to flee to, and it is a little one.* Now, what does "near" mean: Shall we say, physically near and small? But they could see that for themselves! Rather it must mean, Because it was recently settled (i.e., "near" to the present) its sins are little (i.e., few).

Shab. 10b. T.S. 19, 108.

70. Let me escape (na) there.

R. Isaac said: Zoar had been settled fifty-one years, for it says, *Let me escape* (na) *there,* the numerical value of "na" being fifty-one.[1] Sodom was settled fifty-two years, whilst it enjoyed

twenty-six years of peace. For it is written, *Twelve years they served Chedorlaomer, and in the thirteenth year they rebelled. And in the fourteenth year came Chedorlaomer . . . and smote* [them] (14:4f).[2]

Now, further on the narrative relates, *The sun was arisen upon the earth when Lot came* Zoarah (*to Zoar*) (verse 23): Zoar was younger [than Sodom] by the number of days indicated by the word *Zoarah,* viz., 365, which is the one year of its later settlement. Now, *Zoarah* lacks the letter *waw* (six), corresponding to the six hours by which the solar year exceeds the [thirteen months'] lunar year, the former being three hundred and sixty-five days and six hours, neither less nor more.

Shab. 10b; MA. T.S. 19, 109. 119.

71. See, I have granted your petition.[1]

[Scripture writes,] *The Lord lift up His face to you* (Num. 6:26): when you stand and pray, as it says, *See, I have granted your petition.*[2] Now, it follows *a fortiori:* If I granted

2 13:9.
§ 70 [1] Heb. נא. Every Hebrew letter is also a number: נ = 50, + א = 1: total 51.
[2] The 12 years of servitude, 13 of rebellion, and one year of war were not peaceful. This left 26 years of peace before its destruction.
§ 71 [1] Lit., I have lifted up your face.
[2] Just as lifting up the face (see n. 1) here means the granting of one's prayer, so also in the verse quoted.

Zoar.—[23]The sun was risen upon the earth when Lot came unto Zoar. [24]Then the Lord caused to rain upon

COMMENTARY

save.[108] **Zoar. a.** "Little," in reference to Lot's plea, "Is it not a little one?" (verse 20).[109] **b.** Its former name was Bela (14:2).[110] **c.** Little or few; there were too few righteous there that it should be saved; only together with Lot were there sufficient.[111] [23]**The sun was risen,** etc. This is to inform us that Zoar was quite near to Sodom. For Lot left Sodom *"when the morning arose"* (verse 15), and by the time the sun was risen in full strength he was already in Zoar.[112] **when Lot came unto Zoar.** Then *the Lord caused to rain,* etc. (v. 24).[113] [24]**the Lord caused to rain,** etc. **a.** The Angel, Gabriel, the destroyer, is designated by the name of his Master.[114] **b.** "The Lord" . . .

ANTHOLOGY

Lot's petition for the sake of Abraham My friend, shall I not grant your's, both for your own sake, and for the sake of your ancestors? R. Halafta of Caesarea said: If Lot's petition was granted because he honored the angel, shall I not hearken to your prayers for your sake and your ancestors' sake?

Sifre Naso 42; Gen. R. 50, 11. T.S. 19, 110.

72. Hasten, escape there.

R. Simeon said: You can infer *a fortiori:* If the Torah ordered [inanimate] property, which has no understanding to do good or evil, to be burnt because it led the righteous to live together with the wicked;[1] how much the more will he be punished who deliberately seeks to pervert his neighbor and entice him from the good to an evil path. R. Leazar said: Lot is a proof of this. He dwelt in Sodom only on account of his wealth, yet he left it with his hands on his head.[2] That is what our text means: *Hasten, escape there*—it is enough that you save your life.

J. Sanh. 10, 8. T.S. 19, 114.

73. The sun was risen upon the earth.

R. Levi said: This may be compared to a city which had two patrons,[1] one a [small-] townsman and another a citizen of that very city. The king was angry with them [its inhabitants] and desired to chastise them. Said he: "If I chastise them in the presence of that citizen alone, they will say, Were the villager present he would have protected us. While if I chastise them in the villager's presence they will say, If the citizen were present, he would have protected us." Similarly, because some of the Sodomites worshipped the sun and others the moon, the Holy One, blessed is He, said: "If I chastise them by day they will say, Had the moon been present it would have protected us; if I chastise them at night they will say, Had the sun been present it would have protected us. Therefore I will bring retribution upon them on the sixteenth of Nisan, when the sun and moon are visible in the sky [simultaneously]. That is the meaning of our text, *The sun was risen upon the earth when Lot came to Zoar.*[2]

Gen. R. 50, 12. T.S. 19, 115.

74. THE SUN WAS RISEN UPON THE EARTH. [Scripture writes,] *They pass away like a shablul* (AJV: *snail*) (Ps. 58:9): The people of Sodom were swept away like an ear of corn (*shiboleth*) . . . [The verse continues:] *Like the untimely births of a woman, that have not seen the sun:* the people of Sodom did not see the sun. For it says, *The sun was risen upon the earth when Lot came to Zoar;* then we read, *Now, the Lord had* [already] *rained brimstone and fire on Sodom and Gomorrah.*

Tan. Y. Vayyera 17. T.S. 19, 117.

§ 72 [1] See par. 56 and note.
[2] An idiom: Bewailing the loss of all his wealth, which he had to leave behind to be destroyed.
§ 73 [1] Special protectors. The word is taken from the Roman system of patron and client.
[2] On that morning the moon is still visible in the sky.

Sodom and upon Gomorrah brimstone and fire from the Lord out of

COMMENTARY

"from the Lord," etc. Scripture emphasizes that it was *from the Lord,* to make it clear that it was not a natural phenomenon.[115] **c.** Looking over the Dead Sea and its vicinity the observer will notice the volcanic nature of the soil. He will be inclined to classify the destruction of Sodom and Gomorrah as an ordinary natural phenomenon. He will ascribe the origin of the Dead Sea to volcanic eruptions which account for the volcanic nature of the soil. In contrast to this theory stands the Divine word: "God let rain fall—from *God,* from the *sky.*"[116]

brimstone and fire. Miraculously these descended,

ANTHOLOGY

75. Then the Lord rained brimstone and fire.

This is the nature of the Supreme King of kings, the Holy One, blessed is He: when He goes forth in peace, He is accompanied by legions and armies; but when He goes forth to battle, He goes alone. You find it so when He punished the five cities of Sodom:[1] He alone punished them, as it says, *Then the Lord rained brimstone and fire on Sodom and Gomorrah from the Lord out of heaven.*

Sifre Zuta Naso 6, 26. T.S. 19, 120.

76. AND THE LORD RAINED BRIMSTONE AND FIRE. Abba Halafta b. Samki, quoting R. Judah, said: This "Lord" refers to Gabriel;[1] *from the Lord out of heaven* means the Holy One, blessed is He. R. Eleazar said: *And the Lord* always means He together with His [celestial] court. R. Isaac said: In the Torah, the Prophets, and the Writings we find the names of [mere] mortals[2] mentioned twice in one verse, yet you are surprised that the Almighty mentions His name twice in one verse![3]

[Another interpretation:] *And the Lord* intimates that He sat in judgment over them in a Court of seventy-one[4] and pronounced them guilty; then He rained fire on them, and they paid the penalty in fire.

R. Johanan said: The verse teaches that the Holy One, blessed is He, revealed Himself to them together with His celestial Court; their river turned to pitch and their earth became brimstone, which together became a raging fire.

Gen. R. 51, 2; Tan. Y. Vayyera 19; MhG. T.S. 19, 121-2. 124.

77. THE LORD, etc. R. Isaac said: Come and see! Everywhere *Elohim* denotes the God of Judgment and *Adonai* the God of Mercy.[1] Yet even as God of Judgment He displays the quality of mercy, for otherwise the world would be destroyed; it is on account of that quality of Mercy that the world still endures. You find this saving grace[2] in every judgment which He executes. Similarly, when Scripture writes, *The Lord rained brimstone and fire,* etc., a remnant was nevertheless saved.[3]

Zohar Hadash Noah 21. T.S. 19, 123.

78. THE LORD RAINED BRIMSTONE AND FIRE, etc. Should they repent, it would be rain; if not, brimstone and fire. For rain is mentioned

§ 75 [1] Sodom and Gomorrah, Admah, Zeboiim and Zoar; see 14:2 and cf. 19:29, "the cities of the plain"; however, Zoar was spared.

§ 76 [1] As God's messenger, being called here by the name of the Sender.
[2] Lit., commoner.
[3] It is not necessary to assume that different beings are meant, as you interpret.
[4] The Jewish Supreme Court on earth *(Sanhedrin),* which alone could condemn a city, consisted of seventy-one judges (see Sanh. 2a); the Celestial Court is pictured as being the same.

§ 77 [1] Lit., the attribute of Judgment . . . the attribute of Mercy.
[2] Lit., healing, cure.
[3] Zohar 1, 107b states: His mercy is recorded in the sentence, *When God destroyed the cities of the plain, God remembered Abraham, and sent Lot out*—Lot, the ancestor of two nations (Ammon and Moab), and from whom were descended David and Solomon.

ANTHOLOGY

here[1] and in another passage:[2] just as there actual rain is meant, so here too. If so [you might say,] just as here there was brimstone and fire, so there too; therefore it says here, *From the Lord out of heaven*.[3] But Thou didst not finally doom them [the Sodomites] to utter destruction until they filled the measure of their wickedness [by not repenting even then].

Mechilta B'shallach, Parshath ha-Shirah 5. T.S. 19, 125.

79. THE LORD RAINED BRIMSTONE AND FIRE UPON SODOM AND GOMORRAH. [It is written,] *Not to you, all you that transgress [God's] path* (Lam. 1:12).[1] R. Amram, quoting Rab, interpreted: They treated me like those who transgress the Law. For concerning Sodom Scripture writes, *The Lord rained brimstone and fire on Sodom,* and in the case of Jerusalem it is written, *From on high He sent fire into my bones, and it prevailed against them (ibid.* 13).[2] It is also written, *For the iniquity of my people is greater than the sin of Sodom* (4:6).

Sanh. 104b. T.S. 19, 126.

80. THE LORD RAINED BRIMSTONE AND FIRE, etc. It is written, *Let them be as a snail which melts and passes away, like the untimely births of a woman, that have not seen the sun* (Ps. 58: 9). [This applies to the Sodomites, who were] like a snail or a slug which dissolves in excrements; like a mole which never sees the sun until it is dust again; like a married woman who goes out, ashamed of her child [conceived in adultery] being seen, and casts it away at night before the sun can look upon it. In that vein Scripture writes, *The sun had risen upon the earth ... when the Lord had* [already] *rained brimstone and fire,*[1] etc.

Gen. R. 51, 1. T.S. 19, 127.

81. THE LORD RAINED, etc. This may be compared to two countries that revolted against the king, whereupon he ordered: "Let one be burnt at her own cost, and the second at the cost of the exchequer." Similarly, on another occasion Scripture writes, *And her* [Edom's] *streams shall be turned to pitch, and her dust to brimstone* (Isa. 34:9);[1] whereas here *the Lord rained brimstone and fire.*

§ 78 [1] In the verb.
  [2] It does not state which. Probably 7:4 is meant: *I will send rain upon the earth forty days and forty nights*—in the story of the Flood (M.K.).
  [3] It is not clear how this is interpreted; but evidently in such a way as to intimate that only here did brimstone and fire rain down, but not at the Flood.
§ 79 [1] AJV: *Let it not come unto you, all ye that pass by.*
  [2] So Jerusalem was treated in the same way as Sodom. This must be the interpretation on the reading of cur. edd. It is not altogether intelligible, however. Firstly, *"not to you"* does not fit in with this; secondly, "for in the case of Sodom . . . and in the case of Jerusalem" (Heb. ואילו . . . דאילו) should probably be rendered, "for in the case . . . *whereas* in the case," the original implying *contrast,* not agreement. A variant reading in a MS given in Dikduke Soferim yields a better sense: R. Amram, quoting Rab, interpreted: "They *did not* treat me as those who transgress[ed] the law. For in . . . *whereas*" etc. This would indicate that Jerusalem's punishment was not the same (but greater or smaller—it is not clear which). The caption text is then to be rendered: *Not to you* [are to be compared] *all that transgress[ed].* The point of the difference is not clear. If we retain the additional text, *For the iniquity of my people is* greater *than the sin of Sodom,* it must mean that Jerusalem's punishment was greater—perhaps because in Sodom's case God only rained brimstone and fire upon *Sodom;* whereas here He sent fire right into their bones. This again does not agree with the passage that follows, which suggests that Jerusalem's punishment was *less.* According to that, *"for the iniquity"* etc., does not belong here, but is the beginning of the next passage; R. Elijah Gaon does in fact delete "It is also written," making this head the next passage. The lesser punishment will be either that in the case of Sodom God Himself caused it to rain, whereas here the fire was simply sent, by an unstated agency (a very unlikely supposition, since *"the Lord"* is explicitly mentioned in the previous verse, of which this appears to be a continuation); or that Sodom was visited with *brimstone* and fire, where Jerusalem suffered only fire. Nevertheless, the first alternative, viz., that Jerusalem's fate was worse, seems to be more plausible. In that case we must retain "and it is written," and assume that the standpoint of the next passage (*q.v.* in Sanh., Sonc. ed., p. 711) differs from ours.
§ 80 [1] By then the Sodomites were no more—gone before the sun rose.
§ 81 [1] So the materials for her destruction came out of herself.

ANTHOLOGY

R. Abun said: It may be compared to a servant who was taking bread out of the oven. Her mistress's son came and took out a loaf, which she handed to him; but her own son took out burning coals and she let him have them. Similarly, elsewhere we read, Behold, *I will rain bread from heaven for you* (Exod. 6:4); whereas here we read, *Then the Lord rained* brimstone and fire.[2]

Gen. R. 51, 2. T.S. 19, 128-9.

82. THE LORD RAINED, etc. *We have a little sister, and she has no breasts; what shall we do for our sister in the day when she shall be spoken against* (Song 8:8)? This alludes to Sodom, as it says, *Your elder sister is Samaria . . . and your little sister . . . is Sodom* (Ezek. 16:46). *She has no breasts*: she has not suckled (practised) [God's] precepts and good deeds. *In the day when she shall be spoken against*: i.e., in the day that the Celestial Court shall doom her to be destroyed by fire,[1] as our text states.

Song R. 8. T.S. 19, 132.

83. THE LORD RAINED, etc. *I said of laughter, It is mixed* (Eccl. 2:2): how mixed was the laughter of [God's] Attribute of Justice at the people of Sodom.[1] For it says, *A land from which bread came forth—and its site was overturned as by fire. Its stones were the place of sapphires, and it had dust of gold. A path no bird of prey had known* (Job 28:5-7).[2] For when they said, "Let us make the custom of passers-by forgotten among us,"[3] the Holy One, blessed is He, said: "By your life! I will make *you* forgotten by the world," as our text states.[4]

Eccl. R. 2, 1. T.S. 19, 133.

84. THEN THE LORD RAINED, etc. Let our master teach us:[1] If the Beth Din proclaims a public fast for rain, and the rain comes on that very day, must the fast be completed? Thus did our Rabbis learn: If the rain comes before the sun rises in the heavens and whilst they are fasting, they do not complete the fast; if it comes later, they must complete it; this is R. Meir's ruling. R. Judah said: If it comes before midday, the fast is not completed; if after midday, it is. See how effective is repentance! Though a man be burdened with many sins, if he but repents before the Holy One, blessed is He, He regards him as though he had not sinned. This is the proof: When the Almighty sought to destroy Sodom and her sister cities, Abraham arose and supplicated for mercy on their behalf, thinking that there might yet be hope [that they would repent]. But when he found nothing in their favor, the Divine Presence departed . . . and retribution immediately befell them, as our text states.

Tan. Y. Vayyera 16. T.S. 19, 135.

85. THEN THE LORD RAINED, etc. Scripture writes, *He shall rain upon them* bil'humo (Job 20:23). What does *bil'humo* mean? On account of the wars (*b'milhamoth*) which they [the Sodomites] waged against the Almighty.[1]

The Sodomites hardened themselves against Him and deliberately sinned, as it says, *Now the men of Sodom were wicked and sinners against the Lord exceedingly* (13:13). What is related of them? *Then the Lord rained brimstone and fire upon Sodom*: this was in this world; *from the Lord from heaven*—that will be in the next world.

---

[2] Each received what he sought: The Israelites sought bread, and God granted it to them; the Sodomites fire—to burn others—and they too had their desire, to their own destruction.

§ 82 [1] Cf. par. 76.

§ 83 [1] The sense is not quite clear. *Meholal* (mad) is now connected with *mahul*, mixed (as when wine is mixed or adulterated with water—Y.M.). Jast. explains: How abused was the Divine laughter (i.e., the smiling face of good fortune) toward the Sodomites. Or: How balefully Divine Justice laughed at their prosperity, knowing that through their sins it would be so short-lived.

[2] I.e., Sodom was a fertile and rich land, untouched by invaders; yet it was razed. This passage refers the verses to Sodom, and so Rashi *ad loc.*, which this translation follows. AJV differs, *q.v.*

[3] Let us cease all hospitality, so that no traveler will ever visit us, until we forget their very existence.

[4] So that future travelers passing by neither knew nor remembered Sodom: measure for measure.

§ 84 [1] See chap. 18, par. 1, n. 1.

§ 85 [1] This derives *bil'humo* from *laham*, to wage war. AJV: *He shall cause it to rain upon him into his flesh.*

heaven; [25]and He overthrew those cities, and all the Plain, and all the inhabitants of the cities, and that

COMMENTARY

formed without any natural cause.[117] [25]**overthrew.** Lit., turned, reversed. It had been a fertile region, fresh and green: He now completely reversed it, turning it into barren desolation.[118] **all the Plain.**

ANTHOLOGY

Upon the wicked He will rain coals; fire and brimstone and burning wind shall be the portion of their cup (Ps. 11:6). The Holy One, blessed is He, said: "All who exalt themselves will eventually be punished by fire." [So it was with] the people of Sodom, as our text states.

Tan. Y. Vayyera 8; Midrash T'hillim 11; MhG. Sh'moth 130. T.S. 19, 136-8.

86. BRIMSTONE AND FIRE. R. Judan said: Why does a man tremble in his very soul when he smells brimstone? Because it knows that it will be punished with this in the Hereafter.

Gen. R. 51, 3. T.S. 19, 142.

87. BRIMSTONE AND FIRE. The Holy One, blessed is He, said to the wicked: "You say truly that I have sworn never to bring another flood upon the world. Yet by your life! *Judgments are prepared for scorners, and stripes* (mahalumoth) *for the back of fools*" (Prov. 19:29). *Mahalumoth* means *mah lo maweth* (what matter which death?): if I swore not to bring a flood of water, I will bring a flood of fire and brimstone and stones, as our text states.[1]

AB 1, 1. T.S. 19, 143.

88. **From the Lord.**

A Sadducean said to R. Ishmael b. R. Jose: It is written, *Then the Lord rained brimstone and fire upon Sodom from the Lord out of heaven;* surely it should have said, from Him? Said a certain fuller to him [the Rabbi], "Leave him, and I will answer him. Now, it is written, *And Lamech said to his wives: "Adah and Zillah, hear my voice; ye wives of Lamech, hearken to my speech"* (4:23). Surely it should have said, my wives? But that is Scriptural style;

so here too it is Scriptural style." "How do you know this?" he [the Rabbi] asked him. "I heard it at R. Meir's lectures," he replied.

Sanh. 38b. T.S. 19, 145.

89. **From the Lord out of heaven.**

R. Samuel b. Nahmani said: Woe to the wicked, who turn the source of compassion into a source of retribution. For David hymns [God], *Hallelujah; praise the Lord from the heavens* (Ps. 148:1), where there is neither fire, hail, or brimstone. How then does it say, *Then the Lord rained brimstone and fire upon Sodom and Gomorrah from the Lord* out of heaven? Only from the very beginning, when the heavens were created, the Holy One, blessed is He, decreed: Whatever the men deserve, you will be to them: for the people of Sodom and the children of Esau [you must be] brimstone and fire; for Israel, dew.

Why are [the heavens] called hallowed? Because the Name of the Holy One, blessed is He, is hallowed through them. For both [God's] bounty and retribution comes from them. His bounty, as it says, *Behold, I will rain bread* out of heaven *for you* (Exod. 16:4). Retribution, as in our text: *Then the Lord rained brimstone and fire . . .* out of heaven.

Tan. Y. Vayyera 23; Midrash quoted in a Yemenite MS. T.S. 19, 134. 146.

90. **He overthrew those cities.**

R. Levi, quoting R. Samuel b. Nahman, said: These five[1] cities sat on one rock; the angel stretched out his hand and overturned them. So it is written, *He put forth his hand upon the flinty rock; He overturned the mountains by*

§ 87 [1] Cf. chap. 18, par. 182.
§ 90 [1] "Five is mentioned because of the general tradition; see 14:2. However, only four were destroyed, as Zoar was spared. But see par. 108, according to which Zoar too was overthrown after Lot left it.

which grew upon the ground. [26]But his wife looked back from behind him, and she became a pillar of salt.

COMMENTARY

In which Sodom lay.[119] [26]**his wife looked back from behind him. a.** Behind Lot.[120] **b.** She looked back, behind and beyond Lot who was in the rear, shepherding his household in their hasty flight.[121] **c.** The meaning is that she was behind Lot, engaged in saving their cattle and other wealth, when the evil (the fire and brimstone) overtook her.[122] **a pillar of salt.** She looked back and lingered behind, to be overtaken by the brimstone and fire from which the others escaped. A similar fate befell lingering refugees at Pompei. "Her body became encrusted and saturated with a nitrous and saline substance, that very likely preserved it for some time from decay" (De Sola). Ancient writers

ANTHOLOGY

the roots (Job 28:9). One scholar interpreted: with a fifth of the hand; another interpreted: with a fifth of the finger.[2]

Gen. R. 51, 4. T.S. 19, 148.

91. HE OVERTHREW THOSE CITIES. *The wicked are examined,[1] and are not; but the house of the righteous shall stand* (Prov. 12:7). When the Holy One, blessed is He, scrutinizes the deeds of the wicked and examines them, they cannot endure. He examined the deeds of the Sodomites, and they could not endure, as it says, *He examined those cities.*

Tan. Y. Nitsabim 1. T.S. 19, 151.

92. **That which grew upon the ground.**

Even plants of the ground were smitten. R. Joshua b. Levi said: To this very day if one collects rain from the atmosphere of Sodom and pours it into a furrow, it does not promote growth.

Gen. R. 51, 4. T.S. 19, 152.

93. **But his wife looked back from behind him, and she became a pillar of salt.**

[He who sees Lot's wife must offer thanks and praise to the Almighty,] as it says, *But his wife looked back from behind him, and she became a pillar of salt.* This is well in all [the

other instances enumerated], because they were miracles [which wrought salvation].[1] But Lot's wife was a case of punishment? He must say, Blessed be the true Judge.[2] But it says, thanksgiving and praise? It was taught: Two blessings must be recited in respect of Lot and his wife: in respect of his wife, "Blessed be the true Judge"; in respect of Lot, "Blessed be He who remembers the righteous." R. Johanan said: Even in the hour of His anger the Holy One, blessed is He, remembers the righteous, as it says, *And it came to pass, when God destroyed the cities of the Plain, that God remembered Abraham, and sent Lot out in the midst of the overthrow* (verse 29).

Ber. 54b. T.S. 19, 153. 166.

94. BUT HIS WIFE LOOKED BACK FROM BEHIND HIM, AND SHE BECAME A PILLAR OF SALT. Her compassion welled up for her married daughters in Sodom. Looking back to see if they were following her or not, she beheld the Shechinah (Divine Presence) and turned into a pillar of salt, which still stands. Oxen lick it every day until it dwindles down to the toes of her feet; by the morning it has shot up again.

PRE 25. T.S. 19, 155.

95. FROM BEHIND HIM. Scripture should have written, *from behind her?* However, it means

---

[2] By a play on words the ל of חלמיש (flint) is omitted, so that it reads חמיש, a fifth. The thought is that God's power is invincible.

§ 91 [1] *Hafach* ("overthrew") means to turn. Here it is understood in the sense of turning something over and about, to inspect it for soundness, and so the verb in the caption is rendered: He turned these cities round and about, seeking their merits, but found only wickedness. God's punishment is never arbitrary.

§ 93 [1] The passage there enumerates various objects and places where a man must praise God, e.g., the place where the Red Sea was divided or the Jordan was forded.
   [2] This is said on hearing bad news, e.g., the death of a near relation.

²⁷And Abraham got up early in the morning to the place where he had stood before the Lord. ²⁸And he

COMMENTARY

refer to this pillar as being still in existence. Josephus

claims to have seen it.¹²³ ²⁷**Abraham.** After a restless night, his heart heavy with the knowledge of what is about to befall the five cities, he rises early in the morning to gaze with compassionate eyes upon the fulfillment of the Divine decree.¹²⁴ **the place where he had stood before the Lord.** I.e., the place whither he had accompanied the angels. Having failed to find anything more to say in their favor, he now came to plead for mercy

GENESIS XIX, 24

behind the Shechinah. R. Jose interpreted: From behind Lot, whom the destroyer was following. Was he then following him: surely he had sent Lot away? The fact is that wherever Lot went the destroying angel desisted from his work; but where he had already passed and left the destroyer behind him, he overturned the place. Hence he said, *Look not behind you,* for there I am destroying. But his wife looked back and beheld the destroyer; therefore she became a pillar of salt, for the destroying angel does not harm any person whom he does not see; but when she turned back he saw her face, and she became a pillar of salt.

Zohar 1, 108b. T.S. 19, 155 note.

96. SHE BECAME A PILLAR OF SALT. Just as a man cannot take a piece of bread in his mouth when it is excessively salty, so it was with Lot's descendants: since they were the issue of an incestuous union Scripture says of them, *An Ammonite or a Moabite shall not enter into the assembly of the Lord* (Deut. 23:4). Again, everything needs salt, except water. So Ammon and Moab may unite with all nations except Israel.

Midrash Habiur. T.S. 19, 156.

97. **Abraham got up early in the morning.**

A scholar should not go out alone at night... R. Eliezer deduced it from our text.¹

Hul. 91a. T.S. 19, 158.

98. ABRAHAM GOT UP EARLY IN THE MORNING. It was taught: Circumcision may be performed the whole day, but that the zealous hasten early to obey [God's] precepts, as our text states.¹

Pes. 4a. T.S. 19, 159.

99. ABRAHAM GOT UP EARLY, etc. R. Joshua b. Levi said: The institution of daily prayers was learned from our Patriarchs. The morning prayers from Abraham, [of whom it says,] *Abraham got up early in the morning to the place where he had stood before the Lord:* "stood" indicates nought else but prayer, as in the text, *Then* stood up *Phinehas and* prayed (Ps. 106:30).

J. Ber. 4, 1. T.S. 19, 160.

100. **To the place where he had stood before the Lord.**

R. Helbo said, citing R. Huna: The God of Abraham comes to the help of him who always prays in a fixed place, and when he dies he will be eulogized, "Alas! a man of humility; alas! a man of piety, a [true] disciple of our father Abraham." How do we know that Abraham prayed in a fixed place? Because it is written, *Abraham got up early in the morning to the place where he had stood before the Lord:* "stood" means nought else but in prayer, as it says, *Then* stood up *Phinehas and* prayed (Ps. 106:30).¹

Ber. 6b. T.S. 19, 161.

§ 97 ¹ He got up early in the morning, but not before, when it was yet night. He had arisen to go out to pray for Sodom, alone; had it been permitted he naturally would have gone out even earlier, but that it was night.

§ 98 ¹ The proof-text does not refer to circumcision; it is quoted to show that whatever is to be done should be done at the earliest possible moment.

§ 100 ¹ And Abraham was careful to go to that particular place for his prayers.

looked out toward Sodom and Gomorrah, and toward all the land of the Plain, and beheld, and, lo, the smoke of the land went up as the smoke of a furnace. [29]And it came to pass, when God destroyed the cities of the Plain, that God remembered Abraham, and sent Lot out of the midst of the overthrow, when

COMMENTARY

for them.[125] [28]**looked out. a.** To see whether ten righteous men had been found there and the cities spared.[126] **b.** Abraham thought that the appearance of the angels in Sodom would lead the people to repent. He now rose early to see whether this had happened with the consequent sparing of the cities.[127] **and beheld, and, lo, the smoke,** etc. He saw that there was no room for further prayer.[128] [29]**when God destroyed.** I.e., the angel.[129] **God remembered.** God himself.[130] **God remembered Abraham. a.** He remembered that it was only due to Abraham that Lot was in Sodom, for had he not followed Abraham he would still have been in Haran. Therefore God saved him, because it would

ANTHOLOGY

101. BEFORE THE LORD. Hence you learn that he who prays must feel as though the Divine Presence were before him. In this vein it says, *I have set the Lord always before me* (Ps. 16:8).

PZ. T.S. 19, 162.

102. **God was mindful of Abraham.**

R. Berechiah said: When the Holy One, blessed is He, created the world, He desired to show the angels the praiseworthy deeds of the righteous. Said they to Him, *What is man, that Thou art mindful of him* (Ps. 8:5)?—they were alluding to Abraham, as it says, *God was mindful of Abraham.*

Midrash T'hillim 8. T.S. 19, 168.

103. **He sent Lot out of the midst of the overthrow.**

Thus Scripture writes, *The Lord is good, a stronghold in the day of trouble; and He knows them that take refuge in Him* (Nah. 1:7). When a generation angers Him He saves the righteous but destroys the wicked. So it was with the Sodomites, whom He destroyed, as it says, *The Lord rained brimstone and fire on Sodom;* but He rescued Lot, as our text states.

Tan. Y. Bamidbar 32. T.S. 19, 169.

104. HE SENT LOT, etc. [When Balaam, the heathen prophet, came to curse Israel at Balak's request,] the former said to the latter, "We are both alike, for we are both ungrateful. But for their ancestor Abraham there would not have been a Balak, as it says, *And it came to pass, when God destroyed the cities of the plain, that God remembered* Abraham, *and sent Lot out of the midst of the overthrow.* But for Abraham, then, Lot would not have escaped, and you (Balak) are Lot's descendant."

The Holy One, blessed is He, said, "I sent their ancestor Lot out of the overthrow only for Abraham's sake . . . yet they have denied [the bond of] salt:[1] let them revert to their devastation,"[2] as it says, *Therefore as I live, saith the Lord of hosts, the God of Israel: Surely Moab shall be as Sodom, and the children of Ammon as Gomorrah, the breeding-place of nettles, and saltpits,[3] and a desolation for ever* (Zeph. 2:9).

Num. R. 20, 19; MhG. T.S. 19, 170-1.

105. GOD REMEMBERED ABRAHAM, AND SENT LOT OUT. Does God show favoritism: surely it says, *He regards not persons* (Deut. 10:17)? He saved him because Abraham had trained him to righteousness and charity. But He showed no favoritism, seeing that his wife was burnt.[1]

§ 104 [1] I.e., the strong bond of friendship which this should have created between Israel, Abraham's descendants, and Ammon and Moab, Lot's descendants.
[2] Lit., sin, i.e., to the state of devastation by which their sin was punished.
[3] "Saltpits" may have inspired the statement that they denied the bond of salt.

§ 105 [1] Her becoming a pillar of salt is regarded as the same as being burnt up.

He overthrew the cities in which Lot dwelt. [30]And Lot went up out of Zoar, and dwelt in the mountain, and his two daughters with him; for he feared to dwell in Zoar; and he dwelt in a cave, he and his two daughters. [31]And the first-born said

COMMENTARY

not have been fitting that Lot should die on account of his association with Abraham.[131] **b.** He saved him for Abraham's sake, because he was not so righteous as to deserve to be saved for his own.[132] **[30]he feared to dwell in Zoar. a.** Because it was near Sodom.[133] **b.** He knew that Zoar had been spared only because he could not reach the mountain in time. Now that there was time for him to go on, he naturally feared that it too would be destroyed.[134] **c.** Because its inhabitants too were wicked.[135] **he dwelt in a cave.** From Zoar he first took refuge

ANTHOLOGY

R. Simeon said: Any service rendered to a scholar[2] delivers the doer from evil. Moreover, even if he is sinful he is bound to learn of his ways and practise them. Lot is a proof of this: having associated with Abraham, though not following him in all matters, he had learned to show kindness to people, just as Abraham did. It was this that enabled all these cities to exist as long as they did after Lot had settled among them.

Midrash Habiur; Zohar 1, 105a.
T.S. 19, 172 and note.

106.   The cities which Lot inhabited.

They were all wicked, and in none was there anyone meritorious save Lot. From this we learn that every place where the wicked dwell will be destroyed. [Now, the Bible says,] *The cities which Lot inhabited*: but surely he did not inhabit all of them! What it means is that for his sake they remained inhabited and were not destroyed. And that was not due to his own but to Abraham's merit.

Zohar 1, 105a.   T.S. 19, 174.

107.   Lot went up out of Zoar.

This [incestuous union with his daughters] happened to him because he ignored the angel[1] and went further away.

MhG. T.S. 19, 176.

108.   And dwelt in the mountain.

In the extreme limit of Eretz Israel. *And his two daughters with him, for he feared to dwell in Zoar:* he thought, since its doom has been decreed, it cannot be saved. So it was indeed, its inhabitants being swallowed up. *And his two daughters with him:* they were with him alone; therefore he was punished.

Sechel Tob. T.S. 19, 178.

109.   Lot went up out of Zoar . . . and dwelt in the cave.

Thus it is written, *For the Leader: al tasheth [A Psalm] of David; Michtam; when he fled from Saul, in the cave* (Ps. 57:1). "Sovereign of the Universe!" he (David) cried out. "Before I entered this cave Thou wast merciful to others for my sake.[1] Now that I am in the cave, may this be Thy will: destroy not" (*al tasheth*).

Gen. R. 51, 7. T.S. 19, 175.

110.   AND DWELT IN THE CAVE. R. Isaac

said: Wherever dwelling is mentioned trouble is indicated. Here it says, *And dwelt in the cave;* then Scripture writes, *Thus were both the daughters of Lot with child by their father* (verse 36).

MhG Vayyesheb 1. T.S. 19, 177.

111.   There is not a man in the earth.

If the Holy One, blessed is He, judged by men's deeds Lot's daughters should have been

---

[2] In Rabbinic thought scholar is synonymous with righteous.
§ 107   [1] Who told him to go to the mountain: verse 17. See par. 69.
§ 109   [1] Lot was spared because I (David) was to descend from him.

unto the younger: "Our father is old, and there is not a man in the earth to come in unto us after the manner of all the earth. ³²Come, let us make our father drink wine, and we will lie with him, that we may preserve seed of our father." ³³And they made their father drink wine that night. And the first-born went in, and lay with her father;

COMMENTARY

in the mountain; but fearing that the destruction, the brimstone and fire, would spread there too, he sought shelter in a cave.¹³⁶ ³¹**our father is old. a.** He may die or become impotent.¹³⁷ **b.** He cannot

marry again and beget sons, so no male will be left from him.¹³⁸ **c.** Too old to travel to another place where we might find suitable husbands.¹³⁹ **there is not a man in the earth. a.** They thought that the whole world had been destroyed.¹³⁹ᵃ **b.** We will not find any man willing to become kin with one who had lived among people who had deserved such a disaster.¹⁴⁰ **c.** In this region.¹⁴¹ **d.** Some commentators state that Lot's daughters believed that the destruction had been universal, and that but for them the world would be completely depopulated. This explanation is untenable, seeing that they had just left Zoar. Their conduct does not admit of any extenuation: they were true children of Sodom.¹⁴² ³²**that we may preserve seed of our father.** Believing that the destruction was universal, they may have thought that they had been saved that the human race might be rebuilt through them. Marriage with a father was permitted at that time, but their modesty forbade them to propose it; or perhaps though permitted it was looked on with abhorrence.¹⁴³ ³³**wine.** Owing to its abundance, wine used to be stored in caves.¹⁴⁴ **with her father.** Of the younger it is merely said, *with him*. The elder

ANTHOLOGY

burnt in fire [for incest]. But He judged them only for their thoughts and intentions. They said, *Our father is old, and there is not a man in the earth*, etc. They saw, indeed, that there was no man thereabouts. Moreover, they thought that no living being was left on earth, believing that the world had been destroyed just as Sodom and its companion cities had been overturned. It was not their desire to commit incest with their father. Rather, they argued thus: "The Holy One, blessed is He, created man only in order to propagate his kind; but now he has been wiped out like the generation of the Flood; how then can the human race continue? Surely the Almighty saved us only in order to perpetuate mankind through us."

Said the Holy One, blessed is He: "If I judged you by your actions you should be burnt alive. Your intention was only to rebuild the world.

[Therefore I will not condemn you to death;] however, you may not bring [your seed] into the treasury [of humanity]." Therefore *An Ammonite or a Moabite shall not enter into the assembly of the Lord* (Deut. 23:4).¹

AB 25; PR 42. T.S. 19, 180. 184.

112. That we may preserve seed of our father.

It does not say, that we may preserve a son of our father, but *that we may preserve* seed *of our father*, viz., the seed that will issue from a different source,¹ which is the royal Messiah.

Gen. R. 51, 8. T.S. 19, 181.

113. They made their father drink wine that night.

Whence did they obtain wine in the cave? Wine providentially appeared for them for that particular moment.¹ In that spirit it says, *It*

§ 111 ¹ Eleh ha-Debarim Zuta (quoted in T.S. 19, 194) gives this as the reason for God's compassion upon Moab when He bade Moses, *Be not at enmity with Moab, neither contend with them in battle* (Deut. 2:9). See also par. 119.
§ 112 ¹ "Different source" means from different parents.
§ 113 ¹ In Gen. R. 51 the question is asked on verse 32: *Come, let us make our father drink wine.* There the answer is: Since the Sodomites had an abundance of wine they stored it in caves. R. Judah b. R. Simon said: This wine was in the nature of a foretaste of the Hereafter (*var. lec.*, the Messianic days); the same proof-text as in our passage follows.

and he knew not when she lay down, nor when she arose. ³⁴And it came to pass on the morrow, that the first-born said unto the younger: "Behold, I lay yesternight with my father. Let us make him drink wine this night also; and go thou in, and lie with him, that we may preserve seed of our father." ³⁵And they made their father drink wine that night also. And the younger arose,

and lay with him; and he knew not when she lay down, nor when she

COMMENTARY

was the first to commit incest, and so her shame is explicitly stated; but the younger merely followed her example: therefore it is somewhat hidden.[145] ³⁴**this night also.** Heb. *gam*, which in Rabbinic exegesis is regarded as a particle of extension: let us give him *more* tonight than last night, since he had perceived who it was when she arose [see Anthology, par. 115].[146] **that we may preserve seed.** Their purpose was legitimate.[147] ³⁵**the younger arose, and lay with him.** Whereas of the elder it says that she *"went in, and lay with her father."* Possibly, the older sister's action was entirely voluntary, whereas the younger acted under the compulsion of her sister's stronger will; hence

ANTHOLOGY

shall come to pass in that day, that the mountains shall drop down sweet wine (Joel 4:18). If the Holy One, blessed is He, gave so freely to sinners,[2] how much the more [will He give] to those who do His will.

Sifre Ekeb 43. T.S. 19, 183.

114. The first-born went in, and lay with her father.

[It is written,] *The people began to commit harlotry with the daughters of Moab* (Num. 25:1). "Throw a stick up into the air, it falls back to its source."[1] She who first commenced with harlotry—*And the first-born went in, and lay with her father . . . And . . . the first-born said to the younger,* etc.—she taught her harlotry. Therefore the Holy One, blessed is He, spared the younger and did not publicize her [shame], saying only, *And the younger arose, and lay with him* [not explicitly mentioning her father]; whereas of the older it is written,

and lay with her father. She who first practised harlotry, her daughters were the first to surrender to harlotry: thus, *The people began to commit harlotry with the daughters of Moab.*

Tan. Y. Balak 26. T.S. 19, 186.

115. He knew not when she lay down, nor when she arose.

It was taught on the authority of R. Jose b. R. Honi: Why is the *waw* in *ub'kumah* (nor when she arose), referring to the elder daughter, dotted?[1] To tell us that he did not know when she lay down, but he did know when she arose. But what could he do: what was done was done?[2] He should have been warned by that not to drink wine the next evening.[3]

Naz. 23a. T.S. 19, 188.

116. HE KNEW NOT WHEN SHE LAY DOWN, NOR WHEN SHE AROSE. This verse occurs twice, in reference to the elder and the younger respectively. In the case of the elder it is written with

---

² Lit., those who anger Him—by their incest.

§ 114   ¹ A proverb. "Its source" is the ground in which grew the tree from which the stick came.

§ 115   ¹ According to tradition ובקומה is written וּבְקוּמָהּ, with a dot over the second . — There are various readings here; the present is the most likely, and agrees with our Scrolls of the Torah, where it is so written.

    ² Why does Scripture draw attention to it, as though implying a greater shame?

    ³ The same thought is expressed in Y'lamdenu as a comment on "by their father" as implying that he [too] sinned in drinking the second evening when he already knew what had happened. Therefore, it adds, when his disgrace is made public by the Torah reading in the synagogue, he has but himself to blame (quoted in T.S. 19, 193).

arose. ³⁶Thus were both the daughters of Lot with child by their father. ³⁷And the first-born bore a son, and called his name Moab—the same is the father of the Moabites unto this

COMMENTARY

it does not say that she went in.[148] **arose.** The word implies a certain amount of daring and courage: she did not fear that he would not repeat the shame of the previous night.[149] ³⁷**Moab**... ³⁸**Ben-ammi.** They named them so in order to make it clear that they were not the children of promiscuity or lust, but born out of their desire to re-populate the world.[150] **the father of the Moabites ... of**

ANTHOLOGY

a *waw*, which is also dotted, to intimate that the act received assistance from on high, that the royal Messiah might issue thence. Therefore it is written *plene*, with a *waw*. But in the case of the younger it is written defectively, without a *waw*,[1] because no part of the resultant issue belonged to God;[2] [thus her issue was defective,] just as the word is written defectively. R. Simeon said: ["*He knew not*"] means that he did not know that it was God's purpose to raise from her King David, Solomon, and all the other kings, and finally the King Messiah.

Zohar 1, 110b.   T.S. 19, 190.

117.   Thus were both the daughters of Lot with child by their father.

And he [Moses] *said: The Lord came forth from Sinai, and rose from Seir to them; He shone forth from mount Paran* (Deut. 33:2). When the Holy One, blessed is He, came to give the Torah to Israel, He revealed Himself not to Israel alone, but to all the peoples.[1] ... He went to the peoples of Ammon and Moab and asked them, "Will you accept the Torah?" "What is written in it?" they queried. He replied, "*Thou*

shalt not commit adultery" (Exod. 20:13). Said they to Him: "Sovereign of the Universe! The very essence of immorality is ours";[2] as our text states.

Sifre Zoth Hab'rachah 343.   T.S. 19, 191.

118.   THUS WERE BOTH THE DAUGHTERS OF LOT WITH CHILD BY THEIR FATHER. R. Eleazar said: A woman never conceives at the first sexual act. The scholars refuted this: Surely it says, *Thus were both daughters of Lot with child by their father?* Said R. Tanhum: They forced themselves to extrude their hymen, which enabled them to conceive at the first intimacy. R. Nahman b. Hanin said: Whoever burns with immoral passion is eventually fed with his own flesh. R. Judan of Gallia and R. Samuel b. Nahman said, quoting R. Elijah Enene:[1] We would not know whether Lot lusted after his daughters, or vice versa. But when Scripture writes, *He that separates himself seeks lust* (Prov. 18:1), it follows that Lot lusted after his daughters.[2] R. Tanhum b. R. Hiyya, quoting R. Hoshaya, his interpreter,[3] said: There is not a Sabbath when this chapter on Lot is

§ 116   [1] The first is written ובקומה, the second ובקמה.

[2] There was a Divine purpose in the issue of the elder, but not in that of the younger.

§ 117   [1] The verse is interpreted: *He came forth from Sinai*, to give the Torah to Israel; *and rose from Seir*, to give the Torah to Edom (the descendants of Esau—see 36:1, 8); *He shone forth from mount Paran*, having offered the Torah to the Ishmaelites (see 21:21). These two are taken to symbolize all peoples, the Torah having been offered to all. In the light of this it is clear that the benediction, "Blessed art Thou . . . Who hast chosen us from all people and given us the Torah" is not meant in an exclusive sense; God "chose" Israel to give them the Torah only because Israel, unlike the other nations, chose to receive it.

[2] Immorality finds its most essential and concrete expression in us, since it is the very origin of our existence— how then can we accept the Torah? Cf. Vol. II, chap. 16, par. 33.

§ 118   [1] A name not found elsewhere. Perhaps we should simply read, R. Elijah.

[2] The text is applied to Lot, who had separated himself from Abraham (see 13:9ff). The thought may be that his departure from Abraham was responsible for or contributed to his moral downfall.

[3] An official who interpreted the Torah to the congregation at its public reading. Also, when a Rabbi lectured

day. ³⁸And the younger, she also bore a son, and called his name Ben-ammi—the same is the father of the children of Ammon unto this day.

COMMENTARY

the children of Ammon. Because their purpose was legitimate, these children became the progenitors of nations possessing their own territory.[151] **this day. a.** I.e., in the days of Moses, when this was written.[152] **b.** They have retained their identity, not having intermingled with strangers. Or: This fact is known to this very day.[153] **c.** The nations have retained these names to this very day.[154]

ANTHOLOGY

not read.[4] Why so? Because it says, *At every* [assembly of] *wisdom one is disgusted (ibid.)*[5] [by Lot's deed of shame].

Gen. R. 51, 9. T.S. 19, 192.

119. **The first-born bore a son, and called his name Moab . . . and the younger . . . called [her son's] name Ben-ammi.**

R. Hiyya b. Abba, citing R. Johanan, said: The Holy One, blessed is He, does not deprive any creature of his due reward, even if it be only for delicacy of speech. The elder called [her son] Moab [i.e., *me-ab*, by my father]. Wherefore the Holy One, blessed is He, said to Moses: *Be not at enmity with Moab, neither contend with them in battle* (Deut. 2:9)—no

battle, yet he might compel them to service. But the younger one called hers Ben-ammi [a son of my people]. Wherefore God bade Moses: *When you come near over against the children of Ammon, harass them not, nor contend with them (ibid.* 19)—do nothing at all, do not even compel them to service.

R. Hiyya b. Abba also said, quoting R. Joshua b. Karha: Let a man do a good deed at the earliest opportunity. For on account of the one night whereby the elder preceded the younger she preceded [the younger] by four generations [of rulers] in Israel, viz., Obed, Jesse, David, and Solomon.[1] Whereas the younger [had to wait] until Rehoboam, as it is written, *His* [Rehoboam's] *mother's name was Naamah the Ammonitess* (1 Kings 14:21).

B.K. 38b. T.S. 19, 195.

---

to the masses he did not speak to them directly but through an interpreter, whispering to him what he should say. The latter, however, sometimes elaborated and added material of his own. R. Tanhum's quoting of his own interpreter makes it clear that the latter was a man of learning with ideas of his own.

⁴ This is hardly likely, although M. K. and Y. T. assume such indeed to have been the ancient custom. The meaning is probably that the chapter is read on every Sabbath when it is part of the pericope to be read for that Sabbath, and not omitted.

⁵ AJV: *And snarleth against all wisdom.*

§ 119 ¹ Who were all descended from Ruth the Moabitess (see Ruth 4:10, 13, 21-2). This passage is based on the view that their motives were pure, viz., to perpetuate the race (pars. 111, 116). Of these four generations only two were kings; yet she appears in Jewish history four generations before the younger daughter. Both daughters are alternately praised and criticized: the older is praised for her eagerness, but criticized for her disregard of her father's honor. The younger is praised for delicately covering up her father's shame, but criticized for allowing her sister to precede her in a deed of noble motive.

GENESIS
Chapter XX

¹And Abraham journeyed from

COMMENTARY

¹**Abraham journeyed from thence. a.** From the terebinths of Mamre; see 18:1. He journeyed thence to the land of the Philistines in order to dwell successively in the whole country which God had given him.[1] **b.** From Egypt; chronologically this is linked with 13:1 (*q.v.*); here the narrative relates what befell him on the road.[2] **c.** The reason for this journey is not given. Possibly it was at God's command, even though this is not stated, for Scripture does not always state this.[3] **d.** In thus traveling he obeyed God's command, *Arise, walk through the land*, etc. (13:17).[4] **e.** He desired to move about

ANTHOLOGY

1. Abraham journeyed from there.

R. Abin began his lecture thus: *And surely the mountain falling crumbles away* (Job 14: 18): this alludes to Lot, who fell on account of the mountain.[1] *And the rock moves out of its place* (*ibid.*) alludes to Abraham, who left his place. Because when Sodom was destroyed wayfarers ceased; said he, "Why should I allow hospitality to cease from my home?" Thereupon he departed and pitched his tent in Gerar.[2] Hence it is written that *Abraham journeyed from there.*

Gen. R. 52, 1.   T.S. 20, 1.

2. ABRAHAM JOURNEYED FROM THERE. A *brother who leads himself into sin*[1] *is ejected thereby from a strong city* (Prov. 18:19). A *brother* alludes to Lot, the son of Abraham's brother. *Who leads himself into sin:* you sinned against Abraham; you denied him; you were false to him. And what was the result?[2] *Contentions like the bars of a castle* (*ibid.*): he brought contentions[3] upon himself [which shut him out from community with Israel] as the bars of the Temple [shut out the unclean]. For even as we read there, *None that was unclean in any way should enter* (2 Chron. 23:19), so here too, *An Ammonite or a Moabite shall not enter into the assembly of the Lord* (Deut. 23:4). Therefore *Abraham journeyed from there.*[4]

Gen. R. 52, 2.   T.S. 20, 2.

3. ABRAHAM JOURNEYED FROM THERE. *The wise in heart will take good deeds* (Prov. 10:8): this alludes to Abraham. *Will take good deeds:* because the region of Sodom was now desolate and wayfarers had ceased, his stores were never diminished.[1] Said he: "Why should I allow hospitality to cease from my home?" So he went and settled in Gerar. *But the foolish of tongue shall fall* (*ibid.*): this alludes to Lot, who was indeed foolish of tongue. He should have rebuked his daughters: "Shall we perpetrate the same sin on account of which the world was smitten?"[2] What was the result? *He shall fall:* he brought upon himself endless falls. Just as

---

§ 1 [1] The meaning is obscure. Pseudo-Rashi: His moral fall was on account of what happened in the cave in the mountain; this made the separation between himself and Abraham and their respective descendants final and complete; see next two pars. Another possible rendering might be: Who fell from the mountain, "mountain" alluding to Abraham, cf. chap. 19, par. 63—he fell away from Abraham, with tragic results.

[2] It is not enough to practise hospitality when the opportunity comes one's way; one must go out and actively pursue it.

§ 2 [1] This treats the verb as reflexive, and it is apparently so rendered here. The translation follows Rashi *ad loc.*

[2] This is the most likely meaning. Alternatively: Whom did he stir up against himself?

[3] Heb. *midyanim. Var. lec., dinim:* laws.

[4] He departed from the region, in order that neither they nor their descendants should intermingle.

§ 3 [1] No guest diminished his stores.

[2] Sodom was destroyed on account of immorality; see chap. 19, par. 26.

thence toward the land of the South, and dwelt between Kadesh and Shur; and he sojourned in Gerar. ²And

COMMENTARY

rather than dwell in one place in order to spread the knowledge of and belief in the One God.[5] **dwelt between Kadesh and Shur. a.** Where the angels had appeared to Hagar.[6] **b.** Between two large cities, to have the opportunity of making more converts to his faith.[7] **Kadesh.** Usually "Kadesh-Barnea"

(e.g., Deut. 1:2). It is situated on the southeast frontier of Judah.[8] **Shur.** Lit. "the wall," or fortification which protected Egypt on the east from the incursion of raiding Bedouins. Thither Hagar too wandered after her expulsion, it being in the direction of her native land (16:7).[9] **he sojourned in Gerar. a.** Gerar lies between Kadesh and Shur.[10] **b.** His great wealth was disposed between Kadesh and Shur, but he himself stayed in Gerar, the metropolis.[11] **c.** First he dwelt between Kadesh and Shur, and then in Gerar.[12] **dwelt . . . sojourned. a.** These are synonyms.[13] **b.** He settled permanently between Kadesh and Shur, but lived temporarily in Gerar.[14] **Gerar.** Probably the Wady Jerur, 13 miles southwest

ANTHOLOGY

we read elsewhere, *None that was unclean in any way should enter* (2 Chron. 23:19), so here too, *An Ammonite or a Moabite shall not enter into the assembly of the Lord* (Deut. 23:4). Therefore *Abraham journeyed from there.*

Gen. R. 52, 3.   T.S. 20, 3.

4. ABRAHAM JOURNEYED FROM THERE. R. Aha said: I was passing in front of the synagogue[1] of Sepphoris when I heard children reciting, *Abraham journeyed from there.* Said I: Great indeed were the words of the Sages, who taught: Beware of their burning coals, lest you be burnt, for their bite is the bite of a fox, etc.[2] For when Abraham parted from Lot, the parting was forever.[3]

Gen. R. 52, 4.   T.S. 20, 5.

5. ABRAHAM JOURNEYED FROM THERE. In this vein Scripture writes, *I have not dwelt with men of falsehood, neither will I associate with secret evil-doers* (Ps. 26:4). *Men of falsehood* alludes to the people of Sodom and her sister-cities; *secret evil-doers,* to Lot and his daughters. Said Abraham: "I will not associate with secret evil-doers: I have no business with

those of whom it is written, *An Ammonite or a Moabite shall not enter into the assembly of the Lord*" (Deut. 23:4).

AB 25, 2.   T.S. 20, 6.

6. Toward the land of the South (*negeb*).

It has seven names: Darom (South), Negeb (the Dry land), Teman, Yamin (the Right), Hadar (Glory), Yam (Sea) and Sinim. An objection was raised: But it is written, *Nor yet from the wilderness* Harim (Ps. 75:7)?[1] That too is Darom (South).[2]

Gen. R. 52, 4.   T.S. 20, 7.

7. TOWARD THE LAND OF THE SOUTH. All his journeys were toward the side of the South,[1] which, being the side of Wisdom, he preferred to the other sides.

Zohar 1, 111a, b.

8. And dwelt between Kadesh and Shur.

And Moses led Israel onward from the Red Sea, and they went out into the wilderness of Shur (Exod. 15:22). We do not find a wilderness of that name. What then does it mean? Said R. Isaac: [That they went out] in the merit of Abraham, of whom it is written that

§ 4   [1] *Var. lec.,* the Babylonian synagogue.
　　 [2] Aboth 2, 10.
　　 [3] Y.T. When to avoid strife Abraham requested, *"Separate, I pray you, from me"* (13:9), a breach was made for all time, for their descendants too were parted; thus his words were like burning coals.
§ 6   [1] *Harim* ("mountains") is likewise the south. Why then was this name not included?
　　 [2] The name could have been included.
§ 7   [1] "The side of the South" does not refer to the physical south of Canaan. In mystic literature there is a spiritual universe in which the different "sides" are the sources of various spiritual qualities.

Abraham said of Sarah his wife: "She is my sister." And Abimelech king of Gerar sent, and took Sarah. ³But God came to Abimelech in a

COMMENTARY

of Kadesh.[15] ²**my sister. a.** It does not state here that Abimelech's servants saw and took her to the king's palace, as it does in the case of Pharaoh. They were in fact not so immoral here as in Egypt, but Abraham suspected them.[16] **b.** On this occasion he did not ask *her* to say this, as in Egypt. There, where ugliness generally reigned [i.e., the people were dark and swarthy], her beauty was so striking that he felt it necessary for her to speak; Gerar, however, was different: there her beauty was not so outstanding.[17] **c.** "Sister" here means relation, though they understood it literally.[18] **d.** At that time the king had the legal right to take any unmarried woman by force.[19] **Abimelech.** Abimilki is the name of the Egyptian governor of Tyre in the Tell-el-Amarna tablets.[20] **Abimelech . . . sent, etc. a.** Having heard of her beauty he took her to wife.[20a] **b.** It is surprising that in her old age she was still so attractive that kings desired her. Perhaps her physical rejuvenation (chap. 18, par. 65) was accompanied by the restoration of her youthful beauty.[21] **c.** Her beauty is not mentioned here, as in the case of Pharaoh. He took her only because of her distinguished family as the sister of Abraham.[22] **d.** He took her, thinking her unmarried.[23] ³**God came to Abimelech. a.** But did not plague him as He did

ANTHOLOGY

He dwelt between Kadesh and Shur,[1] and whom I promised, [declared the Almighty,] *And also that nation, whom they shall serve, will I judge, and afterward they shall come out with great substance* (15:14).

Exod. R. 24. T.S. 20, 8.

9. **Abraham said of Sarah, his wife: "She is my sister."**

Our Rabbis taught that a man must not rely on miracles: even if the Holy One, blessed is He, has wrought a miracle for him once, let him not expect it again, for miracles do not happen every day. When a man runs into an obvious danger [he may indeed be saved by a miracle, yet] may thereby expend all his previously acquired credits [for good deeds] . . . Now, Abraham had already enjoyed one miraculous deliverance when he went to Egypt; why then did he now court a similar risk by saying, "She is my sister?" In truth, he did not rely on his own merits; but he saw the Divine Presence constantly in Sarah's abode. That gave him the courage to declare, "She is my sister," in the sense of the text, *Say to wisdom, you are my sister* (Prov. 7:4).

Zohar 1, 111b.

10. **Abimelech king of Gerar sent, and took Sarah.**

When the world was created the Shechinah abode here below. [As man sinned it departed to the heavens, each new sin causing it to ascend to a higher heaven, further away from man.] When the Philistines came and sinned, as our text relates,[1] it departed to the seventh heaven. [To counter this] Abraham came and laid up a store of good deeds; then the Shechinah descended from the seventh to the sixth heaven.

PR 5, 18. T.S. 20, 12.

11. **But God came to Abimelech in a dream of the night.**

R. Jose said: The Holy One, blessed is He, reveals Himself to a heathen prophet only when people take leave of each other [at night]. In accordance with this it says, *A word was secretly brought me . . . when men part,*[1] *from the visions*

§ 8 [1] This seems a more than usual far-fetched interpretation. However, the thought may be this: Two reasons have been given for Abraham's departure from his home and settlement between Kadesh and Shur, viz., his desire to practise hospitality, which symbolizes love of humanity, and his recoil from the immorality of Lot. Israel's exodus from Egypt was likewise for the same purpose: To teach and practise love of humanity and to shun anything impure.

§ 10 [1] Abimelech's sin in taking a married woman is here ascribed to his people as a whole.

§ 11 [1] This derives *s'ippim* from *s'if*, a branch—when men branch away from each other. AJV: *in thoughts*.

dream of the night, and said to him: "Behold, thou shalt die, because of the woman whom thou hast taken;

COMMENTARY

Pharaoh, because in truth Abimelech was more righteous.[24] **b.** There was no Divine manifestation, but only a voice.[25] **c.** This was not a prophetic revelation, but a warning from God, to save or to slay him. Therefore Onkelos renders, "there came speech (*memar*) from the Lord," not "the Lord revealed Himself." For the same reason Scripture says, "in a dream," not, "in a vision" of the night.[26]

in a dream of the night. a. Prophetic dreams are vouchsafed to Gentiles to protect the honor of the righteous.[27] **b.** There was no element of prophecy (Divine communication) in this; the whole passage, "God came," etc., merely denotes a true dream.[28] **Behold, thou shalt die.** Because adultery was forbidden as one of the Seven Noachian Laws. ["The Seven Noachian Laws" is a Rabbinic term for a series of laws of universal application, which may be considered fundamental to civilized human society. See Vol. I, chap. 2, par. 134—Ed.].[29] **because of the woman,** etc. You have committed two wrongs (1) You have taken her by force (hence, *whom thou hast taken*—against her will); (2) She is a married woman. The conjunctive *waw* in *w'hi* (AJV: *for she is*) is thus an additional reason, and

ANTHOLOGY

of the night, when deep sleep falls on men (Job 4:12-13). What is the difference between Jewish and heathen prophets? R. Hanina said: It may be compared to a king and his friend together in a chamber, separated by a curtain: when he desires to speak to his friend, he folds the curtain back and speaks to him. [So God speaks to the prophets of Israel.] When, however, He would speak to heathen prophets He does so from behind the curtain, without folding it back. Our Rabbis said: It may be compared to a king who has a wife and a concubine: to the former he goes openly, but to the latter he repairs stealthily. In the same way the Holy One, blessed is He, appears to heathen prophets only at night: *God came to Balaam at night* (Num. 22:20); *God came to Laban the Aramean in a dream of the night* (31:24); *God came to Abimelech in a dream of the night.*

Gen. R. 52, 5. T.S. 20, 13.

12. GOD CAME TO ABIMELECH IN A DREAM OF THE NIGHT. All the miracles wrought for Israel, which simultaneously brought retribution upon the wicked, occurred at night, as our text states.

Num. R. 20, 12. T.S. 20, 14.

13. GOD CAME TO ABIMELECH IN A DREAM OF THE NIGHT. When he had Sarah seized, the Holy One, blessed is He, swiftly bore down on him, as our text relates. R. Johanan said: This was one of the instances where the Pure defiled Himself.[1] For when Abimelech came to enjoy her He immediately appeared and warned him, *Behold, you shall die because of the woman whom you have taken; for she is a man's wife.*

Does the Almighty really come to the wicked? The same question arises in respect to Balaam and Laban, when Scripture tells us, *God came to Balaam* (Num. 22:9), *God came to Laban* (31:24). In all these cases, however, only a heavenly messenger was sent to them; but in carrying out their mission they assumed the name of *Elohim* (God), since they were agents of Justice.[2]

PR 42; Zohar 1, 111b. T.S. 20, 15.

14. **Behold, you shall die, because of the woman whom you have taken; for she is b'ulath baal (a man's wife).**

He [Abimelech] saw[1] all the honor which God paid him [in visiting him], as it says, *God came to Abimelech in a dream of the night.* Said He to him: "You are an incredible fool! You

§ 13 [1] God defiled Himself—if one might speak thus—in communicating with Abimelech.
[2] The Rabbis interpreted *Adonai* (Lord) and *Elohim* (God) as the God of Mercy and the God of Justice respectively, i.e., the former name emphasizes His attribute of mercy, the latter His attribute of justice.
§ 14 [1] Or: See all the honor, etc. However, in that case it would probably say, Come and see, which is the more usual form.

for she is a man's wife." ⁴Now Abimelech had not come near her; and
he said: "Lord, wilt Thou slay even
a righteous nation? ⁵Said he not

COMMENTARY

should be rendered, *and (moreover), she is a man's
wife.*[30] **⁴had not come near her. a.** Prevented
by Divine intervention; see verse 6.[31] **b.** By God's
will he was deprived of desire; or, he suppressed it
when she told him that she was a married woman,

as she undoubtedly did.[32] **c.** He did not approach
her in any way whatsoever; his punishment was because he had taken her.[33] **d.** This is stated because
she conceived Isaac soon after this incident.[34] **righteous. a.** That refrains from immorality.[35] **b.** By
this is meant himself, his household and his people.[36]
c. Probably God had already included his people at
this stage, as is suggested by verse 7, *"You shall
surely die, you and all that are yours."* Similarly,
Abimelech accused Abraham of bringing sin upon
himself *and his kingdom* (verse 9).[37] **d.** Even if I
had sinned, why destroy a whole people? But in
fact I, too, am innocent.[38] **e.** By putting me, its
leader, to death, Thou destroyest the whole
nation.[39] **⁵Said he not himself unto me.** I did

ANTHOLOGY

enjoy so much, yet would die because of a
woman! Know that she is *b'ulath baal.*" What
does this phrase mean? She is superior to her
husband. R. Aha said: Her husband was
crowned through her, but she was not crowned
through him.[2] Our rabbis interpreted: She is her
husband's master.[3] Usually the husband gives
orders; here, however, [God told Abraham,]
*In all that Sarah says to you, hearken to her
voice* (21:12).

> Tan. Y. Vayyera 25; Gen. R. 52, 5.
> T.S. 20, 18. 22.

15. SHE IS B'ULATH BAAL. A wife rises with
her husband, but does not descend with him.[1]
R. Huna said: What text [proves this]? She is
b'ulath baal: she joins in her husband's ascent
(*aliyah*),[2] but not in his descent.

> Keth. 61a. T.S. 20, 21.

16. **Now Abimelech had not come near her.**

Abimelech was credited with having behaved
morally—that he did not touch her. Said our
Rabbis: Happy is he that Scripture wrote, *Now
Abimelech had not come near her.*

[Another view, however, is that he abstained]
because he had been rendered physically impotent.

When the Holy One, blessed is He, said to
him, *"You shall die, because of the woman whom
you have taken,"* Abimelech replied: "Sovereign
of the Universe! Things hidden and revealed
are all manifest to Thee. [Thou knowest that]
I knew her not [as a married woman]; wouldst
Thou then slay me? [Moreover,] I have not
approached her: *Wilt Thou slay even a righteous
nation?"*

> Tan. Y. Vayyera 25; PZ; PR 42.
> T.S. 20, 23-5.

[2] This may simply mean that Abraham derived honor and glory through her, e.g., before Pharaoh (see 12:16),
but she was never honored on his account. A more subtle explanation makes this refer to the change in their
names. Hers was originally שרי (Sarai); the numerical value of *yod*, the last letter of her name, is 10, whilst
heh is 5. God took the *yod* of her name and divided it into two *heh's*; one He put into her name, making it
שרה (Sarah), and the other He added to אברם (Abram), making it אברהם (Abraham). Thus Abraham was
"crowned" through her, since the change was to symbolize his greatness as *"the father of a multitude of
nations"* (17:5), but she was not crowned through him.

[3] This is based on the defective spelling בעלת instead of בעולת. The phrase can now be read *baalath baal*,
her husband's master.

§ 15 [1] If her pecuniary position at marriage is such as to entitle her to certain privileges, she can insist upon them
even if the husband's financial position does not warrant it. Conversely, if she was poor but the husband
wealthy, she can insist upon the position due to his wealth. E.g., if a woman brings two female slaves as part
of her dowry, she is not bound to suckle her child but can demand that her husband engage a wet-nurse, even
if he cannot really afford it. But if he is wealthy she can make the same demand even if she brought no
dowry at all.

[2] This derives *b'ulath* from *alah*, to rise. The literal meaning of the phrase is possessed of, i.e., has cohabited
with, a husband.

himself unto me: She is my sister? and she, even she herself said: He is my brother. In the simplicity of

COMMENTARY

not rely upon the report of my servants but made *personal* enquiries, and he answered me thus.[40]

and she, etc. a. I could not regard his answer as mockery, seeing that she corroborated it.[41] b. I did not rely on his answer, but asked her too.[42] c. Although she did subsequently claim to be Abraham's wife (vs. 4 "had not come near her, comm. b), her words were falsified by her earlier statement.[43] d. Though she told me her true status, I found on enquiring that she informed everyone else in my household that she was Abraham's sister. [This interpretation is based on the wording "and she, even

ANTHOLOGY

17. Wilt Thou slay a nation, also the righteous?[1]

"Sovereign of the Universe!" he cried out. "All are alike before Thee. Job said, *It is all one—therefore I say: He destroys the innocent and the wicked* (Job 9:22). Thou didst destroy the Sodomites [before they sinned]. If Thou didst judge the generation of the Flood and the generation of the Division in the same way [as Thou judgest me], they were indeed righteous."[2] R. Berechiah interpreted: [Abimelech protested:] "If Thou wouldst destroy this nation [myself], Thou shouldst also slay the righteous [Abraham]."[3]

> Tan. Y. Vayyera 25; PR 42; Gen. R. 52, 5. T.S. 20, 26 and note.

18. WILT THOU SLAY EVEN A RIGHTEOUS NATION? To what might Abimelech be compared? To a man who entered the king's palace, purloined his chest in the dark, and went out. But he was seized and the king questioned him, "What have you in your hand?" As he was trembling he asked him, "Why do you tremble? Have you taken anything from the palace?" "No," he replied. "Then what is this box, and who gave it to you?" [he pursued further]. Similarly, Abimelech said to God, "Wilt Thou slay even a righteous nation? Thou knowest that I did not touch her." "Then what is a man's wife doing in your house?" He replied. "Now, let her go, for she is a married woman."

> Exod. R. 20, 1. T.S. 20, 27.

19. WILT THOU SLAY THE NATION, ALSO THE RIGHTEOUS. All the womenfolk of Abimelech's household were barren, so Abimelech had Sarah brought to him, thinking to raise up children from her. The angel Michael descended and drew his sword to slay him. But he protested: Is this a righteous judgment to slay me for something that I did not know? As it says, *Wilt Thou slay even a righteous nation? Said he not himself to me: She is my sister?*

[Another interpretation:] If Thou wilt slay the nation [*sc.* myself], Thou must slay the righteous also. If Thou slayest Abimelech, slay Abraham too. Why? Said R. Berechiah ha-Cohen b. Rabbi: He [Abimelech] pleaded: "I asked him, 'Is she your wife?' to which he replied, 'She is my sister.' Yet in spite of that I still asked the members of his household and they all told me, 'She is his sister.'" [Thus he defended himself:] *Said he not himself to me: "She is my sister?" and she, even she herself said: "He is my brother."* Not she alone, but "*and* she," which means their household too. *In the simplicity of my heart and the innocency of my hands have I done this.*

> PRE 26; PR 42. T.S. 20, 29-30.

20. In the simplicity of my heart and the innocency of my hands, etc.

Scripture informs us that he was more righteous than the people of his realm.

> MhG. T.S. 20, 34.

---

§ 17 [1] Lit. translation, save that "the righteous" is lit. "a righteous."
[2] This makes "nation" and "righteous" refer not to himself but to the various generations and peoples that were destroyed.
[3] Cf. *infra* par. 19.

my heart and the innocency of my hands have I done this." ⁶And God said unto him in the dream: "Yea, I know that in the simplicity of thy heart thou hast done this, and I also withheld thee from sinning against Me. Therefore suffered I thee not to touch her. ⁷Now therefore restore

COMMENTARY

she herself said," but "to me" is lacking—Ed.].⁴⁴ **the innocency of my hands. a.** I am innocent of sin, for I have not touched her.⁴⁵ **b.** I took her honorably, to marry her, and not simply to satisfy my lust.⁴⁶ **c.** "Heart" and "hands" stand metaphorically for thought and deed: I have not sinned in thought or deed.⁴⁷ **d.** Some maintain that because Abimelech had first questioned her God reproved but did not punish him. But Pharaoh did not question her at all; therefore he was smitten with plagues (12:17).⁴⁸ **⁶God said unto him in the dream.** Abimelech's protestations of innocence were made when he awoke, but God's rejoinder was again in the dream.⁴⁹ **Yea, I know,** etc. Your plea is unnecessary; but when I said that you will die (verse 3) I meant if you do not return her immediately.⁵⁰ **in the simplicity of thy heart.** But not "in the innocency of your hands," for you took her by force.⁵¹ **I also withheld thee from sinning.** Because I saw that you did not intend to sin.⁵² **against Me.** Because it was God who enjoined the Noachides against adultery.⁵³ **Therefore,** etc. Because I wished to guard you from sin.⁵⁴ **suffered I thee not. a.** I deprived you of the strength to indulge your lust.⁵⁵ **b.** By quenching your desire. The visitation upon his wives (*infra* verse 18) was in order to make it manifest to all that this (his lack of desire) was Providential and not accidental.⁵⁶ **touch.** Even to

ANTHOLOGY

21. **Yes, I know that in the simplicity of your heart you have done this, and I also withheld you from sinning against Me.**

The Holy One, blessed is He, replied: "In one thing you speak truth; in another you are false. Simplicity of heart—yes; innocency of hands—no."¹ The proof is that it does not say "in the innocency of your hands," but only, "in the simplicity of your heart."² Said the Almighty to him: "You did desire to sin against Me, but that *I also withheld you from sinning against Me.*"

Mehato (from sinning against Me): R. Isaac interpreted: Your potency (*mahtoncha*)³ is in My hands.

Therefore suffered I you not to touch her: This may be compared to a warrior riding a horse at great speed; seeing a child lying in the way he reined in the horse and saved the child. Whom does everyone praise: the horse or the rider? *Therefore suffered I you not to touch her,* because *mahtoncha* (your evil demon), i.e., your evil impulse that incites you to sin, is in my power: I reined you back from sinning: the credit is Mine, not yours.

Tan. Y. Vayyera 25; Gen. R. 52, 7. T.S. 20, 35-6.

22. I ALSO WITHHELD YOU FROM SINNING AGAINST ME. From this our Sages deduced: He who comes to purify himself is helped; he who comes to defile himself [finds that] the door has been opened for him. Hence our Sages said: The Holy One, blessed is He, saves the person who walks in innocence and uprightness from all sin, and the angels guard him from sinning, as it says, *For He will give His angels charge over you, to keep you in all your ways* (Ps. 91:11).

A.Z. 55a; Midrash Habiur; MhG. T.S. 20, 37 and note.

§ 21 ¹ Although you did not defile her, you did mishandle her.
² In Gen. R. *ad loc.* this is deduced from Abimelech's words, *In the simplicity of my heart and the innocency of my hands have I done this*, proving that his hands had somehow been involved.
³ A play on *mehato*—I made it physically impossible for you to sin.

the man's wife; for he is a prophet, and he shall pray for thee, and thou shalt live; and if thou restore her not, know thou that thou shalt surely die, thou, and all that are thine." [8]And Abimelech rose early in the

shall pray for thee. He is near to Me and his prayers will be effective.[58] prophet. This is the first time the word occurs in the Bible. It is here used to denote a man who stands in a specially near relationship to God and is consequently under the Divine protection.[59] live. You will recover from your sickness (see verses 17-18).[60] and all that are thine. a. The unborn children of your wife and maid-servants. [61] b. Your sons and daughters.[62] c. Because a king's sin is ascribed to his entire household.[63] d. Because they all agreed with you; or, because they did not protest.[64] [8]rose early. Because

COMMENTARY

kiss or embrace.[57] [7]for he is a prophet, and he

ANTHOLOGY

23. **Now therefore restore the man's wife, for he is a prophet.**

Is only a prophet's wife to be restored, whereas if she were not a prophet's wife she would not have to be restored? This is what He told him: *Now therefore restore the man's wife*—whoever he might be. And as for your plea, *Wilt Thou slay even a righteous nation? Said he not himself to me: "She is my sister?"*—he is a prophet, and learned from you [that if he had not said so his life would be in danger]: When a visitor comes into a town he is questioned about food and drink [what he needs]; but is he asked, "Is this your wife? is this your sister?"

Mak. 9a. T.S. 20, 38.

24. NOW THEREFORE RESTORE THE MAN'S WIFE, FOR HE IS A PROPHET. "Who will appease him [by assuring him] that I did not touch her?" he asked. "He is a prophet," the Almighty replied, [and knows it without being told]. "And who will make it known to all [that I laid no hand upon her]?" "*He shall pray for you, and you shall live,*" was the answer.[1]

Gen. R. 52, 8. T.S. 20, 39.

25. **He shall pray for you.**

Mishnah: A man who injures his neighbor, even if he pays the five compensations,[1] is not

forgiven until he seeks [his pardon], as it says, *Now therefore restore the man's wife . . . and he shall pray for you.*[2] . . . Gemara: Our Rabbis taught: All these [monetary compensations] which they prescribed[3] are only for humiliation; but for his [the victim's] sorrow [over the assailant's failure to ask his fogiveness],[4] even if he brings all the rams of Nebaioth[5] in the world, he is not forgiven unless he seeks it, as it says, *Now therefore restore the man's wife, for he is a prophet, and he shall pray for you.*

This may be compared to the head of a province who sent his slave to the judge for punishment. When the slave pleaded with the judge [for pardon,] he answered him: "You have not offended against me; let your master say so, and I will let you go." Even so said God: "Abraham has entrusted his rights to Me since yesterday [when you took Sarah], while I have had it written that I *execute judgment for the wronged* (Ps. 146:7). You have wronged him: let him pray on your behalf, and I will let you go."

B.K. 92a; Exod. R. 20. T.S. 20, 41-2.

26. **Know that you shall surely die, you, and all that are yours.**

[This does not mean death literally, but that] it was decreed that they should all be barren.

§ 24 [1] It will naturally be understood from his praying for you.
§ 25 [1] Damages for actual injury sustained; for pain; medical care; loss of time; and humiliation.
[2] Hence in addition to restitution he would have to regain his good will, for only then could he pray for him.
[3] The Mishnah in B.K. 90a gives a table of compensations for various cases of injury.
[4] So Rashi.
[5] The phrase is Biblical, from Isa. 60:7: *The rams of Nebaioth shall minister to you.*

morning, and called all his servants, and told all these things in their ears; and the men were sore afraid. [9]Then Abimelech called Abraham, and said unto him: "What hast thou

the dream had filled him with dread.[65] **the men were sore afraid. a.** His servants who had agreed to his taking Sarah.[66] **b.** That Abraham might refuse to intercede for them.[67] [9]**Abimelech called Abraham.** To hear his explanation and to beg him to intercede.[68] **What hast thou done unto us?** By telling us that she is your sister and so exposing

ANTHOLOGY

[In the same way when] Isaiah said to Hezekiah, *Set your house in order, for you shall die, and not live* (2 Kings 20:1), [he meant] you shall die childless.

[Another interpretation:] You shall surely die—in this world and in the next.[1]

Or Haafelah; PZ. T.S. 20, 44-5.

27. Abimelech rose early in the morning.

He was eagerly awaiting the morning, for the moment when he could arise. [As morning broke] he immediately arose, summoned all his servants and told them, "Thus and thus did the Holy One, blessed is He, speak to me in a dream of the night." Said they to him: "Fear not, dreams speak falsely;[1] would you then be afraid of dreams?" When they spoke thus to him the Holy One, blessed is He, warned him, *If you restore her not, know that you shall surely die* (verse 7); then *the men were sore afraid.*[2] *Then Abimelech called Abraham* (verse 9), [and informed him of what had transpired, to which] Abraham made answer, *Rightly I thought: Surely the fear of God is not in this place* (verse 11).[3]

Tan. Y. Vayyera 26. T.S. 20, 46.

28. The men were sore afraid.

R. Hanin said: Seeing the smoke of Sodom ascending like the smoke of a burning furnace,[1] they thought, Perhaps the same angels who were sent to Sodom have come here, *and the men were sore afraid.*

Gen. R. 52, 9. T.S. 20, 47.

29. THE MEN WERE SORE AFRAID. This man has sinned, they exclaimed, and we are all to die!

PZ. T.S. 20, 48.

30. Then Abimelech called Abraham, and said to him, etc.

What did he mean by *What have you done to us?* [It was a reply to] *Behold, you shall die,* etc. (vs. 3). *Wherein have I sinned against you?* This was his answer to *If you restore her not ... you shall surely die,* etc. (vs. 7). *That you have brought on me and my kingdom a great sin:* wherefore *the Lord had fast closed up all the wombs of the house of Abimelech* (vs. 18). R. Helbo interpreted his complaint, *You have done to me deeds that are not done:* Everywhere plenty preceded you, but here famine preceded you.[1]

Gen. R. 52, 10. T.S. 20, 49.

§ 26 [1] The emphatic "surely" is indicated in Hebrew, as usual, by repeating the verb; this repetition is now interpreted as alluding to both worlds.

§ 27 [1] A slightly changed Biblical text, Zech. 10:2.
  [2] For this interpretation verses 7 and 8 are simultaneous in time, since part of verse 7 belongs in verse 8.
  [3] Your servant's behavior proves that my thoughts were right. AJV: *Because I thought,* etc.

§ 28 [1] Cf. 19:28.

§ 30 [1] Perhaps his coming was actually preceded by famine; R. Helbo, in Gen. R. 40, says that there were two famines in Abraham's days. This first is related in the Bible: It preceded and was the reason for Abraham's visit to Egypt (12:10). Perhaps he holds that one also preceded this present visit. By a slight emendation of the text, reading דאבון instead of רעבון, we get "sorrow": elsewhere prosperity preceded you, but here sorrow (so Radal). The present comment divides the sentence into a series of complaints by Abimelech, each bearing on some different phase of the incident. When he said, *"What have you done to us?"* he asserted that God's threat, *"Behold, you shall surely die,"* was unjustified because his action was the result of what Abraham himself had done. The rest is to be explained similarly.

done unto us? and wherein have I sinned against thee, that thou hast brought on me and on my kingdom a great sin? thou hast done deeds unto me that ought not to be done." [10]And Abimelech said unto Abraham: "What sawest thou, that thou hast done this thing?" [11]And Abraham said: "Because I thought: Surely the fear of God is not in this place; and they will slay me for my wife's

COMMENTARY

us to sin.[69] **and wherein have I sinned against thee?** That you have so requited us.[70] **on me and on my kingdom.** Since the king represents

and personifies the whole nation, hurt to the former affects all.[71] **a great sin. a.** A great punishment.[72] **b.** Adultery.[73] **deeds . . . that ought not to be done. a.** We have suffered in an unheard-of manner because of you.[74] **b.** It is unworthy of a man like yourself to lead us into such a sin.[75] **c.** You have caused harm to people whom you have not known before and with whom you have no quarrel; such deeds are not done.[76] **d.** For a man to describe his wife as unmarried.[77] [10]**Abimelech said.** In the previous verse he upbraided him; here, however, he merely asks him why he behaved so, in a tone of enquiry and appeasement. Therefore "said" is repeated.[78] **What [reason] sawest thou.** What did you see in me to cause you fear; did you ever know my servants or myself to violate married women?[79] [11]**Surely the fear of God is not in this place. a.** When a man enters a city people may question him about his needs, not who is the woman with him.[80] **b.** There was no fear of the ruling authority in that place and so lawlessness prevailed.[81] **c.** Even though the country is good and your people have virtues, I yet see no fear of God.[82] **in this place.** Amongst its people. I.e., I was afraid not of you but of the people.[83] **they will slay me.** For where there is no fear of God there is no deterrent to un-

ANTHOLOGY

31. You have brought on me and on my kingdom a great sin.

Scripture teaches that whoever aids his neighbor to sin is regarded as though he slew him.[1]

MhG. T.S. 20, 50.

32. AND ON MY KINGDOM. Because a king in his realm is like the heart in man. When the heart is sick, the whole body is sick. Similarly, when a king sins his whole realm sins, and he deserves destruction on their account.

MhG. T.S. 20, 51.

33. A GREAT SIN. Hence we learn that immorality[1] (adultery) is the gravest of offences, and particularly where a married woman is concerned.

MhG. T.S. 20, 52.

34. Abimelech said to Abraham: "What [reason] did you see for doing this thing?"

Seeing him meek and lowly in spirit and not answering, he pressed the question: "What reason did you see for doing this thing? You were not compelled, nor are we steeped in immorality like the Egyptians."

Sechel Tob. T.S. 20, 53 note.

35. Surely (rak) the fear of God is not in this place.

[It is a principle of Biblical interpretation that certain words or expressions are limitations.] How is the principle of limitation applied? Three expressions are limitations, viz., *ach* (only), *rak* (save that) and *min* (from or of). An example of *rak* as a limitation: *And Abraham said, "Because I thought, Rak the*

§ 31 [1] Abraham had aided Abimelech to sin by telling him that Sarah was his sister, with the result that he was now threatened with death.
§ 33 [1] I.e., immoral relations with any woman that is forbidden through consanguinity (incest) or marriage (adultery).

sake. [12]**And moreover she is indeed my sister, the daughter of my father, but not the daughter of my mother;**

COMMENTARY

restrained lust.[84] [12]**the daughter of my father.
a.** Such a marriage was permitted to the Noachides (a technical term denoting all who preceded the Revelation at Sinai). She was his brother's daughter, but since grandchildren are looked upon as children, she was considered the daughter of Terah.[85] **b.** It is difficult to see how this plea met Abimelech's complaint. The real answer is given in the previous verse, and this statement is an additional justification: "I spoke the truth," Abraham asserts, "and had the people really been God-fearing they would have asked whether Sarah was also my wife, since one may marry his paternal half-sister."[86] **c.** In those days a brother's daughter was generally called sister.[87] **but not ... my mother.** Her father Haran

ANTHOLOGY

fear of God is not in this place": you might think that they had no fear at all; therefore Scripture writes *rak*.[1] Hence you may deduce that before they heard [a warning] with their own ears they had no fear; but when they heard it with their own ears, they did fear. And Scripture relates just that: *Abimelech . . . called all his servants, and told all these things in their ears; and the men were sore afraid* (verse 8).

B'raitha of 32 Middoth.[2] T.S. 20, 54.

36. SURELY THE FEAR OF GOD IS NOT IN THIS PLACE. Great is fear, for he who fears God may be presumed not to sin, whilst we may presume that he who does not possess the fear of God does not restrain himself from any sin. Thus Scripture says, *That His fear be before you, that you sin not* (Exod. 20:17). But what does it say of the wicked? *The churl has said in his heart: "There is no God." They have dealt corruptly, they have done abominably; there is none that does good* (Ps. 14:1).

MhG; Ned. 20a. T.S. 20, 56.

37. SURELY THE FEAR OF GOD IS NOT IN THIS PLACE. R. Eleazar said: Because the Shechinah does not abide outside the Holy Land (Israel); for that reason he said, *The fear of God is not in this place*, meaning that it was not its [the Shechinah's] natural home, and it did not abide there.

Zohar 1, 141a. T.S. 20, 55.

38. **They will slay me for my wife's sake.**

Thou shalt not murder and *Thou shalt not commit adultery* (Exod. 20:13) are juxtaposed, to teach that he who will commit adultery will certainly[1] commit murder too [if necessary], for should her husband discover him, he [the adulterer] will murder him.

Sechel Tob. T.S. 20, 58.

39. **Moreover she is indeed my sister, the daughter of my father, but not of my mother.**

It was taught: If a man, married to his paternal or maternal sister, becomes a proselyte, he must divorce her: this is R. Meir's ruling. But the Sages say: He must divorce his maternal, but not his paternal sister, because heathens do not recognize paternity[1] ... They refuted him:

---

§ 35   [1] Which indicates that they were not entirely without fear of God.
  [2] I.e., the 32 rules of Scriptural hermeneutics.
§ 38   [1] Emended text, reading בידוע, it is known—that he will murder—instead of זרוע by force.
§ 39   [1] A proselyte is as a new-born babe, who has no relationship whatsoever with his heathen kin. Consequently, in the present instance, his sister is theoretically a stranger to him, and if she too becomes a proselyte he may keep her as his wife. This is the Biblical law as understood by the Rabbis. However, they prohibited those of his pre-conversion relations whom the heathens recognize as forbidden, lest he think that he has passed from a higher degree of sanctity, where such consanguinity is forbidden, to a lower one, where it is permitted. For he cannot be expected to recognize the principle of complete severance of blood ties. R. Meir holds that the heathens recognize both paternal and maternal consanguinity, and therefore both his paternal and maternal sisters are forbidden to him. The Sages hold that they recognize only maternal, but not paternal consanguinity.

ANTHOLOGY

But it says, *Moreover she is indeed my sister, the daughter of my father, but not of my mother?*[2] He answered: Do you consider that proof? It is not, [for consider the end of the verse:] *and she became my wife.*[3]

[R. Akiba holds that a maternal sister is permitted.] Come and hear:[4] *Moreover she is indeed my sister, the daughter of my father, but not of my mother*: this proves that a maternal sister (lit. the mother's daughter) is forbidden. —Now, is this argument logical? Was she then his sister? Surely not: She was his brother's sister;[5] and that being so, it made no difference whether [he was her uncle] by his father or his mother: in either case she was permitted to him. What he [Abraham] told him [Abimelech] was this: "I am fraternally related to her [through my brother] on my father's but not on my mother's side."[6]

[Again,] he answered him according to their own views, whereby a paternal sister (lit. the father's daughter) is permitted, but a maternal sister is forbidden.[7]

J. Yeb. 11, 2; Sanh. 58b;
Gen. R. 52, 11. T.S. 20, 59-60.[8]

40. MOREOVER SHE IS MY SISTER, THE DAUGHTER OF MY FATHER, BUT NOT THE DAUGHTER OF MY MOTHER. Hence our Sages deduced that an idolater has no paternity.[1]

Tan. Y. Vayyera 26. T.S. 20, 62.

41. MOREOVER SHE IS INDEED MY SISTER, etc. R. Simeon lectured on the text, *The lip of truth shall be established for ever; but a lying tongue is but for a moment* (Prov. 12:19). The first part of the verse, he said, alludes to Abraham, whose words were always truth; the other part of the verse, to Abimelech. Twice Abraham said of Sarah, "She is my sister" (see 12:19). The first time he meant the Shechinah, that was with Sarah; he could indeed call the Shechinah "my sister", in the same mystic sense as in the verse, *My sister, my love, my dove, my undefiled* (Song 5:2). Abraham always called her "sister", because he was attached to her inseparably. Later he said: *Moreover she is indeed my sister, the daughter of my father, but not the daughter of my mother.* Was it really so? In truth he was alluding all the time to the Shechinah. At first he said, "She is my sister," in conformity with the admonition, *Say to wisdom, Thou art my sister* (Prov. 7:4). He amplified this: *Moreover she is my sister, the daughter of my father,* i.e., the daughter of Supernal Wisdom, for which reason she is called "my sister" and also Wisdom—*but not the daughter of my mother* —i.e., from the place where is the origin of all, most hidden and recondite. *And so she became my wife,* i.e., by way of fondness and affection, in the sense of the verse, *And his right hand embrace me* (Song 2:6) . . . By calling the Shechinah his sister he claimed the same indissoluble kinship as between brother and sister. For the marital bond can be dissolved, but not the bond between brother and sister . . . The "lying tongue" alludes to Abimelech, who said, *In the simplicity of my heart and the innocency of*

This passage is in J. Yeb. 11, 2. But in the corresponding passage in B. Yeb. 98a R. Meir too is credited with the view that they recognize only maternal relationship.

[2] Which proves that they recognize only maternal relationship.

[3] This is obscure. In the corresponding passage in Sanh. 58b, which follows here, the answer is given that she was not his sister but his fraternal niece, i.e., his brother's daughter. In that case his present distinction was superfluous. The answer then may be this: Consider his saying, *"and she became my wife."* That obviously was superfluous; so was his present distinction, when in fact she was neither. However, this is very forced.

[4] The usual formula introducing a rebuttal.

[5] See 11:29. The Rabbis identified Iscah with Sarah; see Vol. II, chap. 11, par. 48.

[6] Not that she would have been forbidden to him in any case, but merely for the exactness of the record.

[7] But actually it was immaterial, since she was his niece. However, he stated this to explain that in calling her his sister he merely meant that she was fraternally related to him; yet should Abimelech consider such a union forbidden, he pointed out that the relationship was on his mother's side only.

[8] The three passages have been grouped in one for convenience's sake. But, as we have seen, their premises are not identical: the first assumes that she was his sister; the second and third, his niece.

§ 40 [1] Possibly because whilst maternity is indisputable, their paternity is often questionable and uncertain.

and so she became my wife. [13]And it came to pass, when God caused me to wander from my father's house, that I said unto her: "This is thy kindness which thou shalt show unto me; at every place whither we

COMMENTARY

was born of another wife of Terah's.[88] [13]**when God** (*elohim*) **caused me to wander.** (The verb is in the plural.) **a.** From place to place, and I knew that I would often be in the habitation of wicked men.[89] **b.** The verb is in the plural, which is sometimes used when an Israelite speaks to a heathen; cf. also 31:53 and Josh. 24:19. It may also be the "plural of Majesty"; cf. 1:26.[90] **c.** *Elohim* is to be rendered "the gods," i.e., idols: When the idols (i.e., idol-worship) forced me to leave home for an unknown land.[91] **d.** *Elohim* here means the authorities: When the rulers of my country drove me into exile (because I proclaimed the One God) and made me a wanderer.[92] **wander.** (The root idea of the verb is to err, hence here to wander about like one who does not know his way.) **a.** Commanded me to leave home and wander into another country (12:1).[93] **b.** The verb applies to anyone who goes into an unknown country, even though he travels by well-known roads.[94] **from my father's house.** From the home of my brethren and family.[95] **I said unto her. a.** Before arriving in Egypt; or possibly, he asked her before they set out on their wanderings, and repeated his request when they came to Egypt.[96] **b.** Here Abraham explains why Sarah too concurred and actively helped in the deception.[97] **every place. a.** Wherever the ill-repute of the inhabitants will make this stratagem necessary.[98] **b.** The God-fearing are few everywhere, so that wherever I came I feared the same danger. Hence I did the same here

ANTHOLOGY

my hands have I done this. But what was the reply he received? *Yea, I know that in the simplicity of your heart you have done this,* but no mention is made of innocency of hands.[1]

Zohar 1, 111b. 112a.

42. It came to pass, when God caused me to wander from my father's house.

All the names [of God] written in connection with Abraham are holy, except one which is non-holy,[1] viz., *When God caused me to wander,*[2] etc. Some maintain that this too is sacred, the meaning being, But for God, they would have caused me to err [i.e., go astray—from the true faith].[3]

R. Hanan said: Would that we could discharge our duty by interpreting this in three ways:[4] (i) When the heathen nations sought to assail me[5] while I was still in my father's house, the Holy One, blessed is He, protected me. (ii) When they sought to mislead me [into idolatry], He revealed Himself to me and bade me, *Go out of your country,* etc. (12:1). (iii) Finally, when the heathens sought to err from God's paths, He raised two great men from my father's house, viz., Shem and Eber, who warned them.[6]

J. Meg. 1, 5; Gen. R. 52, 11. T.S. 20, 63-4.

§ 41 [1] This is a good example of mystic exegesis, very reminiscent of the Philonic system of interpretation.

§ 42 [1] I.e., in all other cases the name means God, but not here; see n. 6. See also chap. 18, par. 34, though there the name is *Adonai*, while here it is *Elohim*.

[2] The verb is in the plural, whereas verbs relating to Him are always in the singular.

[3] The verse would be rendered as in note 6, ii.

[4] Likewise on account of the difficulty presented by the plural form of the verb.

[5] For my rejection of idolatry.

[6] These are his three renderings:
(i) When they [the nations] erred [and wished to destroy me for rejecting their idolatry], God defended me out of (i.e., whilst I was still in) my father's house.
(ii) When they [the nations] would have misled me, God [took me] from my father's house.
(iii) When the nations erred, God raised up *elohim,* i.e., judges, teachers, out of my father's house, in addition to myself, to guide them in the right path.
Radal observes that for the last interpretation *elohim* does not mean God but judges, teachers. For this rendering of *elohim* cf. Exod. 22:7.

shall come, say of me: He is my brother." [14]And Abimelech took sheep and oxen, and men-servants and women-servants, and gave them unto Abraham, and restored him Sarah his wife. [15]And Abimelech said: "Behold, my land is before thee: dwell where it pleaseth thee." [16]And unto Sarah he said: "Behold, I have given thy brother a thousand pieces of silver; behold, it is for thee a covering of the eyes to all that

COMMENTARY

too, even though conditions here might be different.[99] **of me.** For my sake.[100] [14]**gave them unto Abraham.** To appease and compensate him for the grief and dishonor he had suffered, and also to win his prayers.[101] [15]**my land is before thee. a.** But

Pharaoh, knowing how his people were steeped in immorality, bade him leave the country (12:19).[102] **b.** By permitting him to stay and assuring him of his protection Abimelech sought to make it clear he had not touched her.[103] **dwell where it pleaseth thee.** He recognized Abraham's qualities and desired to make a covenant with him (as he did, in fact—see 21:22 *et sqq.*). Therefore he conferred full citizen rights on him, permitting him to settle wherever he desired.[104] [16]**unto Sarah he said.** To appease her.[105] **I have given. a.** In addition to the gifts enumerated in verse 14.[106] **b.** My gift will prove that I did not touch you. For people will understand that if I had, I would have sent you away immediately.[107] **thy brother. a.** To Abraham, whom you described as your brother.[108] **b.** It was their custom to make gifts to the relations of the bride.[109] **c.** But not to you, because it is indecent to give presents to a woman.[110] **a thousand pieces of silver. a.** The flocks, herds and servants which I have given him are worth that sum of money.[111] **b.** As the dowry paid for a man's daughter or sister. [*a* and *b* make verses 14 and 16 refer to the same thing, and contradict comm. *a* on *I have given*.—Ed.][112] **a covering of the eyes**, etc. **a.** All, knowing that such a dowry is given only to a legitimate wife, will cover their eyes, i.e., not regard you contemptuously as my concubine.[113] **b.** People will not dare to gaze insolently on your

ANTHOLOGY

43. Abimelech took sheep and oxen, and men-servants and maid-servants, and gave them to Abraham.

Whatever Pharaoh gave Sarah, Abimelech gave Abraham,[1] as our text states.

PRE 26.   T.S. 20, 65.

44. Behold, my land is before you.

It is written, *The Philistines stood on the mountain on the one side* (1 Sam. 17:3): the Philistines stood [strong] in the merit of Abimelech [a Philistine king], who had honored Abraham, as it says, *Behold, my land is before you.*

AB 50.   T.S. 20, 67.

45. BEHOLD, MY LAND IS BEFORE YOU. Abimelech was a pious heathen, and desired to be a neighbor to a righteous man.

PZ.   T.S. 20, 68.

46. Behold, it is a covering of the eyes for you.

R. Judah b. R. Ilia explained: [Abimelech said to him:] Make yourself a garment,[1] that people may look at *it*, and not at your beauty; for *a covering of the eyes* means a garment which attracts all eyes. R. Berechiah said: He [Abimelech] elevated her to the aristocracy: [the text means,] a garment which would hide her from the [public] gaze.[2] R. Simeon b. Lakish

§ 43   [1] MhG reads: Whatever Pharaoh gave, he gave to Sarah; whereas everything that Abimelech gave, he gave to Abraham. Hence we may infer that Abimelech was decent; and why did he make these gifts to Abraham? In order to appease him, that he might pray on his behalf. (Whereas Pharaoh, by giving them to Sarah, showed that he still desired her.)
§ 46   [1] *K'suth*, covering, really means garment.
       [2] High-ranking women generally had their faces covered.

are with thee; and before all men thou art righted." [17]And Abraham prayed unto God; and God healed

COMMENTARY

beauty, nor even on your maids, when they realize that even the king had to redeem himself for his action.[114] **c.** *Abraham* is a covering, etc., i.e., the very fact that he is your husband protects your honor, for all know that God would never permit Abraham's wife to be defiled.[115] **d.** This money is to purchase "eye raiment," i.e., garments covering the whole face, leaving only openings for the eyes, for yourself and your maids.[116] **e.** None will insult you to suggest that after I had no more use for you I sent you back empty-handed.[117] **f.** Figurative for "justification"; to make them blind to the wrong which had been done her.[118] **g.** Render: a multi-colored robe.[119] **to all that are with thee.** In the sight of your entire household and all your friends.[120] **thou art righted. a.** Render: you prepared [this unfortunate affair]—i.e., you are responsible for it.[121] **b.** Your honor is clearly proved.[122] **c.** Render: You are reproved—never again call your husband "brother."[123] [17]**healed. a.** Desire and

ANTHOLOGY

said: He wished to incite her anger against her husband, [subtly] implying, "All these years you have been with him [Abraham] and he has made nothing for you, while I have honored you so much on account of a single night."[3]

Gen. R. 52, 12. T.S. 20, 69-70.

47. BEHOLD, IT IS A COVERING OF THE EYES FOR YOU. R. Isaac said: Do not despise an ordinary man's curse, for Abimelech[1] cursed Sarah, and his curse was fulfilled in her descendants. For it says, *Behold, it is a covering of the eyes for you:* Since you covered [the truth] from me, and did not reveal that he is your husband, and so brought all this trouble on me, may you have children of covered eyes (i.e., blind). It was fulfilled in her seed, for it says, *And it came to pass, that when Isaac was old, and his eyes were dim, so that he could not see,* etc. (27:1).

B.K. 93a. T.S. 20, 71.

48. A COVERING OF THE EYES. Take this covering (garment), because you cover your eyes from all men, even from *all that are with you,* for she was wont to cover her face even from Abraham.

Or Haafelah. T.S. 20, 72.

49. **Before all that are with you.**

In addition to what he had given her privately.

MhG. T.S. 20, 73.

50. **Before all men you are righted.**

If anyone asks you whether you are his wife, beware not to answer the same again, lest you become a stumbling-block to people.

MA. T.S. 20, 76.

51. **Abraham prayed to God.**

Mishnah: [If a man injures his neighbor,] even though he compensates him he is not forgiven until he begs his pardon, as it says, *Now therefore restore the man's wife . . . and he shall pray for you* (verse 7).[1] And how do we know that if he does not pardon him he is a cruel man? From our text, *Abraham prayed to God, and God healed Abimelech.*

Let a man always be as pliable as a reed and not as unyielding as a cedar, easy to pacify and hard to anger; and when one who has sinned against him asks his pardon, let him grant it whole-heartedly and eagerly; even if one has sinned greatly against him, let him not avenge or bear malice. Let every man learn from our father Abraham: Is a greater injury imaginable

---

[3] Perhaps he renders: *It is a covering of the eyes*—from Abraham. Turn your eyes away from him; consider rather what I have done for you. The Hebrew is in the third person.
§ 47 [1] Although a king he was, spiritually speaking, a *hediot,* an ordinary man.
§ 51 [1] See par. 25.

Abimelech, and his wife, and his maid-servants; and they bore children. ¹⁸For the Lord had fast closed up all the wombs of the house of Abimelech, because of Sarah Abraham's wife.

COMMENTARY

virility (potency) were restored.[124] **b.** Neither his sickness nor the manner of healing is stated.[125] **c.** The next verse makes the sickness clear.[126] **they bore children.** This refers to Abimelech's wife and maid-servants; their time to give birth had come but they were unable until Abraham prayed on their behalf.[127] ¹⁸**closed up. a.** The women would have aborted had Abimelech not repented.[128] **b.** As a warning of what would befall if Sarah were not returned.[129] **because of Sarah. a.** Because of

ANTHOLOGY

than to take a man's wife forcibly from him? Yet when Abimelech asked his forgiveness he forgave him with a full heart. Not only did he forgive him: he even prayed for mercy on his behalf.

> B.K. 92a; MhG.   T.S. 20, 79 and note.

52. ABRAHAM PRAYED TO GOD. R. Hama b. R. Hanina said: This expression [prayer] is not found from the beginning of the Book [of Genesis] until here. But when Abraham prayed, this knot was untied.[1]

> Gen. R. 52, 13.   T.S. 20, 81.

53. ABRAHAM PRAYED TO GOD. How do we know that a petition for healing is called prayer? —From our text: *Abraham prayed . . . and God healed Abimelech.*[1]

Abraham arose and prayed to God: "Sovereign of the Universe! Thou hast created man to propagate and be fruitful; then let Abimelech and his household indeed be fruitful and multiply!" God granted his entreaty, as our text states.

When Abraham prayed they were all healed of their impotency.[2] Moreover, all Abimelech's household conceived and bore males, as our text states.[3] Abimelech's wife had been barren. How do we know this? Because it says, *God healed*

Abimelech, and his wife: you heal only what was first sick.[4]

> Midrash;[5] PRE 26; PR 42.
> T.S. 20, 82-4.

54. **God healed Abimelech.**

When Abimelech took Sarah God closed up all their fountains, as it says, *For the Lord had fast closed up,* etc. But on his entreating Abraham for forgiveness he was healed, because Abraham prayed on his behalf, as it says, *Abraham prayed to God.* Said the ministering angels to Him: "Sovereign of the Universe! Abraham heals others, and yet himself needs healing. He healed Abimelech and his household and they bore children, as it says, *God healed Abimelech;* yet Thou healest not him." Said the Holy One, blessed is He: "He does indeed merit that I should give him children." [Hence this is immediately followed by, *The Lord remembered Sarah . . . and Sarah conceived* (21:1)].[1]

> Tan. Y. Vayyera 36.   T.S. 20, 85.

55. **For the Lord had fast closed up.**

When Abimelech took Sarah the Holy One, blessed is He, dried up all his orifices—his, his household's and his whole kingdom's.[1] . . . R. Eleazar taught: Young and old, men and women, man-servants and maid-servants—the

§ 52   [1] Probably, from now on one could pray.
§ 53   [1] Hence his "prayer" must have been a petition for healing.
    [2] Lit., their being shut up.
    [3] The text only states that they bore, not that they bore males. This is assumed.
    [4] "Healed" implies that she had been incapable of childbirth.
    [5] Quoted as a Midrash in *Menorath Hamaor* by R. Judah Al-nakawah 2, 132.
§ 54   [1] The bracketed passage is added from Tan. Vayyera 14.
§ 55   [1] Lit., and of all places.

COMMENTARY

the shame she had suffered.[130] **b.** Heb. *al d'bar*= because of the *word* of Sarah, i.e., all this happened because she had told him that she was Abraham's sister.[131]

ANTHOLOGY

Holy One, blessed is He, closed up their fountains: none performed his natural functions; none could even shed a tear; all were shut up, sealed, enclosed. Why did all this happen? *Because of Sarah, Abraham's wife:* to clear her [of the slightest imputation of rape or adultery]. How so? A man, meeting his friend in the morning, said to him: "Do you not know what happened to me at night? So-and-so." His friend replied that he had had the same experience; so they continued their conversation, adding, "By heaven! Another night like this and we are all dead." Yet how was Sarah cleared? Because they continued further, "If this happened to us, who were nowhere near her, need you ask what judgment was meted out on him near whom she slept?" In this sense Scripture writes, *For the Lord had fast shut up . . . because of Sarah, Abraham's wife.*

[That He closed all their orifices may be inferred from] the repetition of the verb.[2] This implies the closing of the mouth, throat, eye, nose, and ear; above and below.

PR 42; Gen. R. 52, 13.   T.S. 20, 88-9.

56.   **All the wombs.**

The School of R. Yannai said: Even the fowls in his house did not lay their eggs.

B.K. 92a.   T.S. 20, 90.

---

[2] The emphatic "fast" is expressed in Hebrew as usual by repeating the verb.

[1]And the Lord remembered Sarah

COMMENTARY

[1]**remembered. a.** Render: *Had* remembered— before He healed Abimelech.[1] **b.** The Hebrew denotes an act of Divine Providence.[2] **c.** This word (*pakad*) is used here because Sarah, being old, required a special Providence to give birth. But Rachel, being young, did not need the intervention

ANTHOLOGY

1. And the Lord remembered Sarah.

R. Eleazar b. Pedath said: Wherever you find the phrase *And the Lord,* it means He together with His court. This teaches that He sat in judgment and asked the ministering angels, "Does Sarah deserve to bear a son?" They all agreed and answered "Yes," and the Almighty sealed their verdict.

The angels argued: "Sovereign of the Universe! It is but right that Abraham be remembered [and granted a son], for if not, Thy Torah will appear false." How so? Said R. Judah ha-Levi in the name of R. Shalom: Abraham was seventy years old when the Almighty spoke to him at the Covenant between the Parts and decreed, *Know of a surety that your seed shall be a stranger in a land that is not theirs . . . and they shall afflict them four hundred years* (15:13), [which meant] From the time you have seed, your children will suffer servitude four hundred years. Now, the Torah preceded the creation of the world; therein is written, *The time that the children of Israel dwelt in Egypt was four hundred and thirty years* (Exod. 12:40).[1] Now, Abraham is a hundred years old today. If Thou dost not remember him now, Thou falsifiest Thy Torah by postponing the redemption;[2] therefore it is necessary for him to be remembered now.

Tan. Y. Vayyera 34; PR 42. T.S. 21, 1 and note.

2. THE LORD REMEMBERED SARAH. R. Judah b. R. Simon said: Although R. Huna said that there is an angel appointed over [the fruits of] desire, Sarah did not need it, for He in His glory [made her conceive,] as it says, *The Lord remembered Sarah.*

Gen. R. 53, 6. T.S. 21, 2.

3. THE LORD REMEMBERED SARAH. Three keys the Holy One, blessed is He, has entrusted to no creature, neither angel nor seraph nor celestial convocation, but has retained in His own hand: the key of rain, the key of resurrection, and the key of the womb (childbirth). The last is inferred from our text, *The Lord remembered Sarah.* In similar vein it is written, *And God remembered Rachel . . . and opened her womb* (30:22).

PR 42. T.S. 21, 3.

4. The Lord visited[1] Sarah.

Sarah, Rachel, and Hannah were remembered on New Year. How do we know this? Said R. Eleazar: The time of "remembering" in one instance is learnt from "remembering" in another; similarly, "visiting" is learnt from "visiting." Concerning Rachel the Bible says, *And God* remembered *Rachel* (30:22); likewise of Hannah, *And the Lord* remembered *her* (1 Sam. 1:19). When these rememberings took place is inferred from the use of the same word re-

§ 1   [1] To reconcile the discrepancy it is assumed that the Covenant between the Parts preceded Isaac's birth by thirty years, whereas the four hundred years of servitude were counted from his birth; see Vol. II, chap. 15, pars. 90-1.
  [2] Thirty years had elapsed since the Covenant between the Parts, for Abraham was seventy years old at the Covenant (see Vol. II, chap. 15, par. 64). If Isaac were not born now, the redemption from Egypt would have to be more than four hundred and thirty years later.

§ 4   [1] I.e., remembered, as AJV. A.V. is given here in order to clarify the passage that follows.

ANTHOLOGY

lating to New Year, of which it is written, *In the seventh month, in the first day of the month,*[2] *shall be . . . a remembering of the blast of horns* (Lev. 23:24). Again, "visiting" in one instance is learnt from "visiting" in another. Of Hannah it is written, *So the Lord visited Hannah* (1 Sam. 2:21); while of Sarah it says, *And the Lord visited Sarah.*

On New Year we read [as the Scriptural Lesson]³ *And the Lord visited Sarah.*

R.H. 11a; T. Meg. 4. T.S. 21, 4-5.

5. THE LORD VISITED[1] SARAH. [The New Year's liturgy must contain "remembrances," i.e., Scriptural texts conveying the idea of remembrance.] We do not recite a "remembrance" that relates to an individual, even one of a happy nature.[2] "Visitations" [i.e., texts which convey the thought of visiting] count as "remembrances," e.g., *The Lord visited Sarah;* or, *I have surely visited you* (Exod. 3:16): this is R. Jose's view. R. Judah maintained that they do not count as such [hence they cannot be recited]. Now, by R. Jose's view, granted that "visitations" count as "remembrances," yet surely *The Lord visited Sarah* relates to an individual? Since many issued from that visitation,[3] it is regarded as relating to the many.

R.H. 32b. T.S. 21, 6.

6. THE LORD VISITED[1] SARAH. It does not say, The Lord remembered Sarah. "Visiting" refers to an occurrence after a long time; "remembering," to one after a short time. E.g., *I have surely* visited *you* (Exod. 3:16) was said only

after four hundred years.[2] Similarly here: *The Lord visited Sarah.* Now, a woman can conceive at the age of twelve, yet Sarah did not give birth until she was over ninety.[3] But "remembering" implies after a short time, e.g., *God remembered Abraham* (19:29).[4] Similarly, David said: *Remember me, Lord, when Thou favorest Thy people; O think of me at* [the time of] *Thy salvation* (Ps. 106:4)—in the Messianic era.

Midrash Habiur. T.S. 21, 10.

7. THE LORD REMEMBERED SARAH. R. Aha said: The Holy One, blessed is He, is a trustee:[1] Amalek deposited bundles of thorns [evil]: He gave him back bundles of thorns [retribution, as it says] *I return*[2] *what Amalek did* (1 Sam. 15:2). Sarah deposited piety and good deeds with Him: He gave her back piety and good deeds,[3] as our text states, *The Lord returned Sarah's deposits.*

Gen. R. 53, 5. T.S. 20, 7.

8. THE LORD REMEMBERED SARAH. R. Isaac said: [Of a woman suspected of infidelity] it is written, *If the woman be not defiled, but be clean, then she shall be cleared, and conceive seed* (Num. 5:28). Now, was it then not logical that this woman [Sarah], who had entered Pharaoh's palace and Abimelech's palace and emerged undefiled, should be remembered [with child]?

Gen. R. 53, 6. T.S. 21, 8.

9. THE LORD REMEMBERED SARAH. [One method of Scriptural interpretation is] the prin-

---

² That is New Year.
³ Since according to the foregoing it happened on that day.
§ 5 ¹ See par. 4, n. 1.
² The Mishnah on 32a states that texts signifying retribution may not be included.
³ Or, from her—Sarah.
§ 6 ¹ See par. 4, n. 1.
² God had foretold to Abraham Israel's servitude in Egypt, which would last four hundred years (15:13); now, after all that time, He visited them—to fulfill His promise of liberation.
³ Hence she waited many years for this visitation.
⁴ To save his nephew Lot—this of course was but a short time after Sodom's destruction; so Abraham had not long to wait for God to remember him.
§ 7 ¹ He connects *pakad* (remembered) with *pikadon,* an article deposited with or entrusted to one's care.
² AJV: *remember.*
³ Probably: The reward for these.

101

ANTHOLOGY

ciple of extension.[1] How so? Three words intimate extension, viz., *eth*,[2] *gam* (also), and *af* (too). An example of *eth* as an extension: *The Lord remembered* eth *Sarah*. If this lacked *eth* I would say that only Sarah was remembered. The addition of *eth* teaches that all barren women were remembered together with her.[3]

B'raitha of 32 Middoth. T.S. 21, 11.

10. THE LORD REMEMBERED SARAH. In allusion to this Scripture writes, *For the fig-tree does not blossom* (Hab. 3:17). Who is meant? Abraham, as in the verse, *I saw* your fathers *as the first-ripe in the* fig-tree *at her first season* (Hos. 9:10). *Neither is there fruit in the vines* (Hab. *ibid.*) this means Sarah, as it says, *Your wife shall be as a* fruitful vine (Ps. 128:3) ... *The fields* (sh'demoth) *yielded no food* (Hab. *ibid.*): those [Sarah's] breasts (*shadayim*) suckled no human. *He cut off the flock from the fold:* Thou raisest not up from her the Community of Israel, who are designated "flock" in the text, *You are My flock* (Ezek. 34:31). *There is no herd in the stalls:* Thou raisest not up from her the Tribe of Ephraim, of whom it is written, *Ephraim is* a heifer *well broken* (Hos. 10:11). Said our mother Sarah: "Nevertheless, *I will rejoice in the Lord* (Hab. 3:18): some say, Sarah cannot bear children; others say, Can Abraham beget? For all that I put my trust in the Lord." Said the Holy One, blessed is He, to her: "You put your trust in Me: by your life! I will remember you"; as it says, *The Lord remembered Sarah*.

Tan. Y. Vayyera 31. T.S. 20, 16.

11. THE LORD REMEMBERED SARAH. Let our master teach us:[1] What is meant by *onaah* [wrong to one's neighbor]? Our masters taught: A man may not wrong his neighbor, e.g., he must not ask him, "What does this cost?" when he does not wish to buy ... Come and see: He who wrongs his neighbor is the first to be punished. But Sarah wronged herself, and she received her reward. For she proposed to Abraham, *"Behold now, the Lord has restrained me from bearing; go in, I pray you, to my handmaid"* (16:2). What is written subsequently? *The Lord remembered Sarah*.

Tan. Vayyera 14. T.S. 21, 17.

12. THE LORD REMEMBERED SARAH. Let our master teach us: If a man has a quarrel with his neighbor, what must he do for the Day of Atonement to make atonement for him? Our masters taught: The Day of Atonement makes atonement for man's sins against God; but not for sins against one's fellow-man, until he becomes reconciled with him. [In turn, the offended party must show compassion and forgive, for] when you have compassion on your neighbor, God has compassion on you. [For showing such compassion] Abraham received his reward immediately, as it says, *Abraham prayed to God* [on behalf of Abimelech] (20:17). What was his reward? His wife was remembered [by God] and bore a son, as our text states.

Raba asked Rabbah b. Mari: What is the source of the Rabbinical teaching, He who prays on his neighbor's behalf, himself being in need of that very thing, is himself answered first? ... Our text: *Abraham prayed to God, and God healed Abimelech and his wife, and his maid-servants; and they bore children*. This is followed by *The Lord had remembered*[1] *Sarah as he* (sic) *had said*: i.e., as *Abraham* had said to Abimelech.[2]

Tan. Y. Vayyera 30; B.K. 92a.
T.S. 21, 12. 18.

§ 9 [1] Cf. chap. 20, par. 35.
  [2] This is the sign of the accusative. In the comment which follows it is treated as an extension.
  [3] Cf. par. 35.
§ 11 [1] See chap. 18, par. 1, n. 1.
§ 12 [1] The pluperfect is required here, since he desires to show that Abraham, having prayed on behalf of Abimelech, was answered himself first.
  [2] That he would pray on his behalf. Cf. chap. 20, par. 54.

as He had said, and the Lord did unto Sarah as He had spoken. [2]And

COMMENTARY

of Providence; hence the verb *zachar* is used in her case (30:22).[3] **remembered . . . spoken.** *Remembered* means that she conceived, and *as He had spoken* denotes that she gave birth.[4] **as He had said. a.** *And God said: "Nay, but Sarah your wife shall bear you a son"* (17:19).[5] **b.** *God said to Abraham . . . "I will give you a son of her"* (ibid. 15f).[6] **c.** Through His angel: *"I will certainly return to you . . . Sarah your wife shall have a son"* (18:10).[7] **d.** She conceived and gave birth at the time promised.[8] **as He had spoken. a.** To Abraham, viz., *the word of the Lord came to Abraham* (15:1), that introduces the promise of a son and the Covenant.[9] **b.** This repetition—it is identical in meaning with "as He had said"—is on account of the marvelous nature of the event, and is not unusual.[10] **c.** She

ANTHOLOGY

13. The Lord remembered Sarah as He had said, and the Lord did to Sarah as He had spoken.

When had He said so?—*And God said: "Nay, but Sarah your wife shall bear you a son"* (17:19). And when had He spoken? *In that day the Lord made a covenant with Abram, saying: "To your seed have I given this land"* (15:18).

R. Judah said: *As He had said* relates to the promise introduced by *amirah* (saying); *as He had spoken* to that prefaced by *dibbur* (speaking).[1] R. Nehemiah interpreted: *As He had said*, through an angel; *as He had spoken*—Himself.[2]

Again, R. Judah expounded: *As He had said*—to give her a son; *as He had spoken*—to bless her with milk. R. Nehemiah demurred: Had she then been informed that she would have milk? Rather, it means that He restored her youthfulness.

> Mechilta Bo 12; Gen. R. 53, 5.
> T.S. 21, 13-14 and note.

14. The Lord remembered Sarah, etc. In allusion to this Scripture writes, *All the trees of the field shall know that I the Lord have brought down the high tree, have exalted the low tree, have dried up the green tree, and have made the dry tree to flourish; I the Lord have spoken and done it* (Ezek. 17:24)[1] . . . *All the trees of the field shall know*, alludes to people in general, as you read, *For the tree of the field is man* (Deut. 20:19). *I the Lord have brought down the high tree*—Abimelech. *I have exalted the low tree*—Abraham. *I have dried up the green tree*—Abimelech's wives, as it says, *For the Lord had fast closed up all the wombs of the house of Abimelech* (20:18). *I have made the dry tree to flourish*—Sarah. *I the Lord have spoken and done it*: R. Judan observed: Not like those who promise but do not perform. R. Berechiah commented: *I the Lord have spoken and done it*: When did He speak? [When He said:] *At the set time I will return to you . . . and Sarah shall have a son* (18:14). *And I have done it*: as our text says, *The Lord did to Sarah as He had spoken*.

> Gen. R. 53, 1.   T.S. 21, 15.

15. The Lord did to Sarah as He had spoken. R. Berechiah, quoting R. Levi, interpreted: [His promise was] to increase [the light of] the luminaries [at Isaac's birth]. For "doing" is employed here: *The Lord did*, etc.; and elsewhere it says, *God made*[1] *the two great lights*: just as there it means that He gave light to the world; so here too it has the same connotation.[2]

> PRK 2.   T.S. 21, 19.

§ 13 [1] This is the same as the previous statement. The first, *Nay, but Sarah*, etc., is prefaced by, *God said*. The second, *In that day*, etc., is introduced by, *The speech (d'bar, same root as dibbur, speech) of the Lord came to Abraham* (15:1).
   [2] See, respectively, 18:10, 14.

§ 14 [1] The dots (. . .) are for an omitted passage, "R. Judan observed," etc., which we have at the end of the paragraph, where it rightly belongs. Its insertion here is an error of dittography.

§ 15 [1] In the Heb. the same verb is used.
   [2] The birth of Isaac, by making possible the continuation of Abraham's teachings, brought increased light to the world.

Sarah conceived, and bore Abraham a son in his old age, at the set time

COMMENTARY

bore a son; not a daughter, which is generally the case when an old woman gives birth.[11] [2]**bore Abraham.** A woman is like the earth, yielding fruit to her husband, and the child is then ascribed to him.[12] **in his old age. a.** She had indeed regained her youth, but he had remained unchanged —an old man.[13] **b.** I.e., in spite of his extreme age; because this was so remarkable it is particularly noted.[14] **at the set time.** Whereof He had told him, *At the set time I will return to you* (18:14): he (the angel speaking in God's name) made a mark on the wall and said to him, "When the sun

ANTHOLOGY

16. THE LORD REMEMBERED SARAH, etc. When Sarah received the tidings of Isaac's birth she prayed to the Omnipresent, blessed is He: "Since Thou givest me seed, why should he suffer such great servitude [in Egypt]?" Said the Holy One, blessed is He: "I will deduct from the set term the combined ages of yourself and Abraham, i.e., 190 years; therefore Israel shall suffer only 210 years of servitude in Egypt." This is what our text means when it says, *The Lord remembered Sarah as He had said, and the Lord did to Sarah as He had spoken.*

MA. T.S. 21, 20.

17. **Sarah conceived and bore a son.**

Her conception and bearing are likened to one another: even as her conception was painless, so was her bearing painless.

Tan. Y. Vayyera 37. T.S. 21, 21.

18. **Sarah conceived and bore a son to Abraham.**

This teaches that she did not steal seed from elsewhere.

Gen. R. 53, 6. T.S. 21, 22.

19. **Sarah . . . Abraham.**

Abram could not beget; Abraham could. Sarai could not bear, Sarah could. Thus it says, *And* Sarah *conceived and bore a son to* Abraham.

AB 37. T.S. 21, 23.

20. SARAH . . . ABRAHAM. Those who interpret words as abbreviations said: The *sin* (ש) of her name stands for *son'ah* (she hated) idolatry; the *resh* (ר) for *roah*: she saw by the Holy Spirit; *he* (ה) for *hirb'thah*: she performed many deeds before the Almighty, for the sake of which she deserved that a miracle should be wrought on her behalf. Abraham (אברהם): the *alef* (א) stands for *abir* (mighty): he was the mighty one of the world; *beth* (ב) for *b'rachah* (blessing): he was the blessing of the world; *resh* (ר) for *rachamim* (compassion): he was the spring whence flowed compassion to the world.[1]

Midrash Habiur. T.S. 21, 24.

21. SARAH . . . ABRAHAM. Just as Sarah was suitable for Abraham, so was Abraham suitable for Sarah. For our Rabbis taught: When a man weds a woman unbecoming to him, the Holy One, blessed is He, binds and Elijah flagellates him, while proclaiming, "Woe to him who make his children unfit and casts a stain on his family!"

B'raitha on Nid. 2, 6. T.S. 21, 25.

22. **A son in his old age.**

This teaches that his [Isaac's] features were like his own.[1]

Gen. R. 53, 6. T.S. 21, 27.

23. IN HIS OLD AGE. When the miracle happened, and Isaac was born to his aged parents, the whole world repaired to Abraham and Sarah,

§ 20 [1] Cf. Vol. II, chap. 17, par. 32. The last probably means that God showed compassion to the world for his sake.

§ 22 [1] A play on words. *Z'kunaw* (his old age) is read *ziv ikunaw*, the luster of his visage—i.e., his general features or physiognomy; cf. par. 37.

**of which God had spoken to him.
³And Abraham called the name of
his son that was born unto him,
whom Sarah bore to him, Isaac.**

COMMENTARY

comes round to this mark next year Sarah will give
birth to a child"; and so it happened.[15] **to him.**
Render: Sarah bore Abraham a son in his old age
at the appointed time: as God had spoken it [viz.,
that she would bear].[16] **b.** Rather, it, i.e., the set
time which God had appointed [other commentators
agree with AJV].[17] **³that was born unto him.
a.** A son fit to be called *his* son, for he would
completely realize the hopes that Abraham placed
in him.[18] **b.** Scripture testifies, *to him*, and to none
other.[19] **whom Sarah bore. a.** Sarah, that aged
woman![20] **b.** He was not a foundling but Sarah's
son.[21] **that was born unto him, whom Sarah
bore to him.** This is to indicate why he was called
Isaac: that was born *unto him*—Abraham laughed
when he was given the tidings of his birth (17:17);
whom *Sarah* bore—she too laughed (18:12) [Isaac
is derived from *tsahak*, to laugh].[22] **Isaac.** He

ANTHOLOGY

and demanded to know what they had done that
so great a thing should be accomplished for
them. Abraham told them all that had happened between Nimrod and himself, how he
had been ready to be burnt for the glory of God,
and how the Lord had rescued him from the
flames. In token of their admiration for Abraham and his teachings they made him their
king; and in commemoration of Isaac's wondrous birth the money coined by Abraham
bore the figures of an aged husband and his
wife on the obverse side, and of a young man
and his wife on the reverse side, for Abraham
and Sarah were both rejuvenated at the birth
of Isaac: Abraham's white hair turned black,
and the lines in Sarah's face were smoothed out.

Ginzberg, Legends 1, 206.

24. **At the set time of which God had spoken
to him.**

R. Judan said: He was born at nine months
[of pregnancy] lest it be said that he was
Abimelech's issue. R. Hunia said: At seven
months, which is nine incomplete months.[1] R.

Huna, quoting R. Hezekiah, said: He was born
at midday. For "set time" *(moed)* is stated
here, whilst in another context we read, *At the
season* (moed) *that you came out of Egypt*
(Deut. 16:6).[2]

Gen. R. 53, 6. T.S. 21, 29.

25. **AT THE SET TIME (MOED).** This teaches
that the day when a son is born is a day of rejoicing, for such is called *moed*, as in the text,
These are moade (plural form of *moed*—the
festivals) *of the Lord* (Lev. 23:4).[1]

Midrash Habiur. T.S. 21, 30.

26. **Whom Sarah bore to him.**

But the verse has already stated, *that was
born to him*: why is "to him" repeated? This
teaches that he was named above [in heaven]
before he was named below [on earth].

Midrash Habiur. T.S. 21, 32.

27. **Yitshak (Isaac).**

[The name signifies:] law went forth (*yatsa
hok*) to the world; a gift was made to the
world.[1] R. Isaac Hipushith interpreted: *Yod,*

§ 24 [1] Seven months and two days: the first and the last days each counted as a month. The seven and nine in
each case means after she left Abimelech's house. Y.T. reads: He was born after seven incomplete months, i.e.,
just over six months.
[2] See Exod. 12:51: *In the middle of that day* (AJV: *the selfsame day*) *the Lord brought the children of
Israel out of the land of Egypt.* Moed is given the same meaning in both cases.
§ 25 [1] Nowadays they celebrate on the day of circumcision, not on the day of birth; see par. 46. Rabah states: It
is a custom to make a feast on the day of a boy's *birth* or circumcision. The present Midrash is apparently
the source of that custom.
§ 27 [1] Law probably refers to the Torah, which is called *hok* in Ps. 81:5: *For it is* hok (*a statute*) *for Israel.* The
"gift" is the blessing that was to come through Abraham and his descendants, made possible now by Isaac's
birth.

⁴**And Abraham circumcised his son Isaac when he was eight days old, as God had commanded him. ⁵And Abraham was a hundred years old,**

COMMENTARY

called him thus on the very day he was born, because

the name had been commanded by God.²³ ⁴**eight days old.** Even though Isaac was probably weak, as is usual when the father is very old, his circumcision was not postponed.²⁴ **as God had commanded him.** Although the father of a child born so unnaturally might have feared the dangers of circumcision, Abraham did not hesitate, but did *as God had commanded him*.²⁵ ⁵**a hundred years old. a.** The Torah frequently repeats important matters to impress them on the memory.²⁶ **b.** This gives the reason for Sarah's declaration in the next

ANTHOLOGY

ten, symbolizes the Ten Commandments; *tsaddi*, ninety, corresponds to, *Shall Sarah, that is ninety years old, bear?* (17:17); *heth*, eight, symbolizes circumcision, which is performed on the eighth day; *kuf*, a hundred, relates to, *Shall a child be born to him that is a hundred years old?*²

Gen. R. 53, 7. T.S. 21, 31.

28. **When he was eight days old, as God had commanded him.**

Where had He instructed him so? *He that is eight days old shall be circumcised among you, every male throughout your generations* (17:12).

Gen. R. 53. T.S. 21, 34.

29. As God had commanded him. Our Rabbis taught: A father must circumcise his son . . . How do we know it? Because it is written, *Abraham circumcised his son Isaac*. How do we know that she [the mother] has no duty [to circumcise her son]?¹ From the text, *As God had commanded him*—him, but not her. Now we know this in respect of a particu-

lar time;² how do we know it for all times? The School of R. Ishmael taught: "Commanding" always intimates an injunction for the immediate present and for all generations.³

Kid. 29a. T.S. 21, 33.

30. **Abraham was a hundred years old when his son Isaac was born to him.**

When He [the Almighty] spoke to Abraham our father at the Covenant between the Parts, he was seventy years old;¹ thirty years elapsed from then until Isaac's birth. This follows from our text.

Seder Olam 1. T.S. 21, 35.

31. Abraham was a hundred years old, etc. Sometimes prayer is answered [only] after one reaches a hundred. We learn this from Abraham, as our text states.¹

Midrash Sh'muel 4. T.S. 21, 36.

32. A hundred years old. There was a weighty reason for Abraham and Sarah to be blessed with offspring only after they had at-

---

² Thus the name symbolized: The power of rejuvenation, as shown in their having a child at such an advanced age; the Ten Commandments—the foundation of social progress; and circumcision, the sign of perfection (see 17:1-2, 10). R. Isaac's comment may be an independent interpretation or a further explanation of the previous one: These constituted the Law and the gift presented to the world.

§ 29 ¹ E.g., in the father's absence.
² That on that occasion only he (Abraham) had been commanded, but not she (Sarah).
³ Therefore the implication of this verse—viz., him and not her—also holds good for all time. It may seem strange that an interpretation which in form is positive and emphasizes and strengthens the obligation, is made to widen the scope of a negative implication. However, R. Ishmael's exegesis was not made on this particular text: it is general in character. But once made it is applied in all cases, even where the result is to *release* one from an obligation.

§ 30 ¹ See Vol. II, chap. 12, par. 58; chap. 15, par. 91.
§ 31 ¹ The point is probably that one should never despair; he may find that his prayer is answered only at a most advanced age.

when his son Isaac was born unto him. [6]And Sarah said: "God hath made laughter for me; every one that heareth will laugh on account

COMMENTARY

verse.[27] [6]laughter. a. A joyous laughter at such an astonishing event.[28] b. It is almost incredible in my eyes.[29] c. Even though the babe is suffering the pains of circumcision, God has filled my heart with joy.[30] d. Abraham has done well to call him Isaac, the name denoting the joy which I have experienced.[31] laughter . . . will laugh. Even though people will laugh at me in derision, that I, an old woman, seek the joys of motherhood, I care not, since God has given me so much happiness.[32] will laugh on account of me. a. That such an amazing thing has happened to me.[33] b. Possibly "me" is emphatic: the happiness is essentially mine, since Abraham already had a son before now.[34] c. Will laugh at *my* skeptical laughter when I first heard

ANTHOLOGY

tained so great an age. It was necessary that Abraham should bear the sign of the covenant upon his body before he begot the son who was appointed to be the father of Israel.

Ginzberg, Legends, 1, 262. Gen. R. 46, 2.

33. God has made laughter [i.e., joy] for me.

Did then God create laughter? Surely laughter is most unseemly? But it means this: Sarah said, "Before I gave birth I would see Ishmael sporting (making laughter) with idols, and my heart ached. But now that this son is born to me my heart rejoices, because he will bring Ishmael's laughter to nought."

Another interpretation: Sarah said: I bore him at ninety, circumcised him at eight [days], and his father begot him at a hundred. This is the significance of the word צחק.[1]

Whenever laughter is mentioned in connection with Abraham and Sarah it connotes amazement . . . "God has done an amazing thing for me." Sometimes laughter is used in connection with sin, as in the verse, *They rose up to make merry* (lit., to laugh.—Exod. 32, 6). Again, it may mean derision, as in the verse, *But he seemed to his sons-in-law as one that made laughter* (19:14).[2] In certain places, however, it denotes great joy, as in our present text.

Midrash Habiur; Sechel Tob. T.S. 21, 37 note. 38.

34. GOD HAS MADE LAUGHTER FOR ME. A particular privilege [granted to Sarah] was responsible for Isaac's birth. This teaches that [she declared:] "The Holy One, blessed is He, took a *yod* from my name and replaced it with *he*, and that *yod* was given to Isaac."[1]

MA. T.S. 21, 39.

35. God has made laughter for me; every one . . . will laugh on account of me.

R. Berechiah, R. Judah b. R. Simon, and R. Hanan, quoting R. Samuel b. R. Isaac, all commented: If Reuben has joy, what does Simeon care about it? Similarly, if Sarah was remembered [with child], what did others care [that they too should laugh and be joyful]? The truth, however, is that when our mother Sarah was remembered, many barren women were remembered at the same time, many deaf gained their hearing, many blind their sight, many insane their sanity. For "making" is stated here; it also appears in the text, *He made a release to the provinces* (Est. 2:18).[1] Even as there "making" means that a gift was granted to the world, so here too it has the same connotation.[2]

§ 33   [1] Cf. par. 27; the *yod* is missing here, as the present is based on צחק.
           [2] Said when Lot urged his family to leave Sodom before its impending doom. They regarded his warnings as derisive.
§ 34   [1] He changed שרי to שרה (17:15); by adding the י thus taken from her name to צחק (laughter) it became יצחק Isaac.
§ 35   [1] Referring to Ahasuerus' remission of taxes in honor of his marriage to Esther.
           [2] Many other women were given cause to rejoice.

of me." ⁷And she said: "Who would have said unto Abraham, that Sarah should give children suck? for I have borne him a son in his old age."

COMMENTARY

the tidings of his birth.³⁵ ⁷**she said.** Explaining why all would laugh.³⁶ **Who would have said. a.** See who promised this, and see who kept His promise!³⁷ **b.** Who could ever have imagined such a thing—surely none but a prophet or an angel!³⁸ **c.** When a man is blessed with a son his friends wish him, "May you have more sons!" But who could

have said this to Abraham (e.g., at Ishmael's birth or after), when we were both so old?³⁹ **d.** "Laughter" refers to Sarah (previous verse), and "Who would have said," to Abraham: for Sarah to give birth was a matter of laughter—incredible; and whilst Abraham's begetting was not so incredible, it was still amazing.⁴⁰ **that Sarah . . . in his old age.** Sarah's rejuvenation to the point where she could suckle children was the greater miracle. Therefore it precedes the lesser miracle of Abraham's begetting.⁴¹ **that Sarah should give children suck.** It is not surprising that I have given birth, for God promised it. But that lactation too should be granted to me is amazing, for this He did not promise.⁴² **children. a.** I.e., if I can suckle Isaac, I can suckle other children.⁴³ **b.** The plural is used generically and is

ANTHOLOGY

R. Berechiah ha-Cohen said: What does "everyone that hears" mean? did then everyone hear of this? But [she said this because] the Holy One, blessed is He, increased the light of the sun and the moon.³ [For making is mentioned here; and] it says, *God made the two great lights* (1:16). Therefore she said, *Everyone that hears will laugh on account of me.*

Gen. R. 53, 8; Tan. Y. Vayyera 37.
T.S. 21, 37. 40.

36. **Who would have said (*millel*) to Abraham, that Sarah should give children suck?**

Amar or *dibber* [the usual Hebrew for said] is not employed here, but *millel*: this was an oblique reference to his [Abraham's] begetting at a hundred [years], which is the numerical value of *millel*.

[Again, she implied] that he now possessed the sap (virility) of youth, which is the root meaning of *millel,* as in the text, *You may pluck sap-rich ears* [of corn] (m'liloth) *with your hand* (Deut. 23:26).

[Another interpretation:] One day my descendants will declaim before the Holy One, blessed is He, at the [Red] Sea, *Who is like unto Thee . . . O Lord* (Exod. 15:11)?¹

Gen. R. 52, 9; Tan. Y. Vayyera 37.
T.S. 21, 42. 44-5.

37. THAT SARAH SHOULD GIVE CHILDREN SUCK. How many children did Sarah suckle? R. Levi said: On the day that Abraham weaned his son Isaac he made a great feast. But all the people derided him, saying: "Have you seen this old man and old woman bring a foundling from the market-place and claim it as their son! Moreover, they make a great feast to corroborate their words." What did our father Abraham do? He invited all the most prominent people of the time, and our mother Sarah invited their wives. Each brought her child, but not the wet-nurse. A miracle happened to Sarah: her teats opened like two springs and she suckled them all. Yet they still derided them: "If Sarah did bear at ninety, could Abraham, a hundred years old, father the child?" Immediately Isaac's features became like Abraham's, whereupon they all exclaimed, *Abraham begot Isaac* (25:19).

Our mother Sarah was excessively modest. Said Abraham to her: "This is not a time for modesty; uncover your teats that all may know that the Holy One, blessed is He, has commenced to perform miracles." She did as she was bid, and the milk gushed forth like two wells. All the noble matrons came and had her suckle their children, exclaiming, "We are not worthy that our children should suck from this saintly woman." Our Rabbis said: Whoever came for

³ A poetic way of saying that Isaac's birth increased the light which Abraham brought to the world (cf. par. 15).
§ 36   ¹ This comment is on the word "who."

[8]And the child grew, and was weaned.

COMMENTARY

applicable to one son too.[44] **c.** With this one child she will bring up "sons," for he will be the corner-stone of the future nation of Abraham. Thus, at this moment, Sarah feels that she is the mother of "sons," mother of an entire nation.[45] [8]**weaned.** At the age of two.[46] **a great feast. a.** The weaning was regarded as a joyous occasion, as we find with Samuel (1 Sam. 1:24): when weaned, his

ANTHOLOGY

the sake of Heaven[1] was imbued with the fear of God. R. Aha said: Even those who did not came for the sake of Heaven were given dominion in the world. But they did not retain it, for the dominion was taken from them when they held aloof at Sinai and would not accept the Torah. Thus it is written, *He looseth the bond of kings, and bindeth their loins with a girdle* (Job 12:18).[2]

Our masters said: All the children whom Sarah suckled became proselytes. Do not wonder at this: you find the same with Eliphaz, Esau's son. Having been reared in Isaac's lap (i.e., home) he became a righteous man and was privileged to have the Holy Spirit rest on him; as it says, *The fruit of the righteous is a tree of life, and the one that is wise wins souls* (Prov. 11:30).

> B.M. 87a; Gen. R. 53, 9; Tan. Y. Vayyera 38. T.S. 21, 46. 47 and note.

38. THAT SARAH SHOULD GIVE CHILDREN SUCK. This teaches that the son that was given her equaled many sons, in the same way as it says, *Am I not better to you than ten sons* (1 Sam. 1:8)? Similarly we read, *I multiplied his [Abraham's] seed, and gave him Isaac* (Josh. 24:3): this too teaches that Isaac equaled many sons. R. Judah said: *wa-arb* (I contended)

is written (*ibid.*) whereas the traditional reading is *wa-arbeh* (I multiplied): this intimates that God declared: "How much did I contend with him before I gave him Isaac!"[1]

> MhG. T.S. 21, 48.

39. **The child grew, and was weaned.**

R. Hoshaya the Elder interpreted: He was weaned from the Evil Tempter.[1] Our Rabbis said: He was weaned from his mother's milk.

> Gen. R. 50, 10. T.S. 21, 49.

40. THE CHILD GREW, AND WAS WEANED. Abraham was the first man to show old age, and the first to suffer . . . How do we know the latter? "Sovereign of the universe!" Abraham pleaded before the Holy One, blessed is He: "Hadst Thou not prospered the Generation of the Flood, they would not have angered Thee; and hadst Thou brought sufferings upon them, they would not have rebelled against Thee." The Almighty replied: "With you I will commence." So he suffered through his son, as it says, *And the child grew, and was weaned.* R. Oshaya and R. Abin disagree: One interpreted, He was weaned from suffering; the other interpreted, He was weaned from evil desire to good desire.[1]

> Tan. Y. Noah 20. T.S. 21, 50.

§ 37 [1] That their children might imbibe a spirit of righteousness with Sarah's milk.
  [2] "Looseth the bond" is understood as depriving of authority.
§ 38 [1] The sense is obscure. "Contention" may mean wrestling in prayer: only after strenuous prayer did I give him Isaac. Possibly, however, *ribin,* here derived from *rib,* contention, may be the masc. plural from of *ribah,* maiden, in which case it might mean: How many young men did I give him in giving him Isaac—i.e., he equaled many other sons. This interpretation would suit the context better, but it is doubtful if the grammatical construction permits it.
§ 39 [1] Either: He turned thirteen, the age when a Jewish boy becomes obligated to fulfill all the commandments of Judaism (so MA). The feast that Abraham made on that occasion may therefore be the origin of the custom to celebrate a boy's thirteenth birthday with a feast—though this does not seem very likely. Or: His education in the Torah now commenced—the Torah being the antidote to evil. See next par.
§ 40 [1] For the latter interpretation see preceding par. "He suffered through his son" and "he was weaned from suffering" are obscure. Perhaps it means that he suffered through the *lack* of a son, and it was *Abraham* who was weaned from suffering, i.e., he now experienced the inner satisfaction of being blessed with a son and seeing him grow up in his ways.

And Abraham made a great feast on the day that Isaac was weaned.

COMMENTARY

mother took him to the Tabernacle at Shiloh.[47] b. To publicize God's wonders.[48] **on the day that Isaac was weaned.** Paternal love reaches its full measure not when the child is born or circumcised but when he is weaned.[49] b. Her flow of milk did not cease until he had to be weaned. In an old woman this itself was a great miracle: the purpose of the feast was to publicize and give thanks for this miracle.[50]

ANTHOLOGY

41. THE CHILD GREW, AND WAS WEANED (VAYYIGAMAL). R. Awira expounded: What is meant by, *The child grew, and was weaned* (vayyigamal)? The Holy One, blessed is He, will make a great feast for the righteous on the day He shows (*yigmol*) His love to Isaac's descendants.[1]

Pes. 119b. T.S. 21, 51.

42. THE CHILD GREW, AND WAS WEANED. Abraham wrote books on the Unity of the Divine Name and taught them to Isaac. The completion of his education is described in the words, *He was weaned,* just as it is written of Samuel, *And when she weaned him, she took him up with her* (1 Sam. 1:24).

Abraham made a great feast. He did this in praise of and gratitude to the great God.

Or Haafelah. T.S. 21, 52.

43. THE CHILD GREW, AND WAS WEANED. He is variously called "the child" and "Isaac": this teaches that before he knew [God][1] he was called child; after he knew [Him] he was called Isaac.[2]

Midrash Habiur. T.S. 21, 53.

44. **Abraham made a great feast.**

R. Judah b. R. Simon said: The Great One of the Universe was there.[1] R. Judah, quoting R. Jose b. R. Hanina, said: [Similarly,] *Then the king made a great feast* (Est. 2:18) means that the Great One of the Universe was there.[2] Thus it is written, *For the Lord will* again *rejoice over you for good* (Deut. 30:9)—in the days of Mordecai and Esther; *as He rejoiced over your fathers* (*ibid.*)—in the days of Abraham, Isaac, and Jacob. R. Judah interpreted: *A great feast* means a feast for the great; for Og together with all his nobles were there.[3] Said they to Og: "Did you not say that Abraham is a sterile mule that cannot beget?" He replied: "Even now, what is his [Abraham's] gift? Is it not puny? If I put my finger on him I can crush him." Said the Holy One, blessed is He, to him: "You despise his gift! By your life: You will see countless myriads of his descendants, and eventually will fall at their hands."

Gen. R. 53, 10. T.S. 21, 54.

45. ABRAHAM MADE A GREAT FEAST. R. Simeon further said: He who rejoices on the festivals but does not give to the Holy One, blessed is He, His due share, is selfish; Satan seeks to injure him and accuses him before Heaven, brings about his downfall, and causes him great sorrow. To give the portion of the Holy One, blessed is He, means to gladden the poor according to one's ability . . . Who was

§ 41 [1] When Israel's sufferings are brought to an end and it is restored to its former glory. The text is interpreted symbolically: the child (Isaac) symbolizes the Jewish people; *vayyigamal*, was weaned, is now connected with *gamal*, to bestow or treat with kindness; hence, when the Jewish people "grow up," i.e., rise to their full stature through God's love and the cessation of persecution, God will make a great feast for the righteous. Possibly the interpretation "was weaned" is retained, in the sense of weaned from suffering, as in the preceding par., save that there it refers to the nation; this is poetically described as God's bestowal of love.

§ 43 [1] Or: Before his intelligence unfolded.
[2] Only then did he begin to have the stature of Isaac.

§ 44 [1] That is the meaning of "*great* feast."
[2] He rejoiced over this feast given in Esther's honor—for this feast laid the ground for the deliverance of the Jews from Haman's future evil machinations against them.
[3] Tan. Y. Vayyishlach 23 states: "Great" teaches that Shem, Eber, and Abimelech were there, though not explicitly named (T.S. 21, 55).

⁹**And Sarah saw the son of Hagar the Egyptian, whom she had borne unto Abraham, making sport.** ¹⁰**Where-**

COMMENTARY

⁹**the son of Hagar the Egyptian. a.** This indicates her contempt: to her he was Hagar's, not Abraham's son.⁵¹ **b.** Sarah assumed that Ishmael's scoffing was the echo of what he had heard from his mother. [This is to explain why he is not mentioned by name but as *the son of Hagar.*—Ed.]⁵²

making sport. a. His behavior was due to the natural envy of an older son who sees himself displaced by a younger.⁵³ **b.** He mocked at the great feast: he too was Abraham's son, yet no feast had been made when *he* was weaned!⁵⁴ **c.** Making merry and lording it over the members of the household as he had done before Isaac was born.⁵⁵ **d.** He derided the whole business, suggesting that Isaac was not Abraham's child at all, but Abimelech's.⁵⁶ **e.** "What nonsense is this!" he jeered. "I am the firstborn and I will be the heir, yet no feast was made at my weaning."⁵⁷ **f.** She saw him spending his time in play (with such things as dice, amours or general dissoluteness), and feared the bad example

ANTHOLOGY

greater than Abraham, whose kindness extended to all creatures? Yet we are told . . . *Abraham made a great feast on the day that Isaac was weaned.* To that grand feast Abraham invited all the great men of the age . . . Satan came and appeared at the door in the guise of a poor man, but no one took notice of him. Abraham was busy with the kings and nobles, while Sarah was suckling all their infants . . . He immediately presented himself before the Holy One, blessed is He, and cried: "Sovereign of the Universe, Thou hast said, *Abraham My friend* (Isa. 41:8); behold, he has made a feast and has not given anything to Thee nor to the poor . . ." The Lord made answer: "Who in this world can be compared to Abraham?" Nevertheless he did not stir from thence until he had spoilt all the festivity; and after that the Lord ordered Abraham to offer Isaac as sacrifice, and it was decreed that Sarah should die from anguish on account of her son's danger—all because Abraham did not give anything to the poor.

Zohar 1, 10b.

46. ABRAHAM MADE A GREAT FEAST ON THE DAY THAT ISAAC WAS WEANED. R. Ishmael said: Abraham did not refrain from anything that He commanded him. When Isaac was born he circumcised him on the eighth day, as our narrative relates. [Later] he offered him on the altar.¹ [On the occasion of his circumcision]

he made a feast of rejoicing. Hence our Sages said: A man should make a feast on the day of his son's circumcision, even as our father Abraham did.

PRE 29. T.S. 21, 56.

47. **Now Sarah saw the son of Hagar the Egyptian [Ishmael] . . . making sport.**

R. Hiyya said: After Isaac's birth Ishmael is never mentioned by name as long as he was in Abraham's house: dross is not mentioned in the presence of gold. Therefore he is described here as *the son of Hagar.* R. Isaac commented: *Sarah saw* indicates that she looked upon him with disfavor, as Hagar's but not Abraham's son . . . Abraham, however, did regard him as his son, as it is written, *The matter was very grievous in Abraham's sight on account of* his *son* (verse 11). R. Simeon said: In this story Scripture tells of Sarah's piety. For what she saw was that he was practising idolatry.¹ Hence she declared: "He is not Abraham's son, for he does not walk in his path, but the son of Hagar, the Egyptian, reverting to his mother's type." . . . Only for that reason did the Holy One, blessed is He, support her demand [that he be sent away], as the story proceeds to relate.

Did she then not see Ishmael making sport until now? Surely, he had been making sport

§ 46   ¹ In זוהר 2, 53 the reading is: Hence you learn that he who brings his son to circumcision is as though he brought a meal-offering and its libations upon the altar. (I.e., he *thereby* offered him on the altar.)

§ 47   ¹ See next par.

fore she said unto Abraham: "Cast out this bondwoman and her son;

COMMENTARY

he might set for Isaac. [This rendering understands the Heb. in the sense of play, not mockery.—Ed.][58]

[10]**this bondwoman and her son. a.** Because the son cannot be left without a mother: therefore they must both be expelled.[59] **b.** If she remains here permanently she will come to be regarded as a real wife whose son has the rights of inheritance.[60] **c.** Both of them, because it was his mother's advice to slander Isaac that he might be the sole heir.[61] **d.** That all may know that Isaac is *your* son.[62]

ANTHOLOGY

for full thirteen years![2] This, however, teaches that she foresaw through the Holy Spirit that some of the Egyptians would become proselytes, leave Egypt together with her descendants, and set up an idol, concerning which it is written, *They rose up to make sport* (Exod. 32:6).[3]

Zohar 1, 118b; Midrash Habiur. T.S. 21, 57 and note.

48. MAKING SPORT. R. Simeon b. Yohai said: R. Akiba expounded: *Making sport* means nothing else but practising idolatry, as it says, *They rose up to* make sport (Exod. 32:6). This teaches that Sarah saw Ishmael build a "high place" [an altar], catch frogs,[1] and offer them to idols. R. Eliezer, son of R. Jose ha-Galilee said: *Making sport* means immorality, as in the text, *The Hebrew servant, whom you brought to us, came in to me to* make sport *of me* (39:17). This teaches that Sarah saw Ishmael rape maidens[2] and ravish women. R. Ishmael said: The term alludes to bloodshed, as in the verses, *Abner said to Joab: "Let the young men, I pray you, arise and* make sport *before us." And Joab said: "Let them arise." Then they arose . . . and caught every one his fellow by his head, and* thrust his sword *in his fellow's side* (2 Sam. 2:14-16). This teaches that Sarah saw Ishmael take arrows and shoot them [as in sport], with intent to kill Isaac; as it says, *As a madman who casts fire-brands, arrows, and death; so is the man that deceives his neighbor, and says: "Am not I in sport"* (Prov. 26:18-19)? But I [, said R. Simeon b.

Yohai,] maintain that the allusion is to inheritance. When Isaac was born people said: "A son has been born to Abraham who will receive a double share [of the inheritance]." But Ishmael made sport of [derided] them, saying: "I am the first-born, and I will receive the double share." I learn this [interpretation] from [Sarah's] demand, for it says, *Wherefore she said to Abraham: "Cast out this bondwoman and her son; for the son of this bondwoman shall not be heir with my son, even with Isaac."*

T. Sot. 6; Gen. R. 53, 11. T.S. 21, 58.

49. **Cast out this bondwoman with her son.**

Once, seeing Isaac sitting alone, he shot an arrow at him to kill him. Sarah saw it and told Abraham: "This is what Ishmael did to Isaac. Arise and bequeath to Isaac everything that the Holy One, blessed is He, swore to give you and your seed. By your life! The son of this bondwoman will not be heir together with my son Isaac." Thus we read, *Cast out this bondwoman.* She demanded: "Write her a bill of divorce and send her away together with her son from my son and myself."

[Another interpretation: Send them away] lest my son learn their ways.

PRE 30; Exod. R. 1. T.S. 21, 60-61.

50. CAST OUT THIS BONDWOMAN WITH HER SON. [I.e.,] in this world; *for he shall not be heir*— in the world to come.

Or Haafelah. T.S. 21, 62.

---

[2] Of his life. He was thirteen years old when Isaac was conceived; cf. 16:16; 17:17; 21:5.

[3] The allusion is to the Golden Calf. The Rabbis assumed that the prime offenders were the "mixed multitude" (see Exod. 12:38). As Ishmael's mother was an Egyptian they were his compatriots; here he is taken to represent them.

§ 48 [1] He was too young to offer the larger animals.

 [2] This involves a textual emendation, reading בנות (daughters) instead of גנות. As it stands the text reads: seize gardens—where women were engaged in working.

for the son of this bondwoman shall not be heir with my son, even with Isaac." [11]And the thing was very grievous in Abraham's sight on account of his son. [12]And God said unto Abraham: "Let it not be grievous in thy sight because of the lad, and because of thy bondwoman; in all that Sarah saith unto thee, hearken unto her voice; for in Isaac

COMMENTARY

shall not be heir. a. He insolently claims to be co-heir! That is why he derides this feast.[63] **b.** Inasmuch as a son takes the status of his mother, not of his father.[64] **with my son, even with Isaac. a.** The addition "with Isaac" was to remind him that God had declared: *"My covenant will I establish with Isaac"* (17:21).[65] **b.** He may not be heir for two reasons: (1) because he is not *my* son—the son of the mistress; (2) because of Isaac's natural superiority.[66] **c.** As against Isaac he does not count

as a son at all.[67] **d.** Delicacy of feeling prevented her from revealing the true cause of Ishmael's derision (see vs. 9, *making sport*, comm. *f*).[68] [11]**on account of his son. a.** His grief was caused not by the prospect of losing the woman but on account of Ishmael.[69] **b.** He was saddened on Hagar's account too, as the next verse shows, but his main grief was on account of Ishmael.[70] **c.** "Son" refers to Isaac: Abraham grieved that Isaac should become the cause, albeit unwillingly, of such cruelty as the expulsion of Hagar and Ishmael.[71] **his son. a.** Whom he loved and pitied as his first-born; moreover, his conduct was decent [this disagrees with some of the views above.—Ed.][72] **b.** He feared the evil consequences that would flow from his son's expulsion: he would take to evil ways and be swallowed up by his new social environment.[73] **c.** Sarah had condemned him as "Hagar's son": but Abraham knew that he was *his* son too.[74] [12]**God said unto Abraham.** Probably in a dream at night.[75] **the lad.** God thus justified Sarah by calling him "the lad," not "your son"—he was not to regard him as his son.[76] **and because of thy bondwoman.** God knew that he grieved on her account too; nevertheless only "son" is mentioned in the previous verse, because he, not Hagar, was the cause of contention between Abraham and Sarah.[77] **hearken unto her voice. a.** Her demand is just.[78] **b.** Though you do not agree with her. To hearken to the voice means to obey, regardless of the nature of the command.[79] **in Isaac,** etc. **a.** The promise

ANTHOLOGY

51. The thing was very grievous in Abraham's sight.

Of all that Abraham suffered this was the worst thing that befell him,[1] as our text implies.

PRE 30. T.S. 21, 64.

52. THE THING WAS VERY GRIEVOUS IN ABRAHAM'S SIGHT. Thus it is written, *He shuts his eyes from perceiving evil* (Isa. 33:15).[1]

Gen. R. 53, 12. T.S. 21, 65.

53. On account of his son.
Because he had launched out on an evil course.

Exod. R. 1. T.S. 21, 66.

54. Let it not be grievous in your sight on account of the lad, and on account of your bondwoman.

R. Judah said: That night the Holy One,

blessed is He, appeared to Abraham and said to him: "Abraham, do you not know that Sarah is a fitting wife for you? she is your companion, and the wife of your youth . . . Hagar is not your wife but your bondmaid. Everything that Sarah has spoken is true."

PRE 30. T.S. 21, 68.

55. In all that Sarah says to you, hearken to her voice.

Sarah had complained to Abraham: "I see Ishmael build an altar, catch frogs and offer them to idols. Will it not be a profanation of the Name of Heaven if he teaches my son Isaac to do the same?" But he replied: "Having promoted a person, does one demote him? Having given her the status of a wife, shall we degrade her from our home! What will people say of

§ 51 [1] The passage adds that this was the ninth of his ten trials. Cf. Aboth 5:3.
§ 52 [1] He deliberately shut his eyes to Ishmael's evil ways; for that reason he was loath to send him away.

shall seed be called to thee. ¹³And also of the son of the bondwoman will I make a nation, because he is

arch's heir; consequently Abraham must act on Sarah's wish and send Ishmael away, to avoid any dispute later concerning the inheritance.⁸¹ ¹³**the son of the bondwoman. a.** He shall bear her name.⁸² **b.** Though he will be called her son, not yours, yet shall I make him a great nation.⁸³ **will I make a nation. a.** God said this to reassure Abraham, who was afraid that harm might befall Ishmael in the desert.⁸⁴ **b.** Distinct from the nation which will grow out of Isaac.⁸⁵ **because he is**

COMMENTARY

that this land shall be yours will be fulfilled through Isaac, not Ishmael.⁸⁰ **b.** Isaac was to be the Patri-

ANTHOLOGY

us?" "Since I say thus, and you say otherwise," she returned, "let the All-Present decide between us." He decided in favor of Sarah, as it says, *In all that Sarah says to you, hearken to her voice.* Now, why does Scripture say "in *all*"? It teaches that He decided in the second matter as in the first: just as the second was on Hagar's account, so was the first on Hagar's account.¹

T. Sot. 5. T.S. 21, 69.

56. HEARKEN TO HER VOICE. Hence you learn that Abraham's prophetic powers were subordinate to Sarah's.¹

Exod. R. 1. T.S. 21, 70.

57. HEARKEN TO HER VOICE. Some hearkened to their wives and profited thereby. Of this Abraham is an example. He was bidden, *In all that Sarah says to you, hearken to her voice.* He did indeed obey her. His profit was that his seed is called after Isaac, as it says, *For in Isaac shall seed be called to you.*

Deut. R. 4, 5. T.S. 21, 71.

58. **In Isaac shall seed be called to you.**

Mishnah. [If a man vows] not to benefit from the seed of Abraham, Israel [Jews] are interdicted to him; but he may benefit from the [Gentile] nations.

Gemara. Is then Ishmael not of Abraham's seed? [Scripture writes,] *In* Isaac *shall seed be called to you.* Is not then Esau of Isaac's seed? Said R. Judan b. Shalom: "*In* Isaac" implies part of Isaac only. R. Huna said: The *beth* (in) stands for two:¹ [God implied: Only] that son who will inherit the two worlds, viz., this world and the next, [will be called your seed]. R. Azariah, quoting b. Hatya, observed: The *beth* implies: He who recognizes the existence of two worlds will inherit the two worlds, and only he shall be called your seed.

J. Ned. 3, 8; Gen. R. 53, 12. T.S. 21, 72-3.

59. **And also the son of the bondwoman.**

The definitive ruling is: Your son by a Jewess is designated *your* son, but your son by a Canaanitish [i.e., Gentile] woman is not called your son but *her* son. For it says, *And also the son of the bondwoman.*¹ That son does not inherit, nor does he free [his father's Jewish wife] from *halitsah* or levirate marriage.²

PZ Pinhas 132. T.S. 21, 76.

60. **And also the son of the bondwoman will I make a nation.**

It is written, *Blessed is the man that trusts in the Lord . . . he shall be as a tree planted*

§ 55 ¹ The sentence contains two statements: (i) *Let it not be grievous in your sight . . . because of your bond-woman;* (ii) *in all that Sarah says to you, hearken to her voice.* The first explicitly refers to Hagar, but the second does not. The second might, e.g., have referred to Ishmael only, since it was his "making sport" that had aroused Sarah's anger. "All," however, in the second shows that it refers also to Sarah's demand for Hagar's expulsion, just as the first explicitly refers to Hagar. This explanation is conjectural.
§ 56 ¹ Otherwise he would not have been told to submit to her.
§ 58 ¹ Every Heb. letter is also a number.
§ 59 ¹ Thus Ishmael was called her son.
　　² See Deut. 25:5-10. The widow of a man who dies childless must either marry his brother (this is called *yibum*, levirate marriage) or perform a ceremony of removing her brother-in-law's shoe from his foot (*halitsah*, drawing off). If he has a child from a Gentile woman his Jewish wife still has the same obligation.

thy seed." [14]**And Abraham rose up early in the morning, and took bread and a bottle of water, and gave it unto Hagar, putting it on her shoulder, and the child, and sent her away; and she departed, and strayed in the wilderness of Beer-sheba.**

COMMENTARY

thy seed. a. For your sake.[86] **b.** Sarah was right in matters concerning the inheritance. But in all other matters which do not affect Isaac he is your seed.[87] [14]**rose up early in the morning. a.** He did not complain, but rose early to obey this as he would any other of His commands, in spite of his natural reluctance.[88] **b.** For "God said" etc. of verse 12 was during the night.[89] **bread and a bottle of water. a.** He gave her food for a couple of days, because she could not carry more. Undoubt-edly he gave them gold and silver too, even though these are not mentioned, for he would not have sent them away empty-handed.[90] **b.** Which one usually gives to slaves.[91] **c.** The necessities for a journey.[92] **a bottle of water.** Sufficient for her needs had she gone straight on to some other settlement.[93] **putting it on her shoulder.** So travelers usually carry it.[94] **and the child. a.** This is the second object of "gave": he gave her bread and water, and the child.[95] **b.** This has the same meaning here as "upon the child": he put the bread and the water upon both the mother and the child.[96] **c.** "Child" is the object of "putting": Ishmael disobeyed his father and refused to go. Therefore he had to bind and place him on her shoulder. Being "a wild ass of a man" (16:12) he would remain in the wilderness once he got there.[97] **d.** "The child" is written instead of "his son," to show that now Abraham conceded that Sarah was right.[98] **and sent her away. a.** Divorced her.[99] **b.** He escorted her.[100] **the wilderness of Beer-sheba. a.** At that time it was not yet called Beer-sheba, which name it received later (see verse 31); Moses, writing the Torah, gives it the name which it bore in his time. Normally she would have gone to Hebron, for

ANTHOLOGY

by the waters . . . whose foliage shall be luxuriant (Jer. 17:7-8): Even the foliage that dropped off from him [Abraham], viz., Ishmael, was luxuriant, as it says, *And also the son of the bondwoman will I make a nation.*

Yelamdenu. T.S. 21, 75.

61. Abraham rose up early, etc.

Abraham rose up early in the morning, wrote a divorce and gave it to her; then he sent her away from himself and his son Isaac. Thus it says, *Abraham rose up early in the morning, and took bread and a bottle of water, and gave it to Hagar, putting it on her shoulder, and the child, and sent her away*—he sent her away with a divorce. He took the water flask and tied it to her loins that it might drag after her, and so people would know that she was a bondwoman.[1]

PRE 30. T.S. 21, 79.

62. And gave it to Hagar.

Because slaves carry pitchers of water on their shoulder.

Gen. R. 53, 13. T.S. 21, 80.

63. And gave it to Hagar; he set [it] on her shoulder.

R. Burka commented: . . . Since it says that *he gave it to Hagar*, why tell us that *he set [it] on her shoulder?* This, however, teaches that he urged her [still] to bear the yoke of faith;[1] it also illumines her original relationship to him.[2] For here is written, *he set [it] on her shoulders;* whilst elsewhere it says, *There He set for them a statute and an ordinance* (Exod. 15:25): just as it refers there to the yoke of the Divine, so here too it has the same meaning.

Zohar Hadash Ruth 82. T.S. 21, 82.

§ 61 [1] Presumably slaves used to carry such water flasks. Abraham desired her rank to be known, lest Ishmael subsequently claim to be his free-born son and therefore his heir as first-born. See next par.

§ 63 [1] Like a burden which one carries on the shoulder.

[2] She was not simply a bondwoman or a wife for the purpose of bearing him a son, but a human personality whom Abraham sought to inspire with faith.

15And the water in the bottle was spent, and she cast the child under one of the shrubs. 16And she went, and sat her down over against him a good way off, as it were a bowshot;

COMMENTARY

which she had sufficient provisions, but that she lost her way.101 **b.** The town Beer-sheba, in the extreme south of Palestine, is situated on the border of the desert.102 15**was spent. a.** Scripture's purpose in narrating this is to teach faith in God even when things look black; also to show how God treats His beloved: even to Abraham's handmaid He sent an angel.103 **b.** For she had lost her way.104 **she cast the child. a.** He had grown weak through thirst and she had to carry him; now that she saw him dying she cast him away.105 **b.** She laid him down and abandoned him.106 **c.** She cast him away in anger, when she recalled that his father too had no pity on him. Nevertheless her maternal feelings were stirred and she wept.107 **the child.** His thirst and sickness had made him weak as a child. Yet the Heb. *yeled* is used even of a man of forty (1 Kings 12:8 ff.).108 **under one of the shrubs.** To protect him from the sun.109 16**a bowshot. a.** But no further, so that she could still see him.110

ANTHOLOGY

64. She departed, and strayed . . . and the water in the bottle was spent, etc.

What did she do? Seeing herself out of Abraham's control, she reverted to her former evil ways. What is written? *She departed, and strayed*—back to idolatry and the images of her father's house. Thus it is written, *They* [the idols] *are vanity, a work that make* [men] *stray* (Jer. 10:15).

[Therefore] *the water in the bottle was spent:* for Abraham's sake the water of the bottle did not diminish. But when she came to the wilderness and strayed after the abominations [idols] of her father's house, the water of the bottle immediately diminished [until there was no more]. For that reason *she cast the child under one of the shrubs.* Ishmael was twenty-four years old when he departed from Abraham's house,1 Isaac being then ten years old.2

Zohar Hadash Ruth 82a; PRE 30. T.S. 21, 83. 85.

65. Under one of the shrubs (sihim).

R. Meir said: It was a juniper tree,1 for these grow in the wilderness. R. Ammi commented: *Under one of the* sihim, intimates that there the ministering angels spoke (*he-sihu*) with her.2

Gen. R. 53, 13. T.S. 21, 86.

66. She went and sat down over against him a good way off (harhek) as the shots (ki-m'tahave) of a bow.

Here it says, *She went and sat down over against him;* and elsewhere we read, *over against it, round about the tent of meeting* (Num. 2:2). Again, here we read, *harhek* (a good way off); whilst in another context we read, *There shall be* rahok [same root as *harhek*— AJV: *a space*] *between you and it, about two thousand cubits by measure* (Josh. 3:4). Thus we infer the meaning of *over against* [in our text] from the same phrase [in the other], and *rahok* from *rahok*.1 R. Isaac said: *As the shots of a bow* indicates two bowshots,2 which are a mile.3

R. Berechiah interpreted: The phrase connotes, as one that hurls (*mateheth*) words against Heaven. "Yesterday," said she, "Thou

§ 64 1 The point is that he was not a child but a young man. However, through illness, the result of an evil eye cast on him by Sarah (see comm. which are drawn from Midrashic literature), he had had to be carried like a child; now, through lack of water, she cast him away.
2 Cf. 16:16 with 21:5, which shows that Ishmael was Isaac's senior by fourteen years.
§ 65 1 Emended text (Radal).
2 MA gives another interpretation: There she spoke against God. See next par.
§ 66 1 She sat two thousand cubits away from him.
2 The plural is always assumed to mean the minimum possible in plural—two.
3 Heb. *mil*, a thousand (paces)—2000 cubits.

for she said: "Let me not look upon the death of the child." And she sat over against him, and lifted up her voice, and wept. [17]And God heard the voice of the lad; and the angel of God called to Hagar out of heaven, and said unto her: "What aileth thee, Hagar? fear not; for God hath heard the voice of the lad where he is. [18]Arise, lift up the lad,

COMMENTARY

b. Within hearing.[111] **Let me not look.** This is not pity but self-love.[112] **she sat over against him.** This is repeated: she went still further off, either because she could still hear the lad's cries, or because she desired to weep out of his hearing.[113] [17]**God heard the voice of the lad. a.** He too wept, even though Scripture has not mentioned it hitherto.[114] **b.** I.e., his suffering and distress; he did not actually cry out.[115] **c.** God has pity on the anguish of the alien slave mother, and hears her prayer no less than that of Abraham.[116] **the angel of God. a.** A heaven-sent prophet; or possibly she dreamt that an angel spoke to her.[117] **b.** An angel speaking from heaven. It was not God Himself, as is shown by his words, "God has heard," etc.[118] **out of heaven.** She heard but did not see him.[119] **What aileth thee?** This question is rhetorical, serving as an introduction.[120] **where he is. a.** In the very place where you cast him away to die, there you will find water.[121] [18]**lift up the lad.** After he drinks; do not despair of nor

ANTHOLOGY

didst say to me, *I will greatly multiply your seed* (16:10); and now he is dying of thirst."

Gen. R. 53, 13. T.S. 21, 87.

67. She lifted up her voice, and wept.

Scripture writes, *Thou hast counted my wanderings; put Thou my tears into Thy flask* (Ps. 56:9): this means, regard them as the tears of that woman who was sent away from her home with a flask—Hagar. *Are they not in Thy book (ibid.)?* For so it is written in the Book of Psalms: *Hear my prayer, O Lord, and give ear to my cry; keep not silence at my tears* (Ps. 39:13): Thou wast not still at Hagar's tears; wilt Thou be silent at mine? Yet if Thou wouldst say, "Because she was a stranger[1] she was more beloved"; surely I am one too: *For I am a stranger with Thee, a sojourner, as all my fathers were (ibid.).*

Three wept, and the Holy One, blessed is He, heard their weeping: Hagar, Esau, and Hezekiah. Whence do we know that Hagar wept? From out text. And how do we know that He heard her weeping? Because it says,

For God has heard the voice of the lad where he is. Arise, lift up the lad (verses 17-18).

Gen. R. 53, 14; ARN Codex 2, 47. T.S. 21, 88 and note.

68. God heard the voice of the lad.

Ishmael's soul was wearied with thirst. He went and threw himself under one of the shrubs of the wilderness and cried out: "Master of all worlds! If it be Thy will to grant me water, let me drink ere I perish with thirst, for death of thirst is the most cruel of all deaths." Then the Holy One, blessed is He, heard his prayer.

PRE 30. T.S. 21, 89.

69. The angel of God called to Hagar.

For Abraham's sake. [When the verse concludes, *God has heard the voice of the lad*] *where he is*, it means for his own sake, for a sick man's prayers on his own behalf are more efficacious than those of any other.

Gen. R. 53, 14. T.S. 21, 90. 92.

70. Where he is.

R. Isaac said: A man is judged only by his

§ 67 [1] She did not belong to Abraham's family. This Rabbinic touch of God's special love for a stranger is enlightening—and characteristic.

and hold him fast by thy hand; for I will make him a great nation." [19]And God opened her eyes, and she saw a well of water; and she went,

COMMENTARY

abandon him.[122] **hold him fast by thy hand. a.** He informed her that soon she would not have to carry him at all, for he would be able to walk himself and she would merely have to hold his hand, or that he might even support her. [This renders: hold your hand fast—i.e., receive support—through him. Ed.][123] **b.** Clasp him in your arms with a mother's love.[124] [19]**God opened her eyes, etc. a.** Possibly the well had been hidden by shrubs, or was too far off for her to see, and now God gave her a sharper eyesight so that she saw it. Alternatively, there had not been a well there until God cleft the ground and caused water to gush forth.[125] **b.** He gave her the intelligence to recognize that there must be a well there, which she now saw. But the verse is not meant in a physical sense: she had not been blind hitherto.[126] **c.** I.e., she now perceived the well of water which was quite near her, but

ANTHOLOGY

deeds at the time [of judgment],[1] for it says, *For God has heard the voice of the lad where he is.*[2]

R. Simeon said: The angels hastened to indict him, pleading with Him: "Master of all worlds! Wilt Thou bring up a well for a man who will one day slay Thy children by thirst?"[3] "But what is he now?" He asked them. "He is righteous,"[4] answered they. To this He replied, "I judge a man only as he is at the moment of judging."

Gen. R. 53, 14; R.H. 53a. T.S. 21, 91. 93.

71. Hold him fast by the hand.

For Abraham took her back for Ishmael's sake.[1]

Or Haafelah. T.S. 21, 94.

72. God opened her eyes, and she saw a well of water.

R. Benjamin b. Levi and R. Jonathan b. Amram said: All are presumed blind until the Holy One, blessed is He, enlightens their eyes. This can be inferred from our text.

Gen. R. 53, 14. T.S. 21, 96.

73. God opened her eyes, and she saw a well of water. [At the destruction of the First Temple] eighty thousand young priests fled through Nebuchadnezzar's armies and made their way to the Ishmaelites (Arabs). Thirsty, they begged for water. Instead, the Ishmaelites brought them salty food and inflated gourds, insisting that they eat first. Having eaten, they put the [air-filled] gourds to their mouths; the air rushed in, penetrated to their stomachs and distended them until they burst open. Thus Scripture writes, *The burden upon Arabia. In the thickets in Arabia shall you lodge, O ye caravans of Dedanim. To him that is thirsty bring water* (Isa. 21:13-14). The interpretation is: Is that how caravans of kinsmen[1] act? When Ishmael was thirsty, was not the text, *To him that is thirsty bring water*, [fulfilled for him]? as we read, *God opened her eyes, and she saw a well of water.*

J. Taan. 4, 5; Lam. R. 2, 2, §4. T.S. 21, 95.

74. She saw a well of water. The well which was created [on the eve of Sabbath] at

§ 70 [1] Not by what he may do in the future.
[2] In his present state.
[3] See Isa. 21:13f: This is interpreted as an unanswered appeal by the Israelites to the Arabs (traditionally Ishmael's descendants). Cf. *infra*, par. 73.
[4] This disagrees with the view in par. 48. Zohar Hadash Bereshith 19 likewise maintains that he was not righteous, but that God does not punish before the age of 20. That again will disagree with par. 64, which states that he was 24 (others maintain that he was 27). The most plausible explanation is that he was righteous as far as the angels' accusation was concerned—so far he had not slain the Israelites by thirst.
§ 71 [1] Either in the past (chap. 16) or later on, 25:1—by Rabbinic tradition Keturah is Hagar; cf. Anth. *ad loc.*
§ 73 [1] Heb. *dedanim* (Dedanites) is by a play on words derived from *dod*, uncle: the Arabs as descendants of Ishmael were kinsmen, children of the uncle of Isaac's children.

and filled the bottle with water, and gave the lad drink. ²⁰And God was with the lad, and he grew; and he dwelt in the wilderness, and became an archer. ²¹And he dwelt in the

COMMENTARY

which in her anguish of mind she had overlooked. "The Hebrew phrase *to open the eyes* is exclusively employed in the figurative sense of receiving new sources of knowledge, not in that of regaining the sense of sight" (Maimonides).[127] ²⁰**God was with the lad. a.** He prospered Ishmael.[128] **b.** As He had promised Abraham.[129] **c.** He saved him from the dangers of the wilderness.[130] **he grew. a.** Literally, under Divine Providence.[131] **b.** In wealth and property.[132] **he dwelt in the wilderness.** He became a desert dweller, fulfilling the prophecy, *He shall be a wild ass of a man* (16:12).[133] **and became an archer** (*robeh kashath*). **a.** He dwelt in the wilderness and robbed travelers, as it is written, *his hand shall be against every man* (ibid.).[134] **b.** *Robeh*=shooter; *kashath*=bow: a shooter of the bow; the term also implies special skill, as though he were a professional in it.[135] **c.** *Robeh*=archer;

ANTHOLOGY

twilight[1] opened for them. They went, drank, and filled their flask with water, as our text relates. They left the well and traveled right through the whole wilderness until they reached the wilderness of Paran, where they found springs of water. There they settled, as it says, *He dwelt in the wilderness of Paran* (verse 21).

PRE 30. T.S. 21, 97.

75. SHE SAW A WELL OF WATER. [When Moses struck the rock for the water to flow, God said to him and Aaron:] *Because you believed not in Me . . . you shall not bring this assembly into the land which I have given them* (Num. 20:12). The Holy One, blessed is He, upbraided Moses: "You should have learned from Hagar, of whom it is written that *she saw a well of water.* If I brought up a well for but a single person [Ishmael], because he had the merit of his father Abraham in his favor, how much the more would I have done so for Israel, who have the merit of their ancestors, the merit of having received the Torah, and the merit of obeying My Commandments."

Yelamdenu. T.S. 21, 100.

76. **She went and filled the flask with water.**
This shows that she lacked faith.[1]

Gen. R. 53, 14. T.S. 21, 98.

77. **God was *eth* (with) the lad.**

R. Ishmael asked R. Akiba: Since you studied twenty-two years under Nahum of Gimzo, who interpreted every *ach* (save that) and *rak* (except) as limitations, and *eth* and *gam* (also) as extensions, what does the *eth* in the present text teach? If it said, God was the lad, he replied, it would be unintelligible; therefore it must say, *God was eth (with) the lad.* [At that reply R. Ishmael] cited, *For it is no empty thing from you* (Deut. 32:47): if you do find this [*eth*] empty, the emptiness comes *from you,* for you cannot interpret aright. Rather, *eth* teaches that God was with him, his ass-drivers, his camel-drivers and his household.[1]

Gen. R. 53, 15. T.S. 21, 101.

78. **He became an archer (*robeh kashath*).**

As he grew (*rabbah*), his cruelty (*kashiuth*) grew with him. Again, while yet a lad (*robeh*) he practised bowmanship. Finally, he was the master (*rab*) of all archers.

Abraham's ninth trial was Ishmael, who was born with the bow and grew up with the bow. . . . He would take a bow and arrow and shoot at birds.[1]

Gen. R. 53, 15; PRE 30. T.S. 21, 102-3.

§ 74 [1] The Rabbis count this well as one of the ten things which were created at that time; Aboth 5:6. The thought is that from the very Creation it was destined that they should be saved through this well.
§ 76 [1] Fearing that its water would dry up.
§ 77 [1] So that here too it is an extension.
§ 78 [1] Ishmael's cruelty was a trial to his father.

wilderness of Paran; and his mother took him a wife out of the land of Egypt. ²²And it came to pass at that time, that Abimelech and Phicol the captain of his host spoke unto

COMMENTARY

kashath=a maker of bows [thus two separate things are meant.]¹³⁶ ²¹**his mother took him a wife.** It was usual for the parents to seek a wife for their son; cf. 24:3f; 34:4.¹³⁷ **out of the land of Egypt.**

a. The idolatrous land of her birth and her upbringing.¹³⁸ **b.** From her own family, since she saw that he had grown apart from his father's family.¹³⁹ ²²**at that time. a.** When Isaac was born, so that Abimelech recognized the miracles wrought for Abraham.¹⁴⁰ **b.** When Sarah gave birth, the kings of the country were convinced that God would keep His oath that the land would one day be Abraham's.¹⁴¹ **Abimelech.** This is not the name of an individual but a royal title, in the same way as all the kings of Egypt were called Pharaoh. Similarly Phicol was not a name but the title of the commander of the forces.¹⁴² **Phicol.** A collective noun meaning all the army generals.¹⁴³ **Abimelech . . . spoke.** He was still in Gerar in the land of the Philistines [the proposal that follows therefore

ANTHOLOGY

79. His mother took him a wife out of the land of Egypt.

R. Isaac said: Throw a stick into the air and it will come back to its source [the earth].¹ Thus, because it is written, *She* [Sarah] *had a handmaid*, an Egyptian, *whose name was Hagar* (16:1), his mother *took him a wife out of the land of* Egypt.

Gen. R. 53, 15. T.S. 21, 104.

80. HIS MOTHER TOOK HIM A WIFE OUT OF THE LAND OF EGYPT. Ishmael had a wife brought to him from the plains of Moab, whose name was Efah. Three years later Abraham went to see his son Ishmael, first having sworn to Sarah that he would not alight from his camel wherever Ishmael dwelt. He arrived about midday, and found Ishmael's wife. On his enquiring where Ishmael was, she informed him that he had gone with his mother to fetch some dates from the wilderness. He then asked her, "Please give me some bread and water, as I am weary from my journey through the desert." She replied, "I have no bread or water." "When Ishmael returns," he rejoined, "tell him what has happened and say that an old man came from the land of Canaan to see you, and he said that the threshold of the house is rotten." When Ishmael returned she told him what had transpired, whereupon he sent her away.¹

Then his mother sent for a wife for him from her father's house [in Egypt], whose name was Patuma [Fatima?]. After three years Abraham went to see his son Ishmael again, having sworn to Sarah, as previously, that he would not alight from his camel wherever Ishmael dwelt. He arrived at midday and found Ishmael's wife. He asked her, "Where is Ishmael?" She replied, "He has gone with his mother to let the camels graze in the desert." "Give me a little bread and water," he requested, "as I am tired from the journey." When she did this Abraham prayed to the Almighty on his son's behalf, and Ishmael's house was filled with every good thing and every blessing. When Ishmael returned and his wife told him what had happened, he realized that his father's compassion was still extended toward him, as it says, *As a father has compassion on children* (Ps. 103:13).

PRE 30. T.S. 21, 104 note.

81. Abimelech and Phicol the captain of his host.

R. Judah said: Phicol was actually his name. R. Nehemiah said: [Phicol was not his name, but only descriptive of his function, for it means] the mouth (*peh*) to whom all (*kol*) his troops rendered obedience [lit., kissed. Another interpretation:] All these troops went

§ 79 ¹ The stick is wood of a tree which grew in the earth.
§ 80 ¹ He understood the hint.

Abraham, saying: "God is with thee in all that thou doest. ²³Now therefore swear unto me here by God that thou wilt not deal falsely with me, nor with my son, nor with my son's son; but according to the kind-

COMMENTARY

was made in the first place by a royal emissary]; hence it does not say that he *went* to Abraham.[144] **God is with thee. a.** As proved by your escape from Sodom (in that you did not choose to live there), your defeat of the kings, and the birth of Isaac in your old age.[145] Only for that reason do I

fear and desire a treaty with you, not because of your wealth or might.[146] **c.** Therefore He will approve any covenant which you make with us.[147] **d.** Abimelech hoped that his own country, the land of the Philistines, would be excluded from the scope of God's promise that Canaan would one day be Abraham's, as a reward for the kindness which he (Abimelech) had shown him and in virtue of the covenant which he now proposed.[148] **in all that thou doest.** You defeated four powerful kings; your wife was saved from two kings; and you were blessed with child in your old age.[149] ²³**here. a.** In your own home, where no charge of coercion can be made, as it might be elsewhere.[150] **b.** In this place, i.e., Beer-sheba.[151] **by God.** The gravest and most binding oath.[152] **deal falsely.** By repaying the kindness which I showed you with evil; such ingratitude constitutes falsity and treachery.[153] **with me, nor with my son, nor with my son's son.**

ANTHOLOGY

out to battle at his command (*peh*), the name having the same meaning as in the verse, *According to your word* (peh) *shall all* (kol) *my people be ruled* (41:40).

Gen. R. 54, 2. T.S. 21, 106-7.

82. ABIMELECH AND PHICOL THE CAPTAIN OF HIS HOST SAID TO ABRAHAM, etc. It is written, *When a man's ways please the Lord, He makes even his enemies to be at peace with him* (Prov. 16:7). This alludes to Abraham, who is called a "man" in the verse, *I am God . . . calling the man of My counsel from a far country* (Isa. 46:9, 11);[1] while *He makes even his enemies to be at peace with him* alludes to Abimelech.

Gen. R. 54, 1. T.S. 21, 105.

83. **God is with you in all that you do.**

The peoples of the world had said, "If he were righteous, would he not have begotten children? 'Tis incredible!" Therefore, when he did beget they said to him, *God is with you.* Again, they argued, "If he were righteous he would not heed his wife"; but when he was

bidden, *In all that Sarah says to you hearken to her voice* (verse 12), they admitted, *God is with you.* Further, "If he were righteous he would not have cast out his first-born son"; but when they saw how he [Ishmael] behaved, they agreed, *God is with you in all that you do.*

Another interpretation: Because the region of Sodom was desolate and travelers had ceased, so that his stores were now never diminished, [he said: "Why should I no more practise hospitality?" Therefore he went and settled in Gerar.][1] Then [everyone exclaimed:] *God is with you in all that you do.*

Gen. R. 54, 2. T.S. 21, 108.

84. **Therefore swear to me.**

From this we learn that a man who adjures his neighbor does it in accordance with his intentions, not the intentions of the adjured.[1]

Midrash Habiur. T.S. 21, 110.

85. **That you will not deal falsely with me, nor with my son, nor with my son's son.**

R. Simeon b. Lakish said: Many texts are

---

§ 82 [1] The Rabbis applied this to Abraham.
§ 83 [1] The bracketed passage is added from Gen. R. 52, 3 (*supra*, chap. 20, par. 3).
§ 84 [1] Its interpretation and length of validity are as meant by the person imposing the oath, and not dependent on the person taking it, and therefore cannot be nullified by the latter. The comment is based on the phrase "*to me.*"

ness that I have done unto thee,
thou shalt do unto me, and to the
land wherein thou hast sojourned."

COMMENTARY

a. Therefore I want you to swear, because I know that your children and grandchildren too will respect your oath.[154] **b.** I.e., that you will not wrest the country from me or from my son or grandson. But he could not demand more, since God had promised that the fourth generation would conquer the country (15:16).[155] **my son. a.** Heb. *nin*, which means the son who will rule and guide his kingdom after him.[156] **b.** *Nin* is used as in Ps. 72:17: *May his name be continued* (yinon) *as long as the sun*: a son is the continuation of his father's light.[157] **kindness. a.** Abraham had been well-treated by him: his only cause for complaint was in fact the theft of the wells—of which Abimelech protested his ignorance.[158] **b.** His gifts and permission to dwell in the country.[159] **c.** Heb. *hesed*; this applies to a pure kindness, which is not in return for benefits received or expected.[160] **do unto me. a.** Show me the kindness to swear on behalf of your children.[161] **b.** When the country is yours do not expel my children.[162] **the land. a.** I.e., its inhabitants.[163] **b.** Literally. Abimelech sought a double promise: one, that he would not expel his children; and two, that he would not destroy the crops of the land.[164]

ANTHOLOGY

[apparently] fit to be burned [as superfluous], yet are vital parts of the Torah. [E.g.,] *The Avvim, that dwelt in villages as far as Gaza, [the Caphtorim, that came forth out of Caphtor, destroyed them, and dwelt in their stead]* (Deut. 2:23). Now, how does this concern us? Because Abimelech adjured Abraham *that you will not deal falsely with me, nor with my son, nor with my son's son*, the Holy One, blessed is He, decreed: Let the Caphtorim expel the Avvim, who are Philistines, that the Israelites may seize their country from the Caphtorim.[1]

Hul. 60b. T.S. 21, 113.

86. THAT YOU WILL NOT DEAL FALSELY WITH ME, NOR WITH MY SON, NOR WITH MY SON'S SON. So far a father's compassion for his son extends.[1] R. Abba b. Kahana said: So far does the partnership of brothers extend.[2]

R. Jose b. R. Hanina commented on the text, *But mine enemies are strong in health* (Ps. 38:20): the time that was given to Abraham for seven generations was given to Abimelech for three generations.[3]

When Israel left Egypt, *God led them not by the way of the land of the Philistines* (Exod. 13:17): why was this? Because his [Abimelech's] grandson was still alive.

Gen. R. 54, 2. T.S. 21, 114.

87. **According to the kindness which I have shown you.**

What kindness did he show him? His offer, *Behold, my land is before you; dwell where it pleases you* (20:15). Yet even so he had not accepted it.[1]

Gen. R. 54, 2. T.S. 21, 115.

§ 85 [1] Thus, only because the Caphtorim had conquered the Avvim was it possible for Israel to conquer it. This apparently superfluous historical note in the Bible is thus seen as a vital element in the conquest of Eretz Israel. The ethical spirit of the passage is worthy of note: Not even the Divine promise that the land would one day belong to the people of Israel could override Abraham's oath made centuries earlier. How different from the light-hearted attitude towards treaties that characterizes so much of history!

§ 86 [1] He does not care what will happen to his descendants after the third generation.
[2] When brothers inherit an estate, it remains in joint partnership for three generations. After that they can insist on a division.
[3] Seven generations (including his own) passed before his descendants entered Eretz Israel, viz.: Abraham, Isaac, Jacob, Levi, Kohath, Amram, and Moses. Yet that whole period was covered by Abimelech in only three generations, as this oath implies: His land was to be inviolate during the lifetimes of himself, his son, and his grandson.

§ 87 [1] See verse 32, which shows that Abraham was not living there. The observation, however, is pointless. A *var. lec.* omits "yet even so," which allows of an entirely different interpretation: What kindness had he shown him? In offering him the hospitality of his country and bearing no malice against him (reading לֹא קִבֵּל instead of לֹא קִבֵּל—in unvocalized Hebrew the two are the same, the subject being Abimelech, not Abraham),

²⁴And Abraham said: "I will swear." ²⁵And Abraham reproved Abimelech because of the well of water, which Abimelech's servants had violently taken away. ²⁶And Abimelech said:

COMMENTARY

²⁴**I will swear. a.** As you request; but your claim to kindness is unjustified, for your servants stole my well.[165] **b.** And you too must give a reciprocal oath.[166] **c.** "I" is emphatic: only I can swear, but I cannot bind my descendants.[167] ²⁵**reproved. a.** For tolerating dishonest servants and enjoying the fruits of their dishonesty.[168] **b.** While agreeing to the suggested alliance, Abraham stated a grievance; cf. Lev. 19:17, *You shall not hate your brother in your heart; you shall surely reprove your neighbor.*[169] **taken away. a.** "From him" is understood.[170] **b.** "From him" is omitted, because his reproof was not in respect of his personal loss

ANTHOLOGY

88. Now therefore swear to me . . . and Abraham said: "I will swear."

Abimelech had an image on his robe, and he requested Abraham to swear by his god on the robe.[1] Abraham, however, replied, *I will swear,* i.e., I will swear by Him who will one day proclaim, *I am the Lord thy God* (Exod. 20:2).

Midrash.[2] T.S. 21, 116.

89. I WILL SWEAR. It should have said, *And Abraham swore?* It is phrased this way in order to teach that when a man engages to swear it is as though he has already sworn, even if he has not. Further, from this we learn that a Jew's word is as binding as an oath.

Midrash Habiur. T.S. 21, 117.

90. Abraham reproved Abimelech.

R. Jose b. R. Hanina said: Reproof leads to love, as it says, *Reprove a wise man, and he will love you* (Prov. 9:8). That agrees with another dictum of his, viz., Love without reproof is not love. Resh Lakish said: Reproof leads to peace; therefore *Abraham reproved Abimelech.* That is in agreement with his general view, which is: Peace without reproof is not peace.

Reproof leads to peace: you find this in the case of Abraham. For after *Abraham reproved Abimelech* we read that *they two made a covenant* (verse 27).

Gen. R. 54, 3; Sifre D'barim 2.
T.S. 21, 118 and note.

91. Because of the well of water which Abimelech's servants had taken in robbery (gazlu).

Who is a robber (*gazlan*)?[1] R. Eleazar, son of Kappara, said: One who robs openly, as in the text, *They robbed all that came along that way by them* (Judg. 9:25): just as a way is public, so is a robber one who acts publicly. R. Simeon b. Johai cited this text: *And you have brought that which was taken in robbery and the lame* (Mal. 1:13): just as lameness is a patent blemish, so is a robber one who steals openly. R. Jose, in R. Abbahu's name; R. Hezekiah quoting R. Abbahu in the name of R. Simeon b. Lakish, said: He who steals in the presence of nine people is a thief (*ganab*); in the presence of ten, is a robber (*gazlan*). R. Tanhuma, quoting R. Huna, said: Only he who snatches from the victim's hand is a robber, as it says, *He snatched* (vayyigzol—root, *gazal*)

---

in spite of the suffering which Abraham had caused him through Sarah. If we retain the present reading the observation has no bearing on the text, but simply points out that Abraham did not take advantage of the offer—perhaps to emphasize that he did not wish to be beholden to any man, as in 14:22-3.

§ 88   ¹ This apparently is the interpretation of *"swear to me."*

      ² Quoted as a Midrash in Tol'doth Yitschak, by Isaac Caro, end of Vayyera. He adds: That is what Abimelech meant when he said, *"Neither yet heard I of it, but today"*—i.e., I know not and have never heard of your God until today.

§ 91   ¹ A man who steals may be either a *ganab* (thief) or a *gazlan* (robber). There is a difference in law: the former, when apprehended, must repay twofold (Exod. 22:3); the latter adds only a fifth (Lev. 5:23-4). Hence the question, When is one a *gazlan*?

"I know not who hath done this thing; neither didst thou tell me, neither yet heard I of it, but to-day." [27] And Abraham took sheep and oxen, and gave them unto Abimelech; and they two made a covenant. [28] And Abraham set seven ewe-lambs of the

COMMENTARY

but dishonesty.[171] [26] **I know not.** Even now; I do not suspect anyone, for I would not harbor such in my court.[172] **I know not who hath done this thing; neither didst thou tell me, neither yet heard I of it.** I did not instruct anyone to do this; when it happened you did not tell me, so that I could punish the offender; nor did I hear it from others.[173] **neither didst thou tell me. a.** Hence you have only yourself to blame.[174] **b.** Had you informed me I would have made investigations to find the guilty party.[175] **neither yet heard I of**

it. Of this alleged theft.[176] [27] **Abraham took sheep and oxen. a.** To give to Abimelech in exchange for the well, thus removing every vestige of a claim that the latter might have.[177] **b.** As payment for the entire field in which the well was situated, because he desired to plant it with trees.[178] **c.** Abraham had received gifts from Abimelech in connection with the incident of Sarah. Now that he was about to make a treaty with him, he wished to be on a level of absolute equality, under no obligation to him whatsoever. Therefore he made him the present gifts in return for those he had received.[179] **sheep and oxen.** An exchange of gifts was customary when making a treaty.[180] **they two made a covenant. a.** By means of these gifts and the oath (verse 31) they made a covenant binding on themselves and their descendants.[181] **b.** Of friendship, in addition to the solemn non-aggression pact which they ratified by the oath.[182] [28] **seven ewe-lambs. a.** These are the sheep mentioned in the preceding verse.[183] **b.** He took seven of the sheep mentioned before.[184] **c.** In addition to the sheep mentioned above. The former were a gift; these seven were in exchange for the well.[185] **seven.** (Heb. *sheba*). **a.** Because *sheba* corresponds to *sh'buah*, oath.[186] **b.** Seven was a sacred number.[187]

ANTHOLOGY

the spear out of the Egyptian's hand (2 Sam. 23:21).

Gen. R. 54, 3. T.S. 21, 119.

92. Abimelech said: "I know not who has done this thing," etc.

Neither did you tell me—by an angel.[1] [Another interpretation:] *Who has done*—hitherto; *I know not*—who is doing this thing now; *neither did you tell me*—in the past; *neither yet heard I of it*—from others; *but to-day*—from you.

Gen. R. 54, 2; MhG. T.S. 21, 120-1.

93. Abraham took sheep and oxen, and gave them to Abimelech.

Why did he not give him slaves and bondmaids, as he [Abimelech] had given him? To teach that a Jew may not allow circumcised slaves or bondmaids who have undergone ritual

immersion,[1] thereby accepting the precepts of Judaism, to pass from his into a Gentile's possession.

Midrash Habiur. T.S. 21, 122.

94. They two made a covenant.

A man should take good care not to make a partnership with a Gentile, nor make a covenant with him. For thus we find that our father Abraham made a partnership, of which the upshot was that he made a covenant with him.

SER 7. T.S. 21, 123.

95. Abraham set seven ewe-lams of the flock, etc.

The Holy One, blessed is He, upbraided him: "You gave him seven lambs without My consent; as you live, I will delay the rejoicing of your descendants seven generations.[1] You gave

§ 92   [1] Or: A messenger.
§ 93   [1] The act whereby a non-Jewess accepts Judaism.
§ 95   [1] See par. 86. They will have to wait seven generations before experiencing the joy of the Promised Land.

flock by themselves. ²⁹And Abimelech said unto Abraham: "What mean these seven ewe-lambs which thou hast set by themselves?" ³⁰And he said: "Verily, these seven ewe-lambs shalt thou take of my hand, that it may be a witness unto me,

COMMENTARY

²⁹**by themselves.** You have already given them to me with the oxen: why do you now place them apart?[188] ³⁰**take of my hand.** In token of the ratification of my rights. This was similar to the ancient practice of removing one's shoe and giving it to the other contracting party (cf. Ruth 4:7).[189] **it. a.** The gift of the sheep.[190] **b.** The covenant. This will be evidence that you admit that I dug the well.[191] **c.** The placing of the sheep apart.[192]

ANTHOLOGY

him seven lambs without My consent; by your life, corresponding to this number they will slay seven righteous of your descendants, viz., Samson, Hofni, Phinehas, Saul and his three sons.[2] You gave him seven lambs: accordingly, they will destroy your descendants' seven Sanctuaries, viz., the Tent of Meeting, the Sanctuaries at Gilgal, Nob, Gibeon, Shiloh, and the two eternal Temples.[3] You gave him seven lambs: My Ark will spend seven months in Philistine country."[4]

Gen. R. 54, 5.   T.S. 21, 124.

96. SEVEN EWE-LAMBS. The three Patriarchs made covenants. Abraham made a covenant with Abimelech, and gave him seven ewe-lambs in ratification. The latter placed these at the entrance to Jerusalem, so that his [Abraham's] descendants might not possess the city of the Jebus [Jerusalem] nor settle in it until David. After these seven lambs died they placed seven iron lambs, which were idolatrous images, at the entrance to Jerusalem; and when the Israelites came to take possession of the city of the Jebusite they showed them Abraham's covenant.

Therefore when David came to attack the city he declared, *"Whosoever will take away these lame and blind[1] shall be the chief."*

They were removed by Joab the son of Zeruiah; and then he captured Jerusalem from the Jebusite.

Or Haafelah.   T.S. 21, 126.

97. **That it may be a witness.**

Our Rabbis said: Abraham's shepherds argued with Abimelech's shepherds, each claiming the well as their own. Said Abraham's shepherds to them: "It belongs to him for whom the water will rise to give drink to his flocks." When the water saw Abraham's flocks it immediately welled up. Said the Holy One, blessed is He, to him: "You are an augury that a well will come up for your children." Thus it is written, *Spring up, O well—sing ye unto it* (Num. 21:17). R. Isaac b. Hakorach said: In our own text proof is not lacking: it does not say, because it was a witness, but, *that it will be[1] a witness for me.*

Gen. R. 54, 5.   T.S. 21, 125.

98. THAT IT MAY BE A WITNESS. This teaches that Abraham set apart seven lambs [and gave them to Abimelech], corresponding to the Seven Precepts which the sons of Noah were commanded,[1] and which were in force at that time. He [Abimelech] placed them apart, so that

---

² See Judg. 16:30; 1 Sam. 4:10-11; *ibid.* 31:6.
³ Some of these were destroyed; others simply fell into disuse.
⁴ A covenant between a true believer and a heathen can only be producive of evil results (Mah.).
§ 96   ¹ Now referred to the iron sheep. This verse is 1 Chron. 11:6, but with *take . . . blind* substituted on the basis of 2 Sam. 5:6, 8.
§ 97   ¹ In the distant future. The verb may be rendered either "may" or "will."
§ 98   ¹ To refrain from: 1. Social injustice (or, disobedience to authority). 2. Blasphemy. 3. Idolatry. 4. Adultery. 5. Murder. 6. Robbery. 7. Eating a limb cut from a living animal. This is the list given in Vol. I, chap. 2, par. 134, *q.v.* and note *ad loc.* There are slight variations in pars. 135 and 136.

that I have digged this well."
³¹Wherefore that place was called
Beer-sheba; because there they
swore both of them. ³²So they made
a covenant at Beer-sheba; and Abimelech rose up, and Phicol the
captain of his host, and they returned into the land of the Philistines. ³³And Abraham planted a
tamarisk-tree in Beer-sheba, and

COMMENTARY

³¹**Wherefore.** In commemoration of the oath and
the agreement on the ownership of the well.¹⁹³ **that
place. a.** The entire locality was thus called, even

though the name strictly speaking applied only to
the well.¹⁹⁴ **b.** Only that place was so named at
that time, but the town received that name only
in the days of Isaac.¹⁹⁵ **Beer-sheba.** The name
has a double significance: the well of the
seven (*sheba*—lambs), and the well of the oath
(*sh'buah*).¹⁹⁶ ³²**they made a covenant. a.** This
summarizes the foregoing.¹⁹⁷ **b.** After swearing
they repeated the covenant, to strengthen it.¹⁹⁸
Abimelech rose up. But Abraham remained there
a few days before returning to his home in Gerar.¹⁹⁹
**they returned into the land of the Philistines.
a.** They were actually there all the time. It means
that they returned from Beer-sheba to Gerar, the
capital.²⁰⁰ **b.** They returned from Beer-sheba, which
was *not* in the land of the Philistines.²⁰¹ **c.** By this
covenant Beer-sheba had passed out of the territory
of the Philistines, where Abraham still lived; hence
"returned". [These interpretations refer "they" to
Abraham and Abimelech, not to Abimelech and
Phicol.—Ed.]²⁰² **d.** They did not return immediately to Gerar but traveled through the country,
informing people of the oath.²⁰³ ³³**planted a
tamarisk-tree** (*eshel*). **a.** To witness that the

ANTHOLOGY

they should be a token, like the heap and
pillar which Jacob set up for Laban.² Whenever
one died Abimelech replaced it with another,
and so on for all time, to serve as a witness of
the covenant.

MhG. T.S. 21, 127.

99. **Abimelech rose up, and Phicol the
captain of his host.**

They did indeed rise [spiritually] in making
peace with the righteous man. *And they returned to the land of the Philistines* in peace.

Sechel Tob. T.S. 21, 128.

100. **Abraham planted an eshel (AJV: tamarisk-tree) in Beer-sheba.**

R. Judah said: *Eshel* is an orchard, the word
denoting, *Sh'al* (request) whatever you desire:
figs, grapes, or pomegranates. R. Nehemiah interpreted: *Eshel* is an inn, the word denoting,

Sh'al (request) whatever you wish: bread (or,
pressed dates), meat, wine or eggs. [How can
you speak of planting in connection with an
inn? Even as in the verse, *He shall* plant the
tents *of his palace between the seas and the
beauteous holy mountain* (Dan. 11:45).]¹ R.
Azariah, quoting R. Judah, interpreted: *Eshel*
is a court of law, as in the verse, *Now Saul was
sitting in Gibeah, under the* eshel (AJV: *tamarisk-tree*) *in Ramah* (1 Sam. 22:6).² Now, by
R. Nehemiah's interpretation that *eshel* is an
inn, Abraham would entertain travelers, and
after they had eaten and drunk he would bid
them, "Now render thanks." When they asked
him what to say he would reply, "Blessed is
the Eternal God, of whose bounty we have
eaten." Hence the text continues, *and called
there on the name of the Lord, the Eternal God.*³

Thus Scripture writes, *Who* [came] *from the
east* [and] *aroused* [the nations] (Isa. 41:2)?
The idolatrous nations slumbered [in their er-

---

² See 31:45 et seqq.

§ 100   ¹ "Plant" is just as suitable for an inn as for a tent. The bracketed passage is added from Sot. 10a. Or Haafelah reads: Some maintain that he made a house of study; read not *eshel* but *sh'al*, ask [knowledge and
wisdom].

² It is assumed that he sat there to render judgments.

³ Sot. 10a adds: Read not *vayyikra*, and called, but *vayyakri*, and inspired [men] to call there, etc.

called there on the name of the
Lord, the Everlasting God. [34]And
Abraham sojourned in the land of
the Philistines many days.

COMMENTARY

well was undisputably his.[204] **b.** For its shade.[205]
c. *Eshel* denotes a house with its surrounding gardens
and trees—he erected these for the benefit of travelers.[206] **d.** As comm. *c*: but its purpose was spiritual
[the wayfarers who would enjoy his hospitality
would at the same time be brought to the understanding of God. See Anthology par. 100—Ed.];
hence the verse states that he *called there on the*
name of the Lord.[207] **called there on the name**
of the Lord, the Everlasting God. a. He prayed
there.[208] **b.** He taught that God is the Ruler and
Guide of the Universe.[209] **c.** He proclaimed the
existence of the One, Incomparable God.[210] **d.** He
taught that God was the "First Cause," the Creator
of a world which was not eternal but had been
created in time.[211] **e.** He gave thanks to the Almighty for bestowing on him such greatness that
kings made covenants with him.[212] [34]**sojourned.**
Possibly, *had* sojourned—he had sojourned many
days in the land of the Philistines before leaving it
for Beer-sheba.[213] **many days. a.** At least until
the Binding of Isaac thirty-eight years later.[214]
b. Having a covenant with Abimelech he feared
no one, whilst the land of the Philistines is generally
one of plenty.[215]

ANTHOLOGY

rors] and did not come under the wings of
the Shechinah;[4] who aroused them to come and
take shelter under the wings of the Shechinah?
Abraham, as it says, *Who* [came] *from the east*
[and] *aroused* [the nations]? Do not think
that he aroused them to this only. Charity
too slumbered, and Abraham awakened it. What
did he do? He built an inn with entrances on
every side and entertained travelers, as it says,
He planted an eshel *in Beer-sheba*. Now, R.
Azariah said: What does *eshel* mean? [It is an
abbreviation standing for] *achilah* (food),
sh'thiah, (drink) and *l'viyyah* (companionship). Hence Scripture continues, *He sum-*
moned charity to his feet.[5]

[After the Flood] Abraham asked Melchizedek,[6] "Through what merit were you privileged to leave the Ark?" "Through the merit of
the charity we performed there," he replied.
"But what charity could you perform there,"
he wondered; "did you have any poor? Surely,
only Noah and his sons were there: to whom
then could you show charity?" "To the animals,
beasts, and birds," he rejoined. "We slept not,
but spent the nights in giving them their food."
"Had these men not shown charity to the animals, beasts and birds, they would not have
left the ark," Abraham exclaimed, "and because
they were charitable to them they left it. How
much the more meritorious is charity to human
beings!" Thereupon *he planted an* eshel *in Beer-*
sheba, i.e., he provided food, drink, and companionship.

> Gen. R. 54, 6; Midrash T'hillim 110, 37.
> T.S. 21, 131. 133; Vol. II, chap. 9, par. 74 note.

101. **Many days.**

More than in Hebron: there he spent twenty-
five years; here he stayed twenty-six years.

> Seder Olam 1. T.S. 21, 137.

---

[4] I.e., did not acknowledge the true God.
[5] AJV: *Who hath raised up one from the east, at whose steps victory attendeth?*
[6] Whom the Rabbis identified with Shem, the son of Noah; Vol. II, chap. 14, par. 49.

GENESIS

CHAPTER XXII

¹And it came to pass after these

COMMENTARY

¹**after these things. a.** After Abraham's treaty with Abimelech, of which God disapproved, for Abraham did wrong in agreeing to leave the land in the latter's possession, when it had been promised to his descendants. God expressed His displeasure by subjecting him to a grievous and most distressing trial.¹ **b.** Enumerated above: after everything that had happened since his circumcision.² **c.** After all the favors which God had shown him, thereby raising him to the great heights to which he attained. He now put him to a trial which would elevate him and his children still higher.³ **d.** After all that he had suffered until he was blessed with a son in his old age, and after that son had grown up (see 21:34: *And Abraham sojourned in the land of the Philistines many days*).⁴ **e.** After the preceding events, which included Ishmael's expulsion. Before that Isaac could not be designated his only

ANTHOLOGY

1. After these things.

After what things? Said R. Johanan, quoting R. Jose b. Zimra: After Satan's words.¹ For it is written earlier, *The child grew, and was weaned. And Abraham made a great feast on the day that Isaac was weaned* (21:8). Satan said to the Holy one, blessed is He: "Master of the world: Thou didst graciously give a son, the fruit of the womb, to this old man at the age of one hundred. Yet of the whole feast which he made he had not one turtle-dove or one pigeon to offer to Thee." He answered: "Surely he made it all for his son's sake: if I bade him, Sacrifice your son, he would do it without hesitation." There and then *God did prove Abraham.*

Another interpretation: After the misgivings of that time.² Who had these misgivings? Abraham. Said he: "I was happy and made all others happy,³ yet did not set aside a single bullock or ram for the Holy One, blessed is He." But God set his mind at rest: "Even if told to offer up your son, you would not refuse."⁴

This may be compared to a king who told a poor friend, "I must make you rich." He gave him money to engage in trade. Later, when he entered the palace, the palace-officials complained, "What right has this man to enter?" Said the king, "Because he is my faithful friend." "Then bid him return your money," they urged. "Give me back what I gave you," the king demanded. He did not withhold it, and the palace-officials were covered with shame. The king then swore to increase his wealth.

Another interpretation: Who pondered? Isaac. For he was arguing with Ishmael, who maintained: "I am older than you and I will inherit the world,⁵ since I am my father's first-born, who always inherits a double portion." Isaac retorted: "Tell me, what has the Almighty from you?" "I will tell you," Ishmael rejoined. "Had I done nothing at all but willingly undergone circumcision at the age of thirteen, when I could have refused, 'twere enough." Said Isaac to him: "Then all that you lent to the Almighty were three drops of blood. But I know that if the Holy One, blessed is He, desired my death as a sacrifice, and bade my father offer me up, though I am now thirty-seven years old,⁶ I would not hinder him."

§ 1   ¹ *D'barim* means both things and words.
    ² A play on words: *ahar* (after) is now connected with *hirhur* (misgiving, after-thought).
    ³ At the feast in honor of Isaac's weaning.
    ⁴ The text reads: On condition that you were told, etc. "On condition" is rather difficult. Possibly it means, I know that. Or: I forgive you, on condition (i.e., provided) that, etc.
    ⁵ Everything that was promised to Abraham.
    ⁶ Sarah was ninety when she gave birth to Isaac, and one hundred and twenty-seven at her death. The Rabbis held that she died from shock on hearing that Abraham had taken Isaac to be sacrificed.

things, that God did prove Abraham,

COMMENTARY

son.[5] **f.** After he had planted an *eshel* (AJV: tamarisk-tree) in Beer-sheba (21:33) for wayfarers. If he was so solicitous for strangers, how much the more for his own son! This then was the very time

for testing him.[6] **g.** After Abraham called on the name of the Lord and proclaimed Him the God of the Universe (21:33).[7] **did prove. a.** A trial of a man's faith is a test from the standpoint of the person tested, but not from that of God, who imposes the test (He knows the result in advance). The purpose of this test, as of all other tests, was to make Abraham's potentialities of sacrifice actual,

ANTHOLOGY

Said the Holy One, blessed is He, to the angels: "This is the hour." Straightway He put Abraham to the test.[7]

> Sanh. 89b; Gen. R. 55, 4; Tan. Y. Vayyera 42; Midrash Abakir quoted in Yalkut Shimoni. T.S. 22, 1-4 and 3 note.

2. AFTER THESE THINGS. When Abraham made a covenant with Abimelech, the angels assembled before God and exclaimed: "Master of all worlds! The one man whom Thou didst choose out of the seventy nations has made a covenant with the nations of the world!" He replied: "I gave him an only son at the age of a hundred, and said to him, *For in Isaac shall seed be called to you* (21:12). I will tell him to offer him up as a burnt-offering. If he obeys, I will know [that this covenant has not impaired his loyalty to Me]; if not, then you speak truly." This we learn from our text, *After these things God tested Abraham,* i.e., after his covenant with Abimelech God tried him. . . . *And He said: "Take now your son,"* etc. . . . *And Abraham stretched out his hand, and took the knife to slay his son* (vss. 2, 10). Yet in spite of that they persecuted and oppressed his children over three hundred years, as a punishment for his having made a covenant with the peoples of the world.[1]

> SER 7. T.S. 22, 6.

3. God tried (*nissah*).

R. Jose ha-Galilee said: It means that He raised him up, like a ship's ensign which flies

aloft. R. Akiba said: He tried him with an unequivocal trial, lest people say that He so dazed and confused him that he knew not what he was doing.[1]

It is written, *Thou hast given* nes (AJV: *a banner) to them that fear Thee,* lehith-noses *(that it may be displayed) for the sake of the truth. Selah* (Ps. 60:6). This means, elevation after elevation, promotion after promotion, in order to make them great and elevate them like a ship's ensign.[2] Now, why did He do all this? *For the sake of the truth,* in order to show that God's justice is true. For should anyone say to you, "God is capricious and arbitrary, enriching, impoverishing, and setting up kings at will—when He desired, He made Abraham a king,[3] and when He desired, He gave him wealth": you can answer him, "Could you do what our father Abraham did?" If he asks, "What did he do?" you may answer: "Abraham was a hundred years old when a son was born to him. After all the anguish of such long childlessness he was bidden, *Take now your son, your only son . . . Isaac . . . and offer him there for a burnt-offering;* yet he did not withhold him."

> Gen. R. 55, 1. 6. T.S. 22, 10. 12.

4. God tried Abraham.

The Lord tries the righteous (Ps. 11:5). R. Jonathan said: A potter does not examine defective utensils, because at a single blow they break. Which does he examine? Only sound ones, which will not break even under many

---

[7] Lit., He sprang upon Abraham.
§ 2 [1] Cf. chap. 21, par. 95.
§ 3 [1] God postponed the sacrifice for a three days' journey, during which time Abraham could reflect and realize clearly what he was doing.
[2] *Nes* and *nissayon* are connected here, in the sense of elevation, like a *nes* (banner, ensign) which flies high above the ship. The text is rendered: God raised Abraham [through Isaac's sacrifice].
[3] Cf. chap. 23, par. 24.

COMMENTARY

that he might be rewarded for deed and not merely for intention.[8] **b.** The purpose was to show to the world, not to God, his steadfast faith in, his great love for and eagerness to serve the Almighty. Thus verse 12, *for now I know that you are a God-fearing man*, really means, now I have made it known.[9] **c.** The test lay in the intentional vagueness of God's command: "take him up for a burnt-offering" (the literal rendering) might mean either, sacrifice *him* as such, or take him up there in order that *he*

(Isaac) should sacrifice or witness the sacrifice of a burnt-offering.[10] **d.** Abraham was tested ten times (Aboth 5:4), but this is the only instance so described. The others were not intended primarily as tests, whereas this was. Again, the others he actually performed, whereas here there was never any intention that he perform.[11] **e.** God's foreknowledge of how man will choose, does not *compel* man, who acts of his free choice.[12] **f.** The purpose was to strengthen Abraham himself in his fear of

ANTHOLOGY

blows. Similarly, the Holy One, blessed is He, does not try the wicked but only the righteous. R. Jose b. R. Hanina said: The more one beats fine flax the better it is and the more it glistens; but inferior flax splits at a single blow.

Gen. 55, 2.　T.S. 22, 11 note.

5. **GOD TRIED ABRAHAM.** Thou[1] *gavest trial to those that fear Thee* (Ps. 60:6). Come and see the difference between the early generations and the later ones. The early generations were tried by the Holy One, blessed is He, Himself, as it says, *God tried Abraham.* Similarly we read of the Generation of the Wilderness, *That I may try them, whether they will walk in My law, or not* (Exod. 16:4). In the same way we read, *That He might afflict you, and that He might try you* (Deut. 8:16). But the later generations were tried through the nations, as it says, *Now these are* the nations *which the Lord left, to try Israel by them* (Judg. 3:1).

Tan. Y. Vayyera 55.　T.S. 22, 14.

6. **GOD TRIED ABRAHAM.** Now that we celebrate New Year for two days, on the first day the Pentateuchal Reading is *The Lord remembered Sarah* (21:1ff.), and on the second day it is *God tried Abraham.* The *Haftorah* (the

Reading from the Prophets) is, *Is Ephraim a darling son to Me* (Jer. 31:20ff.)?[1]

Meg. 31a.　T.S. 22, 15.

7. **GOD TRIED ABRAHAM.** He was tried with ten trials, for the sake of the Ten Commandments,[1] the Ten Plagues which befell their enemies, and the ten miracles in the Temple.[2] The Shechinah (Divine Presence) is found in the midst of ten persons, as it says, *God stands in the congregation of God* (Ps. 82:1).[3] We are forgiven our sins on the tenth of Tishre, and our ancestors were redeemed in the tenth month,[4] which is Tebeth. The priests bathe in ten lavers. *The tenth shall be holy to the Lord* (Lev. 27:32). Asher (Jacob's tenth son) rejoiced: "I will be the High Priest, since I am the tenth." Said the Holy One, blessed is He, to him: "I will start counting not from the eldest but from the youngest, which will make Levi the tenth."

Yelamdenu.　T. S. 22, 16.

8. **GOD TRIED ABRAHAM.** The text demands an explanation. Surely, it should have said that God tried *Isaac* rather than Abraham since Isaac was thirty-seven years old,[1] and his father could not be punished on his account. Had he declared,

§ 5　　[1] In the present passage "Thou" is emphasized.
§ 6　　[1] Cf. chap. 21, par. 4.
§ 7　　[1] I.e., that his descendants might be deemed worthy to receive them.
　　　　[2] See Aboth 5:5.
　　　　[3] "Congregation" is defined as an assembly of ten persons.
　　　　[4] In the days of Esther. In this month she became queen (Esther 2:16); her accession laid the foundation for the salvation of the Jews.
§ 8　　[1] See par. 1, n. 6.

and said unto him: "Abraham"; and he said: "Here am I." ²And He said: "Take now thy son, thine

COMMENTARY

God and desire to serve.[13] **said.** In a vision at night, since verse 3 tells that Abraham rose early in the morning.[14] **Abraham. a.** This call, coming before the command, was to make Abraham understand that His communication was to be of unusual gravity.[15] **b.** It was not repeated, as subsequently when the angel addressed him (verse 11): the repe-

tition denotes great love; but also such imperious urgency that it could have thrown him into such confusion and panic that it might be claimed that his mind was not clear when he carried out His command.[16] **Here am I.** Ready to obey, whatever the order.[17] ²**Take now** (Heb. *na*). **a.** *Na* may mean either now or please: since He had promised that his seed would grow through Isaac (21:12), He could not now *order* him to slay Isaac, but could plead with him, as it were.[18] **b.** Immediately. This was part of the test, that he should not pray for time.[19] **c.** The tone of *na* is so mild that he might have been encouraged or emboldened to beg God to rescind the command, yet he did not.[20] **thy son, thine only son,** etc. The repetition indicates the

ANTHOLOGY

"I refuse to be sacrificed," his father would not have been held responsible. But Scripture says, *God tried Abraham,* because Abraham had to be perfected in character through rigorous justice.[2] Further, although we have observed that the Bible writes, *God tested Abraham,* not Isaac, yet he too is included in this text in a veiled manner, for it says, *God tried* eth[3] *Abraham, eth* is an extension, in the present instance to include Isaac.

> Zohar 1, 119b. T.S. 22, 1 note.

9. Here am I.

R. Joshua b. Karha said: On two occasions Moses compared himself to Abraham, and God chided him, *Glorify yourself not in the presence of the king, and stand not in the place of great men* (Prov. 25:6). Abraham said, *"Here am I"* —here am I, ready for priesthood, here am I, ready for kingship; and he attained to both priesthood and kingship. The priesthood: *The Lord has sworn, and will not repent: you are a priest for ever after the manner of Melchizedek* (Ps. 110:4); kingship: *You are a mighty prince among us* (23:6). Moses too said, *"Here am I"* (Exod. 3:4)—here am I, ready for priesthood, here am I, ready for kingship. To

this God answered, *Approach not* halom (*hither—ibid.* 5): "approaching" refers to nought else but priesthood, as in the text, *And the common man that* approaches *shall be put to death* (Num. 1:51); similarly, *halom* alludes to kingship, as in the text, *Thou hast brought me* halom[1] (*thus far—*2 Sam. 7:18).

> Gen. R. 55, 6. T.S. 22, 17.

10. HERE AM I. This word implies humility and piety, for the humility of the pious always expresses itself in this way.[1]

> Tan. Vayyera 22. T.S. 22, 18.

11. Take, I pray you.

With words, not force.

How could Abraham, an old man, take him by force? Would you say because Isaac was still under his authority—is that then correct?[1] Only it has the same sense as in the text, *Take Aaron and Eleazar his son* (Num. 20:25), which means, Draw them by your words and lead them to the will of God; so here too it means the same.

> Sechel Tob; Zohar 1, 119b. T.S. 22, 20 and note.

---

[2] Although mercy is the highest quality, sometimes one must be capable of justice untempered by mercy, even if it seems cruel. Abraham's test involved his absolute obedience to God even at the cost of completely abandoning compassion.

[3] "*Eth*" is the acc. particle. But Rabbinic exegesis also interpreted it as an amplifying particle, which extends the statement.

§ 9 [1] Spoken by David in reference to the throne.

§ 10 [1] In instant readiness to obey God's command.

§ 11 [1] Surely not—he was now thirty-seven years old.

only son, whom thou lovest, even Isaac, and get thee into the land of Moriah; and offer him there for a

COMMENTARY

intense strain that was being placed upon Abraham's faith, and the greatness of the sacrifice demanded.[21] **thine only son.** "Only," because he was the son of the mistress, and only through him would Abraham's descendants be counted.[22] **the land of Moriah. a.** The land where men worship God. This derives Moriah from *yirah*, fear, worship.[23] **b.** Jerusalem and its adjacent territory. Hence the mountain is called Mount Moriah. Others reverse it, holding that the territory received its name from the mountain.[24] **c.** Moriah=Amorite, with the elision of the *alef*, which is not unusual.[25] **d.** The land of myrrh, so called because myrrh grew there in great profusion.[26] **offer him** (lit., take him up) **there for**

ANTHOLOGY

12. Take, I pray you, your son.

R. Simeon b. Abba said: "I pray you" signifies that He implored him. This may be compared to a human king who waged many victorious wars with the aid of a great general. Later, facing a battle, he begged him: "I entreat you, help me to win this one too, lest it be said that my earlier victories meant nothing."[1] Similarly, the Holy One, blessed is He, said to Abraham, "I tried you with many trials and you acquitted yourself with honor. Now bear this trial successfully for My sake, lest it be said that the earlier trials meant nothing."

Sanh. 89b. T.S. 22, 21.

13. TAKE, I PRAY YOU, YOUR SON. In allusion to this Scripture writes, *My covenant will I not profane, nor alter that which is gone out of My lips* (Ps. 89:35). R. Aha interpreted: *I will not profane My covenant* which I made with Abraham when I said to him, *In Isaac shall seed be called to you* (21:12). *Nor alter that which is gone out of My lips:* When He bade him, *Take now, I pray you, your son,* without hesitation *Abraham built the altar there, and . . . stretched out his hand . . . to slay his son.* But the angel cried out to him, *Lay not your hand upon the lad.* Said Abraham to Him: "Didst Thou not tell me, *Take, I pray you, your son?*" "Did I then order you to slay him?" He replied. That is the point of, *I will not profane My covenant, nor alter that which is gone out of My lips:* it was never My intention to order Abraham to slay his son, even though I told him, *Take, I pray you, your son.* Hence it says, *I will not profane My covenant.*[1]

Scripture writes, *Which I commanded not* (Jer. 19:5)—i.e., I did not order Abraham to slay his son, but on the contrary I told him, *Lay not your hand upon the lad.* The purpose of the trial was to show how Abraham did His will. For the nations of the world said, "Why does the Holy One, blessed is He, love Abraham so much?" Therefore He bade him, *Take, I pray you, your son.* But I certainly *commanded not* Abraham to slay his son.

Tan. Y. Vayyera 40, B'hukothai 7. T.S. 22, 22-3.

14. TAKE, I PRAY YOU, YOUR SON. In allusion to this Scripture writes, *He goes on his way weeping, bearing the measure of seed* (Ps. 126:6). *He goes on his way,* viz., Abraham, when God tried him by bidding him, *Take, I pray you, your son;* in his heart he wept, yet with his mouth he said, "Here am I." *He goes on his way weeping:* when was that? When he was *bearing the measure of seed,* seed alluding to Isaac, as it says, *In Isaac shall seed be called to you.*[1]

Tan. Y. Vayyera 39. T.S. 22, 24 note.

15. TAKE, I PRAY YOU, YOUR SON. *There is one that is alone, and he has not a second; yea, he has neither son nor brother* (Eccl. 4:8). *One* alludes to Abraham, as it says, *Abraham*

§ 12 [1] They were won over weak enemies.
§ 13 [1] Which slaying him would certainly have involved.
§ 14 [1] See par. 25 for the opposite view, that he obeyed with joy.

ANTHOLOGY

was one (Ezek. 33:24). *He has not a second*—there was none other like him. *He has neither son*—when God told him, *Take, I pray you, your son;*[1] *nor brother*—when God had bidden him, *Get you out from your land* (12:1).

Midrash Zuta Koheleth 4, 18. T.S. 22, 25.

16. Your son, your only one, whom you love, even Isaac.

Had the Holy One, blessed is He, desired even Abraham's eyeball, he would have given it to Him. Not his eyeball alone but his very soul, his most precious possession, he would have given Him. For it says, *Take, I pray you, your son, your only one, even Isaac.* Now, do we not know that he was his only son? *Your only one,* however, means the soul, as it says, *Deliver my soul from the sword, mine* only one *from the power of the dog* (Ps. 22:21).

Sifre D'barim 313. T.S. 22, 27.

17. YOUR SON, etc. "Which son?" he asked. *"You only son,"* was the answer. "But each is an only one to his mother?" *"Whom you love,"* He replied. "Has love boundaries?" he countered. *"Even Isaac,"* said He. Now, why did He not reveal it to him immediately? In order to enhance his love for Isaac and reward him for every single word. Another reason was, lest his mind be thrown into a whirl.

Sanh. 89b; Gen. R. 55, 7.
T.S. 22, 28 and note.

18. Isaac.

It is Isaac that I love, said God, because he is the persecuted.[1]

P'sikta. MS. T.S. 22, 29.

19. And go to the land of Moriah.

R. Levi b. Hayyatha said: "Go" is written twice,[1] and we do not know which was more precious in God's sight, the first or the second. But we may deduce that the second was the more precious from our text, *And go to the land of Moriah.*[2]

Gen. R. 55, 7. T.S. 22, 30.

20. TO THE LAND OF MORIAH. R. Hiyya the Elder and R. Yannai interpreted this. One interpreted: To the place whence teaching (*hora-ah*) came to the world.[1] The other: The place whence fear (*yir'ah*) of God came to the world.[2] R. Joshua b. Levi said: From there the Holy One, blessed is He, shoots (*moreh*)[3] at the nations of the world and casts them down into Gehenna. R. Simeon b. Yohai said: To the place that is fitting (*rauy*) for such a sacrifice, as it corresponds to the celestial Temple. R. Ibn (b. Judah) b. Palya said: To the place which was[4] shown (*moreh*) to you. R. Phinehas interpreted: To the seat of world rule (*mar-wetha*). Our Rabbis said: To the place where incense will one day be offered, for Moriah has the same meaning as in the verse, *I will get me to the mountain of myrrh*—Mor (Song 4:6).

R. Yannai and R. Hiyya disagree. R. Yannai said: Moriah denotes the source of light (*orah*) to the world, as it says, *God is light*[5] (nora) [issuing] *out of your holy places* (Ps. 68:36). R. Hiyya said: It means the place whence the Torah shall go forth to the world, as it says, *For out of Zion shall go forth Torah* (Isa. 2:3).

Another interpretation: The place where the righteous instruct (*morin*) the Holy One,

§ 15 [1] He suppressed his fatherly feelings, as though he had no son.
§ 18 [1] By Ishmael. See chap. 21, par. 48.
§ 19 [1] Here and in 12:1, when Abraham was told to leave his home.
[2] It is not clear how this is inferred. Pseudo-Rashi: On the first occasion he was not told where to go, but only *"to the land which I will show you."* The fact that now God told him immediately, *"to the land of Moriah,"* shows that this was more precious in His eyes. Mah.: The first was from outside into Eretz Israel, whereas the second was in Israel itself, to a more sacred spot.
§ 20 [1] Here in later times stood the Chamber of Hewn Stones in the Temple, the seat of the Great Sanhedrin which instructed and gave definite rulings to all Israel on their religious (and civil) duties.
[2] The site of the Temple, the fountainhead of awe and reverence.
[3] Or: Decrees the fate of (lit., instructs about) the nations of the world.
[4] Or: Will be.
[5] This apparently is his translation of *nora*. By the usual rendering, awful, the proof-text is irrelevant.

burnt-offering upon one of the mountains which I will tell thee of."

COMMENTARY

a burnt-offering. a. He did not tell him to sacrifice him.[27] **b.** The purpose of the above interpretation is to answer the difficulty: how could God countermand His own order? It is, however, unnecessary, since the opening statement of the chapter makes it clear that it was only a trial. Hence the literal and usual meaning, *offer him,* is to be retained.[28] **one of the mountains. a.** It was the future site of the Temple, and therefore particularly precious in God's eyes.[29] **b.** There were many mountains in the land of Moriah. His omission to specify which, would necessitate a further revelation later; this would give Abraham more time to think and change his mind if he wished. All these mountains were a considerable distance away, so that nobody need know the purpose of Abraham's journey. Otherwise, when he returned with Isaac unharmed, it might indeed have been thought that at the last moment Abraham's faith failed and he could not carry out God's command.[30] **which I will tell thee of. a.** He did not tell him immediately which it was, in order to show that Abraham's love was

ANTHOLOGY

blessed is He, and He fulfills their instructions,[6] as it says, *Thus were they divided by lot* (1 Chron. 24:5).[7]

Another interpretation: Abraham said to Him: "Master of all worlds! Am I then fit to offer him? Am I a priest? Let Shem, the High Priest, come and receive Isaac from me and offer him." The Almighty answered him: "When you arrive there I will consecrate you as a priest." Thus, what does Moriah connote? Shem's substitute (*temurah*), as it says, *He shall not exchange it, nor put a substitute* (yamir) *for it* (Lev. 27:10).[8]

> Gen. R. 55, 7; Tan. Y. Vayyera 45; PR 40.
> T.S. 22, 31 and note. 32-38.

21. Offer him there for a burnt-offering.

R. Bibi Abba, quoting R. Johanan, said: "Master of all worlds!" cried Abraham to God, "Thou knowest full well that when Thou badest me offer my son Isaac, I could have answered: Only yesterday Thou didst assure me, *In Isaac shall seed be called to you,* yet now Thou tellest me, *Offer him there for a burnt-offering!* Yet heaven forfend! I did not do so, but suppressed my natural feelings and did Thy will. So may it be Thy will, O Lord my God, when the children of my son Isaac are in distress and there is none to plead in their favor, that Thou wilt Thyself be their advocate. Yea, even as I did not answer Thee, but was as though deaf and dumb, *and I heard not, as a deaf man, and was as a mute, who opens not his mouth* (Ps. 38:14); so when Isaac's children are judged before Thee on this day [New Year], even if many accuse them, heed them not, even as I was silent and did not answer Thee."

> J. Taan. 2, 4; PR 40.   T.S. 22, 40; 21, 74.

22. OFFER HIM THERE FOR A BURNT-OFFERING. Abraham had doubts how God's Attribute of Justice would affect him. What did he say? Said R. Levi: "It appears to me that I have already received my reward in this world, since the Holy One, blessed is He, helped me against the kings and delivered me from the fiery furnace." Said the Almighty to him, "You must bring a burnt-offering for having doubted Me"; hence He said, *"Take, I pray you, your son . . . Isaac . . . and offer him there for a burnt-offering."*

> Tan. Y. Lech 13.   T.S. 22, 41.

23. Upon one of the mountains which I will tell you of.

R. Huna said, quoting R. Eliezer: At first the Holy One, blessed is He, puts the righteous in suspense and uncertainty; then He reveals to

---

[6] It is a Rabbinic concept that "the righteous decrees and God fulfills."

[7] This proof-text is hardly relevant, though it could be made so with some strain. PR 40 cites, *Then David and the elders, clothed in sackcloth, fell on their faces* (1 Chron. 21:16)—and prayed for the plague to cease. Their prayer was heard, so that, as it were, God carried out their decree. Y.S. omits this proof-text.

[8] All these interpretations are plays on the word Moriah. See also par. 39.

³**And Abraham rose early in the morning, and saddled his ass, and**

COMMENTARY

so great that he set out on such a grim task without even knowing whither he was bound.[31] **b.** God did tell him later which it was; cf. next verse: *and went to the place which God had told him.*[32] **c.** He did not inform him which; but Abraham recognized it from the cloud (which he perceived to be divine) which hung over it.[33] ³**rose early.** In his eagerness to obey.[34] **in the morning. a.** Lest the townspeople see him and ask embarrassing questions.[34a] **b.** He hastened away lest the matter come to Sarah's ears; she would then surely ask whither they were going and in her grief on learning the truth do herself harm.[35] [he] **saddled.** Himself—he did not wish to arouse the curiosity of his servants by ordering them to saddle his ass so early.[36] **ass.** Not a camel, which was the general mode of travel,

ANTHOLOGY

them His true will. Our present text is an example.

"Master of all worlds," said he, "upon which mountain?" He replied, "Where you will see My glory standing and waiting for you; that will tell you, This is the altar." Hence it says, *Upon one of the mountains which I will tell you of*: it does not say, I told you, but, *I will tell you.*

Another explanation: The mountain where you will see a light shining and a cloud clinging, there are the Shechinah and the place of the sacrifice.

Gen. R. 55, 7; PRE 31; MhG.
T.S. 22, 45. 46 and note.

24. UPON ONE OF THE MOUNTAINS. Hence our Sages said: The Holy One, blessed is He, created seven mountains, and of all these He chose none other than the mountain of Moriah as the site of the Holy Temple. Thus it says, *Why look you askance, you mountains of peaks, at the mountain which God desired as His abode* (Ps. 68:17)?

MhG. T.S. 22, 47.

25. **Abraham rose early in the morning.**

He delights greatly in His commandments (Ps. 112:1): he obeyed the command not under compulsion but with joy, as this verse states. He had bidden him, *Take, I pray you, your son*; and without hesitation *Abraham rose early in the morning.* Thus Scripture says, *I made haste, and delayed not, to observe Thy commandments*

(*ibid.* 119:60), which applies to Abraham, who went swiftly, unlike Lot, his brother's son, of whom we read that *he lingered* (19:16).

When our father Abraham saw the Temple destroyed and burnt . . . he wept bitterly, and demanded of the Almighty, "Sovereign of the Universe! Where are my children?" Said the Holy One, blessed is He, "A cloud descended upon them and carried them away into captivity." "Sovereign of the Universe!" cried he, "Thou gavest me a son at a hundred years in whom I greatly rejoiced. Yet when Thou badest me offer him as a burnt-offering I rejoiced and did not delay," as it says, *Abraham rose early in the morning.* "The ministering angels came before Thee and proposed, Let us go and behold the father who has delivered his son to Thee, showing no compassion upon him. Shouldst Thou not have remembered this Binding[1] in my favor and been merciful to my children?"

Midrash T'hillim 112; AB 31, 3; Echah Zuta
(Version 2) Letter Kaf. T.S. 22, 48 and note.

26. ABRAHAM ROSE EARLY IN THE MORNING. In connection with the Exodus from Egypt we read, *And none of you shall go out of the door of his house until the morning* (Exod. 12:22). This teaches that when you set out on a journey, enter a town when it is light, and go out when it is light. Our early ancestors practised this rule of good society. *Abraham rose early in the morning; Jacob rose up early in the morning* (28:18); *Moses rose up early in the morning* (Exod. 34:4); *Samuel rose early in the morning*

§ 25 ¹ See verse 9. The whole story is generally referred to as the Binding of Isaac.

ANTHOLOGY

to meet Saul (1 Sam. 15:12).[1] Cannot you draw a logical inference? Our fathers and princes were going to do the will of Him who spoke and the world existed,[2] yet they conformed to the usage of society; how much the more should ordinary people do so.

A disciple of the wise should not go out alone at night.[3] . . . R. Abbahu deduced it from our present text.

Mechilta Bo 11; Hul. 91b. T.S. 22, 49. 52.

27. ABRAHAM ROSE EARLY IN THE MORNING. The prayers of the righteous are heard in the morning. Abraham's morning prayer was answered, as it says, *Abraham rose early in the morning.*[1] Isaac's morning prayer, as it says, *They went both of them together* (verse 6): both had arisen in the morning.

Scripture writes, *The Lord said to Moses: "Rise up early in the morning, and stand before Pharaoh, and say to him: Thus says the Lord . . . Let my people go"* (Exod. 9:13). Rise up early, that your mission may be successful through the merit of Abraham who arose early to do My will.

Again, we read: *In the* morning *watch the Lord . . . discomfited the host of the Egyptians* (Exod. 14:24): Abraham and Isaac had uttered prayers in the morning long since, and the merit of these now stood in Israel's favor.

When they saw the Egyptians following them, they were utterly terrified. The ministering angels then proposed to the Almighty: "Let us go down and wreak vengeance on the Egyptians and keep Thy children safe from their hands." "I Myself will go down and guard Israel," He replied, "as a reward for their father Abraham's obedience to My will," as it says, *Abraham rose early in the morning.* At the very hour when Abraham had stood in prayer, the Holy One, blessed is He, looked upon the camp of the Egyptians and discomfited them.

When the Egyptians pursued the Israelites, the latter, together with Moses, lifted up their voices and wept. God's compassion was immediately awakened and He assured Moses: "I remember the prayer of Abraham My beloved when I told him to go and slay Isaac. He accepted My fiat unhesitatingly, and on the morrow rose early to do My will," as we read in our text.

It was extremely difficult for the Almighty to divide the Red Sea. Yet why so: is it not written, *He rebukes the sea and makes it dry* (Nahum 1:4)? *He that calls for the waters of the sea and pours them out upon the face of the earth* (Amos 5:8)?[2] Because . . . Rahab, Egypt's celestial Prince,[3] demanded justice . . . pleading: "Lord of the Universe, why wouldst Thou punish Egypt and divide the Red Sea on behalf of Israel . . . seeing that even as the former are idolaters, so are the latter?"[4] It was indeed difficult for the Almighty to ignore these demands of justice; had He not recalled how Abraham had risen early to sacrifice his only son, they would all have died in the Red Sea.

R. Jose said: The Holy One revealed Himself on Mount Sinai in the morning, and we were taught that this Revelation was afforded to Israel in the very hour that the merit of Abraham, who *rose up early in the morning,* was most efficacious.

MhG Sh'moth 66. 146; Midrash Vayyosha 1. 5; Zohar 2, 81a. 170b. T.S. 22, 50 and note.

28. ABRAHAM ROSE EARLY IN THE MORNING. It is written, *If a woman be delivered, and bear a man-child . . . in the eighth day the flesh of his foreskin shall be circumcised* (Lev. 12:2-3).

§ 26 [1] In all these cases they rose early in the morning, but not before.
[2] The phrase is now liturgical.
[3] This apparently contradicts the first par., which cautions all people not to go out alone at night.
§ 27 [1] This and the rest of the passage assume that he rose in order to pray; cf. chap. 19, par. 99.
[2] Then the dividing of the Red Sea should not have occasioned Him any particular difficulty.
[3] Every nation is regarded by the Rabbis as having a celestial Prince, whose function it is to plead its cause.
[4] The Rabbis held that the Israelites were degraded and corrupted in Egypt, until there was little to choose between them.

took two of his young men with him, and Isaac his son; and he

COMMENTARY

because he wished to conceal the fact that he was going on a journey. The ass might have been to bring some wood or anything else needed at home.[37] **his young men. a.** Those who normally accompanied him to attend to his wants.[38] **b.** He did not summon them first and tell them to prepare for a journey, to avoid awkward questions, but suddenly took them [this explains why it does not say that he called them]. He needed them firstly to carry the wood, and secondly that Isaac should not see anything unusual in their expedition, as would have been the case had they set out alone.[39] **and Isaac his son.** He is mentioned after the two servants: Abraham made it appear as though Isaac was a mere

ANTHOLOGY

This teaches that circumcision may be performed any time during the day, but the eagerly devout perform God's precepts at the earliest possible moment, as our text relates.

> Torath Kohanim Thazria 1. T.S. 22, 51.

29. **Abraham rose early in the morning and saddled his ass.**

He saddled it with joy that he was fulfilling God's will.

R. Simeon b. Yohai said: Love upsets the natural order, and hate upsets the natural order.[1] Love upsets the natural order, for it is written, *Abraham rose early in the morning, and saddled his ass*: did he not possess many slaves?[2] But it is because love[3] upsets the natural order. Hate too upsets the natural order: *Balaam rose in the morning, and saddled his ass* (Num. 22:21): did he not have many slaves? But he did it himself because hate upsets the natural order. . . . Then let Abraham's saddling to fulfill the will of the Omnipresent nullify Balaam's saddling to curse Israel.

> Gen. R. 55, 8; Mechilta B'shallah 2, 1. T.S. 22, 54-5.

30. AND SADDLED HIS ASS. Abraham rose early in the morning, took Ishmael, Eliezer, and his son Isaac, and saddled the ass. That ass was the foal of the she-ass that was created at twilight,[1] as it says, *Abraham rose early in the morning and saddled his ass.* On the same ass Moses rode when he went to Egypt, as it says, *Moses took his wife and his sons, and set them upon the[2] ass,* etc. (Exod. 4:20). On that ass the son of David (i.e., the Messiah) will ride, as it says, *Rejoice greatly, O daughter of Zion, shout, O daughter of Jerusalem; behold, your king comes to you, he is triumphant, and victorious, lowly, and riding on an ass, even on a colt the foal of an ass* (Zech. 9:9).

> PRE 31. T.S. 22, 56.

31. **And took two of his young men with him.**

R. Aibu said: The Torah teaches propriety, that a man should not set out on a journey with less than two attendants; for if he does, he will eventually become a servant to his servant.[1] For R. Aibu said: Two men behaved with propriety —Abraham and Saul. What does it say of Abraham? *Abraham rose early in the morning, and took two of his young men with him.* (Who were they? Ishmael and Eliezer). What does it say of Saul? *He went, he and two men with him* (1 Sam. 28:8). Who were they? Abner and Amasa.[2]

> Lev. R. 26, 7. T.S. 22, 58.

§ 29 [1] Through love or hate a man may do what would otherwise be beneath his dignity.
[2] To saddle his ass; why do it himself?
[3] In this case, his love of God.
§ 30 [1] Aboth 5:6 enumerates ten things which were created on the eve of the Sabbath at twilight.
[2] The Heb. has the def. art., which is probably the basis of the present dictum: *the* ass—the one singled out for the particular purposes enumerated here.
§ 31 [1] His servant may fall sick and he will have to attend to his needs.
[2] Both Abraham and Saul were engaged in missions where privacy was desirable. Hence their only reason for taking two attendants must have been because it would be a breach of propriety for men of their rank to go alone.

cleaved the wood for the burnt-offering, and rose up, and went unto the place of which God had told him. ⁴On the third day Abraham

COMMENTARY

afterthought.⁴⁰ **he cleaved the wood. a.** Only after he was clear from home, lest Sarah's suspicions be aroused.⁴¹ **b.** In his anxiety to obey God he did not wait until reaching the place, in case he did not find any wood there.⁴² **c.** He did this in order that the wood might fix his mind during the whole journey on its fateful purpose.⁴⁰ **rose up, and went.** "Rose up" is added idiomatically to indicate keenness and vigor.⁴⁴ **unto the place. a.** The land of Moriah—he knew not as yet to which mountain.⁴⁵ **b.** Divine guidance led his steps to the chosen spot.⁴⁶ **⁴On the third day. a.** Of the journey. From the land of the Philistines, where he dwelt, to Jerusalem is a distance of fifteen parasangs (Persian miles—one is about 4,000 yards), which is a two-days' journey: hence they reached it on the third morning.⁴⁷ **b.** God did not bid him to sacrifice near home, in order to give him plenty of time for reflection.⁴⁸

ANTHOLOGY

32. He cleaved the wood for the burnt-offering.

R. Hiyya b. R. Jose said, quoting R. Miasha, and the same was said in R. Bannaiah's name: As a reward for the two logs which Abraham split for the burnt-offering,¹ God cleaved (divided) the Red Sea for his descendants, as it says, *And the waters were cleaved* (Exod. 14:21). Said R. Levi: Enough of this!² Abraham did what was in his power, and the Almighty did what was in His.

Gen. R. 55, 8. T.S. 22, 59 note.

33. And rose up, and went.

He was rewarded for rising up and for going.¹

Gen. R. 55, 9. T.S. 22, 61.

34. AND ROSE UP, AND WENT. Abraham went to Sarah and said to her: "How long will your son be so closely attached to you: is he not thirty-seven years old, yet he has attended neither an academy nor a school! Let him go with me, and prepare us provisions for the road, that we may both go to the great academy." She prepared provisions, and the four of them departed.¹

MhG. T.S. 22, 62.

35. On the third day.

Israel never languishes in distress more than three days. For in the case of Abraham it says, *On the third day Abraham lifted up his eyes, and saw the place afar off*.¹

It is written, *After two days He will revive us; on the third day He will raise us up, that we may live in His presence* (Hos. 6:2). [Many a time the third day brought relief and joy, e.g.:] To our tribal ancestors:² *Joseph said to them on the third day: "This do, and live"* (42:18). At the Revelation: *It came to pass on the third day, when it was morning*, etc. (Exod. 19:16). For Joshua's spies: *Hide there three*

§ 32 ¹ The Heb. for wood is here in the plural; hence he must have split at least two logs.
² Either: Do not compare these two incidents, as though they were on a par. Or: Do not suggest that this was his only reward.
§ 33 ¹ For each separate act. Otherwise why state, *and rose up*? It is obvious (M.K.).
§ 34 ¹ Abraham, Isaac, Ishmael, and Eliezer. Tan. *ad loc.* elaborates this: Abraham wondered, "What shall I do? If I inform Sarah, seeing that a woman's mind is weak even in small matters, how much the more in such a serious matter. Yet if I steal away without telling her, she may kill herself when she misses him." What then did he do? He told Sarah, "Prepare us food and drink that we may eat and rejoice." "What is there particular about this day," she asked, "and why this rejoicing?" "The birth of a son to such old people as we is a sufficient cause for eating and drinking and rejoicing, he replied. So she went and prepared the meal. During the meal he said to her, "You know that I recognized my Creator when I was three years old, yet our son is grown up and has not been initiated. There is a place some little distance from us where youths are educated. Let me take him and have him educated there." "Go in peace," she replied. (Quoted in T.S. 22, 51 note.)
§ 35 ¹ His anguish at Isaac's sacrifice was now to give way to joy, when he learnt that it was only a trial.
² Heb. *Sh'batim* (sing. *shebet*), meaning both the tribes (of Israel) and Jacob's sons, the tribal ancestors.

lifted up his eyes, and saw the place

COMMENTARY

c. It was the third day after they reached the mountain range (not the third day of the journey); Abraham wandered about from mountain to mountain, not knowing which God had chosen.[49] **saw the place. a.** He saw the land of Moriah, which was well known, from afar.[50] **b.** God's providence enabled him to see the place from a great distance, and he understood that that was his goal.[51] **c.** He perceived by some intuition that this was the place.[52] **d.** God intimated that this was the site where his

ANTHOLOGY

days (Josh. 2:16). Jonah: *Jonah was in the belly of the fish three days and three nights* (Jonah 2:1). The returning exiles: *We abode there three days* (Ezra 8:32). At Resurrection: *After two days He will revive us.* Esther: *On the third day, Esther put on her royal apparel* (Est. 5:1)—she was invested with ancestral royalty.[3] Through what merit?[4] Our Rabbis said: Through the merit of Revelation which took place on the third day, as stated. R. Levi said: Through the merit of what Abraham did on the third day, as our text states.

Gen. R. 56, 1; Est. R. 9, 2.   T.S. 22, 63. 66.

36. ON THE THIRD DAY. Since it was but a short distance, why did it take three days? Because of several delays. While they were traveling on the road Satan appeared to Abraham in the guise of an old man and asked him whither he was going. "To pray," he answered. "Then why are you carrying wood on your shoulder, and fire and a knife?" he asked. "In case we spend a day or two there," he replied, "we will kill an animal, cook it and eat." "My son," he said, "was I not present when the Enemy told you, *Take, I pray you, your son, your only one . . . and offer him there for a burnt-offering*? Now an old man like yourself would destroy this precious son, this chosen one, whom the Holy One, blessed is He, gave you at the age of a hundred." "It was not the Enemy," he retorted, "but the Almighty Himself, in His glory, who commanded me so." Said Satan, *"Are not your fear, your hope, and the integrity of your ways, your folly?"* (Job 4:6).[1] "Re-

member, I pray you, who ever perished, being innocent, or where were the upright cut off?" (*ibid.* 7) Abraham retorted.

When Satan saw that Abraham and Isaac spurned him, he turned himself into a great river lying athwart their path. Abraham immediately descended into the water, which reached to his knees. "Follow me," he instructed his young men, which they did. When they reached midstream the water reached up to their necks. In that moment Abraham lifted up his eyes to heaven and cried out, "Sovereign of the Universe! Thou didst choose me, Thou didst teach me Thy sovereignty, Thou didst reveal Thyself to me and declare, I am Unique and you are unique: through you shall My name be known in the world; now offer your son Isaac as a burnt-offering to Me. I did not refuse, and lo! I am engaged in fulfilling Thy command. But *the waters have come even unto the soul* (Ps. 69:2): if I or my son Isaac drown, who will fulfill Thy word, and who will assert the unity of Thy name?"[2] Said the Holy One, blessed is He, to him: "By your life! You will assert the unity of My name in the world." There and then He rebuked the spring [Satan]: the river dried up and they stood on dry land.

Midrash Vayyosha; Tan. Vayyera 22.
T.S. 22, 40 note. 64.

37. ON THE THIRD DAY, etc. Why on the third day, and not on the first or the second? Lest the nations of the world say that He so confused him that he went and slew his son.

---

[3] Viz., Saul's (Y.T. and Radal). M.K. and Mah.: She was clothed in the spirit of royalty; or, she fortified herself with the merit of her ancestors.

[4] Was the third day so singled out.

§ 36 [1] This is apparently how the verse is rendered: Your fear [of God], your hopes, your integrity—what else are they but folly, when they lead you to this?

[2] Lit., upon whom will the unity of Thy name be made manifest?

afar off. 5And Abraham said unto his young men: "Abide ye here with the ass, and I and the lad will go

COMMENTARY

descendants would build the Holy Temple; he was now to consecrate that site with the life of his beloved.[53] **afar off. a.** Even though he did not yet know that this was the chosen spot.[54] **b.** He

recognized it either through the presence of a Divine Cloud (see Anthology par. 38) or through some other miraculous revelation.[55] **c.** And then he immediately left the young men, telling them to remain there with the ass.[56] 5**Abide ye here. a.** He gave as an excuse for leaving them that they had to remain with the ass, for which the mountain was too steep to climb.[57] **b.** That they should not attempt to stop him from carrying out the sacrifice.[58] **c.** The intended sacrifice was opposed to all reason and to the concept of a merciful God which he himself had taught. He therefore did not wish his

ANTHOLOGY

Another reason: To chasten him by the long journey, and reward him for every step.

Tan. Vayyera 22; PZ. T.S. 22, 65. 67.

38. Saw the place afar off.

What did he see? He saw a cloud enveloping the mountain. Said he, "That appears to be the place where the All-Present bade me offer my son." He then asked Isaac: "My son, do you see what I see?" "Yes," he replied. On his questioning the two young men, they answered, "No." "Since the ass does not see it, and you do not see it either," he observed, "*Abide you here with the ass.*"

Another account: On the third day they reached Mount Scopus, where he saw the Glory of the Shechinah standing on the mountain, as it says, *Abraham lifted up his eyes, and saw the Place[1] afar off.* He saw a column of fire reaching from earth to heaven. "My son," he asked Isaac, "do you see anything on one of these mountains?" When Isaac replied affirmatively he understood that his son was an acceptable burnt-offering.

Gen. R. 56, 1. 2; PRE 31. T.S. 22, 68. 73.

39. SAW THE PLACE AFAR OFF. How could it be seen afar? This teaches that originally it was in a vale. But when the Holy One, blessed

is He, declared that His Shechinah was to abide there, as the site of the Sanctuary, He said: "It is not for a king to dwell in a vale, but in a high, exalted place, a place beautiful and visible to all." There and then He beckoned to the valley surroundings, bidding the mountains close in so as to form an abode for the Shechinah. For that reason was it called Mount Moriah, because through fear (*yirah*)[1] of the Holy One, blessed and praised is He, it became a mountain. Furthermore, for that very reason it is written *plene*, to indicate that it became a mountain through the fear of the Lord (*mora Yah*).

Tan. Vayyera 22; Midrash Haser V'Yether 19. T.S. 22, 39. 69.

40. SAW THE PLACE AFAR OFF. R. Isaac interpreted: This place would one day be far from its Master.[1] For ever? No: Scripture states, *This is My resting-place for ever; here will I dwell, for I have desired it* (Ps. 132:14): [it will be estranged from Me] only until the advent of him who is described as *lowly, and riding on an ass* (Zech 9:9).[2]

Gen. R. 56, 2. T.S. 22, 71.

41. Abide you here with the ass.

Why did he say this? He prophesied that that place would be the site of the Chosen House,[1]

§ 38   [1] *Ha-makom*, lit., the place; in Rabbinic literature this frequently designates the Almighty, the All-Present.
§ 39   [1] Connected with Moriah.
§ 40   [1] Either: This place, Jerusalem, would one day be spiritually far—i.e., estranged—from God. Or: Far from its rightful owner, the Jewish people, exiled and driven away from Jerusalem.
      [2] The Messiah. *Shebu lachem* (abide) is now rendered, Return (which is quite a possible translation). When? *With the ass*—when he [the Messiah] comes on an ass.
§ 41   [1] The Temple. It was therefore not fitting to ride there on an ass.

yonder; and we will worship, and
come back to you." ⁶And Abraham

COMMENTARY

servants to see it, lest they learn an evil lesson from
it.⁵⁹ **d.** Desiring to be alone with Isaac at the dread
moment of sacrifice.⁶⁰ **yonder.** But a short distance.⁶¹
we will worship. a. We will be gone but a short

time—just sufficient to prostrate ourselves (the lit.
meaning of the Hebrew).⁶² **b.** The word hints at
prayer: we will pray that we come back to you.⁶³
we will come back (literal trans.) **a.** He spoke
thus lest Isaac become suspicious and flee. Actually
by "we" he meant Isaac's bones.⁶⁴ **b.** Because
he said no more, Isaac had a glimmer of understanding, and asked, *"Where is the lamb?"*⁶⁵ **c.** Was
there an undercurrent of conviction that God would
not exact His demand of him? The Rabbis declare

ANTHOLOGY

as it says, *This is My resting-place for ever; here
will I dwell, for I have desired it.* (Ps. 132:14).

Shir Hashirim Zuta 1. T.S. 22, 74.

42. ABIDE YOU HERE WITH (*im*) THE ASS.
Whence do we know that slaves are like animals?¹ From our text: *Abide you here with*
(*im*) *the ass,* which is to be read *am:* the ass-
like people. Our Rabbis inferred this from
the following: *Six days you shall labor . . . but
the seventh day is a Sabbath to the Lord your
God; in it you shall not do any work, you
. . . nor your man-servant, nor your maid-ser-
vant, nor your cattle* (Exod. 20:9-10).

R. Abbahu said: Even a heathen² maidservant
living in Eretz Israel is assured of her portion
in the world to come. For one text says, *Thus
says God the Lord . . . that gives breath to the*
people *upon it* (Isa. 42:5);³ whilst another text
says, *abide you here with* (*im*) *the ass,* which
implies, ye are a *people* like the ass.⁴

Gen. R. 56, 2; Keth. 111a. T.S. 22, 75. 79.

43. **I and the lad will go** *ad koh* **(yonder).**

R. Joshua b. Levi interpreted: We will go
and see what will eventually happen to *koh.*¹

Another interpretation: Why did Abraham
speak thus? He prophesied that here where he
bound his son Isaac, priests would stand and
spread out their hands to bless Israel with the
word *koh—koh (thus) shall you bless the children of Israel* (Num. 6:23).

Whence did Israel earn the priestly blessing?
R. Nehemiah said: From Isaac. For it says, *I and
the lad will go yonder* (*koh*). Therefore the
Omnipresent declared, *Koh (thus) shall you
bless the children of Israel.*

Gen. R. 56, 2; 43, 9; Shir Hashirim Zuta 1.
T.S. 22, 80-2.

44. **We will worship, and** *we* **will come
back to you.**

He thus informed him¹ that Isaac would return unscathed. R. Isaac said: All these things²
happened or will happen through the merit of
worship.³ Abraham returned in peace from
Mount Moriah only through the merit of worship, as our text says, *we will* worship *and we
will come back to you.*

Gen. R. 56, 2. T.S. 22, 83.

45. WE WILL COME BACK TO YOU. R. Johanan
said: How do we know that a covenant has

§ 42 ¹ Legally, e.g., they cannot own or acquire property.
      ² Lit., Canaanitish.
      ³ He renders: That gives breath, i.e., life—the life of the Hereafter—to the people on it, sc. on (in) Eretz Israel.
      ⁴ Hence, even though like an ass, they are still a people. This is a striking example of how an apparently
        derogatory view is turned to precisely the reverse.
§ 43 ¹ God's promise, "*Koh* (so) *shall your seed be*" (15:5)—as numerous as the stars; we will see what will happen
        to that promise, now that I am to sacrifice my son.
§ 44 ¹ Probably: Abraham [unconsciously] informed Isaac. Tan. reads: His mouth informed him [Abraham]—by
        saying, "and *we* will return"—that they would both return unharmed.
      ² A whole list is enumerated *ad loc.*: The Giving of the Torah, the birth of a son (Samuel) to Hannah, the
        Return of the Exiles, the building of the Temple, and Resurrection. Midrash Or Haafelah enumerates: The
        creation of the world, the Temple, and the Hereafter.
      ³ Literally, prostration—then the habitual mode of supplication.

took the wood of the burnt-offering, and laid it upon Isaac his son; and he took in his hand the fire and the knife; and they went both of them together. [7]And Isaac spoke unto Abraham his father, and said: "My

COMMENTARY

that at that moment the Spirit of Prophecy entered into him, and he spoke more truly than he knew.[66] [6]**Abraham took the wood.** From the ass which had carried it until now.[67] **laid it upon Isaac.** **a.** He did not take the ass with him lest the servants think that he was going a distance.[68] **b.** He wanted to break it gently to Isaac: by this act Isaac would perceive that preparations were being made for a sacrifice; he would naturally ask where was the lamb, and thus the truth would gradually dawn on him.[69] **c.** Perhaps he wished to weigh him down with the burden to prevent his running away. It is quite likely that he tied the wood on him.[70] **he took in his hand the fire and the knife.** **a.** Which had been carried hitherto by the servants.[71] **b.** This was a further step in opening Isaac's eyes.[72] **the fire.** I.e., the vessel containing glowing embers, by means of which the wood on the altar was to be kindled.[73] **the knife.** Heb. *maacheleth*: the knife is so called because it makes the meat ritually fit for food (*ochel*, same root).[74] **both of them together.** Abraham, who knew that he was going to sacrifice his son, went with the same joy and good-will as Isaac who knew nought of it.[75] [7]**spoke unto Abraham his father, and said: "My**

ANTHOLOGY

been made with the lips?[1] Because it says . . . *we will worship, and we will come back to you*: by the help of Providence they did both return.

M.K. 18a.   T.S. 22, 84.

46.   Abraham took the wood of the burnt-offering, and laid it on Isaac his son.

Like a man carrying his stake[1] on his shoulder.

Gen. R. 56, 3.   T.S. 22, 85.

47.   He took . . . the *maacheleth* (knife).

R. Hanina said: Why is the knife called *maacheleth*? Because it makes food (*ochlim*) ritually fit.[1] Our Rabbis explained: Whatever Israel enjoys (lit., eats) in this world is only through the merit of that *maacheleth*.[2]

Gen. R. 56, 3.   T.S. 22, 86.

48.   They went both of them together.

One to bind, and the other to be bound; one to slay and the other to be slain.[1]

Gen. R. 56, 3.   T.S. 22, 87.

49.   Isaac spoke to Abraham his father, and said: "My father."

Samael[1] went to our father Abraham and said to him: "Old man, old man! Are you out of your mind? You are going to slay a son given to you at the age of a hundred!" "Yes, even this,"[2] he replied. "And if He tries you even more, can you stand it? *If you be tried in any matter,*[3] *will you be wearied* (Job 4:2)?" "Even more than this," he retorted. "Tomorrow He will tell you that you are a murderer, guilty of shedding your son's blood," Samael urged. "Still I obey Him,"[2] he insisted.

Seeing that he could achieve nothing with him, he went to Isaac. "Son of an unhappy woman!" he exclaimed, "he goes to slay you." "I am content,"[2] he answered. "Then all those fine things which your mother prepared are to be the inheritance of Ishmael, the hated of her house?"[4] he said. When a word does not wholly succeed, it yet has some effect. Therefore Scripture writes, *Isaac spoke to Abraham his*

§ 45   [1] That they unconsciously prognosticate the future.
§ 46   [1] On which he is to be hung or burnt.
§ 47   [1] An animal is not fit for food unless it has been ritually slaughtered.
    [2] As a reward for Abraham's readiness to sacrifice Isaac, and Isaac's acquiescence.
§ 48   [1] Yet they went *together*—both equally ready to obey God's command.
§ 49   [1] The name of a wicked angel, here identified with Satan or the Tempter; cf. Sot. 10b.
    [2] Lit., [my obedience to God is pledged even] on this condition.
    [3] AJV: *If one venture a word unto thee.*
    [4] Or: Shall everything she has done to drive Ishmael out be in vain, and he will inherit after all?

father." And he said: "Here am I, my son." And he said: "Behold the fire and the wood; but where is the lamb for a burnt-offering?" [8]And

COMMENTARY

father." **a.** He repeated "My father" in amazement that preparations were going forward for a sacrifice without the required lamb.[76] **b.** The repetition was to remind him that he was his father—from whom fatherly love and compassion was to be expected. The truth was now becoming apparent to him.[77]

Here am I, my son. **a.** I.e., speak what you wish.[78] **b.** He spoke in tones of love and endearment—in spite of which he was about to sacrifice him.[79] **Behold,** etc. **a.** If you intend going on to a place where you can buy a lamb, you could have bought the wood there too. If not, where will you get the lamb?[80] **b.** You have brought wood, which can easily be obtained on the mountain, yet no lamb, which is much more difficult to find.[81] **the fire and the wood.** But he did not find the knife surprising, because that would normally be carried as a protection against enemies or wild beasts.[82] **but where is the lamb?** Isaac imagined that the idea of his being sacrificed was Abraham's own, as a supreme way of showing his love for God. Had he known that it was God's command he would

ANTHOLOGY

father, and said: "My father." Why is "father" repeated? That he might be filled with compassion for him.[5] *He* [Abraham] *said: "Behold, the fire and the wood"*[6]—may that man be drowned for inciting you! Come what may, *God will provide Himself the lamb*, my son; but if He does not, *the lamb for the burnt-offering* is *my son*."

Gen. R. 56, 4. T.S. 22, 88.

50. Isaac spoke to Abraham his father, and said: "My father." Isaac asked his father, "What are you doing with me?" "I am going to carry out your Maker's will," he replied. Said Isaac to him: "And what will you say to my poor old mother?" "I will tell her that Isaac has been slaughtered," was his answer. Said Isaac to him: "You will kill her and be guilty of her death. Rather, when you have burnt me take my ashes to my mother; may she find consolation in them." "It will be even so," Abraham assured him, and he wept with bitterness of soul at the separation from his son.

Another version: Isaac said to him, "Father, make haste and do the will of your Creator. Burn me thoroughly and take my ashes and place them before my mother. Whenever she sees them she will say, This is my son, whom his

father slew. O my father! What will you both do in your old age?" "My son," he replied, "we know that our death is near: He who comforted us hitherto will comfort us until the day of our death."

He then placed him on the altar. Abraham's eyes gazed into Isaac's, and Isaac's eyes were lifted to the highest heavens. Tears gushed forth from Abraham's eyes until his whole body swam in them. "My son," he cried out, "since you are in anguish at your blood that is to be shed, may your Creator provide you with another sacrifice in your stead." A heart-rending cry of agony burst from his throat; his eyes tremblingly looked to the Shechinah; he raised his voice and cried, *I will lift up mine eyes to the mountains; from whence shall my help come* (Ps. 121:1)?

Midrash;[1] Yalkut Shimoni 1, 101. T.S. 22, 89 and note.

51. **Behold the fire and the wood.**

[*This is the law of the burnt-offering . . . the priest shall kindle wood on it*—the altar—*every morning . . .*] *Fire shall be kept burning upon the altar perpetually* (Lev. 6:2, 5-6). This mystically alludes to the fire of Isaac, as it is written, *Behold the fire and the wood*: that is the perpetual fire, for it will always exist. Again, the

[5] He stressed the relationship as an unspoken appeal.
[6] God's command must be obeyed.
§ 50 [1] From a MS collection of Yemenite Midrashim, Ner Has'chalim.

Abraham said: "God will provide Himself the lamb for a burnt-offering, my son." So they went

not have spoken.[83] **8God will provide** (*yir'eh*) [for] **Himself the lamb for a burnt-offering, my son. a.** The future ("will provide"—*yireh*,

ANTHOLOGY

wood on the altar is the wood that Abraham carried.[1]

Zohar 3, 30b.   T.S. 22, 91.

52.   But where is the lamb for the burnt-offering?

Isaac said to Abraham: *"Behold the fire and the wood, but where is the lamb for the burnt-offering?"* "My son," he replied, "you are to be the burnt-offering." Abraham's face paled with apprehension:[1] I am an old man, thought he, and he is young. Perhaps he will flee; what will then happen to me? Said Isaac to him, "O my father; fear not. May it be the will of the All-Present to accept the measure of my blood.[2] But bind me well, lest I overpower you in an involuntary struggle. And when you go to my mother Sarah, do not tell it to her suddenly, lest she do herself an injury. If she is standing on the roof she may fall down and die. She may be standing by a well, and throw herself into it. Or she may be holding a knife, and commit suicide with it." Isaac, indeed, consented with his lips at that moment, but in his heart he prayed, "Oh that I may be saved from my father's hand. I have no other helper but the Holy One, blessed is He," as it says, *My help comes from the Lord, who made heaven and earth* (Ps. 121:2). The ministering angels said to each other, "Come and see two righteous men: the father slays and the son offers himself to be slain, and neither restrains the other."

ARN MS.   T.S. 22, 92.

53.   Abraham said.

Scripture does not write, His father said, because he was not acting toward him like a father but like an enemy.

Zohar 1, 120a.   T.S. 22, 93.

54.   God will provide Himself the lamb, etc.

He should have said, "will provide (or show) us"? Only, he meant: God will provide for Himself as He needs to; meanwhile there is my son, and no lamb. Without further delay, *they went on, both of them together.*

Zohar 1, 120a.   T.S. 22, 94 note.

55.   GOD WILL PROVIDE HIMSELF THE LAMB FOR THE BURNT-OFFERING, MY SON. It is written, *God sent an angel to Jerusalem to destroy it; and as he was about to destroy, God beheld, and He repented Him of the evil* (1 Chron. 21:15). What did He behold? The blood of Isaac's Binding, as it says, *God will provide Himself the lamb for the burnt-offering,* **my son.**

Mechilta Bo 11.   T.S. 22, 95.

56.   THE LAMB FOR THE BURNT-OFFERING. Satan accosted him on the road and said to him, "Old man, old man, whither are you going? Is it not to bind [and sacrifice] this son of yours?[1] *Should He try you with such a matter that you lose your strength?*[2] ... *Behold, you have instructed many, and have strengthened the feeble hands.... Yet now it* [a trial] *comes to you, so that you are exhausted*"[3] (Job 4:2-3, 5). *"I will walk in my integrity"* (Ps. 26:11),

§ 51   [1] The idea is that the true fire that burns perpetually is the merit and inspiration of Isaac's sacrifice—a flame never to be extinguished.

§ 52   [1] Lit., the features of his face changed.

[2] MhG reads: May my blood be an atonement for all Israel.

§ 56   [1] From "Old man, etc." to here has been added from MS Munich, but is missing in our editions.

[2] Should God have imposed such a severe trial upon you that you lose your strength, i.e., your only son? So Rashi *ad loc.*

[3] You have instructed many, brought them to God, and strengthened their faith. Yet now you undergo such a severe trial that it can only exhaust you, leaving you without an heir.

both of them together. ⁹And they

COMMENTARY

lit., will see) has the force of the present: God sees and knows where the lamb is.⁸⁴ **b.** *Yireh* is to be understood as *yareh*, He will show: God will show us where the lamb is.⁸⁵ **c.** I know that we will not find a lamb on the top of the mountain, but God will choose whatever He desires for the offering.

He was thus hinting that it might not be a lamb at all ("lamb" in the text therefore is to be understood in a general sense: a lamb or anything else that can be offered), from which Isaac might gather that he was to be the sacrifice, since only he and his father would be there. Nevertheless he did not say so outright, desiring to spare his feelings as much as possible.⁸⁶ **So they went both of them together. a.** Even though Isaac now understood, he did not flee but accompanied his father.⁸⁷

ANTHOLOGY

he answered. *"But,"* Satan urged, *"should not your fear be your confidence?"* (Job 4:6).⁴ He retorted, *"Remember, I pray you, who ever perished, being innocent?"* (*ibid.* 7). Seeing that he refused to listen to him, he said, *"Now a word was secretly brought to me* (*ibid.* 12): thus have I heard from behind the Curtain:⁵ *the lamb* will be *for a burnt-offering,* but not Isaac for a burnt-offering." "It is the punishment of a liar," he retorted, "that even when he speaks the truth, he is not heeded."⁶

Sanh. 89b. T.S. 22, 96.

57. **The lamb for the burnt-offering [is yourself], my son.**

When the Temple was destroyed . . . Abraham pleaded with the Holy One, blessed is He, "Sovereign of the Universe! At the age of a hundred Thou gavest me a son. When he was of independent mind, and a young man of thirty seven,¹ Thou didst order me, Offer him to Me as a burnt-offering. I steeled myself to cruelty, and mercilessly bound him myself: shouldest Thou not have remembered this in my favor to have compassion upon my children?" Then Isaac too began to plead: "Sovereign of the Universe! When my father said to me, *God will provide Himself with the lamb for a burnt-offering,* viz., yourself, *my son,* I did not resist Thy command, but with willing heart let myself

be bound on the altar, and I stretched out my throat to the knife: shouldest Thou not have remembered this in my favor to have compassion on my children?"

Midrash Echah Proem 24. T.S. 22. 98.

58. FOR A BURNT-OFFERING, MY SON. *Sing, ye righteous, in the Lord* (Ps. 33:1): When the righteous see the Shechinah of the Holy One, blessed is He, they break straightway into song. When Isaac was bound and he saw the heavens opened, he immediately uttered song. When he asked his father, *"Behold the fire and the wood, but where is the lamb for a burnt-offering?"* Abraham answered him, *"For a burnt-offering, my son"*—you are the lamb for the burnt-offering. Isaac was immediately bound on the fire,¹ and he saw the Shechinah above him in heaven, ready to receive him like a sweet savor. Then Isaac broke forth into song. What song did he utter? The song of sacrifice.

Midrash.² T.S. 22, 99.

59. GOD WILL PROVIDE HIMSELF WITH THE LAMB, etc. For the Passover sacrifice *your lamb shall be without blemish, a male* (Exod. 12:5): this was in memory¹ of Abraham's saying, *God will provide Himself with the lamb.*

Exod. R. 15, 12. T.S. 22, 100.

60. **So they went both of them together.**

He held his hand and they went together, for

---

⁴ Your God-fearingness should have made you completely safe; instead, you are about to sacrifice your son!

⁵ From God's innermost Presence.

⁶ "It is the punishment," etc., may not be Abraham's reply, but an independent comment of the Talmud: He [Abraham] did not listen to him, because it is a liar's punishment to be disbelieved even when he speaks truth.

§ 57 ¹ See par. 1, n. 6.

§ 58 ¹ I.e., on the wood which was to be lit.

² Quoted in *Sefer ha-Pardes,* ascribed to Rashi.

§ 59 ¹ Lit., for the sake of.

came to the place which God had told him of; and Abraham built the altar there, and laid the wood in order, and bound Isaac his son,

COMMENTARY

b. They had stopped walking during the foregoing discussion; now they resumed their march.[88] [9]**which God had told him of.** Which God *now* told him, "This is the mountain of which I spoke to you."[89] **Abraham built the altar . . . laid the wood,** etc. This is told to indicate his steadfast resolution: he performed all these tasks knowing their tragic purpose.[90] **bound. a.** Against his will.[91] **b.** Even though Isaac had consented to the sacrifice, both feared that in the very moment of sacrifice his (Isaac's) resolution might fail him and he would flee. Therefore he bound him with his consent.[92]

ANTHOLOGY

Abraham thought: Isaac may take to his feet and run.[1]

> MhG. T.S. 22, 102.

61. They came to the place . . . and Abraham built the altar there.

R. Ishmael said: When they reached that place the Holy One, blessed is He, showed Abraham with His finger [as it were] and told him, "That is the altar: it is the one on which Adam sacrificed aforetime; it is the same altar on which Cain and Abel sacrificed; and it is the same altar on which Noah and his sons sacrificed. For it says, *Abraham built the altar:* not *an* altar, but *the* altar—the same on which the ancients sacrificed.

Abraham built the altar. It does not say, an altar. This teaches that it was already built from aforetime. There is a universal tradition: David and Solomon built the altar in the threshing-floor of Arawnah on the very same site where Abraham built the altar on which he bound Isaac.

> PRE 31; Or Haafelah.
> T.S. 22, 103 and note.

62. THEY CAME TO THE PLACE. Both of them brought the stones to build the altar, both brought the fire, both brought the wood, Abraham like one arranging his son's marriage feast, and Isaac as though he were setting up his own bridal canopy.

> Midrash quoted in Yalkut Shimoni.
> T.S. 22, 104.

63. ABRAHAM BUILT THE ALTAR THERE. But where was Isaac? Said R. Levi: He had hidden him, lest Satan, the rebuked of God,[1] throw a stone at him and render him unfit for a sacrifice.

> Gen. R. 56, 5. T.S. 22, 105.

64. He bound Isaac his son.

R. Hofni b. Isaac said: Even as Abraham bound his son Isaac here on earth, so did the Holy One, blessed is He, subjugate the heathens' celestial Princes in heaven.[1] But they did not remain subjugated. When Israel became estranged from God in the days of Jeremiah, the Holy One, blessed is He, said to them: What think ye? That their chains will be on them for ever? . . . Not so.

> Gen. R. 56, 5. T.S. 22, 107.

65. HE BOUND ISAAC HIS SON. When Abraham was about to bind him, Isaac said to him, "My father: I am young, and dread that my body tremble in fear of the knife and I grieve you. This will make the ritual act of slaughtering unfit, so that my sacrifice will not count. Therefore bind me well."[1] Straightway *he bound*

---

§ 60 [1] This seems to disagree with previous pars. which state that Isaac went with the same steadfastness and joy to do God's will as Abraham. However, Abraham may well have feared that even so he might not prove equal to the test.

§ 63 [1] See Zech. 3:2.

§ 64 [1] Every nation was conceived as having a celestial patron, "Prince," in heaven. He made them subservient to Israel.

§ 65 [1] Other Midrashim give his reason lest he involuntarily kick him or protest, thereby failing in filial honor and respect.

and laid him on the altar, upon the wood. ¹⁰And Abraham stretched forth his hand, and took the knife to slay his son. ¹¹And the angel of

COMMENTARY

¹⁰**stretched forth his hand.** He summoned up all his resolution to fight against his natural fatherly instincts.⁹³ **to slay his son.** The question might be asked, How could Abraham believe that God had given him a command in such flagrant contradiction

ANTHOLOGY

Isaac his son: could one bind a man thirty-seven years old but with his consent?

Gen. R. 56, 5. T.S. 22, 108.

66. Above the wood.

R. Hanina said: What does "above" indicate? That he erected the altar to correspond exactly to the celestial Throne of Glory above, as it says, *Above it stood seraphim* (Isa. 6:2):¹ this means, above the altar which Abraham had made.

AB 31. T.S. 22, 110.

67. Abraham stretched out his hand.

R. Simeon b. Yohai said: Let the sword in Abraham's hand, which he *stretched out . . . to slay his son*, come and counteract the sword in the wicked Pharaoh's hand when he pursued Israel, as it says, *I will draw my sword, my hand shall destroy them* (Exod. 15:9).¹

Mechilta B'shallah 2, 1. T.S. 22, 111.

68. ABRAHAM STRETCHED OUT HIS HAND. He stretched out his hand to take the knife, while in his fatherly compassion the tears streamed from his eyes into Isaac's. Yet in spite of that he rejoiced to do his Creator's will. The angels mustered in bands on high. What did they cry? *Have the highways lain waste* (Isa. 33:8): does not Abraham entertain travelers [and teach them to worship Thee]?¹ *Ended* [is his merit]

that returned the manner [of menses to Sarah] (*ibid.*), as it is written, *It had ceased to be with Sarah after the manner of women* (18:11).² *He has broken the covenant* (Isa. *ibid.*) of which He said, *My covenant will I establish with Isaac* (17:21). *He has despised the cities* (Isa. *ibid.*), alluding to, *Abraham dwelt between Kadesh and Shur* (20:1).³ *He regards not man* (*ibid.*): does no merit remain in Abraham's favor?⁴

Gen. R. 56, 5. T.S. 22, 112.

69. He took the knife to slay his son.

As he was about to lay the knife on his throat the angels came and wept and cried out to the Holy One, blessed is He, as it says, *Behold, their valiant ones* [the angels] *cry without* (Isa. 33:7). What did they cry? *The highways lay waste? the wayfaring man ceases? He has broken the covenant?* (*ibid.* 8): where is Abraham's reward for making Thee known in the world through the travelers he entertained? *The wayfaring man ceases*: ended is the reward for the wayfarers who would come from all quarters, lodge with Abraham, freely dine and then proclaim Thee as the source of blessings to the world.¹ Instead, *He has broken the covenant?* wilt Thou break the covenant of which Thou saidst to Abraham, *My covenant will I establish with Isaac* (17:21)? Lo, the knife is on his throat! How long wilt Thou wait? R. Berech-

§ 66 ¹ Usually understood to mean, Above God, or above the Heavenly Throne.

§ 67 ¹ See par. 31, which contains the beginning of this passage.

§ 68 ¹ Cf. chap. 21, par. 100.

  ² Long ago she had reached the menopause; but through Abraham's merit her menses resumed and she bore Isaac. If Isaac be now slain, Abraham's merit will have availed nothing. Or: *Ended* (dead) *will be the one whose manner* (of menses) *returned* (Sarah)—when she will learn of this.

  ³ The angels recalled how Abraham had "despised," i.e., rejected, his former residence when it ceased to offer opportunities to practise hospitality; cf. *supra* chap. 20, pars. 1, 3. Another interpretation in T.S.: He [God] has "despised," i.e., has no desire in Jerusalem and the Temple, which He intended for Isaac's descendants.

  ⁴ T.S. (see n. 3) reads: No merit has stood in Abraham's favor; no creature has any value before Him.

§ 69 ¹ Cf. chap. 21, par. 100.

the Lord called unto him out of heaven, and said: "Abraham, Abra-

COMMENTARY

to His promise that his line would continue through Isaac? The answer is that he may have thought that Isaac had sinned and rendered himself unworthy of that high destiny.[94] **11the angel of the Lord called unto him. a.** He received a prophetic communication through an angel; this is the highest degree of prophecy to which one can attain.[95] **b.** The angel speaks in the name of the Lord; therefore he could say, "You did not withhold your son . . . from Me" (not, from Him). Alternatively (following a Rabbinic view in Lev. R. 1, 1), the angel only called his name, to attract his attention; the actual communication came from God.[96] **out of heaven. a.** He heard an actual voice, though he saw nothing.[97] **b.** The matter was too urgent to permit the angel to descend on earth.[98] **Abraham,**

ANTHOLOGY

iah commented on the text, *Behold, their valiant ones cry without*—hutsah: this is written *hitsah:* it is alien *(hitsah)* to Thee to make Abraham slay him with his own hand.[2] At that the Holy One, blessed is He, said to Michael: "Why do you stand? Do not permit him." Then Michael called to Abraham, *"Lay not your hand upon the lad."*

PR 40. T.S. 22, 113.

70. TO SLAY HIS SON. Hence we infer that sacrifices may not be slaughtered save with intention.[1]

Midrash Hahefetz. T.S. 22, 117.

71. TO SLAY HIS SON. R. Meir said: Scripture writes, *You shall love the Lord your God with all your heart* (Deut 6:5)—like Abraham, of whom it says, *For I have known him, to the end that he may command his children and his household after him, that they may keep the way of the Lord, to do righteousness and justice* (18:19).[1] *And with all your soul:* like Isaac, who had himself bound on the altar. *And with all* m'odecha *(your might—ibid.):* acknowledge *(modeh)*[2] your debt to Him as did Jacob when he said, *I am not worthy of all the mercies . . . which Thou hast shown to Thy servant* (32:11).

Sifre D'barim 32. T.S. 22, 118.

72. TO SLAY HIS SON. R. Jose the Galilean said: When the Israelites entered the Red Sea, Mount Moriah, together with the altar built on it for Isaac's sacrifice and the wood that was laid on it, had already been uprooted, as it were, and there were Isaac, as though still bound and lying on the altar, and Abraham, stretching out his hand for the knife to slay his son.[1]

Mechilta B'shallach 1, 3. T.S. 22, 119.

73. **The angel of the Lord called to him . . . out of heaven.**

When the ministering angels saw how the father wholeheartedly bound and the son wholeheartedly allowed himself to be bound, Metatron arose and pleaded with the Almighty: "Master of the Universe! Let not Abraham's seed be wiped out of the world." Then the knife turned to lead.[1] Said the Holy One, blessed is He, to the angels: "Was it not you who approached Me with a subterfuge?[2] Now you plead for compassion!" He beckoned to Metat-

[2] This follows Gen. R. which reads, It is unnatural that he should slay his son with his own hand. But the present text has b'yad'cha, lit., in or by thy hand; here it is rendered "to Thee"—to allow him to slay his son. It may also be rendered: It is unnatural: by Thy hand he [Abraham] slays him.

§ 70 [1] There must be the intention to slay the animal for a sacrifice.

§ 71 [1] This text is quoted in Yalkut Shimoni, but is absent in our version of Sifre. MhG quotes as proof text, *The seed of Abraham, who loves Me*—AJV: *My friend* (Isa. 41:8). This is more suitable, and R. Elijah Gaon emends accordingly.

[2] A play on m'odecha.

§ 72 [1] The idea is that the sea dried up for them as a reward for Isaac's sacrifice; at the moment of their entering the waters it was as though Mount Moriah was uprooted and brought here, and the whole sacrifice re-enacted.

§ 73 [1] It was blunted.

[2] Your own charge of Abraham's ingratitude brought about this trial; see par. 1.

ham." And he said: "Here am I." [12]And he said: "Lay not thy hand upon the lad, neither do thou any

COMMENTARY

Abraham. a. Abraham was so wrapped up in his task that he did not hear his name the first time it was called.[99] **b.** This exclamation ("Abraham, Abraham!") shows the anxiety of the angel of the Lord to hold Abraham back at the very last moment.[100] **Here am I.** He thought that the voice was urging and encouraging him to go on with his task; hence he answered, "Here am I"—engaged in the sacrifice and about to complete it.[101] [12]**he said.** Sc. God, for the angel only called his name [see verse 11, "the angel," etc., b].[102] **neither do thou**

ANTHOLOGY

ron to call him, as it is written, *The angel of the Lord called to him out of heaven.*

MhG. T.S. 22, 120.

74. Abraham, Abraham.

Similarly, others too were so addressed: "Jacob, Jacob"; "Moses, Moses"; "Samuel, Samuel": the repetition expresses love and encouragement: they were the very same in humility after as before He spoke to them; the same after as before they attained greatness.

R. Eliezer b. Jacob said: The repetition teaches that He spoke to him and to future generations. There is no generation without men like Abraham, and no generation without men like Jacob, Moses, and Samuel.[1]

R. Abba b. Kahana said: Whoever has his name thus repeated has a portion in both worlds.

T. Ber. 1; Gen. R. 56, 7; Tan. Sh'moth 18. T.S. 22, 121-2. 124.

75. ABRAHAM, ABRAHAM. The name was repeated because he was hastening to slay him, and so the angel cried out to him, like a man crying out in distress, "What are you doing?" As Abraham turned his face to him he cried out, "What are you doing? *Lay not your hand upon the lad.*"

When the angel called him Abraham asked, "Who are you?" "An angel," he replied. "When the Holy One bade me sacrifice him, He told me so Himself; now therefore I demand that He Himself tell me to do him no harm."

Straightway He opened the heavens and spoke through the thick clouds, as it says, *By Myself have I sworn* (verse 16).

PR 40; Tan. Y. 46. T.S. 22, 123 and note.

76. ABRAHAM, ABRAHAM. The two "Abrahams" are separated by a disjunctive mark, to show that the latter Abraham differed from the former: the latter was Abraham made perfect, whereas the former was still imperfect.[1] We find also "Jacob, Jacob"; "Samuel, Samuel." In their case too there is a disjunctive accent; but when Moses' name is thus repeated (Exod. 3:4) there is no disjunctive. The reason is this: To all other prophets He spoke only at intervals, but He never ceased to speak to Moses all his life.[2]

R. Hiyya said: The angel's repetition of Abraham's name was meant to infuse him with a new spirit, and to spur him to fresh activity with a re-invigorated heart.

Exod. R. 2, 12; Zohar 1, 120a, b. T.S. 22, 125 and note.

77. Lay not your hand upon the lad.

But where was the knife? The angels' tears had fallen upon and dissolved it. "Then I will strangle him," said he. "*Lay not your hand upon the lad,*" he enjoined. "Let me draw a drop of blood from him," he urged. "*Neither do anything*—m'umah—*to him*" answered he, i.e., Do not inflict a blemish—mum—upon him.

§ 74 [1] Every generation would contain such men, whose merit would protect them. The four (including Abraham) stand for love of man, service of God, study of Torah, and civil justice, respectively: these constitute the fundamentals of civilization, and so every age must contain some who practise them (Y.T.).

§ 76 [1] Apparently the thought is that the repetition represented Abraham before his trial, when he was yet imperfect, and Abraham as he now triumphantly emerged from his trial, perfect in obedience.
[2] Therefore there is no "mark of interruption" between the two statements of his name.

thing unto him; for now I know that thou art a God-fearing man,

COMMENTARY

any thing. a. This repeats the first words, "Lay not," etc., for emphasis.[103] **now I know. a.** I.e., I have made known to the world.[104] **b.** Now your potential love for Me has become actual.[105] **c.** This was said by the angel, hence *now* I know. [This disagrees with *b* and the comment on *he said*— Ed.][106] **d.** "Now" refers not to time but to the action: now the action has been performed by which it may be known that you fear God.[107] **e.** The phraseology ("now") is that employed in human speech, which is the usual style of the Torah.[108] **that thou art a God-fearing man. a.** You showed yourself an intimate *friend* of God when you pleaded for Sodom; your unquestioning obedi-

ANTHOLOGY

When Abraham's and Isaac's tears intermingled, tears streamed forth from the angels and dissolved the knife, turning it back to its raw state. For it says, *Lay not your* hand *upon the lad*—hand, not knife. The angels stood before the Almighty and pleaded, "Sovereign of the Universe! Wilt Thou not save his son from the knife as he lies before Thee bound like a beast?" Thus it says, *Man, though he be like a beast,*[1] *Thou preservest, Lord* (Ps. 36:7).

Another account: He took the knife to cut him so that a *rebiith*[2] of his blood might flow out. But Satan came and jogged Abraham's arm and the knife fell out of his hand. As he stretched out his hand to pick it up a Heavenly Voice cried out, *"Lay not your hand upon the lad."* But for that Isaac would already have been slain.

Another version: When Abraham held the knife the angels cried out and wept bitterly before the Almighty. "Master of the world," they urged, "Abraham is about to slay his son, yet Thou didst say, *In Isaac shall seed be called to you* (21:12). To whom wilt Thou declare at Sinai, *I am the Lord your God* (Exod. 20:2)? Or who will sing before Thee at the Red Sea, *This is my God, and I will glorify Him (ibid.* 15:2)?" "I tried Abraham," He replied, "and found his heart in sympathy with Mine. You, who so burdened Me,[3] go down and rescue him." At that He sent an angel of mercy who called to Abraham, *Lay not your hand upon the lad.* "Then I will burn him, or cut him up, limb by limb," said he. *Neither do any thing to him,* he replied.

R. Judah said: When the knife touched his throat, Isaac's soul fled, leaving him lifeless. But when He let His voice be heard from between the two Cherubim,[4] proclaiming, *Lay not your hand upon the lad,* his soul returned to his body. Then Abraham untied him; he stood upon his feet, and Isaac now knew that the Torah assures Resurrection, that all the dead will live again. In that moment he declared, "Blessed art Thou, who resurrectest the dead."[5]

Gen. R. 56, 7; Tan. Vayyera 23; Midrash;[6]
ARN MS; PRE 31. T.S. 22, 127-9. 131-2.

78. For now I know.

"Sovereign of the Universe!" cried Abraham in that moment to the Almighty, "A man tries

---

§ 77 [1] This rendering must be assumed here. AJV: *Man and beast.*

[2] A measure, a quarter of a *log*, the latter being equal to the contents of six eggs. A *rebiith* of blood is the smallest quantity that can sustain life. This, the previous and the following pleas by Abraham are not meant to convey the idea that he wished to harm him, but are intended to emphasize his desire to obey God. Cf. Zohar 1, 120b: Abraham was distressed when the angel enjoined him, *Lay not your hand upon the lad,* for he thought that his offering was imperfect, and that his labor, his preparations, and the altar he had built, were all for nought.

[3] With subjecting him to this trial; see par. 1.

[4] See Exod. 25:22.

[5] This Midrash is given in a different version in *Aggadath T'fillath Sh'moneh Esreh*, printed in Beth Hamidrash Part 5: When Isaac was bound on the altar and became ashes, his dust being strewn over Mount Moriah, the Holy One, blessed is He, poured dew over him and revived him. Therefore did David, peace to him! sing, *"Like the dew of Hermon, that comes down upon the mountains of Zion; for there the Lord commanded the blessing, even life for ever"* (Ps. 133:3), i.e., like the dew which revivified our father Isaac. There and then the angels sang, "Blessed art Thou, O Lord, who resurrectest the dead."

[6] Quoted in Ner Has'chalim MS.

ANTHOLOGY

his neighbor, because he does not know what is in his heart. But didst Thou have to do this to me, Thou who searchest the heart and the reins? Was it not manifest to Thee when Thou badest me offer my son, that I would wholeheartedly and immediately do Thy bidding?" Said the Holy One, blessed is He, to him: "My purpose was to make it known to the peoples that I did not choose you without reason. Yea, now I know you have made it known to all that you love Me."

Another interpretation: Did He then not know beforehand? Surely it is written, *I am God . . . declaring the end from the beginning, and from ancient times things that are not yet done* (Isa. 46:9f.)?—Read not, *yadati* (I know), but *yidati* (I have made known): Now all mortals will know how far the fear of heaven reaches, that a man may sacrifice his only son. All this magnifies His revered and awe-inspiring Name.

Gen. R. 56, 7; Tan. Y. Vayyera 46; Midrash Habiur. T.S. 22, 133-5.

79. That you fear God.

It was taught, R. Meir said: Abraham is described as God-fearing, and Job is too: just as Abraham's fear stemmed from his love of God, so did Job's. But how do we know this of Abraham himself? Because it is written, *The seed of Abraham who loved me* (Isa. 41:8).

What is the difference between love-inspired conduct and that which is inspired by fear? The following, even as it was taught: R. Simeon b. Eleazar said: Love-inspired conduct is greater than conduct inspired by fear, for the latter is effective a thousand generations, whereas the former is effective two thousand generations. Of the former it is written, *I the Lord your God . . . show mercy to thousands* [of generations] *of them that love Me and keep My commandments* (Exod. 20:6); but of the latter it is

written, *And keep His commandment to a thousand generations* (Deut. 7:9). But the latter verse too states, *With them that love Him and keep His commandments?* Each is to be understood by reference to its nearest phrase.[1]

It is written, *Happy is the man that fears the Lord, that delights greatly in His commandments* (Ps. 112:1). Four men are described as fearing God, viz.: Abraham, Joseph, Job, and Obadiah. Abraham: *For now I know that you fear God*; Joseph: *I fear God* (42:18); Job: *A wholehearted and an upright man, one that fears God* (Job 1:8); Obadiah: *I your servant fear the Lord from my youth* (1 Kings 18:12). But did not all the righteous fear God, and did they not walk before Him in integrity? Why then does Scripture single out these? To teach that these feared Him in a spirit of voluntary willingness of heart.

Scripture writes, *It is well with them that fear God* (Eccl. 8:12). Praised be the name of the Supreme King of kings, who rewards well those that fear Him. . . . For of Abraham it is written, *For now I know that you fear God*; in reward for this *Thou madest a covenant with him*, as stated through Ezra (Neh. 9:8), this being preceded by *Thou art the Lord God, who didst choose Abraham* (ibid. 7).

Sot. 31a; Midrash Hahefetz; PZ Sh'moth beginning of Bo. T.S. 22, 136 and note.

80. THAT YOU FEAR GOD. R. Johanan said: More was said of Job than of Abraham. For of Abraham it is written. *Now I know that you fear God*; whereas Job is described as a *man* [that] *was wholehearted and upright, and one that feared God, and shunned evil* (Job 1:1).

R. Abba said: More was said of Obadiah than of Abraham. For it does not say that Abraham feared Him *greatly*, as it does of Obadiah: *Now*

§ 79 [1] The first text reads: *To the thousands* [of generations] *of them that love Me*; thus the "thousands" refer directly to those who love God. But the second reads: *. . . and keep His commandments to a thousand generations*; there the "thousand generations" are linked with those who "keep His commandments." Keeping God's commandments, as distinct from loving Him, may be the result of fear (Rashi).

seeing thou hast not withheld thy son, thine only son, from Me."
[13]**And Abraham lifted up his eyes, and looked, and behold behind him a ram caught in the thicket by his**

COMMENTARY

ence in this instance could only be the result of your fear of God, not your love.[109] **b.** In the light of My former promises you might well have interpreted My command as meaning merely that you are to place him on the altar. The fact that you did not do so proves that you fear God.[110] **c.** You have reached the highest stage possible.[111] **withheld.** Heb. *hasachta*. There are two words in Heb. for

"withhold": *mana* and *hasach*. The former is used of an action that ought to take place, whereas the withholding of it is wrong, e.g., *Withhold not* (al timna, rt. mana) *good from him to whom it is due* (Prov. 3:27). The latter is the reverse and connotes to refrain from or prevent an action that ought not to be done, so that it is right to refrain, e.g., *I also withheld* (wa-ehsoch, rt. hasach) *you from sinning against Me* (20:6). Here *hasach* is used: even though withholding him would have seemed right, you did not do so.[112] **from Me.** I.e., because it was I who commanded. [For other interpretations see verse 11, *the angel*, etc., *b*—Ed.][113] [13]**Abraham lifted up his eyes.** He did not want all his preparations for a sacrifice to go for nought; so he looked about him to see if he could find a suitable animal to sacrifice.[114] **behold . . . a ram.** Passing in front of him.[115] **ahar.** (AJV: *behind him;* but all the following interpretations reject this rendering.) I.e., after that.[116] **caught, etc. a.** After the

ANTHOLOGY

Obadiah feared the Lord greatly (1 Kings 18:3).[1]

B.B. 15b; Sanh. 39b.   T.S. 22, 138-9.

81. **Seeing that you did not withhold your son, your only one.**

Do not say that all ills that do not touch one's own body are not ills:[1] I will regard you as meritorious as if I had commanded you to sacrifice yourself, and you did not refuse.

R. Simeon b. Yohai said: The Holy One, blessed is He, said to him: "By your life! I will ascribe merit to you as though if I had enjoined you to sacrifice yourself, you would not have refused, for My name's sake." For our text says: *Seeing that you did not withhold your son.* Now, this explicitly says who is meant; to what then does "your only one" refer? To yourself, for the soul is called the only one, as in the text, *Deliver my* soul *from the sword, mine* only one *from the power of the dog* (Ps. 22:21). Said Abraham: "Master of all worlds! I

cannot descend from here without a sacrifice"; to which He replied, "Lo! your sacrifice awaits you since the Six Days of Creation.[2] Lift up your eyes and behold the sacrifice behind you." Then *Abraham lifted up his eyes.*

Num. R. 17, 2; PR 40.   T.S. 20, 141. 143.

82. **Behold a ram.**

R. Eliezer said: It came from the mountains where it had been feeding. R. Joshua said: An angel brought it from the Garden of Eden, where it had been feeding under the Tree of Life and drinking from the stream that flows at its foot; its fragrance pervaded the whole world. When had it been placed in the Garden? At twilight on the last day of the Six Days of Creation.

R. Zechariah said: The ram, which had been created at twilight, sped to be offered as a substitute for Isaac. But Samael[1] stood and would thwart it, so that the sacrifice of our father Abraham might be made null, but it was caught

§ 80   [1] According to the Talmud *ad loc.* this Obadiah was a proselyte; some Rabbis in B.B. 15b hold that Job was a Gentile. This may explain why they are both so praised, in the same way as a penitent sinner is said to be higher than the completely righteous (Sanh. 99a).
§ 81   [1] It was a great sacrifice; still, it did not demand his own life.
  [2] Cf. Aboth 5:6, which maintains that the ram which Abraham sacrificed instead of Isaac was created at Sabbath eve at twilight—i.e., it had been ordained since the very Creation that it should be at hand at that moment. On the whole passage cf. par. 16.
§ 82   [1] See par. 49, note 1.

horns. And Abraham went and took

COMMENTARY

angel had bidden him not to harm the lad, he saw

the ram caught in the thicket.[117] **b.** Immediately after seeing it free he saw it caught in the thicket. This indicated to him an act of Divine Providence, in providing a substitute for Isaac. Otherwise he would not have taken it, since it might belong to

ANTHOLOGY

by its two horns between the trees, as it says, *He looked, and behold a ram.* What did the ram do? It stretched out its forefoot and hindfoot into Abraham's cloak. He looked and beheld the ram, took and freed it from its entanglement, and offered it instead of Isaac.

R. Huna, citing R. Hinena b. Isaac, said: All that day Abraham saw the ram passing from tree to bush, from bush to thicket, continually being trapped, freeing itself and again becoming entangled. Said the Holy One, blessed is He, to him: "So will your children be trapped through their sins and entangled by foreign Powers, passing from Babylon to Media, from Media to Greece, and from Greece to Edom" [=Rome]. "Master of all worlds," he cried out; "is it to be thus for all time?" "No," said He to him. "They will be redeemed eventually through the horn of this ram, as it says, *The Lord God will blow the horn, and will go with whirlwinds of the south* (Zech. 9:14).

> Midrash quoted in Yalkut Shimoni 1, 101; PRE 31; J. Taan. 2, 4. T.S. 22, 144-5. 147.

83. **Behold a ram** *ahar* **(AJV: behind).**

What does *ahar* imply? Said R. Judah b. R. Simon: After (*ahar*) many generations.[1] Your children will be seized for their iniquities and entangled in afflictions. Yet will they be redeemed through the horn of a ram, etc.[2]

The Holy One, blessed is He, said to him: "Your children will sin before Me, and I will sit to judge them on New Year. If they wish Me to forgive them, let them sound the shofar before Me on that day." "What is the shofar?" asked Abraham. "Do you really not know?"

said He. "No," was the reply. "Turn around and see," He answered. Thereupon *Abraham lifted up his eyes and looked, and behold a ram behind him caught in the thicket by his horns.* Said He to him: "Let them sound this horn and I will forgive their sins."[3] There and then he praised and gave thanks to the Almighty.

It is written, *This is the law of the* olah (*burnt-offering*—Lev. 6:2). What does *olah* signify? That it ascends (*olah*) to the Almighty and makes atonement for the iniquities of Israel. Now, Abraham sacrificed the ram to God as a burnt-offering, as it says, *Abraham lifted up his eyes and behold a ram,* ahar, etc. Now, what does *ahar* mean? After the Holy One, blessed is He, had seen him about to sacrifice his son Isaac as a burnt-offering with all his heart and with all his soul, He sent him the ram as a substitute. The Sages said that the ram had been in existence ever since the Six Days of Creation to serve as a burnt-offering instead of Isaac.... There the Holy One, blessed is He, assured him that when his children offered burnt-offerings, He would immediately accept them.

Some interpret: After the words of Satan. Others interpret: He saw a ram which had been created after all created things. Hence we infer that it was created on the Sixth Day at twilight.

> J. Taan. 2, 4; Tan. Y. Vayyera 46; Tan. Tsav 13; Midrash.[4] T.S. 22, 146. 149-51.

84. **By his horns.**

All the horns of the wicked will I cut off, but the horns of the righteous shall be lifted

---

§ 83 [1] Gen. R. 56:9 reads: "After all that happened," which EJ explains: After all that God had done for Israel, liberating them from Egypt, etc.

[2] It continues as the end of the previous passage.

[3] Cf. R.H. 16a: R. Abbahu said: Why do we sound the shofar of a ram [on New Year]? In order (says the Almighty) that I may recall the sacrifice of Isaac in your favor, and regard it as though you had bound yourself [for a sacrifice] before Me—(T.S. 22, 156).

[4] Quoted in a MS Yemenite Collection.

the ram, and offered him up for a burnt-offering in the stead of his son. ¹⁴And Abraham called the name

COMMENTARY

someone.¹¹⁸ **c.** He saw the ram after it had been caught.¹¹⁹ **in the stead of his son. a.** He did not offer it in thankfulness for his son's delivery, but as a substitute for him.¹²⁰ **b.** Here we have the irrefutable proof that sacrifices have only symbolic significance. If this were not so, Abraham's sacrifice would be nothing but a ridiculous ceremony: he slaughters an animal that he finds accidentally in the wilderness and that was not even his own, "instead of his son"—at a moment when the dearest possession of his life has been returned to him! It is as if someone received a most generous gift—and picks up a pin from the street and presents it as a token of his gratitude! With this sacrifice, however,

ANTHOLOGY

up (Ps. 75:11). Ten horns the Holy One, blessed is He, gave to Israel . . . one was the horn of Isaac, as it says, . . . *behold a ram behind him caught in the thicket by his horns.*¹

Midrash T'hillim 75. T.S. 22, 153.

85. He took the ram, and offered him up for a burnt-offering instead of his son.

R. Bannai said: He prayed, "Lord of all worlds! Regard the blood of this ram as though it were the blood of Isaac my son; its *emurim*¹ as Isaac's *emurim*." Thus we learned: When a man declares, "This animal be instead of that"; or, "an exchange for that"; or, "a substitute for that"; it is a valid exchange.² R. Phinehas, quoting R. Eleazar, said: He prayed, "Lord of all worlds: Regard it as though I had first sacrificed my son Isaac and then this ram in his stead," *instead* having the same meaning as in the text, *Jotham his son reigned in his stead* (2 Kings 15:7).³

Gen. R. 56, 9. T.S. 22, 154.

86. THE RAM. Ten things were created on the eve of the Sabbath at twilight of the Sixth Day of Creation. . . . Some maintain, Abraham's ram too.

We learnt that that ram was created at twilight, and that it was a yearling, as it is written, [a burnt-offering must be] *a he-lamb of the first year* (Num. 7:63). How then could it have been created at twilight? It means that it was then pre-ordained that the ram should be at hand when Abraham would need it. The same is true of all things which are said to have been created then, which means that it was then pre-ordained that they should appear at the moment that they were needed.

Abot 5, 3; Zohar 1, 120b.
T.S. 22, 155 and note.

87. THE RAM. [When Aaron was consecrated for the High-Priesthood he was commanded to *come into the holy place with . . .*] *a ram for a burnt-offering*" (Lev. 16:3): that means, with the merit of Isaac, to which "ram" esoterically alludes.

PR 47. T.S. 22, 158.

88. AND OFFERED HIM UP FOR A BURNT-OFFERING INSTEAD OF HIS SON. R. Isaac said: Abraham had a ram, called Isaac, which used to run at the head of the flock. Gabriel ran and brought it to him, and he sacrificed it as a burnt-offering instead of his son. That day was New Year, and Abraham fulfilled five pre-

§ 84 ¹ To lift up the horn is a Biblical idiom meaning to exalt, glorify. The Midrash states that God gave ten occasions of such uplifting to Israel. One was the sacrifice of Isaac, symbolized by the horns of the ram offered in his stead; the merit of this sacrifice exalts Israel. We may also have the thought here of forgiveness through the sounding of the horn and recalling Isaac's sacrifice, as in par. 83.
§ 85 ¹ The specially consecrated parts.
² This is a technical term denoting that both the animal originally dedicated and the one now declared as its substitute are holy.
³ There, of course, it means as his successor, not as his substitute. So Abraham prayed that the ram should count as *additional* to Isaac.

of that place Adonaijireh; as it is

COMMENTARY

Abraham vows that his life shall be devoted to the Divine Will, for all time to come.[121] [14]**Adonaijireh** (lit., God will see; or, God will provide). **a.** The plain meaning is: The Lord will see and choose this place for the dwelling of the Divine Presence (i.e., the Temple).[122] **b.** God will see to it for all time that the merit of Isaac's binding shall be credited to his descendants.[123] **c.** He named it so to commemorate his assurance to Isaac, "God will provide," etc. (verse 8), and lo! He has provided.[124] **d.** God will always see and remember my intentions in this place.[125] **e.** Abraham had chosen Mount

ANTHOLOGY

cepts with it. He took its horns and blew upon them. He used the wool for the blue thread;[1] the skin for phylacteries and *mezuzoth*;[2] the thighs for flutes; and the entrails (guts) for harps.[3]

When Isaac lay bound on the altar the Angel of Death crouched before him and declared, "The moment he lays hand on him I will take his soul." But when he saw how all pleaded for Isaac, he said: "None is his enemy; I too then will not touch him." Thus it says, *When a man's ways please the Lord, He makes even his enemies to be at peace with him* (Prov. 16:7).

R. Judah and R. Jose disagreed about this ram. One maintained that it was providentially made to appear at that very moment. The other held that it was the leader of Abraham's flocks, and its name was Isaac, but he did not recognize it. Said the Holy One, blessed is He, "Let Isaac be substituted for Isaac." Now, why a ram and not an ox or a goat? Because seven precepts are performed with it: The two horns are the two trumpets,[4] its two legs are used for the two flutes, the skin for the tabret, the intestines for harps, and the small intestines for viols. R. Joshua observed: In that sense the Sages said: Alive, it has but one voice; dead, it has seven.

R. Hanina b. Dosa said: Nothing of that ram was wasted. The ashes were the foundation on the top of the inner altar, as it says, *Aaron shall make atonement upon the horns of it* [sc. the altar] *once in the year* (Exod. 30:10). The tendons of the ram were ten, corresponding to the ten strings of the viol upon which David played.[5] Of its skin was made the girdle for Elijah's loins, as it says, *They answered him: "He was a hairy man, and girt with a girdle of skin about his loins." And he said: "It is Elijah the Tishbite"* (2 Kings 1:8). As for the ram's horns, the left was sounded by the Holy One, blessed is He, at Sinai, as it says, *There was the sound of the shofar* (horn—Exod. 19:19). The right horn, which is larger than the left, He will sound in the future to call for the Ingathering of the Exiles, as it says, *In that day a great horn shall be blown, and they shall come that were lost in the land of Assyria, and they that were dispersed in the land of Egypt* (Isa. 27:13).

ARN MS; MhG; PRE 31.
T.S. 22, 159 and note.

89. HE OFFERED IT AS A BURNT-OFFERING. When Shem died he transmitted the priesthood to Abraham. Was Abraham then a first-born?

§ 88 [1] See Num. 15:38: *Speak to the children of Israel, and bid them that they make them throughout their generations fringes in the corners of their garments, and that they put with the fringe of each corner a thread of blue.*

[2] See Deut. 6:8-9: *And you shall bind them for a sign upon your hand, and they shall be for frontlets between your eyes. And you shall write them upon the door-posts* (mezuzoth) *of your house and upon your gates.*

[3] Flutes (rather, reed-pipes) and harps were used in the Temple Service. The same is true of the other musical instruments mentioned. It is undoubtedly not meant literally, but that Abraham used the parts of the ram in the same way as his descendants would one day sing the praises of God, accompanied by these instruments; or in anticipating the precepts which God would give his children in the future.

[4] This alludes either to Num. 10:2: *Make you two trumpets of silver . . . for the calling of the congregation, and for causing the camps to set forward;* or to the trumpets which were used in the Temple service: *With trumpets . . . shout before the King, the Lord* (Ps. 98:6). So, too, the other instruments.

[5] Cf. Ps. 144:9: *Upon a psaltery of ten strings will I sing praises to Thee.*

said to this day: "In the mount

COMMENTARY

Moriah because it was the highest in that range; now he named it thus in order that it might be an eternal testimony to Him.[126] **f.** God will see and remember this place for ever.[127] **as it is said to this day,** etc. **a.** Render: As it is said, "Today one must appear on the mountain of the Lord"— the reference is to the pilgrimages which every Jew was obliged to make thrice yearly (Exod. 23:17).[128]

ANTHOLOGY

The birthright was conferred on him because he was righteous, as we see from our text.[1]

Num. R. 4, 6. T.S. 22, 160.

90. **Abraham called the name of that place Adonaijireh (the Lord sees).**

R. Huna, quoting R. Eleazar, said: Why is the Holy One, blessed is He, called "Place"? Because He is the place of the world,[1] as it says, *Behold, the place is with* [i.e., in] *Me* (Exod. 33:21). Abraham too called Him "Place", as it says, *Abraham called the name of that Place[2] Adonaijireh.*

Midrash T'hillim 90. T.S. 22, 164.

91. ADONAIJIREH (the Lord will see). *And when I see the blood, I will pass over you* (Exod. 12:13): I will see the blood of Isaac's sacrifice (binding). That is the blood meant, for it says, *Abraham called the name of that place, "The Lord will see,"* whilst elsewhere it says, *God sent an angel to Jerusalem to destroy it; and as he was about to destroy the Lord beheld, and He repented Him of the evil* (1 Chron. 21:15): what did He behold? The blood of Isaac's sacrifice.[1]

R. Johanan said: He saw the future Temple on it, as it says, *In the mountain of the Lord it shall be seen.* R. Jacob b. Idi and R. Samuel b. Nahmani disagree on this. One maintained that He saw the silver of redemption,[2] while the other held that He saw the Temple. Logic supports the latter view, as we read, *As it is said to this day, In the mountain of the Lord it shall be seen.*

Mechilta Bo 7; Ber. 62b. T.S. 22, 165. 172.

92. ADONAIJIREH (the Lord will see). When they built the First Temple, how did they know the site of the altar? Said R. Eleazar: They saw in a vision the great prince Michael standing and sacrificing on that site. R. Isaac Nappaha[1] said: They saw the ashes of the ram that substituted for our father Isaac lying there, [as it is written, *He called the name of that place Adonaijireh,[2] as it is said to this day: "In the mount of the Lord it shall be seen."[3]*]

Zeb. 62a. T.S. 22, 166.

93. **As it is said to this day.**

What does "this day" indicate? As on this day, for it was New Year.[1]

Scripture tells us that Abraham already knew that here would be the house of service (sacrifice) for future generations.

PR 40; MhG. T.S. 22, 167-8.

§ 89 [1] For only a first-born could perform the sacrifice.
§ 90 [1] The world is in Him, but He is not contained in it.
      [2] Understood now as meaning God Himself.
§ 91 [1] See par. 55.
      [2] The half-shekels given in the wilderness for the building of the Tabernacle. These served the purpose of a census, and also for an atonement. The proof-text *ad loc.* is Exod. 30:16: *And you shall take the atonement-money from the children of Israel.* The Tabernacle was the forerunner of the Temple, so the atonement-money given for it was now seen by God, and the place where the Temple was destined to stand was spared.
§ 92 [1] Or, the smith.
      [2] This is apparently translated, *the Lord with show* (yareh)—the altar site, by preserving there the ashes of Isaac's substitute sacrifice.
      [3] In cur. edd. a different proof-text is quoted. The present reading is given in the Commentary on Sefer Yetsirah by R. Judah of Barcelona, p. 109.
§ 93 [1] I.e., this story will always be retold on this day—New Year.

where the Lord is seen." ⁱ⁵**And the**

COMMENTARY

b. Future generations will say, To this very day the Lord will appear [to His people] in the mountain of the Lord.¹²⁹ **c.** That it may be said today and tomorrow, "In the mountain of the Lord the Lord appeared to Abraham."¹³⁰ **d.** This is an explanation by Moses when writing the Torah, viz., This is the mountain which people designate today, "In the mount where the Lord will be seen," i.e.,

ANTHOLOGY

94.   In the mount of the Lord.

Moses pleaded, *O Lord God . . . Let me go over, I pray Thee, and see . . . that goodly mountain, and Lebanon* (Deut. 3:24-5). All called it [Jerusalem] mountain. Abraham called it mountain, as our text says, *As it is said to this day: "In the mount of the Lord it shall be seen."* David called it mountain, as it says, *Who shall ascend the mountain of the Lord* (Ps. 24:3)? Isaiah called it mountain, as it says, *In the end of days the mountain of the Lord's house shall be established as the top of the mountains* (Isa. 2:2). The nations called it mountain, as it says, *And many nations shall go and say: "Come ye, and let us go up to the mountain of the Lord (ibid. 3)."*¹

Sifre D'barim 28. T.S. 22, 169.

95.   In the mount of the Lord. It is written, *In Salem also is His tabernacle, and His dwelling-place in Zion* (Ps. 76:3). Does then Scripture come to restore her [Jerusalem's] original name?¹ This is the answer: Because it says, *For this city* [Jerusalem] *has been to Me a provocation of Mine anger and of My fury* (Jer. 32:31), you might think that she is still the object of His wrath; therefore Scripture writes, [She is] *the mountain which God has desired for His abode* (Ps. 68:17): thus she is now the object of His desire and yearning, which shows that her destruction made atonement for her. How do we know that the Divine Presence will not return to her until she becomes a mountain? From the text, *In Salem also is His tabernacle, and His dwelling-place in Zion:* Now, we find that when it was known as Salem

it was called Mountain;² hence we learn that the Shechinah will not return there until she becomes a mountain, as it says, *Abraham called the name of that place Adonaijireh, as it is said to this day, "In the mount of the Lord He shall appear."* It also says, *Remember, O Lord, against the children of Edom, the day of Jerusalem* (Ps. 137:7). When will that be? When its foundations will be uprooted, as the text continues, *who said: Rase it, rase it, even to its foundations."*

R. Eleazar said: Why does Scripture say, *And many peoples shall go and say: "Come ye, and let us go up to the mountain of the Lord, to the house of the God of Jacob"* (Isa. 2:3): is He only the God of Jacob, and not the God of Abraham and Isaac? However, it means this: Not as Abraham, in connection with whom "mountain" is written, as in our text, but as Jacob, who called it house, as it says, *And he called the name of that place Beth-el* (the house of God—28:19).³

R. Simeon observed: . . . The heathens will say, Let us go *up,* for heathenism degrades, but cleaving to the Almighty elevates; *to the mountain of the Lord*—i.e., the God of Abraham, who said, *In the mount of the Lord it shall be seen.* Why is Jerusalem called "mountain"? As the mountain is free to all who would climb it, so does this sacred place freely welcome all who come to it. The verse continues, *to the house of the God of Jacob:* because Jacob called this place *the house of God* (28:17). Again, it is called both "mount" and "house": it is a "mount" to the Gentiles, who have to *ascend* it if they would come under the wings of the

---

§ 94   ¹ See next par. for the significance of calling it mountain.
§ 95   ¹ Which was Salem. See 14:18.
        ² I.e., in Abraham's days.
        ³ A mountain is a place visited from time to time only, but a house is a permanent abode.

angel of the Lord called unto Abraham a second time out of heaven,

COMMENTARY

when the nation will enter the Land of Israel the

Lord will choose it for the Temple site.[131] **e.** "To this day" means that it has become a proverbial expression.[132] **f.** Today, when I am on the mount of the Lord, may my deed appear before Him.[133] [15]**the angel of the Lord.** A prophecy is sometimes attributed to the Almighty even when it comes through an angel.[134] **a second time. a.** To inform

ANTHOLOGY

Shechinah; but a "house" to Israel, who is bound to the Shechinah, like a wife to her husband, united in love and joy, the Shechinah protectingly brooding over Israel like a mother over her children.

> T. Ber. 1; Pes. 88a; Ber. 62b; Zohar 2, 69b. T.S. 22, 170 and note. 171.

96. ADONAIJIREH (the Lord sees), etc. This teaches that the Almighty showed him the Temple built, in ruins, and rebuilt in the Messianic era. For it says, *Abraham called the name of that place adonaijireh* (the Lord sees): this alludes to the Temple built, as in the text, *Three times in a year shall your males be seen . . . in the place which He shall choose* (Deut. 16:16). *As it is said to this day: "In the mount":* this alludes to her in ruins, as in the text, *For the mountain of Zion, which is desolate* (Lam. 5:18). *"Where the Lord is seen"* is an allusion to the Temple restored and established for all time in the Messianic era, as in the verse, *When the Lord has* built up Zion, *when He has been* seen *in His glory* (Ps. 102:17).

> Sifre D'barim 352; Gen. R. 56, 10. T.S. 22, 173.

97. **The angel of the Lord called to Abraham.**

It is written, *The Lord called to Moses* (Lev. 1:1). Did He not call Abraham too, as our text indicates? However, it is not degrading for a

king to speak to his host.[1] *The Lord called to Moses:* but not as in the case of Abraham, for there it is written, *The* angel *of the Lord called to Abraham,* i.e., the angel called and the Divine spoke; whereas here, observed R. Abin, the Holy One, blessed is He, declared, "I call and I speak," as it says, I, *even* I, *have spoken, yea, I have called him* (Isa. 48:15).[2]

> Lev. R. 1, 9. T.S. 22, 177.

98. **The angel of the Lord called to Abraham a second time out of heaven.**

When Jacob left home he dreamed, *And behold a ladder set up on earth* (28:12): he saw the virtue of his grandfather Abraham, who had set up a spiritual ladder on earth, by teaching all the Unity of the All-Present. *And the top of it reached to heaven* (ibid.): his virtue reached the Throne of Glory, as we read, *The angel of the Lord called to Abraham a second time out of heaven.*

> PZ 28:13.

99. A SECOND TIME OUT OF HEAVEN. Hence we learn that the Shechinah did not speak to him a third time. So too, when it says, *At that time the Lord said to Joshua: "Make you knives of flint, and circumcise again the children of Israel the second time"* (Josh. 5:2), it implies that they did not have to be circumcised yet a third time.[1]

> MA. T.S. 22, 178.

§ 97 [1] God often allowed His Shechinah to dwell in Abraham's home, so that Abraham was His host, as it were. Therefore there was nothing surprising in His speaking to Abraham.
[2] There is no direct indication that this refers to Moses at all. But the proof-text is cited simply to show that "calling" and "speaking" are two acts, and that (sometimes) God performs both Himself. Mah. explains that the next verse, *From the beginning I have not spoken in secret,* points to the Revelation at Sinai, which was public; hence the verse can rightly be understood as alluding to Moses, since the Revelation was made through him. This is not very plausible.
§ 99 [1] This second circumcision was necessary because it had been suspended altogether in the wilderness (Josh. 5:5). The present passage probably means that never again in Jewish history was it suspended.

[16]**and said: "By Myself have I sworn,**

COMMENTARY

him how his children would be rewarded for this.[135] **b.** The angel now spoke a second time because his first address had been interrupted by the sacrifice of the ram and Abraham's observations on the mountain.[136] [16]**By Myself have I sworn. a.** Even as I am eternal, so is My oath eternal.[137] **b.** Possession of the country had already been promised. Now the oath was an assurance that even if his descendants were expelled on account of sin, they would not forfeit it for all time; nor would they ever be completely destroyed or permanently succumb to the

ANTHOLOGY

100. **"By Myself have I sworn," saith the Lord.**

Why this oath? "Swear to me," he implored Him, "never again to try me or my son Isaac." (This may be compared to one whose garden was swept away by a swollen river, which also carried off his son).[1] Another interpretation: R. Levi, quoting R. Hama b. R. Hanina, said: He implored Him, "Swear never to try me again."[2] This may be compared to a king married to a noble lady. When she bore him his first son he divorced her; the same happened after the second son, the third son, etc.[3] When she had born a tenth son to him they all assembled and demanded, "Swear never to divorce our mother again." Similarly, when Abraham had been tried for the tenth time he demanded, "Swear to me never again to put me to the test."

Gen. R. 56, 11. T.S. 22, 181.

101. BY MYSELF HAVE I SWORN. When He bade him, *Neither do anything to him,* Abraham said, "I will strangle him and so put Thee to the necessity of providing Sarah with another son named Isaac, to fulfill Thy promise to me, *In Isaac shall seed be called to thee* (21:12). Or else swear to me never to try me again. And when Isaac's ashes are heaped up before Thee,[1] let them be a memorial for all generations as though I had actually sacrificed him." The Al-

mighty replied: *"By Myself have I sworn . . . because you have done this thing."* "Nevertheless," rejoined Abraham, "I will not let him go unless Thou givest me Thy seal." "By your life," He replied, "I am lawfully free through the oath by which you adjured Me, seeing that you released Me of any further claims. Yet will I show you My love and fulfill your request. But I will not entrust My seal to you, since Ishmael is your issue. Nor will I give it to Isaac, because Esau will issue from him. I will, however, entrust it to your grandson Jacob, whose couch will be unblemished.[2] In that vein it is written, *Thou wilt give truth to Jacob and love to Abraham* (Micah 7:20). [That is to say, through the love He showed to Abraham He gave truth to Jacob, for "Truth" is God's seal.]

Midrash.[3] T.S. 22, 184.

102. BY MYSELF HAVE I SWORN. When the Israelites sinned with the Golden Calf, Moses pleaded to Him: *"Remember Abraham, Isaac, and Israel, Thy servants, to whom Thou didst swear by Thine own self"* (Exod. 32:13). Hezekiah b. Rabbi said: Moses pleaded, "Hadst Thou sworn to their ancestors by heaven and earth, Thou couldst well destroy their children, for as heaven and earth will cease, so would Thine oath cease. But, O Master of all worlds, not thus Thou didst swear to their an-

§ 100   [1] The bracketed passage is omitted in many editions, as its point is not clear, nor is the rendering certain. However, it may stand, the point being that like the disaster which carried off his field and his son too, so was this a sore trial which tried Isaac as well as himself.
    [2] But he did not plead for Isaac too.
    [3] He remarried her after each divorce.

§ 101   [1] Either, when I have burnt his body after strangling him, if the promise is not made. Or: Let it be considered as though his ashes are heaped up as a burnt-offering.
    [2] All his children will follow Me.
    [3] Quoted as a Midrash by Tosefoth on the Torah in Daath Z'kenim.

saith the Lord, because thou hast done this thing, and hast not withheld thy son, thine only son, [17]that in blessing I will bless thee, and in multiplying I will multiply thy seed

COMMENTARY

enemy. Accordingly, this was a solemn promise of

ultimate redemption.[138] **c.** "By Myself"—it is I that swear, not the angel [even though the words are spoken by the angel].[139] **saith.** Heb. *n'um.* The word is connected with *emunah*, faith, stability, permanence: the oath will remain eternally and absolutely true.[140] **because.** Heb. *yaan*, from the root *anah*, to answer or testify: this thing that you have done will testify [that you have earned the blessing promised in the next verse].[141] **thine only son.** He does not add "from Me" as in verse 12, because now the angel is speaking.[142] **[17]that . . . I will bless thee.** I.e., I have sworn to bless you.[143]

ANTHOLOGY

cestors not to destroy their children, for saidst Thou not to Abraham, *By Myself have I sworn?*" Now, what does this mean? The Holy One, blessed is He, said to Abraham: "Even as I live and endure for ever and to all eternity, so will My oath endure for ever and to all eternity." How rightly then did Moses plead when he said, *to whom Thou didst swear by Thine own self:* do it [forgive them] for the sanctity of Thine own Name, lest it be profaned.

[In the same way, the prayer, *Look forth . . . and bless Thy people Israel . . .*] *as Thou didst swear to our fathers* (Deut. 26:15), alludes to our father Abraham.

Exod. R. 44, 8; T. Maas. Sheni 5. T.S. 22, 180. 182.

103. BY MYSELF HAVE I SWORN. *The Holy One*, blessed is He, said to him: "By My right hand, by My right hand! When your children are in distress I will be with them," as it is written, *I will be with him in trouble* (Ps. 91:15). It also says, *In all their affliction He was afflicted, and the angel of His presence saved them* (Isa. 63:9).

MhG. T.S. 22, 185.

104. **Because you did this thing.**

R. Hanin observed: This was the tenth trial, yet you say, *Because you did* this *thing!* This, however, was the last trial which counter-

balanced all others, and had he not submitted to it, the merit of the others would have been lost.

Gen. R. 56, 11. T.S. 22, 186.

105. **I will surely bless you.**

Here we have a blessing for the father and a blessing for the son. *And I will greatly multiply your seed:* the father and the son will both be blessed with increase.[1] Through this sacrifice Abraham, Isaac, and Jacob received an eternal blessing, for it says, *By Myself*[2] *have I sworn.*

Gen. R. 56, 11. T.S. 22, 188.

106. I WILL SURELY BLESS YOU. R. Berechiah said: The ram's sweet savor ascended to the Throne of Glory, and it was as pleasing to Him as though it were Isaac's sweet savor. He then swore to bless him in this world and in the world to come. For it says, *I will surely bless you and greatly multiply your seed, even as the stars of heaven:* I will surely bless you in this world, and greatly multiply you in the world to come.[1]

PRE 31. T.S. 22, 189.

107. **I will greatly multiply your seed.**

Now, in Joshua we read, *And I multiplied (va-arbeh) his seed* (Josh. 24:3); but though we read it *va-arbeh*, it is written *va-arb* [a shortened and defective form]. This teaches that the Holy One, blessed is He, said to Israel: "Abraham was righteous, yet how much did

§ 105   [1] The emphasis of "surely" and "greatly" is expressed in the original by repeating the verb; the repetition is understood to indicate a double blessing and a double increase.
     [2] See par. 102, where "Myself" emphasizes the eternal nature of the oath.
§ 106   [1] See last par. Here the doubling is made to refer to the two worlds.

as the stars of the heaven, and as the sand which is upon the sea-shore; and thy seed shall possess

as the stars . . . as the sand. Your kings, prophets and saints will shine and be lofty like stars, whilst your masses will be as numerous as the grains of sand.[144] **the sand.** Even as the waves cannot

I multiply him? I gave him but one son. But you I multiplied like the stars of heaven."

Midrash Haser V'Yether. T.S. 22, 192.

108. As the stars of the heaven.

Scripture writes, *When the morning stars sang together, and all the sons of God sang for joy* (Job 38:7). The "morning stars" are Israel who are likened to the stars, as in our text.

As the stars of the heaven means: they will shine like the stars, as it is written, *And they that are wise shall shine as the brightness of the firmament, and they that turn the many to righteousness as the stars for ever and ever* (Dan. 12:3).

When David prayed, *Remember the word unto Thy servant, because Thou hast made me hope* (Ps. 119:49), he meant: I base my hopes on the word which Thou spakest to Thy servant Abraham, viz., *I will greatly multiply your seed as the stars of the heaven.*

Sifre D'barim 206; MhG; Midrash T'hillim 119. T.S. 22, 193 and note.

109. As the sand which is on the sea shore.

R. Judah the Nasi levied taxes on our Rabbis for the maintenance of the city walls. Said Resh Lakish to him: Rabbis do not need the protection of the walls,[1] for it is written, *If I would count them, they are more in number than the sand* (Ps. 139:18). If I would count whom? the righteous: and "they are more numerous than the sand"? Seeing that the whole of Israel is only *as the sand which is on the sea shore,* shall the righteous among them be more

numerous than the sand? Surely then it means, If I should count the deeds of the righteous, they would outnumber the sand. Then if the sand, which is less, affords protection from the sea, surely the deeds of the righteous, which are more numerous, suffice to protect them.

B.B. 7b. T.S. 22, 194.

110. As the sand which is on the sea shore.

Even as the sand walls off the sea, whose furiously raging waves break on the sand, so are Israel: the nations triumph over them, yet ultimately break before them. So it was with Pharaoh, Sisera, Babylon, Haman, and the Greeks. Even so will the Edomites[1] fall one day before them, as it says, *I will lay My vengeance upon Edom by the hand of My people Israel* (Ezek. 25:14).

MA. T.S. 22, 195.

111. As the stars of the heaven, and as the sand which is on the sea shore.

When they do the will of the Holy One, blessed is He, they are as the stars of the heaven, and no kingdom or people can wield dominion over them. But when they flaunt His will, they are as the sand of the sea, trampled by every imperious foot.

Or Haafelah. T.S. 22, 195 note.

112. Your seed shall possess the gate of his enemies.

Rabbi[1] said: This alludes to Tarmod.[2] Happy are they who will see her downfall, for she participated in the destruction of both Temples.

§ 109 [1] A general principle of taxation is laid down *ad loc.* that those who do not benefit are exempt. Since the Rabbis do not need the walls, they should be exempt.
§ 110 [1] This generally means Rome.
§ 112 [1] I.e., R. Judah ha-Nasi.
[2] Palmyra. *Var. lec.,* Tadmor.

the gate of his enemies; [18]and in thy seed shall all the nations of the earth be blessed; because thou hast hearkened to My voice." [19]So Abraham returned unto his young men,

COMMENTARY

sweep the sand away, so will no nation succeed in sweeping away your descendants' greatness of soul and inner strength.[145] **gate.** The "gate" of the city was its most important site; its capture gave one command of the city.[146] [18]**in thy seed shall . . . be blessed. a.** For the sake of your descendants.[147] **b.** Nations will say, "May He bless us even as He has blessed Abraham's seed."[148] **c.** When nations will *call upon the name of the Lord, to serve Him with one consent* (Zech. 3:9), they will seek blessings through your seed and endeavor to become like them.[149] **because thou hast hearkened to My voice. a.** The reward of obeying one precept is the opportunity (or desire) to fulfill another: thus, your reward will be that your descendants will furnish prophets who will teach peoples to worship the true God.[150] **b.** Reward is for obedience to God's command, not for the action which that obedience entails.[151] **c.** When My angel told you *not* to slay him. It must refer to this, because his initial obedience, his readiness to sacrifice him, has already been dealt with in verses 16-17.[152] [19]**Abraham returned. a.** This includes Isaac, who is not mentioned separately because he was part of Abraham's company.[153] **b.** He returned without Isaac, whom

ANTHOLOGY

R. Judan and R. Huna commented. One of them said that at the destruction of the First Temple she provided 80,000 archers [for Nebuchadnezzar's army], and at the destruction of the Second Temple she provided 8,000 archers [for the Roman army].

Gen. R. 56, 11. T.S. 22, 196.

113. In your seed shall all the nations of the earth be blessed.

Just as the world cannot exist without the soil of the earth, without which there can be no trees nor produce, so without Israel the other nations could not exist, for it says, *In your seed shall all the nations of* the earth[1] *be blessed.*

As long as Israel performs righteousness the nations of the earth are blessed for their sake, as our text states.

Had Israel not accepted the Torah the world would have fallen into chaos;[2] all the good that comes to the world is on account of Israel's acceptance of the Torah.

PR 11; Num. R. 2, 13; Midrash Tannaim D'barim 15, 9; MA. T.S. 22, 197-9.

114. Ekeb (because) you hearkened to My voice.

From this you learn that when he was three years old Abraham recognized the voice of the Holy One, blessed is He, and knew his Creator. For his whole life-span was one hundred and seventy-five years, out of which he obeyed God's will one hundred and seventy-two years, which is the numerical value of *ekeb*.[1]

Ned. 32a; MA. T.S. 22, 201.

115. Abraham returned to his young men, etc.

But where was Isaac? Said R. Berechiah, quoting the Rabbis: He sent him to Shem to study Torah. This may be compared to a woman who became rich through her distaff. Said she: "Since this made me rich, it will henceforth never leave my hand." Even so said Abraham: "Everything I have obtained has been only because I occupied myself with Torah and God's precepts; therefore I would not have it ever depart from my descendants."

R. Jose b. R. Hanina said: He sent him away at night for fear of the evil eye.[1] For from the

§ 113 [1] The comment is apparently based on 28:14: *And your seed shall be as the dust* (afar—soil) *of the earth,* spoken to Jacob. But the present proof-text apparently stresses *"the earth."*
    [2] Without the moral order of the Torah cosmos becomes chaos.
§ 114 [1] Hebrew letters are also numbers. He renders: You have hearkened to My voice *ekeb*—one hundred and seventy-two [years].
§ 115 [1] The wonder at his near deliverance might result in an evil eye being cast upon him.

and they rose up and went together to Beer-sheba; and Abraham dwelt

COMMENTARY

he sent home to Hebron by a different route, that he might speedily inform his mother of all that had transpired.[154] **went together.** As equals. In spite of the spiritual heights to which they had attained by their surrender to God's will, they did not allow any distinction between themselves and their servants to show itself.[155] **to Beer-sheba. a.** Temporarily only, for his permanent dwelling was in Hebron.[156] **b.** He now took up his residence there permanently, near the *eshel* (see 21:33) which he had planted.[157]

ANTHOLOGY

moment that Hananiah, Mishael, and Azariah emerged unscathed from the fiery furnace, they are never again mentioned. Whither then had they gone? . . . R. Jose b. R. Hanina said: They died through an evil eye.

R. Eleazar b. Pedath said: Although Isaac did not die, Scripture regards him as though dead, his ashes lying on the altar. Therefore it says, *So Abraham returned* [but not Isaac].

Another explanation: The Holy One, blessed is He, took him into the Garden of Eden, where he stayed three years.[2]

Gen. R. 56, 11; MhG. T.S. 22, 202-4.

116. They went together to Beer-sheba.

Because our father Abraham had experienced spiritual tranquillity in Beer-sheba, he now would not stir from it.

MhG. T.S. 22, 207.

(The following passage briefly summarizes the whole narrative.)

117. Then he took two of his young men with him, and Isaac his son, etc.

Who were these young men? Eliezer, Abraham's slave, and Ishmael. Isaac asked his father, "Whither are we going to worship Him?" "Yonder," he replied, "to a nearby place." *Then Abraham took the wood of the burnt-offering*, etc. (vs. 6). "Father," Isaac exclaimed, "whither are we going alone?" "My son," he rejoined, "to offer a sacrifice." "But Shem is the High Priest," he objected, "and it is for him alone to offer a burnt-offering." In that moment a great fear fell upon Isaac, because he saw nothing at hand for the burnt-offering.

Isaac spoke to Abraham, etc. (vs. 7). He was horror-stricken, trembling in all his limbs, because he now perceived his father's intentions, since Abraham had nought with him. In spite of that, he gathered his strength and said to his father: "You say that God has chosen me: behold, my soul is His!" Thus was Isaac reconciled to his death, in order to obey his Maker's command. Abraham answered, "I know, my son, that you will not oppose your Maker's command and mine." Isaac rejoined, "O my father! Quickly do your Master's will, and may He do yours . . ."

Satan then repaired to Sarah in the guise of an old man and asked her, "Where has Abraham your husband gone?" "To attend to his affairs," she replied. "And whither has your son Isaac gone?" he pursued. "He went with him to learn Torah." "Unhappy old woman!" he exclaimed. "How you must agonize for your son; you know not that he has taken him away to sacrifice him!" At that her loins violently trembled, her limbs were filled with terror and she swooned away. Yet on recovering she mustered her strength and declared, "Whatever the Holy One, blessed is He, has bidden him, let him—peace and life to him!—do." (Here follows the incident of the crossing of a stream; see above, par. 36.)

As he made to slay him an angel called out, *"Do not any thing to him."* Said Abraham to the angel, "The Holy One, blessed is He, commanded me to slay him, yet you tell me not to slay him: When the master and the disciple are in conflict, who is obeyed?" There and then *the angel of the Lord called to Abraham a second*

---

[2] Others: Isaac was hidden in the Garden of Eden two years, to recover from the cut which Abraham had made when he began to kill him.

at Beer-sheba. [20]And it came to pass after these things, that it was told Abraham, saying: "Behold, Milcah, she also hath borne children unto thy brother Nahor: [21]Uz his first-

COMMENTARY

[20]it was told. a. I.e., it had been told (sc. before the Binding of Isaac).[158] b. The main purpose of the passage is to tell of Rebekah's birth.[159] she also. a. Just like Sarah, so she too has borne in her old age.[160] b. "Also"—in addition to the children borne by his concubine.[161] [21]Uz. Job's ancestor.[162]

ANTHOLOGY

time out of heaven, and said: "By Myself have I sworn, saith the Lord, because you did this thing ... I will surely bless you" (verses 15-17). At that he desisted.

Midrash Vayyosha 1. T.S. 22, 208.

118. After these things.

I.e., after deep reflections. Who reflected? Abraham. Had Isaac died at Mount Moriah, he mused, would he have not died childless? What shall I do now? I shall marry him to one of the daughters of Aner, Eshcol or Mamre, who are righteous women; what care I about lineage? Said the Holy One, blessed is He, to him, "You do not need this. Isaac's mate has already been born": Behold, Milcah, she also has borne children, etc.

Another interpretation: Abraham meditated, My son is now consecrated, having been designated for a burnt-offering. How then shall he marry a woman from the land of Canaan? There and then, even as he yet stood on Mount Moriah, he was informed that Isaac's mate had been born.

Another interpretation: After Isaac had been bound and Sarah's death hastened.[1]

Another interpretation: After the ten trials were completed.

Gen. R. 56, 3; PZ; Midrash Habiur. T.S. 22, 209 and note. 211.

119. It was told Abraham.

By a divine communication.

Or Haafelah. T.S. 22, 213.

120. Milcah, she also has borne children.

Milcah and Sarah were sisters, and both were barren. Now, when Isaac was bound on the altar, and God promised, In your seed shall all the nations of the earth be blessed, Abraham reflected: Others are to be blessed for my sake; should then Milcah my kinswoman, Sarah's sister, not be remembered? There and then he was informed, Milcah, she also has borne children.

Yelamdenu.[1] T.S. 22, 215.

121. SHE ALSO. What does "She also" imply? Just as in the case of the one [Sarah] there were eight children by the wife and four by the concubine, so in her case too there were eight children by the wife and four by the concubine.[1]

Gen. R. 57, 3. T.S. 22, 216.

122. Uz his first-born.

When did Job live? R. Simeon b. Lakish, citing Bar Kappara, said: In the days of Abraham. For it is written, There was a man in the land of Uz whose name was Job (Job 1:1), and here we read, Uz his first-born.

The Holy One, blessed is He, said to Abraham, "By your life! Other trials, much more severe, should have befallen you; but now they will not. For all the sufferings which assailed Job should have fallen on Abraham. For immediately following on, After these things, it was told to Abraham, etc., we read, Uz his first-born—who

§ 118   [1] This is based on the view that she died from the shock of learning of his narrow escape.
§ 120   [1] Quoted as a Midrash Yelamdenu in Yalkut Shimoni 1, 766.
§ 121   [1] Jacob, Sarah's grandson, had eight children by his two chief wives, Rachel and Leah, and four by his secondary wives (here called concubines in contrast to the former two). Milcah, the chief wife, likewise bore eight children (verses 21-2), while Reumah, the concubine, bore four (verse 24).

born, and Buz his brother, and Kemuel the father of Aram; [22]and Chesed, and Hazo, and Pildash, and Jidlaph, and Bethuel." [23]And Bethuel begot Rebekah; these eight did Milcah bear to Nahor, Abraham's brother. [24]And his concubine, whose name was Reumah, she also bore

COMMENTARY

the father of Aram. The head of that family—this is interposed here to explain the ancestry of the Arameans, who are frequently mentioned in the Bible.[163] [22]**Chesed.** The ancestor of the Chasdim (Chaldees).[164] [23]**Bethuel begot Rebekah. a.** The whole passage is written only for the sake of Rebekah.[165] **b.** Abraham was thus informed that he could now find a wife for Isaac in his own family, and need not have recourse to a Canaanitish woman.[166] [24]**she also bore,** etc. This indicates that her children (or grandchildren) too belonged

ANTHOLOGY

was in fact Job.[1] . . . Said the Holy One, blessed is He, to Abraham: *Go your way, eat your bread with joy . . . for God has already accepted your works*[2] (Eccl. 9:7).

> J. Sot. 5, 6; Tan. Y. Sh'lach 27. T.S. 22, 218-9.

123. Uz . . . Buz . . . Kemuel.

Our Masters said: All the heathen prophets were descended from Milcah, for it says, *Uz his first-born*, this being Job, as it says, *There was a man in the land of* Uz, *whose name was Job* (Job 1:1); *and Buz his brother*: this was *Elihu the son of Barachel the* Buzite (*ibid.* 32:2). *Kemuel*: this was Balaam. Why was he called Kemuel? Because he arose (*kam*) against the people of God (*el*), for Balaam told Balak: "But for them we (the prophets) would never have arisen."[1] R. Judan and R. Judah b. R. Simon, quoting R. Joshua, identified Kemuel with Laban. Why was he called Kemuel? Because he arose against the people of God.[2]

> Yelamdenu;[3] Gen. R. 57, 4. T.S. 22, 220-1.

124. The father of Aram.

The father of all cheats (*ramai*),[1] viz., Laban.

> Sechel Tob. T.S. 22, 222.

125. Bethuel begot Rebekah.

Before the Holy One, blessed is He, made Sarah's sun set, He made Rebekah's sun rise. First *Bethuel begot Rebekah*; then, *Now the life of Sarah was*, etc. (23:1).

> Gen. R. 58, 2. T.S. 22, 223.

126. Rebekah.

The name is similar in meaning to "*a fatted calf*" (marbek—1 Sam. 28:24).[1] Similarly Rachel means a ewe.

> Sechel Tob. T.S. 22, 224.

127. His concubine . . . she also bore.

When Sarah was remembered with child, all barren women of that generation, even slaves, were remembered at the same time, as it says, *His concubine, whose name was Reumah, she also bore*.

> Midrash.[1] T.S. 22, 225.

---

§ 122 [1] Here follows the same proof-text as already quoted. It is not clear how it is inferred that Job's trials were originally intended for Abraham. Perhaps he interprets: After these things, viz., Abraham's trial with Isaac, it was told to Abraham that Uz (=Job) was now born, and that he would bear all further trials that he (Abraham) should have borne.
  [2] God is satisfied, and will not try you again.
§ 123 [1] Perhaps this is based on the view in par. 120 that Milcah was blessed with child for **Abraham's sake**.
  [2] By pursuing Jacob. Radal substitutes Balaam for Laban.
  [3] Quoted in Yalkut Shimoni 1, 766.
§ 124 [1] The arch-deceiver.
§ 126 [1] It implies well-being, prosperity.
§ 127 [1] Quoted in a Yemenite Yalkut MS.

Tebah, and Gaham, and Tahash, and
Maacah.

COMMENTARY

to Abraham's family, and were therefore included
in his injunction to Eliezer (24:38).[167]

ANTHOLOGY

128. **Tebah . . . Gaham . . . Tahash . . .
Maachah.**

R. Isaac said: All these names signify oppression. Tebah—they slay (*tabhin*); Gaham—they
burn (*gamhin*); Tahash—they silence[1] (*tahshin*); Maachah—they crush (*maachin*).

Another interpretation: Tebah implies that
the Holy One, blessed is He, slew him; Gaham,
that He burned him out of the world; Tahash,
that He sped him out of the world; Maachah,
He crushed him. No nation or family arose
from them, because He destroyed them from
the world.

Gen. R. 57, 4; MA.   T.S. 22, 226-7.

§ 128   1 Or: They speed (peoples to their death).

[1]And the life of Sarah was a hundred and seven and twenty years; these

COMMENTARY

[1]the life of Sarah was a hundred, etc. a. The age of other women in the Bible is not given. Special attention is drawn to her death to connect it with the purchase of the cave of Machpelah; and since her death is mentioned, her age is also recorded.[1] **b.** Her age is given because of her great importance as the first Matriarch.[2] **a hundred years and seven years and twenty years** (literal trans.).

ANTHOLOGY

1. The life of Sarah, etc.

Why does Scripture single out Sarah of all women to state her age? Because an angel had spoken to her.[1] Further, from it we may learn that Isaac was thirty-seven years old when he was bound on the altar.[2]

R. Hiyya said: . . . These thirty-seven years from his birth until his Binding really constituted Sarah's life, for this is the numerical value of *vayyihyu* (her life "was").[3]

Zohar 1, 123a; Or Haafelah.   T.S. 23, 1. 5.

2. The life of Sarah was a hundred years and twenty years and seven years.

The Lord knows the days of them that are without blemish; and their inheritance shall be for ever (Ps. 37:18). As they are whole [without blemish], so are their years whole: at twenty she was like seven in beauty; at a hundred, like twenty in respect of sin.[1]

Why are the years of our early ancestors counted in fragments?[2] To teach that each day was equal to the whole.[3] You find it so in the case of the matriarch Sarah, of whom Scripture writes that she lived a hundred years and twenty years and seven years: at a hundred she had the strength of a woman of twenty; at twenty she was as modest and pure as a child of seven; at seven she had the knowledge of a woman of twenty; and at twenty she had as many good deeds to her credit as another woman of a hundred. Thus the hundred was equal to twenty and [the twenty] to seven; the seven was equal to twenty and the twenty to a hundred.

Gen. R. 58, 1; MhG.   T.S. 23, 2-3.

3. THE LIFE OF SARAH WAS, etc. In this spirit Scripture writes, *The saying of the Lord, who stretches the heavens and lays the foundation of the earth, and forms the spirit of man within him* (Zech. 12:1). This means, when He puts the spirit of life into man He informs him, So many will be the number of your days. Thus we find that the years of the righteous are counted, to teach us that that is the period de-

§ 1   [1] 18:15. This elevated her above all other women.
   [2] See chap. 22, par. 1, n. 6.
   [3] Hebrew letters are also numbers. Only these thirty-seven years could she really be said to have lived, in happiness; for her ninety years of childlessness were not living. Cf. Ned. 64b: Four are accounted as dead . . . he who is childless. Lekah Tob, however, maintains that her entire life was happy (T.S. 23, 9).

§ 2   [1] I.e., sinless, because before the Giving of the Torah the Celestial Court did not punish one for sin before the age of twenty. A woman is more beautiful at twenty than at seven; accordingly Mah. emends: At a hundred she was like twenty in beauty, and at twenty like seven in sin. Hizkuni, however, interprets: At twenty she was as *naturally* beautiful, without paint or rouge, as a child of seven, who does not use cosmetics.
   [2] E.g., Abraham: *a hundred years and seventy years and five years* (25:7), instead of a hundred and seventy-five years. Jacob: *seven years and a hundred and forty years* (47:28).
   [3] Each day was lived fully, a complete life in itself. However, the example given of Sarah rather implies that the meaning is that each stage partook of the nature of another stage in a particular respect.

were the years of the life of Sarah. ²And Sarah died in Kiriath-arba— the same is Hebron—in the land of

COMMENTARY

"Years" is repeated in the usual Biblical style.[3] **the years of the life of Sarah. a.** The repetition is meant to imply that this was her natural life-span, which was not cut short by any untoward mishap. [This contradicts the view in Anthology par. 9.

—Ed.][4] **b.** All of Sarah's years were "years of her life," significant years which met the demands of a life of Mitzvoth, of which not a single day had to be entered as a failure.[5] **²Sarah died.** After the birth of Rebekah, who was to take her place, because the righteous does not die before his successor is born.[6] **Kiriath-** (the city of) **arba. a.** Arba is a proper noun—the name of the city's owner or founder. We find this name in Josh. 15:13, *Kiriath-arba, which Arba was the father of Anak*.[7] **b.** Arba was the name of one of the giants of the city.[8] **the same is Hebron.** I.e., when Moses wrote this it

ANTHOLOGY

termined by the Holy One, blessed is He, for their life's span, as our text states.

Yelamdenu.[1] T.S. 23, 4.

4. A HUNDRED, etc. R. Akiba was lecturing, but the congregation was drowsy. Desiring to wake them he said: Why was Esther privileged to reign over a hundred and twenty-seven provinces?[1] Because it was fitting that Esther, a descendant of Sarah who lived a hundred and twenty-seven years, should reign over the same number of provinces.[2]

Gen. R. 58, 3. T.S. 23, 8.

5. **These were the years of the life of Sarah.**

The Lord knows the days of them that are without blemish; and their inheritance shall be for ever (Ps. 37:18). This applies to Sarah, whose deeds were without blemish. R. Johanan observed: She was like an unblemished calf. *Their inheritance shall be for ever*: now, since the verse commences, *The life of Sarah was a hundred . . . years*, why repeat at the end of the verse, *these were the years of the life of*

Sarah? To teach that the lives of the righteous are precious in the eyes of the Holy One, blessed is He, in this world and in the next.[1]

Gen. R. 58, 1. T.S. 23, 7.

6. **Sarah died in Kiriath-arba—the same is Hebron.**

It had four names: Eshcol, Mamre, Kiriath-arba, and Hebron. Why was it called Kiriath-arba (the City of Four)? 1. Because four righteous men were circumcised there, viz., Abraham, Aner, Eshcol, and Mamre. 2. Because four righteous men, the Patriarchs of the world, were buried there, viz., Adam, Abraham, Isaac, and Jacob.[1] Four Matriarchs too were buried there, viz., Eve, Sarah, Rebekah, and Leah. 3. In reference to its four masters, viz., Anak and his three sons.[2] 4. R. Azariah said: Because from there Abraham sallied forth to pursue four mighty kings.[3] 5. Again, it fell to the lot of four in succession, viz., Judah, Caleb, the Priests, and finally the Levites.[4] 6. Because it is one of the poorest places in Eretz Israel. Which are they? R. Isaac said: Dor, Nofeth Dor, Tim-

§ 3 [1] Quoted as such in a MS Yalkut Torah in Oxford and Munich MS Codex 80.
§ 4 [1] The empire of Ahasuerus, whose queen she became; see Esther 1:1.
  [2] His point may simply be the numerical coincidence. But there may also be an ethical idea: The hundred and twenty-seven years of her life, each filled with good deeds, were fittingly rewarded by her descendant's reign over a like number of countries.
§ 5 [1] The repetition thus refers to her double life—in this world and in the Hereafter—and in this *"their inheritance shall be for ever."* Cf. par 2; there the comment is on *"without blemish,"* which is connected with the first half of our text; here it is on *"their inheritance,"* etc., and bears on the second half.
§ 6 [1] In Erub. 53a R. Isaac states: Four pairs were buried there: Adam and Eve, Abraham and Sarah, Isaac and Rebekah, Jacob and Leah.
  [2] See Num. 13:22; Josh. 15:13.
  [3] Lit., four kings, rulers of the world—the title of the Roman emperors.
  [4] It is not clear how the transfer came about.

Canaan; and Abraham came to mourn for Sarah, and to weep for

COMMENTARY

was called Hebron.[9] **Abraham came. a.** From Beer-sheba.[10] **b.** From elsewhere—the place not being stated.[11] **c.** The phrase is idiomatic, and does not necessarily imply a journey at all: "came" is an idiom for making ready to do something.[12] **d.** He went ("came") into her tent, where she had died.[13] **to mourn. a.** It does not say to bury, because he had no burial-place for her yet.[14] **b.** The Hebrew word indicates the loud wailing still usual in the East as a manifestation of grief.[15] **to mourn for Sarah.**

ANTHOLOGY

nath-serah and Hebron.[5] Our Rabbis said: Dannah, Kiriath-sannah, Timnath-serah and Hebron.[6]

Another interpretation: It was so named because from that city there came forth our father Abraham, of whom it is written, *Who aroused righteousness from the East* (Isa. 41:2), which means that he was like the light which was created on the Fourth Day.[7]

Gen. R. 58, 4; MhG. T.S. 23, 10-11.

7. Kiriath-arba (the city of four).

This name commemorated Sarah's four cries at her death: the cry of grief when she learned what had happened to her son; the cry of woe with which she bewailed him; the cry of the bitterness of her death; and the cry that her rejoicing had been incomplete.[1]

MhG. T.S. 23, 12.

8. SARAH DIED IN KIRIATH-ARBA—THE SAME IS HEBRON. "Sarah died" alludes to the soul, whereof it is said, *Then the Lord God formed man of the dust of the ground, and breathed into his nostrils the soul of life* (2:7). Now,

what is the death of the soul? Its descent from the celestial regions and entrance into the four earthly elements, viz., Fire, Air, Water, and Earth, the components of the animal soul. This is the death of the soul, because it lodges there without Torah. Ere the soul descends into the body, i.e., into the four elements which comprise it, the whole Torah is given to it; but immediately it enters the body, the Torah leaves it.... Yet in spite of this, if a man has the merit to occupy himself with the study of the Torah, *this same* soul *is Hebron*, i.e., the departed Torah is re-united with it.[1]

Zohar Hadash 119a. T.S. 23, 10 note.

9. Abraham came to mourn for Sarah.

Whence did he come? R. Levi said: From Terah's burial to Sarah's. Said R. Jose to him: But Terah's burial preceded Sarah's by two years?[1] Rather, he came from Mount Moriah: Sarah died of the shock [when she learned what had happened there]. Therefore the Binding of Isaac is told in close proximity to Sarah's death.

While Abraham was returning from Mount Moriah, Samael[2] was burning with anger that he had not succeeded in his innermost desire

---

[5] Dor: an ancient city of Canaan (see Josh. 12:23; 17:11), about nine miles from Caesarea of later fame; Nofeth Dor is in its environs. Timnath-serah: the town given to Joshua, where he was also buried (*ibid.* 19:50; 24:30); its exact site is unknown. Hebron: about eighteen miles due south of Jerusalem; it is mentioned very frequently in the Bible.

[6] Dannah: in the hill-country of Judah (Josh. 15:49). Kiriath-sannah has been identified with Debir (*ibid.*); it was not far from Hebron (*ibid.* 10:36-38), but its exact site is not known. The "poorest" means in fertility.

[7] Like the light of the sun which rises in the east, so was the sense of righteousness which he taught to men, illumining their darkness.

§ 7 [1] Or Haafelah MS reads: that her joy had been turned (to sorrow).

§ 8 [1] Deriving Hebron from *hibber*, to unite, and interpreting: It is a [re-]uniting. This passage is an interesting example of the allegorical-mystical mode of Bible interpretation.

§ 9 [1] He was 70 when Abraham was born (11:26) and 205 at his (Terah's) death (*ibid.* 32); hence Abraham was then 135. But since Abraham was ten years Sarah's senior he was 137 when she died at the age of 127.

[2] The angel (to be identified with Satan) who sought to dissuade Abraham and Isaac from obeying God's command. See chap. 18, par. 49.

ANTHOLOGY

to bring Abraham's sacrifice to nought. What did he do? He went to Sarah and said: "Alas, Sarah, have you not heard what has happened?" "No," she replied. "Your aged husband took the young Isaac and offered him as burnt-offering," he exclaimed; "the lad wept and sobbed, but there was none to save him." At that she burst into a fit of tears. Thrice she wept, even as three long blasts are sounded on the shofar; thrice with stabbing sobs, even as three short stabbing blasts are sounded;[3] her soul soared aloft, and she died. When Abraham came home he found her dead, as it says, *Abraham came [only] to mourn . . . and to weep for her.*[4]

Thus Scripture writes, *I said of laughter: It is mad; and of joy: What business has one with it* (Eccl. 2:2)? At the age of a hundred a son was granted to Abraham, in whom he greatly rejoiced. After a time he was tested by being bidden to offer him as a burnt-offering: Accepting the yoke of his Maker's will, he went with gladness to bind his son, but as soon as he stretched out his hand the angel cried out to Abraham, *"Lay not your hand upon him"*: your merit will be as great as though you had indeed offered him entire as a burnt-offering. Moreover, He blessed him and his descendants for all generations, and so his joy was yet further increased; but when he came to tell the good tidings to Sarah, he found her dead. Then was his joy turned to grief. . . . In this vein Scripture writes, *I said of laughter: It is mad; and of joy: What business has one with it?*

Num. R. 58, 5; PRE 32; MhG. T.S. 23, 16 and note.

10. **Abraham came to mourn for Sarah, etc.**

The question was asked: Is the funeral lament in honor of the living or of the dead? What does it matter? If one leaves instructions that he is not to be lamented; or, whether you may compel the heirs to pay for the funeral eulogy.[1] Come and hear: *Abraham came to mourn*[2] *for Sarah and to weep for her*: now, if the eulogy is in honor of the living—could Sarah's burial be delayed to honor Abraham?[3] That does not prove anything: Sarah herself would have desired it in order that Abraham might be honored.

Sanh. 46b. T.S. 23, 18.

11. TO MOURN FOR SARAH AND TO WEEP FOR HER. In this vein Scripture writes, *A woman of valor who can find* (Prov. 31:10)? Of whom was this said? Of Sarah: when *Abraham came to mourn for Sarah* he wept and lamented, "Where will I find one like you?"

R. Abba observed: Of no other woman are the days and years of her life and the place of her burial recorded; this was done in Sarah's case to teach that indeed there was no woman like her in the whole world. Now, the verse states that *Sarah died in Kiriath-arba*: esoterically this means that her death was not caused by the perverse serpent, which has power over all mankind save Moses, Aaron, and Miriam, whose death was caused *by the mouth of the Lord.*[1] It had no power over her too: hence Scripture writes, *And Sarah died by the fate of the Four,* but not through the serpent.[2]

Tan. Y. Hayye Sarah 3; Zohar 1, 125a. T.S. 23, 19 and note.

---

[3] On New Year.

[4] M.A. adds: Therefore we sound the short blasts on the New Year, in prayer that Sarah's death might make atonement for us, for the short blast signifies her sobbing lament.

§ 10 [1] Which was delivered by a professional paid mourner. If the eulogy is in honor of the dead, his instructions are carried out; also, the heirs can be compelled to pay for it. If, however, it is in honor of the living, his instructions must be disregarded, for he cannot deprive them of their due; his heirs, however, can forego the honor, so they cannot be compelled to pay.

[2] This is now understood in its technical sense: to deliver her funeral eulogy.

[3] It is regarded as disrespectful to delay the funeral. If the eulogy is to honor the living (Abraham), surely they had no right to wait for Abraham to come to deliver it.

§ 11 [1] Moses, Deut. 34:5; Aaron, Num. 33:38; on Miriam the Zohar adds parenthetically that the expression is not used out of respect for the Shechinah.

[2] The death of all mankind is ascribed to the snake—i.e., to sin, into which it led Adam and Eve and which every human being since then has committed. The deaths of the three enumerated, however, were not due to

her. ³And Abraham rose up from before his dead, and spoke unto

COMMENTARY

For her sake, i.e., to honor her by mourning for her.[16] **to mourn for Sarah, and to weep for her. a.** When Abraham came and found his household mourning—i.e., eulogizing her in death—because the three days of weeping had already passed, he too joined them in reciting her praises, and after that he wept. [This interpretation is based on M.K. 27b: One weeps for three days, and mourns for seven. According to this the weeping *precedes* the mourning. Hence Riba explains why the order here was reversed.—Ed.][17] **b.** "To mourn" is to eulogize, which naturally leads to weeping.[18] ³**rose up. a.** He rose up because he desired to bow down to those present.[19] **b.** This verb is used because the mourner sat and slept on the ground; see 2 Sam. 12:16, Lam. 2:10.[20] **c.** Scripture teaches here that it is good manners to stand up when addressing a gathering.[21] **from before his dead.** Lit., from

ANTHOLOGY

12. TO MOURN FOR SARAH AND TO WEEP FOR HER. He who indolently neglects to weep for a righteous man deserves to be buried before his time; and the tears shed for the righteous are counted by the Holy One, blessed is He, and stored in His treasure house.

Ner Has'chalim MS. T.S. 23, 21.

13. TO WEEP FOR HER. The *kaf* [of *lib'kothah*—to weep for her] is small,[1] to teach that it is not fitting for a sage to weep in the presence of ordinary people, particularly for women.[2]

Again, it is to teach that he who does not weep for a righteous person is punished by many a *kaf* (hand).[3]

Ner Has'chalim; Midrash Othioth K'tanoth. T.S. 23, 22-3.

14. Abraham rose up from his dead.

He saw the Angel of Death challenging him.[1]

Again, "Abraham" mystically signifies the soul, while "his dead" is the body: [hence, the verse is to be interpreted, The soul rose up out of the body].

Gen. R. 58, 6; Zohar 1, 123a. T.S. 23, 25 and note.

15. ABRAHAM ROSE UP FROM HIS DEAD. Mishnah: He whose dead lies before him is exempt from reciting the Shema,[1] Prayer, Phylacteries,[2] and all Biblical precepts.

Gemara: This implies, only when his dead actually lies before him, but not when his dead does not actually lie before him?[3] . . . R. Ashi said: If one has the responsibility of burial, it is as though his dead lies before him. For we read, *Abraham rose up from his dead*, and further on, *that I may bury my dead out of my sight*: this proves our statement.[4]

R. Johanan said: What is the source of the

sin, but "by the mouth of God," i.e., through the Divine decree dooming man to be mortal. To these Sarah was added as a fourth, and so she shared the fate of the Four. By a play on words Kiriath is connected with *karah*, to befall, and the sentence is rendered: Sarah died through the fate which befell the Four—God's decree; whereas all others died for their sins. This passage, of course, does not imply the doctrine of Original Sin. It merely attests to the facts of human experience, that *"there is not a righteous man upon earth who does [only] good and sins not"* (Eccl. 7:20).

§ 13   [1] It is a tradition that it is written smaller than the other letters.
     [2] Nevertheless Meg. 28b states that Rafram (a certain scholar) pronounced the funeral eulogy on his daughter-in-law. See also Shulhan Aruk Yoreh Deah 340, 6, which rules that a woman must be honored with a funeral eulogy just like a man.
     [3] The sense is obscure. It may be either as rendered, or: many a hand (lit., a *kaf* and a *kaf* and a *kaf*) will be smitten for him—he will die (prematurely) and be bewailed by the smiting of hands, which was the ancient manner of expressing grief.
§ 14   [1] "His dead" is interpreted as though it read "his death"—he saw his own death staring him in the face.
§ 15   [1] "Hear O Israel," etc. (Deut. 6:4-9; 11:13-21).
     [2] *Ibid.* 6:8: *And you shall bind them for a sign upon your hand*, etc.
     [3] A passage follows which states that in the latter case one is also exempt.
     [4] *Rashi ad loc.* explains that she was not actually lying before him at the time, but he spoke thus because he had the responsibility of burying her.

the children of Heth, saying: [4]"I am a stranger and a sojourner with

COMMENTARY

off the face of his dead. **a.** He had actually been lying on her, face to face, bitterly weeping at her departure.[22] **b.** From watching his dead.[23] **c.** In those days it was permitted to kiss one's dead.[24] **d.** He stood *near* her body,

in order to win the sympathy of his audience, so that they might grant his request.[25] **the children of Heth. a.** Heth was Canaan's son. Many people were present, but these, being the leaders, are specifically mentioned.[26] **b.** The Hittites.[27] [4]**a stranger** (*ger*) **and a sojourner** (*toshab*). **a.** A stranger from a foreign land who has settled (*toshab*=settler) among you.[28] **b.** Being a *stranger* here, I have no family sepulchre; but because I want to become a *sojourner* among you, I desire to buy a plot of land.[29] **c.** *Ger* standing alone is a temporarily resi-

ANTHOLOGY

above-mentioned ruling in the Mishnah? Our present text, *Abraham rose up . . . and spoke.*[5]

R. Samuel said: "Arising" refers to nought else but prayer: this teaches that he allowed her burial to override prayer.[6]

[Another interpretation: "Rose up" alludes to the Shema, for] it is said, *And you shall speak of them*[7] *. . . when you rise up* (Deut. 6:7).

> Ber. 18a; Gen. R. 58, 6; MhG; Midrash.[8] T.S. 23, 26-9.

16. And spoke to the children of Heth.

Speaking connotes comfort, as in the text, *Speak to the heart of Jerusalem* (Isa. 40:2).[1] The Writ informs us that when Sarah was alive the people of the country prospered. With her death all beauty departed, everyone was thrown into confusion, and all stood grief-stricken and weeping, in distress. Then arose our father Abraham and spoke words of comfort to them, saying, "My children, be not grieved. This is the way of the world for righteous and wicked alike; as it says, *All things come alike to all; there is one event to the righteous and to the wicked* (Eccl. 9:2). But favor me by granting me a place for burial, not for nought but for payment." So he spoke to them with soft speech.

> MhG. T.S. 23, 32.

17. I am a *ger* (stranger).

Beloved are *gerim* (proselytes), for all the prophets called themselves *gerim*. Abraham: *I am a* ger *and a sojourner*; Moses: *I was a* ger (Exod. 2:22); David: *For I am a* ger *with Thee* (Ps. 39:13).[1]

> MRE 301. T.S. 23, 33.

18. I am a stranger and a sojourner with you.

He who possesses these three traits is of the disciples of our father Abraham: a generous eye, a meek spirit, and a humble soul. How do we know that Abraham possessed a meek spirit? From our text: *I am a stranger and a sojourner with you.*

> ARN 44. T.S. 23, 34.

19. A GER (stranger) AND A TOSHAB (sojourner). But *ger* is a temporary resident, whereas *toshab* connotes a landowner? This is what he meant: "If you agree to my request, I am but a resident; but if not I am the owner of the land, for thus said the Holy One, blessed is He, to me: *To your seed have I given this land*" (15:18).

Observe Abraham's humility! The Holy One, blessed is He, had promised the land to him and his descendants for ever. Yet now he found

---

[5] This implies that until her burial had actually taken place he did nothing else whatsoever but make the necessary arrangements (M.K. and Radal).

[6] Possibly he renders: Abraham arose—i.e., prayed—*after* attending to his dead—but not before.

[7] This is understood to imply the obligation to recite the whole passage in which it occurs, commencing with *Shema* (Hear), daily.

[8] The last par. is quoted as a Midrash in MS Yalkut Mayan Ganim.

§ 16 [1] I.e., speak comfortingly to Jerusalem.

§ 17 [1] Ger, a stranger, is the technical name for a proselyte, which meaning it now bears in the proof-texts.

you; give me a possession of a burying-place with you, that I may bury my dead out of my sight." ⁵And the children of Heth answered Abraham, saying unto him: ⁶"Hear us, my lord: thou art a mighty

COMMENTARY

dent foreigner; when *toshab* is added it means a permanently resident alien.[30] **d.** The two terms are mutually exclusive: in conjunction they imply neither wholly a stranger nor wholly a native.[31] **e.** "And" here="or": you may regard me as a stranger or as a sojourner.[32] **f.** Abraham no longer lived in Hebron. Therefore he was a "stranger." Yet since he had lived there twenty-five years and desired that he and his wife should be buried there, he could call himself a sojourner.[33] **with you.** The Hittites belonged to Transjordan. Only one family (clan), to which Ephron belonged, had settled in Canaan, i.e., the country west of the Jordan. Hence he says *"with you"*—you too are resident aliens here.[34] **give me.** Allow me to purchase a burial-place Permission for this could be granted only with the

consent of the whole city; hence he addressed his request to the whole gathering, not alone to Ephron, the actual owner of the land he desired.[35] **a possession.** I.e., permanent ownership for all time.[36] **a possession of a burying-place. a.** Natives had family sepulchres, whilst there was **a** general cemetery for strangers. Abraham pleaded that since he was a stranger, and hence had no family plot, yet wished to settle there for good, he should be sold a piece of land for that purpose.[37] **b.** He asked only for a burial-place, not fields and vineyards.[38] **c.** This is the first reference in the Bible to burial; and the reverential concern which the Patriarch shows to give honorable sepulchre to his dead has been a distinguishing feature among his descendants. *Meth mitzvah,* care of the unburied body of a friendless man, takes precedence over all other commandments. Burial is the Jewish method of disposal of the dead. Tacitus (Hist. 5, 5) remarked upon the fact that the Jews buried their dead, instead of burning them. Cremation has always been repugnant to Jewish feeling, and is in total variance with the law and custom of Israel.[39] **⁵the children of Heth . . . saying unto him.** They agreed among themselves that one should give this answer on behalf of all.[40] **⁶⁻¹⁸**The bargaining which follows, with grandiloquent phrases and lavish offers, not to be taken too seriously by the person addressed, is still typically Oriental.[41] **⁶my lord**

ANTHOLOGY

no place for burial but at a price, yet he doubted not God's ways, nor did he express resentment. Moreover, he spoke to the citizens of the country with nought but humility, as it says, *I am a stranger and a sojourner.* Said the Holy One, blessed is He: "You have humbled yourself; by your life, I will make you a lord and a prince over them."

Gen. R. 58, 6; MhG. T.S. 23, 35-6.

20. **Give me the possession of a burying-place with you.**

Can you really believe that Abraham desired to be buried among them, among the unclean; or to live in their midst? But he acted with wisdom . . . declaring, "Do not think that I desire to keep aloof from you, as a superior. It

is not so; I desire to be buried in your midst, for I would not shun you."

Zohar 1, 127a, b. T.S. 23, 38 note.

21. GIVE ME THE POSSESSION OF A BURYING-PLACE WITH YOU. What does "with you" mean? In the presence of all of you. Hence our Sages said: If a man sells the site of his funeral eulogy and the place where comforters stand,[1] the members of his family may forcibly dispossess the buyer, for it is an indignity to the family.[2] Only if the whole family consents is the sale valid.[3]

MhG. T.S. 23, 38.

22. **Hear us, my lord.**

R. Jose of Galilee said: Since Scripture places the deeds of Egypt and Canaan on the same

§ 21 [1] The funeral eulogy was apparently delivered on a family plot used especially for that purpose. Again, after the mourners leave the grave their friends take up a stand and arrange themselves in two rows, through which the mourners pass while words of consolation are spoken. This too was done on a family site.
[2] To be without these and have to use land belonging to strangers. The reference is apparently to B.B. 100b, *q.v.*
[3] For that reason Abraham desired all to be present, lest someone subsequently challenge the transaction.

prince among us; in the choice of
our sepulchres bury thy dead; none
of us shall withhold from thee his
sepulchre, but that thou mayest bury

COMMENTARY

(Heb. *adoni*). **a.** The singular "my" (instead of
"our") is used, because one was speaking on behalf
of all.[42] **b.** The *-i* ending is not the usual possessive
suffix "my," but a linguistic addition as in the name
Adoni-zedek (Josh. 10:1).[43] **a prince of God**
(lit. translation). **a.** You are a great man before
the Lord.[44] **b.** You are not "a stranger and sojourner," as you humbly describe yourself, but a
great prince—you have no need to buy.[45] **c.** A term
of greatness—for you are a prophet.[46] **d.** Since we
esteem you highly, choose whichever of our lots you
will to bury your dead, and we will regard it as an
honor that you are thereby joining us.[47] **e.** Above
all, you are a prince of God, for we know the wonders which He has wrought for you.[48] **among us.**
Even though we are of a different faith.[49] **bury
thy dead.** Do not wait until you buy a plot.[50] **his
sepulchre.** Even that which is reserved for him-

ANTHOLOGY

level of wickedness,[1] why were the Canaanites
privileged to dwell an additional forty-seven
years in their country, as it says, *Now Hebron
was built seven years before Zoan in Egypt*
(Num. 13:22)?[2] As a reward for the honor
they paid to Abraham's dead, when they said
to him, *"Hear us, my lord: you are a mighty
prince among us."*

Said the Holy One, blessed is He, to them:
"You have honored My beloved; I will name
the country after you [the land of the Hit-
tites] and give you a country as good as your
own."[3]

R. Simeon b. Gamaliel, quoting R. Judah
b. Lakish, said: It is written, *Now the name of
Hebron beforetime was Kiriath-arba, which
Arba was the greatest man among the Anakim.
And the land had rest from war* (Josh. 14:15).
Because the children of Canaan had honored our
father Abraham, they deserved that the land
should be at rest. For consider our text: *the
greatest man among the Anakim. And the land
had rest from war*: but what connection has
one statement with the other? However, [it
indicates that the land won peace] as a reward
for the honor they showed Abraham when they
said, *Hear us, my lord: you are a mighty prince
among us.*[4] Moreover, a remnant of them remained and settled in Africa. Now, if they
were thus favored as a reward for honoring him,
though they did not walk in his ways nor love
the All-Present, how much the more will be
the reward of his children, who walk in his
ways and perform righteousness and charity.

TK Ahare 1; Mechilta Bo 18; TK.[5]
T.S. 23, 41. 43-4.

23. HEAR US, MY LORD. *I have exalted the
low tree* (Ezek. 17:24): this alludes to Abraham our father, who was lowly in his own
estimation, as it says, *I am but dust and ashes*
(18:27). How was he addressed by all? *Hear
us, my lord.*

MhG. Vayyera 21, 1. T.S. 23, 42.

24. **You are a prince of God among us.**

They told him: "You are a king over us, you
are a prince over us, you are a god to us." He
replied: "The world does not lack its King,
nor does it lack its God."

Gen. R. 58, 6. T.S. 23, 45.

25. YOU ARE A PRINCE OF GOD AMONG US.
Abraham had ten crowns, one of which was

§ 22 [1] In Lev. 18:3: *After the doings of the land of Egypt . . . and . . . the land of Canaan . . . shall you not do.*
[2] The forty-seven years are these seven plus the forty of the Israelites' wanderings in the wilderness, when they
might have gone directly to Canaan from Egypt.
[3] When the time comes for Israel to possess yours.
[4] He renders: Because they recognized Abraham as *"the greatest man among the Anakim,"* the land had rest
from war.
[5] Quoted in Yalkut Shimoni Part 2, 23, but found only in a shorter form in our version of TK.

thy dead." ⁷And Abraham rose up, and bowed down to the people of the land, even to the children of Heth. ⁸And he spoke with them, saying: "If it be your mind that I should bury my dead out of my sight, hear me, and entreat for me to Ephron the son of Zohar, ⁹that he may give me the cave of Machpelah, which he hath, which is in

COMMENTARY

self.⁵¹ ⁷**bowed.** Really, prostrated himself.⁵² **bowed down.** To show that he did not regard himself as a prince but on the contrary recognized their superior position.⁵³ **the people of the land.** Heb. *Am*

ha-aretz, which elsewhere means "the people of the land," and in later Hebrew, "an ignorant person," here means the Council of the Hittites in session. Abraham desired to secure a burial-place that should for ever remain a possession of his family. Such "freehold" purchase was impossible without the assent of the local Hittite Council. "The expression *am ha-aretz* occurs forty-nine times in Scripture. In forty-two of these instances it means neither the nation nor an individual boor, but is simply a technical term of Hebrew Politics and signifies what we would call Parliament."⁵⁴ **to the people of the land, even to the children of Heth. a.** To the people of the land who were the children of Heth.⁵⁵ **b.** To the heads and leaders.⁵⁶ **c.** The *lamed* (to) in the first phrase=*lifne* (before): he bowed to the children of Heth in the presence of the people of the land.⁵⁷ ⁸**entreat for me to Ephron . . . give me.** I know that it is not fitting for a man of his status to sell part of his patrimony; therefore I ask you to entreat him on my behalf to *give* me the land, for though I will pay him for it, I will regard it as a gift.⁵⁸ ⁹**give.** Sell. Possibly "give" is the usual term for "sell" in such circumstances.⁵⁹ **the cave of Machpelah.** Lit., the cave of the double. **a.** It

ANTHOLOGY

that he was called "my lord," as it says, *And he [Eliezer] said: Blessed be the Lord, the God of my lord Abraham* (24:27). Now, should you say that he called him "my lord" because he [Eliezer] was his servant, that is not so, for others too addressed him thus, as it says, *Hear us, my lord.* Another crown: he was called god, as it says, *You are a prince, god,*¹ *among us,* because he taught humanity the fear of God, as it says, *You are a God-fearing man* (22:12).

AB 55. T.S. 23, 48 note.

26. **Abraham rose up, and bowed down, etc.**

From this we learn that one must give thanks for good tidings.

Gen. R. 58, 6. T.S. 23, 50.

27. ABRAHAM ROSE UP, AND BOWED DOWN, etc. Great is humility, the trait for which our father was praised. His contemporaries called

him "a prince of God," but he exalted *them,* as our text states.

MRE 10, 182. T.S. 23, 51.

28. **If it be your mind, etc.**

I will buy it only with your consent, not by force. From this our Sages deduced that a forced sale is not valid.¹

Midrash Habiur. T.S. 23, 52.

29. **Entreat for me.**

Let me meet him, and you act as intermediaries. Yet if he is not willing, beseech him on my behalf.¹

Gen. R. 58, 7. T.S. 23, 53.

30. **The cave of Machpelah.**

Rab and Samuel disagree. One maintained that it consisted of two chambers, one within the other. The other held that it was a chamber with an upper story. Now by the latter view

§ 25 ¹ This is evidently the present Midrashic rendering. Or, a Godly prince.
§ 28 ¹ Cf. B.K. 62a.
§ 29 ¹ *Pig'u* (<*paga*) is given its two meanings, viz., to meet and to entreat.

COMMENTARY

was a double cave, one within the other; or, on top of another.[60] **b.** The whole region was called Machpelah: this follows from verse 17, *So the field of Ephron, which was in Machpelah,* etc. Possibly it

was so called on account of the double cave in it. [This interpretation satisfies both requirements of the text, viz., that Machpelah is the name of the whole region, and yet at the same time it denotes a double

ANTHOLOGY

it is rightly designated *Machpelah.*[1] But if it consisted of an inner and an outer chamber, why is it called Machpelah? Because a series of couples were buried there.[2]

Erub. 53a. T.S. 23, 55.

31. THE CAVE OF MACHPELAH. Adam declared, "While yet on earth I will build me a home for my eternal rest without Mount Moriah." He dug and built a home for his eternal rest. Said Adam: "Even the Tables of stone, which will one day be inscribed with the finger of God, and before which the waters of the Jordan will flee, [will yet be disobeyed]. May then not my body, kneaded by His two hands and animated by His living breath breathed into my nostrils, become an idolatrous image? Therefore will I place my coffin deep below the surface of the cave and in its innermost recesses." For that reason it is called the cave of Machpelah, because it is double, and there sleep Adam and Eve, Abraham and Sarah, Isaac and Rebekah, and Jacob and Leah.

PRE 20. T.S. 23, 56.

32. THE CAVE OF MACHPELAH. R. Juda said: The three Patriarchs, Abraham, Isaac, and Jacob, made a covenant with the people of the land. Abraham did it for this reason: When the angels appeared to him he thought them ordinary travelers. He ran to greet them, and desired to entertain them with a great feast.[1] ... He ran to procure a calf, but it fled into the cave of Machpelah. He followed it and found Adam and Eve lying on couches, asleep; lamps burned near them, and a fragrant, incense-like

odor enveloped them. Therefore he longed for the cave of Machpelah as a family sepulchre. He proposed to buy the cave of Machpelah from the Jebusites at a high price, in gold, ratified by a deed, so that it would be confirmed for all time as a family place of burial.

But were they Jebusites? Surely they were Hittites? They were called Jebusites on account of the city of Jebus in whose vicinity lay this cave. But they rejected his proposal. He prostrated himself and bowed low before them, as it says, *Abraham bowed* (prostrated himself) *before the people of the land.* Said they to him: "We know that the Holy One, blessed is He, will give all these territories to you and your descendants. Make a covenant with us, under oath, that the children of Israel will take possession of the city of Jebus only with the consent of its inhabitants; then you may buy the cave of Machpelah for gold, confirmed in writing as an everlasting holding in perpetuity," as it says, *Abraham hearkened to Ephron,* etc. (verse 16).

PRE 36. T.S. 23, 57.

33. THE CAVE OF MACHPELAH. R. Kisma said: The cave of Machpelah was near the entrance to the Garden of Eden. When Eve died, Adam came to bury her there, permeated as it was with the fragrance of the Garden of Eden.... He would have dug further, but a heavenly voice cried out, "Enough!"[1] So he desisted and dug no further. There he too was buried.

Who attended to his burial? His son Seth, who was *in his own likeness, after his image* (5:3). R. D'romai said: The Holy One, blessed

§ 30 [1] From *kefel,* double.
       [2] See par. 6, note 1; par. 31.
§ 32 [1] 18:1-7.
§ 33 [1] Perhaps the idea is that its walls adjoined the Garden of Eden, which he would have penetrated had he dug further.

the end of his field; for the full price let him give it to me in the midst of you for a possession of a burying-place." [10]Now Ephron was sitting in the midst of the children of Heth; and Ephron the Hittite answered Abraham in the hearing of the children of Heth, even of all that went in at the gate of his city,

COMMENTARY

cave.—Ed.][61] **which is in the end of his field. a.** He desired only the cave. Ephron, however, hinted that it would not befit Sarah's dignity to be buried at the end of a field belonging to another; rather, he should purchase the whole.[62] **b.** Therefore its sale will not impair his estate.[63] **in the midst of you. a.** In your presence—you will be witnesses.[64] **b.** The phrase does not refer to the payment but to the place: let him give me a burial-place in the midst of you.[65] **for a possession of a burying-place. a.** You must all consent that I may use it for this purpose.[66] **b.** Not to build on it.[67] **c.** The Jewish People's first piece of Promised Land were graves, the graves of their fathers and mothers; for this reason alone the land was dear to them.[68] [10]**was sitting, etc. a.** He lived among them.[69] **b.** He was present at this assembly and himself heard Abraham's request [although it was not addressed directly to him].[70] **c.** Presiding over the session of the local Council.[71] **in the hearing, etc.** Aloud and publicly.[72] **of all that went in at the gate of his city. a.** An idiom denoting the entire population, great and small alike.[73] **b.** "The gate of the city" was the place where the courts sat and dispensed judg-

ANTHOLOGY

is He, attended to his creation and attended to him when he died.

None knew of this until Abraham—peace be to him!—came and saw him and smelled the fragrance of the spices wafted from the Garden of Eden and heard the voice of the ministering angels declaring, "Adam is interred here, and Abraham, Isaac and Jacob are destined for this place." He looked upon the lamp burning and departed, immediately filled with longing for this place.

R. Huna said: Many before Abraham sought to be buried there, but the angels kept guard over it; people saw a burning fire, and could not enter, until Abraham came, entered, and bought it.[2]

> Zohar Hadash Ruth 79. T.S. 23, 57 note.

34. For silver (money) to its full value let him give it to me.

Hence the ruling: Land is acquired by money, deed, or a formal act of possession.[1]

> MhG. T.S. 23, 59.

35. In the midst of you.

In the presence of all of you, that none may subsequently dispute it. FOR A POSSESSION OF A BURYING-PLACE: that it be stated in writing that it is a permanent possession.

> MhG. T.S. 23, 60.

36. Now Ephron was sitting (yosheb) in the midst of the children of Heth.

R. Isaac said: Yosheb is written defectively (without a waw): only that day had they ap-

---

[2] In connection with Adam's burial there the following passage is interesting:

> When God decreed Adam's death, He took pity on him and allowed him to be buried near the Garden of Eden, where Adam had previously made a cave and hidden with his wife. . . . When a man is about to die Adam appears and asks him why and in what state he is leaving the world. He answers, "Woe to you that I must die on your account." But Adam retorts: "My son, I disobeyed one commandment and was punished; see how many precepts of your Maker, negative and positive, you have transgressed." . . . R. Yesa said: Adam appears to every man at the moment when he is about to depart from life, to testify that he is dying for his own sins and not Adam's, in accordance with the dictum, "there is no death without sin" (Zohar 1, 57b).

§ 34 [1] Some labor in the field, e.g., digging, threshing, fencing. The deduction in respect to money is inferred from this statement, which is interpreted: By means of the money he will formally give me title to it. In Kid. 26a the proof-text is Jer. 32:44: *Men shall acquire fields with money.*

saying: [11]"Nay, my lord, hear me: the field give I thee, and the cave that is therein, I give it thee; in the presence of the sons of my people give I it thee; bury thy dead." [12]And Abraham bowed down before the people of the land. [13]And he spoke unto Ephron in the hearing of the people of the land, saying:

COMMENTARY

ment.[74] [11]**Nay, my lord. a.** You need not buy it.[75] **b.** Not as you propose to buy it—but I will give it to you; and not the cave alone, as you suggest, but the whole field.[76] **the field . . . and the cave. a.** If I gave you the cave only, without the field, you would have no access to it.[77] **b.** I would not want a field so near to a grave; therefore I give

you both.[78] **c.** I will give you the whole field, because one may sell or give a field for sowing or planting, the cave in it being a mere subsidiary to the field [for that reason alone can I permit it to be used for burial].[79] **I give it.** Lit., I have given. **a.** It is as though I have already given it.[80] **b.** Immediately you spoke I decided to give it.[81] **in the presence of the sons of my people give I it thee. a.** You need have no fear that I will go back on my word, as all *my people* are witnesses of it. Abraham, for his part, did not rely on them, but made sure that *all that went in at the gate of his city* (verse 18), which includes merchants and strangers, witnessed the transaction.[82] **b.** *Only in their presence* do I offer it as a gift; you must understand yourself, however, that I cannot make a gift of all this.[83] [12]**bowed down,** etc. **a.** To *Ephron*, in the presence of the people.[84] **b.** He bowed to the people in gratitude, implying that he recognized that Ephron had consented to sell his field out of respect for them.[85] **c.** He bowed neither to Ephron nor to the people [but to *God*—in gratitude—in the presence of—i.e., "before"—the people; cf. Anth. par. 39.—Ed.].[86] [13]**he spoke unto Ephron.** Directly, without any intermediary.[87] **in the hearing of the people.** All heard his un-

ANTHOLOGY

pointed him chief magistrate, that a great man should not have to buy from one of humble rank.[1]

Gen. R. 58, 7.   T.S. 23, 61.

37.   In the hearing . . . of all that went in at the gate of the city.

R. Phinehas said: This teaches that they had shut their homes to come and extend their sympathy to Abraham.[1]

Gen. R. 58, 7.   T.S. 23, 62.

38.   The field I give to you.

Come and see how the wicked behave. They promise much but do not even little, and would anoint with oil from an empty flask. For Ephron said, "*The field I give to you . . . to you I give it . . . I give it to you.*" Thrice he declares it a gift, yet ends up by taking *money current with the merchant* (verse 16). For they are empty,

their words are empty, and all their deeds are empty. But as for the righteous, they are truth, their words are truth, and all their deeds are truth.

MhG.   T.S. 23, 64.

39.   Abraham bowed down.

He gave thanks to the Divine Name that they had acknowledged him as lord and prince among them. Observe: for the two times that Abraham bowed down to the children of Heth all nations are destined to bow down twice to his descendants: once in the days of Solomon, as it is written, *Yea, all kings shall prostrate themselves before him* (Ps. 72:11); and again in the Messianic era, as it is written, *Kings shall be your foster-fathers, and their queens your nursing mothers; they shall bow down to you with their face to the earth* (Isa. 49:23).

MhG.   T.S. 23, 65.

§ 36   [1] "*Was sitting*" is understood to mean as magistrate, dispensing justice "*at the gate of his city.*" But the defective spelling intimates that he had not enjoyed the dignity long; it had only just been conferred on him.
§ 37   [1] *Var. lec.*, to pay their respects (the Hebrew is the same) to Sarah.

"But if thou wilt, I pray thee, hear me: I will give the price of the field; take it of me, and I will bury my dead there." [14]And Ephron answered Abraham, saying unto him: [15]"My lord, hearken unto me: a piece of land worth four hundred shekels of silver, what is that be-

COMMENTARY

equivocal reply.[88] **if thou wilt** (Heb. *lu*) **hear me. a.** If you really wish to do me a favor, accept my money. [Apparently he renders *lu* "do me a favor."—*N'thinah l'ger.*][89] **b.** All that we have spoken hitherto was for appearances' sake. But if you would really listen to me, without your people as intermediaries, then . . .[90] **I will give the price of the field. a.** The text is literally "I have given," etc.: I wish that I had already paid you for it, so that there could be no question of a gift.[91] **b.** The verb is in the past: I have fully resolved to buy it, and having given my word, it is as though already done.[92] **c.** "I have given" refers back to verse 11: you say, "The field *I have given* (lit. translation) you": [no, rather] the price of the field take from me. The correctness of this rendering is proved by the fact that the Heb. *nathati* has a disjunctive accent; hence it is not read together with "the price of the field."[93] **d.** If you have decided to make me a gift of the field, I on my part desire to make you a gift of the money. Accept my gift, and then I will bury my dead.[94] [14]**saying unto him. a.** "Unto him" is emphasized: his first reply, when he offered the field as a gift, was meant only for the ears of the people. Now, however, he is actually going to talk business: here, then, he really speaks to Abraham.[95] **b.** Lit., to say to him, i.e., he requested another to answer him. The price he asked seems to have been such that Ephron did not dare to present his demands himself![96] [15]**a piece of land worth four hundred shekels of silver.** ("Worth" is not in the original.) **a.** Onkelos (who adds "worth") implies that

ANTHOLOGY

40. I have given [lit. translation] the price of the field.

The word of the righteous is their deed: not "I will give," but *I have given,* says Scripture.

PZ. T.S. 23, 67.

41. I HAVE GIVEN THE PRICE OF THE FIELD. Our father Abraham said: This wicked man is a braggart: if only I should acquire it for a high price, let alone as a gift! Therefore he said to him: *But if you will, I pray you, hear me: I have given the price of the field.* I will not bury her in a place acquired for nought, lest people say, "How worthless was this woman, that she did not even receive a dignified burial."

MhG. T.S. 23, 68.

42. I have given the money of the field; take it of me.

Mishnah: A woman is acquired in marriage in [one of] three ways: by money, deed, or intimacy.

Gemara: How do we know that she can be acquired by money? . . . A Tanna deduces marriage by money as follows: *If any man take a wife* (Deut. 22:13): "taking" is nought else but acquisition by money, as we read, *I have given the* money *of the field; take it of me.*

Kid. 4b. T.S. 23, 69.

43. Four hundred (*meoth*) shekels of silver, etc.

R. Eleazar said: The wicked say much but do not even a little. Whence do we know this? From Ephron. At first it is written that he demanded *four hundred silver shekels,* but in the end it says, *Abraham weighed to Ephron . . . four hundred shekels of silver, current money with the merchant:* he refused anything but *centenaria,* for there is a place where the *tikla*[1] is equated with the *centenarium.*

In this spirit Scripture writes, *He that has an evil eye hastens after riches* (Prov. 28:22): this applies to Ephron, who cast an evil eye on

§ 43 [1] The Aramaic form of shekel. On *centenarium* see par. 46, note 3.

twixt me and thee? bury therefore thy dead." [16]And Abraham hearkened unto Ephron; and Abraham weighed to Ephron the silver, which he had named in the hearing of the children of Heth, four hundred shekels of silver, current money

COMMENTARY

it had a value of this sum. Perhaps he (Onkelos) means that this was its fixed market price. The plain meaning is that Ephron himself or his forebears had paid this sum, for which he was willing to sell it.[97] b. This is according to the value fixed in the Torah: *the sowing of a homer of barley shall*

be valued at fifty shekels of silver (Lev. 27:16).[98] **four hundred shekels of silver.** The value being so little, it is not worth discussing; you could just as well have taken it for nothing.[99] **what is that betwixt me and thee? a.** Between friends such as we it does not count at all.[100] **b.** Between friends such a poor field is hardly worth selling; you could just as well take it for nothing.[101] **c.** In this apparently unconcerned tone the seller indicates the price he wants. The sum demanded, four hundred shekels of silver, is a very substantial sum, perhaps equivalent in purchasing power to from £1,000 to £2,000 in our time. In the contemporary Code of Hammurabi (see on 14:1) the wages of a working-man for a year are fixed at six or eight shekels (Bennett).[102] [16]**Abraham hearkened unto Ephron. a.** The hint was enough.[103] **b.** He accepted Ephron's valuation.[104] **weighed.** There were no coins of standard size and shapes; therefore the pieces of silver had to be weighed before their value could be ascertained. [105] **current money with the**

ANTHOLOGY

that righteous man's wealth; *and knows not that want shall come upon him* (ibid.): the Torah deprived him of a *waw*. Thus it is written, *Abraham hearkened to Ephron, and Abraham weighed to Ephron*, etc.: the second Ephron is spelled defectively.[2]

Furthermore, the cave was ascribed not to him but to the children of Heth, as it says, *the field which Abraham bought from the children of Heth* (25:10): it does not say, from Ephron, but *from the children of Heth*.

> B.M. 87a; Gen. R. 58, 7; Exod. R. 31, 17.
> T.S. 23, 72 note. 75. 92.

44. Abraham weighed to Ephron four hundred shekels.

R. Judan b. R. Simon said: This is one of the three places where the Gentiles cannot besmirch Israel by saying, "You hold stolen property." They are the following: The cave of Machpelah, the site of the Temple, and Joseph's sepulchre. The cave of Machpelah, for it is written, *Abraham hearkened to Ephron, and Abraham weighed to Ephron . . . four hundred shekels.* The site of the Temple, as it is written, *So David*

gave to Ornan for the place six hundred shekels of gold (1 Chron. 21:25). Joseph's sepulchre: *He bought the parcel of ground* (33:19).[1]

> Gen. R. 79, 7.   T.S. 23, 74.

45.   FOUR HUNDRED SHEKELS OF SILVER. Unbounded were the pains which our ancient ancestors took to obtain burial in Eretz Israel. For *a piece of land worth four hundred shekels of silver* as a place for burial he paid four hundred silver *centenaria*.[1]

In this vein Scripture writes, *One may oppress the poor, yet will their gain increase* (Prov. 22:16). This applies to Abraham, who descended into the fiery furnace for the glory of God. What had He told him? *Arise, walk through the land in the length of it and in the breadth of it, for to you will I give it* (13:17). Yet he had no place for burying his dead save by purchase, as our text relates. Now, why was this? In order that his reward in the Hereafter might be great. Thus in him was fulfilled the verse, *One may oppress the poor, yet will his gain increase.*

> PR 1; Yelamdenu MS.   T.S. 23, 76 and note.

---

[2] Which is interpreted as a sign of degradation.
§ 44 [1] Shechem, where Joseph's bones were finally buried; see Josh. 24:32.
§ 45 [1] See par. 46, note 3.

with the merchant. [17]So the field of Ephron, which was in Machpelah, which was before Mamre, the field, and the cave which was therein, and all the trees that were in the field, that were in all the border thereof round about, were

COMMENTARY

merchant. a. Acceptable everywhere.[106] **b.** Who accepts only coins of full weight.[107] **c.** Better, passing over to the merchant. Ephron himself might have been diffident about questioning the correctness of the weight, etc., in view of his exalted position and his own protestations. The money therefore was given to the merchant with whom Ephron generally did business: the former would not have any scruples about drawing attention to any deficiency.[108] **d.** The phrase probably denotes that the silver was in convenient-sized pieces, readily usable in business transactions.[109] [17]**which was in Machpelah.** This indicates that Ephron's field was a part of a region called Machpelah.[110] **which was before Mamre. a.** The field and the cave lay in front of the city.[111] **b.** The field ran the length of the city. Here the city, which was actually Hebron, is called Mamre, whereas in verse 2 it is called Kiriath-arba (literally, the City of the Four). This teaches that Mamre built a town facing Hebron; after his death it fell under the sway of an Anak ("giant") named Arba.[112]

ANTHOLOGY

46. Current money with the merchant.

R. Hanina said: Wherever a shekel of silver is mentioned in the Torah without further specification it means *sela*;[1] in the Prophets it means *litra*;[2] in the Writings it means *centenarium*.[3] The silver shekels mentioned in connection with Ephron, however, were an exception; although they are unspecified, *centenaria* are meant. For Scripture writes, *Four hundred shekels of silver, current with the merchant*; in some places *centenaria* are called *tikle* (shekels).[4]

Bek. 50a. T.S. 23, 77.

47. So the field of Ephron arose (lit. translation).

It had been lowly, and now it rose up. It had belonged to a mean man, and now it became the property of a great man.

Gen. R. 58, 8. T.S. 23, 79.

48. Which was in Machpelah.

This teaches that it was now held by every person in double esteem (*nichp'lah*). Another interpretation: Whoever was buried in it was assured of a double and quadruple reward. R. Abbahu said: The Holy One, blessed is He, bent Adam in double and buried him in it.

Gen. R. 58, 8. T.S. 23, 81.

49. So the field of Ephron passed into Abraham's ownership.

[Title to land is acquired] by money, deed, witnesses and a formal act of possession.

It became his by possession and deed;[1] and so it says in Jeremiah, *I bought the field . . . and weighed the money. . . . And I subscribed the deed, and sealed* (signed) *it, and called witnesses* (Jer. 32:9-10).

Midrash Habiur; Midrash Hahefetz. T.S. 23, 82-3.

50. The field, and the cave which was therein, etc.

Rabbi said: What is the source of what we learnt, One who sells his field must write the distinctive features of its boundaries? Our text: *The field, and the cave which was therein, and*

---

§ 46 [1] 1 *sela*=2 ordinary shekels.
[2] The Roman *libra*, pound; this was both a weight and a coin (since coins were valued by weight).
[3] 25 shekels. But others hold that *litra*=25 shekels and centenarium=100 *manehs*, the *maneh* equalling 25 *selas*; hence a centenarium equals 5,000 shekels.
[4] The phrase *"current with the merchant"* implies that they were universally accepted as shekels, even in those places where centenaria are called shekels.
§ 49 [1] Sc. the act of burying Sarah.

made sure [18]unto Abraham for a possession in the presence of the children of Heth, before all that went in at the gate of his city. [19]And after this, Abraham buried Sarah his wife in the cave of the field of Machpelah before Mamre——the same is Hebron——in the land of Canaan. [20]And the field, and the cave that is

COMMENTARY

c. The exact location is repeated, as is usual in the case of a purchase.[113] **made sure. a.** The plain meaning is that all became Abraham's property.[114] **b.** The deed of purchase was validated by its signatories.[115] **c.** I.e., were assured to Abraham. This verse and the following may well be a citation from the deed of assignment which was drawn up at the purchase. Contracts of this kind, dating from very early Semitic times, have been discovered in large numbers.[116] [18]**unto Abraham . . . children of Heth. a.** It became Abraham's on his payment of the purchase money, but it did not become his possession as a burial-place until he had buried

Sarah in it.[117] **b.** Abraham paid the money; Ephron in turn sold the field and drew up the deed of sale, all in their presence.[118] **c.** Even one's own estate could not be used for a burying-place without the consent of the townspeople. Therefore "the children of Heth" are mentioned.[119] [19]**after this, Abraham buried Sarah.** Not before, because it is degrading to be buried in alien soil. Therefore he first completed the purchase in all its details.[120] **in the cave of the field of Machpelah.** This addition indicates that henceforth the field was not sown but became an appendage, as it were, to Machpelah (the double cave—hence it now became known as the field of Machpelah).[121] **the same is Hebron—in the land of Canaan. a.** The incident is recorded to demonstrate the superiority of the land of Israel over other countries, both for the living and the dead. Moreover, it shows how God's promise that it would be Abraham's heritage began to be fulfilled.[122] **b.** The purpose of the narrative is to indicate that although Abraham came to the country a stranger, God's promise to make his name great (12:2) was fulfilled even in his lifetime, as was demonstrated by the manner in which he was addressed, viz., *my lord* and *a mighty prince* (verse 6). Further, it informs us where the Patriarchs were buried, so that we can honor the place.[123] **in the land of Canaan.** Scripture teaches in this verse that just as that cave was peculiarly favorable for burial, so was Hebron and in fact the whole of Canaan.[124] [20]**the field, and the cave that is**

ANTHOLOGY

all the trees that were in the field, that were in all the border thereof round about.

Gen. R. 58, 8.   T.S. 23, 86.

51.   In the presence of the children of Heth.

R. Eleazar said: How much ink has been used up and how many quills broken to write *the children of Heth* over and over again: no fewer than ten times.[1] These ten correspond to the Ten Commandments, and teach that he who clarifies the purchase of the righteous is as though he has fulfilled the Ten Commandments.[2]

Gen. R. 58, 8.   T.S. 23, 88.

52.   After this, Abraham buried Sarah.

In this vein it is written, *He that pursues righteousness and kindness finds life, prosperity, and honor* (Prov. 21:21). *He that pursues righteousness* applies to Abraham, [who charged his children and his household to] *keep the way of the Lord, to do righteousness and justice* (18:19). *And kindness*: he acted with kindness toward Sarah.[1] *Finds life: And these are the days of the years of Abraham's life which he lived, a hundred threescore and fifteen years* (25:7). *Prosperity and honor*: R. Samuel b. Isaac said: The Holy One, blessed is He, declared to him: "It is My *métier* to dispense kindness; since you have practised My *métier*, come and don

§ 51   [1] Eight times in the present chapter, and again in 25:10; 49:32.
   [2] For such a purchase is honest and put to lofty uses. The most mundane act is sublimated through righteousness.
§ 52   [1] By burying her. The Rabbis called anything done for the dead (which includes attending to the last rites) an act of true kindness, since there is no hope of a favor in return.

therein, were made sure unto Abraham for a possession of a burying-place by the children of Heth.

COMMENTARY

therein, were made sure. a. I.e., since then it has belonged to him and his descendants for a burial-place.[125] **b.** This is redundant, but such repetition is quite usual.[126] **by the children of Heth. a.** They never subsequently disputed his rights.[127] **b.** Their representatives gave their written and sealed consent to the transaction for that particular purpose.[128] **c.** The whole community agreed that it should be his for a burial-place.[129]

ANTHOLOGY

My raiment"; hence, *Abraham was old, well advanced in age* (24:1).[2]

Gen. R. 58, 9. T.S. 23, 89.

53. So the field . . . entered into Abraham's ownership.

How did it become his? Through the formal act of possession (*hazakah*).[1] Hence the rule: When the sale of a field is effected with money, the vendor can retract until the whole purchase price is paid and the deed is written. When it is effected with a deed, the vendor can retract until the money is paid. But immediately one effects ownership by possession the vendor cannot retract.[2] So you learn that possession is the strongest means of acquisition.

MhG. T.S. 23, 91.

---

[2] Old age is, as it were, God's clothing; cf. Dan. 7:13.
§ 53 [1] See par. 34, note 1. The act in this case was his digging the grave.
[2] The sale is binding, the money owing simply being a debt.

GENESIS

CHAPTER XXIV

¹And Abraham was old, well stricken

COMMENTARY

¹**old.** Therefore he wished to see his son married during his lifetime.[1] **well stricken in age** (lit., he had entered into the days). **a.** He had entered the period of life which marks the completion of man's span on earth.[2] **b.** I.e., very old.[3] **c.** He was no longer active and could not travel; therefore he

ANTHOLOGY

1. Abraham was old.

Because he performed a *mitzvah*,[1] viz., Sarah's burial,[2] he was privileged to attain to old age,[3] as her burial is followed by our text, *Abraham was old*. R. Hiyya b. Abba said: All who do acts of kindness attain honor and greatness. This is a logical inference: if Abraham reached old age because he attended to the dead who was, indeed, his obligation; how much the more when one takes trouble over an unattended corpse.[4]

ARN MS. TS. 24, 1.

2. ABRAHAM WAS OLD. Scripture writes, *Her husband was known in the gates, when he sat among the elders of the land* (Prov. 31:23). When Sarah died Abraham quickly aged and he was called an old man, as it says, *Hear us, my lord; you are a mighty prince among us* (23:6); thus *her husband was known in the gates*, and immediately *he sat among the elders of the land*[1]—he became old, as our text says.

Tan. Hayye Sarah 3. T.S. 24, 2.

3. Abraham was old (*zaken*).

What does *zaken* mean? Said R. Simeon b. Yohai: The Holy One, blessed is He, said: "This man has made Me known as the Owner of heaven and earth."[1]

[Another interpretation:] *Zaken* means, This man has acquired wisdom.[2] Again, *zaken* means, This man has acquired both worlds. Three men were crowned with old age and abundant days, and these three, Abraham, Joshua, and David, were each the first of his line. Abraham was the first of the Patriarchs; Joshua was the first of the line of rulers descended from the tribe of Ephraim, as it says, *Out of Ephraim came he whose root* [fought] *against Amalek* (Judg. 5:14), viz., Joshua.[3] David was the first of the royal line of the tribe of Judah.

ARN MS; MA; Gen. R. 59, 6.
T.S. 24, 3. 8-9.

4. ABRAHAM WAS OLD. R. Joshua b. Levi said: Old age is mentioned in connection with the Patriarchs, Kings, and Prophets. The Patriarchs: *Abraham was old*. Kings: *King David was old* (1 Kings 1:1). Prophets: *Now, when Samuel was old* (1 Sam. 8:1). Why was it said of Samuel, but not of Moses, the father of the Prophets? Because it would be unseemly to speak of old age in connection with Moses who ministered before the Holy One, blessed is He. But is was not unseemly to speak thus of Samuel

§ 1   [1] I.e., a precept.
[2] Cf. chap. 23, par. 52, n. 1.
[3] In this and the following passages not only old age is meant, but the venerability and dignity of an elder—who is not necessarily an old man.
[4] Lit., a dead person who[se burial] is an obligation—e.g., a corpse found in a field or in a country road; even a High Priest is obliged to bury him.

§ 2   [1] I.e., Sarah's death, which made it necessary for him to sit among them to request a place for burial, quickly aged him.

§ 3   [1] By a play on words *zaken* is read as *zeh* [*hi*]*knah*, this man has made [Me] the owner.
[2] Reading *zeh kanah*, this man has acquired.
[3] Cf. Exod. 17:8 *et seqq*.

ANTHOLOGY

who ministered before Eli, a mortal of flesh and blood.

ARN MS. T.S. 24, 4.

5. ABRAHAM WAS OLD. R. Hama b. R. Hanina said: Since the days of our fathers the scholar's academy never ceased. . . . Abraham was an elder, sitting in the academy, as it says, *Abraham was old.*[1]

Yoma 28b. T.S. 24, 5.

6. ABRAHAM WAS OLD. Until Abraham there was no indication of old age: whoever saw Abraham thought him to be Isaac, and *vice versa.* Abraham then prayed for visible old age, as it says, *Abraham was old, well stricken in age.*

From the creation of heaven and earth none had gray hairs until Abraham, in whom gray hairs appeared, as it says, *Abraham was old.*[1]

He had indeed prayed for gray hairs. "Sovereign of the Universe!" he pleaded, "when a father and son enter a town, they know not whom to honor; but if a man showed signs of old age he would be recognized." He replied, "By your life! you have asked well, and with you I will begin."

R. Levitas[2] of Yabneh said: Just as a crown lends majesty to the head of a king, so do gray hairs confer glory and majesty upon the aged, as it is said, *The glory of young men is their strength, and the majesty of old men is the hoary head* (Prov. 20:29).

Sanh. 103b; PRE 52;[3] Pirke R. Hakadosh.
T.S. 24, 6-7 and note.

7. **Abraham was old, advanced in age.**

It is written, *The hoary head is a crown of glory, it is found in the way of righteousness* (Prov. 16:31). R. Meir went to Mamla. Seeing all the people black-haired [i.e., young], he said to them, "You would appear to be of the house of Eli, of whom it is written, *All the increase of your house shall die young men*" (1 Sam. 2:33). "Pray for us, Rabbi," they beseeched him. "Go and practise charity,[1] and you will be privileged to enjoy old age." What is the proof? The text, *The hoary head is a crown of glory;* where is it found? *it is found in the way of righteousness* (charity). From whom do you learn this? From Abraham. Of him it is written that *he will command his children . . . that they keep the way of the Lord to do righteousness* (ts'dakah—18:19); therefore he attained old age, as our text states.

Strength and dignity are her clothing, and she laughs at the time to come (Prov. 31:25). That means, strength and dignity are the clothing of the Torah. When are these manifested? When she makes man laugh at the time to come.[2] When does He give its reward?[3] In the Hereafter.[4] From whom may you learn this? From Abraham. Because it is written of him, *He will command his children . . . that they keep the way of the Lord to do righteousness,* he attained to old age.

Length of days are in her right hand; in her left hand are riches and honor (ibid. 3:16). *In her* [the Torah's] *right hand* alludes to the Hereafter; *in her left*—to this world. Even when He would reward man with His left

---

§ 5   [1] I.e., he had gained wisdom (see par. 3)—it is taken for granted by studying at an academy.
§ 6   [1] Gray hairs are assumed a sign of old age.
      [2] This is an interesting example of a Hellenized Hebrew name—an indication of the extent of Hellenization in ancient Israel. Unfortunately there are no data by which his chronology can be fixed, except that he is prior to the compilation of the Mishnah in 219 C.E. He occurs only here (PRE) and in Aboth 4, 4.
      [3] As quoted in Yalkut Hamakiri on Prov. 20:29.
§ 7   [1] Or, righteousness: the same word—ts'dakah—has both meanings, since charity is but one particular manifestation of righteousness.
      [2] When the man who has observed the Torah is seen to face old age and death with fearless serenity, laughing at its terrors.
      [3] For studying and practising the Torah.
      [4] This is probably another interpretation of "the last day" (AJV: *the time to come*).

hand,[5] He grants him riches and honor. From whom do you learn this? From Abraham, etc.

R. Aha lectured: *And even to old age and hoary hairs, O God, forsake me not* (Ps. 71:18). Said R. Aha: Are not "old age" and "hoary hairs" synonymous? The meaning, however, is this: David prayed: "If Thou hast given me old age, give me the dignity of hoary hairs too." From whom do you learn this? From Abraham, etc.

The hoary head is a crown of glory, it is found in the way of righteousness. If you see a man engaged in Torah, good deeds, and kind acts, know that he will be privileged to the crown of a hoary head; therefore it says, *it is found in the way of righteousness.* You may learn this from Abraham. Because he honored the ministering angels,[6] he attained to the crown of the hoary head. Why was he so privileged? Because *it is found in the way of righteousness.* Now, where do we find him practising righteousness? In the text, *He believed in the Lord, and He accounted it to him for righteousness* (15:6).

[Another interpretation:] The Holy One, blessed is He, said to Abraham: "Enough for a servant that he is like his master." This may be compared to a king who had a friend. Said he to him, "What shall I give you? Gold and silver you have; slaves, male and female, fields and vineyards, you have. But I will place the crown of my head on your head." Even so said the Holy One, blessed is He, to Abraham: "Lo, I have already given you gold and silver," as it says, *Abram was very rich in cattle, in silver, and in gold* (13:2). "What then can I give you? The crown of My head."[7] For when Daniel beheld [Him] he said, *The hair of His*

head was [white] *like pure wool* (Dan. 7:9); and so our text, *Abraham was old.*[8]

> Gen. R. 59, 1-3; Midrash Mishle 16, 31; Tan. Hayye Sarah 4. T.S. 24, 11 and note. 12.

8. ABRAHAM WAS OLD, ADVANCED IN YEARS. R. Aha said: One may have the dignity of old age without its years, or the length of days without the dignity of old age. Here, however, the dignity of old age was matched by length of days, and a long life was matched by the dignity of age.

> Gen. R. 59, 6. T.S. 24, 13.

9. ADVANCED IN AGE (lit., *entered into the days*). R. Judah said: He had entered both worlds.[1] R. Abba interpreted: He had set foot on the road that leads to the life of the Hereafter. R. Isaac said: He had entered on those days of which it is written, [*Remember then your Creator in the days of your youth,*] *before the evil days come* (Eccl. 12:1).

He [God] had blessed him with the promise of children and children's children, and had conferred on him this world and the next, as it says, *Abraham was old, advanced in days:* Scripture does not speak of Abraham's days, but refers to one day of this world and one day of the next.[2]

> Gen. R. 59, 6; SER 5. T.S. 24, 14. 16.

10. Abraham was old; he had entered into the days.

R. Judah lectured on the text: *Happy is the man whom Thou choosest and bringest near, that he may dwell in Thy courts* (Ps. 65:5). He interpreted: Happy is the man whose ways are right in the sight of the Holy One, blessed

---

[5] Sparingly, in a lesser measure. Both rendering and interpretation are somewhat conjectural.
[6] The allusion is to 18:2 *et seqq.*
[7] The dignity of old age.
[8] By this interpretation, *The hoary head is a crown of glory* means that it is part of God's glory, given to man as a reward for righteousness. MhG gives a similar comparison, but ends: But I will bless you that there shall not cease from your children and your children's children, to the last generation, one like yourself. Cf. Vol. II, chap. 15, par. 45.
§ 9   [1] He was in this world, but had already earned the joy of the next. Or: Even while in this world he was granted a foretaste of the next. He renders: He had entered into the days [of the Hereafter].
     [2] Hence the plural, days.

in age; and the Lord had blessed Abraham in all things. ²And Abra-

COMMENTARY

sent his servant.⁴ **the Lord had blessed.** The *memra* (word) of the Lord had blessed, etc. [This comment is in line with the ancient distinction between "the Lord" and the *"memra"* (word) of the Lord. See J.E. vol. 8 *s.v.* Memra.—Ed.]⁵ **in all things. a.** With long life, wealth, honor, and child.⁶ **b.** Spiritually: he did not lack a single virtue or ethical quality.⁷ **c.** I.e., a son, because before then he had regarded all his blessings as valueless, as he had exclaimed, *"O Lord God, what wilt Thou give me, seeing I go hence childless?"* (15:8).⁸ [When we give the phrase its plain meaning, as in the first interpretation, the question arises, Why does Scripture mention this? Several reasons are now given:] **d.** To

ANTHOLOGY

is He, so that He delights in bringing him near to Himself. See how Abraham strove to come ever nearer to Him, yearning for Him all his days. Not simply one day, or sporadically from time to time, but advancing steadily through good works from grade to grade, until in his old age he reached the highest grade to which man can attain. Hence Scripture says that when Abraham was old *he had entered into the days*—the days of celestial spirituality which characterize true faith.

Happy are the penitent who in a single day, a single hour, even a single second, can draw as near to the Holy One as the wholly righteous in many years. For Abraham did not reach that nearness until he was old . . . yet the penitent immediately finds entrance and is brought near to the Holy One, blessed is He.

Zohar 1, 129a, b.

11. Abraham was old . . . and the Lord blessed Abraham in all things.

R. Joshua b. R. Nahmani said: Old age springs on man through four things: fear, child-inflicted sorrow, an evil wife, and discord. . . . An evil wife: *Now when Solomon was old,* [for]¹ *his wives turned away his heart after other gods,* etc. (1 Kings 11:4). But Abraham was honored by his wife, who called him "my lord," as it says, *my lord being old* (18:12). Of her it is said, *A virtuous woman is a crown to her husband* (Prov. 12:4). In this sense Scripture writes of him, *The Lord blessed Abraham in all things.*

Tan. Hayye Sarah 2. T.S. 24, 18.

12. THE LORD BLESSED ABRAHAM IN ALL THINGS. Only after Sarah died does Scripture write that He blessed him. Why is that? Lest people say that Abraham was blessed only on account of Sarah; therefore, said God, "I will declare his blessing after her death." Hence our text, *The Lord blessed Abraham in all things.* Why so? *For when he was but one I called him and I blessed him* (Isa. 51:2).

Tan. Hayye Sarah 4. T.S. 24, 19.

13. ABRAHAM WAS OLD . . . AND THE LORD BLESSED ABRAHAM IN ALL THINGS. As long as Abraham lived there was plenty, as it says, *Abraham was old, advanced in days, and the Lord blessed Abraham in all things.* But when he died, what then? *There was a famine in the land* (26:1).

T. Sot. 10. T.S. 24, 20.

14. THE LORD BLESSED ABRAHAM IN ALL THINGS. R. Nehorai said: I will leave every occupation and teach my son nought but Torah . . . which will guard him from all evil in his youth, and give him *a future and a hope* (Jer. 29:11) in his old age. What does it say of one's youth? *They that wait for the Lord shall renew their strength* (Isa. 40:31). Of old age? *They shall still bring forth fruit in old age* (Ps. 92:15). So too it says of our father Abraham, *Abraham was old, and the Lord blessed Abraham in all things.*

Scripture writes, *Though your beginning was small, yet your end will greatly increase* (Job 8:7). This teaches that all who suffer in the

§ 11 ¹ "For" must be added, since the present idea is that he was prematurely aged on account of his wives.

COMMENTARY

show that it was not because the people in Canaan would not give their daughters in marriage to Isaac that he sent his servant to Aram-naharaim, but because he did not want his son to marry a woman of that land.[9] **e.** Scripture tells us that he had *all things*, wealth, honor, long life and children, and now he only lacked grandchildren.[10] **f.** Being old and wealthy, he feared that if he died someone

ANTHOLOGY

beginning enjoy tranquillity in the end. None suffered more than Abraham: he was cast into a fiery furnace; exiled from his father's home; pursued by six kings; tried with ten trials; and he buried Sarah. Yet in the end he enjoyed tranquillity, as our text states, *Abraham was old, advanced in days; and the Lord blessed Abraham in all things.*

> Kid. 4, 14; Tan. Y. Ekeb 5.
> T.S. 24, 21 and note.

15. THE LORD BLESSED ABRAHAM IN ALL THINGS. Abraham blessed all, as it says, *By you shall all the families of the earth be blessed* (Gen. 12:3). Who then blessed Abraham himself? The Holy One, blessed is He, as our text states, *The* Lord *blessed Abraham in all things.*

> Gen. R. 59, 5. T.S. 24, 22.

16. THE LORD BLESSED ABRAHAM IN ALL THINGS. In this vein Scripture writes, *The Lord tries the righteous* (Ps. 11:5). The Holy One, blessed is He, does not promote man to leadership before testing and trying him; when he passes the test, He elevates him to leadership. Thus only after trying our father Abraham with ten trials did He bless him.

> Tan. B'haaloth'cha 8. T.S. 24, 23.

17. IN ALL THINGS. R. Eleazar of Modin said: Our father Abraham was a master of astrology, and all the kings of the east and the west eagerly consulted him. R. Simeon b. Yohai said: A precious stone hung from Abraham's neck: every sick person who but looked upon it was immediately healed; when Abraham died the Holy One, blessed is He, suspended it from the

orb of the sun. Abbaye observed: Hence the popular saying, "As the sun rises high in the sky the sick find relief."

Another interpretation is that Esau did not rebel against God while he [Abraham] was alive. Also, Ishmael returned to God in his [Abraham's] lifetime.

R. Levi explained the phrase as meaning the following three things: He gave him dominion over his evil impulse; Ishmael repented in his lifetime; and his stores were never diminished.[1] R. Levi, quoting R. Hama, said: It means that He never tried him again.

We learnt: R. Berechiah said: It means that His Divine Presence dwelt with him.

> B.B. 16b; Gen. R. 59, 7; Zohar Hadash 25.
> T.S. 24, 24. 26. 32.

18. IN ALL THINGS. Our Rabbis taught: The Holy One, blessed is He, gave three men a foretaste of the Hereafter here on earth, viz., Abraham, Isaac, and Jacob. Abraham, for it is written of him that God blessed him *in all things*; Isaac: *I have eaten of all* (27:33); Jacob: *I have all* (33:11). The Evil Tempter had no power over three, viz., Abraham, Isaac, and Jacob, which is proved by the same texts. Some add David. Our Rabbis taught: The Angel of Death had no power over six,[1] viz., Abraham, Isaac, Jacob, Moses, Aaron, and Miriam. The proof for Abraham, Isaac, and Jacob is as before, etc.[2]

Our Rabbis taught: Seven were not subject to worms and maggots, viz., Abraham, Isaac, Jacob, Moses, Aaron, Miriam, and Benjamin, Jacob's son. The proof for Abraham, Isaac, and Jacob is as above, etc.[2]

> B.B. 17a. T.S. 24, 25.

---

§ 17 [1] Notwithstanding his famed lavish hospitality.
§ 18 [1] They died by the "kiss" of God.
    [2] Proof-texts for the others follow here.

ham said unto his servant, the elder of his house, that ruled over all that he had: "Put, I pray thee, thy hand under my thigh. ³And I will

COMMENTARY

might bribe Eliezer to select an unfit wife for Isaac; hence he had to adjure him.¹¹ ²**the elder of his house. a.** His oldest servant, who had grown old in his service; therefore he was the most fitting person for the mission that he was about to assign to him.¹² **b.** The one who possessed the greatest authority. Although the servant is not named here, it is clear from 15:2 that Eliezer is intended.¹³ **c.** Abraham did not adjure Isaac himself: this proves that a son need not obey his father when the latter forbids him to marry the woman of his choice.¹⁴ **that ruled over all that he had.** Even to the point that Isaac had to obey him.¹⁵ **Put, I pray thee, thy hand under my thigh. a.** This is done when a superior adjures an inferior, such as a master his servant or a father his son, who also owes him

ANTHOLOGY

19. IN ALL THINGS. Why does Scripture state this? Because though Abraham *was very rich in cattle, in silver, and in gold* (13:2), he had no land at first. Now that he had bought the cave Scripture states that he was blessed with everything.¹

Another interpretation: *In all things* means *on account of* land, for once he bought the field of Machpelah he was blessed.²

> Midrash Hahefetz; Midrash Habiur.
> T.S. 24, 29 note.

20. **Abraham said to his servant, the elder of his house.**

This intimates that the luster of Eliezer, his servant's countenance resembled his own.¹

> Gen. R. 59, 8. T.S. 24, 33.

21. THE ELDER OF HIS HOUSE. The elder of Abraham's house was his slave Eliezer. How did he acquire him? When Abraham left Ur of the Chaldees all the great men of the time presented him with gifts; and Nimrod assigned Eliezer to Abraham. He rewarded his loyal service on Isaac's behalf¹ by giving him his freedom. The Holy One, blessed is He, gave him his reward in this world . . . and raised him to the throne, for he was none other than Og king of Bashan.²

> PRE 16. T.S. 24, 34.

22. **That ruled over all he had.**

Eliezer, Abraham's slave, was an elder who sat in the academy of scholars, for he is described as *the elder of his house, that ruled over all he had,* which R. Eleazar interpreted as meaning that he had acquired his master's learning.

[Another interpretation:] He ruled over his Evil Impulse, just like his master.

R. Samuel b. Isaac interpreted: He gave him authority over all his wealth and told him, "Even if you must give all I possess, *you shall take a wife for my son from thence*" (verse 7).

[Another interpretation:] He was generally in charge of all his keys (i.e., to his wealth).

> Yoma 28b; Gen. R. 59, 8; Tan. Y.
> Vayyetse 3; MhG. T.S. 24, 35-8.

23. **Put . . . your hand under my thigh.**

R. Berechiah said: Circumcision was precious to them because it entailed pain; therefore they swore by nought else.

See how highly they prized circumcision. When Jacob adjured Joseph, he too requested, *Put . . . your hand under my thigh* (47:29). Why did they prize it so highly? Because they knew that in the Hereafter it would save their children from Gehenna, as it says, *Therefore the nether-world [Gehenna] has enlarged her desire, and opened her mouth without* hok (AJV:

---

§ 19 ¹ This reflects a deep conviction of the Rabbis: without land to call one's own, one cannot truly be described as blessed.
² Probably: The blessing came after and in virtue of his purchase of land.
§ 20 ¹ By a play on words z'kan, the elder, is read as an abbreviation of ziw ikunin, the luster of countenance.
§ 21 ¹ In securing him a suitable wife.
² Not the Og slain by Moses (Num. 21:25).

make thee swear by the Lord, the God of heaven and the God of the earth, that thou shalt not take a

COMMENTARY

obedience (cf. 47:29).[16] **b.** It was the custom in those days for a servant to swear in this manner, placing his hand under his master's thigh, the latter sitting upon his hand. This signified that the servant was under his master's authority. It is still practised in India.[17] **c.** To signify, Remember the covenant of circumcision to which we have both bound ourselves.[18] **d.** This may be meant figuratively only: put your loyalty, as it were, under my foot, i.e., acknowledge that you owe me loyal service.[19] **e.** He requested two things of him: (1) To acknowledge the fealty due from a servant to his master. (2) To swear to him by the Lord, the God of heaven and earth.[20] **f.** According to the Biblical idiom, chil-

dren are said to issue from the "thigh" or "loins" of their father (cf. 46:26). Therefore the formality of placing the hand under the thigh was taken to signify that if the oath were violated, the children who have issued or might issue from the "thigh" would avenge the act of disloyalty.[21] **[3]I will make thee swear.** He did not adjure Isaac, because he was confident his son would fulfil his wishes without an oath. Possibly too he adjured Eliezer as the executor of his will that a condition of Isaac's inheriting his estate was not to marry a Canaanitish woman. Perhaps that is why Eliezer is described in the previous verse as ruling over all that he had.[22] **the God of heaven and the God of the earth. a.** The Lord is so described here to indicate that marriage on earth is preordained in Heaven.[23] **b.** The God of heaven is also the God who judges what is done on earth: should you violate your oath He will certainly punish you.[24] **c.** The Holy One, blessed is He, is called the God of the land (*earth*) of Israel.[25] **d.** All the prophets treat the spheres and the stars as absolute proof of God's existence.[26]

ANTHOLOGY

measure—Isa. 5:14). What does "without *hok*" mean? *Hok* is nothing else but circumcision, as it says, [The covenant] *which He made with Abraham . . . and He established to Jacob for a hok* (*statute*—Ps. 105:9-10).[1] But Jews, who are circumcised, are delivered from it [Gehenna], as it says, *When you pass through the waters, I will be with you* [. . . *when you walk through the fire, you shall not be burned*] (Isa. 43:2).

> Gen. R. 59, 8; Tan. Y. Hayye Sarah 6. T.S. 24, 39 and note.

24. I will make you swear.

According to my intentions, not yours.[1] *By the Lord:* the oath must be by the Lord and none else, as it says, *By His name you shall swear*

(Deut. 6:13); it also says, *By Myself have I sworn, saith the Lord* (22:16).

> Ner Has'chalim. T.S. 24, 43.

25. By the Lord, the God of heaven.

How do we adjure [a man who must take a judicial oath]? Rab Judah, quoting Rab, said: With the oath that is stated in the Torah, as it is written, *And I will make you swear by the Lord, the God of heaven.* Rabina asked R. Ashi: Is this in agreement with R. Hanina b. Idi who maintains that the Unique Name must be used?[1] He replied: He may even agree with our Rabbis, who hold that only a substitute Name[2] is used, but the practical application of his view is that the person adjured must hold a sacred object in his hand,[3] in conformity with Raba's dictum,

---

§ 23 [1] Thus the covenant, which is always identified with circumcision (17:10), is called *hok*. The proof-text is rendered: Therefore the nether-world . . . has opened her mouth for those that are without *hok*, circumcision.

§ 24 [1] You must swear in the sense that I desire, without any mental reservations or interpretations which would alter the purport of the oath.

§ 25 [1] The "Unique Name" *(shem ha-m'yuhad)* is the Tetragrammaton. The question is whether Rab Judah, by citing the text on Abraham's adjuration of Eliezer, meant that the actual Tetragrammaton must be used in the oath.

[2] But not the actual Tetragrammaton.

[3] Rab Judah did not mean that the name of "the Lord God of heaven" must be employed, but that just as Abraham demanded that Eliezer take the oath whilst holding a sacred object (there, the circumcised *membrum virile*), so must a sacred object (e.g., a Scroll of the Law or phylacteries) be held by all who are adjured.

wife for my son of the daughters of the Canaanites, among whom I dwell. ⁴But thou shalt go unto my country, and to my kindred, and

COMMENTARY

e. Should you prove false to the oath He will punish you in this world (*the earth*) and in the next (*heaven*).[27] **f.** Abraham made his servant swear in the name of the God he himself worshipped; he had converted his servant to the true Faith, as is evidenced by Eliezer's devout conduct throughout the narrative which follows.[28] **daughters of the Canaanites. a.** While the seed of Canaan was cursed (9:25), his seed was blessed (22:18): the two therefore could not mingle.[29] **b.** Other settlers in a country deliberately intermarry with the original inhabitants, in order to acquire estate: I do not need this, since the Almighty has already given me the country.[30] **c.** Who might divert Isaac from the path which his father had mapped out for him. This fear of the evil consequences which would result from intermarriage with heathens is frequently expressed in the Bible; e.g., Deut. 7:3f.[31] **among whom I dwell. a.** Although these include Aner, Eshcol and Mamre, who surpass me in wealth and station, I desire neither their honor nor their gifts.[32] **b.** Even though they are righteous, for I would certainly not dwell among the wicked.[33] **c.** Since I dwell among them presumably my son will too; therefore I have good cause to fear that he may learn from their actions.[34] **⁴thou shalt go.** Do not send anybody else in your stead: you go and you choose whomsoever you think fitting.[35] **my country . . . my kindred. a.** Even in my country, choose only of my kindred.[36] **b.** "My country" means Haran,

ANTHOLOGY

viz., A judge who adjures by "the Lord God of heaven" [without the adjured holding a sacred object] is as one who errs in a Mishnaic law, and his ruling is revocable.[4]

Sheb. 38b. T.S. 24, 42.

26. The Lord, the God of the heaven and the God of the earth.

Before our father Abraham, the Holy One, blessed is He, was only, if one might speak so, the God of heaven,[1] as it says, *The Lord, the God of heaven, who took me from my father's house* (verse 7). But Abraham made His sovereignty acknowledged in heaven and on earth. In this sense it says, *The Lord,* [who is now] *the God of the heaven and the God of the earth.*

R. Isaac observed: Having said, *The Lord,* which is an all-embracing term, why did he add, *the God of the heaven*? Said R. Judah: To teach that He is Sovereign over all things simultaneously, and in a single instant He moves all things, and all are as nought before Him.

Sifre D'barim 313; Zohar Midrash Haneelam 1, 126b. T.S. 24, 44-5.

27. You shall not take a wife, etc.

He exhorted him not to go to the daughters of Aner, Eshcol, and Mamre for a wife.[1]

Gen. R. 58, 8. T.S. 24, 46.

28. The daughters of the Canaanites.

Both the Canaanites and the rest of the Seven Tribes[1] are meant, for they are all called Canaanites. Why did Abraham object to them? Because they were all under the ban, as it says, *You shall utterly destroy them* (Deut. 20:17).

MhG. T.S. 24, 47.

29. Among whom I dwell (*yosheb*).

Yosheb is written *plene*, with a *waw*, because at that time he had full rights of domicile.[1]

Sechel Tob. T.S. 24, 48.

---

[4] If a judge errs where there is no definitely established ruling his judgment is irrevocable, though he may have to make good the consequences of his error (see Sanh. 6a). But if his decision is contrary to a definite Mishnaic law, it is invalid altogether and the case must be retried. In Sanh. *loc. cit.* the same is applied to a decision contrary to amoraic law too. If then a judge ordered an oath without the holding of a sacred object, his ruling is revoked and the oath is administered a second time.

§ 26 [1] Only there was He recognized as God.
§ 27 [1] Sechel Tob adds: Even though they were righteous.
§ 28 [1] Who then inhabited Canaan.
§ 29 [1] Or: He was fully at home.

take a wife for my son, even for Isaac." [5]And the servant said unto him: "Peradventure the woman will not be willing to follow me unto this land; must I needs bring thy son back unto the land from whence thou camest?" [6]And Abraham said

COMMENTARY

where he had lived; "my kindred," Ur of the Chaldees, where he was born.[37] **c.** Aram-naharaim.[38]

d. I do not wish strangers to inherit my estate.[39] **e.** I desire a wife for Isaac preferably of my own family, but at least of my own country: this will ensure that similarity of character and nature which is essential for happy marriage.[40] **a wife for my son, even for Isaac. a.** A wife, unencumbered with property and dowerless.[41] **b.** I.e., a girl who is worthy to become the wife of *my son,* and is suitable for *Isaac* in character and temperament.[42] [5]**to follow me.** She may consider it beneath her dignity and require Isaac to come and fetch her.[43] **bring thy son back. a.** Although Isaac had never been there Eliezer still calls it bringing back, since Isaac's father came from there.[44] **b.** After arranging the marriage shall *I* return with Isaac to fetch her?[45] **whence thou camest.** Which you rejected by

ANTHOLOGY

30. But you shall go to my country, and to my kindred.

R. Isaac quoted:[1] Even though the wheat in your own town is inferior, sow thereof.[2]

But they were all idolaters, as it is written, *Your fathers dwelt of old beyond the River, even Terah, the father of Abraham, and the father of Nahor, and they served other gods* (Josh. 24:2); and Abraham had departed from them? However, Abraham said: "Since I proselytize, let me do so to my kindred and my father's house, who take precedence over all others; moreover, they are already near to penitence." Hence the Sages said: A man's thoughts should always be nearest to his kindred, and if it is in his power, let him act for their benefit. In this sense it is written, *Hide not yourself from your own flesh* (Isa. 58:7).

> MhG; Gen. R. 59, 8. T.S. 24, 49-50.

31. You shall take a wife for my son.

A man has a greater obligation to procreate than a woman. The proof is that Abraham

pressed Eliezer to take a wife for his son Isaac, as our text states, the purpose of which was procreation.

> Tan. Noah 12. T.S. 24, 51.

32. The servant said to him: "Perhaps the woman will not be willing," etc.

Thus it is written, *Canaan*[1] (AJV: *the trafficker*), *the balances of deceit are in his hand:* he sat and weighed his daughter—is she fit to be Isaac's wife or not? *To rob the beloved:*[2] i.e., to rob the beloved of the world, who was Isaac.[3] So he said, *Perhaps the woman will not be willing,* etc., hinting, then I will give him my daughter. Said he [Abraham] to him, "You are accursed,[4] and my son is blessed: the accursed cannot unite with the blessed."

> Gen. R. 59, 10; MhG. T.S. 24, 61-2.

33. Shall I then indeed bring your son back?

Shall I bring him back in your lifetime; shall I bring him back when you are no more?[1]

> Midrash Habiur. T.S. 24, 56.

---

§ 30 [1] Lit., said; but the remark that follows has the ring of a proverb.
[2] And not of other seed. Abraham told him to go to his kindred, even though he might not find there a particularly suitable woman—still, they were his own kin.

§ 32 [1] Canaan was Ham's son, Noah's grandson (10:1, 6), who preceded Abraham by eight generations. The probable meaning here is that Eliezer was a descendant of Canaan. But Mah. points out that actual identification is still possible, for Shem, Canaan's brother, lived 600 years (11:10-11), dying when Jacob was already 50 years old.
[2] AJV: *He loveth to oppress.*
[3] By giving him his own daughter instead of a wife truly fitting for him.
[4] See 9:25.

§ 33 [1] In the Heb. the verb is repeated for emphasis; the comment interprets that repetition.

unto him: "Beware thou that thou bring not my son back thither. ⁷The Lord, the God of heaven, who took me from my father's house, and from the land of my nativity, and who spoke unto me, and who swore unto me, saying: Unto thy seed will I give this land; He will send His angel before thee, and thou shalt

COMMENTARY

leaving it.⁴⁶ ⁶**Beware**, etc. On no account is Isaac to return to Haran, lest he abandon the Land of Promise.⁴⁷ ⁷**the God of heaven**, etc. **a.** He does not mention "the God of the earth," because he is about to refer to His angel ("He will send His angel before you").⁴⁸ **b.** This may be either a prayer (may He send) or an assurance: the God of heaven will certainly send His angel and prosper your mission.⁴⁹ **my father's house . . . the land of my nativity. a.** Haran and Ur of the Chaldees respectively.⁵⁰ **b.** Both refer to Haran.⁵¹ **who spoke unto me. a.** Before I departed thence.⁵² **b.** With the promise "for in Isaac shall seed be called to you" (21:12).⁵³ **spoke . . . and swore.** Even if a mere statement can in certain conditions be abrogated, an oath is eternally binding. The oath is the Covenant between the Parts (15:8 *et seqq.*).⁵⁴ **who swore unto me.** He will therefore certainly enable you to find a suitable wife who will be ready to follow you here.⁵⁵ **Unto thy seed will I give this land.** Therefore I am certain that He does not wish my son to go back there, and I know that *He will send His angel,* etc.⁵⁶ **He will send,** etc. This was a prayer (may He send): had it been a prophecy, why add "and if the woman be not willing," etc.?⁵⁶ᵃ **He will send His angel before thee. a.** An actual angel is meant: either, the angel

ANTHOLOGY

34. That you bring not back my son thither.

Abraham would not let him lose the peculiar sanctity with which he had been invested when he was brought as an offering completely devoted to God.¹

PZ. T.S. 24, 58.

35. THAT YOU BRING NOT BACK MY SON THITHER (*shammah*). Said he: "If you take him back, it is as if you took him to Gehenna." For *shammah* (thither) alludes to nought else but Gehenna, as it says, *There is Pharaoh king of Egypt and all his host; there* (shammah) *is Edom, her kings and her princes* (Ezek. 32:29).¹ Another interpretation: He said to him: "If you take him there, the kingdom of God will revert to its original confined state, when He was only the *Lord, God of heaven.*"²

Another reason for Abraham's refusal was that he was aware that among all the nations none but he alone knew the Holy One, blessed is He. Therefore he would not have Isaac dwell among them but only with him, to learn the ways of God and not deviate from them to the right or the left.

MhG; Zohar 1, 131b. T.S. 24, 59 and note.

36. Who took me from my father's house, etc.

That means literally the house of my father. *From the land of my nativity*: where I lived; *who spoke unto me*: in Haran; *and who swore unto me*: at the Covenant between the Parts.¹

[Another interpretation:] *From my father's house* alludes to idolatry, as it is written, *They say to a stock, "Thou art my father," and to a stone, "Thou hast brought us forth"* (Jer. 2:27); *who spoke to me*—at the Covenant between the Parts; *who swore to me*—at Mount Moriah.

Gen. R. 59, 10; MhG. T.S. 24, 61-2.

§ 34 ¹ Even though it was only a trial, Isaac had thereby become as one devoted to God, consecrated; therefore he would not allow him to go outside the Holy Land.
§ 35 ¹ The reference is to the nether-world. There is no such verse; the second half is as quoted, but the first half, "there . . . host" is a brief summary of the first half of chap. 32.
² His kingdom on earth will be forgotten; see last par.
§ 36 ¹ 15:17f.

take a wife for my son from thence. [8]And if the woman be not willing to follow thee, then thou shalt be clear from this my oath; only thou shalt not bring my son back thither." [9]And the servant put his hand under the thigh of Abraham his master, and swore to him concerning this matter. [10]And the servant took ten camels, of the camels of his master, and departed; having all goodly

COMMENTARY

in charge of marriage; or, the angel whom God sends on any mission required.[57] **b.** An expression denoting that God's protection and aid would be given him; cf. Exod. 23:20.[58] [8]**then thou shalt**

be clear from this my oath. **a.** Then take a wife from the daughters of Aner, Eshcol or Mamre.[59] **b.** You will be free of any further responsibility. However, *this my oath* may mean from the oath to take a wife *from there*, but you will still be bound by the other vow, i.e., not to take a daughter of the Canaanites.[60] **c.** Then use your own discretion.[61] **bring . . . back. a.** "Bring . . . back" is said from the standpoint of Abraham (Isaac, in fact had never been there), who is regarded as the principal character in the narrative.[62] **b.** "*Bring . . . back*" is from the standpoint of Eliezer, who had been there, and who would naturally accompany Isaac.[63] [10]**the servant took**, etc. On his own initiative; he did not have to ask Abraham's permission, because *all the goodly things of his master* [were] *in his hand* —i.e., in his charge.[64] **ten.** This simply means many; cf. 1 Sam. 1:8: *Am I not more to you than ten sons*, where the number is obviously not meant exactly.[65] **the camels of his master.** Of the best. Animals belonging to princes and sheiks are always distinguishable, since they are of the finest. That is the meaning here: they would immediately be recognized as Abraham's—so fine was their quality.[66] **and departed.** He took leave from his master. [*Vayyelech*, went or departed, is repeated in

ANTHOLOGY

37. He will send His angel before you.

R. Dosa said: A particular angel is meant. When our father Abraham said, *He will send His angel before you*, the Holy One, blessed is He, appointed two angels, one to bring Rebekah out to the well, and the other to escort Eliezer on his way.

Not, He will go with you, but, *He will send His angel before you* is written; for, said Abraham, "I will not let the Holy One, blessed is He, depart from me." Not as Saul said to David, *"Go, and the Lord shall be with you"* (1 Sam. 17:37); and what transpired? *Saul was afraid of David, because the Lord was with him, and was departed from Saul* (ibid. 18:12). Moses too spoke in the same vein, *If Thy presence go not with me, carry us not up hence* (Exod. 33:15). He pleaded: "Sovereign of the Universe! Among all the celestial and the terrestrial there is none

but Thee: let Thy glory lead us; do not let us be led by an angel."

Gen. R. 59, 10; MhG. T.S. 24, 64-5.

38. The slave put his hand under the thigh of Abraham his master.

R. Judah said: The slave acted as befit his servile station; the free man as befit his freedom. The slave: *The slave put his hand under the thigh*, etc. The free man: *He* [Joseph] *said: "I will do as you have said."* . . . *And he swore to him* (47:30-1).[1]

Yelamdenu quoted in Yalkut Shimoni, 1st ed. T.S. 24, 68.

39. The servant took ten camels, of the camels of his master.

Abraham's camels were readily distinguished: wherever they went out they were muzzled.[1]

Gen. R. 59, 11. T.S. 24, 69.

§ 38 [1] Jacob had requested him to put his hand under his thigh (verse 29); but he did not do so, for this was not seemly for a free man, but merely gave his word.

§ 39 [1] So as not to graze in strangers' fields. This explains why the Bible states that they were his master's camels, which is obvious.

things of his master's in his hand; and he arose, and went to Aram-naharaim, unto the city of Nahor. [11]And he made the camels to kneel down without the city by the well of water at the time of evening, the time that women go out to draw water. [12]And he said: "O Lord, the

COMMENTARY

this verse. Hence the first is interpreted, took his leave.—Ed.][67] **all goodly things.** ("Things" is not in the original.) **a.** Not literally; it rather means simply a great part of his master's wealth; cf. 41:57, *And the whole earth* (so literally) *came to Egypt.*[68] **b.** The most important members of Abraham's household (cf. verse 54).[69] **c.** Gold and silver, jewels and raiment, to show Abraham's wealth, and thereby encourage a match with his son.[70] **Aram-naharaim. a.** The Aram between the two rivers (*naharaim*), the Tigris and the Euphrates, viz., Iraq (formerly Mesopotamia).[71] **b.** The country where dwelt Abraham's relations.[72] **the city of Nahor. a.** Ur of the Chaldees, where Nahor dwelt after the departure of Terah and Abraham.[73] **b.** It is emphasized that he went to the city of Nahor, because Eliezer knew that Abraham strongly desired a marriage within his own family.[74] [11]**by the well of water.** The place where a stranger seeking information would naturally wait.[75] **the time, etc.** When women draw water for the evening meal.[76]

ANTHOLOGY

40. Having all the goodly things of his master's in his hands.

R. Helbo said: These consisted of a deed of gift.[1]

[Another interpretation:] These were the keys to his treasure-houses.

Gen. R. 59, 11; Yeminite Anth. MS Albihani. T.S. 24, 72-3.

41. He arose, and went to Aram-naharaim.

R. Isaac said: He arrived on the same day. Similarly R. Isaac interprets, *I came this day to the fountain* (verse 42): today I set out, and today I arrived.[1]

Gen. R. 59, 11. T.S. 24, 74.

42. By the well of water.

Why by the well of water? He followed the usual practice: Whoever seeks his neighbor sits at the water and there he finds him; everyone eventually comes to the water. All the righteous who left their homes went to wells. Moses: *He sat down by a well* (Exod. 2:15); Jacob: *And behold a well in the field* (29:2).

MhG; PZ. T.S. 24, 76 and note.

42a. The time that women go out to draw water.

From this our Sages derived: When a man comes to a place and meets maidens coming out of the town, his business will prosper.

Or Haafelah. T.S. 24, 76 note.

43. At the time of evening, the time that women go out to draw water.

R. Huna said: When a man goes to take a wife and he hears dogs barking, he can make them out saying, "*At the time of the evening, the time that women go out to draw water.*"[1]

Gen. R. 59, 12. T.S. 24, 77.

§ 40 [1] Obviously he could not take all of Abraham's possessions. R. Helbo explains that Abraham deeded them to Isaac, and Eliezer took the deed with him. PRE 16 says that he made Isaac his heir, and Eliezer took the will as proof. Sechel Tob explains that he gave him a document showing him (Eliezer) to be steward over all his possessions.
§ 41 [1] This required a miracle.
§ 43 [1] Both translation and meaning are extremely doubtful; the rendering adopted would appear to be the literal translation. Possibly R. Huna's remark is meant humorously: when a man goes seeking a wife, even the dogs will tell him that evening at the well is the best time and place—he will then find a proper mate. Commentators observe that the time and the place are particularly favorable, because he is bound to hear the women gossiping, from which he can learn all the merits and demerits of every woman! The present writer, on the basis of several commentators, has rendered in the Soncino Midrash Rabbah: When a man goes to take a wife and he hears dogs barking, can he then understand what they are saying? [There was just as little

God of my master Abraham, send me, I pray Thee, good speed this day, and show kindness unto my

COMMENTARY

[12]**O Lord, the God of my master Abraham.** **a.** Eliezer did not feel himself worthy to pronounce the Divine Name in all its fullness as Abraham did when he said *"Lord, the God of heaven and the God of the earth"* (verse 3); so he contented himself with the present appellation.[77] **b.** O God, who didst choose Abraham and show him great love, I pray to Thee for his sake.[78] **send me . . . good speed** (lit., make happen) **this day, and show kindness,** etc. **a.** Let it happen as I am about to propose; that will be a sign that Thou wilt show kindness, etc.[79] **b.** What will now transpire may appear a mere co-

ANTHOLOGY

44. O Lord, the God of my master Abraham.

Scripture writes, *A servant that deals wisely shall have rule over a son that puts to shame* (Prov. 17:2). *A servant that deals wisely* applies to Eliezer. What wisdom did he show? He said: My curse is inescapable:[1] some Ethiopian or Barbar[2] may enslave me; better then that I be a slave in this house than in any other. *Shall have rule over a son that puts to shame*: by this Isaac is meant, who put the whole world to shame when he was bound upon the altar.[3] *And shall enjoy inheritance among the brethren*: as these[4] invoked the merit of the Patriarchs,[5] so did he, as it says, *And he said: "Lord, the God of my master Abraham."*

Gen. R. 60, 2. T.S. 24, 78.

45. Send me, I pray Thee, good speed this day.

Today Thou hast commenced;[1] then complete it today.

Gen. R. 60, 2. T.S. 24, 79.

46. SEND ME, I PRAY THEE, etc. How do we know that a man's agent counts as himself? Because Eliezer said, *Send me,*[1] *I pray Thee,* etc.

MRE 153. T.S. 24, 80.

47. SEND ME, I PRAY THEE, GOOD SPEED THIS DAY. Seven Patriarchs slept in eternal glory,[1] free from the worm and the maggot. . . . Seven entered the Garden of Eden alive: Serah (the daughter of Asher; Bathya, Pharaoh's daughter;[2] Hiram King of Tyre; Ebed-melech the Ethiopian, who brought Jeremiah up from the pit; Eliezer, Abraham's servant; the grandson of R. Judah the Nasi (Patriarch); R. Joshua b. Levi; and Jabez.[3] . . . Eliezer, because he served Abraham faithfully. When? When he said, *Send me, I pray Thee, good speed* (hakreh) *this day.* Now elsewhere it says, [*Isaac said to his son:* "How is it that you found it—the venison—*so quickly, my son?" And he said:*] "*Because the Lord your God sent me good speed*" (hikrah—27-20).[4] Now, how do we know [that the foretaste of the Garden of Eden

reason in Eliezer's action] *at the time of the evening, the time that women go out to draw water*—i.e., R. Huna condemned Eliezer's test: one might just as reasonably draw an inference from the barking of dogs!

§ 44 [1] Lit., the curse of that man (meaning himself) is already in his hand. As a descendant of Canaan (see par. 32) he was inevitably fated to slavery. Nevertheless this inevitability of destiny is hardly a characteristic Jewish teaching; see pars. 21, according to which he became a king; 47, 72: through loyal service he entered the category of the blessed instead of the accursed.
 [2] An inhabitant of Barbary, on the African coast.
 [3] Eliezer had rule over him by determining his wife for him.
 [4] The "brethren"—here, Abraham's descendants.
 [5] That is their inheritance—the merit of their ancestors.
§ 45 [1] By miraculously speeding me on the way; see par. 41.
§ 46 [1] He was praying on *Isaac's* behalf, not his own, yet he said, "Send *me,*" etc.
§ 47 [1] They are listed *ad loc.*: Abraham, Isaac, Jacob, Amram the father of Moses, Benjamin, Jesse (David's father) and Caleb. Some add David.
 [2] Who saved Moses (Exod. 2:5ff.).
 [3] This gives eight. One is probably in dispute.
 [4] The use of the same verb (*hikrah*) is understood to imply that both enjoyed the same experience—the foretaste of the Garden of Eden.

master Abraham. ¹³Behold, I stand by the fountain of water; and the daughters of the men of the city come out to draw water. ¹⁴So let it come to pass, that the damsel to whom I shall say: Let down thy pitcher, I pray thee, that I may drink; and she shall say: Drink,

COMMENTARY

incidence; in truth, however, it will be the result of Divine Providence showing kindness to Abraham.[80] **c.** Eliezer proposed the test in order that Abraham's kinsmen might recognize that it was all happening in accordance with a Divine plan, which they did (see verse 50). Otherwise they might object to allowing their daughter to leave home for a distant marriage.[81] **d.** The emphasis is on "this day": let it happen this very day, without the necessity of my spending days in searching for a suitable bride.[82] ¹³**by the fountain. a.** What a girl does at home is no true test of her character, because there she may be under constraint and her mother's orders. Here, however, she will act freely in accordance with her real nature, and so I will be able to judge her.[83] **b.** The fountain was for humans; it is not the same as the *b'er* (well) in verse 20, which was for animals. The two were close together.[84] ¹⁴**to whom I shall say.** He did not leave *everything* to the test: from his own observations he would decide upon a likely-looking girl and start a conversation with her.[85] **that I may drink . . . thy camels.** A request should be moderate, but the response should go beyond it and offer all that is needed.[86] **she shall say: Drink.** There was no

ANTHOLOGY

is alluded to] there? Because it is written, *And he brought him wine,* etc., and then it says, *See, the smell of my son is as the smell of the field which the Lord has blessed (ibid. 25, 27).*[5]

Kallah Rabbathi 3. T.S. 24, 81.

48. Show kindness to my master Abraham.

R. Haggai, quoting R. Isaac, commented: All need kindness. Even Abraham, for whose sake God shows kindness to the world, yet needed kindness himself, as our text intimates.

Gen. R. 60, 2. T.S. 24, 82.

49. The daughters (*b'noth*) of the men of the city came out.

B'noth is written defectively, without a *waw*,[1] intimating that only Rebekah came out just then.

Sechel Tob. T.S. 24, 83.

50. So let it come to pass, that the damsel to whom I shall say: "Let down your pitcher," etc.

R. Samuel b. Nahmani, quoting R. Jonathan, said: Three men asked improperly: two were answered fittingly, and the third unfittingly. They were Eliezer, Abraham's servant; Saul the son of Kish; and Jephtah the Gileadite.[1] Eliezer, Abraham's servant: it is written, *So let it come to pass, that the damsel,* etc.— even if she were lame or blind? But he was answered fittingly, and Rebekah chanced to come out.

Taan. 4a. T.S. 24, 84.

51. The damsel (*naarah*).

Whenever *naarah* occurs in this narrative it lacks a *heh*,[1] because she [Rebekah] was only three years old.[2]

Sechel Tob. T.S. 24, 85.

---

[5] Gen. R. 65, 22, says that Isaac alluded to the fragrance of the Garden of Eden, which entered with Jacob.
§ 49 [1] בנת instead of בנות. Our texts, however, are *plene,* בנות.
§ 50 [1] In Gen. R. 60, 3, the reading is four: Eliezer, Caleb, Saul and Jephtah.
§ 51 [1] Being written נער instead of נערה.
      [2] The lack of a *heh* is understood to indicate immaturity. The calculation is as follows: Sarah died at the age of 127 through the shock of Isaac's Binding (see chapter 23, pars. 1 and 9), so that he was then 37 years of age, since she was 90 at his birth. Abraham was informed of Rebekah's birth at Mount Moriah (22:20-23), while Isaac was 40 years old when he married her (25:20); hence she was 3 years old. However, other views do not link Isaac's Binding with Sarah's death, holding that the latter took place much later. According to these Rebekah would have been considerably older.

and I will give thy camels drink also; let the same be she that Thou hast appointed for Thy servant, even for Isaac; and thereby shall I know that Thou hast shown kindness unto my master." [15]And it came to pass, before he had done speaking, that, behold, Rebekah came out, who was born to Bethuel the son of Milcah, the wife of Nahor, Abraham's brother, with her pitcher upon her shoulder. [16]And the damsel was very fair to look

COMMENTARY

divination or magic in this: it would merely give an indication of the generous hospitality and kind-heartedness essential in Isaac's wife. Nevertheless he did not rely upon it completely and did not give her the presents before ascertaining her family.[87]

let the same be she that Thou hast appointed. [Most commentators explain in accordance with the plain meaning of the text: she is the one whom God has indicated as a fitting mate. The following interpretation is singled out because it differs:] The Hebrew is to be rendered: Her hast Thou taught the right way, and she will make a good wife for Isaac.[88] thereby shall I know. a. This was a prayer: let me know through her.[89] b. If she is of fine character, as the test will show, and is of Abraham's family, I will know, etc.[90] c. I will speak to her after she passes this test, and will then know whether Thou hast shown kindness, etc.,—i.e., whether she is fit to be Isaac's wife.[91] d. This was really a second prayer: if such a girl be found, I will still need her consent; through her, when she accepts my proposal, I will know, etc.[92] e. בה does not refer to the maiden but to the incident: by this test I will know.[93] unto my master. Since I am only acting on his behalf, if it does so transpire it will have been for his sake.[94] [15]it came to pass, before he had done speaking. Or: and thus it was (linking hu—AJV: he—with vayy'hi, instead of killah, [he] had done): before he (not expressed by hu but simply in the verbal form) had done, etc.[95] before he had done speaking. To himself, for all this would naturally not have been said aloud.[96] born to Bethuel the son of Milcah. He was the son of the wife, not of Reumah the concubine (22:24).[97] [16]very fair, etc. Here the reasons are given why Eliezer approached her: (1) She was very

ANTHOLOGY

52. And she shall say, "Drink."

Why did Eliezer make this sign that this would prove her to be the one *whom the Lord has appointed for my master's son* (verse 44)? Because he knew that if she answered thus she would be a righteous woman, eager to show hospitality, just like Abraham and Sarah.

MA. T.S. 24, 86.

53. Now, before he had done speaking, etc.

R. Simeon b. Yohai taught: Three were answered even as they spoke, viz., Eliezer, Abraham's servant; Moses; and Solomon. Eliezer, as our text states.

Even before his petition was ended he was answered. Hence our Sages said: When a man's petition is granted, the Holy One, blessed is He,

answers him even as he is still standing and praying, as it says, *Before they call, I will answer* (Isa. 65:24).

Gen. R. 60, 4; Or Haafelah. T.S. 24, 87-8.

54. Behold, Rebekah went out.

But they were wealthy: did they not have a slave to draw water? It was, however, a miracle: never in her life did she go out save on this day.

Surely Scripture should have written *came out*, not *went out*?[1] It means that the Holy One, blessed is He, made her an exception to all people of the town,[2] for they were all wicked, but not she.

Or Haafelah; Zohar 1, 132a. T.S. 24, 89 and note.

§ 54 [1] AJV: "Came out," but the literal translation of the Hebrew (*yotseth*) is "went (better, goes) out."
[2] I.e., he made her go out, as it were, from their ranks.

upon, a virgin, neither had any man known her; and she went down to the fountain, and filled her pitcher, and came up. [17]And the servant ran to meet her, and said: "Give me to

COMMENTARY

beautiful. (2) No man knew her. Whereas he saw familiarity between the other girls at the well and the men, he recognized that this one was practically a stranger to them. From this he deduced either

that she was of a noble family that generally did not send its daughters to the well, or that her modesty warned men to keep aloof.[98] [16]**neither had any man known her.** Here any undue familiarity is meant.[99] **b.** This is synonymous with "a virgin." An idea is often expressed both affirmatively and negatively; cf. 47:19, *that we may live, and not die.*[100] **and filled her pitcher, and came up.** She did not waste her time in idle chatter, but did her task without delay.[101] [17]**the servant ran to meet her.** Apparently he sat between the well and the town. When she had filled her pitcher she turned to go back to the town whence she had come, and so he ran toward her and asked her for a drink. She gave it to him, without saying, "Why do you not go yourself to

ANTHOLOGY

55. A virgin, neither had any man known her.

R. Johanan said: Rebekah was the first to be intimate with a man who was circumcised at eight days.[1]

Resh Lakish said: Heathen maidens preserved their virginity, yet freely practised unnatural intimacy. She [Rebekah], however, was a *virgin*, her hymen intact, *neither had any man known her* unnaturally.

R. Johanan commented: Does not *a virgin* automatically imply that no man had known her? It means, however, that no man had ever made advances to her, in the spirit of the text, *The rod of wickedness shall not rest upon the lot of the righteous* (Ps. 125:3).

Rebekah was three years and three days old when she left her father's house. For kings' daughters used to submit to their fathers at that age.[2] She, however, did not submit to her father; therefore a miracle was wrought on her behalf, to save her from defilement. For the Arameans used to be intimate with their virgin daughters and then give them in marriage. That is the meaning of the text, *neither had any man known her*, "man" alluding to her father.

Gen. R. 60, 5; Soferim 21. T.S. 24, 93-4.

56. She went down to the fountain, and filled her pitcher, and came up.

All other women went down and drew from the well; in her case, however, the water rose as soon as it beheld her.[1] Said the Holy One, blessed is He, to her: "You have marked out the road[2] for your descendants: just as the waters rose immediately they saw you, so will a well ascend immediately it beholds your descendants." Hence it is written, *Spring up, O well—sing ye unto it* (Num. 21:17).[3]

Gen R. 60, 5. T.S. 24, 95.

57. The servant ran, etc.

To meet her: to welcome her good deeds. *And said: "Give me to drink, I pray you, a little water of your pitcher"*—just a single mouthful.

In this spirit Scripture writes, *The righteous eats to the satisfying of his desire* (Prov. 13:25): this applies to Eliezer, who asked Rebekah for but a mouthful. *But the belly of the wicked shall want (ibid.)* applies to Esau, [who said, *Stuff me with some of this red, red, pottage* (25:30)].[1]

Gen. R. 60, 6; Tan. Pinhas 13. T.S. 24, 96-7.

---

§ 55   [1] Apparently R. Johanan interprets: No man "knew" a woman in the way Rebekah was "known." Cf. 4:1.
      [2] Or: It was the practice of daughters (of other men) to submit to kings, etc.
§ 56   [1] Presumably he renders . . . and filled her pitcher, for it (the *well*) came up.
      [2] Lit., you have provided a token.
      [3] Cf. *supra*, chap. 21, par. 97.
§ 57   [1] The bracketed passage is added from MhG. For "stuff me" AJV has, *let me swallow.*

drink, I pray thee, a little water of thy pitcher." [18]And she said: "Drink, my lord"; and she hastened, and let down her pitcher upon her hand, and gave him drink. [19]And when she had done giving him drink, she said: "I will draw for thy camels also, until they have done drinking." [20]And she hastened, and emptied her pitcher into the trough, and ran again unto the well to draw, and drew for all his camels. [21]And the man looked steadfastly on her; holding his peace, to know whether the Lord had made

COMMENTARY

the well?"[102] [18]**Drink.** Heb. *sh'theh.* This is not the word which Eliezer used, *"hagmiini,"* which means, give me a mouthful. She replied, *"Sh'theh,"* which means, drink as much as you like.[103] **"Drink, my lord"** . . . **and gave him drink.** Thus showing her good breeding and good nature: though she did not know him she called him "my lord," and quickly gave him to drink.[104] [19]**when she had done giving him drink.** Scripture should have said, When *he* had finished drinking. The present indicates that she offered it to him, taking all the labor on herself. Possibly she feared that in his great weariness and thirst occasioned by the journey he might drink more than was good for him; therefore she regulated the amount. Yet lest he think that she merely desired to save herself the trouble she added, "I will draw for your camels also."[105] **when she had done . . . she said.** But not before: it is bad manners to speak to a person while he is eating or drinking.[106] **I will draw for thy camels also.** Now he understood that God had answered his prayer.[107] [20]**she hastened.** Thus showing her respect and regard for him.[108] **the well.** The fountain (*ayin*) was the *natural* spring; the well (*b'er*), the tank or cistern into which the water from the fountain is drawn; whilst the trough (*shoketh*) was the separate receptacle for the animals.[109] [21]**looked steadfastly. a.** Wonderingly and fearfully.[110] **b.** Her assiduousness, intelligence and generosity amazed him and left him speechless.[111] **holding his peace.** He did not say, "Do not take so much trouble," as politeness would have dictated, because he wished *to know,* etc.[112] **holding his peace, to know,** etc. He maintained silence, desirous to know

ANTHOLOGY

58. She said: "Drink, my lord."

The Torah teaches good breeding: Greet everyone warmly and call him, "My master," "My lord." For Rebekah, our matriarch, said to Eliezer, "Drink, my lord."

MhG. T.S. 24, 99.

59. And gave him drink.

He had asked for but a mouthful, but she gave him his fill.

And when she had done . . . she said: "I will draw for your camels also:" See how generous she was! Not enough that she gave him to drink; she went further and said, *"I will draw for your camels also."*

PZ; MhG. T.S. 24, 100-1.

60. The man looked stedfastly at her.

R. Johanan of Sepphoris interpreted: He sipped the water[1] and gazed at her, wondering whether the Lord had prospered his mission.

He scrutinized her, her build and her stature. So some say, "A thin-bearded man is wise; a thick-bearded man is a fool; one who blows the froth off his glass is not thirsty."[2]

Gen. R. 60, 6; MhG. T.S. 24, 104-5.

§ 60 [1] The rendering is conjectural; this derives *mishtaeh* ("looked steadfastly") from *shathah,* to drink. By this interpretation he was not really thirsty, merely toying with the drink, whilst making it an excuse to scrutinize her. Another proposed rendering is: He conversed (with her), which would connect *mishtaeh* with the Aramaic *shutha,* speech, talk.

[2] So his languid drinking showed that he was not really interested in the water but in her. "Some say" is a reference to the Book of Ben Sira, where this saying is found; it is quoted in Sanh. 100b.

his journey prosperous or not. 22And it came to pass, as the camels had done drinking, that the man took a golden ring of half a shekel weight, and two bracelets for her

COMMENTARY

whether without his further request she would really draw water for all his camels.[113] **prosperous or not.** Whether she was motivated by natural kindness or by the hope of reward.[114] **22as the camels had done drinking.** This must have taken a considerable time; when she did not ask for any reward during all this time, he recognized that her motives were entirely altruistic.[115] **took a golden ring,** etc. **a.** Having first asked who she was (see verse 47).[116] **b.** He gave her these ornaments *before* ascertaining her identity, thinking that if she was of Abraham's family they were rightly hers; if not, he would none the less establish a reputation for generosity which would aid him in his search. However, when he related the story to her family he mentioned first that he asked who she was, either because he did not want them to realize his stratagem, or to make them think that he had given her the gifts in honor of the family.[117] **c.** He made

them ready to give, but did not actually give them until he knew who she was. In fact we are merely told that he *took* these ornaments; Scripture *at this stage* does not say that he *gave* them. [This preserves the exact order of the text.—Ed.][118] **d.** It was not necessary to ask her identity, for Abraham had merely insisted that she must be a country-woman of his, but not necessarily of his family.[118a] **e.** He gave them to her before asking her identity, as payment for her labor, [to which she was entitled whoever she might be].[119]* **ring.** Heb. *nezem.* The same word is used of a finger-, nose-, or ear-ring. Here a nose-ring is meant (verse 47).[120] **half a shekel weight. a.** Heb. *beka* is derived from *baka,* to split: hence *half* a shekel.[121] **b.** The shekel weighed about half an ounce. These gifts were both a token of gratitude and a means of obtaining the maiden's favorable opinion.[122] **and two bracelets,** etc. The verse is elliptical, and is to be understood thus: *The man took a gold ring . . . and placed it on her nose and* also placed *two bracelets,* etc.[123] **two bracelets. a.** "Two" refers to the double strand in *each* bracelet: hence it means that he gave her two double-stranded bracelets. [For if "two" referred to the number of bracelets, it is superfluous, since obviously her hands would require two. —Abi Ezer.][124] **b.** Heb. *ts'midim,* sing. *tsamid,* from *tsamad,* to fasten, hence bracelet, which is, as it were, fastened on the hand.[125] **for** (lit., on) **her**

---

* This is not found in Rashi in our edd.—Ed.

ANTHOLOGY

61. As the camels had done drinking.

Then he knew that she possessed the graciousness which fitted her for his master's son, since she showed compassion on dumb animals,[1] as it is written, *A righteous man regards the life of his beast* (Prov. 12:10).

Sechel Tob. T.S. 24, 106 note.

62. A golden ring.

For what purpose did he give it to her? For betrothal.[1] Now, you might think that he gave

her the ring before he knew whose daughter she was; but the text states, *I asked her, and said: "Whose daughter are you?"* . . . *And I put the ring upon her nose* (verse 47): thus from the latter part of the narrative you can learn that first he asked and then gave it to her.[2]

MhG. T.S. 24, 106.

63. A golden ring of half a shekel weight.

R. Huna, citing R. Joseph, said: It was a precious stone weighing half a shekel.[1] Two BRACELETS FOR HER HANDS: in reference to the

---

§ 61 [1] *B'rioth* means living creatures in general, including humans. But the proof-text which follows, and the fact that this comment is based on the camels' drinking, makes it clear that dumb animals are meant here. It is indeed remarkable that her fitness is judged by her behavior to dumb animals; no wonder that the Rabbis stated that it is a Biblical precept not to cause them unnecessary suffering (Shab. 128b).

§ 62 [1] Not merely as a gift; this was actually the ring of betrothal.

[2] Although our text states first that he gave her the ring, and then he enquired about her parentage, we can see from the latter half of the story that the order was the reverse. However, MA holds that he gave her the ring first, because he was certain that Abraham's merit would ensure that a woman of right family would be chosen.

§ 63 [1] Not the ring but the stone weighed half a shekel.

hands of ten shekels weight of gold; [23]and said: "Whose daughter art thou? tell me, I pray thee. Is there room in thy father's house for us to lodge in?" [24]And she said unto him: "I am the daughter of Bethuel the son of Milcah, whom she bore unto Nahor." [25]She said moreover

COMMENTARY

hands. I.e., they fitted her hands exactly.[126] [23]**and said.** I.e., having already said. [This interpretation agrees with the view that he asked her who she was before presenting her with these gifts.—Ed.][127] **Whose daughter,** etc. Only *after* she answered this question did he ask her, "Is there room," etc.?[128] **tell me. a.** Heb. *haggidi.* This verb denotes to give a detailed account: he wanted to know not only her name and her father's name, but all the details of her family.[129] **b.** He adds these words because of the importance of the question.[130] **Is there room.** For guests: in those days houses generally had provisions for accommodating travelers.[131] **for us. a.** For us *only,* not for our camels, which we can stable elsewhere.[132] **b.** "Us" is emphasized: he informed her that he was a member of Abraham's household and required a house free from idolatry.[133] **to lodge** (Heb. *la-lin*). **a.** For a night: *lin* is a verbal noun, viz., a night's lodging. But she answered,

We have room to lodge in (*la-lun*): that is a verb, meaning to lodge (an unspecified time—hence, even many nights).[134] **b.** *La-lin* means many nights' lodging, for which he asked because the animals were weary from the long journey. She answered: We have a place *la-lun,* to lodge *one* night only: you cannot stay long on account of the idolatry in the house [this is the reverse of *a*].[135] **c.** Both *la-lin* and *la-lun* are verbs, save that the former is the "heavy" conjugation (*piel*) while the latter is the "light" form (*kal*). [Abi Ezer, commentator on Ibn Ezra, explains thus: Eliezer, in requesting room for lodging, uses the "heavy" form, indicating that he recognizes that he is asking for something great, which demands a heavy sacrifice; but Rebekah makes light of it—it is but a small thing: hence she employs the *kal*].[136] **d.** There is no difference between *la-lin* and *la-lun;* both the question and the answer were in respect of both man and beast.[137] **e.** *La-lin* is transitive: is there room for us to stable our animals? Thus he merely asked for stabling for the camels, whereas her answer, *la-lun,* embraced the men and their animals.[138] **f.** There is a very fine distinction between *la-lin* and *la-lun:* the former denotes the action without reference to the doer, whereas the latter has specific reference to the doer. Thus Eliezer asked whether they had room for people—anyone—to lodge, as in an inn; she answered, however, that they did not have such a place but only *la-lun,* i.e., a place where *he* and his retinue would be made welcome. Therefore he specified "for us," since the verb itself did not imply it; but she did not say "for you," for that was already implied in *la-lun.*[139] [24]**the son of Milcah.** Who was the *wife* of Nahor, not his concubine . . . She thus in-

ANTHOLOGY

two tables of stone. TEN SHEKELS WEIGHT OF GOLD — in reference to the Ten Commandments.[2]

Again, together these amounted to two hundred and fifty [zuzim]: two hundred for the statutory dowry and fifty as additional.[3] Another interpretation: the half shekel weight corresponded to the half shekel a head (Exod. 38:26).[4]

Gen. R. 60, 6; MA. T.S. 24, 107-8.

64. She said to him: "I am the daughter of Bethuel."

The wise speak of first things first and last things last. This was evidenced by Rebekah. For we read, *He said: "Whose daughter are you? . . . Is there room in your father's house for us to lodge in?" And she said to him: "I am the daughter of Bethuel . . ." She said, moreover, to him: "We have . . . room to lodge in."*[1]

ARN Codex 2, 40. T.S. 24, 110.

[2] The gifts were a prophetic token that she would be the mother of the people that would receive the Two Tables of Stone wherein were engraved the Ten Commandments. Y.T. observes: This interpretation indicates that the purpose of marriage is service to God.

[3] A virgin receives a minimum settlement (*kethubah*) of 200 zuzim, plus whatever additional sum is agreed upon.

[4] Which was levied in the wilderness upon every male Israelite.

§ 64 [1] Her answers were in the same order as the questions.

unto him: "We have both straw and provender enough, and room to lodge in." [26]And the man bowed his head, and prostrated himself before the Lord. [27]And he said: "Blessed be the Lord, the God of my master Abraham, who hath not forsaken His mercy and His truth toward my master; as for me, the Lord hath led me in the way to the house of my master's brethren." [28]And the damsel ran, and told her mother's house according to

COMMENTARY

formed him of her high birth.[140] [25]both straw and provender. For which you did not ask, *and room to lodge in*, which you requested.[141] room to lodge in. a. For yourself and your men.[142] b. She answered first in respect to the animals and then in respect to the men: this is in accordance with the Rabbinic dictum that the needs of animals take precedence.[143] c. She answered that her father was an innkeeper and so had all these.[144] [27]Blessed be the Lord. The term "blessed" when used in reference to God is always either a greeting or praise.[145] who hath not forsaken His mercy, etc. Eliezer knew that God had commanded Abraham to *leave* his family: now that he (Abraham) was seeking a wife for Isaac from out of his family, Eliezer had feared that he would lose God's favor; seeing that he was mistaken and that, on the contrary, God had led him straight to Abraham's family, he gave praise and thanks.[146] His mercy (*hesed*) and His truth (*emeth*). a. *Hesed* is something given as an act of grace; "truth" is one's due. God had given Abraham both his due and more by leading Eliezer to a woman of his own family.[147] b. The phrase is used of an outstanding favor or boon.[148] toward my master. He attributed his good fortune to his master's merit, not to his own.[149] as for me, the Lord hath led me in the way, etc. a. I.e., God has led me in the right direction, into the path that I needed.[150] b. The accentuation necessitates this interpretation: [Behold,] I am [already] on the road to (or, at) the house of my master's brethren, [because] the Lord led me in the way.[151] c. While I was yet on the road, before I even entered the city, He led me to the house, etc.[152] d. The general sense is praise to God for the ease with which he had reached his goal.[153] brethren. Nahor was Abraham's brother, and Milcah was the daughter of Haran, another brother (see 11:27-29); hence the plural "brethren."[154] [28]ran. Joyfully.[155] her mother's house. a. The womenfolk had separate houses where they did their work, and a daughter would only tell her mother about an incident of this kind.[156] b. Her

ANTHOLOGY

65. **The man bowed his head, and prostrated himself before the Lord.**

"She is certainly a suitable match for my master's son," he declared. "She is fit for Abraham's seed, because her deeds are like those of Abraham."

MhG. T.S. 24, 114.

66. **He said: "Blessed be the Lord, the God of my master Abraham."**

He ascribed greatness to whom it belonged.[1]

MhG. T.S. 24, 115.

67. **I being in the way, the Lord led me to the house of my master's brethren.**

Because the road contracted,[1] I knew that *in the way* the Lord *led me to the house*, etc.[2]

Gen. R. 60, 6. T.S. 24, 116.

68. **The damsel (*naarah*) ran.**

This is written *naar*,[1] intimating that she had not yet reached puberty.[2] Another interpretation: She was free of any intimacy.

PZ. T.S. 24, 117.

§ 66 [1] He acknowledged that the success of his mission was due to Abraham, not himself.
§ 67 [1] Lit., leaped before me; see par. 41. This could only have happened by the road itself leaping, as it were.
[2] Such a miracle assured me that I was indeed guided by Him.
§ 68 [1] Though read *naarah*.
[2] Cf. *supra* par. 51.

these words. [29]And Rebekah had a brother, and his name was Laban; and Laban ran out unto the man, unto the fountain. [30]And it came to pass, when he saw the ring, and the bracelets upon his sister's hands, and when he heard the words of Rebekah his sister, saying: "Thus spoke the man unto me," that he

COMMENTARY

narrative included her acceptance of Eliezer's gifts; therefore she told it to her *mother*, not her father, fearing his disapproval.[157] **c.** Her mother was the real head of the house, not her father (the narrative makes it clear that the latter was subordinate even to Laban); therefore she told her mother.[158] **according to these words. a.** The *kaf* ("according to") denotes approximation: her narrative was a

general account, even though she may have changed a word here and there.[159] **b.** She related everything, including Eliezer's reference to his master's brethren, from which she understood that he must be Abraham's servant.[160] [29]**Rebekah had a brother.** This is stated here because he was not mentioned earlier in the account of Nahor's family.[160a] **ran out. a.** He was prompted to do this because *he saw the ring and the bracelets* (next verse); and judging Eliezer to be wealthy, he was anxious to receive rich gifts.[161] **b.** He ran to see the wealthy visitor, but not to offer him hospitality.[162] **c.** This is apparently repeated in the next verse (*when he saw the ring . . . he came to the man*). We are to understand it thus: Even without seeing the gifts Laban would still have gone to see the man who spoke of his master's brethren, but would not necessarily have invited him into his home. Hence Scripture relates that on hearing the story, including the claim to kinship, he went to see the man; and when he saw the gifts he invited him.[163] [30]**when he saw the ring.** Then, not wishing to be ungrateful, *he came to the man*, to invite him into his home; but that was not his original intention.[164] **the words of Rebekah. a.** Apparently Eliezer had informed her of the purpose of his mission, which she now repeated.[165] **b.** Viz., his question whether there was room for

ANTHOLOGY

69. The damsel ran, and told her mother's house.

R. Johanan said: A woman repairs only to her mother's house.[1] An objection was raised: But it is written, *She* [Rachel] *told her father* (29:12)? That was because her mother had died, and she had none to tell but her father.

Gen. R. 60, 6. T.S. 24, 118.

70. His name was Laban.

· R. Isaac interpreted the name in a favorable sense: He was strikingly white. R. Berechiah gave it a derogatory meaning: He was whitened in wickedness.[1]

[Another interpretation:] He whitened the faces of Israel.[2]

[Again:] He turned white with anger the face of every guest who visited him, and shamed him: first he would give him a meal and then demand payment. When he married his daughter to Jacob he invited his fellow citizens, and then seized their outer garments as a pledge for payment. He thus deceived both them and Jacob. Therefore was he called Laban.

Gen. R. 60; MhG; Hemdath Yamim. T.S. 24, 120. 122 and note.

71. When he saw the ring.

Said he: "Has he come to remind us of lust?"[1] for they did indeed refrain from immorality.

He immediately advanced on Eliezer to kill him. Perceiving Laban coming swiftly to harm

§ 69   [1] This has a practical bearing on law; a divorced woman is granted custody of the daughter(s): Keth. 102b; Maim. Hilchoth Ishuth 21, 18; Eben Haezer 82, 7.

§ 70   [1] Laban means white. R. Isaac understands it to refer to his skin, which was exceptionally white and handsome. R. Berechiah explains: He had been brought to white heat in his wickedness—a glib and polished rouge. The word for "strikingly" in the original, פרדיכסוס or פרדוכסוס, is the greek παράδοξος, something striking, marvelous.

[2] With his wickedness. Laban is often described as a type of Israel's enemies. Alternatively: He shamed Israel (with his insults).

§ 71   [1] Thinking that he had defiled his sister and given her the ring in payment.

came unto the man; and, behold, he stood by the camels at the fountain. [31]And he said: "Come in, thou blessed of the Lord; wherefore standest thou without? for I have cleared the house, and made room for the camels." [32]And the man came into the house, and he ungirded the camels; and he

COMMENTARY

them to lodge in her house.[166] **by the camels.** Attending to their needs. Eliezer did not immedi-

ately accompany Rebekah to her home, which would have been bad manners, but remained at the well, waiting for an invitation.[167] [31]**blessed of the Lord. a.** With wealth, as I can see.[168] **b.** With virtue and good breeding.[169] **c.** Laban was smooth-tongued.[170] **wherefore standest thou without? a.** Seeing that you are a kinsman.[171] **b.** You asked only for stabling for your animals (see verse 23, *to lodge*, comm. *c*): why should you wish to remain outside yourself?[172] **I have cleared the house. a.** I have made room for you and your men.[173] **b.** From idols. The Heb. *pinnithi* (cleared) generally refers to clearing away an obstruction or something objectionable (cf. Isa. 57:14: *And He will say: Cast ye up, cast ye up, clear* [pannu—same root] *the way, take up the stumblingblock out of the way of My people*). Hence the ancient commentators related it to the idols, which would be most objectionable to any member of Abraham's household.[174] [32]**the man came into the house, and he ungirded,** etc. "The man" refers to Eliezer,

ANTHOLOGY

him, Eliezer pronounced the Divine Name as an incantation, by which he suspended the camels in the air while he stood upon them.[2] On seeing this Laban recognized him as a righteous man and invited him, *Come in, O blessed of the Lord* (verse 31).

MhG; Midrash Abakir.   T.S. 24, 124-5.

72.   O blessed of the Lord.

He thought he was Abraham, because their features were similar.

R. Jose b. R. Dosa said: Canaan was Eliezer,[1] and because he faithfully served that righteous man he was delivered from the curse and entered the ranks of the blessed,[2] as it says, *Come in, O blessed of the Lord*. R. Jacob said in the name of R. Johanan[3] of Beth Gubrin:[4] He [R. Johanan?] used this for a farewell address:[5] If Eliezer left the category of the cursed and entered that of the blessed because he faithfully served that righteous man; how much

more will Israel be blessed, seeing that they show hospitality with personal service[6] to great and small alike.

[Again] because he himself had said, *Blessed be the Lord* (verse 27), he was privileged to pass out from the ranks of the cursed into those of the blessed.

Gen. R. 60, 7; MA.   T.S. 24, 127-8. 130.

73.   Why do you stand without?

It does not befit your dignity to stay without.

FOR I HAVE CLEARED THE HOUSE. From the defilement of idolatry, AND THERE IS A PLACE FOR THE CAMELS.

Laban said to Eliezer: If you fear to enter on account of idols, I have already removed them for your sake. . . . Why did he add, "*and* [there is] *a place for the camels*"? Laban said to him: Rebekah does not steal idols, and I have cleared the house. Who then does steal?

---

[2] This is based on a literal rendering of the end of the verse: *and, behold, he stood on* (AJV: *by*) *the camels.*

§ 72 [1] See par. 32, n. 1.

[2] Zohar 3, 103a says: Because he (Eliezer) dwelt in the shadow of [Abraham's] faith.

[3] Th. emends: Jonathan.

[4] Eleutheropolis.

[5] It was customary to give a farewell address to one's host in praise of his hospitality.

[6] Lit., with their hands and feet. Y.T.: Giving charity with their hands and running to do good with their feet. It may also mean wholeheartedly.

gave straw and provender for the camels, and water to wash his feet and the feet of the men that were with him. ³³And there was set food

but "he ungirded," etc. to Laban, for it is most unlikely that Eliezer himself set the provender before the animals and the water before his men.[175] **ungirded. a.** He undid the straps of the packs to relieve the camels of their burdens.[176] **b.** Unyoked or

ANTHOLOGY

[She who will hide them] *in the place of the camels,*[1] i.e., Rachel, who will one day steal and hide her booty in the place of the camels, as it says, [*Rachel stole the teraphim—idols—that were her father's.*—31:19.] . . . *Now Rachel had taken the teraphim and put them in the saddle of the camel* (ibid. 34).

Gen. R. 60, 7; AB 67. T.S. 24, 131-2.

74. He gave straw and provender for the camels.

R. Aha said: The talk of the slaves of our Patriarchs' households stands higher than the laws (Torah) of their descendants. The passage on Eliezer takes two or three columns, the narrative being told and repeated.[1] Yet though the uncleanness of a reptile is an integral part of the Torah, it is only from a Biblical extension that we learn that its blood defiles just like its flesh. R. Simeon b. Yohai inferred it from *ha-tame*, where *tame* would have sufficed; R. Eliezer b. R. Jose maintained that it is deduced from the use of *we-zeh* instead of *zeh*.[2]

Gen. R. 60, 8. T.S. 24, 136.

75. HE GAVE STRAW AND PROVENDER FOR THE CAMELS. First he provided fodder for the animals, and only then *was there set food before him to eat* (verse 33). This agrees with the statement of Rab Judah quoting Rab: A man must not eat anything at all before he gives his animal some straw. For it is written, *I will give grass in your fields for* your cattle

(Deut. 11:15), and after that, you *shall eat and be satisfied* (ibid.).

MhG. T.S. 24, 137.

76. Water to wash his feet and the feet of the men that were with him.

R. Aha said: The washing of the feet of the slaves of the Patriarchs' household is more important than the Torah (laws) of their children. For Scripture even finds it necessary to relate how they washed their feet, whereas the uncleanness of a reptile is an integral teaching of the Torah, yet we know that its blood defiles like its flesh only from a Biblical extension, etc.[1]

Gen. R. 60, 8. T.S. 24, 138.

77. THE FEET OF THE MEN THAT WERE WITH HIM. The righteous are greater than angels . . . for angels are sent even when the subordinates of the righteous require them. . . . E.g., many angels escorted Eliezer, Abraham's servant. For it says, *The feet of the men that were with him;* and we do not find that men accompanied him from his master's house. Some maintain that angels escorted him. Others hold that they were literally men, who had come with him to attest his power of attorney,[1] and to keep watch over him on the return journey lest he touch her.

MRE 292; MhG. T.S. 24, 139-40.

78. There was set (*wa-yusam*) food before him.

When they saw the bracelets, they all gath-

§ 73 [1] Lit. translation.
§ 74 [1] First it is related as happening; then repeated through the mouth of Eliezer.
    [2] See Lev. 11:29: *And these* (we-zeh) *are they which are unclean* (ha-tame), "these" being reptiles ("swarming things"). The two Rabbis hold respectively that the *ha* of *ha-tame* and the *we* of *we-zeh* are unnecessary, and therefore to be treated exegetically as extensions.
§ 76 [1] The passage continues as in par. 74.
§ 77 [1] To negotiate on Abraham's behalf. Without their attestation it might have been suspect as a forgery.

before him to eat; but he said: "I will not eat, until I have told mine errand." And he said: "Speak on." [34]And he said: "I am Abraham's servant. [35]And the Lord hath blessed my master greatly; and he

COMMENTARY

untied, the camels having been yoked to each other or to the wagons.[177] [33]**I will not eat,** etc. **a.** Since God had prospered his way, he understood that he must complete his task before eating.[178] **b.** He felt that at present they were under an obligation to him on account of his gifts. This obligation, however, would be materially lessened if he partook of their hospitality, which in turn might decrease the chances of their agreeing to his request.[179] **c.** He did not wish to eat unless they agreed to the marriage.[180] **d.** Although he had been successful so far, there still remained the doubt which he had voiced to his master, viz., whether they would give him the maiden and whether she would consent to go with him. He would not eat until the matter was settled beyond doubt.[181] **he said. a.** Laban or Bethuel.[182] **b.** The head of the house.[183] [34]**I am Abraham's servant. a.** Do not think that all this wealth is mine: it is Abraham's, whose servant I am.[184] **b.** Here he showed his modesty by not claiming friendship or kinship with Abraham.[185] **c.** That is why I do not eat but press so urgently with my business: as Abraham's servant I must carry out my task before anything else.[186] [35]**the Lord hath blessed.** He commenced in this manner in order to make his master's faith clear, viz., he believed in the Lord, and he hoped that his listen-

ANTHOLOGY

ered to kill him. When, however, they saw him take two camels in his two hands and carry them across the stream, they declared, "We cannot kill him." But they set a dish before him containing a deadly poison. For Abraham's sake, however, the dish was changed, and Bethuel (Rebekah's father) ate thereof and died. For *va-yusam* is connected with the word *sam* (poison).

> Midrash quoted in Yalkut Shimoni 1, 109. T.S. 24, 141.

79. I will not eat, until I have said what I have to say.

From this it follows that you must not speak during the meal.

> Midrash Hahefetz. T.S. 24, 142.

80. He said: "I am Abraham's slave."

Raba asked Rabbah b. Mari: What is the source of the popular proverb, "Be the first to tell whatever is degrading in you?"[1] He replied, Our text: He said: "I am Abraham's slave."[2]

> B.K. 92b; Gen. R. 60, 9. T.S. 24, 143.

81. I AM ABRAHAM'S SLAVE. R. Simeon discoursed on the text, *A son honors his father, and a slave his master* (Mal. 1:6). *A son honors his father* applies to Isaac, who honored Abraham. *And a slave his master*: Eliezer honored Abraham, when the latter sent him to Haran; he carried out all Abraham's wishes and also gave him honor, as it is written, *The Lord has blessed my master greatly* (verse 35); it is also written, *He said: "I am Abraham's slave"*—in order to honor Abraham. For a man who brings gold and silver, precious stones and camels, can pretend to be whatever he desires. Yet he did not claim to be Abraham's friend or kinsman, but declared, *"I am Abraham's slave"*—his purpose being to enhance Abraham's stature and honor him in their sight.[1]

Hearing this they hid their faces in the earth [in shame and fear]. Said they, "If the slave is thus, how much more so the master. If you have not seen the lion, look at his whelp! We certainly cannot overcome him." Thereupon they removed the poisoned food.[2]

> Zohar 1, 103a; MhG. T.S. 24, 144-5.

§ 80 [1] Do not wait for others to find it out for themselves.
  [2] He did not wait for them to discover it.
§ 81 [1] By informing them that in spite of all his magnificence he was merely Abraham's slave—by which they could judge the greatness of the master.
  [2] See par. 78.

is become great; and He hath given him flocks and herds, and silver and gold, and men-servants and maid-servants, and camels and asses. ³⁶And Sarah my master's wife bore a son to my master when she was old; and unto him hath he given all that he hath. ³⁷And my master made me swear, saying: Thou shalt not take a wife for my son of the daughters of the Canaanites, in whose land I dwell. ³⁸But thou shalt go unto my father's house, and to my kindred, and take a wife for my son. ³⁹And I said unto my master: Peradventure the woman

COMMENTARY

ers too would accept that faith. This did happen, for when he finished they answered, *"The thing proceeds from the Lord"* (verse 50).[187] **hath blessed my master greatly. a.** Many in our country would be glad to marry into his family, but he will not have them.[188] **b.** So greatly that I, his servant, can travel so richly.[189] **he is become great.** He has acquired great fame.[190] **He hath given him flocks and herds,** etc. His wealth consists not merely of a contented spirit but of actual possessions.[191] ³⁶**all that he hath.** His brothers will not be co-heirs with him.[192] ³⁷**Thou shalt not,** etc. **a.** Unless you first go to my father's house (next verse) and the maiden there refuses.[193] **b.** There is no shortage of women in our country, nor has Isaac any defect which would make them reject him. I am here only because Abraham rejects them.[194] **of the daughters of the Canaanites.** Even if you do not find a fitting wife in my own family.[195] **in whose land I dwell. a.** But Abraham had said, *"among whom* (not, in whose land) *I dwell"* (verse 3), in reliance on God's promise that the land would one day be his. Eliezer, however, regarded only the present.[196] **b.** "Canaanite" includes all the peoples amongst whom Abraham dwells. Therefore there was nothing left for him but to send me here.[197] ³⁸**my father's house . . . my kindred. a.** A wife from my family is more likely to share Isaac's views and general outlook on life.[198] **b.** This is merely a rephrasing of Abraham's more general terms, *my country . . . my kindred* (verse 4).[199] **c.** He did not limit me to his father's house but gave me the wider choice of his family (which is a much broader term = clan); nevertheless his father's house is preferable.[200] ³⁹**Peradventure the woman,** etc. **a.** He repeated the whole

ANTHOLOGY

82. The Lord has blessed my master greatly.

His wealth comes neither from violence nor robbery.

When a man wishes to marry a woman, he tells her his lineage and the lineage of his family, in order to ennoble himself and his family in her eyes. This is what Eliezer did: first he spoke in praise of Abraham, then in praise of Isaac.

PZ; MhG. T.S. 24, 146-7.

83. To him he has given all that he has.

R. Shemaiah said: Abraham willed all his possessions to Isaac in writing. He took the will and gave it to Eliezer his slave, to enhance his desirability in the eyes of his father's house and family.

PRE 16. T.S. 24, 150.

84. ALL THAT HE HAS. He transmitted to him the secret of intercalation.[1]

Ner Has'chalim. T.S. 24, 151.

85. You shall go to my father's house.

To let them know that he still loved them, even though he had departed from them so many years ago.

MhG. T.S. 24, 153.

§ 84 [1] How and when to extend the lunar year to make the seasons correspond to the solar year. This extension by adding a month to the year at certain intervals, determined by astronomical calculations, is called intercalation.

will not follow me. [40]And he said unto me: The Lord, before whom I walk, will send His angel with thee, and prosper thy way; and thou shalt take a wife for my son of my kindred, and of my father's house; [41]then shalt thou be clear from my oath, when thou comest to my kindred; and if they give her not to thee, thou shalt be clear from my oath. [42]And I came this day unto the fountain, and said: O Lord, the God of my master Abraham, if now Thou do prosper my way which I go: [43]behold, I stand by the fountain of water; and let it come to

COMMENTARY

story in order to convince them that Providence willed this marriage, thus delicately hinting that even their refusal would not hinder it.[201] **b.** From this and verse 57 it is evident that whatever the preliminary negotiations in the arrangement of the marriage, the whole matter was contingent on the consent of the maiden.[202] [40]**will send His angel.** I know that they will consent.[203] **my kindred . . . my father's house.** Family (clan) kinship is not enough; she must actually be of my father's house.[204] [41]**my oath** (alathi from alah). Abraham used the word sh'buh (oath): alah is an oath reinforced by a curse; Eliezer used the stronger term alah for greater effect.[205] **my kindred.** Not, my father's house: for if he failed in his father's house he still had to go to the maternal branch of the family.[206] **if they give her not.** Abraham had made it dependent on her consent (verse 8); Eliezer judged it more tactful in speaking to them to put it in the present form.[207] **thou shalt be clear from my oath.** He omitted Abraham's admonition not to return his son there (verse 6), fearing to incur their displeasure at his preference for his newly-found country over the country of his birth.[208] [42]**I came this day,** etc. The purpose of all this repetition was to impress on them that it was all divinely

ANTHOLOGY

86. Perhaps the woman will not follow me.

But insist that your son go to her.

Sechel Tob. T.S. 24, 155.

87. The Lord, before whom I walk.

I.e., in whose fear I have walked.

Why did Eliezer misquote Abraham, who had actually said, *The Lord, the God of heaven, who took me from my father's house* (verse 7)? He acted wisely, to avoid reminding them of what had happened to Haran,[1] as it is written, *Hatred stirs up strifes* (Prov. 10:12). He, however, had come to inspire them with love for Abraham, and one may misquote for the sake of peace.

Midrash Hahefetz; Midrash quoted in Hemdath Yamim. T.S. 24, 156-7.

88. I came this day to the fountain.

From Kiriath-arba to Haran is a seventeen days' journey, which he did in three hours. He was filled with wonder, exclaiming, "To-day I set out and to-day I have arrived!" as it says, *I came* this day[1] *to the fountain*. R. Abbahu said: The Holy One, blessed is He, desiring to show kindness to Isaac, sent an angel before Eliezer and the road contracted, so that in three hours he reached Haran.

PRE 16. T.S. 24, 162.

89. The God of my master Abraham.

He rested his confidence in the merit of the righteous.

PZ. T.S. 24, 163.

§ 87 [1] Who was cast into the fiery furnace and killed after Abraham was miraculously delivered; see Vol. II, chap. 11, par. 46. This was connected with Abraham's departure from his family; hence he refrained from reminding them of it.

§ 88 [1] This very day of my departure.

pass, that the maiden that cometh forth to draw, to whom I shall say: Give me, I pray thee, a little water from thy pitcher to drink; [44]and she shall say to me: Both drink thou, and I will also draw for thy camels; let the same be the woman whom the Lord hath appointed for my master's son. [45]And before I had done speaking to my heart, behold, Rebekah came forth with her pitcher on her shoulder; and she went down unto the fountain, and drew. And I said unto her: Let me drink, I pray thee. [46]And she made haste, and let down her pitcher from her shoulder, and said: Drink, and I will give thy camels drink also. So I drank, and she made the camels drink also. [47]And I asked

COMMENTARY

decreed. Otherwise their immediate consent and declaration, *"The thing comes from the Lord"* (verse 50) would indeed be amazing.[209] [43]**maiden. a.** Heb. *almah*. This denotes a young woman in the strength and vigor of her youth, and is rather more distinguished than *naarah*, the more usual word (as in verse 16).[210] **b.** A different Hebrew word from *naarah*, rendered "damsel," in verse 14. It denotes a girl of marriageable age, and is the word which occurs in Isaiah 7:14.[211] [44]**hath appointed**, etc. As the Rabbis affirm: A heavenly voice proclaims, "The daughter of So and so shall marry So and so."[212] [45]**before I had done speaking.** The immediate answer demonstrated that it was from God.[213] **speaking to my heart. a.** I did not actually say these words but merely thought them.[214] **b.** To make a decision alone is called speaking to one's heart, even if the words of the decision are not actually spoken. "Heart" denotes desire: here it implies that Eliezer wholeheartedly prayed for the success of his mission.[215] **Rebekah.** He had probably heard her name back home; or she had told it to him, even though it is not stated in the narrative (see verse 24).[216] [46]**and said: "Drink."** In his good breeding he modestly omits "my lord" (see verse 18).[217] **I will give thy camels drink.** She had actually said, *"I will draw [water] for your camels also"* (verse 19): before they drank she could speak only of drawing water, since the drinking depended on them; afterwards, however, it could be described as having given them drink.[218] [47]**I asked her**, etc. Actually he gave her the gifts *before* asking about her family (see verses 22-3). Here he reversed the order, fearing that otherwise they might

ANTHOLOGY

90. **She shall say to me: Both drink you, and I will also draw for your camels.**

I know that my master's household is generous; if this woman will be generous, *she is the woman the Lord has appointed for my master's son*, because a man is mated only in accordance with his deeds.

PZ. T.S. 24, 164.

91. **I asked her, etc.**

From this we learn that a man must enquire about a prospective bride's brothers and kinsmen.[1]

MA. T.S. 24, 167.

92. **I ASKED HER**, etc. He did not tell them that he had given her the ring and the bracelets before asking. Because had he told them, they would have rebuked him, "How did you know whether she was of Abraham's family? And had she been of tainted birth or a slave, you would have taken her for Isaac!"[1]

MA. T.S. 24, 168.

§ 91 [1] The narrative does not, in fact, relate that he enquired about her brothers. The present no doubt is influenced by the dictum in B.B. 110a: He who would marry a woman should [first] make enquiries about her brothers, [because] most children resemble their maternal uncle(s).

§ 92 [1] See par. 62, which holds that he did not give her the gifts before making these enquiries.

her, and said: Whose daughter art thou? And she said: The daughter of Bethuel, Nahor's son, whom Milcah bore unto him. And I put the ring upon her nose, and the bracelets upon her hands. [48]And I bowed my head, and prostrated myself before the Lord, and blessed the Lord, the God of my master Abraham, who had led me in the right way to take my master's brother's daughter for his son. [49]And now if ye will deal kindly and truly with my master, tell me; and if not, tell me; that I may turn to the right hand, or to the left."

COMMENTARY

maintain that his gifts were not marriage gifts but merely payment for her labors.[219] [48]and blessed the Lord, etc. He thereby intimated his absolute conviction that God had chosen her, for as long as there was a doubt, blessing Him would have been premature.[220] the Lord, the God of my master Abraham. He was the first to proclaim Him; therefore He is described as his (Abraham's) God.[221] the right way. Lit., "the way of truth": thus was God's promise fulfilled and His word shown to be true.[222] to take my master's brother's daughter. His original statement, my master's brethren (verse 27), referred to the members of the family in general, to whom God had led him. Here, however, when he speaks of "taking" her, viz., in marriage, he is more specific and uses the singular, my master's brother's daughter.[223] brother's daughter. I.e., kinsman's daughter. "Brother" is used here, as in 14:16 and 29:12 to denote "nephew."[224] [49]kindly (hesed) and truly (emeth). a. Hesed refers to action which one is not bound to do; emeth, to keeping the promise of doing hesed.[225] b. Emeth, "truth", is your obligation to show honor to any one of your family and particularly to Abraham, its senior member. But to allow her to go to a distant country will be an act of hesed.[226] c. If you would show kindness to my master to allow your daughter to go so far away, and at the same time consult her true interests.[227] d. Simply: it would be a true act of kindness.[228] tell me . . . tell me. This is repeated: the first is a request for an answer; the second, a request for advice: if you refuse, advise me whether to turn right or left (i.e., who else may be suitable). The verse is to be rendered accordingly.[229] to the right hand, or to the left. I.e., to other members of

ANTHOLOGY

93. **I put the ring on her nose, etc.**

As a gift, not for betrothal.[1]

PZ. T.S. 24, 169.

94. **The ts'midim (AJV: bracelets).**

This is written plene,[1] for a gift is made with all one's heart.[2]

Ner Has'chalim. T.S. 24, 171.

95. **I blessed the Lord.**

He taught them that the Glorious Name should be blessed (praised) for good tidings.

Sechel Tob. T.S. 24, 172.

96. **To the right hand, or to the left.**

To the right hand means to Ishmael; to the left, to Lot, as in the text, If you take the left hand, then I will go to the right (13:9).[1]

[Again] to the left means to Lot, for whose sake my master and I pursued the kings, as it says, He [Abraham] pursued them to Hobah, which is on the left hand of Damascus (14:15).

§ 93 [1] See par. 63, which states that these rings were given for betrothal after he made enquiries. The present passage probably holds that they were given before, as the plain sense of the narrative implies; therefore he pointed out that they were only gifts. But see infra par. 105 for a different reason.

§ 94 [1] צמידים with the yod twice.
[2] This fullness of the gift is suggested by the fullness of the spelling.

§ 96 [1] Lot turned left. The right refers to Ishmael in the wilderness of Paran in the south, which was to the right.

[50]Then Laban and Bethuel answered and said: "The thing proceedeth from the Lord; we cannot speak unto thee bad or good. [51]Behold, Rebekah is before thee, take her, and go, and let her be thy master's son's wife, as the Lord hath spoken." [52]And it came to pass, that, when Abraham's servant heard

COMMENTARY

his family.[230] [50]**Laban and Bethuel. a.** Possibly Bethuel was old and had delegated his affairs in general to Laban; therefore Laban is given precedence.[231] **b.** Perhaps it was always customary to consult the elder brother in such cases; therefore Laban spoke.[232] **we cannot speak unto thee bad or good. a.** We cannot refuse for any reason, good or bad.[233] **b.** By giving precedence to "bad" he showed his character and the natural direction of his thoughts.[234] **c.** It is God's decree, which we can neither annul nor confirm, because it does not depend on us.[235] **d.** I.e., anything at all; cf. 3:22.[236] [51]**take her, and go.** Even without our permission.[237] **as the Lord hath spoken.** He had not

ANTHOLOGY

To the right hand alludes to Ishmael, of whom it is written, *Hold him* [Ishmael] *fast be thy hand* (21:18).

> Gen. R. 60, 9; MA; Midrash Hahefetz. T.S. 24, 173 and note.

97. Then Laban and Bethuel answered.

In his great impudence he [Laban] hastened to speak first.[1]

> PZ. T.S. 24, 174.

98. The thing proceeds from the Lord.

Rab said, quoting R. Reuben b. Itstrobili: We learn from the Torah (the Pentateuch), the Prophets, and the Writings that a woman is destined for a man by the Lord. The Torah: *Laban and Bethuel answered, and said: "The thing proceeds from the Lord."* The Prophets: *But his father and his mother knew not that it was of the Lord* (Judg. 14:4). The Writings: *House and riches are the inheritance of fathers; but a prudent wife is of the Lord* (Prov. 19:14).

> M.K. 18b. T.S. 24, 176.

99. THE THING PROCEEDS FROM THE LORD.
When had it proceeded?[1] R. Joshua b. R. Nehemiah, quoting R. Hanina b. Isaac, said: At

Mount Moriah.[2] Our Rabbis said: [On this very occasion; hence,] *And let her be your master's son's wife, as the Lord has spoken* (verse 51).[3]

> Gen. R. 60, 10. T.S. 24, 177.

100. As the Lord has spoken.

But did they believe in the Lord? surely they were idolaters and diviners?[1] What they meant was, As you and your master Abraham believe the Lord has spoken.

> Mayan Ganim. T.S. 24, 178.

101. We cannot speak to you bad or good.

Granted bad, but why not good? They meant: The good that we would speak is not determined by us but by the Lord.

> PZ. T.S. 24, 180.

102. BAD OR GOOD.
They unconsciously uttered a prophecy, not knowing that she was to give birth to two sons, one evil, viz., Esau, and the other good, viz., Jacob.

> Midrash Habiur. T.S. 24, 179.

103. Behold, Rebekah is before you.

As a reward for Abraham's having said to

§ 97 [1] Though Bethuel was his father. MhG, however, holds that they answered simultaneously.
§ 99 [1] Where and when did God decree this?
[2] There Abraham was informed of this.
[3] The whole narrative convinced them that it was divinely decreed.
§ 100 [1] It is interesting to note that divination, which is forbidden (Lev. 19:26), is automatically linked with idolatry.

their words, he bowed himself down to the earth unto the Lord. [53]And the servant brought forth jewels of silver, and jewels of gold, and raiment, and gave them to Rebekah; he gave also to her brother and to her mother precious things. [54]And they did eat and drink, he and the

COMMENTARY

spoken; but God's clear manifestation is described as His speech.[238] [52]**he bowed.** Rather, prostrated himself, in gratitude and joy.[239] [53]**jewels,** etc. Various articles of women's finery.[240] **precious things. a.** Sweet fruits.[241] **b.** Alternatively: costly raiment.[242] **c.** The Heb. is a general term for gifts of any description, but the usual interpretation of fruit is impossible, since the word appears in contexts which rule out this interpretation, e.g., Ezra 1:6.[243] **d.** Anything costly and precious, but the exact meaning depends in each case on the context.[244] [54]**they did eat and drink.** This was the betrothal

ANTHOLOGY

you, *The Lord, the God of heaven . . . He will send His angel* before you (verse 7).[1]

PZ. T.S. 24, 181.

104. **Take her and go.**

Inwardly they resented it.[1]

Ner Has'chalim. T.S. 24, 182.

105. **The servant brought forth jewels of silver,** etc.

These he gave for betrothal, for the first presents were only gifts.[1] Why so?[2] Because a man may not betroth a woman before making formal arrangements.[3] For Rab flagellated any person who betrothed without the necessary preliminaries (Kid. 12b).

PZ. T.S. 24, 186.

106. JEWELS OF SILVER, etc. From this the Sages deduced that personal finery is more

prized by a woman than any delicacy.

MhG. T.S. 24, 185.

107. **He gave also . . . *migdanoth* (AJV: precious things).**

What is that? R. Huna said: Kunchi.[1] Our Rabbis said: Parched ears of corn and nuts. Were parched ears the most precious things he could give?[2] However, this is to teach that if a man sets out on a journey without his necessary provisions, he is mortifying himself.[3]

What are *migdanoth*? Rab said: Things that awaken desire.[4] Another interpretation: Things worth writing home about,[5] e.g., silks, spices, and pepper.[6]

Gen. R. 60, 11; MhG. T.S. 24, 184. 187.

108. **They ate and they drank.**

Of Rebekah's [betrothal] feast.

PRE 16. T.S. 24, 188.

§ 103 [1] This is based on the phrase *"before you."* Cf. par. 37.
§ 104 [1] Their reply emphasized their helplessness—which implied that they would have prevented it if they could.
§ 105 [1] See pars. 62 and 93 for agreeing and dissenting views.
[2] Why did he not give the first for betrothal?
[3] *Shiduchin* is the formal agreement to marry; *kiddushin* (here rendered betrothal) is not betrothal in our sense, but the first stage of marriage, whereby she becomes his wife, and the marriage tie cannot be broken save by divorce. But the marriage may not be consummated until the *nissuin*, home taking. Nowadays both ceremonies are combined.
§ 107 [1] Jast. doubtfully suggests: pearls. Other suggested renderings: weaving utensils; fish, or salted meat.
[2] That they are mentioned last? Otherwise it is an anti-climax to mention them after the gold and silver. But according to another reading, which omits the next word *ela* ("however"), this is not a question but a statement: "He gave them various dainties, parched ears of corn and nuts, for parched ears were more highly esteemed by them than everything else; he had brought them with him from Eretz Israel" (Sechel Tob). The statement reflects the Rabbis' boundless love for Eretz Israel.
[3] Therein lies the greater importance of dainties over jewels, and not in their intrinsic value.
[4] Lit., the heart. He derives *migdanoth* from *nagad*, to draw, to attract.
[5] Lit., about which people tell (*maggidim*). He derives it from *hagged*, to tell, relate.
[6] All of which were highly prized.

men that were with him, and tarried all night; and they rose up in the morning, and he said: "Send me away unto my master." ⁵⁵And her brother and her mother said: "Let the damsel abide with us a few

COMMENTARY

feast.[245] **he and the men that were with him** (*immo*, from *im*). In verse 32 the Heb. for "with him" is *itto*, from *eth*. *Im* denotes equality; *eth*, subordination. The men with him were of course his subordinates; but they ate together with complete equality, since in matters of food the master may not claim any higher privilege; alternatively,

there cannot be true rejoicing without the feeling of unity which comes from equality.[246] ⁵⁵**her brother and her mother said. a.** Laban, her brother, may have been wise and held in greater respect than Bethuel, her father, and therefore it was the brother who spoke now; similarly, when Scripture records how they agreed to the marriage, Laban is given precedence (verse 50).[247] **b.** Only her brother and mother asked for the delay, but not her father: he was so pleased that she should marry Abraham's son that he was ready to let her go immediately. For the same reason Laban is given precedence earlier, to indicate that her father's consent could almost be taken for granted. [This is the antithesis of the view in Anthology par. 111 that Bethuel had changed his mind and desired to withdraw his consent altogether.—Ed.][248] **Let the damsel abide with us.** In proposing this delay Laban may have hoped for increased gifts as the price for an immediate departure.[249] **a few days**

ANTHOLOGY

109. Tarried all night.

Our Rabbis taught: "Night passes over a judgment and the judgment is annulled."[1] In this sense the narrative continues, *Her brother and her mother said: "Let the damsel abide with us,"* etc.

Yemenite Anth. MS Albihani. T.S. 24, 190.

110. He said: "Send me away to my master."

From this the Sages inferred: A man should never say, "Let me depart for my sake"; but, "Let me depart for the sake of my father"; or, "for the sake of my master."[1]

MhG. T.S. 24, 191.

111. Her brother and her mother said.

But where was Bethuel? He wished to prevent it, and so died suddenly during the night. Thus it is written, *The righteousness of the sincere shall make straight his way, but the wicked shall fall by his own wickedness* (Prov. 11:5). *The righteousness of the sincere* ap-

plies to Isaac; *shall make straight his way*, viz., Eliezer's mission. *But the wicked shall fall by his wickedness* applies to Bethuel, who was smitten at night.

[Another account:] The angel of whom Abraham spoke when he assured Eliezer, *The Lord, the God of heaven . . . He will send His angel before you* (verse 7), exchanged the dish containing poison which had been set before Eliezer[1] and placed it before Bethuel, who ate thereof and died. Some say that Bethuel exercised *le droit de seigneur* over every virgin who was married in that place; therefore an angel killed him lest he exercise it over his daughter Rebekah.

Another interpretation: His townspeople said, "We will now see how he treats his own daughter. If he treats her as he does our daughters, well and good. If not, we will kill him and all that are his." For that reason the angel slew him that night. Therefore was he called Bethuel, because he possessed every virgin (*bethulah*) first.

Gen. R. 60, 12; MA. T.S. 24, 192 and note.

§ 109 [1] This is put in quotes because it has the appearance of a popular proverb. If a court judgment is not immediately carried out, it may well come to nothing. Thus, although they had already agreed to the marriage and told Eliezer to take her and go, yet after sleeping on it they proposed a delay!

§ 110 [1] Lekah Tob comments: Thus Scripture writes, *As the cold of snow in the time of harvest, so is a faithful messenger to him that sends him; [for he refreshes the soul of his master]* (Prov. 25:13).

§ 111 [1] See pars. 78 and 81.

days, at the least ten; after that she shall go." [56]And he said unto them: "Delay me not, seeing the

COMMENTARY

(*yamim*). I.e., "a year" (cf. Lev. 25:29, where *yamim* is used in that sense). They asked for a year, because a virgin required that period to make her preparations for marriage.[250] **ten. a.** I.e., ten months. This proves that *yamim* must mean "a year," not days, for had they asked for a few days, they could not give ten months as an alternative.[251] **b.** They asked for the delay in order to accustom Rebekah to the idea of such a great change in her life.[252] **c.** The Heb. for the adjective ten [days or months understood] is *asarah*, not *asor* as in the text. The latter therefore is a noun, meaning a ten

ANTHOLOGY

112. Let the damsel abide with us *yamim* (AJV: a few days) or ten.[1]

Mishnah: A virgin is given twelve months for her necessary preparations from the time that the husband demands her in marriage.[2]

Gemara: Whence do we know this? Said R. Hisda, From the text, *Her brother and mother said: "Let the damsel abide with us* yamim *or ten."* Now, what does *yamim* mean? Shall we say, two days?[3] Do people speak thus? Having asked for two days, which are refused, they ask for ten! Rather, then, *yamim* must mean a year, as in the verse, yamim (AJV: *a full year*) *shall he have the right of redemption* (Lev. 25:29).[4] But perhaps it means a month, as in the verse, *a month of days* (Num. 11:20)? You may determine the meaning of *yamim,* unspecified, from another text where *yamim* is unspecified; but you cannot determine *yamim,* unspecified, from a text where "a month" is explicitly stated.

Keth. 57b. T.S. 24, 193.

113. DAYS OR TEN. *Days* mean the seven days of mourning for [Bethuel]; or *ten,* the twelve months granted to a virgin to make her preparations.[1]

Gen. R. 60, 12. T.S. 24, 194.

114. DAYS OR TEN. When Bethuel died they proposed that she remain there twelve months in mourning for her father, because it is unseemly to enter into the joy of marriage until twelve months after a father's death.

[Another interpretation:] *Yamim* (days) means a year, etc. (as in par. 112). *Or ten:* the last day of the first month and the first day of the last month, plus ten full months between amount to a full year.[1]

Or Haafelah Ms; MA. T.S. 24, 194 note.

115. OR TEN. Some interpret: Ten months, which would complete a year from the time she had reached puberty. Others interpret: A tenth of a year, the time given to non-virgins for preparations, i.e., approximately thirty days.[1]

MhG. T.S. 24, 195.

116. Delay me not.

He arose early in the morning and saw the angel waiting for him without. Said he to them,

§ 112 [1] Lit. translation. AJV: *At least ten.*
  [2] See par. 105, n. 3. When the husband demands that the *nissuin* (home-taking and consummation of the marriage) shall take place, she is given a year for her preparations, e.g., collecting a trousseau. But see par. 115 and note.
  [3] *Yamim* means days. Since no number is mentioned, the smallest number in the plural must be assumed.
  [4] Thus they were demanding a year for her preparations.
§ 113 [1] It is not clear how *"or ten"* can mean twelve months. E.J.: They argued that she was entitled to twelve months, which, however, they would reduce to ten if he was in a particular hurry. By the present reading this would probably mean in addition to the seven days of mourning.
§ 114 [1] Technically a day sometimes counts as a full month. So they proposed to count the first day as though it were the last day of the first month and make a similar concession for the last month, whereby the year would be practically reduced to ten months.
§ 115 [1] The year stated above is only if she is betrothed immediately she attains puberty. If she has already attained it, she is given up to the year (with a minimum of thirty days); if a year has already passed she is given thirty days, the time normally given to a non-virgin, i.e., a widow or divorcee. Hence we have two views. The first is that Rebekah had attained her puberty two months previously; therefore they demanded ten months. The

Lord hath prospered my way; send me away that I may go to my master." [57]And they said: "We will call the damsel, and inquire at her mouth." [58]And they called Rebekah, and said unto her: "Wilt thou go with this man?" And she said: "I will go." [59]And they sent away

COMMENTARY

[day or month] period.[253] [56]**seeing the Lord hath prospered my way.** Which shows clearly that He does not desire any delay.[254] [57]**We will call the damsel,** etc. **a.** Although God has shown His will (see preceding comm.), it is nevertheless Rebekah's right to decide on these matters.[255] **b.** We will ask her in your presence, lest you think we would unduly influence her.[256] **c.** We will then see if this is really divinely decreed, as you maintain.[257] [59]**they sent.** I.e., they permitted her to depart.[258] **their sister.** "Sister" is used in the sense of kinswoman: hence their, not his (Laban's): all her kinsfolk came to bid her farewell.[259] **they sent**

ANTHOLOGY

Delay me not, seeing the Lord has prospered my way—behold, he is without, waiting for me.[1]
PRE 16. T.S. 24, 197.

117. **Seeing that God has prospered my way.**

By miraculously shortening the road[1] and making everything happen as he had requested.
MA. T.S. 24, 198.

118. **We will call the damsel, and enquire at her mouth.**

From this we learn that a fatherless maiden may not be given in marriage without her consent.
Gen. R. 60, 12. T.S. 24, 199.

119. **The damsel (la-naarah).**

This is written *la-naar*, lacking a *heh*, because she had attained puberty.[1]
MA. T.S. 24, 200.

120. AND ENQUIRE AT HER MOUTH. Even if she is silent [her consent may be assumed].
MhG. T.S. 24, 201.

121. **They said to her: "Will you go?"**

R. Isaac said: They hinted to her, Will you really go?[1] AND SHE SAID: "I WILL GO": in spite of you, and even without your consent.
Gen. R. 60, 12. T.S. 24, 103.

122. **I will go.**

This maiden, who did not know what a man was, accepted her union with Isaac. Why? Because she was destined for him from her very birth by the Omnipotent, as it says, *it is* [decided] *in the balances that they are to rise together* [in marriage], *from* [the time they are] *nothing,* [in the womb] (Ps. 62:10).[1]

When a man gives his daughter in marriage, even to a slave, she is too abashed to say anything. But when they asked Rebekah, *"Will you go with this man?"* she promptly replied, *"I will go."*

The Holy One, blessed is He, brought Israel

---

other, that a year had already elapsed; therefore they asked for thirty days. Both of these views disagree with those in pars. 55 and 68.

§ 116 [1] Sc. the angel whom God had sent to prosper my way by making the road contract before me (see par. 88). Sefer Hasidim observes: There is nothing superfluous in the Torah. From the narrative of Eliezer we learn on the one hand that hospitality must be given with a cheerful countenance; on the other, that a guest may not impose upon his host, as it says, *He said to them, "Do not delay me"* (he did not wish to impose on them longer than was necessary).

§ 117 [1] Cf. *supra* par. 41.

§ 119 [1] The lack of a *heh* indicates that she was no longer a *naarah* but a *bogereth*. See however par. 68 where the reverse is stated: the lack of a *heh* indicates that she had *not* attained puberty.

§ 121 [1] Sechel Tob: They hinted that she should not go with him but insist that Isaac should come to her.

§ 122 [1] This translation follows R. Hiyya in Lev. R. 29, 8. AJV: *If they be laid in the balances, they are together lighter than vanity.*

Rebekah their sister, and her nurse, and Abraham's servant, and his men. [60]And they blessed Rebekah, and said unto her: "Our sister, be thou the mother of thousands of ten thousands, and let thy seed possess

COMMENTARY

away Rebekah their sister . . . and Abraham's servant, and his men. Her kinswomen provided an escort for Rebekah; a similar escort, made up of the prominent men of the town, was provided for Eliezer for part of the way. [This understands "his men" not as referring to the retinue with which he had arrived, but to an escort of honor specially assembled.—Ed.][260] **her nurse.** Of her infancy. It was common for a nurse to remain in a girl's service when she was grown up.[261] [60]**they blessed.** After they had escorted her some distance and were about to take their leave. [This explains why the blessing comes *after* they sent her away, by interpreting the sending of the previous verse as escorting.—Ed.].[262] **be thou the mother,** etc. The pronoun *ath,* which is grammatically unnecessary, denotes emphasis: the multitudes that are to spring

ANTHOLOGY

out of Egypt only for the sake of Sarah, Rebekah, Rachel and Leah . . . as a reward for Rebekah's answer, *I will go,* to their question, *Will you go with this man?* whereby she placed her trust in her Father in Heaven.

PRE 16; MhG; SER 25.   T.S. 24, 205 and note.

123.   **They sent away Rebekah their sister.**

Surely it should have said, his sister? This, however, teaches that all her kinsfolk and the townspeople came to pay their respects and bid her farewell.

Sechel Tob.   T.S. 24, 206.

124.   **Her nurse.**

Sc. Deborah, as we read, *Deborah Rebekah's nurse died* (35:8).

PZ.   T.S. 24, 207.

125.   **They blessed Rebekah.**

R. Aibu said: They were poor and mean, and blessed her with nought but the mouth.[1]

Gen. R. 60, 13.   T.S. 24, 208.

126.   THEY BLESSED REBEKAH. Even as a precentor stands and blesses a bride under her bridal canopy, so did they stand and bless Rebekah.

Baraitha:[1] How do we know that the bridegrooms' benediction[2] is a Scriptural obligation? Because it says, *They blessed Rebekah.* Did they then bless her over a cup of wine?[3] This, however, is merely a support.[4]

PRE 16; Kallah Rabbathi 1.   T.S. 24, 209-10.

127.   **Our sister, be thou the mother of thousands of ten thousands.**

R. Berechiah and R. Levi, quoting R. Hama b. R. Hanina, said: Why did Rebekah not conceive until Isaac prayed for her? Lest the heathen say, Our prayer bore fruit. Rather, she bore because *Isaac entreated the Lord for his wife* (25:21).[1]

Come and see the result of the blessings of the wicked! For twenty years she was barren! Hence our Sages said: The blessing of the wicked is a curse. But when was this blessing fulfilled? In the days of Moses, as it is written, *Return, O Lord, to the ten thousands of the thousands of Israel* (Num. 10:36).

R. Berechiah said, quoting R. Levi: Scrip-

§ 125   [1] Their blessing was the only dowry they gave.
§ 126   [1] A tannaitic teaching not included in the Mishnah.
   [2] Formal benedictions are recited at a marriage.
   [3] These formal benedictions are recited over a cup of wine. But surely they did not do that, their blessing being the natural expression of good wishes, not the formal benediction at all.
   [4] It is not really the source of the practice, but lends support to the idea of a blessing at a marriage.
§ 127   [1] Lekah Tob adds: Nevertheless our Rabbis of blessed memory said: Do not lightly esteem the blessing of the common man.

the gate of those that hate them."
⁶¹And Rebekah arose, and her damsels, and they rode upon the camels,

COMMENTARY

from Isaac in accordance with God's promise, may *you*, not any other wife, be their mother and ancestress.²⁶³ **possess the gate.** I.e., be the councillors and judges, whose functions were carried out at the gate. The blessing was: May your descendants be so wise that even their enemies will recognize and utilize their wisdom.²⁶⁴ **those that hate them** (*son'e*). In the story of the Binding of Isaac (chap. 22) a similar phrase occurs: *your seed shall possess the gate of his enemies* (oyeb—verse 17). *Oyeb* implies one who is an enemy at heart, without outwardly showing it: hence it is a fitting term to be used by God (or an angel, His representative), who knows the heart of man. *Sone*, however, refers to one who expresses his hatred concretely, by overt action: the present blessing was that they should stand in need of the wisdom of Rebekah's descendants [see last note].²⁶⁵ **⁶¹they rode.** They did not mount the camels until their escort had departed, for it would have been unmannerly to ride whilst

ANTHOLOGY

ture writes, *The blessing of the destroyer*² *came upon me* (Job 29:13). *The blessing of the destroyer* applies to Laban the Syrian (Aramean), as it says, *An Aramean would have destroyed my father* (Deut. 26:5).³ *Came upon me*, viz., Rebekah, the blessing being, *Our sister, be thou the mother of thousands* (alfe) *of ten thousands.* There did indeed arise chiefs of thousands (*alufim*) from her through Esau, as it says, *These are the chiefs of* (alufe) *the sons of Esau . . . the* aluf *of Teman, the* aluf *of Omar*, etc. (36:15); *and of tens of thousands* through Jacob, as it says, *I increased you to tens of thousands, even as the growth of the field* (Ezek. 16:7). Some maintain that both blessings were fulfilled through Jacob, as it says, *Return, O Lord, to the* ten thousands *of the* thousands *of Israel.*

> Gen. R. 60, 13; MhG. T.S. 24, 211 and note. 212.

128. Let your seed possess the gate of them that hate you.

Laban prophesied without knowing what he was prophesying. For in this blessing, *Let your seed*, etc., they were cursing themselves and blessing Rebekah.

> ARN Codex 2, 43. T.S. 24, 213.

129. Rebekah arose.

She did indeed rise in leaving an unworthy home and entering a home of sanctity.¹

> PZ. T.S. 24, 214.

130. And her damsels.

But earlier it says that she went with her nurse, and now it says *and her damsels?* In truth, many maidens went to escort Rebekah, and as soon as they were out of sight of the city they declared that they would join Rebekah and go with her.¹

> Or Haafelah. T.S. 24, 215.

131. They rode on the camels.

The School of R. Ishmael taught: One should always use refined language, for the Torah speaks of riding in reference to a *zab*,¹ but of sitting in reference to a woman.² In this sense it says, *Choose the tongue of the skilled* (Job

---

² AJV: *him that was ready to perish.*
³ The Aramean is understood to allude to Laban, who sought to destroy Jacob ("my father") by robbing him of his hard-earned gains (see 31:40-41). AJV: *A wandering Aramean was my father.*
§ 129 ¹ Cf. chap. 23, par. 47.
§ 130 ¹ Cf. par. 123.
§ 131 ¹ A person suffering from gonorrhoea.
² Zab: *And what saddle soever he . . . rides upon shall be unclean* (Lev. 15:9). A menstruant woman: *And if he be . . . on any thing whereon she sits . . . he shall be unclean* (ibid. 23). In these texts Scripture teaches that whatever a zab or a menstruant sits or rides upon becomes unclean and defiles others. In this they are alike; nevertheless the Torah speaks of sitting in connection with a woman, because riding astride is an indecent posture for her.

and followed the man. And the servant took Rebekah, and went his way. ⁶²And Isaac came from the

COMMENTARY

their escort walked (see comm. on verse 59 on *"they sent away,"* etc.).²⁶⁶ **followed the man.** Because he knew the way. [See Anthology par. 133. The present comment points out that in the plain meaning of the text no special significance lies in the fact that they *followed* but did not *precede* him:

they did so simply because he knew the way.—Ed.]²⁶⁷ **the servant took Rebekah. a.** Under his special care.²⁶⁸ **b.** The damsels mentioned earlier in this verse were the escort. When they reached the parting of the ways Eliezer bade them return, after which he took Rebekah and went.²⁶⁹ **c.** In ancient marriage representatives of the bride's father ceremoniously handed her over to representatives of the husband. It was in this latter capacity that Eliezer now received her, whereby he formally became her "servant" too, just as he was Isaac's. Hence he is again called "servant" from this point onward.²⁷⁰ ⁶²**Isaac came,** etc. This tells that Isaac met them on the road, before they entered the city,

ANTHOLOGY

15:5). Yet is not riding mentioned in connection with a woman? Surely our text says, *Rebekah and her damsels arose, and they* rode *upon camels?* There it was natural, through fear of the camels.³

Pes. 3a. T.S. 24, 216.

132. THEY RODE ON THE CAMELS. R. Levi said: That was because camels are bred in the Orient. Our Rabbis said: This was symbolic: as a camel has one characteristic of uncleanness and one of cleanness,¹ so did Rebekah bear one righteous and one wicked son.²

Gen. R. 60, 14. T.S. 24, 217.

133. **And followed the man.**

R. Johanan said: Because it is unseemly for a man to follow a woman.

Thus far he [Eliezer] is spoken of as a man. But when he wished to make improper advances it says, *The* slave *took Rebekah.* Here we see that slaves are untrustworthy.

Gen. R. 60, 14; Or Haafelah. T.S. 24, 218-9.

134. **The slave took Rebekah.**

With words. "Happy are you," said he to her, "to be privileged to wed with a righteous man

whom the Holy One, blessed is He, chose for a complete consecration¹ and blessed him that through him and his seed all the nations of the earth shall be blessed."

Sechel Tob. T.S. 24, 220.

135. **The slave took Rebekah, and departed.**

He departed from Haran at six hours (noon), took Rebekah and Deborah her nurse, and let them ride the camels. Lest the slave be alone with Rebekah at night the road contracted before him, and in three hours, at the time of the Afternoon Prayer, he arrived at Hebron.

PRE 16. T.S. 24, 221.

136. **Isaac came.**

From Mount Moriah.¹

MA. T.S. 24, 222.

137. **Isaac came from coming.**¹

He returned from a mission to fetch someone. Whither had he gone? To *Beer-lahai-roi:* to fetch Hagar—she who had sat at the well (*beer*) and cried out to Him who lives (*lahai*) for ever, "Look upon (*r'eh*) my humiliation."²

R. Oshaya said: When Isaac saw his father send for a wife for him, he thought, "Shall I live with her and leave my father alone? I will

---

³ Because of its height a woman fears to ride side-saddle.
§ 132 ¹ It chews the cud (a mark of cleanness), but has not a parted hoof (a sign of uncleanness); see Lev. 11:4.
     ² MhG: So did Rebekah give birth to a man of blamelessness (*tamim*) and a man of blood (*damim*).
§ 134 ¹ For a burnt-offering, which is completely consecrated to God.
§ 136 ¹ Cf. chap. 23, par. 9. See next par. for a different view.
§ 137 ¹ Lit. translation.
     ² See 16:14.

way of Beer-lahai-roi; for he dwelt in the land of the South. [63]And Isaac went out to meditate in the field at the eventide; and he lifted

COMMENTARY

and how this came about. This apparent chance meeting was similar to Eliezer's meeting with Rebekah at the well, and further strengthens the impression of the divinely-decreed nature of the marriage.[271] **from the way of Beer-lahai-roi. a.** Lit., from coming to Beer, etc. I.e., he did not live there but had been on a visit and was now returning home.[272] **b.** The Heb. *mibo* (lit., from, or, on account of, coming) has a disjunctive accent. We must therefore interpret: Isaac came to Beer-lahai-roi (i.e., went) on account of [Rebekah's] coming (i.e., knowing of her imminent arrival he went out to meet her): this coming was to (the preposition for "to" is omitted, but such omission is not unusual) Beer-lahai-roi.[273] **he dwelt in the land of the South.** Near that Beer (=well).[274] [63]**to meditate** (*la-suah*). **a.** The root is *siah*, tree, i.e., to plant or walk among the trees.[275] **b.** The

ANTHOLOGY

go and bring Hagar back to him, that he may enjoy tranquillity and not cease to procreate." Therefore it says, *Isaac came from his mission to Beer-lahai-roi*, i.e., the well where the Prince of the world (an angel) had appeared to her; for *roi* alludes to Hagar, who said, *Have I even here seen Him that sees me* (roi)? (16:14).

> Gen. R. 60, 14; MhG. T.S. 24, 223-4.

138. Beer-lahai-roi.

Three met their help-mates at or coming from a well: Isaac, Jacob, and Moses. Isaac, as it is written, *Isaac came from his mission at the well of Lahai-roi*. Jacob: *He looked, and behold a well in the field* (29:2). Moses: *He sat down by a well* (2:15).[1]

For Isaac's sake the Almighty delivers people from an unnatural death. For it says, *Isaac came from the well of Lahai-roi*: now "well" means life, as it says, [*They found there*] *a well of living waters* (26:19).

> Tan. Sh'moth 10; Midrash Alpha Bethoth 104. T.S. 24, 225 and note.

139. For he dwelt in the land of the South.

That is Hebron, for it is written, *The same is Hebron—where Abraham and Isaac sojourned* (35:27).

> MhG. T.S. 24, 226.

140. Isaac went out to meditate in the field.

Whence did he go out? From the Garden of Eden [where he had spent the three years that had elapsed since his Binding].[1]

> Midrash quoted in Yalkut Shimoni 1, 109. T.S. 24, 227 and note.

141. TO MEDITATE IN THE FIELD.

It was taught: Isaac instituted the Afternoon Prayer, as it says, *Isaac went out to meditate in the field toward evening*.[1] Now, "meditate" means nought else but pray, as it says, *A prayer of the afflicted when he faints, and pours out his meditation before the Lord* (Ps. 102:1).

Another source: *I pour out my meditation before Him* (ibid. 142:3). Thus it says too, *Evening, and morning, and at noonday, will I meditate and yearn, and He has heard my voice* (ibid. 55:18).

It was taught: R. Eliezer said: A man should first ask for his private needs and then recite the statutory Prayer; as it says, *A Prayer of the afflicted when he faints and pours out his meditation before the Lord*. Now, "meditation" means nought but prayer, as it says, *Isaac went out to meditate in the field*.[2] R. Joshua said: First let him pray and then ask for his private needs, as it says, *I pour out my meditation before Him, I declare before Him my trouble*.[3]

§ 138 [1] Cf. par. 42.
§ 140 [1] Bracketed addition from *Hizkuni*.
§ 141 [1] I.e., in the late afternoon, which is the time of the Afternoon Prayer (*minhah*).
[2] By meditation, i.e., prayer, the statutory Prayer is understood; therefore "a prayer of the afflicted" is interpreted as a petition for one's private needs, and this is given precedence in the text.
[3] "Trouble" likewise means one's private needs.

up his eyes, and saw, and, behold, there were camels coming. [64]And Rebekah lifted up her eys, and when she saw Isaac, she alighted from the camel. [65]And she said unto

COMMENTARY

root is *siah*, to converse: he had gone out to converse with his friends in the cool of the evening.[276] **c.** The word is connected with a root meaning to act without thought: he went out to enjoy an hour of leisure, free from the care of his flocks.[277] **camels.** Not, *the* camels, because he did not recognize them as yet as his own. Nevertheless, expecting the return of Eliezer about this time, he went in their direction.[278] [64]**she saw Isaac.** In his manly dignity, and felt abashed in his presence.[279] **she alighted** (lit., fell) **from the camel. a.** She modestly alighted, because she was riding the camel straddle-wise, and it would have been immodest to allow Isaac to see her in that position.[280] **b.** Rather, she made obeisance from her seat on the camel.[281] [65]**she said,** etc. **a.** Verses 64 and 65 are not consecutive but interlocked, and are to be read thus: She saw Isaac, asked the servant who it was, and on hearing his reply alighted from the camel and

ANTHOLOGY

Isaac went out to pray to his Creator that he should always fear and never try Him.[4] Therefore he went beyond his father; for the latter prayed only in the morning, whereas he went further and instituted the Afternoon Prayer.

Ber. 26b; A.Z. 7b; Num. R. 2; Sechel Tob. T.S. 24, 228 and note.

142. TO MEDITATE IN THE FIELD. Did he have no house or any other place to pray in but that field? It was the field which Abraham had bought near the cave of Machpelah. When Isaac entered he saw the Divine Presence (Shechinah) over it, and from the field there ascended a celestial and holy fragrance. For that reason he prayed there, and made it a permanent practice to repair there for prayer.

Zohar 2, 39b. T.S. 24, 230.

143. He lifted up his eyes, and saw.

The righteous are exalted through their eyes, as it says, *Abraham lifted up his eyes, and looked*, etc. (22:13); also, *He lifted up his eyes and looked* (18:2). Isaac: as in our text.

Tan. Vayyesheb 6. T.S. 24, 231.

144. Behold, there were camels coming.

Sometimes a man goes to his wife; at others, she comes to him. Isaac's spouse came to him, as our text states. Jacob went to his mate, as it says, *Jacob went out from Beer-sheba*, etc.

Gen. R. 68, 3. T.S. 24, 232.

145. She saw Isaac.

R. Huna said: Seeing his hand stretched out in prayer she said to herself, "This must certainly be a great man." Therefore she enquired who he was.

She saw the Shechinah (Divine Presence) above his head; therefore she bowed her head, as it says, *She alighted from the camel.*

Our text is not in natural sequence. Scripture should have said, Rebekah lifted up her eyes and said, "Who is that man?" and the servant said, "It is my master." And she alighted from the camel, took the veil, and covered herself. This disorder teaches that she saw a supernal halo circling his head,[1] whereupon she wonderingly asked, "What man is this"?

Gen. R. 60, 15; Or Haafelah; MhG. T.S. 24, 234-5 and note.

146. She fell[1] from the camel.

Seeing through the Holy Spirit that the wicked Esau was to issue from her, she trembled with horror; as she fell her hymen was torn and she lost her virginal blood. The Holy One, blessed is He, immediately bade Gabriel, "Go

---

[4] Cf. Num. 14:22: *Yet they have tried Me* (AJV: *put Me to the proof) these ten times*, etc. Isaac prayed not to be tempted to do this.

§ 145 [1] Therefore she immediately alighted, before even asking who he was, as might be expected.

§ 146 [1] Lit. translation. Gen. R. *ad loc.*, however, interprets: She descended, as in the verse, *Though he fall, he shall*

the servant: "What man is this that walketh in the field to meet us?" And the servant said: "It is my

COMMENTARY

veiled herself. Or, *she said*, etc., should be rendered, she *had* said, etc., i.e., she saw Isaac and alighted

from the camel, having previously asked Eliezer, etc.[282] **b.** There is no need to alter the sequence of the verses: on seeing the man turn in their direction she instinctively felt that he was Isaac (presumably she was expecting him), and so alighted from the camel. Nevertheless, after alighting she still wished to make sure and so asked Eliezer who he was, and on receiving his reply she veiled herself.[283] **What man is this,** etc. She did not of course ask the identity of every man she saw, but

ANTHOLOGY

down and save the blood from putrefying or becoming tainted."[2]

When Isaac consummated their marriage he found that she lacked her virginity. Suspecting a liaison with Eliezer he demanded, "Where are your tokens of virginity?" "When I fell from the camel my virginity was destroyed," she replied. "You lie," he accused her; "Eliezer must have accosted you." She swore that he had not touched her. They went and found the tree dyed with blood, and Isaac immediately knew that she was undefiled. Said the Holy One, blessed is He: "What shall I do for this slave who was unjustly suspected?" He bade the ministering angels, "Take him alive into the Garden of Eden"; this Eliezer was the son of Nimrod. This indeed was a great wonder: Isaac came out alive from the Garden of Eden, while Eliezer entered alive into the Garden of Eden. [To this R. Judah alluded when he said: May my portion be with the unjustly suspected.][3]

> Midrash quoted in Yalkut Shimoni. T.S. 24, 237.

147. What man is this (*ha-lazeh*)?

R. Hiyya said: She saw his beauty and was seized with wonder, for *ha-lazeh* suggests the

same meaning as in the text, *Behold, this* (ha-lazeh) *dreamer comes* (Gen. 37:19).[1] Our Rabbis said: She saw him and his guardian angel, for *ha-lazeh* means "this other one."[2]

Isaac was as handsome as Joseph, of whom it is written, *Joseph was of beautiful form, and fair to look upon* (39:6).

Ha-lazeh means this tree (*alonzeh*). As Rebekah was coming with Eliezer she saw him, outstandingly beautiful, enrobed in a fringed garment,[3] in appearance like an angel of God. "Who is this man?" she demanded. What does *ha-lazeh* mean? As beautiful as a *luz* (almond tree).

> Gen. R. 60, 15; Midrash T'hillim 90; Tan. Y. Tol'doth 7. T.S. 24, 238 and note. 239.

148. **WHAT MAN IS THIS** (*ha-lazeh*)? *Ha-lazeh* has a *heh* at the beginning and a *heh* at the end of the word. Said she: He must certainly be the man who issued from the twain to whose names a *heh* was added, viz., Abraham and Sarah.[1] The *lamed* and *zayin* left in the word imply, He who was bound for a sacrifice at the age of thirty-seven.[2]

> Midrash.[3]   T.S. 24, 241.

not be utterly cast down (Ps. 37:24)—which the Midrash understands to mean, though he is about to fall, he does not actually fall (T.S. 24, 235).
[2] MA reads: That no animal or bird may devour it.
[3] Bracketed passage added from *Hadar Z'kenim*.

§ 147 [1] See below.
[2] *Alon zeh.* The meaning is doubtful. Either: Who is this one—sc. the angel who accompanied Isaac. Or: This oak—this man who looks as strong as an oak. *Pilsono*, here rendered "his guardian [angel]," may be derived from *palles*, to weigh: he who weighs our actions.
[3] See Num. 15:37-38.

§ 148 [1] Abraham and Sarah were originally Abram and Sarai respectively. In each case the change of name was effected by adding a *heh*.
[2] This being the numerical value of the two letters.
[3] Quoted in Minhath Judah, a commentary on Gen. R.

master." **And she took her veil,
and covered herself.** [66]**And the
servant told Isaac all the things that
he had done.** [67]**And Isaac brought
her into his mother Sarah's tent,
and took Rebekah, and she became**

COMMENTARY

only here, because she realized that he was coming to meet them.[284] **It is my master.** He did not mention Isaac by name, but she saw that he was too young to be Abraham, and understood that it was Isaac.[285] **took her veil, and covered herself. a.** This is told in praise of her modesty and refinement.[286] **b.** Out of fear and chasteness. This reserve characterized her future relationship with her husband; we do not find the same freedom between these two as between Abraham and Sarah or Jacob and Rachel. Both Sarah and Rachel would speak plainly to and upbraid their husbands when the occasion demanded; not so Rebekah.[287] **c.** Rebekah again acted in accordance with Eastern etiquette. It was not necessary for her to have her face veiled in the presence of Eliezer, since he was only a servant.[288] [66]**the servant told Isaac,** etc. That from the whole narrative he might understand that she really was destined for him.[289] [67]**Isaac brought her into his mother Sarah's tent.** In those days husband and wife each occupied a separate tent. Isaac now assigned his mother's tent, which as a mark of respect had remained dismantled since her death, to Rebekah.[290] **Isaac brought her . . . and took Rebekah.** [We would expect the reverse

ANTHOLOGY

149. It is my master.

Straightway she fell, thanking the Almighty and declaring, *"The lines have fallen to me in pleasant places. . . . I will bless the Lord who has counselled me"* (Ps. 16:6-7).

MhG. T.S. 24, 242.

150. She took the veil, and covered herself.

Two covered themselves with a veil, and bore twins: Rebekah and Tamar. Rebekah, as our text states. Tamar: *She covered herself with her veil* (38:14).[1]

Gen. R. 16, 15. T.S. 24, 243.

151. COVERED HERSELF. [As a token of submission,] in fulfillment of the decree, *He shall rule over you* (3:16).

[Another interpretation:] This teaches that he offered her the cup of benediction.[1]

Ner Has'chalim; Midrash Habiur.
T.S. 24, 244 and note.

152. The servant told Isaac all the things he had done.

R. Eleazar said: The general statements in the Torah outnumber its detailed accounts. For one could write several pages on this narrative. Our Rabbis said: He related only the happy incidents, e.g., how the earth contracted before him.

Gen. R. 60, 15. T.S. 24, 245.

153. Isaac brought her into the tent [and lo! she was as] Sarah his mother.[1]

As long as Sarah lived a cloud hung over her tent;[2] when she died, the cloud departed; when Rebekah came, it returned. As long as Sarah lived her doors were wide open; when she died that liberality ceased; when Rebekah came, it returned. As long as Sarah lived her dough was blessed, and a lamp burned in her tent from Sabbath eve to Sabbath eve; when she died, all these ceased; when Rebekah came, the lamp returned. Now, when Isaac saw her following in his mother's footsteps, preparing her dough in ritual purity, he straightway *brought her into the tent* [and lo! she was as] *Sarah his mother.*

Gen. R. 60, 16. T.S. 24, 246.

154. He took Rebekah.

With a formal betrothal (*kiddushin*). *And*

§ 150 [1] The idea is probably that their fruitfulness was a reward for their modesty.
§ 151 [1] Which is given to a bride as she stands veiled.
§ 153 [1] Lit. translation plus the bracketed addition, which is based on what follows.
        [2] Signifying the Divine Presence; cf. Exod. 40:34.

his wife; and he loved her. And Isaac was comforted for his mother.

COMMENTARY

order, viz., Isaac took (i.e., married) Rebekah and (then) led her into Sarah's tent. The following explain the reason for the change.—Ed.]. **a.** *He took Rebekah, and she became his wife.* I.e., he went through the ceremony of marriage and thus she became his wife.[291] **b.** The Bible desires **to** mention Sarah before Rebekah, since Sarah preceded her.[292] **c.** He did not marry her immediately, but first took her into his mother's tent to observe her general conduct, and only when he saw that she was really fit did he marry her.[293] **she became his wife; and he loved her.** Nowadays the love *before* marriage is stressed; the true Jewish view stresses love *after* marriage: thus, the more she became his wife, the more he loved her.[294] **and Isaac was comforted for his mother. a.** A man is attached to his mother during her lifetime; when she dies, he takes comfort in his wife.[295] **b.** Here is a man of forty who is inconsolable at the death of his old mother and who finds consolation in his wife through whom he regains the mother! Here is the supreme concept of woman's dignity—written on a page of the oldest Jewish history![296]

ANTHOLOGY

she became his wife: with *nissuin* (home-taking).[1]

Mayan Ganim.   T.S. 24, 247.

155. Isaac was comforted for his mother.

Our Rabbis said: Three years Isaac mourned for his mother, and whenever he entered her tent and saw it dark he would tear his hair. But when he married Rebekah and led her into his tent, the light returned, as it says, *Isaac brought her into the tent*, "tent" symbolizing light, as it says, *Behold, even the moon has no light*[1] (Job 25:5). Then he was comforted, and it was as though his mother were still alive. Therefore it says, *And Isaac was comforted for his mother.*

Rebekah was patterned after Sarah in all respects. R. Judah said: Just as Isaac's features resembled Abraham's, so did Rebekah's resemble Sarah's. . . . Hence, in very truth, she was "Sarah his mother."[2] R. Eleazar said: Although Sarah was dead, her image had not departed from the house; yet it remained invisible there from the day of her death until Rebekah came. When she entered, Sarah's image became visible, as it says, *He brought her into the tent* [and lo! there was] *Sarah his mother*, which means, Sarah immediately became visible. Yet none saw her save Isaac when he entered. Therefore Scripture does not say that Isaac was comforted after the death of his mother, but *Isaac was comforted after his mother*, which means, after his mother became visible and resumed her place in the home.

MhG; Zohar 1, 133a.   T.S. 24, 248 and note.

§ 154   [1] See par. 105, n. 3. According to this, Eliezer's gifts were not the formal *kiddushin*, in contrast to the view given there. The Talmud (Kid. 41b) states that a man may not betroth a woman without seeing her first. The present view may be based on that prohibition, according to which Isaac could not have permitted Eliezer to betroth her on his behalf, since he had not yet seen her.
§ 155   [1] Heb. *yaahil.* Hence *ohel*, tent, can connote a source of light.
[2] See the translation of our text in the last par.

GENESIS

Chapter XXV

¹**And Abraham took another wife, and her name was Keturah. ²And**

COMMENTARY

¹**Abraham took another wife, and her name was Keturah. a.** One Rabbinic view identifies her with Hagar; others reject it (see Anth. pars. 8, 9). The plain meaning implies that she was not Hagar.[1] **b.** Here he did not insist on a member of his family, as in Isaac's case, because the Covenant (see 17:2, 19) was to be fulfilled only through the descendants of the latter (21:12).[2] **c.** It does not necessarily mean that it was not until after the death of Sarah that he married again. It is quite possible that he

ANTHOLOGY

1. **Abraham took another wife.**

R. Judan said: The Torah teaches propriety, that a man with grown sons should first see them married and then take a wife himself. From whom do you learn this? From Abraham. First *Isaac brought her into his mother Sarah's tent,* and then *Abraham took another wife.*

[Said Isaac: I have taken a wife, but my father is left without one. What did he do? He went and brought a wife for him.][1]

Gen. R. 60, 16.   T.S. 25, 1.

2. **ABRAHAM TOOK ANOTHER WIFE.** Raba asked Rabbah b. Mari: What is the source of the popular saying, "Sixty pains attack the teeth of him who hears his neighbor eating but does not eat himself"? ... It is the text: *Isaac brought her into his mother Sarah's tent, and took Rebekah, and she became his wife; and he loved her. And Isaac was comforted for his mother.* This is immediately followed by, *Abraham took another wife, and her name was Keturah.*[1]

B.K. 92b.   T.S. 25, 2.

3. **Abraham took a wife again.**

After Sarah's death Abraham remarried his divorced wife. For it says, *Abraham took a wife again, and her name was Keturah.* Now, why say, "Abraham took *again*"? Because she had

been his wife once before, and now he took her again.[1]

PRE 30.   T.S. 25, 3.

4. **ABRAHAM TOOK ANOTHER WIFE.** Scripture says, *Remember then your Creator in the days of your youth, before the evil days come, and the years draw nigh when ... the* abiyonah *shall fail* (Eccl. 12:1, 5)—when even desire (*ta-awah*)[1] fails. All these things happen to an old man. But although Abraham is described as old (24:1), his desire did not cease, as our text states.

Happy art thou, Father Abraham. He is one hundred and forty years old, yet he takes a wife, and has children! This teaches that the righteous leave some of their youthful virility for their old age. Not like others to whom applies the verse, *He that commits adultery with a woman lacks understanding; he who does it would destroy his own desire* (AJV: soul—Prov. 6:32).

Tan. Y. Hayye Sarah 7; MhG.
T.S. 25, 4 and note.

5. **ABRAHAM TOOK ANOTHER WIFE.** *In the morning sow your seed, and in the evening withhold not your hand* (Eccl. 11:6). R. Dostai and R. Jannai quoting R. Samuel b. Nahman interpreted: If you have had children in youth, take a wife in old age and have more children.

---

§ 1   [1] Bracketed passage added from Tan. Hayye Sarah 8.
§ 2   [1] The sight of Isaac's joy had made his own loneliness unbearable.
§ 3   [1] See par. 8, where Keturah is identified with Hagar. A different view is taken in par. 9.
§ 4   [1] Connected by a play on words with *abiyonah* (AJV: caperberry).

ANTHOLOGY

From whom may you learn this? From our father Abraham. Though he had children in his younger years, he nevertheless took a wife in his old age and had more children.

Gen. R. 61, 3. T.S. 25, 5.

6. ABRAHAM TOOK ANOTHER WIFE. Let our master teach us:[1] How many times should one pray a day? R. Samuel b. Nahman said: As the day changes three times during its course, one must pray three times. For in the morning the sun is in the east, at noon it stands in mid-heaven, in the afternoon it is in the west.... Now, why did the Sages institute prayers thrice daily? In order that a man might add something to his prayer. This applies not only to prayer; one should continually increase his knowledge of the Torah. Nor is this limited to the Torah: it applies to children too. If you marry a woman and she dies, take another and have children with her. Here is the proof: Abraham, whose wife died, did not remain alone, but took another wife.

Tan. Hayye Sarah 5. T.S. 25, 6.

7. ABRAHAM TOOK ANOTHER WIFE. In this spirit Scripture writes, *And though your beginning was small, yet your end should greatly increase* (Job 8:7). R. Simeon b. Lakish, citing R. Eleazar ha-Kappar, said: From this you learn that the addition given by the Holy One, blessed is He, exceeds the principal. In the beginning Abraham had only Isaac; but when the Almighty gave him more, the addition exceeded the original, as it says, *She bore him Zimran, and Jokshan*, etc.[1]

It is written, *Happy is the man that has not walked in the counsel of the wicked*, etc. (Ps.

1:1). *Happy is the man* applies to Abraham.... *He shall be like a tree planted by streams of water* (*ibid.* 3): the Holy One, blessed is He, planted him in Eretz Israel. *That brings forth its fruit in its season* (*ibid.*)—i.e., Ishmael. *And whose leaf does not wither*—Isaac.[2] *And in whatsoever he does he shall prosper*: this alludes to the children of Keturah.

Gen. R. 61, 1; Tan. Y. Hayye Sarah 10. T.S. 24, 7 and note.

8. **Her name was Keturah.**

R. Judah said: This was Hagar, whom he married by Divine command. Said R. Nehemiah to him, But it is written that *Abraham again took a wife*, which implies a different one? He replied, "Again" has the same meaning here as in the verse, *The Lord spoke to me yet again* (Isa. 8:5).[1] But, he objected, Scripture states that *her name was* Keturah? That means that she blended (*kittrah*) piety with good deeds, he replied. R. Berechiah said: Although it says, *She departed, and strayed in the wilderness* (21:14), lest you think that any man was suspected on her account, it is stated, *Her name was Keturah*, which means that she was like one who seals a treasure and produces it with the seal intact.[2]

Another interpretation: Her deeds were as fragrant as incense (*k'toreth*), and she bore him six sons.

When Hagar left Abraham she relapsed into her ancestral idolatry. Subsequently, however, she turned again to piety and good deeds. Therefore was her name changed to Keturah, signifying that she became attached to good deeds. Then Abraham sent for and married

§ 6 [1] A characteristic opening in the Tanhuma. See chap. 18, par. 1, note 1.
§ 7 [1] The Hebrew literally reads, *Abraham added and took a wife*. The comment apparently is based on the word "added"—the addition exceeded the original, for whereas before he had only one son (or two, including Ishmael, as noted in several different versions of this Midrash), he now begot another six sons. MhG adds: God's addition to a blessing is greater than the blessing itself. How many prayers did Abraham offer before Isaac was granted to him; yet in his old age all these were given to him!
[2] Yalkut Shimoni *ad loc.* reverses this, referring "fruit" and "leaf" to Isaac and Ishmael respectively. This reading is preferable.
§ 8 [1] There "again" clearly intimates a resumption of what had already been started earlier. So here too "again" implies that he resumed marriage with one to whom he had been married earlier, viz., Hagar. Our text seems to be in disorder. The present is based on an attempted restoration.
[2] Deriving Keturah from *kitter*, to tie up, whence to seal.

she bore him Zimran, and Jokshan, and Medan, and Midian, and Ishbak, and Shuah. ³And Jokshan begot Sheba, and Dedan. And the sons of Dedan were Asshurim, and

COMMENTARY

took his secondary wife (in 1 Chron. 1:32 Keturah

is called a "concubine") during her lifetime; and it is only mentioned here in connection with the disposal of the Patriarch's property.³ ²**Medan.** The "Medanites" are referred to in 37:36 as traders with Egypt.⁴ **Midian.** The name of a nomad tribe frequently occurring in the Bible.⁵ **Shuah.** Bildad, one of Job's friends, is described as a Shuhite (Job 2:11).⁶ ³**Jokshan begot.** In some cases Abraham's sons' sons are mentioned, but not in others: possibly they had none, or they (their sons' sons) died before they in turn begot.⁷ **Sheba, and Dedan.** Mentioned in 10:7. The other names are found in

ANTHOLOGY

her. From this we see that a change of name makes atonement for guilt, and for that reason her name was changed.

[Another interpretation:] Keturah was Hagar, Keturah being her real and original name. Why then was she called Hagar? Because after he sent her away she wandered about like a stranger (*ger*), and did not marry until Abraham sent for and remarried her.

> Gen. R. 61, 4; PRE 30; Zohar 1, 133b; Hemdath Yamim. T.S. 25, 8. 10 and note.

9. HER NAME WAS KETURAH. Abraham married three women: Sarah, the daughter of Shem; Keturah, the daughter of Japheth; and Hagar, the daughter of Ham.¹

> Yelamdenu. T.S. 25, 9.

10. **Zimran and Jokshan.**

Ammi b. Ezekiel and our Rabbis disagreed. Ammi b. Ezekiel interpreted: Zimran signifies that they were destroyers (*m'zamm'rin*);¹ Jokshan, that they were cruel (*mith-kashin*). Our Rabbis interpreted: Zimran signifies that they sang hymns (*m'zamm'rin*), accompanied

by the tabret, to idols; Jokshan, that they beat (*ma-kishin*) the tabret in idolatrous worship.

To this you may apply the verse, *And though your beginning was small, yet your end should greatly increase* (Job 8:7). The Holy One, blessed is He, declared: "In this world the righteous beget good and evil, but in the world to come² all shall be righteous," [as it says, *Your people also shall all be righteous...*] *the branch of My planting, the work of My hands* (Isa. 60:21). It also says, *The smallest shall become a thousand, and the least a mighty nation; I the Lord will hasten it in its time* (ibid. 22).³

> Gen. R. 61, 5; Tan. Hayye Sarah 8. T.S. 25, 12-13.

11. **Zimran, and Jokshan, and Medan, and Midian, and Ishbak, and Shuah.**

R. Joshua b. Levi said: The conversation of the people of Eretz Israel is Torah. How so? When one prays on behalf of his neighbor he says to him, "May you be a brother to seven and a father to eight." "A brother to seven" means like Isaac and David, who were brothers to seven; whilst "a father to eight" alludes to Abraham and Jesse.

---

§ 9 ¹ "Daughter" in each case probably means descendant. These were Noah's three sons from whom the world was repopulated after the Flood. The idea is probably that as the "father of a multitude of nations" (17:5) he expressed in himself through these three marriages the ultimate unity of the human race.

§ 10 ¹ Deriving Zimran from *zammer*, to prune, cut down; whence, to destroy (Y.T.; E.J.). Mah. renders: They went through the world singing; he connects it with *zammer*, to sing.
² This apparently means in the Messianic era.
³ Thus the "beginning" of the righteous is "small," for they beget wicked as well as righteous, just as Abraham begot these as well as Isaac. But their "end"—the Messianic era—will show a great "increase"—all will be righteous. This is a striking affirmation of belief in human moral and spiritual progress.

Letushim, and Leummim. ⁴And the sons of Midian: Ephah, and Epher, and Hanoch, and Abida, and Eldaah. All these were the children of Keturah. ⁵And Abraham gave all that he had unto Isaac. ⁶But unto

COMMENTARY

Arabian inscriptions.⁸ **Asshurim, and Letushim. a.** These are the names of the founders of peoples so called.⁹ **b.** Asshurim is derived from a root meaning a man's steps; they were caravan drivers traveling from place to place. Letushim is connected with *natash*, to spread out (the *lamed* and *nun* in the Hebrew are sometimes interchangeable): they were nomad tent-dwellers, whose tents dotted (i.e., spread over) the country.¹⁰ **c.** This does not mean that the children of Dedan were so called, but that these peoples were descended from Dedan. Therefore it says, "and the sons of Dedan *were*," etc., which means that they grew into these peoples.¹¹ ⁴**the sons of Midian,** etc. These were the five "fathers' houses" (clans) which descended from Midian, ruled over by kings; see Num. 31:8.¹² **All these were the children of Keturah.** Sixteen sons and grandsons are enumerated, all of whom apparently were in her own lifetime—possibly too in Abraham's; hence the phrase "All these."¹³ ⁵**Abraham gave,** etc. He distributed his estate during his lifetime

ANTHOLOGY

That is why our Rabbis of blessed memory said¹ that at a circumcision one should say, "May the child live for his father and mother, may he be a brother to seven and a father to eight."

MhG; PZ. T.S. 25, 14 and note.

12. **The sons of Dedan were Asshurim, and Letushim, and Leummim.**

R. Samuel b. Nahman said: Although they¹ render, Merchants, smiths, and heads of peoples, *all* of them were heads of peoples.²

Gen. R. 61, 5. T.S. 25, 15.

13. **Abraham gave all that he had to Isaac.**

R. Judah, R. Nehemiah, and our Rabbis disagreed. R. Judah said: He gave him the birthright. R. Nehemiah said: He gave him the privilege of blessing.¹ Our Rabbis said: It refers to burial in the cave of Machpelah and a deed of gift² to his estate. R. Judah b. R. Simon, R. Berechiah and R. Levi quoting R. Hama b. R.

Hanina said: He did not bless him, but gave him gifts.

R. Isaac said: *All that he had* means the supernal wisdom which he possessed in virtue of his knowledge of the sacred Name of the Holy One, blessed is He.

[Another interpretation:] He transmitted to Isaac the lofty doctrine of the true faith, so that he [Isaac] should be united with his true grade.³

Because the Holy One, blessed is He, had told him, *"In Isaac shall seed be called to you"* (21:12), therefore he gave him all that he had.

He that spares his rod hates his son; but he that loves him instructs him betimes (Prov. 13:24). This applies to Abraham, who instructed Isaac, taught him the Torah, and led him in his own paths. The proof is that at his Binding he was thirty-seven years old, yet Abraham, an old man, bound him like a sheep, without hindrance. Therefore *Abraham gave all that he had to Isaac.*

Gen. R. 61, 6; MA; Tan. Sh'moth 1; Zohar 1, 133b. 223a. T.S. 25, 16-18 and notes.

§ 11 ¹ *Var. lec.*, that is the meaning of our ancestral custom.
§ 12 ¹ The *meturg'manim*, the translators, who translated the public Scriptural readings into Aramaic in the synagogue services.
² Not the last only.
§ 13 ¹ To bless others. This privilege, originally granted to Abraham (see 12:2: *And be a blessing*—which is interpreted, you have the privilege of blessing), he now conferred on Isaac.
² Or: his will.
³ In mystic thought the universe consists of various spiritual grades, and every person has his particular grade; by striving he can rise from a lower to a higher grade.

the sons of the concubines, that Abraham had, Abraham gave gifts;

COMMENTARY

to avert quarrels after his death.[14] [6]**concubines. a.** The word is written defectively, because there was only one, viz., Hagar, who is identified with Keturah. The only difference between a wife and a concubine was that no marriage-settlement was made upon the latter.[15] **b.** Hagar and Keturah.[16] **c.** He had no concubines. The reference is to the concubines of the servants of his household: they are called his because both the servants and their concubines belonged to him. Ishmael and the sons of Keturah are thus not mentioned, but we may assume that he certainly made gifts to them too.[17] **d.** There was no marriage ceremony (*kiddushin*) in the case of a concubine. Further, Hagar and Keturah were not the same person, the former being a concubine, the latter a wife. Hagar was an Egyptian, Keturah a Canaanitish woman. Nevertheless the reference here is to Keturah's sons. She is called a concubine (as in 1 Chron. 1:32), because since Abraham was told, *In Isaac shall seed be called to you* (21:12), he regarded all his other wives as concubines.[18] **gifts. a.** That which he had received on account of Sarah (20:14; 16), because he did not wish to benefit from it.[19] **b.** But he carefully

ANTHOLOGY

14. Abraham gave all that he had to Isaac. But to the sons of the concubines . . . Abraham gave gifts.

We learnt: If a man divides his estate among his sons in his lifetime, gives one more and one less, and places the first-born on the same footing as the rest, his action is valid. That, however, is only if he declares these gifts. If, however, he allots the portions as bequests, we disregard his wishes.[1] That is what Abraham did; he gave one more and another less, but everything as a gift, as it is written, *Abraham gave gifts.*

MhG. T.S. 25, 19.

15. To the sons of the concubines . . . Abraham gave gifts. The Ishmaelites and the Keturites[1] once came in a lawsuit against the Jews before Alexander of Macedon.[2] They pleaded: The Land of Canaan (Israel) belongs to us jointly. For it is written, *These are the generations of Ishmael, Abraham's son* (vs. 12); it is also written, *These are the generations of Isaac, Abraham's son* (verse 19); [further, Ab-

raham took another wife, and her name was Keturah].[3] Said Gebiha b. Pesisa to the Sages: "Allow me to go and argue with them. . . ." Said he to them: "Whence do you bring your proof?" "From the Torah," they replied. "Then I too will argue only from the Torah," he rejoined. "It says, *Abraham gave all that he had to Isaac. But to the sons of the concubines . . . Abraham gave gifts.* Now, if a father gives some of his sons their portion in his lifetime and then sends them away from each other, has one any claim on the other?"

Sanh. 91a. T.S. 25, 20.

16. Gifts. Which gifts? Said R. Jeremiah b. Abba: He transmitted to them the name of Defilement.[1]

R. Abba said: I once chanced to be in a town where dwelt descendants of the "children of the east,"[2] and they taught me some of their ancient wisdom and showed me their books of Wisdom. . . . I said to them, "My children, all this is similar to what we have in our Torah;

§ 14 [1] For then he is bound by the Torah's laws of inheritance, which give the first-born a double portion, whilst the other sons receive equal shares (Deut. 21:17).

§ 15 [1] Abraham's descendants through Keturah. Probably certain Arab tribes or peoples are meant.
[2] The famous world conqueror.
[3] Since we are all Abraham's descendants, we have equal claims to the land. The parallel passage in Gen. R. 61, 7 quotes, *He shall acknowledge the first-born . . . by giving him a double portion* (Deut. 21:17). Ishmael was Abraham's first-born.

§ 16 [1] The meaning is obscure. Apparently it refers to the knowledge of the unhallowed arts, such as sorcery and witchcraft.
[2] See 29:1: *Then Jacob went on his journey, and came to the land of the* children of the east; cf. our text: *he [Abraham] sent them [the sons of his concubines] eastward, to the east country.* The present assumes that the "children of the east" were these sons and the descendants of those whom Abraham had sent eastward.

and he sent them away from Isaac his son, while he yet lived, eastward, unto the east country. ⁷And these

COMMENTARY

avoided describing these gifts as their inheritance.[20] **he sent them away from Isaac.** Lest they quarrel with him over the estate.[21] **eastward.** I.e., to the

east of the land of Israel.[22] **eastward, unto the east country. a.** First the Bible states in general terms that he sent them eastward; it then defines it more specifically, "to [the region known as] the east country," viz., Haran and Ur of the Chaldees. This was his original homeland; there they would find more friendship than elsewhere.[23] **b.** "The east country" is Aram (Syria); cf. *From Aram Balak bringeth me, the king of Moab from the mountains of the East* (Num. 23:7). He sent them there to take possession of the inheritance which

ANTHOLOGY

nevertheless, shun these books, lest you be led astray after the idolatry mentioned in them ... for these books mislead mankind. The ancient children of the east possessed a wisdom which they had inherited from Abraham, who had imparted it to the sons of the concubines, as it is written, *But to the sons of the concubines ... Abraham gave gifts, and he sent them away ... eastward, to the east country.* In the course of time they followed the track of that wisdom into many false roads."[3]

What gifts were they? The sides of the lower grades,[4] and they comprised the names of the powers of the unclean spirit. ... He sent them *eastward, into the east country,* because there are the haunts of the unclean practitioners of sorcery and witchcraft.

Sanh. 91b; Zohar 1, 100b. 133b.
T.S. 25, 22 and note.

17. **He sent them away from Isaac his son ... eastward, to the east country.**

He advised them, Go as far east as you can, lest you be burnt by Isaac's flaming coal.[1] But Esau received his deserts at Jacob's hands because he came and attacked him.[2] Thus it is written, *Is this your joyous city* [that has been

so reduced]? ... *Who has devised this against Tyre, the crowning city* (Isa. 23:7f)? R. Eleazer said: Whenever Tsor (Tyre) is written *plene*, it means the actual province of Tyre; but when it is written defectively,[3] it alludes to Rome.

R. Samuel b. Nahmani said: Our father Abraham, seeing all these hosts [the descendants of his other sons] and knowing that Isaac had no need of them, for they were but as thorns, sent them away to the east. Said he to them: "My son Isaac is delicate, and every people and tongue that will enslave him and his descendants will be hurled into Gehenna. Therefore go and settle in the east away from him, and remain there as long as Isaac's descendants are enslaved amongst the nations. But when you hear that they live in safety and tranquillity, come and serve them, that you may be privileged to hear the blast of the Messianic *shofar*."

Concerning them it says, *The caravans of Tema looked, the companies of Sheba waited for them* (Job 6:19). Now, Sheba alludes to the descendants of Keturah, as it says, *Jokshan begot Sheba.* They dwelt in their homes in the east, until Solomon arose and Israel dwelt in safety, as it says, *Judah and Israel dwelt safely, every man under his vine and under his fig-tree,*

---

[3] This softens the strangeness of the statement that Abraham transmitted to them the "name of Defilement," i.e., the knowledge of the unclean arts. In the light of the present we may interpret it as meaning that he transmitted such wisdom to them which through its abuse led them astray into idolatry and unhallowed rites.

[4] See par. 13, n. 3. "Side" too has a mystic connotation: the "right side" is the source of good, the "left (or, the "other) side" is the source of evil.

§ 17 [1] He advised them that Isaac was a red-hot coal who could burn them up in his righteousness, should they cross him (Y.T.).

[2] In Rabbinical literature Esau generally stands for Rome. The Rabbis here were either speaking in anticipation, or after Rome's downfall.

[3] צר instead of צור; the former can be read צַר, the adversary, and hence was seen as an allusion to Rome, the archenemy of the Jewish people.

are the days of the years of Abraham's life which he lived, a hundred threescore and fifteen years. ⁸And Abraham expired, and

COMMENTARY

was his due from his own parents.²⁴ ⁷**these are the days,** etc. Abraham's life is summed up here,

although he lived on until Jacob was fifteen, in order to complete his story before commencing the story of Isaac. This is the usual method of Biblical narration.²⁵ **a hundred,** etc. Lit., "a hundred years and seventy years and five years": at a hundred he was like seventy and at seventy like five, without sin.²⁶ ⁸**expired. a.** The word implies death in a moment, without pain or lingering.²⁷ **b.** The word denotes the complete loss of the natural powers.²⁷ᵃ **expired, and died.** "Expired" denotes loss of strength (as above); "died," the parting of

ANTHOLOGY

from Dan to Beer-sheba, all the days of Solomon (1 Kings 5:5). Thinking him the King Messiah they all came to pay homage to him, as it says, When malkath (AJV: the queen of) Sheba heard of the fame of Solomon, etc. (2 Chron. 9:1). R. Johanan observed: Whoever believes malkath Sheba to mean a woman [i.e., the queen of Sheba] is in error: read not, malkath Sheba but mal'chuth (the kingdom of) Sheba, the text implying that the whole kingdom of Sheba came in the days of Solomon to serve Israel, as it says, When the kingdom⁴ of Sheba heard of the fame of Solomon because of the name of the Lord (1 Kings 10:1). Now, what does because of the name of the Lord mean? R. Samuel said: Because of the tradition entrusted to them by their ancestor, that the Holy One, blessed is He, would one day manifest His kingship over Israel and grant them to dwell in safety.

When, however, they saw that he was not the Messiah they immediately turned, and went back to their own land (2 Chron. 9:12)—back to their homes. Yet they will come again in the days of the King Messiah, when he reveals himself—may it be speedily, in our days—as it says, The caravan of camels shall cover you, and of the young camels of Midian and Ephah, all coming from Sheba; they shall . . . proclaim the praises of the Lord (Isa. 60:6).

Gen. R. 61, 7; MhG. T.S. 25, 23-4 and note.

18. **These are the days of the years of Abraham's life.**

The Lord knows the days of them that are whole-hearted (Ps. 37:18): this applies to Abraham. And their inheritance shall be for ever (ibid.)—as our text says, These are the days of the years of Abraham's life. The Holy One, blessed is He, cherished the years of the righteous and recorded them in the Torah, that the heritage of their days may be remembered for ever.

Gen. R. 62, 1. T.S. 25, 25.

19. **The years of Abraham's life which he lived.**

Why state which he lived? To teach that all his days were life, and none of them was death.¹

MhG. T.S. 25, 27.

20. **A hundred and seventy-five years.**

He lived to see our father Jacob fifteen years old.¹

He was like a man of seventy [in strength].²

Now, why did the Holy One, blessed is He, deduct five years from his life?³ They corresponded to the five sins which Esau committed: he stole, raped a betrothed maiden, murdered, denied God,⁴ and despised the birthright. Said the Holy One, blessed is He: "I promised

---

⁴ In accordance with R. Johanan's reading.

§ 19 ¹ Living righteously is life; living wickedly is death. Cf. "The righteous even in death are called living; the wicked even in their lifetime are called dead" (Ber. 18a, b).

§ 20 ¹ Since he was a hundred at Isaac's birth, and Isaac was sixty when Jacob was born (verse 26).
² The Heb. reads: A hundred years and seventy years and five years. The repetition of "years" after each number is understood to imply a special teaching for each; cf. chap. 23, par. 2.
³ Isaac lived to a hundred and eighty (35:28).
⁴ Lit., denied the [fundamental] principle.

died in a good old age, an old man, and full of years; and was gathered

COMMENTARY

the soul from the body.[28] **expired . . . and was gathered,** etc. "Expired" refers to the body, in which all movement ceases; "gathered," to the soul, which is gathered to its honorable repose.[29] **in a good old age. a.** In accordance with God's

promise (15:15); and the affliction of his children did not commence in his lifetime.[30] **b.** He lived to see children and grandchildren, and enjoyed happiness and honor throughout his life.[31] **an old man, and full of years. a.** Lit., "satisfied": he saw all the desires of his heart fulfilled, and was satisfied with all that he wished to see and do. Moreover, he was granted the privilege of seeing in his lifetime the reward stored up for him in the world to come.[32] **b.** Satisfied, because all his necessary wants were met, whilst he never desired any superfluous luxuries.[33]

ANTHOLOGY

Abraham, *You shall be buried in a good old age* (15:15):[is this a good old age when he sees his grandson worshipping idols, raping, and murdering? Better let him depart this world in peace]."[5] Therefore He decreased his years, that he might not see his grandson's wickedness.

PZ; MA. T.S. 25, 26. 28.

21. Abraham expired.

R. Judah b. R. Ilai said: The early *hasidim*[1] used to suffer with disease of the bowels about ten or twenty days before they died, which intimates that illness cleanses.[2] R. Judah said: All who are said to have "expired" died of bowel disease.

Gen. R. 62, 2. T.S. 25, 29.

22. Abraham expired and died.

Rab said: On the day that our father Abraham departed this world the great of all nations stood in a row[1] and lamented, "Woe to the world that has lost its leader, and woe to the ship that has lost its pilot."

B.B. 91b. T.S. 25, 30.

23. In a good old age.

R. Simeon b. Lakish said: This phrase occurs in connection with three men: Abraham, who

deserved it; David, who deserved it; and Gideon, who did not deserve it, for *Gideon made an ephod* (Judg. 8:27)—for idolatrous worship.

Gen. R. 62, 2. T.S. 25, 31.

24. An old man, and satisfied with years.

It is written, *Strength and majesty are her clothing, and she laughs at the time to come* (Prov. 31:25). The reward of the righteous is stored up for them for the Hereafter, and while they are still in this world the Holy One, blessed is He, shows them the reward that He will give them; their soul is satisfied, and they sleep. R. Eleazar said: This may be compared to a king who prepared a banquet, invited guests, and showed them what they would eat and drink: their souls were satisfied and they slept. Similarly does the Almighty show the righteous while in this world their reward in the next, so that their soul is satisfied and they sleep. What is the proof? *For now should I have lain still and been quiet; I should have slept; then I had been at rest*[1] (Job 3:14).

Is then any man satisfied with his years? But the text means that he saw his portion in the Garden of Eden (Paradise) and was satisfied. Even as R. Jose said: The righteous does not leave this world until the Almighty shows him his portion in the Garden of Eden, as it says, [The reward for] *your righteousness shall*

---

[5] The bracketed passage is added from Gen. R. 63, 16, quoted in Vol. II, chap. 15, par. 120.

§ 21 [1] Lit., pious men.
[2] Either, from sin; or: It purifies the internal organs, that they may enter on the life of the Hereafter in physical purity.

§ 22 [1] The phrase is taken from the custom of standing in a double row after a funeral, when the mourners pass through and are offered condolences and comfort.

§ 24 [1] He interprets: I should have slept [i.e., died] with the knowledge that then I would have rest in the enjoyment of my reward.

to his people. ⁹And Isaac and Ishmael his sons buried him in the cave of Machpelah, in the field of Ephron the son of Zohar the Hittite, which is before Mamre; ¹⁰the field which Abraham purchased of the children of Heth; there was Abraham buried, and Sarah his wife. ¹¹And it came

COMMENTARY

gathered to his people. a. Some maintain that this is the ordinary idiomatic usage of the language: he traveled the same path as his ancestors and so joined them. Others hold that this refers particularly to the soul: when it is in the body it is, as it were, in isolation; when it leaves the body it rejoins its original source and is gathered back to its glory.[34] **b.** To the members of his family who had died before him. The phrase is used whether the ancestors

were righteous or wicked.[35] **c.** He was gathered into the bond of eternal life together with the righteous of all generations who, being like him in that respect, were *his people*.[36] **d.** This phrase is found only in connection with the righteous.[37] **e.** The word is used of the restoration of anything to its proper place. E.g., Deut. 22:2 *You shall gather it into your home,* in reference to a lost animal: your home, where it will receive proper care, is the right place for it. Similarly, the body is only the soul's *temporary* home; after leaving the body it enters its true, permanent home.[38] ⁹**Isaac and Ishmael his sons buried him. a.** They were older and more respected than his other sons; therefore they alone attended to the burial, even though the sons of Keturah were also present. Alternatively, Abraham may have sent the latter away during his lifetime, just as he had done with the sons of the concubines.[39] **b.** Abraham had informed Ishmael that although he was his son in all respects, God had decreed that *"in Isaac shall seed be called to you"* (21:12). Ishmael loyally abided by this; therefore he did not dispute the inheritance, and for the same reason now gave precedence to Isaac.[40] ¹⁰**the field which Abraham purchased.** Whenever burial in this field is mentioned Scripture adds that he bought it. This is to

ANTHOLOGY

go before you, the glory of the Lord shall be your rear guard (Isa. 58:8). It also says, *Because man goes to his eternal home* (Eccl. 12:5), which means, the home which truly belongs to him.

Gen. R. 62, 2; MhG. T.S. 25, 32 and note.

25. **And was gathered to his people.**

This teaches that his father Terah had repented and his soul was now in Paradise.[1]

What does "his *people*" imply? That every person is gathered in accordance with his peculiar character: the righteous is gathered to the generation of *his* ancestors, and the wicked is hurled to the generation of *his* ancestors; he whose life was silver now eats out of silver utensils, while he whose life was mean eats out of mean utensils.[2]

Sechel Tob; MhG. T.S. 25, 33 and note.

26. **Isaac and Ishmael his sons buried him.**

R. Johanan said: Ishmael repented in his father's lifetime, for it says, *Isaac and Ishmael his sons buried him.* But perhaps Scripture enumerates them in the order of their wisdom? Then when Scripture writes, *Esau and Jacob his sons buried him* (35:29), why does it not enumerate them in their order of wisdom? But since it gives Isaac precedence, Ishmael must have allowed him to take the lead, whence it follows that he had repented.[1]

Scripture describes them as his sons: but do we not know that they were his sons? However, it teaches that they equally paid him honor.

B.B. 16b; MhG; Ner Has'chalim. T.S. 25, 34 and note.

27. **There was Abraham buried and Sarah his wife.**

R. Tanhuma observed: Thirty-eight years

§ 25 [1] "His people" implies that he was reunited with his father.
 [2] Lit., of earthenware. Every man's Hereafter is what he earned in this life.
§ 26 [1] For Ishmael, the elder, would only allow Isaac to lead because he recognized him as more worthy, which he would not have done had he not repented of his evil ways.

to pass after the death of Abraham, that God blessed Isaac his son; and Isaac dwelt by Beer-lahai-roi. [12]**Now these are the generations of Ishmael,**

COMMENTARY

show Abraham's love of and unwavering faith in

God: although He had promised him the entire country, his faith was never shaken even though he had to buy a place for burial.[41] [11]**God blessed Isaac. a.** He prospered the work of his hands.[42] **b.** I.e., the promises made to Abraham were now transferred to him.[43] [12]**generations.** Descendants. Some of the names that follow are found in Assyrian and Arabian inscriptions.[44] **generations of Ishmael.** His generations are enumerated out of respect to Abraham; Scripture tells us that he too, as

ANTHOLOGY

elapsed between Sarah's burial and Abraham's burial; yet you say, *There was Abraham buried and Sarah his wife!*[1] But Scripture teaches that all who paid their last respects to Sarah were privileged to pay their last respects to Abraham.[2]

Gen. R. 62, 3. T.S. 25, 36.

28. It came to pass after the death of Abraham.

R. Simon said: *It came to pass after* always denotes retrogression.[1] Thus, *It came to pass after the death of Abraham* that immediately, *All the wells which his father's servants had digged in the days of Abraham his father, the Philistines stopped them* (26:15). R. Judah said: Had not the Holy One, blessed is He, provided others in their stead, the world would have reverted to its former state, for it says, *It came to pass after the death of Abraham, that . . . Isaac digged again the wells of water* (*ibid.* 18).[2]

Gen. R. 62, 4. T.S. 25, 37.

29. God blessed Isaac.

R. Hama b. R. Hanina said: Why does Scripture say, *After the Lord your God shall you walk* (Deut. 13:5)? is it then possible for man to walk after the Shechinah (Divine Presence), when it is said, *For the Lord your God is a devouring fire* (*ibid.* 4:24)? Only, it enjoins you to imitate His ways. The Holy One,

blessed is He, comforted mourners, as it says, *It came to pass after the death of Abraham that God blessed Isaac;*[1] therefore you must comfort mourners.

Sot. 14a. T.S. 25, 38.

30. GOD BLESSED ISAAC. The righteous with whom it is well is he who is also the son of the righteous. His fathers confer this world on him, while he earns the Hereafter for himself. Abraham's son Isaac is proof of this, for it says, *After the death of Abraham God blessed Isaac his son*: Abraham conferred this world on him, while he earned the Hereafter for himself.

MRE 94. T.S. 25, 39.

31. GOD BLESSED ISAAC. Abraham did not bless Isaac, but gave him gifts. Why did he not bless him? This may be compared to a king who had an orchard, which he entrusted to a gardener. In it were two trees intertwined, one containing a life-giving sap, the other a deadly poison. Said the gardener: "If I water the former, the latter will flourish too, while if I do not water the poisonous tree, how shall the other live?" Then he decided: "I am a gardener; I must do my duty, and whatever the master desires to do, let him do." Similarly, Abraham declared: "If I bless Isaac, I incite the children of Ishmael and Keturah against him;[1] yet if I do not bless the latter, how

§ 27 [1] As though they were buried at the same time.
　　[2] Cf. chap. 23, par. 37.
§ 28 [1] Heb. for after is *ahare*, which by a play on words is rendered as though it were *ahure*, backward: It came to pass that Abraham's death made the world go backward.
　　[2] This is not one consecutive verse; the second half is a chapter later.
§ 29 [1] The blessing is understood to mean that He comforted him.
§ 31 [1] Since Ishmael's hand was to be against everyone (16:12), to bless him could only mean the success of his

Abraham's son, whom Hagar the
Egyptian, Sarah's handmaid, bore
unto Abraham. [13]And these are the
names of the sons of Ishmael, by

COMMENTARY

Abraham's son, begot twelve tribes.[45] **Ishmael,
Abraham's son,** etc. Scripture emphasizes that
Abraham regarded him as a son, even though in
relation to Sarah and Isaac he was merely the son
of the handmaid.[46] **whom Hagar . . . bore.** I.e.,

ANTHOLOGY

am I to bless Isaac?" Then he decided: "I am
but mortal, here to-day and in the grave to-
morrow. I have already done my part; now
let the Holy One, blessed is He, do whatsoever
He desires in His world."[2] When Abraham
died the Almighty revealed Himself to Isaac
and blessed him. Thus it is written, *After the
death of Abraham God blessed Isaac his son.*
Gen. R. 61, 6. T.S. 25, 40.

32. GOD BLESSED ISAAC. From Isaac, who
feared the Almighty from his earliest days,[1]
we learn that God rewards those who fear Him.
He was seventy-five years old when our father
Abraham died. "Woe is me!" he lamented,
"Perhaps I have not good deeds to my credit as
had my father; what then will happen to me?"
There and then the compassion of the Holy
One, blessed is He, was stirred, and He spoke
to him that night, as it says, *After the death of
Abraham,* etc.
SER 23. T.S. 25, 41.

33. GOD BLESSED ISAAC. See how unlike man's
actions are God's. A mortal king has a friend
whom he loves exceedingly. As long as the
friend is alive, his love continues; when he
dies the love is at an end. The Holy One, however, is not so: He loves the righteous and loves
their children, as it says, *Israel, My servant,
Jacob whom I have chosen, the seed of Abraham
My beloved* (Isa. 41:8). As long as he [Abra-
ham] was alive, the Holy One blessed is He,

loved him; when he died, He blessed his son
and loved him.
Early Yelamdenu MS. T.S. 25, 42.

34. **Isaac dwelt by (lit., with) Beer-lahai-
roi.**

With Hagar, his father's widow, who had declared, "It is *Beer lahai roi*" (the well of the
Living One who sees me), i.e., of Him who is
the Life of all worlds.[1]

He dwelt with Hagar, allowing her to stay on
in Abraham's house and be supported from his
estate, as it was taught, A widow is supported
from her husband's estate.

[Another interpretation:] He dwelt with the
knowledge of the Life of all worlds, that he
might attain to such knowledge as none has
attained in this world. Thus it is written, *For
the earth shall be full of the knowledge of the
Lord* (Isa. 11:9).
MA; Or Haafelah; Zohar 1, 130a.
T.S. 25, 44 and note.

35. **Now these are the generations of Ishmael.**

R. Abbahu said: When Scripture writes, *Now
these are* (we-eleh),[1] it adds to the preceding;
when it says, *These are,* it marks a break with
the preceding. Thus, *Now these are the generations of Ishmael the son of Abraham*: this adds
to the preceding, to wit, those who are enumerated above, when it says, *She* [Keturah] *bore*

aggression. Keturah's descendants are regarded here as in the same category. The rendering follows the reading
in Sechel Tob.
[2] The comparison is not quite apt. Here Abraham blessed neither, whereas the gardener presumably watered
both, as it is difficult to see how he would regard watering neither as doing his duty (though the commentaries assume precisely that). The point of the comparison is probably that like the gardener he too treated
both alike, though in the opposite sense.
§ 32 [1] Lit., from the beginning of his works.
§ 34 [1] Cf. 16:13-14; chap. 24, par. 137.
§ 35 [1] With the conjunctive *waw*.

their names, according to their generations: the first-born of Ishmael, Nebaioth; and Kedar, and Adbeel, and Mibsam, [14]and Mishma, and Dumah, and Massa; [15]Hadad, and Tema, Jetur, Naphish, and Kedem; [16]these are the sons of Ishmael, and these are their names, by their villages, and by their encamp-

ments; twelve princes according to

COMMENTARY

as a son of the handmaid, the line of Abraham's descendants did not pass through him.[47] [13]**by their names, according to their generations.** I.e., in order of their birth.[48] **Nebaioth.** Founder of the Nabateans.[49] **Kedar.** In Ps. 120:5 they are cited as a type of hostile neighbors.[50] [16]**these are the sons of Ishmael.** After being enumerated by name they are summed up in a general statement. This is the usual Biblical style.[51] **villages.** Unwalled towns.[52] **encampments. a.** Fortified cities.[53] **b.** Probably a technical term to denote the circular enclosure used by a nomad people.[54] **twelve princes**

ANTHOLOGY

him [Abraham] *Zimran and Jokshan,* etc; so here too, *Now these are the generations of Ishmael . . . Nebaioth,* intimating that they were wicked, just like those enumerated above.

Exod. R. 30, 2. T.S. 25, 45.

36. Now these are the generations of Ishmael the son of Abraham.

R. Hama b. Ukba and our Rabbis were sitting and discussing the question, Why does Scripture give that wicked man's genealogy at this point? Just then R. Levi passed by. Said they, The master of Biblical lore approaches: let us ask him. When R. Levi came up he said, quoting R. Hama b. R. Hanina: To teach your ancestor's age when he was blessed.[1]

[Another reason:] Because he [Ishmael] came from the remote reaches of the wilderness to pay his [last] respects to his father.[2]

Gen. R. 62, 5. T.S. 25, 46-7.

37. The first-born of Ishmael: Nebaioth and Kedar.

These[1] formed the core of Ishmael's kingdom, concerning which David lamented: *Woe is me, that I sojourn with Meshech, that I dwell beside the tents of Kedar* (Ps. 120:5).[2] R. Eleazar said: Thus said David, the Community of Israel cries out, "Woe is me that I must live such a long time[3] beside the tents of Kedar. *I am all peace; but when I speak, they are for war* (*ibid.* 7): daily they issue fresh edicts against me."

We hear their taunts, and hold our peace; we bear their yoke, and are silent.[4] In allusion to them Scripture writes, *Alas, who shall live after God has appointed him* (Num. 24:23)? woe to him who must be under the rule of Ishmael.[5]

MhG. T.S. 25, 50-1.

§ 36 [1] I.e., Jacob was 63 years old when Isaac blessed him. There is a tradition that Jacob received his blessing from Isaac when Ishmael died. Since Ishmael was then 137 years old, Isaac, his junior by 14 years (cf. 16:16; 21:5), was then 123; and as he was 60 at Jacob's birth (verse 26), Jacob was then 63. Cf. par. 39.
[2] Therefore he is rewarded by having his genealogy recorded here.
§ 37 [1] Their descendants.
[2] An allusion to the Islamic persecutions.
[3] *Nimsh'chah* from *mashach,* a play on Meshech.
[4] By a play on words the names are connected with *shama,* to hear, *dom,* to be silent, and *nasa,* to bear.
[5] Rendering: Who shall live after God has appointed (i.e., condemned) him—to be under Ishmael's rule. Maimonides at the end of his *Igereth Teman* writes: Our masters exhorted us to bear Ishmael's lies and falsehoods in silence, finding an allusion to this in these names, Mishma, Dumah, and Massa. Possibly he had the present Midrash in mind. Yalkut Or Haafelah MS reverses the spirit of the interpretation: In these names which Ishmael called his sons he displayed a noble trait of his character, viz., his magnanimity and forbearance, for the names indicate: Let him who is taunted hear and be silent and bear it in patience.

their nations. [17]And these are the years of the life of Ishmael, a hundred and thirty and seven years; and he expired and died; and was gathered unto his people. [18]And they dwelt from Havilah unto Shur that is before Egypt, as thou goest toward Asshur: over against all his brethren he did settle.

COMMENTARY

according to their nations. Each son grew into a "nation," and each nation had its "prince."[55]

[17]**the years of the life of Ishmael. a.** This is recorded as a mark of honor to Abraham.[56] **b.** The age of the righteous is generally stated, and Ishmael was such, since he repented.[57] [18]**from Havilah,** etc. There were two Havilahs: (i) That of the descendants of Cush the son of Ham (10:7), in Ethiopia; (ii) That of Joktan the son of Eber (*ibid.* 29), in Arabia. Therefore the present Havilah is defined as the latter: it lies east of the Red Sea. Further, since Egypt is partially west of the Red Sea it is described as "before Egypt." Shur is mentioned in 20:1: it is in the south of Eretz Israel, east of Egypt.[58] **Asshur.** The reference is probably to the land of Asshurim mentioned in verse 3 [not the well-known Assyria, which does not fit the context].[59] **brethren. a.** Zimran and Jokshan (verse 2).[60] **b.** The sons of Keturah.[61] **over against all his brethren he did settle.** The territory of Ishmael's descendants was as large as that of the descendants of all his brethren together. Thus were fulfilled God's promises, *Behold,*

ANTHOLOGY

38. Twelve princes, according to their nations.

Even as God had told Abraham.[1]

L'umotham (their nations) is written defectively, intimating that all were to become but one nation.

Sechel Tob. T.S. 25, 52 and note.

39. These are the years of the life of Ishmael.

R. Hiyya b. Abba, quoting R. Johanan, said: Why are Ishmael's years counted? In order to estimate Jacob's years. For it is written, *These are the years of the life of Ishmael, a hundred and thirty and seven years.* Now, how much was Ishmael older than Isaac? Fourteen years, as it is written, *Abraham was four score and six years old, when Hagar bore Ishmael to Abram* (16:16); whilst it is also written, *Abraham was a hundred years old, when his son Isaac was born to him* (21:5).[1]

Meg. 17a. T.S. 25, 53.

40. He expired and died, and was gathered to his people.

Wherever death is described as "expiring" ... and being "gathered to one's people," it is the death of the righteous. But Ishmael's death is so described?[1] Said R. Johanan: Ishmael repented.

B.B. 16b. T.S. 25, 54.

41. Upon the face of all his brethren he fell.

He conquered them, and then they furnished him with auxiliary troops.[1]

Another interpretation: This refers to the kingdom of Ishmael, which will fall only after all other kingdoms.

MA; Midrash Habiur. T.S. 25, 55 and note.

42. OVER AGAINST ALL HIS BRETHREN HE FELL. Here you say, "he *fell*"; yet elsewhere we read, *He shall* dwell (16:12)? As long as Abraham lived, he *dwelt*; when he died, he *fell.*

§ 38 [1] 17:20.
§ 39 [1] The full calculation is given in Meg. 17a. It is shown there that according to all the data when Jacob stood before Pharaoh he should have been 116 years old, whereas he gives it as 130 (47:19). The discrepancy is explained by a tradition that when he left home in flight from Esau he spent 14 years in study at the academy of Eber.
§ 40 [1] Though he was wicked.
§ 41 [1] As his vassals. "Fell" is interpreted in the sense of attacked.

COMMENTARY

I have blessed him . . . and I will make him a great nation (17:20); and, *he shall dwell over against his brethren* (16:12).[62] **settle.** Lit., fell. **a.** He dwelt.[63] **b.** "His lot (heritage) fell to him in the presence of all his brethren," i.e., he lived in their midst. Or possibly *fell* means "died": he died during the lifetime of all his brethren, the cause of his death not being stated.[64]

ANTHOLOGY

Before he attacked the Temple, he dwelt; as soon as he attacked the Temple, he fell. In this world he dwells; in the Hereafter, "he *fell*" [will rightly describe him].[1]

Gen. R. 62, 5.

43. *The following passage from the* Sefer Ha-yashar, *a chronological work, brings down the account to the period dealt with so far.*

Now Abimelech, king of the Philistines, died in that year at the age of one hundred and thirty-nine years. Abraham, together with his household, went to Philistia to console all Abimelech's Court, and then returned home.

After Abimelech's death the people of Gerar took his twelve-year-old son Benmelech and set him on his father's throne, giving him the same name as his father, Abimelech, this being the practice in Gerar.

At this same time Lot the son of Haran died, aged one hundred and forty-two years, when Isaac was thirty-nine years old. Lot's two sons by his daughters were Moab and Ben Ammi respectively. They in turn took Canaanitish wives who bore them sons. The sons of Moab were Er, Mayun, Tarsin and Kanoye, who count as the Patriarchs of the Moabites to this very day. The sons of Ben Ammi were Geri, Ushin, Rabboth, Tsilon, and Maya, who count as the Patriarchs of the Ammonites to this very day. These families of Lot were fruitful and multiplied exceedingly, and then went to live wherever they would find the place. They built cities in the lands where they settled, which they called by their own names.

Nahor, the son of Abraham's father Terah, died in those days, when Isaac was forty years old, at the age of one hundred and seventy-two years. He was buried in Haran. On hearing of his brother's death Abraham was sorely grieved, and mourned many days.

Isaac was forty years old when he married Rebekah, the daughter of his uncle Bethuel. At that time Abraham took a second wife in his old age, Keturah of Canaan. She bore him Zimran, Jokshan, Medan, Midian, Jishbak, and Shuah—six sons.

The sons of Zimran: Abihen, Molich, and Mariah. The sons of Jokshan: Sheba and Dedan. The sons of Dedan: Amida, Jub, Gohi, Elisha, and Notah. The sons of Midian: Efah, Efer, Enoch, Abida and Eldaah. The sons of Jishbak: Machiri, Biru and Hator. The sons of Shuah: Bildad, Hemdad, Monan and Meban. All these were the families whom Keturah, the Canaanitish woman, bore to Abraham the Hebrew. Abraham sent them all away and gave them gifts. They departed from his son Isaac and went wherever they listed. All these went to a mountain range in the east and built cities where they live to this very day. However, the children of Sheba, Dedan, and Jokshan did not join their kinsmen in their cities, but are nomads in countries and deserts where they pitch their tents, to this very day.

The children of Midian, Abraham's son, traveled east to the land of Cush (Ethiopia), where they found a great plain and settled. To this day that is the land of Midian. Midian, together with his five sons, lived in the city they had built. The names of these sons, after their cities,[1] were Efah, Efer, Enoch, Abida and Eldaah.

§ 42 [1] Bacher conjectures that this passage alludes either to Aretes, King of Nabatea, who attacked Aristobulus and beseiged Jerusalem (Josephus, Ant. xlv, 2, 1); or to the Arabian Prince who joined Vespasian's army in the assault on the holy city.

§ 43 [1] Lit., to (or, after) their names in their cities. This apparently means that they built cities to which they gave their own names.

The sons of Efah: Metah, Mishuth, Hivvi and Tsalua. The sons of Efer: Ephron, Tsor (Tyre), Eliron and Medin. The sons of Enoch: Reuel, Rekem, Uzzi, Elyushab, and Eled. The sons of Abida: Hor, Melud, Karuy, and Malhi. The sons of Eldaah: Jakir, Reba, Malhiya and Gebel. These are the families of the Midianites, by their clans; afterwards they spread through the land of Midian.

Now, these are the generations of Ishmael, Abraham's son, borne to him by Hagar the Egyptian, Sarah's slave. Ishmael married an Egyptian woman named Ribah, the same being Meribah.[2] Ribah bore him Nebaioth, Kedar, Adbeel, Mibsam, and their sister Basmath. Ishmael divorced his wife Ribah, who left him and returned to her father's house in Egypt; for she was exceedingly wicked in the eyes of Ishmael and his father Abraham.

After that Ishmael took a Canaanitish wife named Malkith. She bore him Mishma, Dumah, and Massa, Hadar, Tema, Jetur, Naphish and Kedmah. These are the sons of Ishmael and these are their names, twelve princes according to their peoples; after that the families of Ishmael spread.

Then Ishmael took his sons and all his possessions and all his household and all that he had, and they went to dwell wherever they should find desirable. They settled near the wilderness of Paran, their habitations stretching from Havilah to Shur that is before Egypt as you go to Asshur. Ishmael and his sons lived in that country; sons were born to them, and they were fruitful and multiplied exceedingly.

These are the names of the sons of Nebaioth, Ishmael's firstborn: Miyud, Suad, and Mayun. The sons of Kedar: Elyon, Ketsem, Hamed, and Eli. The sons of Adbeel: Hamud and Jabin. The sons of Mibsam: Abadiah, Ebed, Melech, and Yeush. These are the families of the sons of Ribah, Ishmael's wife. The sons of Mishma the son of Ishmael: Shamua, Zichron, and Obadiah. The sons of Dumah: Ketsem, Eli, Mahmad, and Amead. The sons of Massa: Malon, Muleh and Ebed-adon. The sons of Hadad: Atsur and Mintsa and Ebed-melech. The sons of Tema: Seir, Saadon and Jachol. The sons of Jetur: Merik and Jaish, Alaw and Poheth. The sons of Naphish: Ebed, Hamid, Abjoseph, and Mir. The sons of Kedmah: Kaliph, Tahtay, and Amir. These were the sons of Malkith, after their families.

All these were the families of Ishmael, after their generations. And they live in the countries which they built for themselves to this very day.

Now, Isaac's wife Rebekah, the daughter of Bethuel, was barren in those days, without child. Isaac lived with his father Abraham in Canaan, and the Lord was with Isaac and with his father Abraham. At that time Arpachshad, the son of Shem the son of Noah, died, when Isaac was forty-eight years old. Now all the days of Arpachshad which he lived were four hundred and thirty-eight years; and he died.

Sefer Hayashar. T.S. 25, 55.

---

[2] Lit., strife.

ADDENDA TO THE ANTHOLOGY*

THE CITIES OF SIN

(on 16:20-21)

1. The inhabitants of Sodom and Gomorrah and the three other cities of the plain [see 14:2] were sinful and godless. In their country there was an extensive vale, where they foregathered annually with their wives and children and all belonging to them, to celebrate a feast lasting several days and consisting of the most revolting orgies. If a traveling merchant passed through their territory, he was besieged by them all, big and little alike, and robbed of whatever he possessed. Each one appropriated a trifle, until the traveler was stripped bare. If the victim ventured to remonstrate with one of them, he would show the merchant that he had taken a mere trifle, not worth talking about. And the end was that they hounded him from the city.

Once it happened that a man journeying from Elam arrived in Sodom toward evening. No one could be found to grant him shelter for the night. Finally a sly fox named Hedor invited him cordially into his house. The Sodomite had been attracted by a rarely magnificent carpet, strapped to the stranger's ass with a rope. He meant to secure it for himself. The friendly persuasions of Hedor induced the stranger to remain with him two days, though he had expected to stay only overnight. When the time came for him to continue on his journey, he asked his host for the carpet and the rope. Hedor said: "You have dreamed a dream, and this is the interpretation of it: the rope signifies that you will have a long life, as long as a rope; the varicolored carpet indicates that you will own an orchard wherein you will plant all sorts of fruit trees." The stranger insisted that his carpet was a reality, not a dream fancy, and continued to demand its return. Not only did Hedor deny having taken anything from his guest, but he even insisted on payment for having interpreted his dream to him. His usual price for such services, he said, was four silver pieces, but in view of the fact that the man was his guest, he would, as a favor to him, content himself with three pieces of silver.

After much wrangling, they put their case before one of the judges of Sodom, Sherek by name, who said to the stranger, "Hedor is known in this city as a trustworthy interpreter of dreams, and what he tells you is true." The stranger declared himself dissatisfied with the verdict, and continued to urge his side of the case. Then Sherek drove both the plaintiff and the defendant from the court room. Seeing this, the inhabitants gathered together and chased the stranger from the city; and lamenting the loss of his carpet, he had to pursue his way.

Sefer Hayashar.

2. As Sodom had a judge worthy of itself, so also had the other cities—Sharkar in Gomorrah, Zabnak in Admah, and Manon in Zeboiim. Eliezer, the bondman of Abraham, made slight changes in the names of these judges, in accordance with the nature of what they did: Sherek he called Shakkara, Liar; Sharkar he called Shakrura, Arch-deceiver; Zabnak he called Kazban, Falsifier; and Manon, Matsle-Din, Perverter of Judgment.

At the suggestion of these judges, the cities set up beds on their commons. When a stranger arrived, three men seized him by the head, and three by his feet, and they forced him upon one of the beds. If he was too short to fit into it exactly, the six attendants pulled and wrenched his limbs until he filled it out; if he was too long for it, they tried to jam him in with all their combined strength, until the victim was on the verge of death. His outcries were met with the words, "Thus will be done to any man that comes into our land."

*The translation of this supplementary material is drawn from L. Ginzberg, *Legends of the Jews,* Vol. I, Phila., 1913.

After a while travelers avoided these cities, but if some poor devil was betrayed occasionally into entering them, the people would give him gold and silver, but never any bread, so that he was bound to die of starvation. Once he was dead, the residents of the city came and took back the marked gold and silver which they had given him, and they would quarrel about the distribution of his clothes, for they would bury him naked.

Once Eliezer, the bondman of Abraham, went to Sodom at the bidding of Sarah, to inquire after the welfare of Lot. He happened to enter the city at the moment when the people were robbing a stranger of his garments. Eliezer espoused the cause of the poor wretch, and the Sodomites turned against him; one threw a stone at his forehead and caused considerable loss of blood. Instantly, the assailant, seeing the blood gush forth, demanded payment for having performed the operation of blood-letting. Eliezer refused to pay for the infliction of a wound upon him, and he was haled before the judge Shakkara. The decision went against him, for the law of the land gave the assailant the right to demand payment. Eliezer quickly picked up a stone and threw it at the judge's forehead. When he saw the blood was flowing profusely, he said to the judge, "Pay my debt to the man and give me the balance."

Sefer Hayashar; Sanh. 109b; MhG.

3. Their laws were calculated to do injury to the poor. The richer a man, the more was he favored before the law. The owner of two oxen was obliged to render one day's shepherd service, but if he had but one ox, he had to give two days' service. One poor orphan, who was thus forced to tend the flocks a longer time than those who were blessed with large herds, killed all the cattle entrusted to him in order to take revenge upon his oppressors, and he insisted, when the skins were assigned, that the owner of two head of cattle should have but one skin, but the owner of one head of cattle should receive two skins, in correspondence to the method pursued in assigning the work.

For the use of the ferry, a traveler had to pay four zuz, but if he waded through the water, he had to pay eight zuz.

Sanh. 109b; MhG.

THE BIRTH OF ISAAC
(on 21:1-7)

4. That Abraham and Sarah were blessed with offspring only after they had attained so great an age, had an important reason. It was necessary that Abraham should bear the sign of the covenant upon his body before he begot the son who was chosen to be the father of Israel. And as Isaac was the first child born to Abraham after he was marked with the sign, he did not fail to celebrate the child's circumcision with much pomp and ceremony on the eighth day. Shem, Eber, Abimelech king of the Philistines, and his whole retinue, Phicol the captain of his host—they all were present, as well as Terah and his son Nahor; in a word, all the great ones round about.

Gen. R. 46, 2; 53, 10; PRE 29; PZ; Deut. R. 1, 25; Sefer Hayashar.

5. To prove that the child was indeed Sarah's, God performed a miracle. Abraham had invited not only men to the celebration, but also the wives of the magnates with their infants. Sarah had enough milk in her breasts to suckle all the babes there, and they who drew from her breasts had much to thank her for. Some mothers harbored only pious thoughts in their minds when they let their infants drink the milk that flowed from the breasts of the pious Sarah; these infants became proselytes when they grew up; and those whose mothers let Sarah nurse them only in order to test her, they grew up to be powerful rulers, who lost their dominion at the revelation on Mount Sinai, because they would not accept the Torah. All proselytes and pious Gentiles are the descendants of these infants.

B.M. 87a; PRK 22; Gen. R. 53, 9.

THE SACRIFICE OF ISAAC
(on 22:3, 10)

6. Abraham persuaded Sarah to let him take Isaac away to study at the academy of Shem

and Eber. But, although she agreed, her heart was heavy. After spending the whole night in weeping on account of Isaac, she got up in the morning and selected a very fine and beautiful garment from those that Abimelech had given her. She dressed Isaac in it, put a turban upon his head, and fastened a precious stone in the top of the turban; then she gave them provisions for the road. Sarah went out with them, and accompanied them upon the road to see them off, and they said to her, "Return to the tent." And when Sarah heard the words of her son Isaac, she wept bitterly, and Abraham wept with her, and their son wept with them, a great sobbing; those of their servants who went with them wept greatly, too. And Sarah caught hold of Isaac, and held him in her arms; she embraced him, and continued to weep with him, saying, "Who knows if I shall ever see you again after this day?"

Sefer Hayashar.

7. Abraham departed with Isaac amid the weeping, while Sarah and the servants returned to the tent. He took two of his young men with him, Ishmael and Eliezer, and while they were walking on the road, the young men spoke to each other. Said Ishmael to Eliezer: "Now my father Abraham is going with Isaac to bring him up for a burnt offering to the Lord, and when he returns, he will give me all that he possesses, to inherit after him, for I am his first-born." Eliezer answered: "Surely, Abraham cast you off with your mother, and swore that you would not inherit anything of all he possesses. Then to whom will he give all that he has, all his precious things, but to his servant who has been faithful in his house—to me, who have served him night and day, and have done all that he desired of me?" The holy spirit answered, "Neither this one nor that one will inherit Abraham."

Sefer Hayashar; PRE 31; Midrash Vayyosha 37.

8. When Abraham stretched forth his hand, and took the knife to slay his son, God spoke to the angels: "Do you see how Abraham my friend proclaims the unity of My Name in the world? Had I hearkened unto you at the time of the creation of the world, when ye spake, *What is man, that Thou art mindful of him? and the son of man, that Thou thinkest of him* (Ps. 8:5)? who would there have been to make known the unity of My Name in this world?"

Midrash Vayyosha 37-8.

THE DEATH OF SARAH
(on 23:1-2)

9. Having heard from Satan what had transpired, Sarah laid her head upon the bosom of one of her handmaids, and became still as a stone. She rose up afterward and went about making inquiries concerning her son, till she came to Hebron, and no one could tell her what had happened to her son. Her servants went to seek him in the house of Shem and Eber, and they could not find him; they sought throughout the land, and he was not there. And, behold, Satan came to Sarah in the shape of an old man, and said to her, "I spoke falsely to you, for Abraham did not kill his son, and he is not dead"; when she heard that, her joy was so exceedingly violent that her soul went out through joy.

When Abraham returned with Isaac to Beersheba, they sought for Sarah and could not find her; and when they made inquiries concerning her, they were told that she had gone as far as Hebron to seek them. Abraham and Isaac went to her to Hebron; when they found that she was dead, they cried bitterly over her, and Isaac said: "O my mother, my mother, how have you left me, and whither have you gone? O whither have you gone, and how have you left me?" And Abraham and all his servants wept and mourned over her a great and heavy mourning, so much so, that Abraham did not pray, but spent his time in mourning and weeping over Sarah.

Sefer Hayashar; PRE 32; MhG on 23:3.

THE BURIAL OF SARAH
(on 23:19)

10. When Abraham entered the cave to place the body of Sarah within, Adam and Eve re-

fused to remain there, "Because," they said, "as it is, we are ashamed in the presence of God on account of the sin we committed; and now we shall be even more ashamed on account of your good deeds." Abraham soothed Adam. He promised to pray to God for him, that the need for shame be removed from him. Adam resumed his place, and Abraham entombed Sarah, and at the same time he carried Eve, resisting, back to her place.

Zohar 1, 128a-b.

THE LAST YEARS OF ABRAHAM
(on 25:1-5)

11. Rebekah first saw Isaac as he was coming from the way of Beer-lahai-roi, the dwelling-place of Hagar, whither he had gone after the death of his mother, for the purpose of reuniting his father with Hagar, or, as she is also called, Keturah.

Gen. R. 60, 14; T.J. 25:1.

12. Hagar bore him six sons, who, however, did scant honor to their father, for they all were idolaters. Abraham, therefore, during his own lifetime, sent them away from the presence of Isaac, lest they be burnt by the glowing ember of Isaac, and gave them the instruction to journey eastward as far as possible. There he built a city for them, surrounded by an iron wall, so high that the sun could not shine into the city. But Abraham provided them with huge gems and pearls, their lustre more brilliant than the light of the sun, which will be used in the Messianic time when *the moon shall be confounded and the sun ashamed* (Isa. 24:23). Also Abraham taught them the black art, wherewith they held sway over demons and spirits. It is from this city in the east that Laban, Balaam, and Balaam's father Beor derived their powers of sorcery.

Gen. R. 61, 5; 61, 7; Midrash T'hillim 92, 13; Soferim 21, 9; Sanh. 91a; Zohar 1, 133b.

13. Epher, one of the grandsons of Abraham and Keturah, invaded Lybia with an armed force, and took possession of the country. From this Epher the whole land of Africa has its name. Aram is also a country made habitable by a kinsman of Abraham. In his old age Terah contracted a new marriage with Pelilah, and from this union sprang a son Zoba, who was the father in turn of three sons. The oldest of these, Aram, was exceedingly rich and powerful, and the old home in Haran was not large enough for him and his kinsmen, the sons of Nahor, the brother of Abraham. Aram and his brethren and all that belonged to him therefore departed from Haran, settled in a vale, and built themselves a city there which they called Aram-Zoba, to perpetuate the name of the father and his first-born son. Another Aram, Aram-naharaim, on the Euphrates, was built by Aram son of Kemuel, a nephew of Abraham. Its real name was Petor, after the son of Aram, but it is better known as Aram-naharaim. The descendants of Kesed, another nephew of Abraham, a son of his brother Nahor, established themselves opposite to Shinar, where they founded the city of Kesed, the city whence the Chaldees are called Kasdim.

Josephus, *Antiqui*, I, 15, 1; Sefer Hayashar Vayyera.

14. Though Abraham knew full well that Isaac deserved his paternal blessing beyond all his sons, yet he withheld it from him, that no hostile feelings be aroused among his descendants. He said: "I am but flesh and blood, here to-day, to-morrow in the grave. What I was able to do for my children I have done. Henceforth let come what God desires to do in His world," and it happened that immediately after the death of Abraham God Himself appeared unto Isaac, and gave him His blessing [25:11].

Gen. R. 61, 6; Tan. Y. Naso 17; Num. R. 11, 2; Midrash T'hillim 1, 5.

15. Abraham's activity did not cease with his death, and as he interceded in this world for the sinners, so will he intercede for them in the world to come. On the day of judgment he will sit at the gate of hell, and he will not suffer those who kept the law of circumcision to enter therein.

Erub. 19a; MhG on 17:10

NOTES TO THE COMMENTARY

CHAPTER XVIII

1. T.J.
2. Rashbam
3. Ibn Ezra
4. Rashbam
5. Ibn Ezra. Maim.
6. Ramban
7. Sforno
8. Hirsch
9. T.J.
10. Ramban
11. Onk.
12. Radak. Akedath Yitzhak
13. Ramban
14. Idem
15. Rashbam
16. Rashi. K'li Yakar
17. Abrabanel
18. Sechel Tob
19. Rashi
20. Tol'doth Yitzhak
21. Ibn Ezra
22. Bahya
23. Abrabanel
24. Ramban
25. Sforno
26. Rashi
27. Haamek Dabar
28. Ramban
29. Sforno
29a. Ramban. Sforno
30. Akedath Yitzhak
31. Rashi
32. Ramban
33. Abrabanel
34. Sforno
35. Or Hahayyim
36. Abrabanel
37. Homath Anach
38. Malbim
39. Radak
40. Idem
41. Reggio
42. Hertz
43. Reggio
44. Idem
45. Alshech
46. T.J. as explained by Perush Jonathan. Rashi
47. Hizkuni
48. Idem
49. Ibn Ezra
50. Ramban

51. Abrabanel
52. Idem
53. Haamek Dabar
54. Hizkuni
55. Ramban; cf. Anthology par. 81
56. Rashi
57. Rashbam
58. Ramban
59. Halifoth S'maloth interpreting Onk. and T.J.
60. Hizkuni
61. Gordon
62. Radak
63. Rashbam
64. Ramban
65. Astruc
66. Rashbam
67. Hertz
68. Idem
69. Rashbam. Sforno
70. Rashi
71. Idem
72. Radak
73. Onk. T.J.
74. Radak
75. Rashbam
76. Idem
77. Sforno
78. Radak
79. Idem
80. Abrabanel
81. Malbim
82. Rashi
83. Malbim
84. Daath Z'kenim. Alshech
84a. Radak
85. Ramban
86. Sforno
86a. Idem (alternative explanation)
87. Minhah B'lulah
88. Onk. Rashi
89. Rashi. Hak'tav v'Hakabalah
90. Abrabanel
91. Radak. Bahya
92. Har'chasim L'bikah
93. Ramban
94. Radak
95. Abrabanel
96. Hizkuni
97. Alshech
98. Or Hahayyim
99. Sforno

100. Idem
101. Rashbam
102. Sforno
103. Abrabanel
104. Sforno
105. Abrabanel
106. Alshech
107. Malbim
108. Ramban
109. Sforno
110. B'chor Shor
111. Sforno
112. Astruc
113. Abrabanel
114. Alshech
115. Rashi
116. Ramban
117. Ralbag
118. Onk. T.J.
119. Ralbag. Ibn Caspi
120. Sforno
121. Rasag
122. Rashi
123. Ramban
124. Idem
125. Bahya
126. Meshech Hochmah
127. Rashbam
128. Abrabanel
129. Sforno
130. Abrabanel
131. Maim. Guide, 3, 51
132. Hertz
133. Hirsch
134. Maim. Hilchoth Matnoth Aniyyim 10, 1.
135. Hirsch
136. Radak
137. Maim. Guide, 3, 43
138. Rashbam
139. Ibn Ezra
140. Ramban
141. Abrabanel
142. Sforno
143. Ibn Ezra. Ramban
144. Alshech
145. Ibn Ezra
146. Malbim
147. Reggio
148. Ramban
149. Abrabanel
150. Ramban
151. Radak

152. Hertz
153. Rasag
154. Rashi
155. Rashbam
156. Ralbag
157. Rashi
158. Ramban. Ralbag
159. Abrabanel
160. Astruc
161. Rashbam
162. Radak
163. Sforno
164. Radak
165. Sforno
166. Ramban
167. Akedath Yitzhak
168. Hertz
169. Rashi
170. Ramban
171. Radak
172. Malbim
173. Alshech
174. Abrabanel
175. Haamek Dabar
176. Ibn Ezra. Radak
177. Minhah B'lulah
178. Rashi
179. Or Hahayyim
180. Bahya
181. Haamek Dabar
182. Rashbam
183. Sforno
184. Dibre David
185. Reggio
186. Hertz
187. Bahya
188. Rashi
189. Rawah
190. Ibn Ezra
191. Ramban
192. Malbim
193. Rawah
194. Radak
195. Rawah
196. Sforno
197. Rawah
198. Sforno
199. Malbim
200. Bahya. Rasag
201. Radak
202. Astruc
203. Ramban
204. Radak. Astruc
205. B'chor Shor
206. Onk. Tan. Y. Vayyera 13; T.S. 297.
207. Haamek Dabar

208. Ibn Ezra. Bahya
209. Radak
210. Bahya
211. Minhah B'lulah quoting Maim.
212. Alshech

CHAPTER XIX

1. B'chor Shor
2. Abrabanel
3. Or Hahayyim
4. Reggio
5. B'chor Shor
6. Hertz
7. Bahya
8. Sforno
9. Abrabanel
10. Sforno
11. Rashi
12. Ralbag
13. Abrabanel
13a. B'chor Shor
14. Abrabanel
15. Hertz
16. Radak
17. Ramban. Or Hahayyim
18. Ramban
19. Akedath Yitzhak
20. Hertz
21. Radak
22. Sforno
23. Hirsch
24. Radak
25. Idem
26. Or Hahayyim
27. Rashi
28. Radak
29. Hertz
30. Ibn Ezra
31. Radak
32. Ramban
33. Baal Haturim
34. Radak
35. Akedath Yitzhak
36. Radak
37. Ramban
38. Abrabanel
39. Hizkuni
40. Astruc
41. Rashi
42. Rasag
43. Hizkuni
44. Abrabanel
45. Dibre David
46. Jacob Isserlein
47. Abrabanel
48. Ramban
49. Sforno

50. T.S. 61 notes.
51. Hertz
52. Rashbam
53. Sforno
54. Rashi
55. Abrabanel
56. Rashi
57. Ramban
58. Ibn Ezra
59. Radak
60. Idem
61. Ramban
62. Radak. Abrabanel
63. Radak
64. Sforno
65. Sechel Tob
66. Rashi
67. Ibn Ezra
68. B'chor Shor
69. Rashbam
70. Abrabanel
71. Idem
72. Sforno
73. Rashi
74. Abrabanel
75. Hertz
76. Ibn Ezra
77. Ramban
78. Idem
79. Sforno
80. Radak
81. Idem
82. Hizkuni
83. Sechel Tob
84. Hertz
85. Rashi
86. Idem
87. Sforno
88. Ramban
89. B'chor Shor
90. Abrabanel
91. Idem
92. Rashi
93. Hertz on 14:10.
94. Sechel Tob
95. Ibn Ezra
96. Radak
97. Minhah B'lulah
98. Abrabanel
99. Ramban
100. Hizkuni
101. Hertz
102. Radak
103. Rashi
104. Idem
105. Radak
106. B'chor Shor

107. Abrabanel
108. Rashi
109. Idem
110. Radak
111. Abrabanel
112. Idem
113. Radak
114. Radak. Ramban
115. Sforno
116. Hirsch
117. Abrabanel
118. Idem
119. Har'chasim L'bikah
120. Rashi
121. Ramban
122. Abrabanel
123. Hertz
124. Idem
125. Sforno
126. Rashbam
127. Abrabanel quoting Ran
128. Sforno
129. Bahya
130. Idem
131. Ramban
132. Radak
133. Rashi
134. Rashbam
135. Radak
136. Abrabanel
137. Rashi
138. Radak
139. Sforno
139a. Rashi
140. Radak
141. Sforno
142. Hertz
143. Ramban
144. Mechilta B'shallah
145. Rashi
146. Sechel Tob
147. Idem
148. Daath Z'kenim
149. Har'chasim L'bikah
150. Rashi
151. Abrabanel
152. Sforno
153. Rashbam
154. Ibn Ezra
155. B'chor Shor

Chapter XX

1. Radak
2. Homath Anach on verse 2.
3. Mishneh Kesef
4. Panim Yafoth
5. Malbim

6. Sechel Tob
7. Sforno
8. Hertz on 14:7.
9. Idem on 16:7.
10. Radak
11. Haamek Dabar
12. Malbim
13. Radak
14. Hirsch
15. Hertz
16. Ramban
17. Or Hahayyim
18. Rasag quoted in T.S. 10.
19. Malbim
20. Hertz
20a. Radak
21. Ramban
22. Reggio
23. Sechel Tob
24. Ibn Ezra
25. Sforno
26. Maim.
27. Radak
28. Malbim
29. Ts'ror Hamor
30. Malbim
31. Rashbam
32. Radak
33. Lekah Tob
34. Hizkuni
35. Ralbag
36. Rasag
37. Ibn Ezra
38. Ralbag
39. Ibn Caspi
40. Ibn Ezra
41. Radak
42. Abrabanel
43. B'chor Shor
44. Haamek Dabar
45. Alshech
46. Rashi
47. Radak. Bahya
48. Malbim
49. Hizkuni
50. Haamek Dabar
51. Reggio
52. Malbim
53. M'yuhas
54. Radak
55. Hizkuni
56. Rashi
57. Radak
58. Idem
59. Idem
60. Malbim
61. Hertz

62. Sforno
63. Rashbam
64. Abrabanel
65. Radak
66. Idem. Malbim
67. Radak
68. Idem
69. Haamek Dabar
70. Radak
71. Idem
72. Idem
73. Abrabanel
74. Ralbag
75. Abrabanel
75a. Rashi
76. Radak
77. Sforno
78. Sechel Tob
79. Alshech
80. Abrabanel
81. Rashi
82. Sforno
83. Radak. Malbim
84. Rasag. Homath Anach
85. Haamek Dabar
86. Rashi
87. Ramban
88. Radak
89. Rashi
90. Idem
91. Hertz
92. B'chor Shor. Hak'tav v'Hakabalah
93. Hizkuni. Minhah B'lulah
94. Rashbam
95. Akedath Yitzhak
96. Radak
97. Ramban
98. B'chor Shor
99. Radak
100. Minhah B'lulah. Haamek Dabar
101. Ibn Ezra
102. Rashi
103. Idem
104. Malbim
105. B'chor Shor. Reggio
106. Rashi
107. Radak
108. Rashi
109. Hizkuni
110. Ts'ror Hamor
111. Ramban
112. Sforno
113. Rashbam
114. Ramban
115. Ralbag
116. Abrabanel

117. Sforno
118. Hertz
199. Sforno
120. Idem
121. Ibn Janah
122. Rashi
123. R. Jacob of Vienna. Hizkuni
124. Radak
125. Ramban
126. Ibn Caspi
127. Ibn Ezra
128. Sforno
129. Rasag
130. Panim Yafoth
131. Alshech

CHAPTER XXI

1. Rashi. Rawah
2. Abrabanel
3. Baal Haturim. R. Jacob of Vienna
4. Rashi
5. Rashi
6. Sforno
7. Lekah Tob
8. Radak
9. Rashi
10. Radak
11. Sforno
12. Radak
13. Idem
14. Abrabanel. Ts'ror Hamor
15. Rashi
16. Rasag
17. Reggio. M'yuhas
18. Or Hahayyim
19. Sechel Tob
20. Ts'ror Hamor
21. Homath Anach
22. Reggio
23. Radak. Abrabanel
24. Tol'doth Yitzhak
25. Abrabanel
26. Ibn Caspi
27. Reggio
28. Rashbam
29. Radak
30. Sforno
31. Ralbag
32. Ts'ror Hamor. Akedath Yitzhak
33. Radak
34. Ralbag
35. Abrabanel
36. Haamek Dabar
37. Rashi
38. Ramban. Ralbag
39. Haamek Dabar
40. Tol'doth Yitzhak

41. Reggio
42. Abrabanel
43. Radak
44. Maase Hashem
45. Hirsch
46. Rashi
47. Rashbam
48. Sechel Tob
49. Bahya
50. Abrabanel
51. Idem
52. Sforno
53. Ibn Ezra
54. Ralbag
55. Abrabanel
56. Sforno
57. Tol'doth Yitzhak
58. Mishneh Kesef
59. Ramban
60. Abrabanel
61. Sforno
62. Haamek Dabar
63. Radak
64. Sforno
65. Radak
66. Abrabanel
67. Haamek Dabar
68. Har'chasim L'bikah
69. Ramban
70. Mishneh Kesef
71. Rawah
72. Radak
73. Or Hahayyim. Hak'tav v'Hakabalah
74. Haamek Dabar
75. Hertz
76. Or Hahayyim
77. Radak
78. Sforno
79. Hirsch
80. Rashbam
81. Hertz
82. Or Hahayyim
83. Reggio
84. Ramban
85. Sechel Tob
86. Reggio
87. Haamek Dabar
88. Abrabanel
89. Mishneh Kesef
90. Idem
91. Abrabanel
92. Akedath Yitzhak
93. Rashbam
94. Sechel Tob
95. Ramban
96. Abrabanel

97. Idem quoting Ran
98. Or Hahayyim
99. Sechel Tob
100. Sforno
101. Reggio
102. Hertz
103. Radak
104. Abrabanel
105. Ibn Ezra
106. Ramban
107. Minhah B'lulah
108. Hak'tav v'Hakabalah
109. Abrabanel
110. Radak
111. Hertz
112. Hirsch
113. Rashi
114. Radak
115. Abrabanel
116. Hertz
117. Ralbag
118. B'chor Shor
119. Radak
120. Reggio
121. Rashbam. Bahya
122. Abrabanel
123. Haamek Dabar
124. Reggio
125. Radak
126. Sforno
127. Hertz
128. Radak
129. Reggio
130. Malbim
131. Idem
132. Radak
133. Malbim
134. Rashi
135. Radak. Haamek Dabar
136. Ramban
137. Hertz
138. Rashi
139. Radak
140. Rashbam
141. Hizkuni
142. B'chor Shor
143. Abrabanel
144. Radak
145. Rashi
146. Sforno
147. Malbim
148. Reggio
149. Rashi. Abrabanel
150. Malbim
151. Hertz
152. Malbim
153. Abrabanel. Reggio

154. Radak
155. Abrabanel. Hizkuni
156. Haamek Dabar
157. Pashteh Dik'ra
158. Ramban
159. Hertz
160. Malbim
161. Sforno
162. B'chor Shor
163. Radak
164. Bahya
165. Sforno
166. Radak
167. Abrabanel
168. Sforno
169. Hertz
170. Comm.
171. Haamek Dabar
172. Sforno
173. Abrabanel
174. Radak
175. Haamek Dabar
176. Sforno
177. Abrabanel
178. Malbim
179. Ts'ror Hamor
180. Ralbag
181. Radak
182. Haamek Dabar
183. Sechel Tob
184. Radak
185. Akedath Yitzhak
186. Radak
187. Malbim
188. Sechel Tob
189. Sforno
190. Radak
191. Sforno
192. Sechel Tob
193. Malbim
194. Akedath Yitzhak
195. Hizkuni
196. Mishneh Kesef
197. Reggio
198. Haamek Dabar
199. Radak
200. Ramban
201. Sforno
202. Malbim
203. Haamek Dabar
204. Radak
205. Ralbag
206. Abrabanel
207. Bahya
208. Rashbam
209. Ramban
210. Maim. Guide, 2, 13

211. Bahya. Abrabanel
212. B'chor Shor
213. Reggio
214. Akedath Yitzhak
215. Radak

Chapter XXII

1. Rashbam
2. Abrabanel
3. Idem. Haamek Dabar
4. Or Hahayyim
5. Idem
6. K'tav Sofer
7. Homath Anach
8. Ibn Ezra. Ramban
9. Ibn Ezra
10. Ralbag
11. Abrabanel. Malbim
12. Akedath Yitzhak
13. Reggio
14. Radak
15. Or Hahayyim
16. Malbim
17. Abrabanel
18. Idem
19. Or Hahayyim
20. Akedath Yitzhak
21. Hertz
22. Ramban
23. Onk. Rasag. Bahya
24. Rashi. Radak. Bahya
25. Rashbam
26. Ramban
27. Rashi
28. Ibn Ezra
29. Ramban
30. Abrabanel
31. Radak
32. B'chor Shor
33. Haamek Dabar
34. Rashi
34a. Abrabanel
35. Radak. Alshech
36. Alshech
37. Abrabanel
38. Radak
39. Abrabanel
40. Alshech
41. Ibn Ezra
42. Ramban
43. Homath Anach
44. Akedath Yitzhak
45. Radak
46. Haamek Dabar
47. Ibn Ezra
48. Radak
49. Abrabanel

50. Ramban
51. Sforno
52. Abrabanel
53. Radak
54. Idem
55. Shadal
56. Ralbag
57. Abrabanel
58. Sforno. Hizkuni
59. Malbim
60. Hertz
61. Rashi
62. Abrabanel
63. Panim Yafoth
64. Ibn Ezra
65. R. Jacob of Vienna
66. Hertz
67. Sechel Tob
68. Radak
69. Abrabanel. Alshech
70. Akedath Yitzhak
71. Sechel Tob
72. Abrabanel
73. Hertz
74. Tos'foth
75. Rashi
76. Michlal Yofi
77. Minhah B'lulah
78. Abrabanel
79. Alshech
80. Abrabanel
81. Alshech
82. Abrabanel
83. Alshech
84. Onk. M'yuhas
85. Rasag
86. Reggio
87. Abrabanel
88. Shadal
89. Ramban
90. Abrabanel
91. Ibn Ezra
92. Radak
93. Hak'tav v'Hakabalah
94. Ralbag
95. Maim. Guide, 2, 45
96. Sefer Hab'rith al Hatorah. Hak'tav v'Hakabalah
97. Radak. Abrabanel
98. Baal Haturim
99. Hak'tav v'Hakabalah
100. Hertz
101. Abrabanel
102. Alshech
103. Radak
104. Rasag
105. Ramban

106. Sforno
107. Reggio
108. B'chor Shor
109. Haamek Dabar
110. Astruc
111. Reggio
112. Hak'tav v'Hakabalah
113. Abrabanel
114. Radak. Idem
115. Rashbam
116. Idem
117. Rashi
118. Rambam. Hizkuni. Sforno
119. Ibn Ezra
120. Abrabanel
121. Hirsch
122. Rashi
123. Bahya
124. Radak. Abrabanel
125. Abrabanel
126. Maim. Guide, 3, 45
127. M'yuhas
128. Rasag
129. Rashi
130. Rashbam
131. Reggio
132. Hertz
133. Bahya
134. Maim. Guide, 2, 41
135. Radak
136. Ts'ror Hamor
137. Radak
138. Ramban
139. Ts'ror Hamor
140. Hak'tav v'Hakabalah
141. Ibn Ezra
142. Sechel Tob
143. Sforno
144. Abrabanel. Malbim
145. Haamek Dabar
146. Hertz
147. Onk.
148. Radak
149. Sforno
150. Idem
151. Sefer Hab'rith al Hatorah
152. Mishneh Kesef
153. Ibn Ezra. Radak
154. Abrabanel
155. Yalkut Pirushim al Hatorah
156. Rashi
157. Mizrahi. Akedath Yitzhak
158. Abrabanel
159. Radak
160. Baal Haturim
161. Sforno
162. Pashteh Dik'ra

163. Reggio
164. Radak
165. Rashi
166. Sforno
167. Ramban. Sforno

CHAPTER XXIII

1. Rashbam
2. B'chor Shor
3. Ramban
4. Abrabanel
5. Hirsch
6. Sforno
7. Rashbam
8. Ibn Ezra
9. Reggio
10. Rashi
11. Radak
12. Rashbam
13. Ramban
14. Baal Haturim
15. Hertz
16. Sforno
17. Riba
18. Tol'doth Yitzhak
19. Hadar Z'kenim
20. Hertz
21. Bahya
22. Abrabanel
23. Ahavath Jonathan
24. Ts'ror Hamor
25. Hak'tav v'Hakabalah
26. Radak
27. Hertz
28. Rashi
29. Rashbam
30. Ibn Ezra
31. Mishneh Kesef
32. Reggio
33. Haamek Dabar
34. T'cheleth Mord'chai
35. Rashbam
36. Radak
37. Ramban
38. Akedath Yitzhak
39. Hertz
40. Radak. Or Hahayyim
41. Hertz
42. Radak
43. Or Hahayyim
44. Onk.
45. Rashbam
46. Ibn Ezra
47. Haamek Dabar
48. Reggio
49. Homath Anach
50. Sforno

51. Radak
52. Rawah
53. Or Hahayyim
54. Hertz, quoting Judge Mayer Sulzberger, *The Am ha-aretz, the Ancient Hebrew Parliament,* Philadelphia, 1910.
55. Sechel Tob
56. Astruc
57. Homath Anach
58. Ramban
59. T.J. Ramban
60. Ibn Ezra. Ralbag
61. Rashbam. Radak
62. Ramban
63. Sforno
64. Rashbam
65. Reggio
66. Rashbam
67. Sechel Tob
68. Hirsch
69. M'yuhas
70. Mishneh Kesef
71. Hertz
72. Radak
73. Idem
74. R'bid Hazahab
75. Rashi
76. Radak
77. Sforno
78. B'chor Shor
79. Malbim
80. Rashi
81. Sechel Tob
82. Ramban
83. Haamek Dabar
84. Rashbam
85. Sforno
86. Mishneh Kesef
87. Sechel Tob
88. Haamek Dabar
89. Onk.
90. Ts'ror Hamor
91. Rashi
92. Sechel Tob
93. Hizkuni
94. Or Hahayyim
95. Ts'ror Hamor
96. Hirsch
97. Ramban
98. T'cheleth Mord'chai
99. Ramban
100. Rashi
101. Rashbam
102. Hertz
103. Rashbam
104. Sforno

105. Hertz
106. Rashbam
107. Ibn Ezra
108. Akedath Yitzhak. Tol'doth Yitzhak
109. Hertz
110. Ibn Shoib
111. Radak
112. Hizkuni
113. Sechel Tob
114. Rashi
115. Sforno. Maim. Guide, 1, 12
116. Hertz
117. Rashbam
118. Radak
119. Ralbag
120. Haamek Dabar
121. Malbim
122. Ibn Ezra
123. Ramban
124. Haamek Dabar
125. Ibn Ezra
126. M'yuhas
127. Bahya
128. Hizkuni
129. Sforno

CHAPTER XXIV

1. Rashbam
2. Radak
3. Ramban
4. Hizkuni
5. T.J.
6. Ibn Ezra
7. Astruc
8. Akedath Yitzhak chap. 22
9. Rashbam
10. Ramban
11. Sforno
12. Radak. B'chor Shor
13. Hertz
14. Meshech Hochmah citing Caro and Isserles
15. Malbim
16. Rashbam
17. Ibn Ezra
18. Abrabanel
19. B'chor Shor
20. Bahya
21. Hertz
22. Ramban
23. Ibn Ezra
24. Radak
25. Ramban
26. Maim. Guide, 2, 19
27. Sforno
28. Hertz

29. Radak
30. B'chor Shor
31. Hertz
32. Abrabanel
33. Ts'ror Hamor
34. K'li Yakar
35. Haamek Dabar
36. Rashbam
37. Ibn Ezra
38. Radak
39. Hizkuni
40. Abrabanel
41. Abrabanel
42. Hirsch
43. Abrabanel
44. Rashbam
45. Abrabanel
46. Sforno
47. Hertz
48. Abrabanel
49. B'chor Shor
50. Rashi
51. Ramban
52. Radak
53. Sforno
54. Haamek Dabar
55. Sforno
56. Rashbam
56a. Ibn Ezra
57. Haamek Dabar. Minhah B'lulah
58. Hertz
59. Rashi
60. Ramban
61. B'chor Shor
62. Ibn Ezra
63. Tos'foth
64. Hizkuni. Astruc
65. Or Hahayyim
66. Hizkuni. Tol'doth Yitzhak
67. Sforno
68. Radak
69. Rashbam
70. Radak
71. Rashi. Hertz
72. Abrabanel
73. Radak
74. Abrabanel
75. Hertz
76. Sechel Tob
77. Abrabanel
78. Reggio
79. Radak
80. Abrabanel
81. Hak'tav v'Hakabalah
82. Abrabanel
83. B'chor Shor. Hizkuni
84. Haamek Dabar

85. Radak. B'chor Shor
86. Sforno
87. Rashi. Hizkuni
88. Sforno
89. Rashi
90. Radak
91. Abrabanel
92. Haamek Dabar
93. Reggio
94. Haamek Dabar
95. Hak'tav v'Hakabalah
96. Mishneh Kesef
97. Ramban
98. Haamek Dabar
99. Rashbam
100. Ibn Caspi
101. Minhah B'lulah
102. Abrabanel
103. Or Hahayyim
104. Radak
105. Or Hahayyim
106. Sforno
107. Rashbam
108. Sforno
109. Reggio
110. Rashi
111. Abrabanel
112. Sforno
113. Ralbag
114. Sforno
115. Idem
116. Rashbam
117. Astruc. Hizkuni
118. R. Jacob of Vienna
118a. Malbim
119. Rashi quoted by Abrabanel, but not found in our edd.
120. Ibn Ezra. Ts'ror Hamor
121. Ibn Ezra
122. Hertz
123. Ibn Janah
124. Ibn Ezra
125. Reggio
126. Or Hahayyim
127. Bahya
128. Har'chasim L'bikah
129. Haamek Dabar
130. Reggio
131. Sforno
132. Olath Shabbath
133. Pardes Joseph
134. Rashi
135. Daath Z'kenim
136. Ibn Ezra
137. Radak
138. Sforno
139. Hak'tav v'Hakabalah

140. Rosh
141. Rashbam
142. Sforno
143. Hak'tav v'Hakabalah. Rosh
144. Haamek Dabar
145. Hizkuni
146. Reggio
147. Radak. Ralbag
148. Har'chasim L'bikah
149. Ts'ror Hamor
150. Rashi
151. Hak'tav v'Hakabalah
152. Astruc
153. Haamek Dabar
154. Radak
155. Idem
156. Rashi
157. Astruc
158. Haamek Dabar
159. Radak
160. Abrabanel
160a. Idem
161. Rashi
162. Sforno
163. Haamek Dabar
164. Sforno
165. Radak
166. Sforno
167. Idem. Radak
168. Radak
169. Ts'ror Hamor
170. Reggio
171. Abrabanel
172. Sforno
173. Idem
174. Hak'tav v'Hakabalah
175. Ramban
176. Rashbam
177. Ramban
178. Rashbam
179. Ralbag
180. Abrabanel
181. Ts'ror Hamor
182. Radak
183. Abrabanel
184. Radak
185. Ts'ror Hamor
186. Hadar Z'kenim
187. Minhah B'lulah
188. Rashbam
189. Radak
190. Haamek Dabar
191. Idem
192. Rashbam
193. Rashi
194. Sforno. Minhah B'lulah
195. Reggio

196. Daath Z'kenim
197. Haamek Dabar
198. Ralbag
199. Mishneh Kesef
200. Haamek Dabar
201. Radak
202. Hertz
203. Rashbam
204. Haamek Dabar
205. Idem
206. Baal Haturim
207. Haamek Dabar
208. Reggio
209. Rashbam. Hizkuni
210. Malbim
211. Hertz
212. Sforno
213. Idem
214. Sechel Tob
215. Hak'tav v'Hakabalah
216. Ramban
217. Bahya
218. Reggio
219. Or Hahayyim
220. Haamek Dabar
221. Lekah Tob
222. Rashbam
223. Hizkuni
224. Hertz
225. Ibn Ezra
226. Radak
227. Sforno
228. Haamek Dabar
229. Hefetz
230. Rashbam
231. Radak
232. Ts'ror Hamor
233. Rashi
234. Bahya
235. Sforno
236. Hertz
237. Sforno
238. Hak'tav v'Hakabalah
239. Radak. Haamek Dabar
240. Rashbam
241. Rashi
242. Ibn Ezra
243. Ibn Janah
244. Reggio
245. MhG. T.S. 188.
246. Malbim. Haamek Dabar
247. Ibn Ezra
248. B'chor Shor
249. Reggio
250. Rashi
251. Idem
252. Sforno

253. Radak. Har'chasim L'bikah
254. Rashbam
255. Idem. Radak
256. Radak
257. Ts'ror Hamor
258. Reggio
259. Anthology par. 123. Radak
260. M'yuhas
261. Ibn Ezra
262. Radak
263. Sforno
264. Haamek Dabar
265. Idem
266. Radak
267. Ramban
268. Ramban
269. R. Jacob of Vienna
270. Sforno
271. Radak
272. Ramban
273. Hak'tav v'Hakabalah
274. Rashi
275. Rashbam. Ibn Ezra
276. Ramban
277. Hak'tav v'Hakabalah
278. Reggio
279. Rashi
280. Rashbam
281. Ramban
282. Hizkuni. Radak
283. Mishneh Kesef
284. Rashbam
285. Reggio
286. Akedath Yitzhak
287. Haamek Dabar
288. Hertz
289. Rashbam
290. Radak
291. Idem
292. Bahya
293. Malbim
294. Hirsch
295. Rashi
296. Hirsch

CHAPTER XXV

1. Rashbam
2. Ramban
3. Hertz
4. Idem
5. Idem
6. Idem
7. Radak
8. Hertz
9. Rashi
10. Idem. Ramban
11. Reggio

12. Idem
13. Radak
14. Idem
15. Rashi
16. Rashbam
17. Radak
18. Ramban
19. Rashi
20. Sforno
21. Radak
22. Ibn Ezra
23. Radak
24. Hizkuni
25. Reggio
26. Rashi
27. Ibn Ezra
27a. Akedath Yitzhak
28. Malbim

29. Hak'tav v'Hakabalah
30. Rashbam
31. Radak
32. Ramban
33. Bahya
34. Ibn Ezra. Idem
35. Radak
36. Sforno
37. Reggio
38. Hak'tav v'Hakabalah
39. Radak
40. Haamek Dabar
41. Radak
42. Idem
43. Hertz
44. Idem
45. Radak
46. Haamek Dabar

47. Rashbam
48. Rashi
49. Hertz
50. Idem
51. Radak
52. Rashi
53. Radak
54. Hertz
55. Radak
56. Rashbam
57. Ramban
58. Reggio
59. Hertz
60. Ibn Ezra
61. B'chor Shor
62. Reggio
63. Rashi
64. Ibn Ezra

SOURCES OF THE COMMENTARY [1]

ABRABANEL: R. Isaac b. Judah Abrabanel, Bible exegete and religious philosopher, 1497-1508. Used and paraphrased many other commentaries in his work on Scriptures.

AHAVATH JONATHAN: Homiletic commentary on the *haftaroth* (Prophetic portions read after the *sidroth*) by the Talmudist and Cabalist R. Jonathan Eybeschutz, 1690-1764.

AKEDATH YITZHAK (AKEDAH): A homiletical biblical commentary by R. Isaac Arama, c. 1420-1494.

ALSHECH: R. Moses Alshech, author of *Torath Moshe*, Bible commentary based on his weekly lectures; fl. in Safed, second half of 16th century.

BAAL HATURIM: R. Jacob b. Asher, German author of a four-part code of Jewish law (*Arba Turim*) and two commentaries on Pentateuch; d. Toledo, Spain, before 1340.

BAHYA: R. Bahya b. Asher b. Halawa, Spanish biblical exegete and Cabbalist, c. 1255-1340.

B'CHOR SHOR: Biblical commentary by R. Joseph B'chor Shor, French Tosafist and exegete of the second half of the 12th century. (Leipzig, 1855.)

BENAMOZEGH: R. Elijah Benamozegh, rabbi, theologian and apologist; author of *Em L'mikrah*, Livorno, 1862; 1823-1900.

BIUR: Commentary on the Pentateuch by Moses b. Nahman Mendelssohn (philosopher and translator, 1729-1786) and others.

BOTSER OL'LOTH: Commentary on Scripture by R. Simeon b. Meïr Santo, Fürth 1824.

CARO, R. Joseph, 16th century codifier, mystic, and exegete.

CASSUTO: Prof. Umberto Cassuto, hebraist and historian, author of *Me-Adam ad Noah*, Jerusalem, 1944 b. 1883.

COMM.: Many commentators, generally.

DAATH Z'KENIM: A commentary ascribed traditionally to the *Tosafists*, 12-14th century French Talmudists.

DIBRE DAVID: A supercommentary on Rashi by R. David b. Shmuel Halevi. (Dhyrenfurt, 1689.)

EMDEN: R. Jacob b. Zvi Ashkenazi Emden, Talmudist and author, 1697-1776.

FUERST: Julius Fürst, bibliographer and lexicographer, 1805-1873.

GORDON: Samuel Loeb Gordon, translator; author of a modern commentary on Scripture, Warsaw and Tel Aviv, 1900-1930; b. 1867.

GRE: Rabbi Elijah of Vilna (called the Vilna Gaon) renowned Lithuanian Talmudist, 1720-1797.

HAAMEK DABAR: Commentary on the Pentateuch by R. Naftali Ts'vi Yehuda Berlin (N'tsiv), pub. 1881.

HADAR Z'KENIM: A Bible commentary similar to *Daath Z'kenim, q.v.* (Livorno, 1840.)

HAK'TAV V'HAKABALAH: A logical commentary on the Pentateuch by R. Jacob Z'vi Hirsch of Meklenburg (1831-1865), 4th ed., Frankfurt a. M., 1880 (1st., Leipzig, 1839).

HALIFOTH S'MALOTH: Commentary on the Scriptural translation of Onkelos (*q.v.*) by R. Ben Zion Berkowitz. (Vilna, 1874.)

HAR'CHASIM L'BIKAH: A commentary "to clarify and illuminate the apparently unintelligible verse of Scripture," by R. Levi Shapiro of Frankfort. (Altona, 1815.)

HEFETZ, R. Moses, author of *M'lecheth Mahsheveth*, Venice, 1710.

HEIDENHEIM: See Rawah.

HERTZ, J. H.: Joseph Herman Hertz, British chief rabbi, author of *The Pentateuch and Haftorahs with Commentary*, 1872-1946.[2]

HIRSCH, S. R.: Commentary in German on the Pentateuch by R. Samson Raphael Hirsch, late nineteenth-century leader of Orthodox Jewry in Germany.

HIZKUNI: Commentary on Scripture by R. Hezekiah b. Manoah (French exegete of the 13th century), Venice, 1524. It is based upon about twenty other commentaries, principally Rashi.

---

[1] The following lists but a part of the many works consulted in the preparation of the Commentary—i.e., those directly and frequently quoted. It should also be noted that many more explanations on the Biblical verses than are given in the Commentary are to be found in the Talmudic-Midrashic passages cited in the Anthology.

[2] Rev. Dr. J. H. Hertz cites most of the modern commentators on the Bible in his Pentateuch. We have drawn on his work for all their important and significant interpretations.

254

HOFFMANN: R. David Zvi Hoffmann, Talmudist and biblical exegete, 1843-1921.

HOMATH ANACH: Exegetical work on the Pentateuch by R. Hayyim Joseph David Azulai, prolific Sephardic rabbinic author, ca. 1724-1807.

IBN CASPI: R. Joseph ibn Caspi, philosophical commentator on Scripture, 1297-1340.

IBN EZRA: R. Abraham b. Meir ibn Ezra, Hebrew poet and biblical commentator, 1093-1167.

IBN JANAH: R. Jonah ibn Janah, greatest Hebrew philologist of the Middle Ages, c. 985-c. 1050.

IBN SHOIB: R. Joshua ibn Shoib, author of *D'rashoth al Hatorah* ("Homilies on the Pentateuch"); fl. ca. 1328.

ISSERLES: R. Moses Isserles, known as "the ReMA," noted Talmudist and codifier, Cracow, 1520-1572.

JACOB, Benno: German-Jewish biblical commentator; b. 1862.

R. JACOB OF VIENNA: 14th century Austrian author of Bible commentary. (Mainz, 1868.)

JOSEPHUS: Josephus Flavius, military leader, historian and apologist, 37-105.

KAHANA, Abraham: Edited a critical Hebrew commentary on the Bible, of which he wrote several volumes; 1874-1946.

KIR'TSON ELYON, by R. Judah Moses, author of *Ham'vaer*, Warsaw, 1871.

K'LI YAKAR: Annotations on the Pentateuch by R. Shlomo Ephraim of Lencziza, preacher and sermonist, d. 1619.

K'TAV SOFER: Commentary on the Pentateuch by R. Abraham Samuel Benjamin Schreiber, 1815-1872.

LEKAH TOB: Midrashic commentary on Scripture by R. Tobiah b. Eliezer, fl. 11th century; also called *P'siktha Zutratha*.

MAASEH HASHEM, by R. Eliezer Ashkenazi, 1583; pupil of R. Joseph Caro.

MAIM. (RAMBAM): R. Moishe b. Maimon (Maimonides), famous theologian, metaphysician, commentator and codifier; 1135-1204.

MALBIM: Rabbi Meir Loeb b. Jehiel Mikael Malbim, Russian rabbi and Hebraist, author of *Hatorah v'Hamitsvah*, commentary on the Bible, 1809-1879.

MECHILTA: Tannaitic Midrash on Exodus, ascribed to the school of R. Ishmael.

MESHECH HOCHMAH: Comments on Pentateuch by R. Meir Simha Hacohen of Dvinsk, latter-day Talmudist. (Jerusalem, 1947.)

MHG: *Midrash Hagadol* ("the Great Midrash"), a compilation on Pentateuch discovered in Yemen at the end of the 19th century; the work dates from ca. 14th century.

MICHLAL YOFI: Commentary by R. Solomon b. Melech, Constantinople, 1549.

MIKRA M'FORASH by R. Nehemiah Moses Borlaga of Odessa.

MINHAH B'LULAH: Commentary on the Pentateuch by R. Menahem Abraham b. Jacob Ha-cohen Rapa (d. 1596), Cremona, 1582.

MIZRAHI: Elijah b. Abraham Mizrahi, rabbi and Talmudist, author of a commentary on Rashi to Pentateuch, 1455-1526.

MORTARA, R. Mordecai, author of *Ho'il Moshe*, Leghorn, 1881.

M'YUHAS: Commentary on the Pentateuch by the Sephardic R. M'yuhas b. Elijah. (London, 1909.)

NAHLATH JACOB, by Jacob Abraham b. Raphael of Cracow; d. 1699.

OLATH SHABBATH: Sermons on the weekly portions of Scripture by R. Joel ibn Shoib, 15th century Spanish preacher and commentator. (Venice, 1577.)

OR HAHAYYIM: Rabbi Hayyim ibn Attar, Talmudist and Cabbalist, author of *Or Ha-hayyim*, commentary on Scripture, 1696-1743.

PANIM YAFOTH: Cabalistic commentary on the Pentateuch by R. Phinehas Levi Horowitz, ca. 1731-1805.

PHILO: Greek-Jewish philosopher and author of voluminous allegorical commentaries on Scripture; 30 B.C.E.-40 C.E. Extracts of an edition of his selected writings (ed. Lewy, East and West Library) have been included.

RABAD: R. Abraham b. David of Posquieres (1125-1198). Talmudist and Halachist, famous for his keaen criticism of Maimondes in *Hasagoth ha-Rabad*.

RADAK: Rabbi David Kimhi, Hebrew grammarian and exegete, 1160-1235.

RALBAG: R. Levi b. Gershon (Gersonides), philosopher, exegete, mathematician and astronomer, 1288-1344.

RALASH: See Har'chasim L'bikah.

RAMBAM: See Maim.

RAMBAN: R. Moshe b. Nahman (Nahmanides), rabbi, Talmudist and Cabbalist, 1194-1270.

RAN: R. Nissin b. Reuben Gerondi, Spanish halachist, astronomer and physician, fl. ca. 1340-1380.

RANHAW: Naphtali Herz Weassely, Hebrew poet and educationalist, 1725-1805.

RASAG: R. Saadyah (b. Joseph) Gaon, celebrated Jewish scholar, 882-942.

RASHAD: R. Solomon Dubno, Bible commentator, grammarian, and poet; b. Dubno, 1738; d. Amsterdam, 1813.

RASHBAM: R. Samuel b. Meir, grandson of Rashi, biblical exegete, 1085-1174.

RASHI: R. Solomon b. Isaac, author of the most popular commentaries to Scripture and Talmud, 1040-1105.

RAWAH: R. Wolf Heidenheim, grammarian and exegete, 1757-1832.

R'BID HAZAHAB: Cabalistic-halachic commentary on the Bible by R. Dob Ber b. Judah Treves, d. 1803.

REGGIO: R. Isaac Samuel Reggio, Austro-Italian scholar, author of *Sefer Torath Elokim* on the Pentateuch; 1784-1855.

RIBA: R. Judah b. Eliezer, 14th century scholar, author of *Minhath Judah*.

RoSH: R. Asher b. Jehiel, outstanding codifier and Talmudist, 1250-1327.

SECHEL TOB: Biblical commentary by R. Menahem b. Shlomo, written 1139, apparently in Italy. (Berlin, 1900.)

SFORNO: R. Obadiah Sforno, exegete, philosopher and physician, c. 1475-1550.

SHADAL: Samuel David Luzzatto, scholar and philologian, 1800-1865.

T'CHELETH MORD'CHAI: A work on the Bible and the commentaries of Rashi and Ibn Ezra, by R. Mord'chai Drucker. (Lemberg, 1894.)

TOL'DOTH YITZHAK: Commentary on the Bible which stresses the literal meaning, by R. Isaac b. Joseph Caro, Spanish Talmudist of the 15-16th century.

TOS'FOTH: Commentary on the Bible similar to *Daath Z'kenim, q.v.*

T.S.: *Torah Shelemah*, the Hebrew encyclopedia of biblical interpretation by Rabbi Menahem M. Kasher, on which this work is based.

TS'ROR HAMOR: Mystical commentary on Pentateuch by R. Abraham Saba, 15th century Spanish preacher.

YAHUDA, A. S., Egyptologist, author of *The Language of the Pentateuch*.

TRANSLATIONS

ONK.: Aramaic translation by Onkelos the *Ger* (proselyte), 1st century C.E.

PESHITA: Ancient Syriac translation of the Bible.

SAMARITAN PENTATEUCH: An Aramaic version of Scripture produced by Samaritan Jewry, which contains many of their traditional interpretations.

SEPTUAGINT: A Greek translation, widespread among Egyptian Jewry since the 3rd century C.E. Traditionally it was written by seventy-two Sages to the order of one of the Ptolmey's.

SYMMACHUS: Translator of the Bible into Greek; lived in the second half of the second century.

TARGUM JERUSHALMI: An abridged verson of *Targum Jonathan, q.v.,* called Targum Jerushalmi II.

T.J.: Targum Jonathan. A free, expanded translation into Aramaic of Scripture, ascribed to R. Jonathan b. Uziel, called also Targum Jerushalmi I.

VULGATE: Latin translation by Jerome, made c. 383 C.E.

RABBINICAL AND SUBJECT INDEX

GENESIS XVIII-XXI

First figures indicate pages; second figures, after a dash—, indicate paragraph numbers. Thus 18—71 means page 18, paragraph 71. Where only figures are given for the rabbis quoted, the comment there is verbal rather than topical.

Simeon, R., b. Yohai, Abraham as healer, 188—17; execution, 55—3; gazlan, 123—91; love and hate, 137—29; Moriah, 133—20; Torah, 38—151; zaken, 184—3; 112—48; 147—67; 152—81; 198—53; 206—74

Simlai, R., on God's love, 1—1

Sisera, 161—110

Sodom (and Gomorrah), 72f—79f; 241-2—1-3; angels, 54f—1f; downfall, 3—11; judges, 56—10; overturn, 7—25; 33—135-6; 39-40—154-8; 42—168; 44f—173f; 48—184; 51-2—197-8; 65f—50f; 67—62; 83—3; 121—83

Sodomites, 30—125; 32—130; 47—182; 72—80; 73—85; et passim

Soferim, 15—53; 42—165n

Solomon, 198—53; 230—17

Song of Songs, God and Israel, 3—8n

Tamar, twins, 223—150

Tanhum, R., on angels, 54—2; Lot and daughters, 81—118

Tanhum, R., b. Hanilai, "When in Rome," 20—79; ashes, 50—190

Tanhuma, R., Abraham's burial, 233—27; angels, 54—2; gazlan, 123—91; 40—158; 64—45

Tarmod (Rome) downfall, 161—112

Ten Comandments, 21—82

Terebinths of Mamre, 45—14-15

Tobiah, R., b. R. Isaac, daughters, 65-6—53

Torah, acceptance, 162—113; 21—82

Three righteous men, 7f—22f

Transjordan, 17—67n

Tree, as Torah, 13—46

Tyre, and Rome, 230—17

Unity, 110—42

Water, for feet, 11-13—39-42

World to Come, 9—32

Yannai, R., on Gehenna, 6—19; Moriah, 133—20

Yannai, R., b. R. Ishmael, on washing feet, 13—42

Yannai, School of R., 99—56

Y'lamdenu, Midrash Tanhuma, 1—1n

Zabdi b. Levi, on Sarah's child, 24—96

Zadok, R., at wedding, 8—29

Zechariah, R., 152—82

Zeira, R., on dawn, 65—50

Zoar, 69—70; 74—90n; 78—107-8

Zohar, 43—168n